Lecture Notes in Computer Science 3357

Commenced Publication in 1973
Founding and Former Series Editors:
Gerhard Goos, Juris Hartmanis, and Jan van Leeuwen

Helena Handschuh   M. Anwar Hasan (Eds.)

Selected Areas in Cryptography

11th International Workshop, SAC 2004
Waterloo, Canada, August 9-10, 2004
Revised Selected Papers

 Springer

Volume Editors

Helena Handschuh
Gemplus, Issy-les-Moulineaux, France
E-mail: Helena.Handschuh@gemplus.com

M. Anwar Hasan
University of Waterloo, Waterloo, Ontario, Canada
E-mail: ahasan@ece.uwaterloo.ca

Library of Congress Control Number: 2004117402

CR Subject Classification (1998): E.3, D.4.6, K.6.5, F.2.1-2, C.2, H.4.3

ISSN 0302-9743
ISBN 3-540-24327-5 Springer Berlin Heidelberg New York

Springer is a part of Springer Science+Business Media

springeronline.com

© Springer-Verlag Berlin Heidelberg 2005
Printed in Germany

Typesetting: Camera-ready by author, data conversion by Scientific Publishing Services, Chennai, India
Printed on acid-free paper   SPIN: 11376224   06/3142   5 4 3 2 1 0

Preface

SAC 2004 was the eleventh in a series of annual workshops on Selected Areas in Cryptography. This was the second time that the workshop was hosted by the University of Waterloo, Ontario, with previous workshops being held at Queen's University in Kingston (1994, 1996, 1998 and 1999), Carleton University in Ottawa (1995, 1997 and 2003), the Fields Institute in Toronto (2001) and Memorial University of Newfoundland in St. John's (2002). The primary intent of the workshop was to provide a relaxed atmosphere in which researchers in cryptography could present and discuss new work on selected areas of current interest. This year's themes for SAC were:

- Design and analysis of symmetric key cryptosystems.
- Primitives for symmetric key cryptography, including block and stream ciphers, hash functions, and MAC algorithms.
- Efficient implementation of cryptographic systems in public and symmetric key cryptography.
- Cryptographic solutions for mobile (web) services.

A record of 117 papers were submitted for consideration by the program committee. After an extensive review process, 25 papers were accepted for presentation at the workshop (two of these papers were merged). Unfortunately, many good papers could not be accommodated this year. These proceedings contain the revised versions of the 24 accepted papers. The revised versions were not subsequently checked for correctness.

Also, we were very fortunate to have two invited speakers at SAC 2004.

- Eli Biham arranged for some breaking news in his talk on "New Results on SHA-0 and SHA-1." This talk was designated as the Stafford Tavares Lecture.
- Yevgeniy Dodis enlightened us with "Basing Cryptography on Biometrics and Other Noisy Data."

We are very grateful to the program committee and to the numerous external reviewers for their hard work and precious help. They collectively produced over 380 review reports in less than two months, which was quite a challenge. We have tried to list all of them in these proceedings and we sincerely hope we did not omit anyone.

We are also indebted to the University of Waterloo, Queen's University Kingston, Mitsubishi Electric Corporation, and Research in Motion Ltd. for their financial support of the workshop.

Special thanks are due to K.U.Leuven for kindly providing the Webreview software, Julien Brouchier for running both the submission server and Webreview, Janet Bullock for perfectly handling registrations, and Jaewook Chung and the local arrangements committee from the University of Waterloo for setting up the website and organizing a very nice and entertaining workshop.

Last but not least we would like to thank all submitters and all the participants who made this year's workshop a great success.

November 2004   Helena Handschuh and M. Anwar Hasan

11th Annual Workshop on Selected Areas in Cryptography

August 9–10, 2004, Waterloo, Ontario, Canada

Program and General Chairs

Helena Handschuh .... Gemplus, France
M. Anwar Hasan .... University of Waterloo, Canada

Program Committee

Carlisle Adams .... University of Ottawa, Canada
Henri Gilbert .... France Télécom, France
Mike Just .... Carleton University, Canada
Charanjit Jutla .... IBM, USA
Arjen Lenstra .... Lucent Technologies, USA
and T.U. Eindhoven, The Netherlands
Stefan Lucks .... Universität Mannheim, Germany
Mitsuru Matsui .... Mitsubishi Electric, Japan
Alfred Menezes .... University of Waterloo, Canada
Shiho Moriai .... Sony Computer Entertainment Inc., Japan
Kaisa Nyberg .... Nokia, Finland
Bart Preneel .... Katholieke Universiteit Leuven, Belgium
Matt Robshaw .... Royal Holloway University of London, UK
Douglas R. Stinson .... University of Waterloo, Canada
Serge Vaudenay .... EPFL, Switzerland
Michael Wiener .... Cryptographic Clarity, Canada

Local Arrangements Committee

Janet Bullock, Jaewook Chung, Agustin Dominguez, M. Anwar Hasan, Arash Reyhani-Masoleh, and Siavash B. Sarmadi

Sponsors

University of Waterloo
Mitsubishi Electric Corporation
Research in Motion Ltd.
Queen's University Kingston

External Referees

Frederik Armknecht
Gildas Avoine
Steve Babbage
Thomas Baignères
Lejla Batina
Come Berbain
Florent Bersani
Eli Biham
Olivier Billet
Antoon Bosselaers
Eric Brier
Jaewook Chung
Carlos Cid
Jean-Sébastien Coron
Nicolas Courtois
Paolo D'Arco
Christophe De Cannière
Nevine Ebeid
Soichi Furuya
Guang Gong
Louis Goubin
Shai Halevi
Darrel Hankerson

Jason Hinek
Daisuke Inoue
Tetsu Iwata
Shaoquan Jiang
Antoine Joux
Pascal Junod
Masayuki Kanda
John Kelsey
Kazukuni Kobara
Matthias Krause
Ulrich Kühn
Joseph Lano
Yi Lu
Jonathan Lutz
Kazuhiko Minematsu
Serge Mister
Jean Monnerat
Sumio Morioka
James Muir
Sean Murphy
Junko Nakajima
Kazuomi Oishi
Sıddıka Berna Örs

Matthew Parker
Kenny Paterson
Josyula R. Rao
Arash Reyhani-Masoleh
Pankaj Rohatgi
Taiichi Saito
Fumihiko Sano
Akashi Satoh
Werner Schindler
Jasper Scholten
Kyoji Shibutani
Takeshi Shimoyama
Taizo Shirai
Dirk Stegemann
Daisuke Suzuki
Jacques Traoré
Dai Watanabe
Brecht Wyseur
Yongjin Yeom
Erik Zenner
Robert Zuccherato

Table of Contents

Secret Key Cryptography I

Cryptanalysis

Cryptographic Protocols

Secret Key Cryptography II

An Improved Correlation Attack on A5/1

Alexander Maximov[1], Thomas Johansson[1], and Steve Babbage[2]

[1] Dept. of Information Technology, Lund University, Sweden
[2] Vodafone Group R&D, UK

Abstract. A new approach to attack A5/1 is proposed. The proposed attack is a refinement of a previous attack by Ekdahl and Johansson. We make two important observations that lead to a new attack with improved performance.

1 Introduction

The security of GSM conversation is based on usage of the A5 family of stream ciphers. Many hundred million customers in Europe are protected from the over-the-air piracy by the stronger version in this family, the A5/1 stream cipher. Other customers on other markets use the weaker version A5/2. The approximate design of A5/1 was leaked in 1994, and in 1999 the exact design of both A5/1 and A5/2 was discovered by Briceno [1]. As the result, a lot of investigations of the A5 stream ciphers were done.

The first analysis of the A5/1 cipher resulted in "Guess-and-Determine" type of attacks [2]. Then a time-memory trade-off attack was proposed by Biryukov, Shamir, and Wagner [3], which in some cases can break A5/1 in seconds. Unfortunately, it needs to use a huge precomputational time and about $4 \times 73\text{Gb}$ of hard memory. The attack complexity grows exponentially depending on the length of the LFSRs in the design of the cipher. Another attack was presented by Biham and Dunkelman [4]. Their attack breaks the cipher within $2^{39.91}$ A5/1 clocking assuming $2^{20.8}$ bits of keystream available. This attack has expensive assymptotic behaviour. In 2002, Krause, [5] presented a general attack on LFSR-based stream ciphers, called BDD-based cryptanalysis. This attack requires computation complexity of $n^{O(1)}2^{an}, a < 1$ polynomial time operations, where a is a constant depending on the cipher and n is the combined shift registers length. For A5/1, the attack achieves $a = 0.6403$, so the complexity is again exponential in the shift registers length.

A completely different way to attack A5/1 was proposed by Ekdahl and Johansson in 2001 [6]. The attack needs a few minutes for computations, and 2-5 minutes of conversation (plaintext). The idea behind the attack came from correlation attacks. This is the only attack for which the complexity does not grow exponentially with the shift register length.

Finally, very recently Barkan, Biham and Keller [7] investigated the usage of the A5 ciphers in GSM. They demonstrated an active attack where a false base station can intercept a conversation and perform a man in the middle attack. By asking for usage of the weak A5/2 algorithm in the conversation with the

H. Handschuh and A. Hasan (Eds.): SAC 2004, LNCS 3357, pp. 1–18, 2005.

base station and then breaking it, the false base station finds the session key which is also used in the A5/1 protected conversation with the mobile unit. In [7] the authors also propose the passive memory-time trade-off ciphertext only attack. As one of the examples, if 5 minutes of conversation is available, then the attack needs one year of precomputations with 140 computers working together, 22×200GBs hard discs. Then the attack can be done in time 2^{28} by one PC. Obviously, the authors did not try to implement the attack and the complexity was just estimated.

In this paper a new approach to attack the A5/1 stream cipher is proposed. We consider the Ekdahl-Johansson attack as the basis, and apply several new improvements. As the result, the new attack now needs only less then 1 minute of computations, and a few seconds of known conversation. It does not need any notable precomputation time, and needs reasonable space of operation memory.

For the case of a ciphertext-only attack on A5/1, we use the fact that some redundancy is part of the plaintext. There are at least two kinds of redundancy that are explicit and may be used in an attack where only ciphertext is available. *The first* kind is the fact that coding is done before encryption, which results in linear relationships in the plaintext since the parity check symbols are also encrypted. This observation was used in [7]. *The second* kind of redundancy is the fact that during silence, a special frame including a large number of zeros is sent [8]. Silence occurs very often, but unfortunately these frames used for silence are transmitted less frequently, one to initialise a period of silence and then two each second. The attack that we propose can be considered in a ciphertext-only scenario, in which case we use this redundancy during silence to get some known outputs from the cipher.

Although several of the previous attacks are sufficient to break A5/1 in a known plaintext attack, we believe that further progress is very important. The A5/1 stream cipher is perhaps the most used cipher in the world, and from the wireless communication channel interception of the communication is very easy. Mobile base stations are not expensive to buy and they can be used to record GSM conversations.

The paper is organized as follows. In Section 2 a short description of the cipher A5/1 is given. The basic Ekdahl-Johansson attack on A5/1 is briefly described in Section 3. Then, in Section 4, we give new ideas to improve the attack in general. The details and particulars of the attack simulations are described in Section 4.2. Then in Section 5 the results of our simulations are presented.

2   Description of A5/1

A GSM conversation between A and B is a sequence of frames, each sent in about 4.6 milliseconds. Each frame consists of 228 bits – 114 bits of which is the message from A to B, and the second half bits are representing communication from B to A. One session is encrypted with a secret *session key K*. For the jth frame the running key generator is initialised with mixture of K and the publicly known *frame counter*, denoted by F_j. It then generates 228 bits of running key for the current frame. The ciphertext is a binary xor of the running key and the plaintext.

A5/1 consists of 3 LFSRs of lengths 19, 22, and 23, which are denoted R_1, R_2, and R_3, respectively. The LFSRs are clocked in an irregular fashion. Each of them has one tap-bit, C_1, C_2, and C_3, respectively. In each step, 2 or 3 LFSRs are clocked, depending on the current values of the bits C_1, C_2, and C_3. Thus, the clocking control device imple-

values of			clocking		
C_1	C_2	C_3	R_1	R_2	R_3
$1 \oplus c$	c	c	×	√	√
c	$1 \oplus c$	c	√	×	√
c	c	$1 \oplus c$	√	√	×
c	c	c	√	√	√

ments the majority rule, shown in the table on the right. Note, for each step the probability that an individual LFSR is being clocked is 3/4.

After the initialisation procedure for the LFSRs, 228 bits of running key are produced, using irregular clocking. In each step one bit of the running key is calculated as the binary xor of the current output bits from the LFSRs.

The initialisation process uses the session key K and the known frame counter F_n. First the LFSRs are initialised to zero. They are then clocked 64 times, ignoring the irregular clocking, and the key bits of K are consecutively xored in parallel to the feedback of each of the registers. In the second step the LFSRs are clocked 22 times, ignoring the irregular clocking, and the successive bits of F_n are again xored in parallel to the feedback of the LFSRs. Let us call the state of LFSRs at this time the *initial state* of the frame. In the third step the LFSRs are clocked 100 times *with* irregular clocking, but ignoring outputs. Then, the LFSRs are clocked 228 times with the irregular clocking, producing 228 bits of the running key. For a more detailed description of A5/1 we refer to [1].

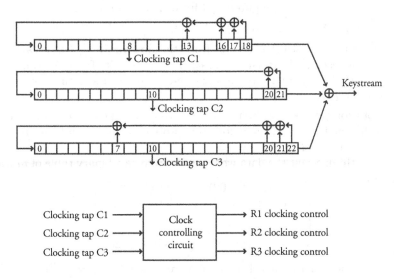

Fig. 1. The structure of A5/1 cipher

3   A Short Description of the Ekdahl-Johansson Attack on A5/1

This attack was proposed in 2002 by Ekdahl and Johansson. The idea behind the attack came from correlation attacks, and is based on the linearity of the initialisation procedure. The attack needs a set of m frames (about 20000-50000 in their attack), during one session, i.e., when the session key K is not changed.

For notation purposes, let the key $K = (k_1, \ldots, k_{64})$, and the frame counter $F_j = (f_1, \ldots, f_{22})$, where $k_i, f_j \in \mathbf{F}_2$, $i = 1..64, j = 1..22$. Denote by $u_1^j(l_1)$, $u_2^j(l_2)$, and $u_3^j(l_3)$ the output bits of LFSRs, if they are independently *clocked* l_1, l_2, and l_3 times, respectively, *after* the LFSRs being in the initial state, and when the current frame is number j. The 228 bits of the running key are then denoted as $v^j(101), \ldots, v^j(100+228)$, and every $v^j(t) = u_1^j(l_1) \oplus u_2^j(l_2) \oplus u_3^j(l_3)$, for *some unknown* l_1, l_2, l_3.

Note, that $u_1^j(l_1)$ is a linear combination of K and F_j bits, since all operations before the initial state are linear. I.e., $u_1^j(l_1)$ can be represented as $u_1^j(l_1) = X_{1,l_1}(F_j) + Y_{1,l_1}(K)$, where $X_{1,l_1}(F_j)$ is a known fixed value and $Y_{1,l_1}(K) = \sum_{i=1}^{64} y_{1,l_1,i} \cdot k_i$ is a linear function with known coefficients $y_{1,l_1,i} \in \mathbf{F}_2$.

With the same arguments we define

$$u_1^j(l_1) = X_{1,l_1}(F_j) + Y_{1,l_1}(K),$$
$$u_2^j(l_2) = X_{2,l_2}(F_j) + Y_{2,l_2}(K),$$
$$u_3^j(l_3) = X_{3,l_3}(F_j) + Y_{3,l_3}(K),$$

where $X_{a,l_a}(F_j)$ and the coefficients $y_{a,l_a,i} \in \mathbf{F}_2$, for $a = 1, 2, 3$, $l_a = 0, 1, \ldots, 100+228$, $i = 1, \ldots, 64$ are precomputed and fixed. Let us write

$$s_1(l_1) = Y_{1,l_1}(K), \qquad s_2(l_2) = Y_{2,l_2}(K), \qquad s_3(l_3) = Y_{3,l_3}(K). \tag{1}$$

Our target is to estimate 19 bits from the first LFSR $s_1(0), \ldots, s_1(18)$, 22 bits from the second LFSR $s_2(0), \ldots, s_2(21)$, and 23 bits from the third LFSR $s_3(0), \ldots, s_3(22)$. These 64 bits map one-to-one to 64 bits of the key K, if the frame counter F_j is given.

For notation purposes we write $E \overset{p}{=} \hat{E}$, when $\hat{E}$ appears to be an estimator for E, such that $\Pr\{E = \hat{E}\} = p$, for some probability p. $\hat{E}$ can be derived from accessible data, or assumed (guessed).

One can think about the data we have access to as a binary table of m frames in the form

$$\begin{pmatrix} v^1(101) & v^1(102) & \ldots & v^1(100+228) \\ v^2(101) & v^2(102) & \ldots & v^2(100+228) \\ & \vdots & & \\ v^m(101) & v^m(102) & \ldots & v^m(100+228) \end{pmatrix}.$$

The idea behind the attack is to observe that $v^j(101) \overset{p}{=} s_1(l_1) + s_2(l_2) + s_3(l_3) + X_{1,l_1}(F_j) + X_{2,l_2}(F_j) + X_{3,l_3}(F_j)$ for some $p \neq 1/2$, if l_1, l_2, l_3 are chosen properly. The probability $p = \frac{1}{2} + \frac{1}{2}\Pr\{(l_1, l_2, l_3)$ at time $t\}$, where $\Pr\{(l_1, l_2, l_3)$ at time $t\}$ is the probability that at time 101 the LFSRs were regularly clocked exactly l_1, l_2, l_3 times, respectively. The probability that at time $t \in \{101 \ldots 100 + 228\}$, the LFSRs have been clocked (l_1, l_2, l_3) times is

$$\Pr\{(l_1, l_2, l_3) \text{ at time } t\} = \frac{\binom{t}{t-l_1}\binom{t-(t-l_1)}{t-l_2}\binom{t-(t-l_1)-(t-l_2)}{t-l_3}}{4^t}. \qquad (2)$$

Let us now define the known value $\hat{O}^j_{l_1, l_2, l_3}(t) = v^j(t) \oplus X_{1,l_1}(F_j) \oplus X_{2,l_2}(F_j) \oplus X_{3,l_3}(F_j)$. Then

$$\hat{O}^j_{l_1, l_2, l_3}(t) \overset{p}{=} s_1(l_1) \oplus s_2(l_2) \oplus s_3(l_3). \qquad (3)$$

The case when $\hat{O}^j_{l_1, l_2, l_3}(t)$ is equal to the value $s_1(l_1) \oplus s_2(l_2) \oplus s_3(l_3)$ can happen only in two ways,

a) The LFSRs are really clocked l_1, l_2, l_3 at time t, happening with probability $\Pr\{(l_1, l_2, l_3) \text{ at time } t\}$. If so, the expression will be true with probability 1.
b) If the condition in a) is not fulfilled, the expression will still be true with probability $1/2$.

This means that the relation (3) is biased ($p > 1/2$).

From the given frames we can estimate many of the linear combinations $s_1(l_1) \oplus s_2(l_2) \oplus s_3(l_3)$ for different triples (l_1, l_2, l_3). But we only need 64 correct estimates in order to recover the key K uniquely.

To minimise the amount of frames m and perform the estimation with low probability of error, Ekdahl and Johansson suggested to use the values of $v^j(101), \ldots, v^j(164)$ for all j for better estimation of $s_1(l_1) \oplus s_2(l_2) \oplus s_3(l_3)$. They used the expression

$$\Pr\{s_1(l_1) \oplus s_2(l_2) \oplus s_3(l_3) = 1, \text{ for the frame } j\} = p^j_{(l_1, l_2, l_3)} =$$

$$= \sum_{t \in \{101 \ldots 164\}} \Pr\{(l_1, l_2, l_3) \text{ at time } t\} \cdot \left[\hat{O}^j_{l_1, l_2, l_3}(t) = 0\right]$$

$$+ 1/2 \cdot \left(1 - \sum_{t \in \{101 \ldots 164\}} \Pr\{(l_1, l_2, l_3) \text{ at time } t\}\right).$$

This probability gives the estimation of the corresponding linear combination for one frame j. We will increase the possibility to estimate the value of $s_1(l_1) + s_2(l_2) + s_3(l_3)$ correctly, when m frames (samples) $v^1(101 \ldots 328), \ldots, v^m(101 \ldots 328)$ are given, as each of them provides some small contribution. By calculating the likelihood ratio

$$\Lambda_{l_1, l_2, l_3} = \sum_{j=1}^{m} \log_2 \left[\frac{p^j_{(l_1, l_2, l_3)}}{1 - p^j_{(l_1, l_2, l_3)}}\right]$$

we achieve a likelihood value (estimate) which is taken over all m frames. This can be turned into a binary estimate by

$$s_1(l_1) \oplus s_2(l_2) \oplus s_3(l_3) \overset{p}{=} \begin{cases} 0 \text{ if } \Lambda_{l_1, l_2, l_3} \geq 0 \\ 1 \text{ if } \Lambda_{l_1, l_2, l_3} < 0 \end{cases},$$

where $p > 0.5$ depends mainly on m. In [6] the authors finally examine different strategies for implementing the recovery of the key bits as efficient as possible.

4   Explaining the New Attack

In this section we describe our discovered improvements in general. Our main purpose is to reduce the number of frames m, which is needed for the attack.

4.1   Statistical Analysis of m Frames

We mentioned before that we have identified two general ideas for improving the previous results. The first is the fact that it is beneficial to study the derivative sequences instead of the sequences themselves. Assume that at time t the LFSRs are clocked l_1, l_2, and l_3 times, respectively. Then we also assume that at time $t+1$ the third LFSR is not clocked. In this case we have the equalities,

$$\hat{O}^j_{l_1,l_2,l_3}(t) = s_1(l_1) \oplus s_2(l_2) \oplus s_3(l_3),$$
$$\hat{O}^j_{l_1+1,l_2+1,l_3}(t+1) = s_1(l_1+1) \oplus s_2(l_2+1) \oplus s_3(l_3). \tag{4}$$

Then the probability $\Pr\{\hat{O}^j_{l_1,l_2,l_3}(t) \oplus \hat{O}^j_{l_1+1,l_2+1,l_3}(t+1) = s_1(l_1) \oplus s_2(l_2) \oplus s_1(l_1+1) \oplus s_2(l_2+1)\} = \frac{1}{4} \cdot \Pr\{(l_1,l_2)$ at time $t\}$, where

$$\Pr\{(l_1,l_2) \text{ at time } t\} = \frac{\binom{t}{t-l_1}\binom{l_1}{t-l_2}}{2^{3t-(l_1+l_2)}}.$$

Note, that $\frac{1}{4} \cdot \Pr\{(l_1,l_2)$ at time $t\} > \Pr\{(l_1,l_2,l_3)$ at time $t\}$ so it gives us a larger bias when estimating the value of linear combinations of $s_i(l_i)$'s. Below is a comparison of these probabilities.

$(l_1,l_2,l_3),t$	$\Pr\{(l_1,l_2,l_3)$ at $t\} \cdot 10^4$	$\frac{1}{4}\Pr\{(l_1,l_2)$ at $t\} \cdot 10^4$
$(76,76,76), 101$	9.7434	22.1207
$(79,79,79), 105$	9.2012	21.2840
$(80,80,80), 105$	6.6388	19.3778
$(79,80,81), 106$	8.3858	20.8899
$(82,82,82), 109$	8.7076	20.5083

The first idea to improve the attack is then to consider two consecutive expressions (4). Their sum only depends on two LFSRs, and the probability of the event is higher than before. We also note that we can similarly assume that LFSR-1 and LFSR-2 are not clocked at some time t. This gives us 3 *cases*. We define

$$_1\hat{z}^j_{l_2,l_3}(t) = \hat{O}^j_{l_1,l_2,l_3}(t) \oplus \hat{O}^j_{l_1,l_2+1,l_3+1}(t+1) \overset{p}{=} s_2(l_2) \oplus s_3(l_3) \oplus s_2(l_2+1) \oplus s_3(l_3+1),$$
$$_2\hat{z}^j_{l_1,l_3}(t) = \hat{O}^j_{l_1,l_2,l_3}(t) \oplus \hat{O}^j_{l_1+1,l_2,l_3+1}(t+1) \overset{p}{=} s_1(l_1) \oplus s_3(l_3) \oplus s_1(l_1+1) \oplus s_3(l_3+1),$$
$$_3\hat{z}^j_{l_1,l_2}(t) = \hat{O}^j_{l_1,l_2,l_3}(t) \oplus \hat{O}^j_{l_1+1,l_2+1,l_3}(t+1) \overset{p}{=} s_1(l_1) \oplus s_2(l_2) \oplus s_1(l_1+1) \oplus s_2(l_2+1). \tag{5}$$

The case when $_3\hat{z}^j_{l_1,l_2}(t)$ is equal to the value $s_1(l_1) \oplus s_2(l_2) \oplus s_1(l_1+1) \oplus s^j_2(l_2+1)$ can happen in two ways,

a) The first and the second LFSRs are indeed clocked l_1, l_2 times at time t occuring with probability $\Pr\{(l_1, l_2) \text{ at time } t\}$, **AND** at time $t+1$ the third LFSR *is not clocked*, with probability $1/4$. The expression is always true in this case.

b) If the condition in a) is not fulfilled the expression will still be true with probability $1/2$.

The second idea is to consider d consecutive estimators jointly as one d-dimension estimator. If we look at the sequence of d estimators of the form $_3\hat{z}^j_{l_1, l_2}(t), \ldots, _3\hat{z}^j_{l_1+d-1, l_2+d-1}(t+d-1)$, then we note that they are dependent on each other. To use this fact we suggest to consider not binary expressions, but vectors of d bits. Introduce a new d-bits vector, derived from the frame j,

$$_3\hat{Z}^j_{l_1, l_2}(t) = \begin{pmatrix} _3\hat{z}^j_{l_1, l_2}(t) \\ _3\hat{z}^j_{l_1+1, l_2+1}(t+1) \\ \vdots \\ _3\hat{z}^j_{l_1+d-1, l_2+d-1}(t+d-1) \end{pmatrix} \tag{6}$$

$$= \begin{pmatrix} v^j(t) & \oplus\, v^j(t+1) \oplus & X_{1,l_1}(j) & \oplus & X_{2,l_2}(j) & \oplus X_{1,l_1+1}(j) \oplus X_{2,l_2+1}(j) \\ v^j(t+1) & \oplus\, v^j(t+2) \oplus & X_{1,l_1+1}(j) & \oplus & X_{2,l_2+1}(j) & \oplus X_{1,l_1+2}(j) \oplus X_{2,l_2+2}(j) \\ & & \vdots & & & \\ v^j(t+d-1) & \oplus\, v^j(t+d) \oplus X_{1,l_1+d-1}(j) & \oplus X_{2,l_2+d-1}(j) & \oplus X_{1,l_1+d}(j) \oplus X_{2,l_2+d}(j) \end{pmatrix}.$$

Define the d-dimension vector $_3\mathcal{S}_{l_1, l_2}$ (which is unknown for the attacker) as

$$_3\mathcal{S}_{l_1, l_2} = \begin{pmatrix} s_1(l_1) & + & s_2(l_2) & + s_1(l_1+1) + s_2(l_2+1) \\ s_1(l_1+1) & + & s_2(l_2+1) & + s_1(l_1+2) + s_2(l_2+2) \\ & & \vdots & \\ s_1(l_1+d-1) & + s_2(l_2+d-1) & + s_1(l_1+d) + s_2(l_2+d) \end{pmatrix}. \tag{7}$$

Then, from (5) it follows that

$$_3\mathcal{S}_{l_1, l_2} \overset{p}{=} {}_3\hat{Z}^j_{l_1, l_2}(t), \tag{8}$$

with some biased probability p. Note that the symbols are now of alphabet size 2^d.

Examining this in more detail, consider d consecutive irregular steps. The total number of possible scenarios is 4^d, since in each step one of four types of irregular clockings can be chosen, according to the bits C_1, C_2, C_3. If we assume that at time t the first and the second LFSRs are clocked exactly l_1, l_2 times, then we can classify the bits of the vector $_3\hat{Z}^j_{l_1, l_2}(t)$. They can be either **C***orrect* (i.e., the next clocking is the required one so the bit has the same value as the corresponding bit in the vector $_3\mathcal{S}_{l_1, l_2}$), or **R***andom* (i.e., the bit can be 0 or 1, with probability $1/2$). For each possible pattern $\{\mathbf{C}orrect, \mathbf{R}andom\}^d$ we calculate the corresponding number of scenarios out of 4^d possible, by exhaustively trying all the scenarios. For example, when $d = 4$, we have the following distribution:

Condition	$3\hat{Z}^j_{l_1,l_2}(t)$				Probability	Event
	$3\hat{z}^j_{l_1,l_2}$ (t)	$3\hat{z}^j_{l_1+1,l_2+1}$ $(t+1)$	$3\hat{z}^j_{l_1+2,l_2+2}$ $(t+2)$	$3\hat{z}^j_{l_1+3,l_2+3}$ $(t+3)$		
Assumption is NOT correct	Random	Random	Random	Random	$1-P_0$	E_R
Assumption is correct	Correct	Correct	Correct	Correct	$P_0 \cdot 1/2^8$	E_0
	Random	Correct	Correct	Correct	$P_0 \cdot 1/2^8$	E_1
	Correct	Random	Correct	Correct	$P_0 \cdot 1/2^8$	E_2
	Random	Random	Correct	Correct	$P_0 \cdot 1/2^8$	E_3
	Correct	Correct	Random	Correct	$P_0 \cdot 1/2^8$	E_4
	Random	Correct	Random	Correct	$P_0 \cdot 1/2^8$	E_5
	Correct	Random	Random	Correct	$P_0 \cdot 1/2^8$	E_6
	Random	Random	Random	Correct	$P_0 \cdot 1/2^8$	E_7
	Correct	Correct	Correct	Random	$P_0 \cdot 3/2^8$	E_8
	Random	Correct	Correct	Random	$P_0 \cdot 3/2^8$	E_9
	Correct	Random	Correct	Random	$P_0 \cdot 3/2^8$	E_{10}
	Random	Random	Correct	Random	$P_0 \cdot 3/2^8$	E_{11}
	Correct	Correct	Random	Random	$P_0 \cdot 11/2^8$	E_{12}
	Random	Correct	Random	Random	$P_0 \cdot 11/2^8$	E_{13}
	Correct	Random	Random	Random	$P_0 \cdot 43/2^8$	E_{14}
	Random	Random	Random	Random	$P_0 \cdot 171/2^8$	E_{15}

where $P_0 = \Pr\{(l_1,l_2)$ at time t$\}$ and the assumption is that the first two LFSRs have clocked (l_1,l_2) at time t.

Let us assume that we have received the vector $3\hat{Z}^j_{l_1,l_2}(t) = (0,1,1,0)^T$ at time t from the frame j. If we consider the hypothesis that $3\mathcal{S}_{l_1,l_2} = (0,0,1,1)$, then the error pattern is $\mathcal{E}_d = 3\mathcal{S}_{l_1,l_2} \oplus 3\hat{Z}^j_{l_1,l_2}(t) = (0,1,0,1)$. This *error pattern* $\mathcal{E}_d$ can be the result of one of the following events: $E_R, E_{10}, E_{11}, E_{14}, E_{15}$. Thus, the conditional probability $\Pr\{3\mathcal{S}_{l_1,l_2} = (0,0,1,1)|3\hat{Z}^j_{l_1,l_2}(t) = (0,1,1,0)\} = \Pr\{\mathcal{E}_d = (0,1,0,1)\} = \frac{\Pr\{E_R\}}{2^4} + \frac{\Pr\{E_{10}\}}{2^2} + \frac{\Pr\{E_{11}\}}{2^3} + \frac{\Pr\{E_{14}\}}{2^3} + \frac{\Pr\{E_{15}\}}{2^4} = (1-P_0)/2^4 + P_0 \cdot 275/2^{12}$. Continuing in this way, the complete table for $\Pr\{\mathcal{E}_d\}$ can be derived. The distribution for $d=4$ is given as in the table on the right.

$\mathcal{E}_d = 3\mathcal{S}_{l_1,l_2} \oplus 3\hat{Z}^j_{l_1,l_2}(t)$	
$\mathcal{E}_d$	$\Pr\{\mathcal{E}_d\}$
$(0,0,0,0)$	$(1-P_0)/2^4 + P_0 \cdot 431/2^{12}$
$(1,0,0,0)$	$(1-P_0)/2^4 + P_0 \cdot 229/2^{12}$
$(0,1,0,0)$	$(1-P_0)/2^4 + P_0 \cdot 293/2^{12}$
$(1,1,0,0)$	$(1-P_0)/2^4 + P_0 \cdot 183/2^{12}$
$(0,0,1,0)$	$(1-P_0)/2^4 + P_0 \cdot 341/2^{12}$
$(1,0,1,0)$	$(1-P_0)/2^4 + P_0 \cdot 199/2^{12}$
$(0,1,1,0)$	$(1-P_0)/2^4 + P_0 \cdot 263/2^{12}$
$(1,1,1,0)$	$(1-P_0)/2^4 + P_0 \cdot 173/2^{12}$
$(0,0,0,1)$	$(1-P_0)/2^4 + P_0 \cdot 377/2^{12}$
$(1,0,0,1)$	$(1-P_0)/2^4 + P_0 \cdot 211/2^{12}$
$(0,1,0,1)$	$(1-P_0)/2^4 + P_0 \cdot 275/2^{12}$
$(1,1,0,1)$	$(1-P_0)/2^4 + P_0 \cdot 177/2^{12}$
$(0,0,1,1)$	$(1-P_0)/2^4 + P_0 \cdot 323/2^{12}$
$(1,0,1,1)$	$(1-P_0)/2^4 + P_0 \cdot 193/2^{12}$
$(0,1,1,1)$	$(1-P_0)/2^4 + P_0 \cdot 257/2^{12}$
$(1,1,1,1)$	$(1-P_0)/2^4 + P_0 \cdot 171/2^{12}$

For each frame j and for each vector $(b_0, \ldots, b_{d-1})^T$ we calculate

$$\Pr\{{}_3\mathcal{S}_{l_1,l_2} = (b_0, \ldots, b_{d-1})^T \text{ in } j\text{th frame}\} = {}_3p^j_{l_1,l_2}(b_0, \ldots, b_{d-1})$$

$$= \sum_{t \in \{101\ldots164\}} \Pr\{(l_1, l_2) \text{ at time } t\} \cdot \Pr\{\mathcal{E}_d = {}_3\hat{\mathcal{Z}}^j_{l_1,l_2}(t) \oplus (b_0, \ldots, b_{d-1})^T\}$$

$$+ \frac{1}{2}\left(1 - \sum_{t \in \{101\ldots164\}} \Pr\{(l_1, l_2) \text{ at time } t\}\right). \tag{9}$$

All the m frames give us a more precise estimation:

$$\Pr\{{}_3\mathcal{S}_{l_1,l_2} = (b_0, \ldots, b_{d-1})^T\} = {}_3p_{l_1,l_2}(b_0, \ldots, b_{d-1})$$

$$= \prod_{j=1}^{m} {}_3p^j_{l_1,l_2}(b_0, \ldots, b_{d-1}) = 2^{\sum_{j=1}^{m} \log_2\left({}_3p^j_{l_1,l_2}(b_0,\ldots,b_{d-1})\right)}. \tag{10}$$

In this formula the last two values should both be divided by a factor equal to their sum over all possible values of $(b_0, \ldots, b_{d-1})$. This factor has been left out because we are really interested in the relative values of the probabilities for different values of $(b_0, \ldots, b_{d-1})$. To simplify numerical calculations, ${}_3p_{l_1,l_2}(b_0, \ldots, b_{d-1})$ can be normalised through division by any constant.

We have just found the way how to calculate the probability $\Pr\{{}_3\mathcal{S}_{l_1,l_2} = (b_0, \ldots, b_{d-1})^T\}$, for every d-dimension value $(b_0, \ldots, b_{d-1})^T$. In a similar fashion, based on the equation (5), we can derive the d-dimension vectors ${}_1\hat{\mathcal{Z}}^j_{l_2,l_3}(t)$ and ${}_2\hat{\mathcal{Z}}^j_{l_1,l_3}(t)$, and then define the vectors ${}_1\mathcal{S}_{l_2,l_3}$ and ${}_2\mathcal{S}_{l_1,l_3}$. The formulas to calculate $\Pr\{{}_1\mathcal{S}_{l_2,l_3} = (b_0, \ldots, b_{d-1})^T\}$ and $\Pr\{{}_2\mathcal{S}_{l_1,l_3} = (b_0, \ldots, b_{d-1})^T\}$ are similar to equations (9) and (10).

Finally, we have a set of h tables like $\Pr\{{}_r\mathcal{S}_{l_i,l_j} = (b_0, \ldots, b_{d-1})\}$. If we "guess" the key $\hat{K}$, then in each such distribution table one row (probability) can be selected, corresponding to $\hat{K}$. *The measure of likelihood acceptance of $\hat{K}$ is the product of the selected probabilities through all the h tables.*

Our task is then to select a set of "guessed" keys $\hat{K}$ with maximum probabilities, and then perform a test whether the real key K can be one of the selected. More details depend on the exact structure of simulations, which we discuss in the next section.

4.2   Creating Candidate Tables of $s(l)$-Sequences

In the previous subsection we have found how to create a distribution table for d-dimension random variables ${}_r\mathcal{S}_{l_i,l_j}$. If we have h such distributions, then a "guessed" key $\hat{K}$ is measured by its probability, as described above. We are now faced with the problem of how to select the most likely $\hat{K}$'s in an efficient way. For this purpose we partly use the idea that was introduced in the Ekdahl-Johansson attack, but in a modified way. In this section we show the technical details of searching for the best $\hat{K}$'s, and focus on computation aspects.

The idea is that first we choose some interval $\mathcal{I}_1 = [I_{1,a} \ldots I_{1,b}]$ and then we construct h_1 distribution tables for $_3\mathcal{S}_{l_1,l_2}$, where $l_1, l_2 \in \mathcal{I}_1$. I.e., the number of distribution tables will be $h_1 = (I_{1,b} - I_{1,a} + 1)^2$, and the number of $s_1(l)$'s and $s_2(l)$'s that are involved in the linear expressions for $_3\mathcal{S}_{l_1,l_2}$ is $2 \cdot (I_{1,b} - I_{1,a} + 1 + d)$, see formula (7).

Let us consider some choice of values for $s_1(I_{1,a}), \ldots, s_1(I_{1,b} + d), s_2(I_{1,a}), \ldots,$ $s_2(I_{1,b} + d)$ to be a pair of vectors $(\mathcal{S}_{1,\mathcal{I}_1}, \mathcal{S}_{2,\mathcal{I}_1})$ (note, the vector of interest ends with $I_{1,b} + d$, rather then $I_{1,b} + d - 1$; the reason can be seen from (7), where $l_1, l_2 \in \mathcal{I}_1$), i.e.,

$$(s_1(I_{1,a}), \ldots, s_1(I_{1,b} + d), s_2(I_{1,a}), \ldots, s_2(I_{1,b} + d)) \stackrel{p}{=} (\mathcal{S}_{1,\mathcal{I}_1}, \mathcal{S}_{2,\mathcal{I}_1}). \quad (11)$$

The measure of the choice is the probability mass defined as

$$\prod_{l_1, l_2 \in \mathcal{I}_1} \Pr\{_3\mathcal{S}_{l_1,l_2} | (\mathcal{S}_{1,\mathcal{I}_1}, \mathcal{S}_{2,\mathcal{I}_1})\}. \quad (12)$$

Now, by exhaustive search the most likely r pairs $(\mathcal{S}_{1,\mathcal{I}_1}, \mathcal{S}_{2,\mathcal{I}_1})$ form a set $_3\mathcal{T}_{\mathcal{I}_1} = \{(\mathcal{S}_{1,\mathcal{I}_1}, \mathcal{S}_{2,\mathcal{I}_1})\}$. The size of the exhaustive search is $2^{2 \cdot (I_{1,b} - I_{1,a} + 1 + d)}$. In a similar way we can perform the same exhaustive search to create the sets $_1\mathcal{T}_{\mathcal{I}_1} = \{(\mathcal{S}_{2,\mathcal{I}_1}, \mathcal{S}_{3,\mathcal{I}_1})\}$ and $_2\mathcal{T}_{\mathcal{I}_1} = \{(\mathcal{S}_{1,\mathcal{I}_1}, \mathcal{S}_{3,\mathcal{I}_1})\}$, each containing the r most likely candidates.

To understand better how the exhaustive search for $_3\mathcal{T}_{\mathcal{I}_1}$ is done, one can think of the matrix multiplication:

$$\begin{pmatrix} 1\,1\,0 \ldots 0\,0 \ldots 0\,0\,0 \ldots 0\,0 & 1\,1\,0\ 0 \ldots 0\,0\,0 \ldots 0\,0\,0 \ldots 0\,0 \\ 0\,1\,1 \quad 0\,0 \quad 0\,0\,0 \quad 0\,0 & 0\,1\,1\ 0 \quad 0\,0\,0 \quad 0\,0\,0 \quad 0\,0 \\ \vdots \ \ddots \ \vdots \quad \vdots \quad \vdots & \vdots \ \ddots \quad \vdots \quad \vdots \quad \vdots \\ 0\,0\,0 \ldots 1\,1 \ldots 0\,0\,0 \ldots 0\,0 & 0\,0\,0\ 0 \ldots 1\,1\,0 \ldots 0\,0\,0 \ldots 0\,0 \\ 1\,1\,0 \ldots 0\,0 \ldots 0\,0\,0 \ldots 0\,0 & 0\,1\,1\ 0 \ldots 0\,0\,0 \ldots 0\,0\,0 \ldots 0\,0 \\ 0\,1\,1 \quad 0\,0 \quad 0\,0\,0 \quad 0\,0 & 0\,0\,1\ 1 \quad 0\,0\,0 \quad 0\,0\,0 \quad 0\,0 \\ \vdots \ \ddots \ \vdots \quad \vdots \quad \vdots & \vdots \quad \ddots \ \vdots \quad \vdots \quad \vdots \\ 0\,0\,0 \ldots 1\,1 \ldots 0\,0\,0 \ldots 0\,0 & 0\,0\,0\ 0 \ldots 0\,1\,1 \ldots 0\,0\,0 \ldots 0\,0 \\ \vdots & \vdots \\ 0\,0\,0 \ldots 0\,0 \ldots 1\,1\,0 \ldots 0\,0 & 0\,0\,0\ 0 \ldots 0\,0\,0 \ldots 1\,1\,0 \ldots 0\,0 \\ 0\,0\,0 \quad 0\,0 \quad 0\,1\,1 \quad 0\,0 & 0\,0\,0\ 0 \quad 0\,0\,0 \quad 0\,1\,1 \quad 0\,0 \\ \vdots \quad \vdots \quad \vdots\ \ddots\ \vdots & \vdots \quad \vdots \quad \vdots \quad \ddots\ \vdots \\ 0\,0\,0 \ldots 0\,0 \ldots 0\,0\,0 \ldots 1\,1 & 0\,0\,0\ 0 \ldots 0\,0\,0 \ldots 0\,0\,0 \ldots 1\,1 \end{pmatrix} \cdot \begin{pmatrix} s_1(I_a) \\ \rule{1cm}{0.4pt} \\ s_1(I_b + d) \\ \hline s_2(I_a) \\ \vdots \\ s_2(I_b + d) \end{pmatrix} = \begin{pmatrix} _3\mathcal{Z}_{I_a,I_a} \\ \rule{1cm}{0.4pt} \\ _3\mathcal{Z}_{I_a,I_a+1} \\ \hline \vdots \\ \rule{1cm}{0.4pt} \\ _3\mathcal{Z}_{I_b,I_b} \end{pmatrix},$$

where for every "guessed" vector $(\mathcal{S}_{1,\mathcal{I}_1}, \mathcal{S}_{2,\mathcal{I}_1})$ (exhaustive search) the set of vectors $_3\mathcal{S}_{l_1,l_2} \stackrel{p}{=} {}_3\mathcal{Z}_{l_1b,l_2}$ is determined uniquely by the matrix multiplication. We can then calculate the value of our choice by formula (12). After that, the most likely r pairs are selected and stored in the list (or table) $_3\mathcal{T}_{\mathcal{I}_1}$.

Recall that to recover the key K uniquely, we need to have 64 bits: 19 bits of $s_1(l)$'s, 22 bits of $s_2(l)$'s, and 23 bits of $s_3(l)$'s. It means that for $d = 4$ it might be enough to have only one interval $\mathcal{I}_1$ of size 19. When we try to reduce the number of frames m needed for the attack, then there are two reasons for why this simple scenario is not working:

a) to create one likelihood table $_3\mathcal{T}_{\mathcal{I}_1}$ the exhaustive search will be of size $2^{2\cdot(19+4)} = 2^{46}$ – this is practically impossible;

b) when the number of frames m is reduced, then the number of candidates r must be increased significantly, so that the correct pairs are present in the tables $_1\mathcal{T}_{\mathcal{I}_1}, _2\mathcal{T}_{\mathcal{I}_1}$, and $_3\mathcal{T}_{\mathcal{I}_1}$. Otherwise, the joint intersection of these sets will not give us the correct triple $(\mathcal{S}_{1,\mathcal{I}_1}, \mathcal{S}_{2,\mathcal{I}_1}, \mathcal{S}_{3,\mathcal{I}_1})$.

To overcome these problems, we could take $\mathcal{I}_1$ of a short size, and introduce one more interval, $\mathcal{I}_2 = [I_{2,a} \ldots I_{2,b}]$, and then we construct two kinds of tables $_*\mathcal{T}_{\mathcal{I}_1}$ and $_*\mathcal{T}_{\mathcal{I}_2}$ each of size r. We need to take $\mathcal{I}_2$ such that it intersects $\mathcal{I}_1$, otherwise the intersection would be r^2, and, hence, r cannot be large. Now in a similar way we can create the sets $_1\mathcal{T}_{\mathcal{I}_2} = \{(\mathcal{S}_{2,\mathcal{I}_2}, \mathcal{S}_{3,\mathcal{I}_2})\}$, $_2\mathcal{T}_{\mathcal{I}_2} = \{(\mathcal{S}_{1,\mathcal{I}_2}, \mathcal{S}_{3,\mathcal{I}_2})\}$, and $_3\mathcal{T}_{\mathcal{I}_2} = \{(\mathcal{S}_{1,\mathcal{I}_2}, \mathcal{S}_{2,\mathcal{I}_2})\}$, each containing the r most likely pairs, the measure of which is calculated similar to the formula (12). Due to the intersection

$$\mathcal{S}_{i,\mathcal{I}_1} \times \mathcal{S}_{i,\mathcal{I}_2} = \begin{cases} \mathcal{S}_{i,\mathcal{I}_1 \cup \mathcal{I}_2}, & \text{if the end of } \mathcal{S}_{i,\mathcal{I}_1} \text{ corresponds to the beginning of } \mathcal{S}_{i,\mathcal{I}_2} \\ \emptyset, & \text{otherwise} \end{cases}$$

the intersection of these two sets is

$$_3\mathcal{T}_{\mathcal{I}_1 \cup \mathcal{I}_2} = {_3\mathcal{T}_{\mathcal{I}_1}} \cap {_3\mathcal{T}_{\mathcal{I}_2}} = \left\{ (\mathcal{S}_{1,\mathcal{I}_1 \cup \mathcal{I}_2}, \mathcal{S}_{2,\mathcal{I}_1 \cup \mathcal{I}_2}) : \begin{cases} (\mathcal{S}_{1,\mathcal{I}_1}, \mathcal{S}_{2,\mathcal{I}_1}) \in {_3\mathcal{T}_{\mathcal{I}_1}} \\ (\mathcal{S}_{1,\mathcal{I}_2}, \mathcal{S}_{2,\mathcal{I}_2}) \in {_3\mathcal{T}_{\mathcal{I}_2}} \\ \mathcal{S}_{1,\mathcal{I}_1} \times \mathcal{S}_{1,\mathcal{I}_2} \neq \emptyset \\ \mathcal{S}_{2,\mathcal{I}_1} \times \mathcal{S}_{2,\mathcal{I}_2} \neq \emptyset \end{cases} \right\}.$$

The larger the intersection of the intervals $\mathcal{I}_1$ and $\mathcal{I}_2$, the smaller the intersection set, i.e. $|_3\mathcal{T}_{\mathcal{I}_1 \cup \mathcal{I}_2}| \ll |_3\mathcal{T}_{\mathcal{I}_1}| \cdot |_3\mathcal{T}_{\mathcal{I}_2}| = r^2$. Let us call this type of intersections as *horizontal* intersection. Similar horizontal intersections are $_1\mathcal{T}_{\mathcal{I}_1 \cup \mathcal{I}_2}$ and $_2\mathcal{T}_{\mathcal{I}_1 \cup \mathcal{I}_2}$.

By *vertical* intersection we call the intersections of the form:

$$_{1,2}\mathcal{T}_{\mathcal{I}_i} = {_1\mathcal{T}_{\mathcal{I}_i}} \cap {_2\mathcal{T}_{\mathcal{I}_i}} = \left\{ (\mathcal{S}_{1,\mathcal{I}_i}, \mathcal{S}_{2,\mathcal{I}_i}, \mathcal{S}_{3,\mathcal{I}_i}) : \begin{cases} (\mathcal{S}_{2,\mathcal{I}_i}, \mathcal{S}_{3,\mathcal{I}_i}) \in {_1\mathcal{T}_{\mathcal{I}_i}} \\ (\mathcal{S}_{1,\mathcal{I}_i}, \mathcal{S}_{3,\mathcal{I}_i}) \in {_2\mathcal{T}_{\mathcal{I}_i}} \end{cases} \right\},$$

and $_{2,3}\mathcal{T}_{\mathcal{I}_i}$, $_{1,3}\mathcal{T}_{\mathcal{I}_i}$ are defined in a similar way. One more *triple vertical* intersection is defined as

$$_{1,2,3}\mathcal{T}_{\mathcal{I}_i} = {_1\mathcal{T}_{\mathcal{I}_i}} \cap {_2\mathcal{T}_{\mathcal{I}_i}} \cap {_3\mathcal{T}_{\mathcal{I}_i}} = \left\{ (\mathcal{S}_{1,\mathcal{I}_i}, \mathcal{S}_{2,\mathcal{I}_i}, \mathcal{S}_{3,\mathcal{I}_i}) : \begin{cases} (\mathcal{S}_{2,\mathcal{I}_i}, \mathcal{S}_{3,\mathcal{I}_i}) \in {_1\mathcal{T}_{\mathcal{I}_i}} \\ (\mathcal{S}_{1,\mathcal{I}_i}, \mathcal{S}_{3,\mathcal{I}_i}) \in {_2\mathcal{T}_{\mathcal{I}_i}} \\ (\mathcal{S}_{1,\mathcal{I}_i}, \mathcal{S}_{2,\mathcal{I}_i}) \in {_3\mathcal{T}_{\mathcal{I}_i}} \end{cases} \right\}.$$

4.3   Design of Intervals

Let us take one interval $\mathcal{I}_1' = [87 \ldots 97]$. Two extreme situations are when $(l_1, l_2) = (87, 87)$ and $(l_1, l_2) = (97, 97)$. In each frame j there are only 228 bits are accessible $v^j(101), \ldots, v^j(100 + 228)$. In Figure 2 we see that the probability $\Pr\{(l_1, l_2) \text{ at time } t\}$ for this interval gets its maximum value on around

$t \approx (116 \dots 129)$. Hence, the bits around $v(116) \dots v(129)$ give us the most information about the d-dimension vectors, when $l_1, l_2 \in \mathcal{I}_1$. We can also say that for this interval the informative bits are around $v(105) \dots v(145)$, because for any other v's the probability is almost 0.

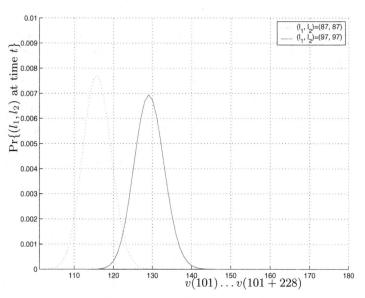

Fig. 2. The density of $\Pr\{(l_1, l_2)$ at time $t\}$ when $(l_1, l_2) = (87, 87)$ and $(l_1, l_2) = (97, 97)$

Let us now consider three more intervals $\mathcal{I}'_2 = [63 \dots 73]$, $\mathcal{I}'_3 = [165 \dots 175]$, and $\mathcal{I}'_4 = [231 \dots 241]$. In Figure 3 the bounded densities for each interval are shown. The interval $\mathcal{I}'_2$ is moved to the left below $t < 101$, where the valuable v's are unaccessible for us. It means that this choice is not appropriate. On the other hand, the interval $\mathcal{I}'_4$ is moved to the right and very close to the right border of accessible v's. This interval can be considered as the last appropriate interval. Also note that as the interval is moved to the righ the amplitute decreases, i.e. the error probability of the random variables estimation is higher.

In our simulations we decided to choose the size of each interval to be 11. Independently of the parameter $d \geq 1$ in each table $_3\mathcal{T}_{\mathcal{I}_i}$ we store only the pairs $(\mathcal{S}_{1,\mathcal{I}_i}, \mathcal{S}_{2,\mathcal{I}_i})$ of vectors each of size 12 bits only. The schematical structure of intervals is depicted below in Figure 4.

Two neighbour intervals intersect in 6 positions, whereas the last $d - 1$ positions are assumed to be badly estimated (tail bits). I.e., any horizontal intersection of two tables $_3\mathcal{T}_{\mathcal{I}_i}$ and $_3\mathcal{T}_{\mathcal{I}_{i+1}}$ will be done by 12 bits (6 bits are $s_1(\mathcal{I}_{i+1})$, $\dots$, $s_1(\mathcal{I}_{i+1} + 5)$, and similar 6 bits are $s_2(\mathcal{I}_{i+1})$, $\dots$, $s_2(\mathcal{I}_{i+1} + 5)$). Also note that any vertical intersection will be done in 12 bits also. The choice of this structure of the intervals allowed us to introduce several efficient strategies to intersect the tables.

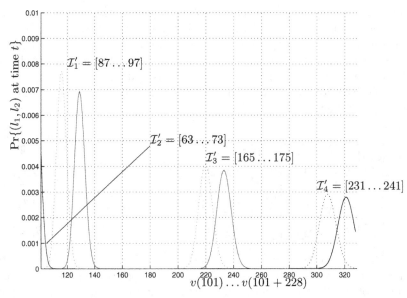

Fig. 3. The bounded densities for $\mathcal{I}'_1 = [87\ldots97]$, $\mathcal{I}'_2 = [63\ldots73]$, $\mathcal{I}'_3 = [165\ldots175]$, and $\mathcal{I}'_4 = [231\ldots241]$

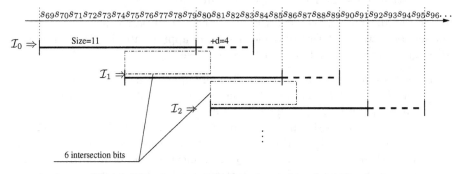

Fig. 4. The structure of intervals used in simulations

Since the size of each interval is 11, it means that the number of distribution tables of $_*\mathcal{S}_{l_i,l_j}$-random variables is $11^2 = 121$. When $d = 4$, the number of variables involved in $_*\mathcal{S}_{l_i,l_j}$'s is $2 \cdot (11 + 4) = 30$. Hence, to create one $_*\mathcal{T}_{\mathcal{I}_i}$-set of the r most likelihood pairs, we need to perform an exhaustive search of size 2^{30}. The number of such sets $_*\mathcal{T}_{\mathcal{I}_i}$ is 9 (3 intervals times 3 cases for '*').

In our simulations we have considered 28 intervals:

$$\begin{cases} \mathcal{I}_0 = [69\ldots79] \\ \mathcal{I}_k = 6 \cdot k + \mathcal{I}_0 \quad \text{for } k = 1, 2, \ldots, 27. \end{cases} \tag{13}$$

So, the last interval is $\mathcal{I}_{27} = [231\ldots241]$ (see also Figure 3). When for a chosen interval $\mathcal{I}_i$ we estimate the probability $\Pr\{_3\mathcal{S}_{l_1,l_2} = (b_0, \ldots, b_{d-1})^T\}$ with the formula (9), then we only need to look through the bits v^j that are valuable for $\mathcal{I}_i$. Let us set the "window" of valuable bits to be of size 64, then, for example, for the interval $\mathcal{I}_1$ on the Figure 3 the "window" is $t_1 = [101 \ldots 164]$, for $\mathcal{I}_3 \Rightarrow t_3 = [203 \ldots 266]$, and for $\mathcal{I}_4 \Rightarrow t_4 = [266 \ldots 329]$. Actually, the "window" can be less, but 64 bits completely cover the most valueable v's for any interval $\mathcal{I}_i$.

The likelihood sets $_*\mathfrak{T}_{\mathcal{I}_i}$, each containing r pairs, can be presented in the following table:

	$\mathcal{I}_0$	$\mathcal{I}_1$		$\ldots$	$\mathcal{I}_{27}$
Case 1	$_1\mathfrak{T}_{\mathcal{I}_0} =$ $(\mathcal{S}_{2,\mathcal{I}_0}, \mathcal{S}_{3,\mathcal{I}_0})$	$_1\mathfrak{T}_{\mathcal{I}_1} =$ $(\mathcal{S}_{2,\mathcal{I}_1}, \mathcal{S}_{3,\mathcal{I}_1})$			$_1\mathfrak{T}_{\mathcal{I}_{27}} =$ $(\mathcal{S}_{2,\mathcal{I}_{27}}, \mathcal{S}_{3,\mathcal{I}_{27}})$
Case 2	$_2\mathfrak{T}_{\mathcal{I}_0} =$ $(\mathcal{S}_{1,\mathcal{I}_0}, \mathcal{S}_{2,\mathcal{I}_0})$	$_2\mathfrak{T}_{\mathcal{I}_1} =$ $(\mathcal{S}_{1,\mathcal{I}_1}, \mathcal{S}_{2,\mathcal{I}_1})$			$_2\mathfrak{T}_{\mathcal{I}_{27}} =$ $(\mathcal{S}_{1,\mathcal{I}_{27}}, \mathcal{S}_{2,\mathcal{I}_{27}})$
Case 3	$_3\mathfrak{T}_{\mathcal{I}_0} =$ $(\mathcal{S}_{1,\mathcal{I}_0}, \mathcal{S}_{2,\mathcal{I}_0})$	$_3\mathfrak{T}_{\mathcal{I}_1} =$ $(\mathcal{S}_{1,\mathcal{I}_1}, \mathcal{S}_{2,\mathcal{I}_1})$			$_3\mathfrak{T}_{\mathcal{I}_{27}} =$ $(\mathcal{S}_{1,\mathcal{I}_{27}}, \mathcal{S}_{2,\mathcal{I}_{27}})$

The time complexity to form these data is $O(3 \cdot 28 \cdot (11^2 \cdot 2^d \cdot m \cdot 64 + 2^{22+2d}))$. This is because there are 84 sets $_*\mathfrak{T}_i$; to create each set requires 11^2 distribution tables of size 2^d; to calculate each value in the table requires $m \cdot 64$ operations; and the exhaustive search complexity for each set is 2^{22+2d}.

4.4   Strategies for Intersection of the Tables $_*\mathfrak{T}_{\mathcal{I}_i}$

When the first part of the attack is done, the second part is just intersection of the sets until we get the set of triples $_{1,2,3}\mathfrak{T}_*$ of appropriate size. Here are several strategies that we can follow to achieve our goal:

I. *Intersection of 9 tables, large r.* Try all triples of intervals $(\mathcal{I}_k, \mathcal{I}_{k+1}, \mathcal{I}_{k+2})$, for $k = 0, 1, \ldots, 25$. The intersection of 9 tables gives us the table $_{1,2,3}\mathfrak{T}_{\mathcal{I}_k \cup \mathcal{I}_{k+1} \cup \mathcal{I}_{k+2}}$ of triples $(\mathcal{S}_{1,\mathcal{I}_k \cup \mathcal{I}_{k+1} \cup \mathcal{I}_{k+2}}, \mathcal{S}_{2,\mathcal{I}_k \cup \mathcal{I}_{k+1} \cup \mathcal{I}_{k+2}}, \mathcal{S}_{3,\mathcal{I}_k \cup \mathcal{I}_{k+1} \cup \mathcal{I}_{k+2}})$. Each $\mathcal{S}$ contains 24 bits, but we need only 19, 22, and 23 bits for LFSR-1, LFSR-2, and LFSR-3, respectively. We can do first vertical intersections and get $_{1,2,3}\mathfrak{T}_{\mathcal{I}_i}$, and then perform horizontal intersection. Since any of the intersections is done by 12 bits, the number of the most likely pairs in $_*\mathfrak{T}_{\mathcal{I}_i}$ can be quite large. For this strategy we can safely use $r \approx 50000$;

II. *Intersection of 6 tables, medium r.* The same as Strategy I, but for each interval one table is discarded. We just assume that the discarded tables do not contain the correct pairs. Then perform the intersection of the remaining 6 tables. The number of assumptions is 3^3. The parameter r is about $r \approx 30000$.

III. *Intersection of 4 tables, small r.* Try all pairs of intervals $(\mathcal{I}_k, \mathcal{I}_{k+2})$, for all $k = 0, 1, \ldots, 25$. We assume also that one of the tables $_*\mathfrak{T}_{\mathcal{I}_k}$ and one of $_*\mathfrak{T}_{\mathcal{I}_{k+2}}$ do not contain the correct pair. The number of assumptions is 3^2. For the remaining 4 tables we perform the intersection. Note, there is no horizontal intersection, but only 2 vertical intersections, one for $\mathcal{I}_k$ and one for $\mathcal{I}_{k+2}$. Due to this the critical value for the parameter r is about

$r \approx 10000$. The appropriate choice of the intersection scheme made this strategy work.

IV. *Intersection of 4 tables, small r, version 2.* The same as Strategy III, but the pairs of intervals $(\mathcal{I}_{k_1}, \mathcal{I}_{k_2})$ can be so that $k_1 = 0, 1, \ldots, 25$, and $k_2 = k_1 + 2, \ldots, 28$. Unfortunately, it can happen that *some* outputs from LFSR's in the second interval $\mathcal{I}_{k_2}$ will be a linear combination of $s(l)$'s from $\mathcal{I}_{k_1}$. For LFSR-1, the size of which is 19, it is not very critical because we achieve 24 bits of information. It means that even if 5 bits will depend on others, we still have a full rank in translation from $s(l)$'s to 19 bits of the key K. It is more critical for LFSR-3, which is of length 23. Anyway, if the system will not be of full rank, then some bits we can just guess. That makes this strategy work in general (implementation is then more complicated).

V. *Heuristic procedure, r is dynamic.* Can be introduced in the following way: If in some step for some intersection $\mathcal{T}' \cap \mathcal{T}''$ we get $\emptyset$, or a very small set, then increase the value r for $\mathcal{T}'$ and $\mathcal{T}''$ selectively, until their intersection give us a set of size at least r_0, for some threshold value. Thus, we can start creating the sets $_*\mathcal{T}_{\mathcal{I}_i}$ with a small value of r, and then increase it selectively, when necessary.

So, here is a wide choice to choose a strategy. In our simulations we have tried several of them.

5   Simulation Results

The attack can basically be divided into three steps,

1) Statistical analysis of m frames,
2) Decoding process and generating the tables $_*\mathcal{T}_{\mathcal{I}_i}$,
3) Intersection of the tables and check estimated keys $\hat{K}$.

For the first two steps we present the actual time. The attack was implemented on Pentium-4, CPU 2.4GHz, 256Mb RAM, OS Windows XP Pro SP1.

1st step/ 2nd step	m=2000	m=5000	m=10000
d=1	11 sec/ 18 sec	26 sec / 18 sec	58 sec / 18 sec
d=2	14 sec/ 8 min	32 sec / 8 min	72 sec / 8 min
d=4	40 sec/ 7 hrs	94 sec / 7 hrs	190 sec / 7 hrs

The measure of "goodness" of the attack can be expressed in terms of the number of frames m needed and its success rate. The attack was successfully implemented on a usual PC-computer, and it performs the attack from several seconds to several minutes, depending on the choice of strategy, and parameters m, d, and r.

Success rate of the attack depends on the choice of the design parameters d and r, and the strategy that is used. For some values of m and d here we present in Figure 5 the plots for the probabilities:

$$\Pr\{ \text{ the correct vector } is \ in \ _*\mathcal{T}_{\mathcal{I}_i}, \text{ for given parameter } r\}.$$

When the tables are constructed, in the intersection process it is very important that the correct pair is present in the corresponding table. Otherwise, the intersection will never give us a correct key.

In Figure 5 we show the real estimated success rates for different strategies, with different number of frames m and the attack design parameter d. In Figure 5 (upper left) consider the curve corresponding to $d = 1$ and to Strategy I, when $m = 10000$ frames. For $r = 15000$ we have the success rate of the attack around 58%, whereas for Strategies II-IV the success rate is almost 100%.

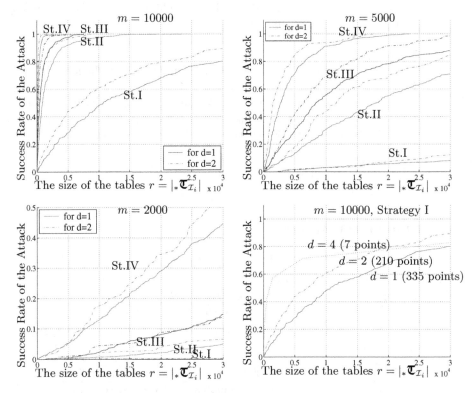

Fig. 5. Strategies comparison for $m = 10000$ (top left), $m = 5000$ (top right), and $m = 2000$ (down left). The effect of d on the success rate on the example when $m = 10000$ and Strategy I is applied (down right)

From the plots below the Strategy IV looks the most attractive. In this strategy we need to intersect only 4 tables, but the disadvantage is that there is no horizontal intersection. And then after two vertical intersections we need to try all possible combinations of elements in two tables. One more disadvantage is that we could get some equation dependencies between two intervals, so then the actual time complexity will grow. On the contrary, strategy III looks the next the most attractive, and there are no problems with intervals. Since there are no horizontal intersections in these strategies, this forces us to reduce the parameter r significantly. The critical value of this parameter is $r_{cr} = 10000$, and the optimal is $r_{opt} = 2000$ from the computational and memory points of view. Strategy II avoids such problems mostly because of the presence of vertical intersections, which are intersecting on 12 bits.

A practical solution to overcome the time-memory problems related to intersections of the tables can be the use of the Heuristic Strategy V, combined with one of the previous strategies. The idea of Heuristic is to control the size of the intersection. If the size is likely to be increased by some threshold criteria, then try to increase the initial parameter r until the limit is reached, or solution is found. Heuristic can also control the size of the tables independently, and this will give the best performance of the attack.

Dramatic advantage of use the proper design parameter d is seen in the same Figure 5. To make the advantage clearer, the bottom right subplot shows how much we gain when d is 1, 2, and 4. When $r = 15000$, the change of the parameter d from $d = 1$ to $d = 2$ significantly increases the success rate from 58% to 70%. These simulations were done for $m = 10000$ frames, and with the application of Strategy I.

Finally, we show the advantage of our attack in comparison with the previous Ekdahl-Johansson attack in the following two tables:

Success Rate/	Ekdahl-Johansson Attack (2002)		
(Time of the Attack)	Number of Frames/(time of GSM conversation in min/sec)		
Configuration	30000	50000	70000
	(2m30s)	(3m45s)	(5m20s)
3 Intervals of size 7	0.02/(1min)	0.13/(2min)	0.49/(3min)
3 Intervals of size 8	0.02/(2min)	0.20/(3min)	0.57/(4min)
2 Intervals of size 9	0.03/(3min)	0.33/(4min)	0.76/(5min)

Success Rate/	Our Proposed Attack		
(Time of the Attack)	Number of Frames/(time of GSM conversation in min/sec)		
Configuration	2000	5000	10000
	(9sec)	(43sec)	(46sec)
St.I, d=2, r=10K	0.01/(8min)	0.05/(8min)	0.60/(8min)
St.II, d=1, r=5K	0.01/(29sec)	0.15/(44sec)	0.93/(76sec)
St.III, d=2, r=5K	0.02/(8min)	0.40/(8min)	0.99/(8min)
St.IV, d=2, r=5K	0.05/(10min)	0.85/(10min)	0.9999(10min)

6   Conclusions

We have demonstrated how two new ideas provide improved performance for a correlation attack against A5/1. In simulation we get a high success rate for only 2000-5000 frames, using very little computation. But there is still deviation in performance depending on the strategies we choose, which means that there may very well be further improvements to come if we can find the best attack strategies. Another interesting topic is to examine how small m can be made if we allow a substantial increase in attack complexity. If m can be decreased a bit further, ciphertext only attack may be practically possible, as discussed briefly in the introduction of the paper.

Acknowledgments

We thank Eli Biham for his useful comments on the paper.

References

1. M. Briceno, I. Goldberg, and D. Wagner. A pedagogical implementation of A5/1. Available at http://jya.com/a51-pi.htm, Accessed August 18, 2003, 1999.
2. J.D. Golić. Cryptanalysis of alleged A5 stream cipher. In W. Fumy, editor, *Advances in Cryptology—EUROCRYPT'97*, volume 1233 of *Lecture Notes in Computer Science*, pages 239–255. Springer-Verlag, 1997.
3. A. Biryukov, A. Shamir, and D. Wagner. Real time cryptanalysis of A5/1 on a PC. In B. Schneier, editor, *Fast Software Encryption 2000*, volume 1978 of *Lecture Notes in Computer Science*, pages 1–13. Springer-Verlag, 2000.
4. E. Biham and O. Dunkelman. Cryptanalysis of the A5/1 GSM stream cipher. In B. E. Roy and E. Okamoto, editors, *Progress in Cryptology—INDOCRYPT 2000*, volume 1977 of *Lecture Notes in Computer Science*, pages 43–51. Springer-Verlag, 2000.
5. M. Krause. BDD-based cryptanalysis of keystream generators. In L.R. Knudsen, editor, *Advances in Cryptology—EUROCRYPT 2002*, volume 2332 of *Lecture Notes in Computer Science*, pages 222–237. Springer-Verlag, 2002.
6. P. Ekdahl and T. Johansson. Another attack on A5/1. In *Proceedings of International Symposium on Information Theory*, page 160. IEEE, 2001.
7. E. Barkan, E. Biham, and N. Keller. Instant ciphertext only cryptanalysis of GSM encrypted communication. In D. Boneh, editor, *Advances in Cryptology—CRYPTO 2003*, volume 2729 of *Lecture Notes in Computer Science*, pages 600–616. Springer-Verlag, 2003.
8. ETSI EN 300 963 v8.0.1 (2000-11) Standard. Digital cellular telecommunications system (Phase 2+) (GSM); Full rate speech; Comfort noise aspect for full rate speech traffic channels (GSM 06.12 version 8.0.1 Release 1999), 2000.

---

[0] The work described in this paper has been supported in part by Grant VR 621-2001-2149, in part by the Graduate School in Personal Computing and Communication PCC++, and in part by the European Commission through the IST Program under Contract IST-2002-507932 ECRYPT.

The information in this document reflects only the author's views, is provided as is and no guarantee or warranty is given that the information is fit for any particular purpose. The user thereof uses the information at its sole risk and liability.

Extending the Resynchronization Attack[*]

Frederik Armknecht[1,**], Joseph Lano[2,***], and Bart Preneel[2]

[1] Universität Mannheim, Theoretische Informatik,
68131 Mannheim, Germany
armknecht@th.informatik.uni-mannheim.de
[2] Katholieke Universiteit Leuven,
Dept. Elect. Eng.-ESAT/SCD-COSIC,
Kasteelpark Arenberg 10, 3001 Heverlee, Belgium
{joseph.lano, bart.preneel}@esat.kuleuven.ac.be

Abstract. Synchronous stream ciphers need perfect synchronization between sender and receiver. In practice, this is ensured by a resync mechanism. Daemen et al. [10] first described attacks on ciphers using such a resync mechanism. In this paper, we extend their attacks in several ways by combining the standard attack with cryptanalytic techniques such as algebraic attacks and linear cryptanalysis. Our results show that using linear resync mechanisms should be avoided, and provide lower bounds for the nonlinearity required from a secure resync mechanism.

1 Introduction

Synchronous stream ciphers generate a key stream independently from the plaintext. They typically consist of a finite state machine from which at each iteration a key stream bit is generated by an output function. Synchronous stream ciphers have the advantage that there is no error propagation. On the other hand, perfect synchronization between sender and receiver is required. In order to prevent synchronization loss or to restore synchronization after synchronization loss is detected, a resynchronization mechanism is used. Such a mechanism generates a new initial state for the finite state machine from the secret key and a unique initialization vector IV and thus prevents the reuse of key stream. For the sake of efficiency the resynchronization mechanism should be as fast as possible.

Daemen, Govaerts and Vandewalle [10] observed that this resynchronization mechanism can lead to a new type of attacks on synchronous stream ciphers. They also showed an efficient attack on nonlinearly filtered systems using a linear resynchronization mechanism and using an output Boolean function with few

* This work was supported by the Concerted Research Action (GOA) Mefisto-2000/04 of the Flemish Government.
** This work has been supported by grant 620307 of the DFG (German Research Foundation).
*** Research financed by a Ph.D. grant of the Institute for the Promotion of Innovation through Science and Technology in Flanders (IWT-Vlaanderen).

H. Handschuh and A. Hasan (Eds.): SAC 2004, LNCS 3357, pp. 19–38, 2005.
© Springer-Verlag Berlin Heidelberg 2005

inputs. Golic and Morgari [13] extended this attack to the case where the output function is unknown. Borissov et al. [7] showed that a ciphertext-only attack is also possible in some cases.

In this paper, we extend the resynchronization attack to overcome some limitations of the original attack of Daemen *et al.* We achieve this by further refining the original resynchronization attack and by combining the attack with other attack methodologies, notably with algebraic attacks. We do not show practical applications of our attacks in this article, but describe such attacks on $E0$, $A5$ and the summation generator in the extended version of our paper [2].

The paper is organized as follows. In Sect. 2, we present some preliminary notions: Boolean functions, the general framework of a stream cipher, algebraic attacks and resynchronization attacks. In Sect. 3 we present the Daemen *et al.* attack and its limitations. In Sect. 4 we show how to perform the Daemen *et al.* attack in real-time by precomputation. In Sect. 5 we describe several methods to mount a resync attack when the number of resyncs is small. Section 6 describes methods to mount attacks when the output function has many inputs. In Sect. 7, we describe attacks on stream ciphers with memory and in Sect. 8 we discuss attacks on stream ciphers with nonlinear resynchronization mechanism. We conclude in Sect. 9.

2   Preliminaries

2.1   Boolean Functions and Related Inputs

In this section we repeat some definitions and known facts about Boolean functions. Additionally, we provide some theorems about Boolean functions and related inputs. All calculations are done over the finite field $GF(2)$.

Definition 1. *For* $\alpha = (\alpha_1, \ldots, \alpha_n)$ *and* $x = (x_1, \ldots, x_n) \in \{0,1\}^n$, *we define* $m_\alpha(x) := \prod_i x_i^{\alpha_i}$ *and the degree* $\deg m_\alpha := |\alpha| := \#\{i | \alpha_i = 1\}$.

Theorem 2. *(Algebraic Normal Form) Let* $f : \{0,1\}^n \rightarrow \{0,1\}$ *be a Boolean function. Then,* $f(x)$ *can be written as* $f(x) = \bigoplus_{\alpha \in \{0,1\}^n} c_\alpha \cdot m_\alpha(x)$ *for unique coefficients* $c_\alpha \in \{0,1\}$. *Hence, the value* $\max\{\deg m_\alpha | c_\alpha \neq 0\}$ *is unique and is called the degree* $\deg f$ *of* f.

Definition 3. *For* $\alpha = (\alpha_1, \ldots, \alpha_n), \alpha' = (\alpha'_1, \ldots, \alpha'_n) \in \{0,1\}^n$ *we say that* $\alpha' \leq \alpha$ *if* $\forall i : \alpha'_i \leq \alpha_i$ *(treated as integers). Consequently, we say that* $\alpha' < \alpha$ *if* $\alpha' \leq \alpha$ *but* $\alpha' \neq \alpha$. *For* $\alpha' \leq \alpha$ *we define* $\alpha - \alpha' := (\alpha_1 - \alpha'_1, \ldots, \alpha_n - \alpha'_n)$.

Obviously, $\alpha' \leq \alpha$ (resp. $\alpha' < \alpha$) implies $\deg m_{\alpha'} \leq \deg m_\alpha$ (resp. $\deg m_{\alpha'} < \deg m_\alpha$).

Lemma 4. *Let* $\alpha, \delta^{(1)}, \delta^{(2)} \in \{0,1\}^n$ *be arbitrary. For* $i = 1, 2$ *it holds that* $m_\alpha(x \oplus \delta^{(i)}) = \bigoplus_{\alpha' \leq \alpha} m_{\alpha'}(x) m_{\alpha - \alpha'}(\delta^{(i)})$ *and* $m_\alpha(x \oplus \delta^{(1)}) \oplus m_\alpha(x \oplus \delta^{(2)})$ *has a degree* $\leq \deg m_\alpha - 1$.

Proof. The first equation is obvious. The second one is because of:

$$m_\alpha(x + \delta^{(1)}) + m_\alpha(x + \delta^{(2)})$$
$$= \sum_{\alpha' \leq \alpha} \left(m_{\alpha'}(x) m_{\alpha - \alpha'}(\delta^{(1)}) + m_{\alpha'}(x) m_{\alpha - \alpha'}(\delta^{(2)}) \right)$$
$$= \underbrace{m_\alpha(x) + m_\alpha(x)}_{=0} + \sum_{\alpha' < \alpha} \left(m_{\alpha'}(x) m_{\alpha - \alpha'}(\delta^{(1)}) + m_{\alpha'}(x) m_{\alpha - \alpha'}(\delta^{(2)}) \right) . \qquad \square$$

Theorem 5. *Let f be a Boolean function with $\deg f = d$. Then, $f(x \oplus \delta^{(1)}) \oplus f(x \oplus \delta^{(2)})$ has a degree $\leq d - 1$.*

Proof. By Theorem 2 we can write $f(x)$ as $\sum_{\alpha, |\alpha| \leq d} c_\alpha m_\alpha(x)$. Then, by lemma 4 it is $f(x \oplus \delta^{(1)}) \oplus f(x \oplus \delta^{(2)}) = \bigoplus_{\alpha, |\alpha| \leq d} c_\alpha \underbrace{\left(m_\alpha(x \oplus \delta^{(1)}) \oplus m_\alpha(x \oplus \delta^{(2)}) \right)}_{\deg \leq d-1}. \quad \square$

The following corollary is obvious:

Corollary 6. *For any even number m and any vectors $\delta^{(1)}, \ldots, \delta^{(m)}$, the degree of the function $\bigoplus_{i=1}^m f(x \oplus \delta^{(i)})$ is $\leq \deg f - 1$.*

Theorem 7 is a special case of theorem 5 and will be of use in this paper:

Theorem 7. *Let f be a Boolean function with $\deg f = d$. Let $e_i \in \{0,1\}^n$ be the unit vector with its only 1 in position i. Then the function $f_1(x') = f(x) \oplus f(x \oplus e_i)$ has degree $\leq d - 1$, where $x' = (x_1, \ldots, x_{i-1}, x_{i+1}, \ldots, x_n) \in \{0,1\}^{n-1}$.*

Proof. We first split the function $f(x)$ into two parts, the first part consisting of the monomials containing x_i, and the second part consisting of the monomials not containing x_i as a factor:

$$f(x) = x_i \cdot f_1(x') \oplus f_2(x'), \qquad (1)$$

where it is straightforward to see that $\deg f_1 \leq d - 1$ and $\deg f_2 \leq d$. We do the same for the function $f(x \oplus e_i)$:

$$f(x \oplus e_i) = (x_i \oplus 1) \cdot f_1(x') \oplus f_2(x'). \qquad (2)$$

Taking the XOR of the equations (1) and (2) and eliminating terms occurring twice yields: $f(x) \oplus f(x \oplus e_i) = f_1(x')$. $\qquad \square$

2.2   General Framework for Synchronous Stream Ciphers

We consider a synchronous stream cipher with n-bit state S updated by a linear function represented by a matrix L (*e.g.*, one or more LFSRs) over $\mathbb{Z}_2$, and with a nonlinear output function f that takes φ input bits coming from S to produce one output bit z_t. Some designs (*e.g.*, the combiners with memory) also include a m-bit memory M that has a nonlinear update function h. This results in the following general framework for a synchronous stream cipher:

$$\begin{cases} z_t = f(S_t, M_t) \\ c_t = p_t \oplus z_t \\ S_{t+1} = L \cdot S_t \\ M_{t+1} = h(S_t, M_t), \end{cases} \qquad (3)$$

where p_t, z_t and c_t are respectively the plaintext, the key stream and the ciphertext at time $t = 0, 1, 2 \ldots$

The initial state (S_0, M_0) is determined by the resynchronization mechanism, which combines a k-bit secret key K and a ι-bit known initialization vector IV^i with an initialization function f_{init}, i.e., $(S_0, M_0) = f_{init}(K, IV^i)$.

2.3   Algebraic Attacks

In this section we repeat some facts about algebraic attacks against LFSR-based key stream generators. We describe the general attack on combiners with memory introduced in [3] as this includes the special case of memoryless combiners [8].

An algebraic attack works as follows: first find a Boolean function $F \not\equiv 0$ (called an ad-hoc equation) such that for all t

$$0 = F(L^t \cdot K, \ldots, L^{t+r-1} \cdot K, z_t, \ldots, z_{t+r-1}). \tag{4}$$

Such a function F can be found with the algorithm of [3] if $\varphi \cdot r$ is not too large.

Secondly, recover the secret key K by solving this system of equations. For this purpose, several methods (Linearization, XL, XSL, Groebner bases algorithms such as F4 and F5,...) exist. Amongst them only the linearization method allows a general estimation of the work effort. We give now a description of the linearization method. Due to the linearity of L, all equations (4) have degree $\leq d := \deg F$. Therefore, the number $\mathcal{M}$ of different monomials occurring is upper bounded by $\beta(k, d) := \binom{k}{0} + \ldots + \binom{k}{d}$.

By replacing each monomial by a new variable, the attacker gets a linear system of equations in $\mathcal{M}$ unknowns. It can be solved by Gaussian elimination or more refined methods like the one by Strassen [27]. As $\beta(k, d) \in O(k^d)$, the lower the degree d, the faster the attack.

2.4   Resynchronization Attacks

For a synchronous stream cipher, perfect synchronization between sender and receiver is required. The aim of the resynchronization mechanism is to achieve this in a secure fashion.

A first solution is *fixed resync*. In this scenario, the message is divided into frames, and each frame i is encrypted with a unique IV^i, a frame counter updated in a deterministic way. An attack under this scenario is called a *known IV resynchronization attack*. The frequency at which resynchronization should occur depends on the risk of synchronization loss. Examples of stream ciphers that use fixed resync are the $E0$ algorithm used in the Bluetooth [6] wireless communication standard, and A5 [1] used in GSM cellular voice and data communication.

A second scenario is that the receiver sends a resynchronization request to the sender as soon as synchronization loss is detected. This is called *requested resync*. In this scenario, the receiver may be allowed to choose the nonce IV^i used in the frame. This may enable a *chosen IV resynchronization attack*, as described e.g. by Joux and Muller [16]. Security under the chosen IV attack scenario implies security under the known IV attack scenario. Hence, a good resynchronization mechanism should be resistant against a chosen IV attack.

We now describe a first resynchronization attack by Daemen et $al.$ [10] on a simplified version of this framework and point out its limitations.

3   The Daemen et $al.$ Resynchronization Attack

3.1   Description

The resynchronization attack of Daemen et $al.$ is a known plaintext attack for the special case of a simple memoryless combiner with a linear resynchronization mechanism.

The framework of the attack can be described as follows:

$$\begin{cases} S_0^i = A \cdot K \oplus B \cdot IV^i \\ z_t^i = f(\varPi \cdot S_t^i) \\ S_{t+1}^i = L \cdot S_t^i . \end{cases} \tag{5}$$

In these equations, A, B, L and $\varPi$ are known binary matrices, $A \in \mathbb{Z}_2^{n \times k}$, $B \in \mathbb{Z}_2^{n \times \ell}$, $L \in \mathbb{Z}_2^{n \times n}$ and $\varPi \in \mathbb{Z}_2^{\varphi \times n}$. The matrices A and B represent the fact that the resync mechanism is linear, the projection matrix $\varPi$ shows that the output function f uses only a subset of φ bits of S_t^i. The initialization vector of the ith frame is IV^i, and z_t^i is the key stream bit at time t of the ith frame.

We introduce the key-dependent unknown values κ_t and the known values IV_t^i as follows:

$$\begin{cases} \kappa_t = \varPi \cdot L^t \cdot A \cdot K \\ \mathrm{IV}_t^i = \varPi \cdot L^t \cdot B \cdot IV^i . \end{cases} \tag{6}$$

The attacker can set up a system of equations built as follows:

$$z_t^i = f(\kappa_t \oplus \mathrm{IV}_t^i) \quad \text{for } 0 \le i \le R-1,\ 0 \le t \le T-1 , \tag{7}$$

where R is the number of resynchronizations and T is the number of key stream bits we know in each frame. We try to find a solution of this system of equations for each t. Assume without loss of generality that $t = 0$. If φ is not too large, we can perform an exhaustive search over κ_0, and check whether the guess satisfies the R equations for $t = 0$. If $R \ge \varphi$, it is expected that a unique solution for κ_0 exists. Hence the correct value of κ_0 has been found, and thus φ linear equations in the bits of the secret key. This is repeated for $t = 1, 2, ..., p-1$, such that $p = \lceil k/\varphi \rceil$, until the entire secret key is deduced.

The complete attack requires on average $\lceil k/\varphi \rceil \cdot 2^\varphi$ evaluations of the function f, at least φ resyncs and about k bits of key stream in total (φ frames of length $\lceil k/\varphi \rceil$). Note that the computational complexity of the attack increases exponentially with the number φ of inputs of the Boolean function f.

3.2   Limitations

The Daemen et $al.$ attack can be seen as a divide-and-conquer attack. Standard cryptanalytic attacks such as correlation and algebraic attacks work chronologically on a key stream, which corresponds to the output of one frame. On the contrary, the Daemen *et al.* attack tries to solve the system by working on one specific time over all frames. One of the motivations of the paper is to combine both approaches. Of special interest is the combination of the resynchronization attack with algebraic attacks.

In many cases, it is not obvious whether the approach by Daemen *et al.* works or not. We have identified the following limitations:

1. The attack does not work in real time.
2. The number of resyncs R has to be at least the number φ of input bits of the output function f.
3. The complexity is prohibitively large for large values of φ.
4. The divide-and-conquer approach does not work if the key stream generator uses additional memory.
5. The initialization function f_{init} has to be linear.

In this paper, we will address each of these limitations and show how to overcome them.

4   Real-Time Attack

The attack of Daemen *et al.* shows that ciphers that use a linear resynchronization mechanism and that have a Boolean function f with few inputs are insecure. This enables a passive attack on such designs. A real-time attack in which the attacker can discover the plaintext immediately (and even modify it in a controlled way) is not possible, because the time required to perform the p exhaustive searches will be too high. Here we show how to easily replace this iterated exhaustive search by a precomputation step. This enables real-time active attacks on such ciphers.

We start from the realistic assumption that the IV^is are chosen in a deterministic way, for instance by a counter or a fixed update mechanism. In the precomputation step, we first calculate the values IV_t^i for $0 \leq i \leq \varphi - 1$ and $0 \leq t \leq T - 1$. Then we calculate the following φ bits, and repeat this for all values of G_t (a guess for K_t) going from 0 to $2^\varphi - 1$, and this for all t.

$$\begin{cases} f(\mathrm{G}_t \oplus \mathrm{IV}_t^0) = b_{\mathrm{G}_t,t}^0 \\ f(\mathrm{G}_t \oplus \mathrm{IV}_t^1) = b_{\mathrm{G}_t,t}^1 \\ ... \\ f(\mathrm{G}_t \oplus \mathrm{IV}_t^{\varphi-1}) = b_{\mathrm{G}_t,t}^{\varphi-1} . \end{cases} \tag{8}$$

For each time t, we obtain 2^φ sequences $b_{\mathrm{G}_t,t}^0 b_{\mathrm{G}_t,t}^1 \dots b_{\mathrm{G}_t,t}^{\varphi-1}$. Because the length of these sequences is φ, every value of G_t is expected to correspond with a unique sequence $b_{\mathrm{G}_t,t}^0 b_{\mathrm{G}_t,t}^1 \dots b_{\mathrm{G}_t,t}^{\varphi-1}$. We then sort the G_t values based on the numerical value of the corresponding sequence, and store this in memory.

The attack now goes as follows. We group the outputs observed at say $t = 0$ in a sequence $z_0^0 z_0^1 ... z_0^{\varphi-1}$. We jump to this position in our table built for $t = 0$, and the value found there is the correct value of K_0. We do the same for the times $t = 1, 2, ...p - 1$, and we have then found the necessary K_i to directly determine the secret key K.

The total complexity of the precomputation step is about $k \cdot 2^\varphi$ evaluations of f (but this can of course be replaced by 2^φ evaluations of f and $k \cdot 2^\varphi$ table look-ups). The memory requirement is about $k \cdot 2^\varphi$ bits, which is feasible for many stream ciphers (*e.g.*, for a secret key of $k = 256$ bits, and a Boolean function with $\varphi = 20$ inputs, 32 Mbyte is required).

5   Attack with a Small Number of Resynchronizations

In [10], the authors made the assumption that the number of solutions converges to 1 if $R \gtrsim \varphi$. Actually, the number of required resyncs depends on the cipher and the observed public parameters IV^i. In [15], Golic and Morgari discussed the number of IVs that are needed for the Daemen *et al.* attack to work. They showed that with a non-negligible probability more than φ known IVs are necessary. This results in an increased attack complexity, both for the original attack and for the precomputation attack.

We will here follow different approaches. We want the attacks to work in any case and with a minimal number of known IVs. Simulations on various Boolean functions have confirmed that the standard resynchronization attack does not always work in practice with φ IVs. This is due to two reasons, the first being imperfect behavior of the function f. However, this effect is not very important because in most stream ciphers the function f has good statistical properties, which typically include balancedness and high nonlinearity. A second reason is that sometimes collisions occur between two values IV_t^a and IV_t^b where $a \neq b$. We will show several ways to overcome this problem.

5.1   Computational Approach

Two-Phase Attack. We implement the algorithm in two steps. The first step, the resynchronization attack, retains a set of values for each of the $K_0, K_1 \ldots K_{p-1}$. In a second step, we then search through all possible combinations until we have found the correct secret key.

Simulations have shown that for φ (or more) known IVs, the time complexity of the second step is negligible. In other words, the resynchronization attack (extended with the fast search step) is always successful under realistic assumptions with φ known IVs.

Using this two-step algorithm, one can also mount a resynchronization attack with $R < \varphi$ known IVs. The time complexity of the second step can then be shown to be about $2^{(\varphi - R) \cdot \frac{k}{\varphi}}$. Even if this complexity increases exponentially with decreasing R, this shows that a resynchronization attack is still feasible for R smaller than (but close to) φ.

Overlapping Bits. There is also another interesting way to perform a resynchronization attack when $R < \varphi$. Let's take the case $R = \varphi - 1$. For K_t, we will get two possibilities after the exhaustive search. But looking at the bits of these two possibilities $K_{t,1}$ and $K_{t,2}$, about half of these will be equal, and will therefore certainly be the correct values for these bits of κ_t. This implies that we have still found $\varphi/2$ linear equations in K, and we will just need frames that are twice as long as in the standard attack, *i.e.*, have length $T \geq 2k/\varphi$ each. This is still very realistic in most cases. We can develop a similar reasoning for smaller values of R, but the length of the frames and the complexity required increases rapidly: they can be shown to be $2^{2^{\varphi-R}-1} \cdot k/\varphi$ and $2^{2^{\varphi-R}-1} \cdot k/\varphi \cdot 2^{\varphi}$ respectively (see the extended version of this paper [2]).

5.2   Using Algebraic Attacks

The resync scenario implies the following system of equations:

$$z_t^i = f(\kappa_t \oplus \mathrm{IV}_t^i), \quad 0 \leq i \leq R-1,\ 0 \leq t \leq T-1. \tag{9}$$

Hence, another possibility is to try to solve it as a whole instead of working time per time. The linearization method described in Sect. 2.3 requires that the number of linearly independent equations exceeds the number $\mathcal{M}$ of occurring monomials. This requires $T \cdot R \geq \mathcal{M}$. As $\mathcal{M}$ is upper bounded by $\beta(k, d') \in O(k^{d'})$ with $d' = \deg f$, the lower the degree of the equations the faster the attack. In the literature [8, 9, 19, 5], several conditions and methods are described for transforming (9) into a new system of equations

$$g(\kappa_t \oplus \mathrm{IV}_t^i, z_t^i) = 0, \quad 0 \leq i \leq R-1,\ 0 \leq t \leq T-1. \tag{10}$$

with $d := \deg g < \deg f$. Next, we will show how to use the resync setting to decrease the degree of (10) further.

The Degree-d-1 Attack. The first approach is to construct new equations of degree $\leq d - 1$. We express g by

$$g(\kappa_t \oplus \mathrm{IV}_t^i, z_t^i) = \bigoplus_j g_j(\kappa_t \oplus \mathrm{IV}_t^i) \cdot \tilde{g}_j(z_t^i). \tag{11}$$

Observe that the functions g_j and $\tilde{g}_j$ depend only on g and are all known to the attacker. The idea is to find appropriate linear combinations of (11) to reduce the degree. Let $I := \{j \mid \deg g_j = d\}$ and rewrite (11) to

$$g = \underbrace{\bigoplus_{j \in I} g_j \cdot \tilde{g}_j}_{\deg g_j = d} \oplus \underbrace{\bigoplus_{j \notin I} g_j \cdot \tilde{g}_j}_{\deg g_j < d}. \tag{12}$$

Theorem 8 provides a method for decreasing the degree at least by 1:

Theorem 8. *Let g be expressed as described in (11). For any known $\mathrm{IV}_t^0, \ldots, \mathrm{IV}_t^{|I|}$ and corresponding known outputs z_t^i, coefficients $c_0, \ldots, c_{|I|} \in \{0,1\}$ with at least one $c_i \neq 0$ can be computed such that the degree of $\bigoplus_{i=0}^{|I|} c_i \cdot g(\kappa_t \oplus \mathrm{IV}_t^i, z_t^{(i)})$ is $\leq \deg g - 1$.*

Proof. We set $g_j^i := g_j(\kappa_t \oplus \mathrm{IV}_t^i)$ and $\tilde{g}_j^i := \tilde{g}_j(z_t^i) \in \{0,1\}$. With (11), we can write

$$\bigoplus_{i=0}^{|I|} c_i \cdot g(\kappa_t \oplus \mathrm{IV}_t^i, z_t^i) = \bigoplus_{j \in I} \bigoplus_{i=0}^{|I|} c_i \cdot \tilde{g}_j^i \cdot g_j^i \oplus \bigoplus_{j \notin I} \bigoplus_{i=0}^{|I|} c_i \cdot \tilde{g}_j^i \cdot g_j^i.$$

The second part of the right hand side has a degree $\leq d - 1$ by definition of I. The idea is to find coefficients $c_0, \ldots, c_{|I|} \in \{0,1\}$ such that the first part of the right hand side has degree $\leq d - 1$ too. By Corollary 6, it is sufficient that $\sum_{i=0}^{|I|} c_i \cdot \tilde{g}_j^i$ (treated as an integer) is an even number for all $j \in I$.

We show now that it is always possible. For each i we define the vector $\vec{V}_i := \left(\tilde{g}_1^{(i)}, \ldots, \tilde{g}_{|I|}^{(i)}\right) \in \{0,1\}^{|I|}$. Then the assumption above is equivalent to $\bigoplus_i c_i \cdot \vec{V}_i = \vec{0}$. By the theory of linear algebra, the $|I|+1$ vectors of the $|I|$-dimensional vector space $\{0,1\}^{|I|}$ are linearly dependent. Therefore, such coefficients c_i exist. $\square$

Let $\mathcal{M}_e$ be the number of monomials of degree $\leq e$ occurring in (10). The attack complexity is as follows. First we have to calculate (for a fixed clock t) the coefficients c_i. This requires $O(|I|^3)$ operations. Then, the computation of the function of degree $\leq d - 1$ is equivalent to the summation of (several) vectors of size $\mathcal{M}_{d-1}$. The two steps have to be repeated about $\mathcal{M}_{d-1}$ times to get enough linearly independent equations of degree $\leq d-1$. The final step is to use Gaussian elimination to solve the linearized system of equations $\approx (\mathcal{M}_{d-1})^3$. Therefore the overall number of operations is about $\left(|I|^3 + \mathcal{M}_{d-1}\right) \cdot \mathcal{M}_{d-1} + (\mathcal{M}_{d-1})^3$. Because of $\mathcal{M}_e \leq \beta(k, e)$, an upper bound is $\left(|I|^3 + \beta(k, d-1)\right) \cdot \beta(k, d-1) + \beta(k, d-1)^3$. Note that it may happen that $\bigoplus_i c_i \cdot g(\kappa_t \oplus \mathrm{IV}_t^i, z_t^i)$ is equal to zero for some t.[1]

As opposed to fast algebraic attacks [9,4], this approach does not require the highest-degree monomials to be independent of the key stream bits. Moreover, the number of key stream bits required is $\leq \beta(k, d-1) + |I|$ instead of $\leq \beta(k, d)$. On the other hand, fast algebraic attacks benefit from the fact that the most time consuming part can be sourced out in a precomputation step. This is not possible here. Another advantage is that its applicability is independent of the values of IV_t^i and z_t^i and that it does not require φ to be low.

The Degree-e Attack. So far, we concentrated only on decreasing the degree by 1. But clever combinations may reduce the degree even further. In the worst case these combinations may be linear, even if the degree of g is high. This is for example the case for the E_0 key stream generator.[2] We develop now the theory how to compute the lowest possible degree. In the following, we treat κ as φ unknowns.

Definition 9. *We set $S(g) := \{g(\kappa \oplus \mathrm{IV}, z) \mid \mathrm{IV} \in \{0,1\}^\varphi, z \in \{0,1\}\}$ and define by $< g >:=< S(g) >$ the linear span of $S(g)$ (i.e., all possible linear combina-*

---

[1] For example, this cannot be avoided if g is linear. But in this case, the cipher is weak anyhow.

[2] The best before was a system of equations of degree 3 (see [9]).

tions). $<g>$ is a vector space over the finite field GF(2). By $\dim g$ we define the dimension of $<g>$ and by $B(g)$ an arbitrary basis of $<g>$. Further on we set $\mathcal{M}_d(g)$ to be all monomials of degree $\leq d$ which occur in $S(g)$.

From the theory of linear algebra, the following theorem is obvious:

Theorem 10. *A function of degree $\leq e$ exists in $<g>$ only if the vectors in $B(g) \cup \mathcal{M}_e(g)$ are linearly dependent.*

Let $\mathcal{S}$ be a set of Boolean functions. We now describe an algorithm to compute a linearly independent set of functions $<\mathcal{S}>$ with the lowest possible degree e: We treat the functions in $\mathcal{S}$ as rows of a matrix where each column reflects one occuring monomial. Then, we apply Gaussian elimination in such way that the monomials with the highest degree are eliminated first and so on. Finally, we just pick those functions in the result with the lowest degree.

If $\mathcal{S} = B(g)$, the algorithm computes the lowest possible value for e. Let $\tilde{B} := \{g(\mathrm{K}_t \oplus \mathrm{IV}_t^i, z_t^i) \mid 0 \leq i \leq R-1\}$ be the set of functions available to the attacker. $<\tilde{B}>$ might be only a subset of $<g>$. In this case, the lowest possible degree can be higher.

We try now to estimate the complexity of the Degree-e attack. The first step is to find an appropriate linear combination in $\tilde{B}$. The effort is about $(\dim g)^2 \cdot |\mathcal{M}_d(g)|$ to find the linear combination and about $\mathcal{M}_e$ to compute the corresponding vector of size $\mathcal{M}_e$. This has to be repeated at least $\mathcal{M}_e$ times. Finally, a system of equations in $\mathcal{M}_e$ has to be solved ($\approx \mathcal{M}_e^3$). Hence, the overall number of operations is about $((\dim g)^2 \cdot |\mathcal{M}_d(g)| + \mathcal{M}_e) \cdot \mathcal{M}_e + \mathcal{M}_e^3$. Because of $\mathcal{M}_e \leq \beta(k,e)$ and $\dim g \leq \mathcal{M}_d \leq \beta(k,d)$, the following expression is an upper bound for the complexity $(\beta(\varphi,d)^3 + \beta(k,d)) \cdot \beta(k,e) + \beta(k,e)^3$.

In the individual case, the applicability of this attack depends on many parameters: the function g, the number R of accessible frames and the corresponding values of IV^i and z_t^i. Hence the attack does not work in every case. On the other hand, it puts on the designer the responsibility of making sure that these attacks are not feasible.

Moreover, if the set $\tilde{B}$ is a basis of $<g>$, then an equation of the lowest possible degree can be constructed. What is the probability that this happens? Let $s := \dim g$ and $R \geq s$. If we assume that each expression $g(\mathrm{K}_t \oplus \mathrm{IV}_t^i, z_t^i)$ is a random vector in $\{0,1\}^s$ then by [30], the probability that $\tilde{B}$ is a basis of $<g>$ is $\mathrm{Prob} = \prod_{i=R-s+1}^{m} (1 - 1/2^i)$.

6   Resynchronization Attacks with Large φ

The Daemen *et al.* attack only works when the number φ of inputs to the Boolean function is not too large. However, we will show in this section that using a linear resynchronization mechanism will inevitably induce weaknesses into stream ciphers, even when φ is very large. We will show a chosen *IV* attack, a known *IV* attack and an algebraic attack.

6.1   A Chosen *IV* Attack

The standard attack has a large time complexity of $\lceil n/\varphi \rceil \cdot 2^\varphi$ evaluations of the function f, but it only requires φ resyncs. We will now show that a tradeoff is possible.

Let κ_t in (7) consist of the bits $k_0, k_1, \ldots k_{\varphi-1}$. We make the reasonable assumption that in the chosen *IV* attack, the attacker can control the values of iv_t^i, consisting of the bits $iv_0, iv_1, \ldots iv_{\varphi-1}$. We now start the chosen *IV* attack. We first take a constant C. We then perform resyncs with all the values $\text{iv}_t^i = C \oplus i$, where we let i take all values[3] going from 0 $(00\ldots 0)$ to $2^u - 1$ $(00\ldots 011\ldots 1)$ for some u. Let's consider the first two values of our resynchronization attack. We denote $k_i \oplus iv_i$ as x_i. We know that:

$$\begin{cases} f(x_0, x_1, \ldots x_{\varphi-1}) = z_0^0 \\ f(x_0, x_1, \ldots x_{\varphi-1} \oplus 1) = z_0^1 . \end{cases} \tag{13}$$

By XORing both equations and using Theorem 7 we get:

$$f_1(x_0, x_1, \ldots x_{\varphi-2}) = z_0^0 \oplus z_0^1, \tag{14}$$

where the Boolean function f_1 has many properties that are desirable for an attacker. The degree of f_1 is lower, it has fewer monomials and it depends on less variables than f. This makes many attacks much easier.

In our attack, we will apply this method with 2^u chosen *IV*s in an iterative way. As an illustration, these are the equations for $u = 2$.

$$\left. \begin{matrix} \left. \begin{matrix} f(\ldots x_{\varphi-2}, x_{\varphi-1}) = z_0^0 \\ f(\ldots x_{\varphi-2}, x_{\varphi-1} \oplus 1) = z_0^1 \end{matrix} \right\} \Rightarrow \begin{matrix} f_1(\ldots x_{\varphi-2}) = \\ z_0^0 \oplus z_0^1 \end{matrix} \\ \left. \begin{matrix} f(\ldots x_{\varphi-2} \oplus 1, x_{\varphi-1}) = z_0^2 \\ f(\ldots x_{\varphi-2} \oplus 1, x_{\varphi-1} \oplus 1) = z_0^3 \end{matrix} \right\} \Rightarrow \begin{matrix} f_1(\ldots x_{\varphi-2} \oplus 1) = \\ z_1^2 \oplus z_0^3 \end{matrix} \end{matrix} \right\} \Rightarrow \begin{matrix} f_2(x_0 \ldots x_{\varphi-3}) = \\ z_0^0 \oplus z_0^1 \oplus z_0^2 \oplus z_0^3 \end{matrix}$$

$$\tag{15}$$

The basic attack requires at every time $2^u \cdot \varphi$ resyncs, in order to obtain $\varphi - u$ equations in the Boolean function $f_u(x_0 \ldots x_{\varphi-u-1})$ which can then be used in a normal resynchronization attack.

In practice, however, we note that the number of monomials, variables and the degree of the equation decreases very rapidly, making the attack work with very small complexity.

6.2   A Known *IV* Attack

We now describe another attack, which shows that the linear resynchronization mechanisms introduces weaknesses in the fixed resync setting for all Boolean functions.

---

[3] The impact of this choice of i is that the last u input bits of f will take all possible values. Of course we can do the same with any combination of u bits by choosing i as needed.

The principle of the attack is similar to the linear cryptanalysis method, developed by Matsui for attacking block ciphers [18]. First we search for a linear expression for the Boolean function that holds with probability $p \neq 0.5$. We then collect sufficiently many resyncs such that we can determine key bits using a maximum likelihood method. We will now describe this in more detail.

Our starting point is the fact that for any φ-input nonlinear Boolean function f, we can always find a subset $S \subset \{0, 1, \ldots \varphi - 1\}$ for which the equation

$$\bigoplus_{i \in S} x_i = f(x_0, \ldots x_{\varphi - 1}) \tag{16}$$

holds with probability $0.5 + \epsilon$, where $\epsilon \neq 0$. Suppose that the best bias we have found is ϵ ($0 < \epsilon \leq 0.5$). For each time t, with R known IVs, we get the following equations:

$$\begin{cases} \bigoplus_{i \in S} k_i = \bigoplus_{i \in S} iv_i^0 \oplus z_t^1 \\ \vdots \\ \bigoplus_{i \in S} k_i = \bigoplus_{i \in S} iv_i^{I-1} \oplus z_t^{I-1}, \end{cases} \tag{17}$$

each of which holds with probability $0.5 + \epsilon$. We now count for how many of these equations the right hand side is 1 respectively 0. We assume then that the correct right hand side is the value (0 or 1) that occurs most if $\epsilon > 0$, and the value that occurs least if $\epsilon < 0$.

We now have found one linear equation in the state bits that is true with some probability. This probability increases with the value of R and is dependent on the magnitude of ϵ. As in [18], the probability that the equation is correct, given R resyncs and a bias ϵ, is equal to:

$$\int_{-2 \cdot \sqrt{R} \cdot |\epsilon|}^{\infty} \frac{1}{\sqrt{2 \cdot \pi}} \cdot e^{-x^2/2} \cdot dx = 0.5 + 0.5 \cdot erf(\sqrt{2 \cdot R} \cdot |\epsilon|), \tag{18}$$

where erf is the error function. If we want the probability of correctness to approach one, we need the number of resyncs R to be $c \cdot \epsilon^{-2}$ for a small constant value c.

The output of a Boolean function is correlated to at least one linear function of the inputs, see Xiao and Massey [29]. The smallest bias ϵ that can be found[4] is at least $2^{-\frac{\varphi}{2}-1}$. This implies that any linear resynchronization mechanism with a φ-input Boolean function f can be broken by this resynchronization attack using at most about $2^{\varphi+2}$ known IVs.

How to search for the best linear approximation has been well-studied. The Walsh-Hadamard transform can be used to find the best linear approximation,

---

[4] This lower bound for ϵ follows from the universal nonlinearity bound for Boolean functions. Equality applies to the so-called bent functions. Stream ciphers typically do not use bent functions because they are not balanced. The size of the smallest bias to be found in balanced Boolean functions is still an open problem, but some bounds have been presented, see [12] for an overview. For simplicity, we take the bias of bent functions, but the bias for actual functions will be higher and therefore less resyncs will be needed in practice.

see [24] for a thorough treatment. In the context of correlation attacks, such linear approximations have been studied in the literature, both for memoryless combiners and nonlinear filter generators [24] as for combiners with memory [13, 20].

The biases found in actual Boolean functions used in stream ciphers will be much higher than the lower bounds described above. This is due to several reasons: the functions have to be balanced, they have to be easily implementable, and for combiners they will also have to take into account the trade-off that has to be made between nonlinearity and resilience, see Sarkar and Maitra [26]. It can be expected that most Boolean functions used in practice are vulnerable to this known IV attack on a linear resynchronization mechanism.

6.3   An Algebraic Attack

As said in Sect. 5.2, the goal is to find a solution to the system of equations as described in (10). Again, the approaches to reduce the degree as described in Sect. 5.2 can be also applied here.

If all bits of κ_t are uniquely specified by the equations, use Gröbner bases or the linearization method to solve (10) clock by clock. If the degree of the equations is low (e.g., Toyocrypt), it might be faster and require less IVs than the approach described in Sect. 6.2.

6.4   The Degree-1 Attack

Another approach is to apply the methods described in Sect. 5.2 if $e = 1$ is possible. In this case, we get at least one linear equation in the bits of κ_t directly. If we repeat this for enough values of t the corresponding K can be reconstructed by solving a system of linear equations.

The exact effort depends on many parameters: the function g, the number R of frames, the corresponding values of IV^i and z_t^i and so on (see also Sect. 1). The number of operations is about $((\dim g)^2 \cdot |\mathcal{M}_d(g)| + k) \cdot k + k^3$ or more general $(\beta(\varphi, d)^3 + k) \cdot k + k^3$. This indicates that the approach might be feasible if the degree d is small.

7   Attacks on Combiners with Memory

Many stream ciphers use their linear state in conjunction with a (small) non-linear memory in order to avoid the trade-off between correlation immunity and nonlinearity for the combining function, see Rueppel [23].

In this section we demonstrate that resynchronization attacks can also be performed on stream ciphers with memory. Note that the known IV attack of Sect. 6 can also be applied on combiners with memory.

7.1   A Standard Resynchronization Attack

We will use the following model based on the general case of the combiners with memory:

$$S_0^i = A \cdot K \oplus B \cdot IV^i \tag{19}$$
$$M_0^i = \text{const} \tag{20}$$
$$S_{t+1}^i = C \cdot S_t^i \tag{21}$$
$$M_{t+1}^i = h(D \cdot S_t^i, M_t^i) = h(\kappa_t \oplus IV_t^i, M_t^i) \tag{22}$$
$$z_t^i = f(D \cdot S_t^i, E \cdot M_t^i) = f(\kappa_t \oplus IV_t^i, E \cdot M_t^i). \tag{23}$$

In practice, some designs only start outputting key stream when $t = \mu$; this results in an improved diffusion of the key and the initialization vector into the nonlinear state. We will discuss both the cases $\mu = 0$ and $\mu > 0$. Note that in some designs M_0^i is also dependent on the key and the IV. This can in our model be treated in the same way as the case $\mu > 0$.

$\boldsymbol{\mu = 0.}$ In the case $\mu = 0$, the resynchronization attack can easily be adapted to work also with combiners with memory. We again describe the attack with φ resyncs.

The first series of outputs can be written as $z_0^i = f(\kappa_0 \oplus IV_0^i, M_0^i)$. Because M_0^i is known, the attacker can recover κ_0 by exhaustive search. He can then determine M_1^i for all the resyncs using (22). Now he knows all inputs to (23) for $t = 1$ except κ_1, which he can again recover through exhaustive search, and so on. All complexities of this attack are exactly the same as for the case without memory. The only difference is that each step now consists of one evaluation of f and of φ evaluations of h.

$\boldsymbol{\mu > 0.}$ The attacker does not know the initial contents of the m-bit memory M. Moreover, this memory is different for each resync. The attack now works exactly as above, except that the attacker will first have to guess the contents of M at $t = \mu$. The time complexity of the attack now becomes $2^{\varphi \cdot m} \cdot \lceil n/\varphi \rceil \cdot 2^\varphi$ evaluations of the f and h function. As φ and m are quite small in most actual designs, the attacks are feasible.

Let's take as an example a combiner consisting of 5 LFSRs with total length 320 bits, and with 5 memory bits. The complexity of the resynchronization attack is then equal to 2^{36} function evaluations.

Practical Considerations of the Attack. As for the case without memory, we would like that the attack always works with φ resyncs. At some times, we will have several possible values for κ_i. In a second phase, we cannot use the exhaustive search method of the memoryless case, because we would then have to try all possible values for updating the memory bits, which would increase the complexity enormously.

This problem can be easily overcome by implementing the algorithm with a depth-first search. When at some time t we have several possibilities for K_t, we pick the first one and go to $t + 1$. If we have no solution at time t, we go back to $t - 1$ and try the next possibility there. When we have arrived at time $\lceil k/\varphi \rceil$, we have found a sufficient number of values and we check if we have found the correct key. Simulations indicate that when the number of resyncs R is equal to or larger than φ, the attack will find the correct values very quickly and has to search very few states.

The same approach can also be used when the attacker disposes of less than φ resyncs, i.e., $R < \varphi$. In the case $\mu > 0$ this may even be advantageous from a complexity viewpoint, because we have to perform an exhaustive search over less than φ initial memory states. But again the complexity of the search algorithm will increase exponentially with decreasing R, making this attack feasible only when R is close to φ.

A particularity is the case when the Boolean output function f is linear. In that case we don't get new information at each new resync, because all equations $z_0^i = f(K_0 \oplus IV_0^i, M_0^i)$ are equivalent. This problem can be easily overcome by using the memory update function h to do the checks during the search. An example of such a linear output function is $E0$.

7.2   Using Ad-Hoc Equations

Another possibility is the use of ad-hoc equations which have been introduced in [3]. The authors showed that for a combiner with memory with m memory bits M_t, an equation

$$F(S_t^i, \ldots, S_{t+m}^i, z_t^i, \ldots, z_{t+m}^i) = 0 \tag{24}$$

of degree $\leq \lceil \frac{\varphi \cdot (m+1)}{2} \rceil$ always exists which is completely independent of the memory bits. They also propose an algorithm to find ad-hoc equations

$$G(S_t^i, \ldots, S_{t+r-1}^i, z_t^i, \ldots, z_{t+r-1}^i) = 0 \tag{25}$$

with the lowest possible degree d if $\varphi \cdot r$ is not too large. For example, an ad-hoc equation of degree 4 using $r = 4$ successive clocks exists for the E_0 key stream generator.

As (25) is independent of the memory bits, these equations can be used for *all* attacks described in the previous sections. An additional requirement is now that the attacker knows enough successive key stream bits.

If $\varphi \cdot r$ is small the Daemen *et al.* attack is applicable. The number of operations is about $\lceil k/(\varphi \cdot r) \rceil \cdot 2^{\varphi \cdot r} + k^3$. The methods described in Sect. 5.2 to reduce the degree of the equations can be easily adapted to the case of ad-hoc equations.

8   Attacks on Stream Ciphers with Nonlinear Resynchronization

In this section, we will show that stream ciphers with a nonlinear resynchronization mechanism can also be vulnerable to resynchronization attacks. A first attack is a chosen *IV* attack; its principle is similar to that of Daemen *et al.* The second attack is a known *IV* attack that uses the principle of linear approximations as used in the known *IV* attack of Sect. 6.2. We will demonstrate these attacks on the two-level memoryless combiner. The framework of the attack is shown in Fig. 1. In a first level, the key and an *IV* are linearly loaded into the LFSRs. The input to f at time t of the level 1 initialization is denoted x_t. The following holds:

$$x_t = (x_t^0, x_t^1, \ldots, x_t^{\varphi-1}) = K_t \oplus IV_t = (k_t^0 \oplus iv_t^0, k_t^1 \oplus iv_t^1, \ldots, k_t^{\varphi-1} \oplus iv_t^{\varphi-1}). \quad (26)$$

The output y_i of level 1 is collected and is used as the initial state for the level 2 generator. We use here the simplified setting shown in the figure. Level 2 generates the key stream z_i.

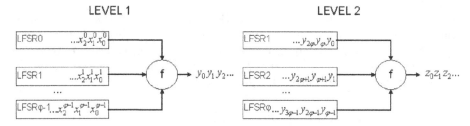

Fig. 1. Model for a two-level combiner

8.1   A Chosen *IV* Attack

We will show an attack scenario on this construction which holds under the assumption that the attacker can choose the value of the IVs which go into the Boolean function (this is for instance the case when the initial state equals the XOR of the key and the initialization vector).

We start with $t = 0$. We let IV_0 take j different values, while keeping the other IVs constant. We obtain the following equations:

$$\begin{cases} f(f(K_0 \oplus IV_0^1), y_1, \ldots y_{\varphi-1}) = z_0^1 \\ f(f(K_0 \oplus IV_0^2), y_1, \ldots y_{\varphi-1}) = z_0^2 \\ \ldots \\ f(f(K_0 \oplus IV_0^j), y_1, \ldots y_{\varphi-1}) = z_0^j. \end{cases} \quad (27)$$

Denote the vector $(y_1, \ldots y_{\varphi-1})$ by R. In half of the cases, we will see that all z_0^i are equal (either all 0 or all 1). This is due to the fact that $f(0, R) = f(1, R)$. In the other half of the cases, which is of interest here, the z_0^i take both the values 0 and 1 in a random-looking way; which is due to the fact that $f(0, R) \neq f(1, R)$.

Assume that we are in the latter case. We now guess the $\varphi - 1$ bits of R, let's call this guess G. If $f(0, G) = f(1, G)$, then our guess is certainly not correct and we proceed to the next guess. If $f(0, G) \neq f(1, G)$, the guess is possible; we now get j equations in K_0 of the form:

$$f(K_0 \oplus IV_0^i) = z_0^i \oplus f(0, G). \quad (28)$$

The equations we have obtained are exactly the same as in the case of the linear resynchronization mechanism. If j is large enough, we expect to find a unique solution for κ_0 over all the guesses for G. It can be shown that we need about $2 \cdot \varphi$ chosen IVs to achieve this.

In the same way, we can also recover $\kappa_1, \kappa_2, \ldots$ which gives us the whole secret key of the system. The attack requires a total of about $2 \cdot k$ chosen IVs and has a time complexity of $\lceil k/\varphi \rceil \cdot 2^{2 \cdot \varphi - 1}$. This attack has been implemented on various 8-bit Boolean functions, and we can easily recover the key.

8.2   A Known IV Attack

In this attack, we extend the approach in which we search a bias in the φ-input Boolean function (see the known IV attack in Sect. 6) in a straightforward way to the case of the two-level combiners. Each bit now goes twice through the function f, but we can show that a bias still persists. The equation we want to hold is as follows:

$$\bigoplus_{j \in BS} k_j = \bigoplus_{j \in BS} iv_j^i \oplus z_0^i , \tag{29}$$

where the set BS consists of the bits of the set S involved in the linear bias, for all times $t \in S$ of the first level of the combiner. Similar equations can be written for the next iterations. Let's denote the cardinality of the set S by s. Of course it holds that $s \leq \varphi$. The cardinality of the set BS is then evidently s^2.

The piling-up lemma [18] learns that the probability that this equation holds is equal to $1/2 + 2^s \cdot \epsilon^{s+1}$, where ϵ is the bias of the Boolean function. The bias of this equation is thus $2^s \cdot \epsilon^{s+1}$, which means we need $R = 2^{-2 \cdot s} \cdot \epsilon^{-2 \cdot s - 2}$ resyncs to break this system by a known IV attack.

We will show what this implies for actual Boolean functions. We take Boolean functions with φ inputs and resilience ρ. We will use two well-known lower bounds for the bias ϵ:

$$\begin{cases} \epsilon \geq 2^{-\varphi/2 - 1} \\ \epsilon \geq 2^{\rho + 1 - \varphi} , \end{cases} \tag{30}$$

where the first bound is due to Parseval's relation and the second to the trade-off between nonlinearity and resilience, see [28]. The cardinality of the set S is now[5] $s = \rho + 1$. We can calculate an upper bound for the number of resyncs needed for a successful attack as a function of φ and of the resilience ρ. This is shown in Fig. 2 for some values of φ. These graphs show that memoryless combiners with few inputs cannot be made resistant against resynchronization attacks on a two-level combiner. For larger functions it should be checked whether the Boolean

---

[5] We conjecture that we will find the bias for $\rho + 1$ in practice. We will certainly find a bias for $\rho + 1$, as f is ρ-th order correlation immune but not $\rho + 1$-th order correlation immune. As the cases we discuss are optimal from a designer's point of view, we expect the Walsh spectrum to be flattened as much as possible over the values with Hamming weight $> \rho$ and therefore to find a bias (very close) to ϵ for Hamming weight $\rho + 1$. This conjecture can be easily verified for a popular class of functions, the plateaued functions [31].

function is strong enough to withstand the above attack. The bounds given here may be refined by a more careful examination of the properties of the various classes of Boolean functions.

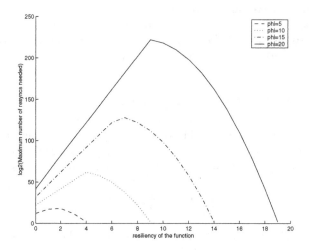

Fig. 2. Upper bound for the number of resyncs as a function of the resilience ρ with as parameter the number φ of input bits of the Boolean function

8.3   Implications of the Attacks

The known IV attack described above for the two-level memoryless combiner can be easily extended to other nonlinear resynchronization mechanisms. It is also possible to apply the attack on other designs, such as combiners with memory, nonlinearly filtered generators and irregularly clocked shift registers. We can use techniques as described by Golic [13, 14] to find suitable linear approximations. Our attack can be used to evaluate the strength of any resynchronization mechanism, and resistance against this attack is a minimum requirement for any design. We are currently investigating the impact of this attack on some actual designs, such as the resynchronization mechanisms of $E0$ and the NESSIE [22] candidates.

9   Conclusions

In [10], Daemen, Govaerts and Vandewalle presented the original resynchronization attack on synchronous stream ciphers. In this paper, we have extended this resynchronization attack in several directions, by using new attack methods and by combining the attack with cryptanalytic techniques such as algebraic attacks and linear cryptanalysis.

Our attacks on linear resynchronization mechanisms show that a linear resynchronization mechanism should never be used in practice. Even if the system uses few resyncs, has an input function with many inputs and has a non-linear memory, it will still very likely contain weaknesses that can be exploited by one of our attack scenarios.

Nowadays, resynchronization mechanisms are typically designed in an *ad hoc* manner, by making them nonlinear to an extent that seems to be sufficient. Our attacks on nonlinear resynchronization mechanisms lead to a better understanding of the strength of such mechanisms and can be used to provide a lower bound for the nonlinearity required from a secure resynchronization mechanism. This allows designers to consider the trade-offs between the speed and the security of a resynchronization mechanism.

Acknowledgements

The authors would like to thank An Braeken, Joe Cho, Matthias Krause, Stefan Lucks, Erik Zenner and the anonymous referees for helpful comments and discussions.

References

1. R. Anderson, *A5 (Was: Hacking Digital Phones)*, sci.crypt post, June 1994.
2. F. Armknecht, J. Lano, B. Preneel, *Extending the Resynchronization Attack (extended version)*, Cryptology ePrint Archive, Report 2004/232, 2004.
3. F. Armknecht, M. Krause, *Algebraic Attacks on Combiners with Memory*, Crypto 2003, LNCS 2729, D. Boneh, Ed., Springer-Verlag, pp. 162-176, 2003.
4. F. Armknecht, *Improving Fast Algebraic Attacks*, FSE 2004, LNCS 3017, B. Roy, W. Meier, Eds., Springer-Verlag, pp. 65–82, 2004.
5. F. Armknecht, *On the Existence of Low-degree Equations for Algebraic Attacks*, Cryptology ePrint Archive, Report 2004/185, 2004.
6. Bluetooth S.I.G., *Specification of the Bluetooth System, Version 1.2*, available from www.bluetooth.org/spec, 2003.
7. Y. Borissov, S. Nikova, B. Preneel, J. Vandewalle, *On a Resynchronization Weakness in a Class of Combiners with Memory*, SCN 2002, LNCS 2576, S. Cimato, C. Galdi, G. Persiano, Eds., Springer-Verlag, pp. 164–173, 2002.
8. N. Courtois, W. Meier, *Algebraic Attacks on Stream Ciphers with Linear Feedback*, Eurocrypt 2003, LNCS 2656, E. Biham, Ed., Springer-Verlag, pp. 345–359, 2003.
9. N. Courtois, *Fast Algebraic Attacks on Stream Ciphers with Linear Feedback*, Crypto 2003, LNCS 2729, D. Boneh, Ed., Springer-Verlag, pp. 177–194, 2003.
10. J. Daemen, R. Govaerts, J. Vandewalle, *Resynchronization Weaknesses in Synchronous Stream Ciphers*, Eurocrypt 1993, LNCS 765, T. Helleseth, Ed., Springer-Verlag, pp. 159–167, 1993.
11. S. Fluhrer, *Improved key recovery of level 1 of the Bluetooth Encryption System*, Cryptology ePrint Archive, Report 2002/068, 2002.
12. C. Fontaine, *Contribution à la Recherche de Fonctions Booléennes Hautement Non Linéaires, et au Marquage d'Images en Vue de la Protection des Droits d'Auteur*, PhD Thesis, Paris University, 1998.
13. J. Golic, *Correlation via Linear Sequential Circuit Approximation of Combiners with Memory*, Eurocrypt 1992, LNCS 658, R. Rueppel, Ed., Springer-Verlag, pp. 113–123, 1992.

14. J. Golic, *Linear Cryptanalysis of Stream Ciphers*, FSE 1994, LNCS 1008, B. Preneel, Ed., Springer-Verlag, pp. 154–169, 1994.
15. J. Golic, G. Morgari, *On the Resynchronization Attack*, FSE 2003, LNCS 2887, T. Johansson, Ed., Springer-Verlag, pp. 100–110, 2003.
16. A. Joux, F. Muller, *A Chosen IV Attack against Turing*, SAC 2003, LNCS 3006, M. Matsui, R. Zuccherato, Eds., Springer-Verlag, pp. 194–207, 2003.
17. D. Lee, J. Kim, J. Hong, J. Han, D. Moon, *Algebraic Attacks on Summation Generators*, FSE 2004, LNCS 3017, B. Roy, W. Meier, Eds., Springer-Verlag, pp. 34–48, 2004.
18. M. Matsui, *Linear Cryptanalysis Method for DES Cipher*, Eurocrypt 1993, LNCS 765, T. Helleseth, Ed., Springer-Verlag, pp. 386–397, 1993.
19. W. Meier, E. Pasalic, C. Carlet, *Algebraic Attacks and Decomposition of Boolean Functions*, Eurocrypt 2004, LNCS 3027, C. Cachin, J. Camenisch, Eds., Springer-Verlag, pp. 474–491, 2004.
20. W. Meier, O. Staffelbach, *Correlation Properties of Combiners with Memory in Stream Ciphers (extended abstract)*, Eurocrypt 1990, LNCS 473, I. Damgard, Ed., Springer-Verlag, pp. 204–213, 1990.
21. M. Mihaljević, H. Imai, *Cryptanalysis of Toyocrypt-HS1 stream cipher*, IEICE Transactions on Fundamentals, vol. E85-A, pp. 66–73, Jan. 2002. Available at http://www.csl.sony.co.jp/ATL/papers/IEICEjan02.pdf.
22. New European Schemes for Signature, Integrity and Encryption, http://www.cryptonessie.org
23. R. Rueppel, *Correlation Immunity and the Summation Generator*, Crypto 1985, LNCS 218, H. Williams, Ed., Springer-Verlag, pp. 260–272, 1985.
24. R. Rueppel, *Analysis and Design of Stream Ciphers*, Springer-Verlag, Berlin, 1986.
25. M. Saarinen, *Bluetooth und E0*, sci.crypt post, February 2002.
26. P. Sarkar, S. Maitra, *Nonlinearity Bounds and Constructions of Resilient Boolean Functions*, Crypto 2000, LNCS 1880, M. Bellare, Ed., Springer-Verlag, pp. 515–532, 2000.
27. V. Strassen, *Gaussian Elimination is Not Optimal*, Numerische Mathematik, vol 13, pp. 354–356, 1969.
28. Y. Tarannikov, *On Resilient Boolean Functions with Maximum Possible Nonlinearity*, Indocrypt 2000, LNCS 1977, B. Roy, E. Okamoto, Eds., Springer-Verlag, pp. 19–30, 2000.
29. G. Xiao, J. Massey, *A Spectral Characterization of Correlation-immune Combining Functions*, IEEE Trans. Inf. Theory, Vol. IT-34, pp. 569–571, 1988.
30. K. Zeng, C. Yang, T. Rao, *On the Linear Consistency Test (LCT) in Cryptanalysis with Applications*, Crypto 1989, LNCS 435, G. Brassard, Ed., Springer-Verlag, pp. 164–174, 1990.
31. Y. Zheng, X. Zhang, *Plateaued Functions*, ICICS 1999, LNCS 1726, V. Varadharajan, Y. Mu, Eds., Springer-Verlag, pp. 284–300, 1999.

A New Simple Technique to Attack Filter Generators and Related Ciphers

Håkan Englund and Thomas Johansson

Dept. of Information Techonolgy, Lund University,
P.O. Box 118, 221 00 Lund, Sweden

Abstract. This paper presents a new simple distinguishing attack that can be applied on stream ciphers constructed from filter generators or similar structures. We demonstrate the effectiveness by describing key recovery attacks on the stream cipher LILI-128. One attack on LILI-128 requires 2^{47} bits of keystream and a computational complexity of roughly 2^{53}. This is a significant improvement compared to other known attacks.

1 Introduction

Much work has been put into trying to understand the security of stream ciphers. Stream ciphers can be made very efficient in software and in hardware, but their security has not been as widely studied as for example block ciphers. In this paper we investigate filter generators, a linear feedback shift register (LFSR) from which the output is filtered by a nonlinear filter function. This output is added modulo two to the plaintext. See for example [18] for more details on filter generators.

Several different kinds of attacks can be considered on stream ciphers. We usually consider the plaintext to be known, i.e. the keystream is known and we try to recover the key. A popular technique is to exploit some correlation in the keystream. This idea was introduced by Siegenthaler [23] in 1984, a consequence of this attack is that designers of nonlinear functions must use functions with high nonlinearity. This attack was later followed by the fast correlation attack by Meier and Staffelbach [17]. Since then many improvements have been introduced on this topic, see [1, 2, 14, 13, 15]. In a fast correlation attack one first try to find a low weight parity check polynomial of the LFSR and then apply some iterative decoding procedure.

Algebraic attacks have received much interest lately. These attacks try to reduce the key recovery problem to the problem of solving a large system of algebraic equations [6, 5].

Another class of key recovery attacks on filter generators was proposed by Golić, the so-called inversion attacks, see [10, 11, 12]. In an inversion attack one tries to "invert" the nonlinear function and recover the initial state.

A distinguishing attack is a different type of attack. Here we try to distinguish the output of the cipher from a truly random source. In some specific cases these

H. Handschuh and A. Hasan (Eds.): SAC 2004, LNCS 3357, pp. 39–53, 2005.

attacks can be used to create a key recovery attack. Distinguishing attacks have received a lot of attention recently, see for example [8, 4].

In this paper we present a very simple distinguishing attack that can be applied on stream ciphers using a filter generator or a similar structure as a part of the cipher.

Recently, Leveiller et. al. [16] proposed methods involving iterative decoding and the use of vectors instead of the binary symmetric channel. We use a similar idea, but much simpler in its form and more powerful in its performance, to mount a distinguishing attack. In the basic algorithm we first find a low weight multiple of the LFSR. We then consider the entries of the parity check equation as a vector. Such vectors, regarded as random variables, are non-uniformly distributed due to the parity check, and this is the key observation that we use to perform a distinguishing attack. This allows us to detect statistical deviations in the output sequence, creating the distinguishing attack. We can also present ideas on how to improve the performance by using slightly more complex algorithms.

In order to demonstrate the effectiveness of the proposed ideas, we apply them on a recently proposed cipher called LILI-128. The attack is a *key recovery attack*. LILI-128 has one LFSR controlling the clock of another LFSR. Our approach is to guess the first 39 bits of the key, those bits that are used in the LFSR that controls the clocking. If our guess is correct we will be able to detect some bias in the output sequence through the proposed distinguishing attacks. The complexity for one of the proposed attacks is roughly 2^{53} binary operations and it needs about 2^{47} keystream bits, a significant improvement compared to other known attacks.

The paper is organized as follows. In Section 2 we give a basic description of filter generators. In Section 3 we present some theory on hypothesis testing. After this we describe our new distinguishing attack in Section 4, here we also present some ideas on how to improve this distinguishing attack. In Section 5 we turn this attack into a key recovery attack on LILI-128. Finally in Section 6 some future work and conclusions are discussed.

2   Preliminaries

In this paper we consider binary stream ciphers where the output from a LFSR is filtered by a nonlinear function. The keystream generator is divided into two parts, one linear, i.e., the LFSR, and one nonlinear function. LFSRs are known to produce long pseudo-random data sequences and can be made very efficient in both hardware and software. Usually the feedback polynomial of the shift register is primitive and the LFSR sequence will have maximum period. Since the initial state of an LFSR is very simple to recreate from the output stream we need to destroy the linearity in the keystream. This is the purpose of the nonlinear function. Much work on nonlinear functions has been done, see for example [21].

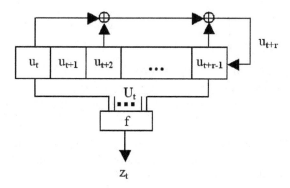

Fig. 1. Description of a filter generator

A filter generator can be described as follows. Let $u_t, u_{t+1}, \ldots$ denote the output sequence from a length r LFSR with feedback polynomial $g(x)$. Let f denote the nonlinear function as can be seen in Figure 1. At each time t this function takes d input values from the LFSR register and produces on output bit z_t. The variables used as inputs to f at time t are the entries in the vector $\mathbf{U}_t = (u_{t+t_1}, u_{t+t_2}, \ldots, u_{t+t_d})^T$. We denote the output sequence from the Boolean function, i.e., the keystream, by $z_t, z_{t+1}, \ldots$. We thus have $z_t = f(\mathbf{U}_t)$. This is modeled in Figure 1.

3   Hypothesis Testing

In a distinguishing attack we try to decide whether the data origins from the considered cipher or from a random source. To make this decision we use hypothesis testing. The problem stated above can be reformulated. We have two hypotheses, where H_0 denotes the hypothesis that the observed data comes from our cipher and H_1 that the data origins from a random source. We will now shortly explain how the decision is made and how we can calculate the number of samples we need to make a correct decision. For a more thorough description of hypothesis testing, see [7].

Assume that we have a sequence of m independent and identically distributed (i.i.d.) random variables $X_1, X_2, \ldots, X_m$ taken from the alphabet $\mathcal{X}$. The distribution of the random variables, X_i, are denoted $P(x) = \Pr(X_i = x), 1 \leq i \leq m$, where $x_1, x_2, \ldots, x_m$ denotes observed values. If we denote the distribution of X_i under hypothesis H_0 with P_0 and the uniform distribution by P_1, we can write our hypothesizes as $H_0 : P = P_0$ and $H_1 : P = P_1$. To perform the actual hypothesis test we use the Neyman-Pearson lemma.

Lemma 1. *(Neyman-Pearson lemma) Let $X_1, X_2, \ldots, X_m$ be drawn i.i.d. according to mass function P. Consider the decision problem corresponding to the hypotheses $P = P_0$ vs. $P = P_1$. For $T \geq 0$ define a region.*

$$\mathcal{A}_m(T) = \left\{ (x_1, x_2, \ldots, x_m) : \frac{P_0(x_1, x_2, \ldots, x_m)}{P_1(x_1, x_2, \ldots, x_m)} > T \right\}.$$

Let $\alpha = P_0(\mathcal{A}_m^c(T))$ and $\beta = P_1(\mathcal{A}_m(T))$ be the error probabilities corresponding to the decision region $\mathcal{A}_m$, ($\mathcal{A}_m^c$ denotes the complement of the region $\mathcal{A}_m$). Let $\mathcal{B}_m$ be any other decision region with associated error probabilities α^* and β^*. If $\alpha^* \leq \alpha$, then $\beta^* \geq \beta$.

The region $\mathcal{A}_m(T)$ minimizes α and β. In our case we set α and β to be equal and hence $T = 1$. As all x_n are assumed independent we can rewrite the Newman-Pearson as a log-likelihood test,

$$I = \sum_{n=1}^{m} \left(\log_2 \frac{P_0(x_n)}{P_1(x_n)} \right) > 0 \ ? \tag{1}$$

We also need to know how many keystream bits we need to observe in order to make a correct decision. In [4] the *statistical distance* is used. The statistical distance, denoted ϵ, between two distributions P_0, P_1 defined over the finite alphabet $\mathcal{X}$, is defined as

$$\epsilon = |P_0 - P_1| = \sum_{x \in \mathcal{X}} |P_0(x) - P_1(x)|, \tag{2}$$

where x is an element of $\mathcal{X}$. Since $0 \leq \epsilon \leq 2$ we use the more natural $\varepsilon = \epsilon/2$. If the distributions are smooth, the number of variables N we need to observe is $N \approx 1/\varepsilon^2$, see [4]. Note that the error probabilities are decreasing exponentially with N.

4   Description of the New Attack

In this section we will give a description of the different steps of our attack. If the feedback polynomial of the LFSR is of low weight from the beginning, we can apply our attack directly. Usually this is not the case, and our first step is then to try to find a low weight multiple of the feedback polynomial.

4.1   Finding a Low Weight Multiple

There exist many methods for finding low weight multiples (of weight w) of a feedback polynomial $g(x)$. Because the degree of the multiple gives a lower bound of the number of samples we need to observe, we wish to minimize this degree. In [9] it is stated that the critical degree when the polynomial multiples of weight w starts to appear is $(w-1)!^{1/(w-1)} 2^{r/(w-1)}$, where r is the degree of the original feedback polynomial. In [9] an algorithm to find multiples is described. First one calculates the residues $x^i \bmod g(x)$, then one computes the residues $x^{i_1} + \ldots x^{i_k} \bmod g(x)$ for all $\binom{n}{k}$ combinations $1 \leq i_1 \leq \ldots \leq i_k \leq n$, with n

being the maximum degree of the multiples. Use fast sorting to find all of the zero and one matches of the residues from the second step. The complexity of this algorithm is approximately $O(S \log S)$ with $S = \frac{(2k)!^{1/2}}{k!} 2^{r/2}$ for odd multiples of weight $w = 2k+1$, and $S = \frac{(2k-1)!^{k/(2k-1)}}{k!} 2^{rk/(2k-1)}$ for even multiples of weight $w = 2k$.

Wagner [24] presented a generalization of the birthday problem, i.e., given k lists of r-bit values, find a way to choose one element from each list, so that these k values XOR to zero. This algorithm finds a multiple of weight $w = k+1$ with lower complexity, $k \cdot 2^{r/(1+\lfloor \log k \rfloor)}$, than [9] but with higher degrees, $2^{r/(1+\lfloor \log k \rfloor)}$, on the multiples. Since the number of samples is of high concern to us we have chosen to work with the method described in [9]. Continuing, we now assume that the LFSR sequence is described by a low weight recursion.

4.2 Building a Distinguisher

The technique we use for building a distinguisher is inspired by the work in [16]. However in [16] the authors describe a key recovery attack and use iterative decoding methods, etc. We construct instead a very simple distinguisher. A usual description of a stream cipher is to model it as a binary symmetric channel (BSC), using linear approximations. But we proceed differently. Instead we write the terms in the weight w parity check equation as a length w vector. This way we use our knowledge of the nonlinear function better than in the BSC model. Assume that we have a LFSR of weight w with the parity check equation

$$u_t + u_{t+\tau_1} + \ldots + u_{t+\tau_{w-1}} = 0. \tag{3}$$

We write the terms in this relation as a vector, and by noticing that $u_{t+\tau_{w-1}}$ is fully determined by the sum of the other components we get ($\tau_0 = 0$),

$$(u_t, u_{t+\tau_1}, \ldots, u_{t+\tau_{w-1}}) = (u_t, u_{t+\tau_1}, \ldots, \sum_{i=0}^{w-2} u_{t+\tau_i}). \tag{4}$$

From the LFSR, d different positions are taken as input to the nonlinear function f. For each of these positions, where $t_1, t_2, \ldots, t_d$ denotes its position relative to time t, we can write a vector similar to (4). If we consider the following matrix,

$$A_t = \begin{pmatrix} u_{t+t_1} & u_{t+t_1+\tau_1} & \cdots & \sum_{i=0}^{w-2} u_{t+t_1+\tau_i} \\ u_{t+t_2} & u_{t+t_2+\tau_1} & \cdots & \sum_{i=0}^{w-2} u_{t+t_2+\tau_i} \\ \vdots & \vdots & & \vdots \\ u_{t+t_d} & u_{t+t_d+\tau_1} & \cdots & \sum_{i=0}^{w-2} u_{t+t_d+\tau_i} \end{pmatrix},$$

then by writing $\mathbf{U}_{t+\tau_l} = (u_{t+t_1+\tau_l}, u_{t+t_2+\tau_l}, \ldots, u_{t+t_d+\tau_l})^T$ we get

$$A_t = (\mathbf{U}_t, \mathbf{U}_{t+\tau_1}, \ldots, \sum_{i=0}^{w-2} \mathbf{U}_{t+\tau_i}). \tag{5}$$

In the attack we will not have access to the LFSR output, instead we have access to the output bits from the nonlinear function f. The output values $(z_t, z_{t+\tau_1}, \ldots, z_{t+\tau_{w-1}})$, denoted by $\mathbf{Z_t}$, can be described as

$$\mathbf{Z_t} = (z_t, z_{t+\tau_1}, \ldots, z_{t+\tau_{w-1}}) = (f(\mathbf{U}_t), f(\mathbf{U}_{t+\tau_1}), \ldots, f(\sum_{i=0}^{w-2} \mathbf{U}_{t+\tau_i})). \quad (6)$$

As we run through $\mathbf{U}_t, \mathbf{U}_{t+\tau_1}, \ldots, \mathbf{U}_{t+\tau_{w-1}}$ in a nonuniform manner (not all values of $\mathbf{U}_t, \mathbf{U}_{t+\tau_1}, \ldots, \mathbf{U}_{t+\tau_{w-1}}$ are possible), we will (in general) generate a nonuniform distribution of $(z_t, z_{t+\tau_1}, \ldots, z_{t+\tau_{w-1}})$. In [16] it is shown that the distribution of these vectors only depends on the parity. If the number of output bits is large enough, we can perform a hypothesis test according to Section 3. In this hypothesis test we need the probability distribution $P_0(\mathbf{Z_t})$. This distribution can be calculated by running through all different values of $\mathbf{U}_t, \mathbf{U}_{t+\tau_1}, \ldots, \mathbf{U}_{t+\tau_{w-1}}$. If d and w are large, the complexity for such a direct approach is too high. Then we can use slightly more advanced techniques based on building a trellis, that have much lower complexity.

The new basic distinguishing attack is summarized in Figure 2.

---

1. Find a weight w multiple of $g(x)$.
2. Calculate the distribution $P_0(\mathbf{Z}_t)$.
3. Calculate the length N we need to observe.
4. **for** $t = 0 \ldots N$
      $\mathbf{Z}_t = (z_t, z_{t+\tau_1}, \ldots, z_{t+\tau_{w-1}})$
end for
5. Calculate $I = \sum_{t=0}^{N} \left(\log_2 \frac{P_0(\mathbf{Z}_t)}{1/2^w} \right)$.
6. **if** $(I > 0)$
      output "cipher" otherwise "random".

Fig. 2. Summary of the new basic distinguishing attack

4.3 Example of the Attack Applied on a Filter Generator

To really show the simplicity of the attack we will demonstrate with an example. We use an example from [16] in which we consider a three weight multiple from which the output is filtered by an 8-input, 2-resilient plateaued function.

$$f(x) = x_1 + x_4 + x_5 + x_6 + x_7 + x_1(x_2 + x_7) + x_2 x_6 + x_3(x_6 + x_8) + $$
$$+x_1 x_2(x_4 + x_6 + x_7 + x_8) + x_1 x_3(x_2 + x_6) + x_1 x_2 x_3(x_4 + x_5 + x_8).$$

For a parity of weight three and using the notation from Section 4.2 we can write the vectors as

$$(z_t, z_{t+\tau_1}, z_{t+\tau_2}) = (f(\mathbf{U}_t), f(\mathbf{U}_{t+\tau_1}), f(\mathbf{U}_t + \mathbf{U}_{t+\tau_1})).$$

If we try all possible inputs to this function and determine the distribution $P_0(z_t, z_{t+\tau_1}, z_{t+\tau_2})$ we get Table 1. Since we know that the probability only

Table 1. The probability distribution $P_0(z_t, z_{t+\tau_1}, z_{t+\tau_2})$

$z_t, z_{t+\tau_1}, z_{t+\tau_2}$	$P_0(z_t, z_{t+\tau_1}, z_{t+\tau_2})$
000	$8320/2^{16}$
001	$8064/2^{16}$
010	$8064/2^{16}$
011	$8320/2^{16}$
100	$8064/2^{16}$
101	$8320/2^{16}$
110	$8320/2^{16}$
111	$8064/2^{16}$

depends on the parity of these vectors we translate these probabilities into binary probabilities. Using the binary probabilities we can calculate the bias, $\varepsilon = P(z_t + z_{t+\tau_1} + z_{t+\tau_2} = 0) = 4 \cdot \frac{8320}{2^{16}} - \frac{1}{2} = 7.8125 \cdot 10^{-3}$. As described before we use the thumb rule, $N \approx 1/\varepsilon^2$, for the number of output bits we need to observe in order to make a correct decision in the hypothesis test. This means that we need approximately 16384 bits to distinguish the cipher from a truly random source. Of course, we can use several weight three recursions (using squaring technique) and decrease the number of required bits. However, there are more powerful possibilities, as we will show in the next section.

4.4   Using More Than One Parity Check Equation

The distinguishing attack described in the previous section is in a very simple form. We can improve the performance by using a slightly more advanced technique. If we can find more than one low weight parity check equation, we can use them simultaneously to improve performance. Assume that we have the two parity check equations, $u_t + u_{t+\tau_1} + \ldots + u_{t+\tau_{w-1}} = 0$ and $u_t + u_{t+\tau_w} + \ldots + u_{t+\tau_{2w-2}} = 0$, giving rise to

$$\begin{aligned}
\mathbf{U}_t + \mathbf{U}_{t+\tau_1} + \ldots + \sum_{i=0}^{w-2} \mathbf{U}_{t+\tau_i} = \mathbf{0}, \\
\mathbf{U}_t + \mathbf{U}_{t+\tau_w} + \ldots + \sum_{i=w}^{2w-3} \mathbf{U}_{t+\tau_i} = \mathbf{0}.
\end{aligned} \tag{7}$$

We introduce in this case

$$\mathbf{Z_t} = (z_t, z_{t+\tau_1}, \ldots, z_{t+\tau_{2w-2}}).$$

In this case two of the variables are totally determined by the other variables,

$$\mathbf{Z_t} = (f(\mathbf{U}_t), \ldots, f(\sum_{i=0}^{w-2} \mathbf{U}_{t+\tau_i}), f(\mathbf{U}_{t+\tau_w}), \ldots, f(\mathbf{U}_t + \sum_{i=w}^{2w-3} \mathbf{U}_{t+\tau_i})). \tag{8}$$

In a similar manner we can use more than two parity checks in the vectors. Assume that we have N parity check equations. Then we have N positions in the vector that are fully determined by other positions. This means a more skew distribution of the output vector in (8). For the particular case of two parity check equations, the algorithm is described in Figure 3.

> 1. Find two weight w multiples of $g(x)$.
> 2. Calculate the distribution $P_0(\mathbf{Z}_t)$.
> 3. Calculate the length, N we need to observe.
> 4. **for** $t = 0 \dots N$
> $$\mathbf{Z}_t = (z_{t_t}, z_{t+\tau_1}, \dots, z_{t+\tau_{2w-2}})$$
>   **end for**
> 5. Calculate $I = \sum_{t=0}^{N} \left(\log_2 \frac{P_0(\mathbf{Z}_t)}{1/2^w} \right)$.
> 6. **if** $(I > 0)$
>   output "cipher" otherwise "random".

Fig. 3. Summary of the new distinguishing attack using two parity check equations

4.5 Example of the Attack Applied on a Filter Generator, Cont'd

In this section we consider the same example as in Section 4.3, but we use two recursions as described in Section 4.4. Hence we observe the keystream vectors

$$(z_t, z_{t+\tau_1}, \dots, z_{t+\tau_4}) = (f(\mathbf{U}_t), f(\mathbf{U}_{t+\tau_1}), f(\mathbf{U}_t + \mathbf{U}_{t+\tau_1}), f(\mathbf{U}_{t+\tau_3}), f(\mathbf{U}_t + \mathbf{U}_{t+\tau_3})),$$

when $(\mathbf{U}_t, \mathbf{U}_{t+\tau_1}, \mathbf{U}_{t+\tau_3})$ runs through all values. In this case we use statistical distance, as defined in Section 3, in order to determine the number of vectors N we need to make a correct decision. The statistical distance is approximately $\varepsilon = 0.01172$ and hence we need $N \approx 1/\varepsilon^2 = 7282$ vectors to distinguish the key stream. We see that the result is a significant improvement. If we extend the reasoning and use three weight three recursions we get $\varepsilon = 0.01276$ and hence we need $N \approx 1/\varepsilon^2 = 6145$ vectors. The gain of using three recursions instead of two is smaller.

4.6 The Weight Three Attack

If we can find many multiples of weight three of a feedback polynomial we can simplify the description of our attack. With a d-input nonlinear function we write one parity check as

$$\mathbf{U}_t + \mathbf{U}_{t+\tau_1} + \mathbf{U}_{t+\tau_2} = \mathbf{0}.$$

If $\mathbf{U}_t = \mathbf{0}$ we notice that $\mathbf{U}_{t+\tau_1} = \mathbf{U}_{t+\tau_2}$. If this is the case, then obviously $z_{t+\tau_1} = z_{t+\tau_2}$ (we assume that $f(\mathbf{0}) = 0$). Now, we have m weight three parity checks, say

$$\mathbf{U}_t + \mathbf{U}_{t+\tau_1} + \mathbf{U}_{t+\tau_2} = \mathbf{0},$$
$$\mathbf{U}_t + \mathbf{U}_{t+\tau_3} + \mathbf{U}_{t+\tau_4} = \mathbf{0},$$
$$\vdots$$
$$\mathbf{U}_t + \mathbf{U}_{t+\tau_{2m-1}} + \mathbf{U}_{t+\tau_{2m}} = \mathbf{0}.$$

Again assuming $\mathbf{U}_t = \mathbf{0}$ we see that we must have $z_{t+\tau_1} = z_{t+\tau_2}$, $z_{t+\tau_3} = z_{t+\tau_4}$, $\dots$, $z_{t+\tau_{2m-1}} = z_{t+\tau_{2m}}$. So, since $P(\mathbf{U}_t = \mathbf{0}) = 2^{-d}$ we will have

$$P(z_{t+\tau_1} = z_{t+\tau_2}, z_{t+\tau_3} = z_{t+\tau_4}, \dots, z_{t+\tau_{2m-1}} = z_{t+\tau_{2m}}) > 2^{-d}. \tag{9}$$

For a purely random sequence, however, this probability is 2^{-m}. It is important to note that when (9) holds for some t, it is very probable that $\mathbf{U}_t = \mathbf{0}$, i.e., *we have recovered a part of the key*. Since all output bits from the LFSR can be written as a linear combination of the initial state, $u_{t+t_i} = \sum_{i=0}^{r-1} a_i u_i$, $i = 1\ldots d$ where $a_i \in \{0,1\}$ are constants, we get d equations of the kind $u_{t+t_i} = \sum_{i=0}^{r-1} a_i u_i = 0$ for each $\mathbf{U}_t = \mathbf{0}$. Finding another value of t for which (9) holds gives more expressions describing the key. Since a full rank of the system of equations would only lead to the all zero solution, we need to guess at least one bit of the key. Then simple Gauss elimination can be applied to the system to deduce the other key bits. So we have described a *key recovery attack*. This attack has major consequences for any filter generator, as well as for nonlinear combining generators, and possibly also others. Basically, any filter generator of length r where the number of inputs d is smaller than $r/2$ can be broken very easily if we have access to a bit more than $2^{r/2}$ output symbols.

This leads to an attack as described in Figure 4.

---

1. Find m weight three multiples of $g(x)$.
2. Calculate the length N we need to observe.
3. **for** $t = 0 \ldots N$
       if $z_t = 0$ and
   $$z_{t+\tau_1} = z_{t+\tau_2}$$
   $$z_{t+\tau_3} = z_{t+\tau_4}$$
   $$\vdots$$
   $$z_{t+\tau_{2m-1}} = z_{t+\tau_{2m}}$$
       then assign $\mathbf{U}_t = \mathbf{0}$.
4. Guess at least one u_t and then recover $u_1, u_2, \ldots$ by linear algebra.

Fig. 4. Summary of the weight three key recovery attack

5   A Key Recovery Attack on LILI-128

In 2000 a project called NESSIE was initialized. The aim of this project was to collect a strong portfolio of cryptographic primitives. After a open call for proposals the submissions were thoroughly evaluated. One proposed candidate in the stream cipher category was called LILI-128 [3]. The cipher is very simple and its design is shift register based and uses a key of length 128 bits.

5.1   Description of LILI-128

LILI-128 has the structure of a filter generator. The only difference is that LILI-128 use an irregular clocking. LILI-128 consists of a first LFSR, called $LFSR_c$, that via a nonlinear function clocks a second LFSR, called $LFSR_d$, irregularly. The structured can be viewed in Figure 5. LILI-128 use a key length of 128 bits, the key is used directly to initialize the two binary LFSRs from left to right. Since

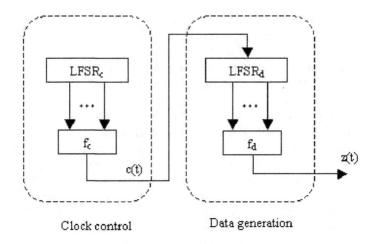

Fig. 5. Overview of LILI keystream generator

the the first shift register, $LFSR_c$ is a polynomial of length 39, the leftmost 39 bits of the key is used to initialize $LFSR_c$. The remaining 89 bits are used in the same manner to initialize $LFSR_d$. The feedback polynomial for $LFSR_c$ is given by

$$x^{39} + x^{35} + x^{33} + x^{31} + x^{17} + x^{15} + x^{14} + x^2 + 1 \ .$$

The Boolean function f_c takes two input bits from $LFSR_c$, namely the bit in stage 12 and the bit in stage 20 of the LFSR. The Boolean function f_c is chosen to be

$$f_c(x_{12}, x_{20}) = 2 \cdot x_{12} + x_{20} + 1 \ . \tag{10}$$

The output of this function is used to clock $LFSR_d$ irregularly. The reason for using irregular clocking [3], was that regularly clocked LFSRs are vulnerable to correlation and fast correlation attacks. The output sequence from f_c is denoted $c(t)$ and $c(t) \in \{1, 2, 3, 4\}$, i.e., $LFSR_d$ is clocked at least once and at most four times between consecutive outputs. On average, $LFSR_d$ is clocked $\bar{c} = 2.5$ times.

$LFSR_d$ is chosen to have a primitive polynomial of length 89 which produces a maximal-length sequence with a period of $P_d = 2^{89} - 1$. The feedback polynomial for $LFSR_d$ is

$$x^{89} + x^{83} + x^{80} + x^{55} + x^{53} + x^{42} + x^{39} + x + 1 \ .$$

Ten bits are taken from $LFSR_d$ as input to the the function f_d, these bits are taken from the positions (0,1,2,7,12,20,30,44,65,80) of the LFSR. The function f_d is given as a truth table, see [3].

5.2 The Attack Applied on LILI-128

In this chapter we will give a description of how we turn our new ideas described in Section 4 into a key recovery attack on LILI-128. The different steps of our attack can be summarized as follows:

- First we find a multiple of low weight of the $LFSR_d$, see Section 4.1.
- Secondly, we guess the content of $LFSR_c$. For each guess we perform a distinguishing attack on the output keystream. If the guessed key is the correct, we will detect a certain a bias in the output.
- When we have found the correct starting state of $LFSR_c$, we recover the initial state of $LFSR_d$ by just applying some well known attack, e.g. a time-memory tradeoff attack, or the weight three attack described in this paper.

After calculation of one (or several) multiple(s) of the feedback polynomial of $LFSR_d$, our first step is to guess the initial state of $LFSR_c$. If we guess the correct key the clocking of $LFSR_d$ is correct and we should be able to detect some bias in the keystream. To detect this bias we apply our distinguishing attack on the keystream. If we instead made an incorrect guess, the output sequence will have properties like a random source. For each guess of $LFSR_c$ we need to make a decision whether this is the correct key or not. LILI-128 uses 10 bits as input to the Boolean function f_d. For a w-weight multiple we get

$$(z_t, z_{t+\tau_1}, \ldots, z_{t+\tau_{w-1}}) = (f_d(\mathbf{U}_t), f_d(\mathbf{U}_{t+\tau_1}), \ldots, f_d(\sum_{i=0}^{w-2} \mathbf{U}_{t+\tau_i})), \qquad (11)$$

where $\mathbf{U}_{t+\tau_i}$ is a column vector including the ten inputs to f_d. If we consider the fact that we have an irregularly clocked LFSR, not all of the terms in (4) will be used to produce an output bit. If so, we cannot use this relation. Thus we will need more keystream to be able to get the required number of valid vectors $\mathbf{Z_t}$ we want. As $LFSR_d$ is clocked on average 2.5 times between consecutive outputs we can expect that we need to increase the keystream by roughly a factor $(2/5)^{w-1}$. (This is valid for the case of one weight w parity check. If we would consider all weight w parity checks up to a certain length, we do not need to increase the keystream length at all in the case of irregular clocking.)

5.3   Results with Weight Three Multiple

We first use the method described in Section 4.1 on LILI-128 to find a multiple of weight three. In this case we have the degree of the original feedback $r = 89$ and $w = 3$, hence the degree of the multiple is approximately $2^{44.5}$. The complexity to find one multiple of weight three according to [9] is approximately 2^{50}. If we use the distinguishing attack described above on a regularly clocked $LFSR_d$, the bias is $\varepsilon = 1.953 \cdot 10^{-3}$ which is greater than we would usually expect. This means that we will need approximately $1/\varepsilon^2 = 2^{18}$ keystream bits to distinguish it from a stream of random data. We thus need about slightly more than $2^{44.5}/2.5$ bits of received sequence. The complexity for the attack is $2^{38} \cdot 2^{18} \cdot 2.5^2$ since we search through the initial states of $LFSR_c$, each of these states takes 2^{18} bits to distinguish. To get 2^{18} sample values, we need to use $2^{18} * 2.5^2 \approx 2^{21}$ parity checks in the case of irregular clocking. The total complexity is about 2^{60}.

5.4   Results with Weight Four Multiple

To find a multiple of weight four we use the same method as before. In this case we have the degree of the original feedback $r = 89$ and $k = 4$, hence the degree of the multiple is approximately $2^{29.67}$. The complexity to find this multiple is 2^{65}. The bias is calculated to $\varepsilon = 1.862 \cdot 10^{-3}$, see [20] for an explanations on why weight three and weight four multiples give almost the same bias. We will need approximately $1/\varepsilon^2 = 2^{18.14}$ keystream bits in the case when all parities are available. We use the same argument as in the 3-weight case for the uncertainty of positions actually appearing in the output stream and we get that we in total need 2^{22} bits. Since the degree of the polynomial is 2^{30} we will need about $2^{30}/2.5$ bits to detect the bias. The complexity for the attack is about 2^{61}.

5.5   Results with Weight Five Multiple

To find a multiple of weight five we need a degree of the multiple of approximately $2^{17.8}$ and it takes about 2^{50} time. With a multiple of weight five the bias decreases significantly to $\varepsilon = 7.182 \cdot 10^{-6}$ and hence we will need approximately $1/\varepsilon^2 = 2^{34}$ available checks. We need in total 2^{40} bits to perform the distinguishing attack. The complexity for the attack is around 2^{79}.

5.6   The Weight Three Attack

We can improve the results above by using several low weight parity checks as described in Section 4.4. We do not present the results here, but consider only the modified attack described in Section 4.6. In earlier sections we have stated that the multiples of weight three start to appear at degree $2^{44.5}$. If we use about 15 valid parity equations in the weight three attack, the probability that we make an incorrect decision is low. The total complexity for this attack is roughly 2^{53} since we still guess the contents of $LFSR_c$ 2^{38} times on average, and for each guess we need to test whether the set of equalities $z_{t+\tau_1} = z_{t+\tau_2}, \ldots$ is true. Since the probability of such an event occurring for the correct key is $> 2^{-10}$ we run through a bit more, say 2^{12} such t values. As all but one test correspond to the random case, the equalities will hold with probability $1/2$. Hence we need very few comparisons on average (say 2). We also need to include the fact that not all positions are present, a factor 2.5^2. The required keystream length to find 15 valid weight three parity checks is roughly 2^{47}.

5.7   Summary

In Table 2 we summarize our result. Note that the work to synchronize positions for each guessed $LFSR_c$ state was not considered in previous work, but can be done without increasing the overall complexity by choosing states in the order they appear in the $LFSR_c$ cycle, see also [19].

We compare with the best attacks so far, summarized in Table 3. Here we have recalculated the complexity of [22] to bit operations.

Table 2. The sequence length and the complexity for different weights, the basic attack is described in Section 5.2, and the weight three attack is described in Section 5.6

	Sequence length	Complexity
Weight three attack	2^{47}	2^{53}
Basic attack with weight 3	2^{43}	2^{60}
Basic attack with weight 4	2^{29}	2^{61}
Basic attack with weight 5	2^{34}	2^{79}

Table 3. Comparison of our attack with the best known attacks

Attack by	Our	[6]	[22]	[5]
Sequence length in bits	2^{47}	2^{18}	2^{46}	2^{60}
Attack complexity	2^{53}	2^{96}	2^{60}	"

6   Conclusions and Future Work

We have presented a new simple attack philosophy on filter generators and related ciphers. We demonstrated the efficiency by attacking LILI-128. We can recover the key using 2^{47} keystream bits with complexity around 2^{53}, an improvement compared to previous attacks. The weight three attack is a very powerful key recovery attack on any filter generator, if enough output symbols are available. It also applies to any filter generator with a weight three feedback polynomial, by the squaring method.

It is an open problem to examine whether these techniques can be applied on stronger designs like LILI-II and word-oriented stream ciphers.

Finally, we mention that related work has independently been done by Molland and Helleseth [20].

References

1. A. Canteaut and M. Trabbia. Improved fast correlation attacks using parity-check equations of weight 4 and 5. In *Advances in Cryptology—EUROCRYPT 2000*, volume 1807 of *Lecture Notes in Computer Science*, pages 573–588. Springer-Verlag, 2000.
2. V. Chepyzhov, T. Johansson, and B. Smeets. A simple algorithm for fast correlation attacks on stream ciphers. In *Fast Software Encryption 2000*, volume 1978 of *Lecture Notes in Computer Science*, pages 181–195. Springer-Verlag, 2001.

3. A. Clark, E. Dawson, J. Fuller, J. Golic, H-J. Lee, William Millan, S-J. Moon, and L. Simpson. The LILI-128 keystream generator. In *Selected Areas in Cryptography—SAC 2000*, volume 2012 of *Lecture Notes in Computer Science*. Springer-Verlag, 2000.

4. D. Coppersmith, S. Halevi, and C.S. Jutla. Cryptanalysis of stream ciphers with linear masking. In M. Yung, editor, *Advances in Cryptology—CRYPTO 2002*, volume 2442 of *Lecture Notes in Computer Science*, pages 515–532. Springer-Verlag, 2002.

5. N. Courtois. Fast algebraic attacks on stream ciphers with linear feedback. In D. Boneh, editor, *Advances in Cryptology—CRYPTO 2003*, volume 2729 of *Lecture Notes in Computer Science*, pages 176–194. Springer-Verlag, 2003.

6. N. Courtois and W. Meier. Algebraic attack on strem ciphers with linear feedback. In E. Biham, editor, *Advances in Cryptology—EUROCRYPT 2003*, volume 2656 of *Lecture Notes in Computer Science*, pages 345–359. Springer-Verlag, 2003.

7. T. Cover and J.A. Thomas. *Elements of Information Theory*. Wiley series in Telecommunication. Wiley, 1991.

8. P. Ekdahl and T. Johansson. Distinguishing attacks on SOBER-t16 and SOBER-t32. In J. Daemen and V. Rijmen, editors, *Fast Software Encryption 2002*, volume 2365 of *Lecture Notes in Computer Science*, pages 210–224. Springer-Verlag, 2002.

9. J.D. Golić. Computation of low-weight parity-check polynomials. *Electronic Letters*, 32(21):1981–1982, October 1996.

10. J.D. Golić. On the security of nonlinear filter generators. In D. Gollman, editor, *Fast Software Encryption'96*, volume 1039 of *Lecture Notes in Computer Science*, pages 173–188. Springer-Verlag, 1996.

11. J.D. Golić, A. Clark, and E. Dawson. Inversion attack and branching. In J. Pieprzyk, R. Safavi-Naini, and J.Seberry, editors, *Information Security and Privacy: 4th Australasian Conference, ACISP'99*, volume 1587 of *Lecture Notes in Computer Science*, pages 88–102. Springer-Verlag, 1999.

12. J.D. Golić, A. Clark, and E. Dawson. Generalized inversion attack on nonlinear filter generators. 49(10):1100–1109, 2000.

13. T. Johansson and F. Jönsson. Fast correlation attacks based on turbo code techniques. In *Advances in Cryptology—CRYPTO'99*, volume 1666 of *Lecture Notes in Computer Science*, pages 181–197. Springer-Verlag, 1999.

14. T. Johansson and F. Jönsson. Improved fast correlation attacks on stream ciphers via convolutional codes. In *Advances in Cryptology—EUROCRYPT'99*, volume 1592 of *Lecture Notes in Computer Science*, pages 347–362. Springer-Verlag, 1999.

15. T. Johansson and F. Jönsson. A fast correlation attack on LILI-128. In *Information Processing Letters*, volume 81, pages 127–132, 2002.

16. S. Leveiller, G. Zémor, P. Guillot, and J. Boutros. A new cryptanalytic attack for pn-generators filtered by a boolean function. In K. Nyberg and H. Heys, editors, *Selected Areas in Cryptography—SAC 2002*, volume 2595 of *Lecture Notes in Computer Science*, pages 232–249. Springer-Verlag, 2003.

17. W. Meier and O. Staffelbach. Fast correlation attacks on stream ciphers. In C.G. Günter, editor, *Advances in Cryptology—EUROCRYPT'88*, volume 330 of *Lecture Notes in Computer Science*, pages 301–316. Springer-Verlag, 1988.

18. A. Menezes, P. van Oorschot, and S. Vanstone. *Handbook of Applied Cryptography*. CRC Press, 1997.

19. H. Molland. Improved linear consistency attack on irregular clocked keystream generators. In *Fast Software Encryption 2004*.

20. H. Molland and T. Helleseth. An improved correlation attack against irregular clocked and filtered keystream generators. In *Advances in Cryptology—CRYPTO 2004*.
21. E. Pasalic. *On Boolean Functions in Symmetric-Key Ciphers*. PhD thesis, Lund University, Department of Information Technology, P.O. Box 118, SE–221 00, Lund, Sweden, 2003.
22. M-J.O. Saarinen. A time-memory tradeoff attack against LILI-128. In J. Daemen and V. Rijmen, editors, *Fast Software Encryption 2002*, volume 2365 of *Lecture Notes in Computer Science*, pages 231–236. Springer-Verlag, 2002.
23. T. Siegenthaler. Correlation-immunity of non-linear combining functions for cryptographic applications. *IEEE Transactions on Information Theory*, 30:776–780, 1984.
24. D. Wagner. A generalized birthday problem. In M. Yung, editor, *Advances in Cryptology—CRYPTO 2002*, volume 2442 of *Lecture Notes in Computer Science*, pages 288–303. Springer-Verlag, 2002.

[0] The work described in this paper has been supported in part by the European Commission through the IST Programme under Contract IST-2002-507932 ECRYPT. The information in this document reflects only the author's views, is provided as is and no guarantee or warranty is given that the information is fit for any particular purpose. The user thereof uses the information at its sole risk and liability

On XTR and Side-Channel Analysis

Daniel Page and Martijn Stam

Dept. Computer Science, University of Bristol,
Merchant Venturers Building, Woodland Road,
Bristol, BS8 1UB, United Kingdom
{page, stam}@cs.bris.ac.uk

Abstract. Over the past few years, there has been a large volume of work on both attacking elliptic curve cryptosystems (ECC) using side-channel analysis and the development of related defence methods. Lenstra and Verheul recently introduced XTR, a cryptosystem that can compete with ECC in terms of processing and bandwidth requirements. These properties make XTR ideal for use on smart-cards, the devices that suffer most from vulnerability to side-channel attack. However, there are relatively few papers investigating the side-channel security of XTR and although some ECC techniques can be re-used, there are also notable differences. We aim to fill this gap in the literature. We present the first known SPA attack against XTR double exponentiation and two defence methods against such an attack. We also investigate methods of defending XTR against DPA attack.

Keywords: XTR, LUC, finite field, power analysis, side channel attack.

1 Introduction

In 2000 Lenstra and Verheul introduced XTR [16], a cryptosystem using (a sub-group of) the multiplicative group of $\mathbf{F}_{p^6}$ but with a compact representation based on the trace over $\mathbf{F}_{p^2}$ that allows highly efficient arithmetic. Given the current state of affairs in breaking the discrete logarithm problems over either finite fields or elliptic curves, XTR can compete with elliptic curve cryptography (ECC) in terms of both speed and bandwidth. This makes XTR suitable for deployment on similar sorts of constrained devices as ECC, where computational power and storage capacity are both very limited.

Side-channel analysis [13, 12] moves the art of cryptanalysis from the mathematical domain into the practical domain of implementation. Such attacks are based on the assumption that one can observe an algorithm being executed on a processing device and infer details about the internal state of computation from the features that occur. Although timing attacks are the classic example of this technique, in the context of ECC, power analysis is a popular method of monitoring the activity of the processor since smart-cards which commonly implement ECC cryptography draw power from an external and hence accessible source. Using simple equipment, an attacker can collect power profiles from a target smart-card and break the security of a system if the implementation does not include defences mechanisms. Techniques such as electromagnetic (EM) radiation based side-channels are growing in popularity but in this paper we limit our scope to attacks using simple (SPA) and differential (DPA) power analysis.

H. Handschuh and A. Hasan (Eds.): SAC 2004, LNCS 3357, pp. 54–68, 2005.

Due to wide spread use on devices such as smart-cards, there has been a large volume of work on side-channel attacks against ECC and also on defending against these attacks. Conversely, there are relatively few, if any papers addressing the side-channel security of XTR. Although one can borrow some defence methods from ECC and successfully apply them to XTR, there are also notable differences. For instance, ECC techniques based on curve isomorphisms or curve isogenies do not seem to apply, while others, such as exponent splitting, do apply but may not be the best engineering solution. We aim to fill this gap in the literature by investigating possible weaknesses of XTR against side-channel attacks and evaluating different defence techniques.

The paper is organised as follows. We use Section 2 to briefly recap on features of side-channel attacks that relate to subsequent discussion before presenting the XTR cryptosystem in Section 3. In Section 4 we describe an SPA attack against XTR, including some experimental results. We then describe methods for defending XTR against SPA and DPA attack in Sections 5 and 6 respectively.

2 Side-Channel Analysis

At the heart of power analysis is the concept of power traces. When a smart-card performs an operation, it consumes power in proportion to a number of factors such as which computational units are active and the Hamming weights of data involved. The power trace is a profile of how much power is being consumed at a given point in time during execution. Since the power supply on smart-cards is part of the reader terminal, it is both easily controllable and inspected by the attacker unless masking devices are used [23].

Attackers can harness such traces in two main ways. In an SPA attack the attacker executes the algorithm once and gleans information from the types of operation that are performed, focusing mainly on control flow. The attacker uses an operation trace that is constructed by spotting known operation profiles in the power trace. For example, suppose it is possible to differentiate between when a squaring and when a more general group multiplication is performed during an exponentiation using some secret exponent. Using a shorthand of A and D to represent squaring and multiplication, or addition and doubling in the additive case of elliptic curves, this leads to a sequence we call an operation trace. Let us consider the example of a left-to-right binary exponentiation algorithm used to perform ECC point multiplication. From a single trace, the secret exponent can be read immediately if the addition and doubling operations are distinguishable. For example, the operation trace DADD corresponds to an exponent of $(((1 \cdot 2) + 1) \cdot 2) \cdot 2 = 12_{10} = 1100_2$. By simply noting where an addition follows a doubling in the operation trace, the attacker can directly read the secret exponent and hence break the presumed security without needing to resort to solving a discrete logarithm problem.

DPA is a more powerful technique that may break systems that are secure against SPA attack. It also filters out noise from a power trace. By running the algorithm many times and focusing mainly on the value of data items used in each execution, the attacker applies statistical techniques to correlate the secret information with features in the collected profiles. To perform these statistical methods on an exponentiation algorithm for example, large numbers of power traces using the same exponent are required. If the exponentiation is suitably randomised, the samples will be too uncorrelated to provide useful information. However, if no randomised defence measures are in place DPA can be used to break the exponentiation, potentially using a small number of traces. Recent advances in DPA type analysis have seen address calculation as well as actual data values being examined in order to break table or window based exponentiation algorithms [6].

3 XTR

3.1 Description of XTR

XTR [16] is based on the assumed hardness of the discrete logarithm problem in the multiplicative group of $\mathbf{F}_{p^6}$. Using Pohlig-Hellman-like techniques, Lenstra [15] argues that the hardness of the DLP in $\mathbf{F}_{p^6}^*$ must in fact reside in the part that does not lie in any proper subfield. This is called the cyclotomic subgroup and denoted G_{p^2-p+1} since it has order $p^2 - p + 1$. Moreover a subgroup G_q of large prime order q is chosen in this cyclotomic subgroup to prevent further Pohlig-Hellman attacks on the smooth part of $p^2 - p + 1$.

In XTR elements of G_{p^2-p+1} are represented by their trace over $\mathbf{F}_{p^2}$. For $g \in \mathbf{F}_{p^6}^*$ the trace $\mathrm{Tr}(g)$ over $\mathbf{F}_{p^2}$ is defined as the sum of the conjugates over $\mathbf{F}_{p^2}$ of g

$$\mathrm{Tr}(g) = g + g^{p^2} + g^{p^4} \in \mathbf{F}_{p^2} .$$

Because the order of g divides $p^6 - 1$, the trace over $\mathbf{F}_{p^2}$ of g equals the trace of the conjugates over $\mathbf{F}_{p^2}$ of g, hence XTR makes no distinction between an element g and its conjugates over $\mathbf{F}_{p^2}$. If $g \in G_{p^2-p+1}$ then the element g, or one of its conjugates, can be retrieved from $c = \mathrm{Tr}(g)$ by determining a root of the cubic polynomial $X^3 - cX^2 + c^p X - 1$. Lenstra and Verheul also show that any given $c \in \mathbf{F}_{p^2}$ is the trace of some element in G_{p^2-p+1} if the aforementioned cubic polynomial is irreducible over $\mathbf{F}_{p^2}$. This tightly and provably links the discrete logarithm problem for XTR to that of the corresponding subgroup $G_q \in \mathbf{F}_{p^6}^*$, and heuristically to that in the entire field $\mathbf{F}_{p^6}^*$.

Henceforth, let p and q be primes with q dividing $p^2 - p + 1$. Suggested lengths to provide adequate levels of security are $k = \lg q \approx 160$ and $l = \lg p \approx 170$. Also, let g be a generator of G_q and let $c = \mathrm{Tr}(g)$. Lenstra and Verheul [17] show how p, q and c can be found quickly. In particular, there is no need to find an explicit representation of $g \in \mathbf{F}_{p^6}$.

Throughout this article, c_n denotes $\mathrm{Tr}(g^n) \in \mathbf{F}_{p^2}$, for some p and g of order q dividing $p^2 - p + 1$ as above. Note that $c_0 = 3$ and $c_1 = c$. Efficient computation of c_n given p, q and c depends on the recurrence relation

(1) $$c_{n+m} = c_n c_m - c_m^p c_{n-m} + c_{n-2m} ,$$

which simplifies for $n = m$ to

$$c_{2n} = c_n^2 - 2c_n^p .$$

Lenstra and Verheul note that the simplification of c_{2n} allows for a considerable speedup of its computation. This speedup will be responsible for providing different traces for A corresponding to c_{n+m} and D corresponding to c_{2n}. We will occasionally abuse notation and use A and D denote the cost of the operations as well, where A $\approx$ 2D.

3.2 Binary Exponentiation

Algorithm 1 was introduced by Lenstra and Verheul alongside XTR. They already noted that regardless of the bit being read in Step 3, two doublings and one addition are being performed. Hence the operation trace contains no Shannon information on the exponent apart from its length, provided that for both cases in Step 3 the same order is used [5] (cf. [21, 10] for similar subtleties for the binary Lucas left-to-right algorithm [14]). The algorithm can be slightly adapted to output the triple (c_{n-1}, c_n, c_{n+1}), but care has to be taken (e.g., by adding a dummy operation) that the least significant bit of n is not leaked. The runtime of the algorithm is basically $A + 2D$ per exponent bit.

Algorithm 1: Left-to-Right Binary Exponentiation.

On input n and c this algorithm returns c_n or the triple $(c_{2\lfloor \frac{n}{2} \rfloor}, c_{2\lfloor \frac{n}{2} \rfloor+1}, c_{2\lfloor \frac{n}{2} \rfloor+2})$. It maintains as invariant

$$0 \le j < k, \quad a = 1 + \sum_{i=j+1}^{k-1} n_i 2^{i-j}, \quad S_a = (c_{a-1}, c_a, c_{a+1}) .$$

(a is carried along for expository purposes only).

1. [Initialization] Set $j \leftarrow k - 1, a \leftarrow 1$ as well as $S_a \leftarrow (3, c, c_2)$.
2. [Finished?] If $j = 0$ terminate with output c_{a-1} if $n_0 = 0$ and with output c_a otherwise.
3. [Decrease j] If $n_j = 0$, set $S_a \leftarrow (c_{2(a-1)}, c_{(a-1)+a}, c_{2a})$ and set $a \leftarrow 2a - 1$; else ($n_j = 1$) set $S_a \leftarrow (c_{2a}, c_{(a+1)+a}, c_{2(a+1)})$ and set $a \leftarrow 2a + 1$. Decrease j by one and go back to the previous step.

3.3 Euclidean Exponentiation

A faster exponentiation routine for XTR was described by Stam and Lenstra [24]. It is based on an adaptation of a Euclidean algorithm by Montgomery [20] using Lucas chains. For ease of notation, we will momentarily use ordinary exponentiation in our description instead of the third order XTR recurrence. The algorithm is based on the invariant relation $A^d B^e = g^n h^m$, where the left-hand side are variables in the algorithm and the right-hand side is the exponentiation to be performed. It is easy to initialise the variables by $(d, e) = (n, m)$ and $(A, B) = (g, h)$. The algorithm then reduces d and e in a way depending on the current values of d and e, updating A and B applying multiplication and squaring operations as execution progresses. Finally, when $e = 0$, the algorithm outputs A and the unprocessed part of the exponent d.

Algorithm 2: Euclidean Double Exponentiation.

Given bases $c_\kappa, c_\lambda, c_{\kappa-\lambda}$, and $c_{\kappa-2\lambda}$ and positive exponents n, m, this algorithm outputs $u = \gcd(n, m)$ and $c_{(n\kappa+m\lambda)/u}$. It uses invariant

$$d > 0, \quad e \ge 0, \quad ad + be = n\kappa + m\lambda, \quad \gcd(d, e) = \gcd(n, m),$$
$$A = c_a, \quad B = c_b, \quad C = c_{a-b}, \quad D = c_{a-2b} .$$

(a and b are carried along for expository purposes only).

Table 1. Two tables that describe the operation of Euclidean exponentiation

Type	Condition	Substitution	Trace
Substitutions if $d \geq e$			
X1	$d \leq 4e$	$(e, d-e)$	A
X2	d even	$(d/2, e)$	ADD
X3	d, e both odd	$((d-e)/2, e)$	ADD
X4	e even	$(e/2, d)$	DD
Substitutions if $e \geq d$			
X5	$e \leq 4d$	$(d, e-d)$	A
X6	e even	$(e/2, d)$	DD
X7	d, e both odd	$((e-d)/2, d)$	ADD
X8	d even	$(d/2, e)$	ADD

(a) A table describing the operations performed by the Euclidean exponentiation algorithm and the SPA trace produced as a result. Note the ordered constraints on values of d and e that dictate the algorithm execution

Type	Condition	Substitution	Trace
Substitutions if $d \geq e$			
X1	$0 \leq e \leq 3d$	$(d+e, d)$	A
X2	$e < \frac{1}{2}d$ and e odd	$(2d, e)$	ADD
X3	$e < \frac{2}{3}d$ and e odd	$(2d+e, e)$	ADD
X4	$e > 8d$ and e odd	$(e, 2d)$	DD
Substitutions if $e \geq d$			
X5	$0 \leq e \leq 3d$	$(d, d+e)$	A
X6	$e < \frac{1}{2}d$ and e odd	$(e, 2d)$	DD
X7	$e < \frac{2}{3}d$ and e odd	$(e, 2d+e)$	ADD
X8	$e > 8d$ and e odd	$(2d, e)$	ADD

(b) A reverse engineering of Euclidean exponentiation which shows the operations used if the algorithm is run in reverse, starting with the pair $(1, 1)$ and moving towards the initial exponent values

1. [Initialization] Let $a = \kappa$, $b = \lambda$, and set $d \leftarrow n$, $e \leftarrow m$, $A \leftarrow c_\kappa$, $B \leftarrow c_\lambda$, $C \leftarrow c_{\kappa-\lambda}$, and $D \leftarrow c_{\kappa-2\lambda}$.
2. [Both even?] Set $f_2 \leftarrow 0$. As long as d and e are both even, replace (d, e) by $(d/2, e/2)$ and f_2 by $f_2 + 1$.
3. [Finished?] If $e = 0$ terminate with output $d2^{f_2}$ and A.
4. [Decrease (d, e)] Substitute (d, e) using the first applicable rule in Table 1a. Update a, b, A, B, C and D accordingly, in order to maintain the invariant. Go back to the previous step.

Table 1a contains the rules that are used to decrease the pair (d, e), including the operations-trace that is left by any particular rule. We have left out the optional ternary rules described by Stam and Lenstra, because the speedup achieved is based upon a clearly recognisable tripling operation and we believe the resulting increase of side-channel leakage is likely to outweigh the gain in speed. On average, the algorithm takes $1.39A + 1.1D$ per exponent bit.

A single exponentiation routine can be based on the double exponentiation routine by writing $g^n = g^{n-r}g^r$ where r can be chosen arbitrarily. A sensible way to do this is described in Algorithm 3, where we have thrown out some speedups proposed by Montgomery based on the factorisation of the exponent, since we deem them to vulnerable to attack. If r is chosen as in Step 3 below coprime to the exponent n, the call to Algorithm 2 will result in approximately $0.72 \lg n$ applications of X1 after which a random $(\lg n)/2$-bit random double exponentiation follows. Overall, a single exponentiation will take $1.41A + 0.55D$.

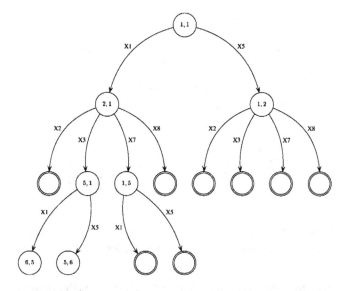

Fig. 1. A parse tree generated by the SPA trace AADDA corresponding to the initial pair $(5, 6)$. Note that the edges are marked with operations that are applied by the exponentiation algorithm to move between the nodes that contain intermediate (d, e) pairs

Algorithm 3: Single Exponentiation.

Given a base c and an exponent n, this algorithm computes c_n.

1. $[d = 1?]$ If $d = 1$, the algorithm terminates with output A.
2.   [Initialise new GCD calculation] Set $r \leftarrow \lceil \frac{d}{\phi} \rceil$ and set $(d, e) \leftarrow (r, d - r)$.
3.   [Compute "A^p"] Run Algorithm 2 on input $(c, c, 3, c^p)$ and exponents (d, e). Let the output be u and $\tilde{A}$. Set $d \leftarrow u$ and $A \leftarrow \tilde{A}$. Go back to step 1.

4   SPA Attack

Since the single exponentiation routine starts off with a fairly predictable part after which a random double exponentiation takes part, we direct our efforts into analysing the double exponentiation (with coprime exponents). Curiously, attacking double exponentiation algorithms has only received limited attention in the literature so far, although they are essential if precomputation is used and of potential benefit if exponent splitting is used to defend against SPA and DPA.

From the view of an adversary, the Euclidean algorithm starts with unknown values for (d, e) but ends with the known pair $(1, 0)$. In their analysis, the adversary can attempt to run the algorithm backwards by trying to predict which step led to a certain pair (d, e). For instance, $(1, 0)$ is certain to be preceded by $(1, 1)$ which will be our starting point henceforth. We can view the second-guessing of which operations were performed as movement within a tree of choices where nodes represent (d, e) pairs and edges represent

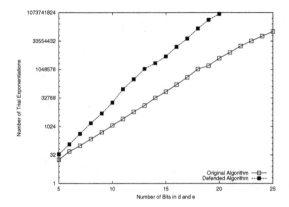

Fig. 2. A graph showing the results of implementing an SPA guided search attack against the original and defended versions of Euclidean exponentiation

the operations performed. As such, there will be a single path through the tree from the initial (d, e) pair to the root of the tree which will be the pair $(1, 1)$. Each leaf in the tree corresponds to a potential exponent. The adversary needs to check the exponents until he has found the correct one, so in order to improve the efficiency of the attack we want to minimise the number of leaves.

By using the collected SPA trace, we can prune the search tree considerably. For example, if we notice the sequence DD we know that neither operation X1 nor X5 will have generated it. We can therefore refine the full tree into what one might call a parse tree derived from the operations observed in the SPA trace. That is, we include only those paths that match what has been observed and prune the rest. Figure 1 shows an example tree for the parse A, ADD, A of a trace AADDA corresponding to the initial pair $(5, 6)$.

As well as using the SPA trace to eliminate impossible paths, we can work from the known root of the tree towards the leaves and use constraints on (d, e) pairs to eliminate operations that could not have occurred. Table 1b illustrates such transformations and constraints, which are essentially the postconditions that follow from the preconditions and the transformations in Table 1a. One can see that rule X6 is almost superfluous: none of the eight steps can actually lead to its precondition, so it can be called at most once from the start in a double exponentiation routine. Also note that X4 is always followed by either X7 or X8 and that the observation of ADDDD implies the last two D's originate from X4. As a more concrete example of pruning based on Table 1b, consider that we arrive at pair $(1, 2)$ and see the sequence ADD. We would ordinarily need to search the paths for operations X2, X3, X7 and X8 but since we know that e must be odd for any of these operations to have occurred, we can eliminate the impossible paths from our search. In Figure 1, empty nodes with double rings denote nodes that are pruned using this method. Using a brute force search of the key space, one might perform around 2^6 trial exponentiations in the worst case since the pair $(5, 6)$ represents six unknown bits. Using the SPA trace to prune this search, we perform only two trials due to the number of false or impossible paths eliminated. However, with such small values of d and e, it is not clear how the method might perform in the face of recommended key sizes.

In order to empirically investigate this technique with larger parameters, we implemented the search mechanism and ran a large number of experiments. Ambiguity of parses, such as the choice of A, ADD, A over A, A, DD, A from the trace AADDA is managed inline with our search so that accumulated work is not wasted. We also added two search heuristics to guide the selection of valid paths that rely on us first generating a large number of random keys and constructing some tables from the probability of generating a given trace. These tables allow us to order our selection of paths through the tree based on the probability of their occurrence in our analysis phase. Specifically, we maintain a path history from the root and use it to guide subsequent choices. For example, at node $(2, 1)$ we might descend down edge X3 before edge X7 since that has shown to be a more probable path to target nodes.

From the graph of results in Figure 2 we can see that the average number of trial exponentiations is roughly given by $2^{1.09 \cdot k}$ where k is the length of the exponents. Put more simply, this implies that if an attacker can capture an SPA trace the system is only as secure as where the exponents are about half as long. For example, given 80-bit values of d and e, the attack can recover their value in the same time a naive exhaustive search would take if they were around each around 43-bits. Although not totally devastating for large keys, care must be taken to guard against smaller values of d and e being vulnerable to such an attack. This is especially true since it might be attractive to use such smaller values in constrained environments so as to balance performance against available resources.

For a single exponentiation of a k-bit exponent, this implies the attack succeeds after roughly $2^{0.55 \cdot k}$ trials. Although this is still more than using the Pollard rho method, it is worryingly close. Moreover, it is not unthinkable that in significantly less time part of the exponent can be recovered.

5   SPA Countermeasures

5.1   Adapting the Euclidean Algorithm

Precomputing r. For a fixed exponent, it is possible to precompute r in Algorithm 3 and store this value alongside the exponent. A clever choice of r might increase the number of A's in the operation trace without significantly increasing the total costs. For instance, Montgomery conjectured the existence of an r with only 1,2 and 3 in the continued fraction of n/r. Precomputation of such an r would yield an SPA-resistant algorithm since it would only call rules X1 and X5. We did not attempt to find such a conjectured r, but instead opted for generating a large number of r's coprime to the fixed exponent and picked the one that used the least number of steps in the Euclidean algorithm without binary steps. We formed our r's by dividing n by a deviation of the golden ratio ϕ. The golden ratio has as continued fraction an infinite number of ones. Our deviations also allow 2's and some 3's in the initial part of the continued fraction. For 160-bit exponents we examined about hundred thousand possible values of r per exponent. On average, the cost of the exponentiation, after this precomputation, is about 1.7A per exponent bit.

As a result, for fixed exponents we achieve a SPA-resistant algorithm for hardly any extra work, not taking into account the precomputation. Working harder during precomputation might result in a faster routine, potentially even faster than the unprotected algorithm (this was observed for some smaller bitlengths). Essentially, a small addition chain of a special type is being sought. In principal, similar techniques could apply to ordinary exponentiation with a fixed exponent as well, although we are not aware of any particular family of small addition chains that is resilient against SPA attacks yet having a short certificate (although storing the description of the entire chain might be an option).

This SPA countermeasure excludes several DPA countermeasures from Section 6. This is unfortunate since the SPA countermeasure only makes sense if the same exponent is reused over and over. For random exponents DPA is not an issue, but this particular SPA countermeasure does not work. For random, fresh exponents one could consider constructing the exponent by means of a randomly generated continued fraction with sufficiently small entries. We did not explore this avenue, but it undoubtedly will skew the probability distribution of the exponents in some way.

Choice Randomisation. Making the operation choices non-deterministic is a fairly simple task that to some extent follows work in ECC where addition chains are traversed in random patterns [22]. In order to implement this measure, we propose to relax the bounding conditions that dictate when an operation is selected and then introduce some random factor into the decision making process. For example, one might set the conditions for X1 and X4 to be $d < 2e$ and $2e < d < 4e$ but only execute the later with probability of a half. Although this acts to randomise calculation and help to thwart DPA attack, clearly some investigating of how this might effect security in the context of SPA is required.

We implemented the defense strategy and mounted our search attack from Section 4 against it with results again shown in Figure 2. The introduction of non-determinism clearly hampers the search with the number of trial exponentiations now given by about $2^{1.52 \cdot k}$. This improvement in security is fairly inexpensive; a double exponentiation now takes on average about $1.29A + 1.53D$ per exponent bit corresponding to a 3.2% overhead for a single exponentiation. Given the low cost of the method, one might implement further similar transformations that introduce more non-determinism should higher degrees of resistance to SPA attack be required.

For ordinary binary algorithms, using randomization to prevent SPA can actually weaken the algorithm if a small number of traces using the same exponent are known due to attacks based on hidden Markov models [11]. The Euclidean algorithm does not seem to be susceptible to this kind of attack, since a different random choice at one point makes it extremely unlikely that further on in the algorithm the same state is going to occur.

5.2   SPA-Resistant Trace Operations

In ECC the doubling and addition operations are mathematically quite different, so distinguishable traces for them are hard to avoid. Even so, there are some uniform solutions, although they have additional problems [18, 8, 1, 7]. In contrast, for XTR obtaining indistinguishable operations is really only a matter of choice beween accelerated and normal arithmetic. An obvious way to hinder SPA is therefore to not bother speeding things up and hope that the power traces of a real c_{n+m} and a less general c_{n+n} will be indistinguishable. However, there is no need to compromise since we can have SPA-resistant trace operations that largely preserve the speedup and also make the trace of two applications of c_{2n} indistinguishable to one application of c_{n+m}. Similar techniques have been described to do this in the context of ECC [26, 4].

For efficiency purposes, Lenstra and Verheul propose to pick $p \equiv 2 \bmod 3$ and use $\{\zeta_3, \zeta_3^2\}$ as a basis for $\mathbf{F}_{p^2}$, where ζ_3 is a root of the third cyclotomic polynomial $x^2 + x + 1$. Later it was noted by Stam and Lenstra [25] that if $p \equiv 3 \bmod 4$, then one can use $\{1, \zeta_4\}$ without significant loss of efficiency, where ζ_4 is a root of the fourth cyclotomic polynomial $x^2 + 1$. Using these bases, the costs of applying c_{2n} are dominated by two modular multiplications, whereas performing c_{n+m} is twice as expensive, costing four modular multiplications and several additions (cf. [16–Lemma 2.1.1], [24–Lemma 2.2], [2–Case $p = 3$], and [2–Case $p^k = 4$]).

The 4:2 ratio in modular multiplications leads us to attempt to try and make two applications of c_{2n} indistinguishable from one application of c_{n+m}. In the Appendix we describe how to do this based on the field representation given by Lenstra and Verheul if p is congruent to 2 modulo 3; and then for the alternative representation if p is congruent to 3 modulo 4. We assume that modular addition and modular subtraction are indistinguishable. We also assume that in the base field computing $a + (a + 2)$, or more generally $a + (b + c)$ where c is very small, is indistinguishable from computing $a + b$. These are all modular additions and if some carry fiddling is allowed, the assumption should hold. However, using Montgomery arithmetic might hamper things, in that 2 has to be represented by the full fledged $2R \bmod p$ where R is the Montgomery radix. In this case an Add' will be equivalent to two ordinary modular additions and some extra dummy additions have to be added to c_{n+m} routine to make up for this.

6 DPA Countermeasures

The algorithms presented in Section 3 are deterministic in their use of data and are therefore likely to be vulnerable against DPA type attacks. One way to prevent DPA attacks is to inject randomness into both the behaviour of the algorithm and the data items it operates on, so that correlation between executions is more difficult. Such techniques have been well studied within the context of ECC and here we describe their applicability for use with exponentiation routines in XTR.

6.1 Binary Exponentiation

Exponent Randomisation. One of the easiest ways to randomise an exponentiation is to add a random multiple of the group order to the original exponent and run the algorithm using the result [12, 3]. That is, one picks a random r and computes c_{n+rq} before recovering the required result at the end, a technique sometimes called exponent blinding. This method is clearly applicable to XTR but suffers from the same significant performance problems as when used in ECC and is therefore not ideal. For example, for a group of 160 bits in size if r is chosen to be 20 bits long, the exponentiation is slowed down by around 12.5%.

Exponent Splitting. A related technique to randomising the exponent is splitting it into two parts by picking a random $r \in \mathbf{Z}_q$ and rewriting the exponent as $(n - r) + r$. The values $(n - r)$ and r are then used to compute two single exponentiations that are multiplied together to reconstruct the required result. This final multiplication is troublesome in XTR because although c_{n-r} and c_r are known, the required differences c_{n-2r} and c_{n-3r} are typically not and explicitly computing c_{n-2r} and c_{n-3r} alongside other calculations effectively quadruples the cost of a conventional exponentiation. One can bypass this problem by computing g^{n-r} and g^r in $\mathbf{F}_{p^6}$, multiply these two values and trace back the result, but this would be outside the realm of XTR and we do not expect it to be particularly efficient. The final possibility is to use a double exponentiation routine that directly leads to c_n. Stam and Lenstra [24] present a double exponentiation version of the binary algorithm that is suitable for this purpose. In essence, the exponent is rewritten as

$$n \equiv \frac{r}{2^k}\left(2^k + \frac{(n-r)2^k}{r}\right) \bmod q,$$

after which the binary algorithm is called twice on exponents $\frac{(n-r)2^k}{r} \bmod q$ and $\frac{r}{2^k} \bmod q$. Hence this countermeasure doubles the execution time required for an exponentiation and can hardly be recommended.

Note that the problems just described also complicates the use of techniques such as meet-in-the-middle [19], where one picks a random point in the binary expansion of an exponent before using a left-to-right algorithm to compute one half and a right-to-left algorithm for the other half.

Base Randomisation. Another method is to randomise the base value by operating modulo some random multiple of the real modulus p and converting back only at the end of an exponentiation. This method applies to XTR although the costs are harder to pin down, since it requires comparing modular multiplications of different length exponents.

Field Randomisation. Han et al. [5] suggest using a field randomisation as a countermeasure, mimicking an ECC countermeasure by Joye and Tymen [9]. Although theoretically XTR works for any field representation, it is essential for its efficiency that the Frobenius endomorphism can be computed almost for free without aversely affecting the costs of an ordinary field multiplication. This combined requirement severely limits the number of field representations that can be used, so using randomised field representations as a countermeasure against DPA will probably be expensive.

Order Randomisation. One could consider randomising the order in which operations are called within Step 3 of the algorithm, for instance using the sequence DDA with probability a half and ADD with probability a half. Although this does randomise the traces in some sense, it does not alter any of the intermediate triples S_a and typically it is leakage such as the Hamming weight of these data items that allows successful DPA attacks. As a consequence, we doubt this countermeasure is suitable to defend against

DPA and note that it has the additional drawback of complicating parallel implementation of the computation required in Step 3.

6.2   Euclidean Exponentiation

Most countermeasures discussed for binary exponentiation apply in equal measure to Euclidean exponentiation (where exponent randomisation takes place before calling Algorithm 3). The main difference is that exponent splitting is actually a very attractive choice now, since it is a necessity part of the Euclidean exponentiation algorithm anyway. If we replace ϕ in Step 2 of Algorithm 3 by a deviation of the golden ratio where the first 20 values in the continued fraction are independently changed to two with probability a half, the runtime of the single exponentiation increases by less than one percent. We believe this to be an efficient and adequate DPA countermeasure.

7   Conclusions

Previous work has shown that the public key cryptosystem XTR can be a high performance alternative to ECC and is especially suited for implementation on constrained, mobile devices such as smart-cards. In this paper, we have presented an analysis of several security issues that are important if XTR is to be used on such devices. By examining issues of side-channel security relating to the double exponentiation used in XTR, we fill a gap in the literature left open by other work in this area.

We presented the first known SPA attack against XTR double exponentiation and two defence methods against such an attack. The first method used a novel randomisation of the exponentiation algorithm while the second borrowed a technique from ECC to construct indistinguishable arithmetic. Finally, we investigated methods of defending XTR against DPA attack, noting that adapting ECC specific techniques require several subtle alterations to cope with the XTR group structure.

As a result, for security against currently known side-channel methods we propose the use of the Euclidean method in Algorithm 2 coupled with indistinguishable arithmetic to guard against SPA and exponent splitting to cope with DPA. This offers a very low performance overhead defence method while achieving a high level of security against side-channel attack. In further work we intend to investigate this security level in physical SPA and DPA experiments and also to explore defence methods for the explicit, i.e. nontrace based, version of XTR.

The authors would like to thank Bart Preneel for his opposition, which led to this research, and Arjen K. Lenstra for his encouragement and proofreading.

References

1. É. Brier and M. Joye. Weierstraß elliptic curves and side-channel attacks. *PKC'02*, LNCS **2274**, pages 335–345.
2. H. Cohen and A. K. Lenstra. Supplement to implementation of a new primality test. *Mathematics of Computation*, 48(177): S1–S4, 1987.

3. J.-S. Coron. Resistance against differential power analysis for elliptic curve cryptosystems. *CHES'99*, LNCS **1717**, pages 292–302.
4. C. H. Gebotys and R. J. Gebotys. Secure elliptic curve implementations: An analysis of resistance to power-attacks in a dsp processor. *CHES'02*, LNCS **2523**, pages 114–128.
5. D.-G. Han, J. Lim, and K. Sakurai. On insecurity of the side channel attack on xtr. In *The 2004 Symposium on Cryptography and Information Security (SCIS'04)*, page To appear. The Institute of Electronics, Information and Communication Engineers, 2004.
6. K. Itoh, T. Izu, and M. Takenaka. Address-bit differential power analysis of cryptographic schemes OK-ECDH and OK-ECDSA. *CHES'02*, LNCS **2523**, pages 129–143.
7. T. Izu and T. Takagi. Exceptional procedure attack on elliptic curve cryptosystems. *PKC'03*, LNCS **2567**, pages 224–239.
8. M. Joye and J.-J. Quisquater. Hessian elliptic curves and side-channel attacks. *CHES'01*, LNCS **2162**, pages 93–100.
9. M. Joye and C. Tymen. Protection against differential power analysis for elliptic curve cryptography – an algebraic approach. *CHES'01*, LNCS **2162**, pages 377–390.
10. M. Joye and S.-M. Yen. The Montgomery powering ladder. *CHES'02*, LNCS **2523**, pages 291–302.
11. C. Karlof and D. Wagner. Hidden markov model cryptanalysis. *CHES'03*, LNCS **2779**, pages 17–34.
12. P. C. Kocher. Timing attacks on implementations of Diffie-Hellman, RSA, DSS, and other systems. *Crypto'96*, LNCS **1109**, pages 104–113.
13. P. C. Kocher, J. Jaffe, and B. Jun. Differential power analysis. *Crypto'99*, LNCS **1666**, pages 388–397.
14. D. H. Lehmer. Computer technology applied to the theory of numbers. *Studies in Number Theory*, volume 6 of *MAA Studies in Mathematics*, pages 117–151. Math. Assoc. Amer. (distributed by Prentice-Hall, Englewood Cliffs, N.J.), 1969.
15. A. K. Lenstra. Using cyclotomic polynomials to construct efficient discrete logarithm cryptosystems over finite fields. *ACISP'97*, LNCS **1270**, pages 127–138.
16. A. K. Lenstra and E. R. Verheul. The XTR public key system. *Advances in Cryptography— Crypto'00*, LNCS **1880**, pages 1–19.
17. A. K. Lenstra and E. R. Verheul. An overview of the XTR public key system. *The proceedings of the Public-Key Cryptography and Computational Number Theory Conference*, pages 151–180. Verlages Walter de Gruyter, 2001.
18. P.-Y. Liardet and N. P. Smart. Preventing SPA/DPA in ECC systems using the Jacobi form. *CHES'01*, LNCS **2162**, pages 391–401.
19. T. S. Messerges, E. A. Dabbish, and R. H. Sloan. Power analysis attacks on modular exponentiation in smartcards. *CHES'99*, LNCS **1717**, pages 144–157.
20. P. L. Montgomery. Evaluating recurrences of form $X_{m+n} = f(X_m, X_n, X_{m-n})$ via Lucas chains. Revised (1992) version from ftp.cwi.nl: /pub/pmontgom/Lucas.ps.gz, 1983.
21. K. Okeya and K. Sakurai. Power analysis breaks elliptic curve cryptosystems secure against timing attack. *Indocrypt'00*, LNCS **1977**, pages 178–190.
22. E. Oswald and M. Aigner. Randomized addition-subtraction chains as a countermeasure against power attacks. *CHES'01*, LNCS **2162**, pages 39–50.
23. A. Shamir. Protecting smart cards from passive power analysis with detached power supplies. *CHES'00*, LNCS **1965**, pages 71–77.
24. M. Stam and A. K. Lenstra. Speeding up XTR. *Asiacrypt'01*, LNCS **2248**, pages 125–143.
25. M. Stam and A. K. Lenstra. Efficient subgroup exponentiation in quadratic and sixth degree extensions. *CHES'02*, LNCS **2523**, pages 318–332.
26. E. Trichina and A. Bellezza. Implementation of elliptic curve cryptography with built-in counter measures against side channel attacks. *CHES'02*, LNCS **2523**, pages 98–113.

A   SPA-Resistant Trace Operations

A.1   Field Representation for $p \equiv 2 \bmod 3$

This is the original XTR field representation. Let p be a prime congruent to 2 mod 3, then p generates $\mathbf{Z}_3^*$ and $\Phi_3(x) = x^2 + x + 1 \mid (x^3 - 1)$ is irreducible in $\mathbf{F}_p$. Let ζ_3 denote a root of $\Phi_3(x)$, then $\zeta^n = \zeta_3^{(n \bmod 3)}$ and in particular $\zeta_3^p = \zeta_3^2$. Hence $\{\zeta_3, \zeta_3^2\}$ is an optimal normal basis of $\mathbf{F}_{p^2}$ over $\mathbf{F}_p$.

Let $c_n \in \mathbf{F}_{p^2}$ be represented by $(c_{n,1}, c_{n,2}) \in (\mathbf{F}_p)^2$, i.e., $c_n = c_{n,1}\zeta_3 + c_{n,2}\zeta_3^2$ (similarly for c_m, c_{n-m} and c_{n-2m}). Using Fermat's little theorem we have that $c_{n,1}^p = c_{n,1}$ etc. and hence $c_n^p = c_{n,2}\zeta_3 + c_{n,1}\zeta_3^2$. We need to consider the computation of c_{2n} and c_{n+m}. The first one is easiest, since

$$c_{2n} = (c_{n,2} - 2(c_{n,1} + 1))c_{n,2}\zeta_3 + (c_{n,1} - 2(c_{n,2} + 1))c_{n,1}\zeta_3^2 .$$

Computation of c_{n+m} boils down to computing

$$c_{n+m} = ((c_{n-m,1} - (c_{n-m,2} + c_{m,2}))c_{n,1} + (c_{n-m,2} + c_{m,2} - c_{m,1})c_{n,2} + c_{n-2m,1})\zeta_3 +$$
$$+ ((c_{n-m,2} - (c_{n-m,1} + c_{m,1}))c_{n,2} + (c_{n-m,1} + c_{m,1} - c_{m,2})c_{n,1} - c_{n-2m,2})\zeta_3^2 .$$

If c_{2m-n} is known instead of c_{n-2m} the required Frobenius operation can be easily incorporated into the formula above by swapping the roles of $c_{n-2m,1}$ and $c_{n-2m,2}$. This is especially handy for the binary exponentiation algorithm.

	One c_{n+m} call	Operation		Two c_{2n} calls
1.	$t_1 = c_{n-m,2} + c_{m,2}$	Add	Add'	$t_1 = c_{n,1} + (c_{n,1} + 2)$
2.	$t_2 = c_{n-m,1} - t_1$	Sub	Sub	$t_2 = c_{n,2} - t_1$
3.	$t_3 = c_{n,1} \cdot t_2$	Mul	Mul	$c_{2n,1} = c_{n,2} \cdot t_2$
4.	$t_4 = c_{n-2m,1} + t_3$	Add	Add'	$t_4 = c_{n,2} + (c_{n,2} + 2)$
5.	$t_2 = t_1 - c_{m,1}$	Sub	Sub	$t_2 = c_{n,1} - t_4$
6.	$t_3 = c_{n,2} \cdot t_2$	Mul	Mul	$c_{2n,2} = c_{n,1} \cdot t_2$
7.	$c_{n+m,1} = t_3 + t_4$	Add	-	
8.	$t_1 = c_{n-m,1} + c_{m,1}$	Add	Add'	$t_1 = c_{m,1} + (c_{m,1} + 2)$
9.	$t_2 = c_{n-m,2} - t_1$	Sub	Sub	$t_2 = c_{m,2} - t_1$
10.	$t_3 = c_{n,2} \cdot t_2$	Mul	Mul	$c_{2m,1} = c_{m,2} \cdot t_2$
11.	$t_4 = t_3 - c_{n-2m,2}$	Sub	Add'	$t_4 = c_{m,2} + (c_{m,2} + 2)$
12.	$t_2 = t_1 - c_{m,2}$	Sub	Sub	$t_2 = c_{m,1} - t_4$
13.	$t_3 = c_{n,1} \cdot t_2$	Mul	Mul	$c_{2m,2} = c_{m,1} \cdot t_2$
14.	$c_{n+m,2} = t_3 + t_4$	Add	-	

Fig. 3. Indistinguishable arithmetic for $p \equiv 2 \bmod 3$

A.2   Field Representation for $p \equiv 3 \bmod 4$

Lenstra and Stam remark that the representation below can be used for XTR as well. Let p be a prime congruent to 3 mod 4. Then p generates $\mathbf{Z}_4^*$ and $\Phi_4(x) = x^2 + 1$ is irreducible in $\mathbf{F}_p$. Let ζ_4 denote a root of $\Phi_4(x)$, then $\{1, \zeta_4\}$ is a basis of $\mathbf{F}_{p^2}$ over $\mathbf{F}_p$.

Let $c_n \in \mathbf{F}_{p^2}$ be represented by $(c_{n,0}, c_{n,1}) \in (\mathbf{F}_p)^2$, i.e., $c_n = c_{n,0} + c_{n,1}\zeta_4$ (similarly for c_m, c_{n-m} and c_{n-2m}). Using Fermat's little theorem we have that $c_{n,0}^p = c_{n,0}$ etc. and hence $c_n^p = c_{n,0} - c_{n,1}\zeta_4$. Below we list the formulae for c_{2n} and c_{n+m} based on the current field representation

$$c_{2n} = ((c_{n,0} + 1 + c_{n,1})(c_{n,0} + 1 - c_{n,1}) - 1) + 2(c_{n,0} - 1)c_{n,1}\zeta_4 .$$

$$c_{n+m} = ((c_{n-m,0} + c_{m,0})c_{n,0} + (c_{n-m,1} - c_{m,1})c_{n,1} + c_{n-2m,0}) +$$
$$+ ((c_{n-m,0} + c_{m,0})c_{n,1} - (c_{n-m,1} - c_{m,1})c_{n,0} + c_{n-2m,1})\zeta_4 .$$

In Figure 4 we show how to make two applications of c_{2n} indistinguishable from one application of c_{n+m}. Note that we are doing some double work for the latter (1 and 7, 3 and 9) and are once more depending on additions with minor carry fiddling (and more so than previously).

	One c_{n+m} call	Operation		Two c_{2n} calls
1.	$t_1 = c_{n-m,1} - c_{m,1}$	Sub	Sub'	$t_1 = c_{n,0} + c_{n,0} - 2$
2.	$t_2 = c_{n,1} \cdot t_1$	Mul	Mul	$c_{2n,1} = t_1 c_{n,1}$
3.	$t_1 = c_{n-m,0} + c_{m,0}$	Add	Add'	$t_1 = c_{n,0} + c_{n,1} + 1$
4.	$t_3 = c_{n-2m,0} + t_2$	Add	Sub'	$t_2 = c_{n,0} - c_{n,1} + 1$
5.	$t_4 = c_{n,0} \cdot t_1$	Mul	Mul'	$c_{2n,0} = t_1 t_2 - 1$
6.	$c_{n+m,0} = t_3 + t_4$	Add	-	
7.	$t_1 = c_{m,1} - c_{n-m,1}$	Sub	Sub'	$t_1 = c_{m,0} + c_{m,0} - 2$
8.	$t_2 = c_{n,0} \cdot t_1$	Mul	Mul	$c_{2m,1} = t_1 c_{m,1}$
9.	$t_1 = c_{n-m,0} + c_{m,0}$	Add	Add'	$t_1 = c_{m,0} + c_{m,1} + 1$
10.	$t_3 = c_{n-2m,1} + t_2$	Add	Sub'	$t_2 = c_{m,0} - c_{m,1} + 1$
11.	$t_4 = c_{n,1} \cdot t_1$	Mul	Mul'	$c_{2m,0} = t_1 t_2 - 1$
12.	$c_{n+m,1} = t_3 + t_4$	Add	-	

Fig. 4. Indistinguishable arithmetic for $p \equiv 3 \bmod 4$

Provably Secure Masking of AES

Johannes Blömer[1], Jorge Guajardo[2], and Volker Krummel[1]

[1] University of Paderborn, D-33095 Paderborn, Germany
{bloemer, krummel}@upb.de
[2] Infineon Technologies, Secure Mobile Solutions, 81609 Munich, Germany
Jorge.Guajardo@infineon.com

Abstract. A general method to secure cryptographic algorithms against side-channel attacks is the use of randomization techniques and, in particular, masking. Roughly speaking, using random values unknown to an adversary one masks the input to a cryptographic algorithm. As a result, the intermediate results in the algorithm computation are uncorrelated to the input and the adversary cannot obtain any useful information from the side-channel. Unfortunately, previous AES randomization techniques have based their security on heuristics and experiments. Thus, flaws have been found which make AES randomized implementations still vulnerable to side-channel cryptanalysis. In this paper, we provide a formal notion of security for randomized maskings of arbitrary cryptographic algorithms. Furthermore, we present an AES randomization technique that is provably secure against side-channel attacks if the adversary is able to access a single intermediate result. Our randomized masking technique is quite general and it can be applied to arbitrary algorithms using only arithmetic operations over some finite field. To our knowledge this is the first time that a randomization technique for the AES has been proven secure in a formal model.

1 Introduction

The security of the Advanced Encryption Standard (AES) [27] against Simple (SPA), Differential (DPA), Higher Order Differential Power Analysis (HODPA) [14,15], and Timing (TA) attacks [16] has received considerable attention since the beginning of the AES selection process. Koeune and Quisquater [17] describe timing attacks against careless implementations of AES. [3,6] discuss DPA attacks on the AES candidates in software based solutions. Örs et al. [21] describe the first (documented) power analysis-based attack on a dedicated AES ASIC implementation and Mangard [18] discusses an SPA attack on the key schedule of the AES.

As a result of these attacks, numerous hardware and algorithmic countermeasures have been proposed. Hardware methodologies were proposed right from the beginning. They include randomized clocks, memory encryption/decryption schemes, (see [5], [10]), power consumption randomization [6], and decorrelating the external power supply from the internal power consumed by the chip.

H. Handschuh and A. Hasan (Eds.): SAC 2004, LNCS 3357, pp. 69–83, 2005.

Moreover, the use of different hardware logic, such as complementary logic [6], sense amplifier based logic (SABL), and asynchronous logic [8, 20] has also been proposed. Some of these methods soon proved to be ineffective while other more successful countermeasures are very costly in terms of development, area and power. For example, the techniques in [6, 23, 24, 8, 20] require about twice as much area and will consume twice as much power as an implementation that is not protected against power attacks. In addition, hardware countermeasure will only protect against known techniques and attacks. They cannot provide security in some precisely defined mathematical sense. Hence, although hardware countermeasures are an important defense against side-channel attacks, they should be complemented by mathematically analyzed algorithmic countermeasures.

In this paper, we concentrate on algorithmic countermeasures against timing and power attacks on AES. In general, algorithmic countermeasures against timing and power attacks are based on randomization techniques. Here the problem is to guarantee that all information that can be gained via side-channels is random and hence useless to the attacker. More precisely, one has to guarantee that intermediate results of the computation look random to an adversary. Furthermore, the randomization must be used in such a way that, at the end of the algorithm, the correct encryption or signature corresponding to the input plaintext is obtained. Randomized algorithmic countermeasures against timing and power attacks include secret-sharing schemes, proposed by Goubin and Patarin [11] and independently by Chari et al. [4] as well as methods based on the idea of masking all data and intermediate results during an encryption operation, originally introduced by Messerges in [19].

The first algorithmic countermeasure against power attacks customized for the AES was the transformed masking method [2] by Akkar and Giraud. This method was further simplified by Trichina et al. [26]. It was noticed in [26, 9] that the multiplicative masking introduced in [2] masked *only* non-zero values, i.e., a zero byte will not get masked because of the multiplicative nature of the mask. This feature renders the method of Akkar and Giraud vulnerable to DPAs. A second masking technique for AES is the random representation method by Golić and Tymen [9]. Similar to Akkar and Giraud, Golić and Tymen do not try to show that their technique randomizes all intermediate results. Instead, the authors argue experimentally that using their methods the Hamming weights of all intermediate results are distributed in roughly the same way, independent of the plaintext and secret key. We conclude that so far customized randomization techniques for AES were based on empirical assumptions about the power of potential adversaries. Then these assumptions were used to define some ad-hoc-model in which to analyze and argue the security of the methods. We believe that this is a potentially dangerous approach. Therefore, in this paper

- *We start with a mathematically precise security notion in which we discuss randomization techniques.* For our security notion we only make some inevitable assumptions: First, we assume that some (small) part of the computation runs in a protected environment. Secondly, we limit the number of intermediate results that an adversary has access to. Note that previous methods made at least these assumptions. On the other hand, we assume that arbitrary differences in the distribution of an intermediate result that depends on the plaintext or secret key of the cryptosystem can be used to break the system completely. Accordingly, our security notion requires that the distribution of any intermediate result is independent of the secret key being used and independent of the plaintext. This requirement was already briefly sketched by Golić in [10]. In the sequel, we call an algorithm *an order d perfectly masked* algorithm if the joint distribution of any d intermediate results is independent of the secret key and the plaintext. This notion of security strengthens the security notion proposed in [4] which only required distributions of intermediate results to be indistinguishable by an adversary. Since our security notion assumes that even tiny differences in the distribution of intermediate results completely break an implementation of a cryptosystem, this notion is strong and often unrealistic. On the other hand, we will argue that our security notion implies security against most side-channel attacks.

– *Based on this security notion we develop an order* 1 *perfectly masked algorithm for AES*. Hence this algorithm is secure against any adversary that gets pairs of plain- and cipher-texts and *a single* intermediate result for each of those pairs. The main problem here is to describe a secure algorithm for the inversion operation that is the main ingredient of the AES SubBytes transformation. Our solution is based on a general technique to turn an arbitrary algorithm using arithmetic operations defined over some finite field into a randomized algorithm that securely computes the same function. Our method can be combined with standard d-out-of-d secret sharing schemes to obtain order d perfectly masked algorithms for AES. However, at this point the exact costs of this approach are not clear. We will present these algorithms in a subsequent work.

– *Show that masking countermeasures are inexpensive to implement in hardware*. The countermeasures shown here amount to only a 20% increase in the overall area required for an AES hardware implementation when compared to dual-rail logic type countermeasures. To show this, we provide a detailed cost comparison of the different methods. Because our method is based on the usage of multipliers and adders over any binary field, designers might use this method to implement DPA-safe circuits which utilize previously designed multiplier and adder blocks. Moreover, the method is modular and encourages reusability.

The paper is organized as follows. Sections 2 and 3 introduce and discuss our security notion. In Sect. 5, we show how to compute the SubBytes transformation in the AES in a way that is provably secure in our model. We finish with a discussion of a possible hardware implementation of our method and compare its cost with the costs of other (less secure) countermeasures.

2   Security Notion

In this section we describe our notion of security. To do so, we first need to describe what we consider a successful attack. To simplify the exposition, we assume that we are given some encryption function enc that we want to evaluate in a side-channel resistant manner. The inputs to the function enc are a plaintext x and a secret key k.

Given an algorithm that evaluates the function enc, for each plaintext x and key k, we view the computation of $enc(x, k)$ as a sequence of *intermediate results* $I_1(x, k, r), \ldots, I_t(x, k, r) = enc(x, k)$. Each intermediate result may depend on the plaintext x, on the secret key k, and some $r \in \{0, 1\}^*$. The element r is used to randomize the computation and is chosen uniformly at random from $\{0, 1\}^*$. The ciphertext $enc(x, k)$ only depends on x and k and not on r.

We consider an adversary that knows plaintext/ciphertext pairs $(x, enc(x))$. Additionally, we assume that for each pair $(x, enc(x))$ the adversary gets several intermediate results $I_1(x, k, r), \ldots, I_d(x, k, r)$. The adversary may get different intermediate results for different plaintext/ciphertext pairs. If the adversary can get at most d intermediate results for each pair $(x, enc(x))$ of plaintext and ciphertext, we call this an *order d adversary*. In any case, the goal of the adversary is to compute parts of the secret key k.

Intuitively, we say that the algorithm computing enc is insecure or that an adversary is successful, if the joint distribution of the intermediate results that an adversary gets depends on the plaintext x and on the secret key k. To formalize this, fix some d-tuple $I_1, \ldots, I_d$ of intermediate results. For a pair (x, k) of plaintext and key we denote by $D_{x,k}(R)$ the joint distribution of $I_1, \ldots, I_d$ induced by choosing r uniformly at random in $\{0, 1\}^*$.

Definition 1 (perfect masking). *An algorithm that evaluates an encryption function enc is order d perfectly masked if for all d-tuples $I_1, \ldots, I_d$ of intermediate results we have that $D_{x,k}(R) = D_{x',k'}(R)$ for all pairs $(x, k), (x', k')$. For $d = 1$ we say that an algorithm is perfectly masked.*

3   Discussion of Security Notion

Our notion of security is very strong. Basically, we assume that an adversary can determine the secret key even from tiny differences in the (joint) distribution of intermediate results. In many realistic cases this may not be true. However, we do not want to base our security model on assumptions about technical abilities or limitations adversaries currently have. Instead we want to provide a precise mathematical notion that captures security against current side-channel attacks as well as future ones. Our notion of security strengthens the security notion in [4]. We require that for any two pairs $(x, k), (x', k')$ of plaintext and key the joint distributions $D_{x,k}(R), D_{x',k'}(R)$ of d intermediate results induced by these pairs must be identical. Chari et al., on the other hand only demand that the distributions $D_{x,k}(R), D_{x',k'}(R)$ must be indistinguishable by an adversary. As Chari et al. argue in their paper, if the joint distributions of d intermediate results induced by different plaintext/key pairs are indistinguishable for an adversary then power analysis and timing attacks using information about at most d intermediate results cannot be mounted. Clearly, identical distributions are indistinguishable. Hence, an algorithm that is order d perfectly masked is secure against timing and power analysis attacks using information about d intermediate results.

In this paper, we will concentrate on methods to achieve a perfectly masked algorithm to compute AES. From the discussion above it follows that the perfectly masked algorithm for AES that we describe is secure against timing and power analysis attacks using a single intermediate result. As can easily be seen, our algorithm is not secure, if an adversary has access to two or more intermediate results. Notice that most countermeasures proposed so far also assume an adversary with access to a single intermediate result (see [2, 9, 25]).

Notice that without further assumptions even a perfectly masked algorithm is impossible. To see this, note that the secret key k itself can be considered as an intermediate result. This intermediate result clearly does not satisfy the condition stated in Definition 1. Hence, to achieve a perfectly masked algorithm we must assume that some parts of the computation run in a guaranteed secure environment. In other words, some intermediate results cannot be accessed by an adversary. At least implicitly, all previously proposed countermeasures against side-channel attacks have made the same assumption. Clearly, our goal has to be to design perfect maskings that require only few intermediate results to be inaccessible by an adversary. Moreover, we must be able to identify those intermediate results that have to be computed in a secure environment. Note that on modern smartcards, protected by different sensors and encrypted memories, the assumption that at least some computations are done in a secure environment is realistic. Like all other countermeasures, we also assume that we have a true random number generator (TRNG) and that the adversary is not able to manipulate the random bits.

So far we have been talking of intermediate results without specifying what we consider as possible intermediate results that an adversary may get. We consider an algorithm as a sequence of operations that are treated as encapsulated modules. This leads to a classification of intermediate results into different levels down to the bit level:

1. *Text level:* The whole algorithm is treated as a module. This level is the one of classical cryptography. The only information available to the adversary is the plaintext and the ciphertext.
2. *Block level:* Each part or subroutine of the algorithm is treated as a module. In the case of a block cipher such as the AES, each transformation within a round is treated as a module (SubBytes, ShiftRows, MixColumns and AddRoundKey).
3. *Unit level:* Each arithmetic operation is treated as a module. These operations work on the atomic units of information in the cipher. For example, the AES units of information are bytes; no operation acts on bits or nibbles. In hardware terms this level is based on the contents of registers.

4. *Bit level:* Each bit manipulation is treated as a module, for example XOR, shift etc.

Every output of such a module is an *intermediate result*. In this paper we concentrate on intermediate results at the unit level. For AES this seems to be a natural choice. Basically all operations in AES are arithmetic operations on bytes. Therefore timing, power and fault attacks on AES have focused on these operations as well. Moreover it is not hard to see that security on the unit level implies security on the bit level since the distributions of inputs and outputs of arithmetic operations are identical for all inputs of the algorithm.

4   Additive Masking and the AES

In [19], Messerges introduced the idea of masking all intermediate values of an encryption operation as an effective countermeasure against DPA and SPA type attacks. Randomizing the computation of a function f is, thus, achieved as $f(u')$ where $u' = u + r$ and r is a randomly chosen mask. If the function is linear, one can recover the desired value $f(u)$ from $f(u') = f(u) + f(r)$. A similar computation will recover $f(u)$ if the function f is affine. For non-linear functions, the previous equation does not hold true and it is necessary to come up with a series of computations dependent only on r and u' such that we obtain the value of $f(u)$ without leaking any information.

We notice that in the case of the AES [27], the only non-linear function in the algorithm is the AES SubBytes transformation. In particular, most researchers have concentrated their efforts on efficient methods to perform inversion over $\mathbb{F}_{256}$ in a secure manner via masking countermeasures, i.e., computing $u^{-1} + r$ from $u + r$ without compromising the value of u. In this context, three masking methods have been proposed: two of them [2, 9] are based on the idea of combining Boolean and multiplicative masking operations and the third one is based on the idea of masking the individual logic operations required to compute a $\mathbb{F}_{256}$ inverse. A simplification of [2] was introduced in [26] but it has been recently found in [1] that the simplifications lead to further vulnerabilities against DPA. Thus, we do not consider it any further in this work. In the following, we shortly summarize the previously mentioned countermeasures.

The Transform Masking Method (TMM). In [2], Akkar and Goubin introduce the Transform Masking Method (TMM) and algorithms to transform between boolean mask (XOR operation) and multiplicative masking (multiplication in $\mathbb{F}_{256}$) which is compatible with inversion in $\mathbb{F}_{256}$. [2] solves the problem using Algorithm 1, where r_2 is a non-zero random value and all variables and results are 8-bit long. However, as noticed in [26, 9], this countermeasure is susceptible to first-order DPA if $u = 0$ because zero cannot be masked with a multiplicative mask. It is clear that because of the special nature of the zero value, multiplicative masking cannot lead to perfect masking.

Algorithm 1 Transform Masking Method

Input: $u' = u + r_1$, r_2
Output: $u^{-1} + r_1$
1: $t_1 \leftarrow u' \cdot r_2$; $t_2 \leftarrow r_1 \cdot r_2$ $\qquad\qquad\qquad\qquad\qquad\qquad$ $\{t_1 = (u + r_1) \cdot r_2\}$
2: $t_1 \leftarrow t_1 + t_2$; $t_3 \leftarrow r_2^{-1}$ $\qquad\qquad\qquad\qquad\qquad\qquad$ $\{t_1 = u \cdot r_2\}$
3: $t_1 \leftarrow t_1^{-1}$; $t_2 \leftarrow t_3 \cdot r_1$ $\qquad\qquad\qquad\qquad$ $\{t_1 = (u \cdot r_2)^{-1}; t_2 = r_1 \cdot r_2^{-1}\}$
4: $t_1 \leftarrow t_1 + t_2$ $\qquad\qquad\qquad\qquad\qquad$ $\{t_1 = (u \cdot r_2)^{-1} + (r_1 \cdot r_2^{-1})\}$
5: $t_1 \leftarrow t_1 \cdot r_2$ $\qquad\qquad\qquad\qquad\qquad\qquad\qquad$ $\{t_1 = u^{-1} + r_1\}$

Embedded Multiplicative Masking (EMM). The basic idea in [9] is to embed the field $\mathbb{F}_{256}$ in the ring $\mathcal{R}_k = \mathbb{F}_2[x]/(pq) \cong \mathbb{F}_{256} \times \mathbb{F}_{2^k}$, where q is another irreducible polynomial of degree k that is co-prime to p. The field $\mathbb{F}_{256}$ is now a subring of the ring $\mathcal{R}_k$ with the isomorphism defined by $v \mapsto (v_p, v_q)$, where $v_p \equiv v \bmod p$ and $v_q \equiv v \bmod q$. [9], then, suggests to use a random mapping ρ_k defined by $v \mapsto v + rp \bmod pq$ and modified inversion I' defined as $v^{254} \bmod pq$, where r is a randomly chosen polynomial of degree less than k. In this way, arithmetic operations remain compatible with $\mathbb{F}_{256}$ and the zero value gets mapped to one of 2^k random values. Thus, it is harder to detect the zero value as k becomes larger. From a security point of view, however, the approach in [9] does not yield perfect masking since the sets of representatives of different values are pairwise disjoint. From an implementation point of view, we show in Section 6.2 that this method is too expensive to implement in hardware. This is important since our method can be implemented with less than half the hardware resources and, at the same time, yield perfect masking.

Combinational Logic Design for AES S-Box on Masked Data. To the authors' knowledge, Trichina [25] is the first to consider embedding a masking countermeasure directly in hardware. [25] allows for a modified inversion function which on input $u + r_1$ outputs $u^{-1} + r_2$, where r_1 and r_2 need not be the same. In addition, [25] reduces the masking problem for inversion in $\mathbb{F}_{2^k}$ to the problem of masking a logical AND operation since masking XOR operations is, in principle, trivial. In particular, given masked bits $u' = u + r_1$, $v' = v + r_2$ and corresponding masks r_1, r_2, we compute $(u \wedge v) + r_3$, where r_3 is the output mask. According to [25] and setting $r_3 = r_1 + r_2$ this can be accomplished as:

$$(u \wedge v) + r_3 = (u \wedge v) + (r_1 \wedge r_2) = (u' \wedge v') + ((r_1 \wedge v') + (r_2 \wedge u')) \qquad (1)$$

where the parenthesis indicate the order in which intermediate results are computed. Equation (1) implies that we can compute the AND operation of two bits u, v without using the actual bits but rather their masked counterparts u', v' and corresponding masks r_1, r_2. We notice that if $u = v = 0$, the intermediate value $(r_1 \wedge v') + (r_2 \wedge u')$ is always equal to zero for any value of r_1 and r_2. This implies that (1) does not lead to perfect masking.

5   Perfectly Masking AES Against First-Order Side-Channel Attacks

As mentioned before, in order to obtain a perfectly masked algorithm for AES we concentrate on the problem of computing multiplicative inverses in $\mathbb{F}_{256}$ because

$$INV(x) = \begin{cases} x^{-1}, \text{ if } x \in \mathbb{F}_{256}^{\times} \\ 0, \quad \text{ if } x = 0 \end{cases}$$

is the main step of the SubBytes-transformation. In this section we present an algorithm that is secure against an adversary that is able to get one intermediate result. However this solution can easily be generalized to higher order attacks by using more randomness.

Let r, r' be independently and uniformly distributed random masks. We start with an additively masked value $u + r$ and would like to calculate $INV(u) + r'$. However a direct application of INV leads to $INV(u + r)$ that is of no use because of the non-linearity of inversion.

5.1   Idea

The basis of our idea is to calculate $INV(x)$ as x^{254} by using the square-and-multiply algorithm or an optimal addition chain. In general the multiplicative inverse of an element over an arbitrary finite field $\mathbb{F}_{p^m}$ can always be calculated by raising it to the $(p^m - 2)$-th power. This can be efficiently done using only squarings and multiplications. Since our inputs are additively masked values $(u + r)$ we correct the result of every single operation in the square-and-multiply algorithm in order to obtain the desired result. Our invariant is that at the end of each step our result has the form $(u^e + r')$ for some e. Hence, the problem is to correct the intermediate results without revealing any information about u.

5.2   Method

We introduce some variables: We name $r_{j,i}$ the jth random mask used in Step i of our algorithm. All $r_{j,i}$ are independently and uniformly distributed masks. The direct result of an operation (squaring or multiplication) in Step i performed on some masked values is called f_i. Furthermore, we need the auxiliary terms $s_{1,i}$ and $s_{2,i}$ to correct f_i. The variable $t_{1,i}$ is the intermediate result that appears during the correction and t_i is the final result of Step i which complies with our invariant, i.e., it is of the form $u^e + r_{1,i}$ for some e.

The input to our modified inversion algorithm is the masked value $(u + r_{1,0})$. Next, we describe how to perform multiplications and squarings in a perfectly masked manner. The security analysis is shown in Sect. 5.3. We distinguish between squaring and multiplication because the former can be done more efficiently.

Squaring. The squaring operation in Step i is described in Algorithm 2. The input $t_{i-1} = u^e + r_{1,i-1}$ is squared in Step 1. In order to compute the output that respects our invariant we have to change the mask to $r_{1,i}$. To do so in Steps 2 and 3 we use the auxiliary term $s_{1,i}$ and compute the desired output $t_i = u^{2e} + r_{1,i}$.

Algorithm 2 Perfectly Masked Squaring (PMS)

Input: $x = u^e + r_{1,i-1}$
Output: $u^{2e} + r_{1,i}$
1: $f_i \leftarrow x^2$ $\{f_1 = u^{2e} + r_{1,i-1}^2\}$
2: $s_{1,i} \leftarrow r_{1,i-1}^2 + r_{1,i}$ {auxiliary term to correct f_i}
3: $t_i \leftarrow f_i + s_{1,i}$ $\{t_i = u^{2e} + r_{1,i}\}$

Multiplication. Our perfectly masked multiplication (PMM) method is described in Algorithm 3. The input are two intermediate results: The output of the previous step and a freshly masked value derived by securely changing the masked value from $u + r_{1,0}$ to $u + r_{2,i}$. In Step 1 we calculate the product f_i of two intermediate results. f_i contains the desired power of u as well as some disturbing terms. In Steps 2-5 we compute the auxiliary terms $s_{1,i}$ and $s_{2,i}$. In the end (Steps 6 and 7) we eliminate the disturbing parts of f_i and transform it according to our invariant. This is done by simply adding up the two auxiliary terms $s_{1,i}$, $s_{2,i}$ and f_i.

Algorithm 3 Perfectly Masked Multiplication (PMM)

Input: $x = u^e + r_{1,i-1}$, $x' = u + r_{2,i}$
Output: $u^{e+1} + r_{1,i}$
1: $f_i \leftarrow x \cdot x'$ $\{f_i = u^{e+1} + u^e \cdot r_{2,i} + u \cdot r_{1,i-1} + r_{1,i-1} \cdot r_{2,i}\}$
2: $v_{1,i} \leftarrow x' \cdot r_{1,i-1}$ $\{v_{1,i} = u \cdot r_{1,i-1} + r_{1,i-1} \cdot r_{2,i}\}$
3: $v_{2,i} \leftarrow v_{1,i} + r_{1,i}$ $\{\, v_{2,i} = u \cdot r_{1,i-1} + r_{1,i-1} \cdot r_{2,i} + r_{1,i}\}$
4: $s_{1,i} \leftarrow v_{2,i} + r_{1,i-1} \cdot r_{2,i}$ $\{s_{1,i} = u \cdot r_{1,i-1} + r_{1,i}\}$
5: $s_{2,i} \leftarrow x \cdot r_{2,i}$ $\{s_{2,i} = u^e \cdot r_{2,i} + r_{1,i-1} \cdot r_{2,i}\}$
6: $t_{1,i} \leftarrow f_i + s_{1,i}$ $\{t_{1,i} = u^{e+1} + u^e \cdot r_{2,i} + r_{1,i-1} \cdot r_{2,i} + r_{1,i}\}$
7: $t_i \leftarrow t_{1,i} + s_{2,i}$ $\{t_i = u^{e+1} + r_{1,i}\}$

5.3   Security Analysis

As defined in our security model we have to look at all intermediate results. For Algorithms 2 and 3 we only have to analyze the distributions of the following intermediate results: $f_i, s_{1,i}, s_{2,i}, t_i, t_{1,i}, v_{1,i}, v_{2,i}$ where $1 \leq i \leq 13$. These are the results that depend on u. We can neglect intermediate results such as $r_{1,i}^2$ since they do not depend on u.

Our security analysis is based on the following 2 lemmas that characterize the distributions of intermediate results.

Lemma 1. *Let* $u \in \mathbb{F}_{256}$ *be arbitrary. Let* r *be uniformly distributed over* $\{0, \ldots, 255\}$ *independent of* u. *Then* $I(u, r) = u + r = Z$ *is uniformly distributed.*

Lemma 2. *Let* $u, u' \in \mathbb{F}_{256}$ *and* $r, r' \in \mathbb{F}_{256}$ *be independently and uniformly distributed over* $\{0, \ldots, 255\}$. *Set* $I_1 = u + r$ *and* $I_2 = u' + r'$. *Then the product* $Z = I_1 \cdot I_2$ *is distributed according to*

$$Pr(Z = i) = \begin{cases} (2^9 - 1)/2^{16} \,, \text{if } i = 0 \\ (2^8 - 1)/2^{16} \,, \text{if } i \neq 0 \end{cases}$$

The proofs of these lemmas are straightforward and therefore omitted. For our security analysis we also need the following observation.

Remark 1. In any finite field of characteristic 2 squaring is a one-to-one mapping.

Analysis of f_i. We have to look at the intermediate result f_i in the two cases of squaring and multiplication.

- **Squaring:** The calculation is $f_i \leftarrow t_{i-1}^2 = u^{2e} + r_{1,i-1}^2$ for some $2 \leq e \leq 254$. Since $r_{1,i-1}$ is chosen uniformly at random, Remark 1 together with Lemma 1 shows that f_i is uniformly distributed for all u.
- **Multiplication:** $f_i \leftarrow (u^e + r_{1,i-1}) \cdot (u + r_{2,i}) = u^{e+1} + u^e r_{2,i} + u r_{1,i-1} + r_{1,i-1} r_{2,i}$. Here the terms $u^e + r_{1,i-1}$ and $u + r_{2,i}$ are independently (because of the independence of $r_{1,i-1}$ and $r_{2,i}$) and uniformly distributed (Lemma 1). So by Lemma 2, f_i is distributed according to D_0 for all u.

Analysis of $s_{1,i}, s_{2,i}$

- **Squaring:** Here $s_{1,i}$ can be neglected since it does not depend on u.
- **Multiplication:** $s_{1,i}$ is calculated by adding or multiplying independent masks on the term $(u + r_{2,i})$ leading to the term $u r_{1,i-1} + r_{1,i}$. So $s_{1,i}$ is obviously uniformly distributed. $s_{2,i} \leftarrow (u^e + r_{1,i-1}) r_{2,i}$ is the product of two independently uniformly distributed variables each of which is distributed independently of u. So independent of the value of u, the variable $s_{2,i}$ is distributed according to D_0.

Analysis of $t_{1,i}, t_i$. All these intermediate results are sums of some part depending on u and an independent additive mask. So all of them are uniformly distributed by Lemma 1.

Hence corresponding intermediate results are always identically distributed independent of the value of u. This implies that the whole computation is perfectly masked. The analysis on the bit level is similar to the analysis on the unit level. Instead of looking at the distributions of bytes one has to look at the distributions of single bits.

5.4   Simplified Version

Previously we assumed that for each step we generate new random masks. In the special case of first order side channel attacks we can reuse random masks because the adversary is allowed to choose only one intermediate result. Thus, we can reduce the number of random masks needed to only three masks (r_1, r_2, r_3). To achieve this we modify our calculations such that after each step we switch back to our original mask. This can be done by simply adding our original mask and then adding our temporarily used mask. Because of the independence of the masks this has no impact on security.

6   Implementation and Costs

Throughout the paper, we have only considered a theoretical implementation of the inversion algorithm according to the square-and-multiply algorithm. However, our method is compatible with any implementation that combines additions, multiplications, and squarings in a field or ring. More precisely, an arbitrary straight-line program over some finite field using only additions and multiplications can be transformed to an equivalent program that is perfectly masked. In this work, we do not consider software implementations of the presented countermeasures. However, we notice that for constrained environments previous works have based their software implementations of side-channel countermeasures on table look-ups. From a hardware point of view, the most area efficient ASIC hardware implementation is the one described in [22] based on composite fields. We will discuss a possible implementation of our countermeasure based on composite fields and will provide area and delay estimates in the next section.

6.1   Efficient Hardware Implementation Over $GF(((2^2)^2)^2)$

First we describe in some detail how to implement an inverter over $GF(((2^2)^2)^2)$, so that it is clear how we obtained our area and delay estimates. This methodology is nothing new and it is well known in the literature. We assume a composite field representation $GF(((2^2)^2)^2) \cong \mathbb{F}_{256}$ for the inverse transformation using the following irreducible polynomials:

$$
\begin{array}{ll}
GF(2^2) & : P(x) = x^2 + x + 1, \ \ P(\alpha) = 0 \\
GF((2^2)^2) & : Q(y) = y^2 + y + \alpha, \ \ Q(\beta) = 0 \\
GF(((2^2)^2)^2) & : R(z) = z^2 + z + \lambda, \ \ \lambda = (\alpha + 1)\beta
\end{array}
$$

We use the PMM and PMS algorithms from Sect. 5 instead of the normal ones to build our inversion circuit and, thus, render it secure against side-channel attacks. Based on [13, 12], [22] notices that for $A \in GF(((2^2)^2)^2)$, A^{-1} can be computed as $A^{-1} = (A^{17})^{-1} A^{16}$, where $A^{17} \in GF((2^2)^2)$. Notice that the Itoh and Tsujii algorithm can be recursively applied to $B = A^{17} \in GF((2^2)^2)$, thus obtaining $B^{-1} = (B^4 \cdot B)^{-1} \cdot (B^4)$ where $B^5 \in GF(2^2)$. In the following, we write $B = B_1\beta + B_0 \in GF((2^2)^2)$ with $B_i \in GF(2^2)$. Then, we can minimize the area requirement of the implementation using the following "tricks":

- $B^4 \in GF((2^2)^2)$ can be computed as $B^4 \equiv B_1\beta + (B_1 + B_0)$, i.e., only one addition over $GF(2^2)$.
- $B^5 \in GF(2^2)$ can be computed as $B^5 \equiv B_0 \cdot B_1 + B_0^2 + B_1^2 \cdot \alpha$, where $B_1^2 \cdot \alpha$ requires only wires for its implementation (no gates).
- Given $C = c_1\alpha + c_0 \in GF(2^2)$, $C^{-1} \equiv c_1\alpha + (c_1 + c_0)$, i.e., it requires one $GF(2)$ adder.
- Thus, computing $B^{-1} = B^{-5} \cdot B^4 \in GF((2^2)^2)$ requires 3 $GF(2^2)$ multipliers, 1 $GF(2^2)$ squarer, and 4 $GF(2^2)$ adders. Inversion in $GF(((2^2)^2)^2)$ can then be implemented according to [22] with 2 adders, 3 multipliers, 1 inverter, and 1 squarer followed by multiplication by $\lambda = (\alpha + 1)\beta$, all over $GF((2^2)^2)$.

The hardware implementation of the perfectly masked version can be implemented similarly except that now instead of using the normal adders, multipliers, squarers, and inverters, we use circuits which implement the algorithms from Sect. 5.

6.2   Cost and Comparison to Previous Countermeasures

Area and delay estimates for circuits with and without countermeasures are provided in the appendix. The estimates are given in terms of the area and delay of 2-input AND gates, 2-input XOR gates, and NOT gates. The complexity and specific implementation of these circuits is taken from [28]. In addition, we provide complexity estimates in terms of normalized area and delay. The normalization is done with respect to the area and delay of a NOT gate. We have assumed that the areas of a 2-input AND gate and 2-input XOR gate are twice and 3 times that of an inverter, respectively. Similarly, it is assumed that the delays of NOT, AND, and XOR gates are equal. Notice that the assumptions regarding the gates' area and delay are not arbitrary but based on the actual sizes of several standard cell libraries. Finally, we point out that [22] which describes AES ASIC implementations over $GF(((2^2)^2)^2)$ does not provide the actual circuits used to implement the AES S-box.

Table 1 provides a cost comparison among the different masking countermeasures. We did not consider the method from [9] because its hardware implementation requires too many hardware resources. We can estimate the cost of [9] with $k = 8$ by simply considering the cost of a multiplier and an inverter over $\mathbb{F}_2[x]/(pq) \cong \mathbb{F}_{256} \times \mathbb{F}_{2^k}$. According to [7], such a multiplier requires 289 2-input AND gates and 272 2-input XOR gates. The map I' can also be implemented with a multiplier (a squarer requires only wires). Thus, we would need at least 1 multiplier and 1 inverter over $\mathbb{F}_2[x]/(pq)$ and 3 multipliers and 1 inverter over $\mathbb{F}_{256}$. This results in a circuit which requires at least 731 AND and 766 XOR_2 or about twice as many gates as our method. We can see from Table 1 that

Table 1. Hardware cost comparison for different inversion circuits with side-channel countermeasures

Arithmetic Operation	A	$A/A_{Normal\ Inv.}$	T	$T/T_{Normal\ Inv.}$	$A \cdot T$
Inversion over $GF(((2^2)^2)^2)$ [22]	312	1	17	1	1
Inversion with DPA countermeasure from [25] according to (1)	1071	3.4	26	1.5	5.3
$GF(((2^2)^2)^2)$ PM inverter (this paper)	1704	5.5	21	1.2	6.7
Inversion with DPA countermeasure from [25])	1341	4.3	34	2	8.6
Inversion with countermeasure from [2]	1784	5.7	34	2	11.4

the countermeasure of [25] implemented according to (1) has the best area/time product of all the implementations. However, as we have shown in Section 4, this countermeasure is susceptible to DPA attacks if the input byte is zero and, thus, it does not provide perfect masking. If we then consider the best area/time product of the countermeasures that offer DPA resistance, the implementation presented in this work has the best area/time product. This result comes from the reduced critical path in the circuit presented here. In addition, our design encourages re-usability of previously designed blocks. In other words, since the masking method depends only on multipliers and adders, if one has multiplier and adder blocks already designed, they can be used immediately to build a perfectly masked circuit (with the work from [25], implementation of the masking countermeasure would require a complete circuit redesign). Finally, we estimate the cost that our masking countermeasure would have on an AES hardware implementation. To do this, we assume that the implementation would follow the architecture described in [22] where the SubBytes transformation occupies about 22% of the design with 4 S-Boxes in parallel. In SubBytes, the inverse transformation accounts for 60% or about 14% of the total area. We also assume that the remaining circuits require twice as much area as an implementation without masking countermeasures. Then, our new inversion circuit would need about 2.5 times the area that an AES hardware implementation without countermeasures would need. Of this 31% would correspond to the inverter circuit. The required area is only 20% larger than an implementation that used hardware countermeasures based on the usage of different hardware logic. Such methods double the hardware resources when compared to an implementation using standard (single-rail) logic.

In addition to time and area, other costs are also of importance. For example, the amount of randomness is very important since its generation is quite expensive. In our simplified algorithm we only need 3 random masks in order to compute $INV(x)$ in a secure manner. Another important cost factor is the number of operations that have to be protected by hardware means. Our approach needs this inevitable protection only for one intermediate result. Hence it is optimal with respect to this cost measure.

7   Conclusions and Recommendations for Further Research

A natural way to extend this research is to consider more powerful adversaries which can access more than one intermediate result at the time and develop methods which would withstand such attacks. Here a major challenge is to design methods which are "practical", in the sense, that they can be implemented at a reasonable hardware cost. Another interesting problem is to see whether for less powerful adversaries secure algorithms exist that require less randomness or are more efficient than the algorithms presented in this paper. A further question is if we can find more efficient methods to implement side-channel attack safe circuits for the AES in hardware or software with respect to time or area. We believe that, using masking methodologies, the best we could hope for is to use twice as much area as a circuit without countermeasures (imagine simply that the circuit could be implemented using only XOR gates). Is this bound possible to achieve in practice? Related to this last question is the need for random masks. Can we reduce the randomness requirement without affecting security?

References

1. M.-L. Akkar, R. Bévan, and L. Goubin. Two Power Analysis Attacks against One-Mask Methods. In *11th International Workshop on Fast Software Encryption — FSE 2004*, volume LNCS 3017. Springer-Verlag, 2004.
2. M.-L. Akkar and C. Giraud. An Implementation of DES and AES, Secure against Some Attacks. In *Workshop on Cryptographic Hardware and Embedded Systems — CHES 2001*, volume LNCS 2162, pages 309–318. Springer-Verlag, May 14-16, 2001.
3. E. Biham and A. Shamir. Power Analysis of the Key Scheduling of the AES Candidates. In *Proceedings of the Second AES Candidate Conference (AES2)*, Rome, Italy, March 1999.
4. S. Chari, C. S. Jutla, J. R. Rao, and P. Rohatgi. Towards Sound Approaches to Counteract Power-Analysis Attacks. In *Advances in Cryptology — CRYPTO '99*, volume LNCS 1666, pages 398–412. Springer-Verlag, August 1999.
5. C. Clavier, J.S. Coron, and N. Dabbous. Differential Power Analysis in the Presence of Hardware Countermeasures. In *Workshop on Cryptographic Hardware and Embedded Systems — CHES 2000*, volume LNCS 1965, pages 252–263. Springer-Verlag, August 17-18, 2000.
6. J. Daemen and V. Rijmen. Resistance Against Implementation Attacks: A Comparative Study of the AES Proposals. In *Proceedings of the Second AES Candidate Conference (AES2)*, Rome, Italy, March 1999.
7. G. Drolet. A New Representation of Elements of Finite Fields $GF(2^m)$ Yielding Small Complexity Arithmetic Circuits. *IEEE Transactions on Computers*, 47(9):938–946, September 1998.
8. J.J.A. Fournier, S. Moore, H. Li, R. Mullins, and G. Taylor. Security Evaluation of Asynchronous Circuits. In *Workshop on Cryptographic Hardware and Embedded Systems — CHES 2003*, volume LNCS 2779, pages 125–136. Springer-Verlag, September 7-10, 2003.
9. J.Dj. Golić and C. Tymen. Multiplicative Masking and Power Analysis of AES. In *Workshop on Cryptographic Hardware and Embedded Systems — CHES 2002*, volume LNCS 2523, pages 198–212. Springer-Verlag, 2002.
10. Jovan Dj. Golić. DeKaRT: A New Paradigm for Key-Dependent Reversible Circuits. In *Cryptographic Hardware and Embedded Systems - CHES 2003*, volume LNCS 2779, pages 98–112. Springer Verlag, 2003.
11. L. Goubin and J. Patarin. DES and Differential Power Analysis, "The Duplication Method". In *Workshop on Cryptographic Hardware and Embedded Systems — CHES 1999*, volume LNCS 1717, pages 158–172. Springer-Verlag, 1999.
12. J. Guajardo and C. Paar. Itoh-Tsujii Inversion in Standard Basis and Its Application in Cryptography and Codes. *Design, Codes, and Cryptography*, 25(2):207–216, February 2002.
13. T. Itoh and S. Tsujii. A Fast Algorithm for Computing Multiplicative Inverses in $GF(2^m)$ Using Normal Bases. *Information and Computation*, 78:171–177, 1988.
14. P. Kocher, J. Jaffe, and B. Jun. Introduction to Differential Power Analysis and Related Attacks. Technical Report, Cryptography Research, Inc., 1998.
15. P. Kocher, J. Jaffe, and B. Jun. Differential Power Analysis. In *Advances in Cryptology — CRYPTO '99*, volume LNCS 1666, pages 388–397. Springer-Verlag, 1999.
16. Paul C. Kocher. Timing attacks on implementations of Diffie-Hellman, RSA, DSS and other systems. In *Advances in Cryptology - Proceedings of CRYPTO 1996*, volume LNCS 1109, pages 104–113. Springer Verlag, 1996.

17. Francois Koeune and Jean-Jacques Quisquater. A timing attack against Rijndael. Technical Report CG-1999/1, Université Catholique de Louvain, 1999.
18. S. Mangard. A Simple Power-Analysis (SPA) Attack on Implementations of the AES Key Expansion. In *Proceedings of the 5th International Conference on Information Security and Cryptology (ICISC 2002)*, volume LNCS 2587, pages 343–358. Springer-Verlag, 2002.
19. T.S. Messerges. Securing the AES Finalists Against Power Analysis Attacks. In B. Schneier, editor, *7th International Workshop on Fast Software Encryption — FSE 2000*, volume LNCS 1978, pages 150–164. Springer-Verlag, 2001.
20. S. Moore, R. Anderson, R. Mullins, G. Taylor, and J.J.A. Fournier. Balanced Self-Checking Asynchronous Logic for Smart Card Applications. *Journal of Microprocessors and Microsystems*, 27(9):421–430, 2003.
21. S.B. Örs, F. Gürkaynak, E. Oswald, and B. Preneel. Power-Analysis Attack on an ASIC AES Implementation. In *Proceedings of the 2004 International Symposium on Information Technology (ITCC 2004)*. IEEE Computer Society, 2004.
22. A. Satoh, S. Morioka, K. Takano, and S. Munetoh. A Compact Rijndael Hardware Architecture with S-Box Optimization. In *Advances in Cryptology — ASIACRYPT 2001*, volume LNCS 2248, pages 239–254. Springer-Verlag, 2001.
23. K. Tiri, M. Akmal, and I. Verbauwhede. A Dynamic and Differential CMOS Logic with Signal Independent Power Consumption to Withstand Differential Power Analysis on Smart Cards. In *28th European Solid-State Circuits Conference (ESSCIRC 2002)*, 2002.
24. K. Tiri and I. Verbauwhede. Securing Encryption Algorithms against DPA at the Logic Level: Next Generation Smart Card Technology. In C.D. Walter, Ç. K. Koç, and C. Paar, editors, *Workshop on Cryptographic Hardware and Embedded Systems — CHES 2003*, volume LNCS 2779, pages 125–136. Springer-Verlag, 2003.
25. E. Trichina. Combinational logic design for aes subbyte transformation on masked data. Cryptology eprint archive: Report 2003/236, IACR, November 11, 2003.
26. E. Trichina, D. De Seta, and L. Germani. Simplified Adaptive Multiplicative Masking for AES. In *Workshop on Cryptographic Hardware and Embedded Systems — CHES 2002*, volume LNCS 2523, pages 187–197. Springer-Verlag, 2002.
27. U.S. Department of Commerce/National Institute of Standard and Technology. *FIPS PUB 197, Specification for the Advanced Encryption Standard (AES)*, November 2001. Available at http://csrc.nist.gov/encryption/aes.
28. P. Voigtländer. Entwicklung einer Hardwarearchitektur für einen AES-Coprozessor. Diplomarbeit, Fachbereich Informatik, Mathematik und Naturwissenhaften, Technische Informatik, HTWK Leipzig, Germany, May 2, 2003.

Perfect Diffusion Primitives for Block Ciphers
Building Efficient MDS Matrices

Pascal Junod and Serge Vaudenay

École Polytechnique Fédérale de Lausanne, Switzerland
{pascal.junod, serge.vaudenay}@epfl.ch

Abstract. Although linear perfect diffusion primitives, i.e. MDS matrices, are widely used in block ciphers, e.g. AES, very little systematic work has been done on how to find "efficient" ones. In this paper we attempt to do so by considering software implementations on various platforms. These considerations lead to interesting combinatorial problems: how to maximize the number of occurrences of 1 in those matrices, and how to minimize the number of pairwise different entries. We investigate these problems and construct efficient 4×4 and 8×8 MDS matrices to be used e.g. in block ciphers.

1 Introduction

Block ciphers are cascades of diffusion and confusion layers [9]. We usually formalize confusion layers as application of substitution boxes which are defined by lookup tables. Since those tables must be as small as possible for implementation reasons, confusion layers apply substitution in parallel on pieces of informations, e.g. elements whose values lie in a set $\mathcal{K}$ of size 256. The goal of diffusion is to mix up those pieces. One possibility for formalizing the notion of perfect diffusion is the concept of *multipermutation* which was introduced in [8, 10]. By definition, a diffusion function f from $\mathcal{K}^p$ to $\mathcal{K}^q$ is a multipermutation if for any $x_1, \ldots, x_p \in \mathcal{K}$ and any integer r such that $1 \leq r \leq p$, the influence of modifying r input values on $f(x_1, \ldots, x_p)$ is to modify at least $q - r + 1$ output values. Another way to define it consists of saying that the set of all words consisting of $x_1, \ldots, x_p$ concatenated with $f(x_1, \ldots, x_p)$ is a code of $(\#\mathcal{K})^p$ words of length $p + q$ with minimal distance[1] $q + 1$. This notion matches the Singleton bound which relates to MDS codes. Indeed, if $\mathcal{K}$ is a finite field, a linear multipermutation is equivalent to an MDS code expressed in a systematic way, i.e. an arbitrary word of length p is encoded by concatenating it with the linear mapping applied to the word. Since this notion of perfect diffusion was introduced, several block ciphers used the so-called "MDS-matrix" primitive, e.g. AES [2,5], Twofish [6,7], Khazad [1], or FOX [3], to name a few examples. It is furthermore noteworthy that very few MDS codes are known and they are seldom used in practice. In this paper, we will adopt the following definition of a linear multipermutation.

---

[1] Here the notion of distance is the number of different $\mathcal{K}$-entries.

H. Handschuh and A. Hasan (Eds.): SAC 2004, LNCS 3357, pp. 84–99, 2005.

Definition 1. *Let $\mathcal{K}$ be a finite field and p and q be two integers. Let $x \mapsto M \times x$ be a mapping from $\mathcal{K}^p$ to $\mathcal{K}^q$ defined by the $q \times p$ matrix M. We say that it is a linear multipermutation (or an MDS matrix) if the set of all pairs $(x, M \times x)$ is an MDS code, i.e. a linear code of dimension p, length $p + q$ and minimal distance $q + 1$.*

The following theorem [4, Theorem 8 (page 321)] is another way to characterize an MDS matrix.

Theorem 1. *A matrix is an MDS matrix if and only if every sub-matrix is non-singular.*

It is very difficult to define what is "an optimal matrix" in terms of implementation performances, since there exists a large number of criteria which are very dependent of the platform. In this paper we investigate the problem of constructing MDS matrices whose implementation is *very efficient* on most low-cost platforms. For this, we isolate a few criteria which seemed important to us, and we derive several optimality results on these criteria. Note that we only considered one direction, which renders somewhat easier the problem of finding good matrices. Their inverses may not be very efficient but this is not important if we use these matrices with self-inverting constructions, like the Feistel or the Lai-Massey schemes.

2   Performances of Linear Multipermutations

We consider linear multipermutations from $\mathcal{K}^p$ to $\mathcal{K}^q$ where $\mathcal{K}$ is a finite field of characteristic 2. Typically, $\mathcal{K}$ is GF(256). We let M denote a matrix of type $q \times p$ whose elements lie in $\mathcal{K}$. We let $M_{i,j}$ denote the element on row i and column j with $1 \leq i \leq q$ and $1 \leq j \leq p$. The multipermutation is simply $x \mapsto y = M \times x$ where x and y column vectors, i.e.

$$y_i = \sum_{j=1}^{p} M_{i,j} x_j \qquad \text{for } i = 1, \ldots, q.$$

We consider several implementation strategies depending on the platform.

2.1   Software Implementation on 32/64-Bit Platforms

Modern 32-bit (or 64-bit) microprocessors with large cache memory[2] lead to well-known and quite simple implementation strategies. Indeed, columns of M can be partitioned into several sub-columns whose size correspond to the word size (or less). We let w denote the size of the words in terms of $\mathcal{K}$ elements. Then

---

[2] By "cache memory", we mean the fastest available cache memory, i.e. L1 cache. Most modern CPUs have 16 kB available or more (current versions of the Intel Pentium 4, having 8 kB available, are an exception).

all possible multiplications can be precomputed and put in a table. This means that we consider M as a block matrix of type $\lceil q/w \rceil \times p$, y as a block vector of $\lceil q/w \rceil$ elements, and where every block are vectors of w elements of $\mathcal{K}$, except the blocks in the last row which may be smaller if w does not divide q.

For instance, let us consider 32-bit words, the set $\mathcal{K}$ of bytes (i.e. $w = 4$ and $\#\mathcal{K} = 256$), and $p = q = 8$. We let $T_{k,j}$ be a table of 256 4-words vectors such that

$$T_{k,j}(u) = \begin{pmatrix} M_{4k-3,j} \cdot u \\ M_{4k-2,j} \cdot u \\ M_{4k-1,j} \cdot u \\ M_{4k,j} \cdot u \end{pmatrix}$$

for all $u \in \mathcal{K}$ and $k = 1, 2$. Then we can compute $y = M \times x$ by computing $v_k = T_{k,1}(x_1) \oplus \cdots \oplus T_{k,p}(x_p)$ for $k = 1, 2$. Then y is simply the concatenation of v_1 and v_2. Using this approach, we can implement the computation of the linear multipermutation by using $\lceil q/w \rceil \times p$ tables of $\#\mathcal{K}$ entries where each entry is of $w \log_2 \#\mathcal{K}$ bits. For typical applications such as $p = q = 8$, $\#\mathcal{K} = 256$ and $w = 4$ or 8, we have tables of $p \times q \times \#\mathcal{K}$ bytes, i.e. 16 kB of tables. This fits in the fast cache memory of nowadays microprocessors. So this means that we can compute y from x by using only $(p-1) \times \lceil q/w \rceil$ XOR operations, i.e. 14 XORs for $w = 4$ or 7 XORs for $w = 8$, and table lookups. With this approach, performances only depends on $p, q, w, \#\mathcal{K}$ and are independent on the structure of M.

2.2   Software Implementation on 8-Bit Platforms

Low-cost 8-bit microprocessors cannot afford to use precomputed data with a size of 16 kB: the matrix multiplication has to be computed on-the-fly. Obviously no $M_{i,j}$ elements can be equal to zero, since this would lead to a singular submatrix of type 1×1 in M and thus would contradict Theorem 1; so we really have to implement $p \times q$ operations. For $\#\mathcal{K} = 256$ we cannot even consider all multiplication tables since this would require naively 64 kB of memory. Another solution would be to express each element x of $\mathcal{K}$ as $x = g^i$, where g is a generator of $\mathcal{K}^*$, and to store the precomputed mappings $x \mapsto i$ and $i \mapsto x$ (one needs 512 bytes of memory). Any multiplication in $\mathcal{K}$ can then be computed using 3 table lookups and 1 addition. However, this approach remains costly. Some multiplication tables are quite simple though. For instance the multiplication by 1 — the neutral element in $\mathcal{K}^*$ — is trivial. Since we need to make multiplications by $M_{i,j}$ only, we may need a small number of tables. Our basic approach is to have all multiplication tables by $M_{i,j}$ elements except for the multiplication table by 1. This leads to the following definitions.

Definition 2. *Let $\mathcal{K}^*$ be a set including a distinguished one denoted 1. Let M be a $q \times p$ matrix whose entries lie in $\mathcal{K}^*$.*

1. *We let $v_1(M)$ denote the number of (i,j) pairs such that $M_{i,j}$ is equal to 1. We call it the* number of occurrences of 1.
2. *We let $c(M)$ be the cardinality of $\{M_{i,j}; i = 1, \ldots, q; j = 1, \ldots, p\}$. We call it the* number of entries.

3. *If $v_1(M) > 0$ we let $c_1(M) = c(M) - 1$. Otherwise we let $c_1(M) = c(M)$. We call it the* number of nontrivial entries.

With this basic implementation approach we need tables of total size $c_1(M) \times \#\mathcal{K}$ entries in $\mathcal{K}$ in order to implement M. The number of operations consists of $(p-1) \times q$ XORs and number of table lookup's which is equal to $c_1(M_{1,.}) + \cdots + c_1(M_{q,.})$ where $M_{i,.}$ denotes the ith row of M. Indeed, for each row we can look at all equal entries, XOR the corresponding x_j element, look up at the appropriate table, and XOR everything. So the number of CPU operations is within the order of $pq - q + qc_1(M)$. Hence the key metrics for this implementation approach are $c_1(M)$ (for the memory complexity) and $v_1(M)$ (for the time complexity). Note that we may save extra multiplication tables using "efficient GF elements". Here are four typical examples.

- With $\mathcal{K} = \mathrm{GF}(256)$ we can represent a polynomial $a_0 + a_1x + \cdots + a_7x^7$ by the bitstring $a_7 \cdots a_1 a_0$. The multiplication by the x element can be implemented by a shift by one bit to the left and a conditional XOR with a constant when a carry bit is set[3].
- Similarly, the multiplication by the x^{-1} element can be implemented by a shift by one bit to the right and a conditional XOR with a constant when a carry bit is set.
- If M includes two elements α and $\alpha + 1$, we can omit the multiplication table by $\alpha + 1$. Multiplication by $\alpha + 1$ is performed by one table lookup (a multiplication by α) and a XOR.
- If M includes two elements α and α^2, we can omit the multiplication table by α^2. Multiplication by α^2 is performed by two consecutive table lookup's.

We can also optimize implementations afterward.

3   Bi-regular Arrays as Candidates for MDS Matrices

In this section we concentrate on making MDS matrices with high v_1 and low c. The following definition introduces *bi-regular arrays* which are useful objects to build MDS matrices.

Definition 3. *Let $\mathcal{K}^*$ be a set including a distinguished one denoted 1.*

1. *We say that a 2×2 array with entries in $\mathcal{K}^*$ is* bi-regular *if at least one row and one column have two different entries.*
2. *We say that a $q \times p$ array with entries in $\mathcal{K}^*$ is* bi-regular *if all 2×2 sub-arrays are bi-regular.*
3. *An array which is not bi-regular is called* bi-singular.
4. *Two arrays are* equivalent *if we can obtain the second by performing a finite sequence of simple operations on the first one. Simple operations are permutation of rows, columns, transpose, and permutation of $\mathcal{K}^*$ elements for which 1 is a fixed point.*

---

[3] With a special care about side-channel attacks.

Note that an MDS matrix is necessary a bi-regular one (otherwise one 2×2 sub-determinant is singular). Equivalence keeps the bi-regularity. Finally, equivalent arrays have the same v_1 and c metrics. So we can first focus on making bi-regular arrays with high v_1 and low c.

Definition 4. *Let $\mathcal{K}^*$ be a set including a distinguished one denoted 1. We let $v_1^{q,p}$ (resp. $c^{q,p}$) be the maximal (resp. minimal) value of $v_1(M)$ (resp. $c(M)$) for a bi-regular array M of type $q \times p$.*

Note that when $\mathcal{K}^*$ has not enough elements for bi-regular arrays to exist, then $v_1^{q,p}$ and $c^{q,p}$ are undefined. Otherwise $v_1^{q,p}$ and $c^{q,p}$ do not depend on $\mathcal{K}^*$ at all.

One approach for constructing MDS matrices with high v_1 and low c_1 is first to construct a bi-regular array, second to assign elements to some non-zero field values until we get an MDS matrix. We can e.g. look at random values until it succeeds or concentrate on efficient GF elements.

3.1   Highest v_1 for Bi-regular Arrays

Here are easy facts about $v_1^{q,p}$.

1. We have $v_1^{q,p} = v_1^{p,q}$ since we can transpose bi-regular arrays.
2. We have $v_1^{1,p} = p$ for $p \geq 1$.
3. $v_1^{q,p}$ increases with p and q.

Lemma 1. *The following facts hold:*

- $v_1^{2,p} = p + 1$ *for any $p \geq 1$.*
- $v_1^{3,p} = p + 3$ *for any $p \geq 3$.*
- $v_1^{4,4} = 9$, $v_1^{4,5} = 10$, *and* $v_1^{4,p} = p + 6$ *for any $p \geq 6$.*
- $v_1^{5,5} = 12$, $v_1^{5,6} = 13$, $v_1^{5,7} = 14$, $v_1^{5,8} = 17$, $v_1^{5,9} = 18$, *and* $v_1^{5,p} = p + 10$ *for any $p \geq 10$.*

Proof. For the 2 rows case, the $2 \times p$ array

1	1	1	$\cdots$	1
1	a_2	a_3	$\cdots$	a_p

is bi-regular when $1, a_2, \ldots, a_p$ are pairwise different. We cannot have more occurrences for 1, otherwise we must have two different columns whose entries are only 1, which leads to a bi-singular 2×2 sub-array.

For the 3 rows case, if one column has three occurrences of 1, all other columns must have at most one occurrence of 1 which leads to $p+2$ in total. If no column has three occurrences of 1, we notice that at most three columns can have two occurrences, which leads to the following construction with $p + 3$ occurrences in total.

1	1	a_1	1	1	$\cdots$	1
1	a_1	1	a_2	a_3	$\cdots$	a_{p-2}
a_1	1	1	a_3	a_4	$\cdots$	a_{p-1}

For the 4 rows case, we similarly prove that no column has four occurrences of 1 in optimal solutions. We cannot have two different columns with 3 occurrences of 1 so we easily notice that the constructions below are optimal.

a_1	1	1	1
1	a_1	a_2	1
1	a_2	1	a_2
1	1	a_2	a_1

a_1	1	1	1	1
1	a_1	a_2	1	a_3
1	a_2	1	a_2	a_3
1	1	a_2	a_1	a_3

When we have more than 5 columns we notice that we get better results when we limit the occurrence number to 2 in every column as done in the following construction.

1	1	1	a_1	a_2	a_3	1	1	1	$\cdots$
1	a_3	a_1	1	1	a_2	a_4	a_5	a_6	$\cdots$
a_1	1	a_2	1	a_3	1	a_5	a_6	a_7	$\cdots$
a_2	a_1	1	a_3	1	1	a_6	a_7	a_8	$\cdots$

For the 5 rows case, we similarly prove that having five occurrences of 1 in the same row leads to sub-optimal solutions. Having a single row with four occurrences, four others with two occurrences, and the others with a single occurrence yields $v_1^{5,5} = 12$, $v_1^{5,6} = 13$, and $v_1^{5,7} = 14$. We can have at most two columns with three occurrences and up to four others with two occurrences, all others being limited to a single occurrence. If we keep a single column with three occurrences then we can have up to seven other columns with two occurrences, all others being limited to a single occurrence. This yields $v_1^{5,8} = 17$. Finally, limiting the occurrences number to two is optimal when we have more than 8 columns since we achieve $v_1^{5,9} = 18$, and $v_1^{5,p} = p + 10$ for any $p \geq 10$.   □

We could continue the proof further and obtain $v_1^{6,6} = 16$, $v_1^{6,7} = 18$, $v_1^{6,8} = 19$, $v_1^{7,7} = 21$, $v_1^{7,8} = 22$, $v_1^{8,8} = 24$. The optimal solutions with 6 rows consist of the following array. (For 6 or 7 columns, restrict on the first columns.) Blank cells need to be filled with elements other than 1.

1	1			1			1
1		1			1		
1			1			1	
	1	1				1	
	1		1		1		
		1	1	1			

The optimal solutions with 7 rows and 7 or 8 columns, and 8 rows and columns are the first rows and columns of the following array.

1	1	1					1
1			1	1			
1					1	1	
	1		1		1		
	1			1		1	
		1	1			1	
		1		1	1		
			1				1

The following lemma (with $\alpha = 2$) indicates that $v_1^{n,n}$ can be close to $n\sqrt{n}$ since we can put $\sqrt{n}$ occurrences of 1 in every row.

Lemma 2. *If p is a prime power, for any integers $\alpha > 1$ and $q \leq p^{\alpha-1}(p^\alpha - 1)/(p-1)$ we have $v_1^{q,p^\alpha} \geq q \times p$.*

Proof. This comes from the following construction. We let $\mathcal{K} = \mathrm{GF}(p)$ and we consider the affine space $\mathcal{K}^\alpha$. We have $p^{\alpha-1}(p^\alpha - 1)/(p-1)$ straight lines in total each containing exactly p points. We consider that every column corresponds to a point and that every row corresponds to a straight line. We put 1 in cells in which the corresponding point belongs to the straight line. We fill other cells so that it does not introduce bi-singular sub-arrays. Since straight lines intersect to at most one point, we have a bi-regular array. □

The following lemma provides optimal constructions for small p and q.

Lemma 3. *We have $v_1^{q,p} \geq p + 2q - 3$ for any p,q such that $q \leq p$.*

Proof. This lemma comes from the following construction:

a_{p-1}	1	1	1	1	$\cdots$
1	1	a_2	a_3	a_4	$\cdots$
1	a_{p-1}	1	a_2	a_3	$\cdots$
1	a_{p-2}	a_{p-1}	1	a_2	$\cdots$
1	a_{p-3}	a_{p-2}	a_{p-1}	1	$\cdots$
$\vdots$	$\vdots$	$\vdots$	$\vdots$	$\vdots$	$\ddots$

□

In summary, Table 1 gives the first values of $v_1^{q,p}$. Underlined numbers are obtained with the construction of Lemma 3.

3.2   Lowest c for Bi-regular Arrays

Here are easy facts about $c^{q,p}$.

1. We have $c^{q,p} = c^{p,q}$ since we can transpose bi-regular arrays.
2. We have $c^{1,p} = 1$ for $p \geq 1$. Indeed, the $1 \times p$ array

1	1	1	$\cdots$	1

   is bi-regular and we cannot have more occurrences for 1.
3. $c^{q,p}$ increases with p and q.

Table 1. Values of $v_1^{q,p}$

	2	3	4	5	6	7	8
2	3	4	5	6	7	8	9
3	4	6	7	8	9	10	11
4	5	7	9	10	12	13	14
5	6	8	10	12	13	14	17
6	7	9	12	13	16	18	19
7	8	10	13	14	18	21	22
8	9	11	14	17	19	22	24

Let us now demonstrate other results.

Lemma 4. *We have $c^{2,p} = \lceil \sqrt{p} \rceil$ for any integer $p \geq 1$.*

So we deduce that $c^{q,p} \geq \lceil \sqrt{p} \rceil$ for any $q \geq 2$ and any $p \geq 1$.

Proof. Let $s = \lceil \sqrt{p} \rceil$. Let $a_0, \ldots, a_{s-1}$ be pairwise different. For any $j = 1, \ldots, p$ we first let $j - 1 = qs + r$ be the Euclidean division of $j - 1$ by s, i.e. $0 \leq r < s$. Note that $0 \leq q < s$. We set $M_{1,j} = a_q$ and $M_{2,j} = a_r$. We notice that M is a $2 \times p$ bi-regular array. We have $v_1(M) = s$ and $c(M) = s$. Hence $c^{2,p} \leq s$.

Given an arbitrary $2 \times p$ bi-regular array, let us assume that there are no more than $s - 1$ pairwise different elements in the first row. Since we have more than $s(s-1)$ columns, one element at least occurs at least s times. Let us extract a $2 \times s$ sub array whose first row is a constant element. Note that this sub-array must be bi-regular as well. Obviously the second row must have pairwise different elements. So there are at least s pairwise different elements in the array. Hence $c^{2,p} \geq s$. □

Lemma 5. *For any $k > 1$ we have $c^{k^2 - k + 1, k! + 2} > k$.*

As an application we deduce that $c^{3,4} > 2$ and $c^{7,8} > 3$.

Proof. Let M be a $(k^2 - k + 1) \times (k! + 2)$ array of k elements. We notice that the first column must have an element a with k occurrences. Let us extract the $k \times (k! + 2)$ sub-array M' corresponding to these occurrences. All elements in the first column of M' are equal. If M was bi-regular, M' would be bi-regular as well, so no other column could have two occurrences of the same element b. Hence all columns but the first one would be permutations of the set of elements. Since there are k elements and $k!$ permutations, then two of the other columns would be equal which would contradict the bi-regular property. □

Lemma 6. *For any k we have $c^{2k-1, 2k-1} \leq k$.*

As an application we deduce that $c^{3,3} \leq 2$, $c^{5,5} \leq 3$, $c^{7,7} \leq 4$, and $c^{9,9} \leq 5$.

Proof. We construct a bi-regular $(2k - 1) \times (2k - 1)$ array by using matrices. Let A^r be the $(2k - 1) \times (2k - 1)$ matrix with integral elements defined by

$$A^r_{i,j} = \begin{cases} 1 \text{ if } |i + j - 2k| = 2k - r - 1 \text{ or } |i - j| = r \\ 0 \text{ otherwise.} \end{cases}$$

Note that the (i, j) coordinates which lead to $A^r_{i,j} = 1$ lie in a rectangle whose edges are parallel to the diagonals of the matrix and whose (virtual) corners have coordinate

$$\left(\frac{1}{2}, r + \frac{1}{2}\right), \left(2k - r - \frac{1}{2}, 2k - \frac{1}{2}\right), \left(2k - \frac{1}{2}, 2k - r - \frac{1}{2}\right), \left(r + \frac{1}{2}, \frac{1}{2}\right).$$

Finally we let

$$M = a_1 A^0 + a_2 A^2 + \cdots + a_k A^{2k-2}$$

with pairwise different $a_1, \ldots, a_k$. As examples, here are the 5×5 and 9×9 arrays obtained with $k = 3$ and $k = 5$.

a	b	b	c	c
b	a	c	b	c
b	c	a	c	b
c	b	c	a	b
c	c	b	b	a

a	b	b	c	c	d	d	e	e
b	a	c	b	d	c	e	d	e
b	c	a	d	b	e	c	e	d
c	b	d	a	e	b	e	c	d
c	d	b	e	a	e	b	d	c
d	c	e	b	e	a	d	b	c
d	e	c	e	b	d	a	c	b
e	d	e	c	d	b	c	a	b
e	e	d	d	c	c	b	b	a

We first notice that for any $1 \leq i, j \leq 2k - 1$ there exists a single even r such that $A^r_{i,j} = 1$. Thus for every cell in M there exists one and only one A^r matrix with r even with the corresponding cell containing 1.

Second we consider a 2×2 sub-array corresponding to positions (i, j), (i, j'), (i', j) and (i', j'). We assume that $M_{i,j} = M_{i,j'}$ and $M_{i',j} = M_{i',j'}$ and we want to lead to a contradiction.

If $i \equiv j \equiv j' \pmod 2$ then $|i - j| = |i - j'|$. Since $j \neq j'$ we deduce $j + j' = 2i$. If $i \not\equiv j \equiv j' \pmod 2$ then $|i + j - 2k| = |i + j' - 2k|$. Since $j \neq j'$ we deduce $j + j' = 4k - 2i$. Since $i \leq 2k - 1$, we obtain that $j \equiv j' \pmod 2$ implies $i = k - |(j+j')/2 - k|$. The same holds for i'. Since $i \neq i'$ we have a contradiction for the $j \equiv j' \pmod 2$ case.

If $i \equiv j \not\equiv j' \pmod 2$ then $|i - j| = 2k - 1 - |i + j' - 2k|$. So we have $2i = j - j' - 1$. Similarly, if $i \not\equiv j \not\equiv j' \pmod 2$ then $2i = j' - j - 1$ thus if $j \not\equiv j'$ $\pmod 2$ we have $2i = |j - j'| - 1$. The same holds for i'. Since $i \neq i'$ we have a contradiction for the $j \not\equiv j' \pmod 2$ case as well.

So we cannot have $M_{i,j} = M_{i,j'}$ and $M_{i',j} = M_{i',j'}$. By using the transpose, we cannot have $M_{i,j} = M_{i',j}$ and $M_{i,j'} = M_{i',j'}$. So M is bi-regular and $c(M) = k$. □

Lemma 7. *We have $c^{4,6} \geq 4$.*

Proof. The proof can be found in the Appendix.

Lemma 8. *Let q be a prime power. We have $c^{q,q^2-q+1} \leq q$.*

As an application we deduce that $c^{3,7} \leq 3$, $c^{4,13} \leq 4$.

Proof. Let $\mathcal{K}$ be a finite field of cardinality q. We let f be a bijective mapping from $\{2, \ldots, q^2 - q + 1\}$ to $\mathcal{K}^* \times \mathcal{K}$. We let $f(i) = (a_i, b_i)$ for $i = 2, \ldots, q^2 - q + 1$. We let $x_1, \ldots, x_q$ be a numbering of all $\mathcal{K}$ elements. We define $M_{i,1} = 1$ and $M_{i,j} = a_i x_j + b_i$ for $i = 1, \ldots, q$ and $j = 2, \ldots, q^2 - q + 1$. Obviously M is a $q \times (q^2 - q + 1)$ array of q elements. As an example, here is the array with $q = 3$.

a	a	a	b	b	c	c
a	b	c	c	a	a	b
a	c	b	a	c	b	a

Since $a_i \neq 0$ the $x \mapsto a_i x + b_j$ mappings are permutations so all 2×2 sub-array containing the first column are bi-regular. Let us now consider a 2×2 sub-array containing columns j and j' such that $1 < j < j'$. Assuming that $a_i x + b_i = a_{i'} x + b_{i'}$ and $a_i y + b_i = a_{i'} y + b_{i'}$ we have $(a_i - a_{i'})(x - y) = 0$. Since $(a_i, b_i) \neq (a_{i'}, b_{i'})$ we must have $x = y$. Hence the sub-array is bi-regular.   □

Lemma 9. *We have $c^{3,8} \geq 4$.*

Proof. Here we must have at least one column which is not a permutation of (abc). Let us assume without loss of generality that the first column is (aax). Then for every other column the entries at row 1 and 2 must be different. But there are only 6 possibilities which is not enough to fill all columns.   □

Lemma 10. *We have $c^{6,8} \geq 5$.*

Proof. Assuming that we have a 6×8 array with $c \leq 4$ then for every column we can produce at least two different pairs $\{i, j\}$ corresponding to two equal elements in row i and row j. If the array were bi-regular all pairs would be pairwise different so we would have 16 pairs in total. But we have only $\binom{6}{2} = 15$ possible pairs in total so this is impossible.   □

In summary Table 2 provides the obtained $c^{q,p}$ values. Underlined numbers are obtained from Lemma 4, 5, 6, 7, 8, 9, and 10. Other value come from basic properties such as symmetry and monotonicity. The missing element $c^{5,8} \leq 4$ result is obtained by the following construction.

a	a	a	a	d	d	b	b
a	d	c	b	b	a	a	d
b	a	d	c	b	c	d	c
c	b	a	d	a	b	d	a
d	c	b	a	c	b	c	d

4   MDS Matrices Constructions for $p = q = 4$

We study constructions with $p = q = 4$ over the field $\mathcal{K} = \mathrm{GF}(256)$. Elements are represented as polynomials of degree at most 7 over $\mathrm{GF}(2)$. The $a_0 + a_1 x + \cdots + a_7 x^7$ polynomial is represented by the bitstring $a_7 \cdots a_1 a_0$. Formally, x represents a root of an irreducible polynomial of degree 8.

Table 2. Values of $c^{q,p}$

	2	3	4	5	6	7	8
2	2	2	2	3	3	3	3
3	2	2	3	3	3	3	4
4	2	3	3	3	4	4	4
5	3	3	3	3	4	4	4
6	3	3	4	4	4	4	5
7	3	3	4	4	4	4	5
8	3	4	4	4	5	5	5

4.1   The AES Matrix

Here is the MDS matrix[4] taken from AES [2, 5] with $a = x$ and $b = x + 1$:

$$\begin{pmatrix} a & b & 1 & 1 \\ 1 & a & b & 1 \\ 1 & 1 & a & b \\ b & 1 & 1 & a \end{pmatrix} \tag{1}$$

Multiplication by a is a shift and a conditional XOR. In this case, $c = 3$ is optimal according to our criteria, but $v_1 = 8$ is not. As described in [2], a multiplication by (1) can be implemented (in a pseudo-C notation) using 15 XORs, 4 table lookups and 3 temporary variables:

```
t = a[0] ^ a[1] ^ a[2] ^ a[3]; /* a is the input vector */
u = a[0];
v = a[0] ^ a[1]; v = time[v]; a[0] = a[0] ^ v ^ t;
v = a[1] ^ a[2]; v = time[v]; a[1] = a[1] ^ v ^ t;
v = a[2] ^ a[3]; v = time[v]; a[2] = a[2] ^ v ^ t;
v = a[3] ^ u;    v = time[v]; a[3] = a[3] ^ v ^ t;
```

Note that AES also requires to implement the inverse MDS matrix.

4.2   An Efficient Matrix

As we have seen, $v_1^{4,4} = 9$ and $c^{4,4} = 3$ and we can hit both optimal criteria with the array of Lemma 3 (M_1 in (2)); let us furthermore consider a second matrix M_2, which is a permuted version of M_1.

$$M_1 = \begin{pmatrix} a & 1 & 1 & 1 \\ 1 & 1 & b & a \\ 1 & a & 1 & b \\ 1 & b & a & 1 \end{pmatrix} \qquad M_2 = \begin{pmatrix} a & 1 & 1 & 1 \\ 1 & a & 1 & b \\ 1 & b & a & 1 \\ 1 & 1 & b & a \end{pmatrix} \tag{2}$$

---

[4] In order to check that this is indeed an MDS matrix, we compute all sub-determinants. They can be expressed as polynomials in terms of x. We can check that none of these polynomials is zero. Since they are all of degree at most 4 and that x is of degree 8, they cannot vanish so we have an MDS matrix.

One can easily verify that necessary conditions for M_2 being a MDS matrix are, for any $a \neq b$ which are not equal to 0 or 1, $a \neq b^2$, $a \neq b+1$, and $a^2 \neq b$. If we dispose of two multiplication tables (namely, by $a+1$ and by $b+1$), we can implement a multiplication by M_2 in the following way:

```
u    = a[0] ^ a[1] ^ a[2] ^ a[3]; /* a is the input vector */
a[0] = u ^ timeap1[a[0]];       v    = timeap1[a[1]];
a[2] = timeap1[a[2]];           a[3] = timeap1[a[3]];
a[1] = u ^ v ^ timebp1[a[3]]; a[3] = u ^ a[3] ^ timebp1[a[2]];
a[2] = u ^ a[2] ^ timebp1[v];
```

This implementation needs 10 XORs, 2 temporary variables, 7 table lookups in two tables. This allows us to decrease the overall number of temporary variables and of operations (at the cost of a supplementary precomputed table), if the XOR operations and table lookups generate identical costs. Note that the same matrix (up to a permutation) forms the diffusive block of FOX64 [3].

5   MDS Matrices Constructions for $p = q = 8$

Here, we give explicit constructions with $p = q = 8$ over $\mathcal{K} = \mathrm{GF}(256)$.

5.1   Circulating-Like Matrix

By using the construction of Lemma 3 with $p = q = 8$, we obtain $v_1 = 21$ and $c = 7$ which, are not optimal. Many different possibilities for filling the coefficients exist; we give here as illustration two different examples.

$$\begin{pmatrix} f & 1 & 1 & 1 & 1 & 1 & 1 & 1 \\ 1 & 1 & a & b & c & d & e & f \\ 1 & f & 1 & a & b & c & d & e \\ 1 & e & f & 1 & a & b & c & d \\ 1 & d & e & f & 1 & a & b & c \\ 1 & c & d & e & f & 1 & a & b \\ 1 & b & c & d & e & f & 1 & a \\ 1 & a & b & c & d & e & f & 1 \end{pmatrix}$$

For GF(256) represented by the irreducible polynomial $x^8 + x^4 + x^3 + x^2 + 1$ over GF(2), a possible combination is given by $a = x+1$, $b = x^3 + 1$, $c = x^3 + x^2$, $d = x$, $e = x^2$ and $f = x^4$. Note that we need a single precomputed table, namely the multiplication by x. If we can afford two precomputed multiplication tables (by x and by x^{-1}, in this case), when using $x^8 + x^7 + x^6 + x^5 + x^4 + x^3 + 1$ as field representation, another possible combination is $a = x+1$, $b = x^{-1} + x^{-2}$, $c = x$, $d = x^2$, $e = x^{-1}$ and $f = x^{-2}$. An implementation using 29 table lookups, 71 XORs is given in Appendix. Note that the same matrix (up to a permutation) forms the diffusive block of FOX128 [3].

5.2   Matrix with Rectangle Patterns

We use the construction of Lemma 6 with $k = 5$ and we remove the first row and the last column. We obtain $v_1 = 15$ and $c = 5$ so this is optimal for c.

$$\begin{pmatrix} b\ a\ c\ b\ d\ c\ 1\ d \\ b\ c\ a\ d\ b\ 1\ c\ 1 \\ c\ b\ d\ a\ 1\ b\ 1\ c \\ c\ d\ b\ 1\ a\ 1\ b\ d \\ d\ c\ 1\ b\ 1\ a\ d\ b \\ d\ 1\ c\ 1\ b\ d\ a\ c \\ 1\ d\ 1\ c\ d\ b\ c\ a \\ 1\ 1\ d\ d\ c\ c\ b\ b \end{pmatrix}$$

Representing GF(256) with $x^8+x^7+x^6+x^5+x^4+x^3+1$ as irreducible polynomial, a possible combination is given by $a = x^{-3}+x^{-1}$, $b = x^{-2}+x^{-1}+1$, $c = x^4+x$ and $d = x$. With $x^8 + x^4 + x^3 + x^2 + 1$ as irreducible polynomial, a valid combination is $a = x + 1$, $b = x^4 + 1$, $c = x^4 + x$ and $d = x$. Using these coefficients, we are able to implement this matrix multiplication with the same amount of table lookups (i.e. 16), 54 XORs instead of 56 and two less temporary variables than the matrix used by the designers of Khazad (as described in [1]), for instance. We might do even better by dedicated optimizations.

6   Conclusion

MDS matrices are a well-known way to build linear multipermutations, i.e. optimal diffusion components which can be used as building blocks of cryptographic primitives, like block ciphers and hash functions. Although their implementation is quite straightforward on 32/64-bit architectures, which have large data L1 caches and thus allow to store large precomputed tables, we need to evaluate the matrix multiplication on-the-fly on low-cost 8-bit architectures, and we can afford only a very limited amount of precomputed data. In this paper, we have studied MDS matrices under the angle of efficiency, defined mathematical criteria and proven several optimality results relatively to these criteria; furthermore, we give new constructions of efficient 4×4 and 8×8 matrices over GF(256).

Future potential investigations may go in the direction of hardware implementations of linear multipermutations, which are not covered by this paper. Furthermore, we may extend our mathematical considerations with criteria specifically dedicated to SPNs; such matrices must have inverses which are also efficient, for fast decryption operations. Finally, we studied bi-regularity of matrices as a necessary condition for being MDS. It is however not sufficient. We indeed have found optimal bi-regular arrays but no instances which are MDS. This problem is left as future work.

Acknowledgments. The work presented in this paper was initiated by a project supported by MediaCrypt AG, and supported (in part) by the National Competence Center in Research on Mobile Information and Communication Systems

(NCCR-MICS), a center supported by the Swiss National Science Foundation under grant number 5005-67322.

References

1. P. Barreto and V. Rijmen. The Khazad legacy-level block cipher. First Open NESSIE Workshop, Leuven, 2000. See https://www.cryptonessie.org.
2. J. Daemen and V. Rijmen. *The Design of Rijndael*. Information Security and Cryptography. Springer, 2002.
3. P. Junod and S. Vaudenay. FOX: a new family of block ciphers. In *Proceedings of SAC'04*. Springer-Verlag, 2004.
4. F. MacWilliams and N. Sloane. *The theory of error-correcting codes*. North-Holland, 1977.
5. National Institute of Standards and Technology, U. S. Department of Commerce. *Advanced Encryption Standard (AES)*, 2001.
6. B. Schneier, J. Kelsey, D. Whiting, D. Wagner, C. Hall, and N. Ferguson. Twofish: A 128-bit block cipher. In *The First AES Candidate Conference*. National Institute for Standards and Technology, 1998.
7. B. Schneier, J. Kelsey, D. Whiting, D. Wagner, C. Hall, and N. Ferguson. *The Twofish encryption algorithm*. Wiley, 1999.
8. C. Schnorr and S. Vaudenay. Black box cryptanalysis of hash networks based on multipermutations. In A. De Santis, editor, *Advances in Cryptology - EUROCRYPT '94. Proceedings*, volume 950 of *LNCS*, pages 47–57. Springer-Verlag, 1995.
9. C. Shannon. Communication theory of secrecy systems. *Bell System Technical Journal*, 28(4), 1949.
10. S. Vaudenay. On the need for multipermutations: cryptanalysis of MD4 and SAFER. In B. Preneel, editor, *Fast Software Encryption. Proceedings*, volume 1008 of *LNCS*, pages 286–297. Springer-Verlag, 1995.

A   Proof of Lemma 7

First we demonstrate that a 4×6 bi-regular array such that $c = 3$ has no column equivalent to the pattern $(aabb)$. Indeed, let M be a 4×6 array of 3 elements a, b, and c whose first column is $(aabb)$. If the first row has two other occurrences of a and two occurrences of another element x, we can permute columns in order to get a first row equal to $(aaaxx\cdot)$. Then $M_{2,2}$ and $M_{2,3}$ must be pairwise different, and different from a for M to be bi-regular. Similarly, either $M_{2,4}$ or $M_{2,5}$ must be equal to a. We may permute columns 2 and 3, and columns 4 and 5 and obtain the array below.

a	a	a	x	x	
a	b	c	a		
b	?	?	?		
b	?	?	?		

Positions with question mark cannot be equal to b, so we must fill them with a and c elements. We have three pairs of question marks. Since we only have two elements, either two different pairs are equal, or one pair consists of the same element twice. In both case we contradict the bi-regular property. This means that row 1 cannot be equivalent to $(aaaxx\cdot)$. Obviously row 1 cannot be equivalent to $(aaaa\cdot\cdot)$ (otherwise we have not enough elements to put in row 2 below the a occurrences). For similar reasons row 1 cannot be equivalent to $(axxx\cdot\cdot)$. Thus row 1 must be equivalent to $(aabbcc)$. Since the same arguments hold for row 2, both rows are equivalents. Now let us assume that row 1 is $(aabbcc)$. Looking at what we can put in row 2 we obtain (after potential column permutations) the following array.

a	a	b	b	c	c
a	?	a	c	a	b
b					
b					

So row 2 cannot be equivalent to $(aabbcc)$ which leads to a contradiction. Hence no column can be equivalent to $(aabb)$ in a 4×6 bi-regular array of three elements.

Second, we show that no column can be equivalent to $(xxxy)$. Indeed, if the first column is $(xxxy)$, the elements in row 1, 2, and 3 must be pairwise different in every other column, which leads to 6 possibilities. Let us assume without loss of generality that the array is

x	a	a	b	b	c
x	b	c	a	c	a
x	c	b	c	a	b
y	?				

If the entry at the position of the question mark is b, then the entry at position $(4,3)$ must be different from b and different from the entry at position $(2,3)$, i.e. it must be a. Similarly, if the entry at the position of the question mark is c, the entry at position $(4,3)$ must also be a. After an eventual permutation of column 2 and 3 we can assume that the entry at the position of the question mark is a. But then entries at position $(4,4)$ and $(4,5)$ must be c and a respectively which lead to a singular sub-array.

In conclusion all column must be equivalent to $(xxyz)$. Let us assume that we have the following shape.

x	x'	x''	?		
x	y'	y''	?		
y	x'	z''	?		
z	z'	x''	?		

Then all entries in column 4 must be pairwise different, which is impossible.

B   Implementation of the Circulant Matrix

The input is in x[0..7], and the output in y[0..7]. We use two precomputed tables,
namely xtime[.] (multiplication by x) and xm1time[.] (division by x).

```
y[0] = x[0]^x[1]^x[2]^x[3]^x[4]^x[5]^x[6]^xtime[x[7]];
y[1] = x[1]^x[0]^x[7]^xtime[x[1]^x[3]^xtime[4]]^
       xm1time[x[2]^x[5]^xm1time[x[2]^x[6]]];
y[2] = x[0]^x[6]^x[7]^xtime[x[0]^x[2]^xtime[3]]^
       xm1time[x[1]^x[4]^xm1time[x[1]^x[5]]];
y[3] = x[6]^x[5]^x[7]^xtime[x[6]^x[1]^xtime[2]]^
       xm1time[x[0]^x[3]^xm1time[x[0]^x[4]]];
y[4] = x[5]^x[4]^x[7]^xtime[x[5]^x[0]^xtime[1]]^
       xm1time[x[6]^x[2]^xm1time[x[6]^x[3]]];
y[5] = x[4]^x[3]^x[7]^xtime[x[4]^x[6]^xtime[0]]^
       xm1time[x[5]^x[1]^xm1time[x[5]^x[2]]];
y[6] = x[3]^x[2]^x[7]^xtime[x[3]^x[5]^xtime[6]]^
       xm1time[x[4]^x[0]^xm1time[x[4]^x[1]]];
y[7] = x[2]^x[1]^x[7]^xtime[x[2]^x[4]^xtime[5]]^
       xm1time[x[3]^x[6]^xm1time[x[3]^x[0]]];
```

C   Implementation of the Matrix with Rectangle Patterns

The input is in x[0..7], and the output in y[0..7]. We use two precomputed tables,
namely xtime[.] (multiplication by x) and x4time[.] (multiplication by x^4).

```
t0 = x[0]^x[1]; t1 = x[0]^x[2]; t2 = x[3]^x[5];
t3 = x[1]^x[4]; t4 = x[2]^x[4]; t5 = x[5]^x[7];
t6 = x[3]^x[6]; t7 = x[4]^x[6];
r1 = t1^t5; r2 = t2^t4; r3 = t3^t6; r4 = t2^t6;
y[0] = t0^t6^xtime[t3^t5^x[2]]^x4time[t1^t2];
y[1] = r1^x[4]^xtime[t6^x[1]^x[2]]^x4time[t0^t7];
y[2] = r4^t3^xtime[r1^t2]^x4time[t0^t5];
y[3] = r2^x[6]^xtime[t0^x[4]^x[7]]^x4time[t1^x[6]];
y[4] = r2^x[7]^xtime[t1^x[5]^ x[6]]^x4time[x[2]^x[3]^x[7]];
y[5] = r3^xtime[r1^x[7]]^x4time[t4^x[7]];
y[6] = r1^xtime[r3^x[7]]^x4time[r4];
y[7] = t0^x[6]^x[7]^xtime[r2]^x4time[t5^t7];
```

Security of the MISTY Structure in the Luby-Rackoff Model: Improved Results

Gilles Piret and Jean-Jacques Quisquater

UCL Crypto Group,
Place du Levant, 3, B-1348 Louvain-la-Neuve, Belgium
{piret, jjq}@dice.ucl.ac.be

Abstract. In this paper we consider the security of the Misty structure in the Luby-Rackoff model, if the inner functions are replaced by involutions without fixed point. In this context we show that the success probability in distinguishing a 4-round L-scheme from a random function is $O(m^2/2^n)$ (where m is the number of queries and $2n$ the block size) when the adversary is allowed to make adaptively chosen encryption queries. We give a similar bound in the case of the 3-round R-scheme. Finally, we show that the advantage in distinguishing a 5-round scheme from a random permutation when the adversary is allowed to adaptively chosen encryption as well as decryption queries is also $O(m^2/2^n)$. This is to our knowledge the first time involutions are considered in the context of the Luby-Rackoff model.

1 Introduction

Proving the security of block ciphers has been a long-standing problem, and it is not solved yet. In their seminal paper [4], M. Luby and C. Rackoff introduced a model that permits the assessment of the security of some block cipher constructions. In this model, only the high-level structure of a block cipher is considered, while the lower-level operations are replaced by random functions. This last hypothesis is pretty strong, but at least it permits to guarantee that the basic structure of a block cipher is not flawed from the beginning.

More precisely, the model works as follows: let $\Phi(f_1, ..., f_r)$ be a construction which to r functions $f_1, ..., f_r : \{0,1\}^n \rightarrow \{0,1\}^n$ associates one function $F : \{0,1\}^{2n} \rightarrow \{0,1\}^{2n}$. We consider a distinguishing algorithm $\mathcal{A}$ which has unbounded computation capabilities, and can make a certain number of adaptively chosen encryption queries to an oracle function $\mathcal{O} : \{0,1\}^{2n} \rightarrow \{0,1\}^{2n}$ he received as an input[1]. Based on the answers he obtains to his queries, $\mathcal{A}$ outputs either 0 or 1. Let $p = \Pr[\mathcal{A}^{\Phi(f_1^*, ..., f_r^*)} = 1]$ and $p^* = \Pr[\mathcal{A}^{F^*} = 1]$ denote the probability that $\mathcal{A}$ outputs 1 when $\mathcal{O}$ is respectively a function of the form

---

[1] The size of the input and output spaces of $\mathcal{O}$ are often $2n$ bits, where n is the size of the inner functions. However these constraints are absolutely not mandatory; the input and output sizes do not even need to be the same.

H. Handschuh and A. Hasan (Eds.): SAC 2004, LNCS 3357, pp. 100–113, 2005.

$\Phi(f_1^*, ..., f_r^*)$, where $f_1^*, ..., f_r^*$ are **perfect** random functions (i.e. functions randomly chosen with respect to the uniform distribution), or $\mathcal{O}$ itself is a perfect random function F^*. We are interested in the *advantage* $\mathcal{A}$ has in distinguishing $\Phi(f_1^*, ..., f_r^*)$ from F^*: $\text{Adv}_{\mathcal{A}}(\Phi(f_1^*, ..., f_r^*), F^*) = |p - p^*|$. A security proof in the Luby-Rackoff model consists in upper bounding this advantage (as a function of the number of queries m and the block size $2n$) for all possible distinguishers $\mathcal{A}$. If for n big enough, and for all distinguishing algorithms $\mathcal{A}$ of which the number of queries m is polynomial in n, $\text{Adv}_{\mathcal{A}}$ is polynomially small, then Φ is said to be **pseudorandom**. If this criteria still holds when *decryption* queries are allowed as well, then Φ is said to be **superpseudorandom**. As a shortcut, an algorithm allowed to make adaptive encryption queries only will often be called **pseudorandom distinguisher**, and an algorithm allowed to make both adaptive encryption and adaptive decryption queries will be called **superpseudorandom distinguisher**.

Luby and Rackoff's paper initiated a significant amount of research in the area: in 1992 Patarin [11, 12] made explicit the link between the advantage and the transition probability associated with a given structure Φ (see section 2.3); this gives a practical way of upper bounding the advantage. The same year, Maurer showed how to generalise undistinguishability results to *locally* random functions. More recently, Ramzan and Reyzin introduced a new model which assumes that the attacker has oracle access to some of the round functions [16]. Besides, the Feistel structure (first examined by Luby and Rackoff) was widely studied. On the one hand, its security bounds were tried to be improved [11, 13, 14, 15]. On the other hand, slightly modified constructions were examined: constructions were some of the round functions are identical [12], or are replaced by hash functions for example [5, 10]. Moreover some other constructions were also examined [9, 19].

Recently, constructions used in the block ciphers Misty [6] and Kasumi were examined. In 1997, Sakurai and Zheng [17] presented several negative results (i.e. non-pseudorandomness and non-superpseudorandomness) on these schemes. Then Gilbert and Minier [8] showed in 2001 that the 4-round Misty construction (called *L-scheme*) is pseudorandom, while 3 rounds of its inverse (called *R-scheme*) is sufficient to obtain pseudorandomness. Moreover they showed that 5 rounds of these constructions are necessary to obtain superpseudorandomness. The same year, Iwata et al. [3] showed that some of the 5 inner permutations can be replaced by uniform ϵ-XOR universal permutations without losing superpseudorandomness; moreover, following the model of Ramzan and Reyzin [16], they show that oracle access to some specific inner permutations does not change superpseudorandomness either. Finally, the next year about the same authors showed that the second inner permutation of a 5-round Misty does not need to be cryptographic at all to guarantee superpseudorandomness: it can be a constant and public transformation g, provided g satisfies $g(x) \oplus x \neq g(x') \oplus x'$ [2].

In this paper, we consider another restriction on the inner functions: namely, we assume that all of them are random involutions (i.e. permutations c such that $\forall x : c(c(x)) = x$) without fixed point. For implementation reasons, involutions were a basis of the design of several recent block ciphers (see e.g. Khazad [1], Anubis, Noekeon, ICEBERG [18]), hence the interest of such hypothesis. We show that the pseudorandom character of Misty constructions is preserved under this constraint (the number of rounds considered remaining unchanged).

2   Preliminaries

2.1   The Misty L- and R-Schemes

We describe two basic schemes: the L-scheme has been used in the Misty [6] and Kasumi block ciphers, the R-scheme is almost its inverse (we follow the terminology used by Gilbert and Minier [8]).

We define a 1-round L-scheme as a $2n$-bit permutation ψ_L taking a n-bit permutation c as a round function and such that:

$$\psi_L(c)(L, R) = (R, c(L) \oplus R)$$

It is depicted in Figure 1. An r-round L-scheme is simply the composition of r 1-round L-schemes, transforming r n-bit permutations $c_1, ..., c_r$ into a $2n$-bit permutation:

$$\psi_L(c_1, c_2, ..., c_r) = \psi_L(c_r) \circ ... \circ \psi_L(c_1)$$

A 1-round R-scheme transforms a n-bit permutation c into a $2n$-bit permutation $\psi_R(c)$ too. It is defined as (see Figure 1):

$$\psi_R(c)(L, R) = (c(L) \oplus R, c(L))$$

The composition of r 1-round R-schemes is a r-round R-scheme:

$$\psi_R(c_1, c_2, ..., c_r) = \psi_R(c_r) \circ ... \circ \psi_R(c_1)$$

In this paper we consider variants of the ψ_L and ψ_R schemes, where the last XOR operation is omitted, as well as the last swap. We call them ψ'_L and ψ'_R.

Remark 1. Cryptographically speaking, ψ'_L and ψ'_R are equivalent respectively to ψ_L and ψ_R.

Remark 2. $\psi'_L(c_1, c_2, ..., c_r)$ and $\psi'_R(c_r^{-1}, c_{r-1}^{-1}, ..., c_1^{-1})$ are inverses of each other. It implies that their security against superpseudorandom distinguishers is the same.

2.2   Notations

Throughout this paper we use the following notations:

- I_n denotes the $\{0, 1\}^n$ set.
- $I := I_n^m$ (where m is the number of plaintext-ciphertext pairs considered).
- For $\mathbf{X}, \mathbf{Y} \in I$: $\mathbf{X} \sim \mathbf{Y}$ informally means that $\mathbf{X}$ and $\mathbf{Y}$ could be the inputs and outputs of a permutation. More formally: $\forall i, j \in [1...m] : X_i = X_j \Leftrightarrow Y_i = Y_j$.

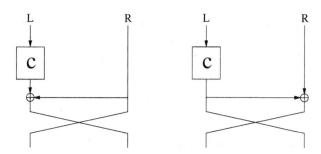

Fig. 1. 1-round L-scheme at left, 1-round R-scheme at right

- $I^{\neq} := \{\mathbf{X} \in I | \nexists i \neq j \in [1...m] : X_i = X_j\}$ $I^{=} := I \backslash I^{\neq}$.
- Let $\mathcal{X}$ be the subset of I_{2n}^m such that $\forall ((X_i, Y_i))_{i \in [1..m]} \in \mathcal{X} : \forall i \neq j :$ $(X_i, Y_i) \neq (X_j, Y_j)$. Then the m inputs to ψ_L (or ψ_R) are assumed[2] to belong to $\mathcal{X}$ and denoted by $(\mathbf{L}, \mathbf{R}) = ((L_i)_{i \in [1..m]}, (R_i)_{i \in [1..m]}) \in \mathcal{X}$. Similarly the m corresponding outputs are denoted by $(\mathbf{S}, \mathbf{T}) = ((S_i, T_i))_{i \in [1..m]} \in \mathcal{X}$.
- f^* always denotes a perfect random function (or permutation, or involution without fixed point, depending on the context), i.e. one which is chosen in accordance with the uniform probability distribution.

2.3   Patarin's Coefficient H Technique

Let $\mathcal{P}_{(\mathbf{S},\mathbf{T})}^{(\mathbf{L},\mathbf{R})}$ be the probability for a structure $\Phi(f_1, ..., f_r)$ to be such that $\Phi(f_1, ..., f_r)(\mathbf{L}, \mathbf{R}) = (\mathbf{S}, \mathbf{T})$ (computed over all possible $f_1, ..., f_r$). Not surprisingly, this probability plays a big role in upper bounding the advantage an algorithm $\mathcal{A}$ has in distinguishing Φ from a perfect random function F^*. The link between $\mathcal{P}_{(\mathbf{S},\mathbf{T})}^{(\mathbf{L},\mathbf{R})}$ and the best advantage has been quantified by Patarin [11, 12][3]:

Theorem 1 (Patarin). *Let* $F : I_{2n} \rightarrow I_{2n}$ *be a random function; let* $F^* :$ $I_{2n} \rightarrow I_{2n}$ *be a perfect random function. Let* m *be an integer. If there exists a subset* $\mathcal{Y}$ *of* I_{2n}^m *and two positive real numbers* ϵ_1 *and* ϵ_2 *such that*

1. $|\mathcal{Y}| > (1 - \epsilon_1) \cdot |I_{2n}|^m$
2. $\forall (\mathbf{L}, \mathbf{R}) \in \mathcal{X}$ $\forall (\mathbf{S}, \mathbf{T}) \in \mathcal{Y} : \mathcal{P}_{(\mathbf{S},\mathbf{T})}^{(\mathbf{L},\mathbf{R})} \geq (1 - \epsilon_2) \cdot \frac{1}{|I_{2n}|^m}$

Then for any distinguisher $\mathcal{A}$ *using* m *encryption queries*

$$Adv_{\mathcal{A}}(F, F^*) \leq \epsilon_1 + \epsilon_2$$

Theorem 1 deals with pseudorandom distinguishers. A similar theorem holds for superpseudorandom distinguishers:

---

[2] This hypothesis reflects the fact that the distinguisher is assumed not to make two times the same query. As the distinguisher would learn nothing more when repeating a query, there is no loss of generality.

[3] We particularized Patarin's theorem to the case where the input and output sizes are both $2n$, but it holds for any size.

Theorem 2 (Patarin). *Let $C : I_{2n} \to I_{2n}$ be a random permutation; let C^* : $I_{2n} \to I_{2n}$ be a perfect random permutation. Let m be an integer, and $\epsilon > 0$. If for all $(\mathbf{L}, \mathbf{R}) \in \mathcal{X}$, and all $(\mathbf{S}, \mathbf{T}) \in \mathcal{X}$: $\mathcal{P}_{(\mathbf{S},\mathbf{T})}^{(\mathbf{L},\mathbf{R})} \geq (1 - \epsilon) \cdot \frac{1}{|I_{2n}|^m}$ then for any distinguisher $\mathcal{A}$ using m encryption or decryption queries: $Adv_{\mathcal{A}}(C, C^*) \leq \epsilon + \frac{m(m-1)}{2 \cdot 2^{2n}}$*

3   The 4-Round L-Scheme

We consider a 4-round L-scheme were the inner permutations $c_1^*, ..., c_4^*$ are perfect random involutions without fixed point. In section 4 we will prove the following lemma:

Lemma 1. *Let $m, n > 0$. Let $(\mathbf{L}, \mathbf{R}) \in \mathcal{X} \subset I_{2n}^m, (\mathbf{S}, \mathbf{T}) \in I \times I^{\neq}$. Then the probability for a 4-uple (c_1, c_2, c_3, c_4) of involutions without fixed point to satisfy $\psi_L'(c_1, ..., c_4)(\mathbf{L}, \mathbf{R}) = (\mathbf{S}, \mathbf{T})$ is lower bounded by*

$$\left[1 - \frac{15m^2}{2^n} - \frac{9}{32} \sum_{k=2}^{\infty} \left(\frac{16m^2}{2^n} \right)^k \right] \cdot \frac{1}{2^{2nm}} \geq \left(1 - \frac{24m^2}{2^n} \right) \cdot \frac{1}{2^{2nm}}$$

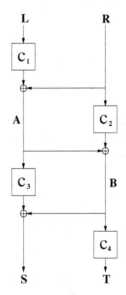

Fig. 2. 4 rounds L-scheme

It allows to prove the following theorem:

Theorem 3. *Let $c_1^*, ..., c_4^*$ be independent perfect random involutions without fixed point on I_n. Let $C := \psi_L(c_1^*, ..., c_4^*)$. Let $F^* : I_{2n} \to I_{2n}$ be a perfect* *random function. Then for any pseudorandom distinguisher $\mathcal{A}$ allowed to make m queries, we have:*

$$Adv_{\mathcal{A}}(C, F^*) \leq \frac{31m^2}{2 \cdot 2^n} + \frac{9}{32} \sum_{k=2}^{\infty} \left(\frac{16m^2}{2^n}\right)^k \leq \frac{49m^2}{2 \cdot 2^n}$$

Thus $\psi_L(c_1^*, ..., c_4^*)$ is pseudorandom, and secure as long as $m \ll 2^{n/2}$.

Proof. It is an immediate application of theorem 1. The constraint $\mathbf{T} \in I^{\neq}$ in lemma 1 implies a non-zero ϵ_1. More precisely, ϵ_1 is equal to the probability for a (perfect) random $\mathbf{T} \in I$ to belong to $I^{=}$. It can be shown to be smaller than $\frac{m^2}{2 \cdot 2^n}$:

$$\Pr[\mathbf{T} \in I^{=}] = \Pr[\bigvee_{i<j} T_i = T_j] \leq \sum_{i<j} \Pr[T_i = T_j] \leq \frac{m^2}{2 \cdot 2^n}$$

Lemma 1 gives the corresponding ϵ_2.

4   Proof of Lemma 1

For a given $(\mathbf{L}, \mathbf{R}, \mathbf{S}, \mathbf{T})$, we define λ and ρ as the number of independent equalities of the form $L_i = L_j$ and $R_i = R_j$ ($i \neq j$), respectively. We also define two intermediate states during the computation of $\psi_L'(c_1, ..., c_4)$, namely $\mathbf{A} := c_1(\mathbf{L}) \oplus \mathbf{R}$ and $\mathbf{B} := c_2(\mathbf{R}) \oplus \mathbf{A}$ (see Figure 2). Let $\mathcal{P}_{(\mathbf{S},\mathbf{T})}^{(\mathbf{L},\mathbf{R})}$ be the probability that a random 4-uple (c_1, c_2, c_3, c_4) is such that $\psi_L'(c_1, c_2, c_3, c_4)(\mathbf{L}, \mathbf{R}) = (\mathbf{S}, \mathbf{T})$. Then

$$\mathcal{P}_{(\mathbf{S},\mathbf{T})}^{(\mathbf{L},\mathbf{R})} = \sum_{\mathbf{A},\mathbf{B} \in I} \Pr[(c_1(\mathbf{L}) \oplus \mathbf{R} = \mathbf{A}) \wedge (c_2(\mathbf{R}) \oplus \mathbf{A} = \mathbf{B}) \tag{1}$$
$$\wedge (c_3(\mathbf{A}) \oplus \mathbf{B} = \mathbf{S}) \wedge (c_4(\mathbf{B}) = \mathbf{T})]$$

We consider the following conditions $(\mathcal{C})$ on $(\mathbf{A}, \mathbf{B})$:

($\mathcal{C}$1) $\mathbf{A} \oplus \mathbf{R} \sim \mathbf{L}$ and $\nexists i, j$ s.t. $L_i = A_j \oplus R_j$.
($\mathcal{C}$2) $\mathbf{A} \oplus \mathbf{B} \sim \mathbf{R}$ and $\nexists i, j$ s.t. $R_i = A_j \oplus B_j$.
($\mathcal{C}$3) $\mathbf{B} \oplus \mathbf{S} \in I^{\neq}$ and $\nexists i, j$ s.t. $A_i = B_j \oplus S_j$.
($\mathcal{C}$4) $\nexists i, j$ s.t. $B_i = T_j$.

Then equation (1) implies:

$$\mathcal{P}_{(\mathbf{S},\mathbf{T})}^{(\mathbf{L},\mathbf{R})} \geq \sum_{\substack{\mathbf{A},\mathbf{B} \in I^{\neq} \\ (\mathbf{A},\mathbf{B}) \text{ satisfies } (\mathcal{C})}} \Pr[(c_1(\mathbf{L}) \oplus \mathbf{R} = \mathbf{A})] \cdot \Pr[c_2(\mathbf{R}) \oplus \mathbf{A} = \mathbf{B}] \tag{2}$$
$$\cdot \Pr[c_3(\mathbf{A}) \oplus \mathbf{B} = \mathbf{S}] \cdot \Pr[c_4(\mathbf{B}) = \mathbf{T}]$$

The number of $\mathbf{A}$ such that $(\mathcal{C}1)$ is satisfied is $\frac{(2^n - m + \lambda)!}{(2^n - 2m + 2\lambda)!}$. For a (perfect) random such $\mathbf{A}$ we have:

$$\Pr[\mathbf{A} \in I^{\neq}|(\mathcal{C}1)] \geq 1 - \sum_{i<j} \Pr[A_i = A_j|(\mathcal{C}1)] \tag{3}$$

Consider given $1 \leq i < j \leq m$, and assume $L_i \neq L_j$ and $R_i \neq R_j$. As there are $(2^n - m + \lambda)(2^n - m + \lambda - 1)$ possible values for (A_i, A_j) satisfying $(\mathcal{C}_1)$, among which $2^n - m + \lambda$ satisfy $A_i = A_j$, we get

$$\Pr[A_i = A_j | (\mathcal{C}_1)] = \frac{2^n - m + \lambda}{(2^n - m + \lambda)(2^n - m + \lambda - 1)} \leq \frac{2}{2^n} \tag{4}$$

If $L_i = L_j$ or $R_i = R_j$, it is easy to see that $\Pr[A_i = A_j | (\mathcal{C}1)] = 0$.
Then we have

$$\Pr[\mathbf{A} \in I^{\neq} | (\mathcal{C}1)] \geq 1 - \frac{m(m-1)}{2} \cdot \frac{2}{2^n} \geq 1 - \frac{m^2}{2^n} \tag{5}$$

Similarly, the number of $\mathbf{B}$ such that $(\mathcal{C}2)$ is satisfied is $\frac{(2^n - m + \rho)!}{(2^n - 2m + 2\rho)!}$, and $\Pr[\mathbf{B} \in I^{\neq} | (\mathcal{C}2)] \geq 1 - \frac{m^2}{2^n}$. Finally for a (perfect) random $(\mathbf{A}, \mathbf{B})$ we compute:

$\Pr[\mathbf{B} \text{ satisfies } (\mathcal{C}3) \wedge \mathbf{B} \text{ satisfies } (\mathcal{C}4) \wedge \mathbf{A} \in I^{\neq} \wedge \mathbf{B} \in I^{\neq} | (\mathcal{C}1) \wedge (\mathcal{C}2)]$

$$\geq 1 - \Pr[\bigvee_{i<j} B_i \oplus S_i = B_j \oplus S_j | (\mathcal{C}1) \wedge (\mathcal{C}2)]$$

$$- \Pr[\bigvee_{i,j} A_i = B_j \oplus S_j | (\mathcal{C}1) \wedge (\mathcal{C}2)] - \Pr[\bigvee_{i,j} B_i = T_j | (\mathcal{C}1) \wedge (\mathcal{C}2)] - 2 \cdot \frac{m^2}{2^n}$$

$$\geq 1 - \frac{m(m-1)}{2} \cdot \frac{2}{2^n} - \frac{4m^2}{2^n} - 2 \cdot \frac{m^2}{2^n} \geq 1 - \frac{7m^2}{2^n}$$

Thus the number of $(\mathbf{A}, \mathbf{B}) \in I^{\neq}$ satisfying $(\mathcal{C})$ can be lower bounded by:

$$\frac{(2^n - m + \lambda)!}{(2^n - 2m + 2\lambda)!} \cdot \frac{(2^n - m + \rho)!}{(2^n - 2m + 2\rho)!} \cdot (1 - \frac{7m^2}{2^n}) \tag{6}$$

Under these conditions on $(\mathbf{A}, \mathbf{B})$ we can evaluate

$$\Pr[(c_1(\mathbf{L}) \oplus \mathbf{R} = \mathbf{A})] \cdot \Pr[c_2(\mathbf{R}) \oplus \mathbf{A} = \mathbf{B}] \cdot \Pr[c_3(\mathbf{A}) \oplus \mathbf{B} = \mathbf{S}] \cdot \Pr[c_4(\mathbf{B}) = \mathbf{T}]$$

and we obtain:

$$\frac{\frac{(2^n - 2m + 2\lambda)!}{2^{2n-1} - m + \lambda \cdot (2^{n-1} - m + \lambda)!} \cdot \frac{(2^n - 2m + 2\rho)!}{2^{2n-1} - m + \rho \cdot (2^{n-1} - m + \rho)!} \cdot \left[\frac{(2^n - 2m)!}{2^{2n-1} - m \cdot (2^{n-1} - m)!} \right]^2}{\left[\frac{2^n!}{2^{2n-1} \cdot (2^{n-1})!} \right]^4} \tag{7}$$

After multiplication of (7) by the number of terms (6):

$$\frac{2^{4m - \lambda - \rho} \cdot (2^n - m + \lambda)! \cdot (2^n - m + \rho)!}{(2^{n-1} - m + \lambda)! \cdot (2^{n-1} - m + \rho)!} \cdot \frac{(2^{n-1}!)^4}{(2^n!)^4} \cdot \left[\frac{(2^n - 2m)!}{(2^{n-1} - m)!} \right]^2 \cdot (1 - \frac{7m^2}{2^n})$$

$$= 2^{4m - \lambda - \rho} \cdot \frac{\prod_{i=0}^{m-\lambda-1} \frac{2^{n-1} - i}{2^n - i} \cdot \prod_{i=0}^{m-\rho-1} \frac{2^{n-1} - i}{2^n - i} \cdot \left(\prod_{i=0}^{m-1} \frac{2^{n-1} - i}{2^n - i} \right)^2}{\left(\prod_{i=m}^{2m-1} 2^n - i \right)^2} \cdot (1 - \frac{7m^2}{2^n})$$

By lower bounding the products, this expression can be shown to be greater or equal than:

$$2^{4m-\lambda-\rho} \cdot \left(\frac{2^{n-1} - m}{2^n - m}\right)^{4m-\lambda-\rho} \cdot \frac{1}{2^{2nm}} \cdot \left(1 - \frac{7m^2}{2^n}\right) \tag{8}$$

It is easy to show that $\frac{2^{n-1} - m}{2^n - m} = \frac{1}{2} - \frac{1}{2}\sum_{k=1}^{\infty} \frac{m^k}{2^{nk}}$. Then (8) is greater or equal than:

$$\left(1 - \sum_{k=1}^{\infty} \frac{m^k}{2^{nk}}\right)^{4m} \cdot \frac{1}{2^{2nm}} \cdot \left(1 - \frac{7m^2}{2^n}\right) \tag{9}$$

By evaluating the first factor using the binomial theorem, we can show

$$\left(1 - \sum_{k=1}^{\infty} \frac{m^k}{2^{nk}}\right)^{4m} \geq 1 - \frac{1}{2}\sum_{k=1}^{\infty} \left(\frac{16m^2}{2^n}\right)^k \tag{10}$$

Finally, immediate calculations show that (9) is greater or equal than:

$$\left[1 - \frac{15m^2}{2^n} - \frac{9}{32}\sum_{k=2}^{\infty} \left(\frac{16m^2}{2^n}\right)^k\right] \cdot \frac{1}{2^{2nm}} \geq \left(1 - \frac{24m^2}{2^n}\right) \cdot \frac{1}{2^{2nm}} \tag{11}$$

which concludes the proof.

5   The 3-Round R-Scheme

A result similar to theorem 3 can be proved for a 3-round R-scheme:

Theorem 4. *Let c_1^*, c_2^*, c_3^* be independent perfect random involutions without fixed point on I_n. Let $C := \psi_R(c_1^*, c_2^*, c_3^*)$. Let $F^* : I_{2n} \to I_{2n}$ be a perfect random function. Then for any pseudorandom distinguisher A allowed to make m queries, we have:*

$$Adv_A(C, F^*) \leq \frac{11m^2}{2^n} + \frac{5}{8}\sum_{k=2}^{\infty} \left(\frac{8m^2}{2^n}\right)^k \leq \frac{13m^2}{2^n}$$

Thus $\psi_R(c_1^*, c_2^*, c_3^*)$ is pseudorandom, and secure as long as $m \ll 2^{n/2}$.

6   The 5-Round Scheme

The following lemma is proved in the next section:

Lemma 2. *Let $m, n > 0$. Let $(\mathbf{L}, \mathbf{R}), (\mathbf{S}, \mathbf{T}) \in \mathcal{X} \subset I_{2n}^m$. Then the probability for a 5-uple $(c_1, c_2, c_3, c_4, c_5)$ of involutions without fixed point to satisfy $\psi_L'(c_1, ..., c_5)(\mathbf{L}, \mathbf{R}) = (\mathbf{S}, \mathbf{T})$ is lower bounded by*

$$\left(1 - \frac{12m^2}{2^n}\right) \cdot \frac{1}{2^{nm}}$$

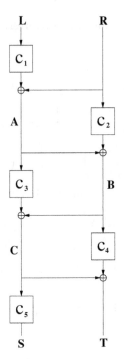

Fig. 3. 5 rounds L-scheme

Using theorem 2, it implies superpseudorandomness for a 5-round scheme:

Theorem 5. *Let $c_1^*, c_2^*, ..., c_5^*$ be independent perfect random involutions without fixed point of I_n. Let C^* be a perfect random permutation of I_{2n}. Let $C := \psi_L(c_1^*, c_2^*, ..., c_5^*)$ (resp. $C := \psi_R(c_1^*, c_2^*, ..., c_5^*)$). Then for any superpseudorandom distinguisher $\mathcal{A}$ allowed to make m queries:*

$$Adv_{\mathcal{A}}(C, C^*) \leq \frac{12m^2}{2^n} + \frac{m^2}{2 \cdot 2^n}$$

Thus $\psi(c_1^*, c_2^*, ..., c_5^*)$ is superpseudorandom, and secure as long as $m \ll 2^{n/2}$.

The proof of lemma 2 will require the following lemma. Proving it is easy, it is why we do not give the proof here.

Lemma 3. *Let $x, y \in I_n, 0 \neq \Delta \in I_n$. The probability for a random involution without fixed point c to satisfy*

$$c(x) \oplus c(y) = \Delta$$

is at most $4/2^n$.

7   Proof of Lemma 2

We use the intermediate states $\mathbf{A} := c_1(\mathbf{L}) \oplus \mathbf{R}$, $\mathbf{B} := c_2(\mathbf{R}) \oplus \mathbf{A}$ and $\mathbf{C} := c_3(\mathbf{A}) \oplus \mathbf{B}$ (see Figure 3). Let $\mathcal{P}_{(\mathbf{S},\mathbf{T})}^{(\mathbf{L},\mathbf{R})}$ be the probability that a random 5-uple $(c_1, c_2, c_3, c_4, c_5)$ of involutions is such that $\psi'_L(c_1, c_2, c_3, c_4, c_5)(\mathbf{L}, \mathbf{R}) = (\mathbf{S}, \mathbf{T})$. Then:

$$
\mathcal{P}_{(\mathbf{S},\mathbf{T})}^{(\mathbf{L},\mathbf{R})} = \sum_{\mathbf{A},\mathbf{B},\mathbf{C} \in I} \Pr[(c_1(\mathbf{L}) \oplus \mathbf{R} = \mathbf{A}) \wedge (c_2(\mathbf{R}) \oplus \mathbf{A} = \mathbf{B})
$$
$$
\wedge (c_3(\mathbf{A}) \oplus \mathbf{B} = \mathbf{C}) \wedge (c_4(\mathbf{B}) \oplus \mathbf{C} = \mathbf{T}) \wedge (c_5(\mathbf{C}) = \mathbf{S})]
\tag{12}
$$

We define the following three conditions $(\mathcal{C})$ on $(\mathbf{A}, \mathbf{B}, \mathbf{C})$:

$(\mathcal{C}1)$ $\nexists i, j : L_i = A_j \oplus R_j$ and $\nexists i, j : R_i = A_j \oplus B_j$
$(\mathcal{C}2)$ $\nexists i, j : A_i = B_j \oplus C_j$ and $\nexists i, j : B_i = C_j \oplus T_j$
$(\mathcal{C}3)$ $\nexists i, j : C_i = S_j$

Then $\mathcal{P}_{(\mathbf{S},\mathbf{T})}^{(\mathbf{L},\mathbf{R})}$ is greater or equal than

$$
\sum_{\substack{\mathbf{A},\mathbf{B} \in I^{\neq} \\ \mathbf{A},\mathbf{B}\ \text{satisfy}\ (\mathcal{C}1)}} \left(\Pr[(c_1(\mathbf{L}) \oplus \mathbf{R} = \mathbf{A}) \wedge (c_2(\mathbf{R}) \oplus \mathbf{A} = \mathbf{B})] \right.
$$
$$
\left. \cdot \sum_{\substack{\mathbf{C} \in I \\ \mathbf{C}\ \text{satisfies}\ (\mathcal{C}2),(\mathcal{C}3)}} \Pr[c_3(\mathbf{A}) \oplus \mathbf{B} = \mathbf{C}] \cdot \Pr[c_4(\mathbf{B}) \oplus \mathbf{C} = \mathbf{T}] \cdot \Pr[c_5(\mathbf{C}) = \mathbf{S}] \right)
\tag{13}
$$

We first evaluate the inner sum for given $\mathbf{A}, \mathbf{B} \in I^{\neq}$ satisfying $(\mathcal{C}1)$. Adding constraints $\mathbf{C} \sim \mathbf{S}$, $\mathbf{C} \oplus \mathbf{T} \in I^{\neq}$ and $\mathbf{B} \oplus \mathbf{C} \in I^{\neq}$ only removes zero terms from the sum. Thus it is equal to:

$$
\sum_{\substack{\mathbf{C} \sim \mathbf{S} \\ \mathbf{C} \oplus \mathbf{T} \in I^{\neq},\ \mathbf{B} \oplus \mathbf{C} \in I^{\neq} \\ \mathbf{C}\ \text{satisfies}\ (\mathcal{C}2),(\mathcal{C}3)}} \Pr[c_3(\mathbf{A}) \oplus \mathbf{B} = \mathbf{C}] \cdot \Pr[c_4(\mathbf{B}) \oplus \mathbf{C} = \mathbf{T}] \cdot \Pr[c_5(\mathbf{C}) = \mathbf{S}]
\tag{14}
$$

It is easy to see that $|\{\mathbf{C} \in I : \mathbf{C} \sim \mathbf{S} \wedge (\mathcal{C}3)\}| = \frac{(2^n - m + \sigma)!}{(2^n - 2m + 2\sigma)!}$. Moreover we compute:

$$
\Pr[\mathbf{C} \oplus \mathbf{T} \in I^{\neq} \wedge \mathbf{B} \oplus \mathbf{C} \in I^{\neq} \wedge (\mathcal{C}2)|\mathbf{C} \sim \mathbf{S} \wedge (\mathcal{C}3)]
$$
$$
\geq 1 - \sum_{i<j} \Pr[C_i \oplus T_i = C_j \oplus T_j | \mathbf{C} \sim \mathbf{S} \wedge (\mathcal{C}3)]
$$
$$
- \sum_{i<j} \Pr[B_i \oplus C_i = B_j \oplus C_j | \mathbf{C} \sim \mathbf{S} \wedge (\mathcal{C}3)])
$$
$$
- \sum_{i,j} \Pr[A_i = B_j \oplus C_j | \mathbf{C} \sim \mathbf{S} \wedge (\mathcal{C}3)] - \sum_{i,j} \Pr[B_i = C_j \oplus T_j | \mathbf{C} \sim \mathbf{S} \wedge (\mathcal{C}3)]
$$

We evaluate the first sum. For given $1 \leq i < j \leq m$, if $S_i \neq S_j$ and $T_i \neq T_j$, then the probability is smaller than $\frac{2}{2^n}$. If $S_i = S_j$ or $T_i = T_j$, it is easy to see that it is 0. Therefore

$$\sum_{i<j} \Pr[C_i \oplus T_i = C_j \oplus T_j | \mathbf{C} \sim \mathbf{S} \wedge (\mathcal{C}_3)] \leq \frac{m(m-1)}{2} \cdot \frac{2}{2^n} \leq \frac{m^2}{2^n} \tag{15}$$

The second sum can be bounded similarly.

We now consider the third sum. Let $1 \leq i, j \leq m$. As there are $2^n - m + \sigma$ possible values of C_j satisfying $\mathbf{C} \sim \mathbf{S}$ and $(\mathcal{C}_3)$, we obtain $\Pr[C_j = A_i \oplus B_j | \mathbf{C} \sim \mathbf{S} \wedge (\mathcal{C}_3)] = \frac{1}{2^n - m + \sigma} \leq \frac{2}{2^n}$. Therefore

$$\sum_{i,j} \Pr[A_i = B_j \oplus C_j | \mathbf{C} \sim \mathbf{S} \wedge (\mathcal{C}_3)] \leq m^2 \cdot \frac{2}{2^n} \tag{16}$$

The fourth sum can be bounded similarly.

Putting these inequalities together, we finally get

$$\Pr[\mathbf{C} \oplus \mathbf{T} \in I^{\neq} \wedge \mathbf{B} \oplus \mathbf{C} \in I^{\neq} \wedge (\mathcal{C}_2) | \mathbf{C} \sim \mathbf{S} \wedge (\mathcal{C}_3)] \geq 1 - \frac{6m^2}{2^n} \tag{17}$$

The probabilities in (14) are easy to evaluate. Thus (14) is lower bounded by:

$$\frac{\left[\frac{(2^n - 2m)!}{2^{2^n - 1 - m} \cdot (2^n - 1 - m)!}\right]^2 \cdot \left[\frac{(2^n - m + \sigma)!}{2^{2^n - 1 - m + \sigma} \cdot (2^n - 1 - m + \sigma)!}\right]}{\left[\frac{2^n!}{2^{2^n - 1} \cdot (2^n - 1)!}\right]^3} \cdot \left(1 - \frac{6m^2}{2^n}\right) \tag{18}$$

which is greater or equal than

$$2^{3m - \sigma} \cdot \left(\frac{2^{n-1} - m}{2^n - m}\right)^{3m - \sigma} \cdot \frac{1}{2nm} \geq \left(1 - \sum_{k=1}^{\infty} \frac{m^k}{2^{nk}}\right)^{3m} \cdot \frac{1}{2nm} \tag{19}$$

It remains to evaluate

$$\sum_{\substack{\mathbf{A}, \mathbf{B} \in I^{\neq} \\ \mathbf{A}, \mathbf{B} \text{ satisfy } (\mathcal{C}1)}} \Pr[(c_1(\mathbf{L}) \oplus \mathbf{R} = \mathbf{A}) \wedge (c_2(\mathbf{R}) \oplus \mathbf{A} = \mathbf{B})] \tag{20}$$

which is equal to

$$\Pr[c_1(\mathbf{L}) \oplus \mathbf{R} \in I^{\neq} \wedge c_1(\mathbf{L}) \oplus c_2(\mathbf{R}) \oplus \mathbf{R} \in I^{\neq}$$
$$\wedge \not\exists i, j : c_1(L_i) = L_j \wedge \not\exists i, j : c_2(R_i) = R_j]$$
$$\geq 1 - \sum_{i<j} \Pr[c_1(L_i) \oplus c_1(L_j) = R_i \oplus R_j]$$
$$- \sum_{i<j} \Pr[c_1(L_i) \oplus c_2(R_i) \oplus R_i = c_1(L_j) \oplus c_2(R_j) \oplus R_j]$$
$$- \sum_{i<j} \Pr[c_1(L_i) = L_j] - \sum_{i<j} \Pr[c_2(R_i) = R_j]$$

Let $1 \leq i < j \leq m$. $\Pr[c_1(L_i) \oplus c_1(L_j) = R_i \oplus R_j]$ is easy to evaluate. If $R_i \oplus R_j = 0$, then $L_i \neq L_j$ and the probability is 0. If $R_i \oplus R_j \neq 0$, we can apply lemma 3. Thus in any case

$$\Pr[c_1(L_i) \oplus c_1(L_j) = R_i \oplus R_j] \leq 4/2^n \tag{21}$$

For shortness, let us denote $Z(R_i, R_j) := c_2(R_i) \oplus c_2(R_j) \oplus R_i \oplus R_j$. The terms of the second sum can be written:

$$\begin{aligned}
&\Pr[c_1(L_i) \oplus c_1(L_j) = Z(R_i, R_j)] \\
&= \Pr[c_1(L_i) \oplus c_1(L_j) = Z(R_i, R_j)|Z(R_i, R_j) = 0] \cdot \Pr[Z(R_i, R_j) = 0] \\
&\quad + \Pr[c_1(L_i) \oplus c_1(L_j) = Z(R_i, R_j)|Z(R_i, R_j) \neq 0] \cdot \Pr[Z(R_i, R_j) \neq 0] \\
&= \Pr[c_1(L_i) \oplus c_1(L_j) = 0] \cdot \Pr[Z(R_i, R_j) = 0] \\
&\quad + \Pr[c_1(L_i) \oplus c_1(L_j) = Z(R_i, R_j)|Z(R_i, R_j) \neq 0] \cdot \Pr[Z(R_i, R_j) \neq 0]
\end{aligned}$$

If $R_i = R_j$ then $L_i \neq L_j$ and the first term is 0. Else by lemma 3 it is not greater than $4/2^n$. Using lemma 3 again, the second term is also not greater than $4/2^n$. The conclusion is that

$$\Pr[c_1(L_i) \oplus c_2(R_i) \oplus R_i = c_1(L_j) \oplus c_2(R_j) \oplus R_j] \leq \frac{8}{2^n} \tag{22}$$

Finally using (21) and (22), (20) is greater or equal than

$$1 - \frac{m(m-1)}{2} \cdot \frac{4}{2^n} - \frac{m(m-1)}{2} \cdot \frac{8}{2^n} - 2 \cdot \frac{m(m-1)}{2 \cdot (2^n - 1)} \geq 1 - \frac{8m^2}{2^n} \tag{23}$$

Multiplying (19) and (23), we get

$$\mathcal{P}_{(\mathbf{S,T})}^{(\mathbf{L,R})} \geq \left(1 - \sum_{k=1}^{\infty} \frac{m^k}{2^{nk}}\right)^{3m} \cdot \frac{1}{2nm} \cdot \left(1 - \frac{8m^2}{2^n}\right) \tag{24}$$

which is greater or equal than (see proof of lemma 1)

$$\left(1 - \frac{1}{2} \sum_{k=1}^{\infty} \left(\frac{8m^2}{2^n}\right)^k\right) \cdot \left(1 - \frac{8m^2}{2^n}\right) \cdot \frac{1}{2nm} = \left(1 - \frac{12m^2}{2^n}\right) \cdot \frac{1}{2nm} \tag{25}$$

8   Conclusion and Open Problems

In this paper we showed that replacing the inner permutations of a Misty structure by involutions without fixed point, without changing the number of rounds, did not significantly affect the previously known security bounds.

Several open problems remain: first, one could wonder whether the hypothesis "without fixed point" is important. Intuitively it is clearly not, as taking the inner permutations from a (much) bigger set increases the variety of functions one can generate, and hence the difficulty to distinguish them from perfect random functions.

Also, it is an open question whether in some cases involutions achieve significantly weaker security bounds than permutations. It should be interesting to consider involutions as inner functions of structures different from the Misty ones.

Finally, being able to do security proofs when the inner functions are even more specific (i.e. drawn from a smaller set) than involutions without fixed point would be nice, as it could maybe pave the way to security proofs on structures closer to real-life block ciphers.

References

1. P.S.L.M. Barreto and V. Rijmen. The Khazad Legacy-Level Block Cipher. Submitted as a NESSIE Candidate Algorithm. Available at http://www.cryptonessie.org.
2. T. Iwata, T. Yoshino, and K. Kurosawa. Non-cryptographic Primitive for Pseudorandom Permutation. In Joan Daemen and Vincent Rijmen, editors, *Fast Software Encryption, 9th International Workshop, FSE 2002, Leuven, Belgium, February 4-6, 2002*, volume 2365 of *Lecture Notes in Computer Science*, pages 149–163. Springer-Verlag, 2002.
3. T. Iwata, T. Yoshino, T. Yuasa, and K. Kurosawa. Round Security and Super-Pseudorandomness of MISTY Type Structure. In Mitsuru Matsui, editor, *Fast Software Encryption, 8th International Workshop, FSE 2001, Yokohama, Japan, April 2-4, 2001*, volume 2355 of *Lecture Notes in Computer Science*, pages 233–247. Springer-Verlag, 2002.
4. M. Luby and C. Rackoff. How to construct pseudorandom permutations from pseudorandom functions. *SIAM Journal on Computing*, 17(2):373–386, 1988.
5. S. Lucks. Faster Luby-Rackoff Ciphers. In Dieter Gollmann, editor, *Fast Software Encryption, Cambridge, UK, February 21-23, 1996*, volume 1039 of *Lecture Notes in Computer Science*, pages 189–203. Springer-Verlag, 1996.
6. M. Matsui. New Block Encryption Algorithm MISTY. In Eli Biham, editor, *Fast Software Encryption, 4th International Workshop, FSE '97, Haifa, Israel, January 20-22, 1997*, volume 1267 of *Lecture Notes in Computer Science*, pages 54–68. Springer-Verlag, 1997.
7. M. Minier. *Preuves d'Analyse et de Sécurité en Cryptologie à Clé Secrète*. PhD thesis, LACO, Université de Limoges, September 2002.
8. M. Minier and H. Gilbert. New Results on the Pseudorandomness of Some Blockcipher Constructions. In Mitsuru Matsui, editor, *Fast Software Encryption, 8th International Workshop, FSE 2001, Yokohama, Japan, April 2-4, 2001*, volume 2355 of *Lecture Notes in Computer Science*, pages 248–266. Springer-Verlag, 2002.
9. S. Moriai and S. Vaudenay. On the Pseudorandomness of Top-Level Schemes of Block Ciphers. In Tatsuaki Okamoto, editor, *Advances in Cryptology - ASIACRYPT 2000, Kyoto, Japan, December 3-7, 2000*, volume 1976 of *Lecture Notes in Computer Science*, pages 289–302. Springer-Verlag, 2000.
10. M. Naor and O. Reingold. On the Construction of Pseudorandom Permutations: Luby-Rackoff Revisited. *Journal of Cryptology*, 12(1):29–66, 1999.

11. J. Patarin. *Etude des Générateurs de Permutations Basés sur le Schéma du DES.* PhD thesis, Université Paris VI, November 1991.
12. J. Patarin. How to Construct Pseudorandom and Super Pseudorandom Permutations from one Single Pseudorandom Function. In Rainer A. Rueppel, editor, *Advances in Cryptology - EUROCRYPT '92, Balatonfüred, Hungary, May 24-28, 1992*, volume 658 of *Lecture Notes in Computer Science*, pages 256–266. Springer-Verlag, 1993.
13. J. Patarin. About Feistel Schemes with Six (or More) Rounds. In Serge Vaudenay, editor, *Fast Software Encryption, Paris, France, March 23-25, 1998*, volume 1372 of *Lecture Notes in Computer Science*, pages 103–121. Springer-Verlag, 1998.
14. J. Patarin. Generic Attacks on Feistel Schemes. In Colin Boyd, editor, *Advances in Cryptology - ASIACRYPT 2001, Gold Coast, Australia, December 9-13, 2001*, volume 2248 of *Lecture Notes in Computer Science*, pages 222–238. Springer-Verlag, 2001.
15. J. Patarin. Luby-Rackoff: 7 Rounds Are Enough for $2^{n(1-\epsilon)}$ Security. In Dan Boneh, editor, *Advances in Cryptology - CRYPTO 2003, Santa Barbara, USA, August 17-21, 2003*, volume 2729 of *Lecture Notes in Computer Science*, pages 513–529. Springer-Verlag, 2003.
16. Z. Ramzan and L. Reyzin. On the Round Security of Symmetric-Key Cryptographic Primitives. In Mihir Bellare, editor, *Advances in Cryptology - CRYPTO 2000, Santa Barbara, USA, August 20-24, 2000*, volume 1880 of *Lecture Notes in Computer Science*, pages 376–393. Springer-Verlag, 2000.
17. K. Sakurai and Y. Zheng. On Non-Pseudorandomness from Block Ciphers with Provable Immunity Against Linear Cryptanalysis. *IEICE Trans. Fundamentals*, E80-A(1), January 1997.
18. F.-X. Standaert, G. Piret, G. Rouvroy, J.-J. Quisquater, and J.-D. Legat. ICE-BERG : an Involutional Cipher Efficient for Block Encryption on Reconfigurable Hardware. In Bimal K. Roy and Willi Meier, editors, *Fast Software Encryption, 11th International Workshop, FSE 2004, Delhi, India, February 5-7, 2004*, volume 3017 of *Lecture Notes in Computer Science*, pages 279–299. Springer-Verlag, 2004.
19. S. Vaudenay. On the Lai-Massey Scheme. In Kwok-Yan Lam, Eiji Okamoto, and Chaoping Xing, editors, *Advances in Cryptology - ASIACRYPT '99, Singapore, November 14-18, 1999*, volume 1716 of *Lecture Notes in Computer Science*, pages 8–19. Springer-Verlag, 1999.

FOX : A New Family of Block Ciphers

Pascal Junod and Serge Vaudenay

École Polytechnique Fédérale de Lausanne, Switzerland
{pascal.junod, serge.vaudenay}@epfl.ch

Abstract. In this paper, we describe the design of a new family of block ciphers based on a Lai-Massey scheme, named FOX. The main features of this design, besides a very high security level, are a large implementation flexibility on various platforms as well as high performances. In addition, we propose a new design of strong and efficient key-schedule algorithms. We provide evidence that FOX is immune to linear and differential cryptanalysis, and we discuss its security towards integral cryptanalysis, algebraic attacks, and other attacks.

Keywords: Block ciphers, Lai-Massey scheme.

1 Introduction

Why do we need another block cipher? First of all, industry is still requesting; second, recent advances in the cryptanalysis field motivate new designs. The AES [1] and NESSIE [27] efforts, among others, have resulted in a number of new proposals of block ciphers. It is noteworthy that there exists a clear trend in direction of lightweight and fast key-schedule algorithms, as well as substitution boxes based on purely algebraic constructions. In a parallel way, we observe that, on the one hand, several of the last published attacks against block ciphers take often advantage of exploiting "simple" key-schedule algorithms (a nice illustration is certainly Muller's attack [24] against Khazad), and, on the other hand, algebraic S-boxes are helpful to Courtois-Pieprzyk algebraic attacks [8], and lead to puzzling properties as shown by [2, 10, 25].

In this paper, we describe the design of a new family of block cipher, named FOX and designed upon the request of MediaCrypt AG [23]. The main features of this design, besides a very high security level, are a large flexibility in terms of use and of implementation on various platforms, as well as high performances. The family consists in two block ciphers, one having a 64-bit block size and the other one a 128-bit block size. Each block cipher allows a variable number of rounds and a variable key size up to 256 bits. The high-level structure is based on a Lai-Massey scheme, while the round functions consist of Substitution-Permutation Networks with no algebraic S-boxes. In addition, we propose a new design of strong and efficient key-schedule algorithms.

Our main motivations are the following: our first goal is to offer a serious alternative to block ciphers following present trends; we have explicitly chosen

H. Handschuh and A. Hasan (Eds.): SAC 2004, LNCS 3357, pp. 114–129, 2005.
© Springer-Verlag Berlin Heidelberg 2005

to *avoid a lightweight key-schedule and a pure algebraic construction as S-boxes*. Our second goal is to reach the highest possible flexibility, being in terms of round number, key size, block size and in terms of implementation issues. For instance, we feel that it is still useful to propose a 64-bit block size flavour for backward-compatibility reasons. Finally, our last motivation was to design a family of block ciphers which compares favourably with the performances of the fastest block ciphers on hardware, 8-bit, 32-bit, and 64-bit architectures. This paper is organized as follows: in §2, we give a formal description of the block ciphers, then we successively discuss the rationales in §3 the security foundations in §4 and several implementations aspects in §5. Test vectors are available in Appendix A. The full version of this paper is [14].

Notations: A variable x indexed by i with a length of ℓ bits is denoted $x_{i(\ell)}$. A C-like notation is used for indexing i.e. indices begin with 0.

Representation of $\mathrm{GF}\left(2^8\right)$: Some of the internal operations used in FOX are the addition and the multiplication in the $\mathrm{GF}(2^8)$ finite field. Elements of the field are polynomials with coefficients in $\mathrm{GF}(2)$ in α, a root of the irreducible polynomial $P(\alpha) = \alpha^8 + \alpha^7 + \alpha^6 + \alpha^5 + \alpha^4 + \alpha^3 + 1$: the 8-bit binary string $s = s_{0(1)}\|s_{1(1)}\|s_{2(1)}\|s_{3(1)}\|s_{4(1)}\|s_{5(1)}\|s_{6(1)}\|s_{7(1)}$ represents $s_{0(1)}\alpha^7 + s_{1(1)}\alpha^6 + s_{2(1)}\alpha^5 + s_{3(1)}\alpha^4 + s_{4(1)}\alpha^3 + s_{5(1)}\alpha^2 + s_{6(1)}\alpha + s_{7(1)}$.

2   Description

The different members of this block cipher family are denoted as follows:

Name	Block size	Key size	Rounds number
FOX64	64	128	16
FOX128	128	256	16
FOX64/k/r	64	k	r
FOX128/k/r	128	k	r

In FOX64/k/r and FOX128/k/r, the number r of rounds must satisfy $12 \le r \le 255$, while the key length k must satisfy $0 \le k \le 256$, with k multiple of 8. Note that a generic instance of FOX has 16 rounds.

2.1   High-Level Structure

The 64-bit version of FOX is the $(r-1)$-times iteration of a *round function* lmor64, followed by the application of a slightly modified round function called lmid64. For decryption, we replace lmor64 by lmio64. The encryption $C_{(64)}$ by FOX64/k/r of a 64-bit plaintext $P_{(64)}$ is defined as

$$C_{(64)} = \mathsf{lmid64}(\mathsf{lmor64}(\ldots(\mathsf{lmor64}(P_{(64)}, RK_{0(64)}),\ldots,RK_{r-2(64)}),RK_{r-1(64)})$$

where $RK_{(64r)} = RK_{0(64)}||RK_{1(64)}|| \ldots ||RK_{r-1(64)}$ is the subkey stream produced by the key schedule algorithm from the key $K_{(k)}$ (see §2.3). The decryption $P_{(64)}$ by FOX64/k/r of a 64-bit ciphertext $C_{(64)}$ is defined as

$$P_{(64)} = \mathsf{lmid64}(\mathsf{lmio64}(\ldots(\mathsf{lmio64}(C_{(64)}, RK_{r-1(64)}), \ldots, RK_{1(64)}), RK_{0(64)})$$

In the 128-bit version of FOX, we simply replace lmor64, lmid64, and lmio64 by elmor128, elmid128, and elmio128, respectively. lmor64, illustrated in Fig. 1(a), is built as a Lai-Massey scheme [19, 18] combined with an orthomorphism[1] or, as described in [30]. This function transforms a 64-bit input $X_{(64)}$ split in two parts $X_{(64)} = X_{0(32)}||X_{1(32)}$ and a 64-bit round key $RK_{(64)}$ in a 64-bit output $Y_{(64)} = Y_{0(32)}||Y_{1(32)}$ as $Y_{(64)} = $ or $\left(X_{0(32)} \oplus \phi\right)||\left(X_{1(32)} \oplus \phi\right)$ with $\phi = \mathsf{f32}\left(X_{0(32)} \oplus X_{1(32)}, RK_{(64)}\right)$. lmid64 and lmio64 are defined like for lmor64 but for or, which is replaced by the identity function and io (the inverse of or), respectively. elmor128, illustrated in Fig. 1(b), is built as an *Extended Lai-Massey scheme* combined with two orthomorphisms or. This function transforms a 128-bit input $X_{(128)}$ split in four parts $X_{(128)} = X_{0(32)}||X_{1(32)}||X_{2(32)}||X_{3(32)}$ and a 128-bit round key $RK_{(128)}$ in a 128-bit output $Y_{(128)}$. Let $F_{(64)} = (X_{0(32)} \oplus X_{1(32)})||(X_{2(32)} \oplus X_{3(32)})$. Then,

$$Y_{(128)} = \mathsf{or}\left(X_{0(32)} \oplus \phi_L\right) \big|\big| \left(X_{1(32)} \oplus \phi_L\right) \big|\big| \mathsf{or}\left(X_{2(32)} \oplus \phi_R\right) \big|\big| \left(X_{3(32)} \oplus \phi_R\right)$$

where $\phi_L||\phi_R = \mathsf{f64}\left(F_{(64)}, RK_{(128)}\right)$. In elmid128, resp. elmio128, the two orthomorphisms or are replaced by two identity, resp. io functions. The orthomorphism or is a function taking a 32-bit input $X_{(32)} = X_{0(16)}||X_{1(16)}$ and returning a 32-bit output $Y_{(32)} = Y_{0(16)}||Y_{1(16)}$ which is in fact a one-round Feistel scheme with the identity function as round function; it is defined as $Y_{0(16)}||Y_{1(16)} = X_{1(16)}||\left(X_{0(16)} \oplus X_{1(16)}\right)$.

2.2   Definition of f32 and f64

The round function f32 builds the core of FOX64/k/r. It is built of three main parts: a *substitution* part, denoted sigma4, a *diffusion* part, denoted mu4, and a *round key addition* part (see Fig. 2(a)). Formally, the f32 function takes a 32-bit input $X_{(32)}$, a 64-bit round key $RK_{(64)} = RK_{0(32)}||RK_{1(32)}$ and returns a 32-bit output $Y_{(32)} = \mathsf{sigma4}(\mathsf{mu4}(\mathsf{sigma4}(X_{(32)} \oplus RK_{0(32)})) \oplus RK_{1(32)}) \oplus RK_{0(32)}$.

The function f64, building the core of FOX128/k/r, is very similar to f32 (see Fig. 2(b)): it takes a 64-bit input $X_{(64)}$, a 128-bit round key $RK_{(128)} = RK_{0(64)}||RK_{1(64)}$ and returns $Y_{(64)} = \mathsf{sigma8}(\mathsf{mu8}(\mathsf{sigma8}(X_{(64)} \oplus RK_{0(64)})) \oplus RK_{1(64)}) \oplus RK_{0(64)}$.

The mapping sigma4 (resp. sigma8) consists of 4 (resp. 8) parallel computations of a non-linear bijective mapping (see §3.1 for a description and the table in §B). The diffusive parts of f32 and f64, mu4 and mu8, consider an input

---

[1] An orthomorphism o on a group $(\mathcal{G}, +)$ is a permutation $x \mapsto \mathsf{o}(x)$ on $\mathcal{G}$ such that $x \mapsto \mathsf{o}(x) - x$ is also a permutation.

$X_{0(8)} || \ldots || X_{n(8)}$ as a vector $(X_{0(8)}, \ldots, X_{n(8)})^T$ over GF (2^8) and multiply it with a matrix to obtain an output vector of the same size. The two matrices are the following:

$$\text{mu4} : \begin{pmatrix} 1 & 1 & 1 & \alpha \\ 1 & z & \alpha & 1 \\ z & \alpha & 1 & 1 \\ \alpha & 1 & z & 1 \end{pmatrix} \qquad \text{mu8} : \begin{pmatrix} 1 & 1 & 1 & 1 & 1 & 1 & 1 & a \\ 1 & a & b & c & d & e & f & 1 \\ a & b & c & d & e & f & 1 & 1 \\ b & c & d & e & f & 1 & a & 1 \\ c & d & e & f & 1 & a & b & 1 \\ d & e & f & 1 & a & b & c & 1 \\ e & f & 1 & a & b & c & d & 1 \\ f & 1 & a & b & c & d & e & 1 \end{pmatrix}$$

where $z = \alpha^{-1} + 1 = \alpha^7 + \alpha^6 + \alpha^5 + \alpha^4 + \alpha^3 + \alpha^2 + 1$, and where $a = \alpha + 1$, $b = \alpha^7 + \alpha$, $c = \alpha$, $d = \alpha^2$, $e = \alpha^7 + \alpha^6 + \alpha^5 + \alpha^4 + \alpha^3 + \alpha^2$ and $f = \alpha^6 + \alpha^5 + \alpha^4 + \alpha^3 + \alpha^2 + \alpha$.

2.3   Key-Schedule Algorithms

A FOX key $K_{(k)}$ must have a bit-length k such that $0 \leq k \leq 256$, and k must be a multiple of 8. Depending on the key length and the block size, a member of the FOX block cipher family may use one among three different key-schedule algorithm versions, denoted KS64, KS64h and KS128. The following table defines which variant is used, as well as a constant ek.

Cipher	Block size	Key size	Key-Schedule Version	ek
FOX64	64	$0 \leq k \leq 128$	KS64	128
FOX64	64	$136 \leq k \leq 256$	KS64h	256
FOX128	128	$0 \leq k \leq 256$	KS128	256

The three different versions of the key-schedule algorithm are constituted of four main parts: a padding part, denoted P, expanding $K_{(k)}$ into ek bits, a mixing part, denoted M, a diversification part, denoted D, whose core consists mainly in a linear feedback shift register denoted LFSR, and finally, a non-linear part, denoted NLx, which is actually the only part which differs between the different versions: we denote the three variants NL64, NL64h and NL128. When $ek = k$, the P and M parts are omitted.

Definition of P. The P-part, taking ek and k as input, is a function expanding a bit string by $\frac{ek-k}{8}$ bytes; it concatenates the key $K_{(k)}$ with the first $ek - k$ bits of a constant, pad, giving $PKEY$ as output. The constant pad is defined as being the first 256 bits of the hexadecimal development of $e - 2 = \sum_{n=0}^{+\infty} \frac{1}{n!} - 2$:

pad = 0xB7E151628AED2A6ABF7158809CF4F3C762E7160F38B4DA56A784D9045190CFEF

Definition of M. The M-part mixes the padded key $PKEY$ with the help of a Fibonacci-like recursion. It takes as input a key $PKEY$ with length ek (expressed in bits) seen as an array of $\frac{ek}{8}$ bytes $PKEY_{i(8)}, 0 \leq i \leq \frac{ek}{8} - 1$, and is processed according to $MKEY_{i(8)} = PKEY_{i(8)} \oplus (MKEY_{i-1(8)} + MKEY_{i-2(8)} \bmod 2^8)$, for $0 \leq i \leq \frac{ek}{8} - 1$, assuming that $\text{MKEY}_{-2(8)} = $ 0x6A and $\text{MKEY}_{-1(8)} = $ 0x76.

Definition of D *and* LFSR. The D-part takes a key $MKEY$ having a length in bits equal to ek, the total round number r, and the current round number i, with $1 \leq i \leq r$; it modifies $MKEY$ with the help of the output of a 24-bit Linear Shift Feedback Register (LFSR) denoted LFSR. More precisely, $MKEY$ is seen as an array of $\lfloor \frac{ek}{24} \rfloor$ 24-bit values $MKEY_{j(24)}$, with $0 \leq j \leq \lfloor \frac{ek}{24} \rfloor - 1$ concatenated with one residue byte $MKEYRB_{(8)}$ (if $ek = 128$) or two residue bytes $MKEYRB_{(16)}$ (if $ek = 256$), and is modified according to, for $0 \leq j \leq \lfloor \frac{ek}{24} \rfloor - 1$,

$$DKEY_{j(24)} = MKEY_{j(24)} \oplus \mathsf{LFSR}\left((i-1) \cdot \left\lceil \frac{ek}{24} \right\rceil + j, r\right)$$

and the $DKEYRB_{(8)}$ value ($DKEYRB_{(16)}$) is obtained by XORing the most 8 (16) significant bits of $\mathsf{LFSR}((i-1) \cdot \left\lceil \frac{ek}{24} \right\rceil + \lfloor \frac{ek}{24} \rfloor, r)$ with $MKEYRB_{(8)}$ ($MKEYRB_{(16)}$), respectively. The remaining 16 (8) bits of the LFSR routine output are discarded. The stream of pseudo-random values is generated by a 24-bit linear feedback shift register, denoted LFSR. It takes two inputs: the total number of rounds r and the number of preliminary clockings. It is based on the following primitive polynomial of degree 24 over GF(2): $\xi^{24} + \xi^4 + \xi^3 + \xi + 1$. The register is initially seeded with the value $\mathtt{0x6A}\|r_{(8)}\|\overline{r_{(8)}}$, where $r_{(8)}$ is expressed as an 8-bit value.

Definition of NL64, NL128, *and* NL64h. We describe here the NL64 and NL128 processes, respectively. Basically, the $DKEY$ value passes through a substitution layer, made of four parallel sigma4 (sigma8) functions, a diffusion layer, made of four parallel mu4 (mu8) functions and a mixing layer called mix64 (mix128), respectively. Then, the constant $\mathsf{pad}_{[0...127]}$ ($\mathsf{pad}_{[0...255]}$) is XORed and the result is flipped if and only if $k = ek$. The result passes through a second substitution layer, it is hashed down to 64 (128) bits using two exclusive-or operations and the resulting value is encrypted first with a lmor64 (elmor128) round function, where the subkey is the left half of the $DKEY$ value and second by a lmid64 (elmid128) function, where the subkey is the right half of $DKEY$. The resulting value is defined to be the 64-bit (128-bit) round key, respectively. Detailed descriptions may be found in Fig. 3(a) and Fig. 3(b), respectively. In the case of NL64h, the process is very similar than for NL128; the difference is that the sigma8 (mu8) functions are replaced by two concatenated sigma4 (mu4) functions, respectively, that mix128 is replaced by mix64h, and that one uses *three* lmor64 round functions, where the respective subkeys are the three left quarters of the $DKEY$ value and a lmid64 function, where the subkey is the rightmost quarter of $DKEY$. The resulting value is defined to be the 64-bit round key. Fig. 3(c) illustrates the NL64h process whose construction is similar to those of NL64 and of NL128.

Definition of mix64, mix64h *and* mix128. Given an input vector of four 32-bit values, denoted $X = X_{0(32)}\|X_{1(32)}\|X_{2(32)}\|X_{3(32)}$, the mix64 function consists in processing it by the following relations, resulting in an output vector denoted $Y = Y_{0(32)}\|Y_{1(32)}\|Y_{2(32)}\|Y_{3(32)}$. More formally, mix64 is defined as $Y_{i(32)} =$

$\bigoplus_{j \neq i} X_{j(32)}$ for $0 \leq i, j \leq 3$. The mix64h and mix128 functions use identical relations operating on 64-bit values.

3 Rationales

3.1 sbox Transformation and Linear Multipermutations

As outlined in the introduction, our primary goal was to avoid a purely algebraic construction for the S-box; a secondary goal was the possibility to implement it in a very efficient way on hardware using ASIC or FPGA technologies. The sbox function is a bijective non-linear mapping on 8-bit values. It consists of a Lai-Massey scheme with 3 rounds taking three different substitution boxes as round function; these "small" S-boxes are denoted S_1, S_2 and S_3, and their content is given in §B. The orthomorphism[2] or4 used in the Lai-Massey scheme is a single round of a 4-bit Feistel scheme with the identity function as round function. We describe now the generation process of the sbox transformation. First a set of three different candidates for small substitution boxes, each having a LP_{max} and a DP_{max} (with the common notations[3] [22]) smaller than 2^{-2} were pseudo-randomly chosen. Then, the candidate sbox mapping was evaluated and tested regarding its LP_{max} and DP_{max} values until a good candidate was found. The chosen sbox satisfy $DP_{max}^{sbox} = LP_{max}^{sbox} = 2^{-4}$ and its algebraic degree is equal to 6.

Both mu4 and mu8 are *linear multipermutations*. This kind of construction was early recognized as being optimal for which regards its diffusion properties [28, 29]. A linear application defined by a matrix A is a multipermutation if and only if $\det(A) \neq 0$ and if the determinant of each submatrix of A is different of zero as well. It is well-known that linear multipermutations are equivalent to MDS linear codes (i.e. Maximum Distance Separable codes). Not all constructions are very efficient to implement, especially on low-end smartcard, which have usually very few available memory and computational power (see [15]). In order to be efficiently implementable, the elements of the matrix, which are elements of $GF(2^8)$, should be efficient to multiply to[4].

3.2 Key-Schedule Algorithms

The FOX key-schedule algorithms were designed with several rationales in mind: first, the function, which depends on the block size, taking a key K and the round number r in output and returning r subkeys should be a cryptographic pseudo-random, collision resistant and one-way function. Second, the sequence

---

[2] The orthomorphism of the third round is omitted.

[3] Where $DP^{sbox}(a, b) = \Pr[sbox(X \oplus a) = sbox(X) \oplus b]$ and where $LP^{sbox}(a, b) = (2 \cdot \Pr[a \cdot X = b \cdot sbox(X)] - 1)^2$ with $\cdot$ being the inner dot-product on $GF(2)^n$, $DP_{max}^{sbox} = \max_{a \neq 0, b} DP^{sbox}(a, b)$, and $LP_{max}^{sbox} = \max_{a, b \neq 0} LP^{sbox}(a, b)$.

[4] The only really efficient operations are the addition, the multiplication by α and the division by α. Note that $\alpha^7 + \alpha = \alpha^{-1} + \alpha^{-2}$, $\alpha^7 + \alpha^6 + \alpha^5 + \alpha^4 + \alpha^3 + \alpha^2 = \alpha^{-1}$, and that $\alpha^6 + \alpha^5 + \alpha^4 + \alpha^3 + \alpha^2 + \alpha = \alpha^{-2}$.

of subkeys should be generated in any direction without any complexity penalty. Third, all the bytes of $MKEY$ should be randomized even when the key size is strictly smaller than ek. Finally, the key-schedule algorithm should resist *related-cipher attacks* as described by Wu in [33].

We are convinced that "strong" key-schedule algorithms have significant advantages in terms of security, even if the price to pay is a smaller key agility; in the case of FOX, we believe that the time needed to compute the subkeys (about equal to the time needed to encrypt 6 blocks[5] of data) remains acceptable. The second central property of FOX key-schedule algorithms is ensured by the LFSR construction. The third property is ensured by our "Fibonacci-like" construction (which is a bijective mapping). Furthermore, $MKEY$ is expanded by XORing constants depending on r and ek with *no overlap* on these constants sequences (this was checked experimentally). Finally, the fourth property is ensured by the dependency of the subkey sequence to the actual round number of the algorithm instance for which the sequence will be used.

4   Security Foundations

4.1   Luby-Rackoff-Like Security

Although less popular than the Feistel scheme or SPN structures, the Lai-Massey scheme offers similar (super-) pseudorandomness and decorrelation inheritance properties, as was demonstrated by Vaudenay [30]. Note that we will indifferently use the term "Lai-Massey scheme" to denote both versions, as we can see the Extended Lai-Massey scheme as a Lai-Massey scheme[6]. From this point, we will make use of the following notation: given an orthomorphism o on a group $(\mathcal{G}, +)$ and given r functions $f_1, f_2, \ldots, f_r$ on $\mathcal{G}$, we note a r-rounds Lai-Massey scheme using the r functions and the orthomorphism by $\Lambda^{\circ}(f_1, \ldots, f_r)$. Then the following results are two Luby-Rackoff-like [21] results on the Lai-Massey scheme. We refer to [30,31] for proofs thereof.

Theorem 1.   *1. Let f_1^*, f_2^* and f_3^* be three independent random functions uniformly distributed on a group $(\mathcal{G}, +)$. Let o be an orthomorphism on $\mathcal{G}$. For any distinguisher[7] limited to d chosen plaintexts, where $g = |\mathcal{G}|$ denotes the cardinality of the group, between $\Lambda^{\circ}(f_1^*, f_2^*, f_3^*)$ and a uniformly distributed random permutation c^*, we have $\mathrm{Adv}(\Lambda^{\circ}(f_1^*, f_2^*, f_3^*), c^*) \leq d(d-1)(g^{-1} + g^{-2})$.*

---

[5] In the case of FOX64 with keys strictly larger than 128 bit, it takes the time to encrypt 12 blocks of data.

[6] We can prove this by swapping the two inner inputs and noting that the function $(x, y) \mapsto \mathrm{or}32(x) \| \mathrm{or}32(y)$ builds an orthomorphism.

[7] A distinguisher $\mathcal{A}$ is a probabilistic Turing machine with unlimited computational power. It has access to an oracle $\mathcal{O}$ and can send it a *limited* number of queries. At the end, the distinguisher must output "0" or "1". The advantage for distinguishing a random function f from a random function g is defined by $\mathrm{Adv}(f, g) = |\mathrm{Pr}\left[\mathcal{A}^{\mathcal{O}=f} = 1\right] - \mathrm{Pr}\left[\mathcal{A}^{\mathcal{O}=g} = 1\right]|$.

2. *If* $f_1, \ldots, f_r$ *are* $r \geq 3$ *independent random functions on a group* $(\mathcal{G}, +)$ *of order* g *such that* $\mathrm{Adv}(f_i, f_i^*) \leq \frac{\epsilon}{2}$ *for any adaptive distinguisher between* f_i *and* f_i^* *limited to* d *queries for* $1 \leq i \leq r$ *and if* $\circ$ *is an orthomorphism on* $\mathcal{G}$, *we have* $\mathrm{Adv}(\Lambda^{\circ}(f_1, \ldots, f_r), c^*) \leq \frac{1}{2}(3\epsilon + d(d-1)(2g^{-1} + g^{-2}))^{\lfloor \frac{r}{3} \rfloor}$.

Basically, the first result proves that the Lai-Massey scheme provides pseudorandomness on three rounds unless the f_i's are weak , like for the Feistel scheme [9]. Super-pseudorandomness corresponds to cases where a distinguisher can query chosen ciphertexts as well; in this scenario, the previous result holds when we consider $\Lambda^{\circ}(f_1^*, \ldots, f_4^*)$ with a fourth round. The second result proves that the decorrelation bias of the round functions of a Lai-Massey scheme is inherited by the whole structure: provided the f_i's are strong, so is the Lai-Massey scheme[8]; in other words, a potential cryptanalysis will not be able to exploit the Lai-Massey's scheme only, but it will have to take advantage of weaknesses of the round functions' internal structure.

4.2 Linear and Differential Cryptanalysis

It is possible to prove some important results about the security of both f32 and f64 functions towards linear and differential cryptanalysis, too. As these functions may be viewed as classical *Substitution-Permutation Network* constructions, we will refer to some well-known results on their resistance towards linear and differential cryptanalysis proved in [12] by Hong *et al.* As the mu4 (mu8) mapping is a $(4, 4)$-multipermutation $((8, 8)$-multipermutation$)$, one is ensured that at least $n_d = 5$ $(n_d = 9)$ S-boxes before and after mu4 will be active, respectively. Then, by Theorem 1 of [12], we have $\mathrm{DP}_{max}^{f32} \leq (\mathrm{DP}_{max}^{sbox})^4$ and $\mathrm{DP}_{max}^{f64} \leq (\mathrm{DP}_{max}^{sbox})^8$. Similar results can be obtained with respect to linear cryptanalysis. By taking into account the fact that in a Lai-Massey scheme, any differential or linear characteristic on two rounds must involve *at least one round function*, we obtain the following result; its complete proof can be found in [14].

Theorem 2. *The differential (resp. linear) probability of any single-path characteristic in* FOX64/k/r *is upper bounded by* $(\mathrm{DP}_{max}^{sbox})^{2r}$ *(resp.* $(\mathrm{LP}_{max}^{sbox})^{2r})$. *Similarly, the bounds are* $(\mathrm{DP}_{max}^{sbox})^{4r}$ *(resp.* $(\mathrm{LP}_{max}^{sbox})^{4r})$ *for* FOX128/k/r.

Since $\mathrm{DP}_{max}^{sbox} = \mathrm{LP}_{max}^{sbox} = 2^{-4}$, we conclude that it is impossible to find any useful differential or linear characteristic after 8 rounds for both FOX64 and FOX128. Hence, a minimal number of 12 rounds provides a minimal safety margin.

4.3 Integral Attacks

Integral attacks [17] apply to ciphers operating on well-aligned data, like SPN structures. As the round functions of FOX are SPNs, one can wonder whether it

---

[8] One should not misinterpret these results in terms of the overall block cipher security: FOX's round functions are far to be indistinguishable from random functions, as it is the case of DES round functions, for instance: the fact that DES is vulnerable to linear and differential cryptanalysis does not contradict Luby-Rackoff results.

is possible to find an integral distinguisher on the whole structure. We consider now the case of FOX64: let us denote the input bytes by $X_{i(8)}$ with $0 \leq i \leq 7$. Let $X_{3(8)} = a$, $X_{7(8)} = a \oplus c$, and $X_{i(8)} = c$ for $i = 0, 1, 2, 4, 5, 6$, where c is a constant. We consider plaintext structures $x^{(j)}$ for $1 \leq j \leq 256$ where a takes all 256 possibles byte values. Let us denote the output of the third round lmid64 by $Y_{i(8)}$ with $0 \leq i \leq 7$. Then, $\bigoplus_{j=1}^{256} Y_{i(8)}^{(j)} = \bigoplus_{j=1}^{256} Y_{i+4(8)}^{(j)}$ for $0 \leq i \leq 3$. Note that we have still two such equalities if we replace the last round by a lmor64 round. This integral distinguisher[9] can be used to break (four, five) six rounds of FOX64 (by guessing the one, two, or three last round keys and testing the integral criterion for each subkey candidate on a few structures of plaintexts) with a complexity of about $(2^{64}, 2^{128})$ 2^{192} operations. A similar property may be used to break up to 4 rounds of FOX128 (by guessing the last round key) with a complexity of about 2^{128} operations.

4.4   Other Attacks

Statistical Attacks. Due to the very high diffusion properties of FOX's round functions, the high algebraic degree of the sbox mapping, and the high number of rounds, we are strongly convinced that FOX will resist to known variants of linear and differential cryptanalysis (like differential-linear cryptanalysis [20, 4], boomerang [32] and rectangle attacks [5]), as well as generalizations thereof, like Knudsen's truncated and higher-order differentials [16], impossible differentials [3], and Harpes' partitioning cryptanalysis [11], for instance.

Slide and Related-Key Attacks. Slide attacks [6, 7] exploit periodic key-schedule algorithms, which is not a property of FOX's key-schedule algorithms. Furthermore, due to very good diffusion and the high non-linearity of the key-schedule, related-key attacks are very unlikely to be effective against FOX.

Interpolation and Algebraic Attacks. Interpolation attacks [13] take advantage of S-boxes exhibiting a simple algebraic structure. Since FOX's non-linear mapping sbox does not possess any simple relation over $GF(2)$ or $GF(2^8)$, such attacks are certainly not effective. One of our main concerns was to avoid a pure algebraic construction for the sbox mapping, as it is the case for a large number of modern designs of block ciphers. Although such S-boxes have many interesting non-linear properties, they probably form the best conditions to express a block cipher as a system of sparse, over-defined low-degree multivariate polynomial equations over $GF(2)$ or $GF(2^8)$; this fact may lead to effective attacks, as argued by Courtois and Pieprzyk in [8]. Not choosing an algebraic construction for sbox does not necessarily ensure security towards algebraic attacks. Note that we base our non-linear mapping on "small" permutations, mapping 4 bits to 4 bits, and that, according to [8], *any* such mapping can always be written as an overdefined

---

[9] Note that one could extend it to four rounds using large precomputed tables, and thus reduce the overall complexity by a factor of 2^{64}.

system of *at least* 21 quadratic equations. Indeed, we checked that S_1, S_2, and S_3 cannot be described by a system with more than 21 quadratic equations over GF (2); furthermore, we are not aware of any quadratic relation over GF (2^8) for sbox. Following the very same methodology than [8], it appears that XSL attacks *would* break members of the FOX family within a complexity[10] of 2^{171} to 2^{192}, depending on the block size and the round numbers. However, one should interpret these figures with an extreme care: on the one hand, the real complexity of XSL attacks is by no means clear at the time of writing and is the subject of much controversy [26]; on the other hand, we feel that the advantages of a small hardware footprint overcome such a (possible) security decrease.

5   Implementation Issues

Hardware. The size of the small S-boxes allows to implement FOX very efficiently on hardware using ASIC or FPGA technologies (which can usually implement any 4-bit to 4-bit mapping very efficiently). Projects are currently in process. We expect that FOX results in very high performances on hardware.

8-Bit Platforms. Obviously, the most intensive computations are related to the evaluation of the sbox mapping and of mu4 and mu8. Different strategies may be applied: when extremely few memory is available, one computes on-the-fly the sbox mapping, as it is described in §3.1, and all the operations in GF (2^8). The sole needed constants are the small substitution boxes S_1, S_2 and S_3 (see §B) and the constants needed by the key-schedule algorithm. A significant speed gain can be obtained if one precomputes the sbox mapping, the finite field operations being all computed dynamically. A third possibility is to precompute two more mappings: multiplication in GF (2^8) by α and by α^{-1}. Finally, in the case of FOX128, a further speed gain may be obtained by tabulating two more mappings: multiplication by α^2 and by α^{-2}.

32/64-Bit Platforms. The f32 and f64 functions can be implemented very efficiently using a classical combinations of table-lookups and XORs. For a fully precomputed implementation, one needs 8'192 bytes of memory space for FOX64, as well as 32'768 bytes for FOX128. Depending on the target processor, the nearest cache (i.e. the fastest memory) size may be smaller than 32 kB. In this case, one can spare half of the space (at the cost of a few masking operations) by noting that the S-boxes are "embedded" in the tables combining the S-box and the diffusion layer; this allows to reduce the fast memory needs to 4'096 and 16'384 bytes, respectively.

Performance Results. The following table summarizes the results obtained so far by our optimized implementations of the FOX family (in clock cycles to encrypt one block, with precomputed subkeys):

---

[10] Under the unchecked hypothesis that XSL can use Gaussian elimination within a complexity equal to $n^{2.376}$.

Cipher	Architecture	Implementation	$r = 12$	$r = 16$
FOX64/k/r	Intel Pentium 3	C (gcc)	316	406
FOX64/k/r	Intel Pentium 3	ASM	220	295
FOX64/k/r	Intel Pentium 4	C (gcc)	388	564
FOX64/k/r	AMD Athlon-XP	C (gcc)	306	390
FOX64/k/r	Alpha 21264	C (Compaq cc)	360	480
FOX128/k/r	Intel Pentium 3	C (gcc)	636	840
FOX128/k/r	AMD Athlon-XP	C (gcc)	544	748
FOX128/k/r	Alpha 21264	C (Compaq cc)	440	588

We note that FOX64 is extremely fast on 32-bit architectures, while FOX128 is competitive on 64-bit architectures. Namely, according to the Nessie project [27], FOX64/12 is the fourth fastest 64-bit block cipher on Pentium 3 behind Nimbus, CAST-128 and RC5. It is 19% faster than Misty1 (NESSIE's choice), 39% faster than IDEA, 57% faster than DES and about three times faster than TDES. The generic version of FOX64 (with 16 rounds) is still 8% faster than IDEA. On Alpha 21264, a 64-bit architecture, FOX128/12 is the third fastest block cipher behind Nush and AES, according to [27], while FOX128 (16 rounds) with 256-bit keys is still 30% faster than Camellia, which is one of NESSIE's choices.

Finally, we have an implementation of FOX64/12 (resp. FOX64/16) on 8051, a typical low-cost 8-bit architecture, needing 16 bytes of RAM, 896 bytes of ROM (precomputed data and precomputed subkeys) and 575 bytes of code size encrypting one block in 2958 (resp. 3950) clock cycles.

6   Conclusion

Obviously, proposing a new block cipher family leads to new open problems. We *strongly* encourage the development of attacks against full or reduced versions of any member of the FOX family.

Another very interesting open problem is the definition of new linear multi-permutations which can be implemented efficiently on low-cost 8-bit smartcards. Some proposals have been done in connection with the design of block ciphers based on SPNs, where the inverse multipermutation also has to be implemented; using them in a self-inverting structure, *e.g.* a Feistel or a Lai-Massey scheme, allows to relax this condition. Hence, the linear mapping can be optimized.

Acknowledgments

We would like to thank MediaCrypt AG, for having motivated and supported this work, as well as Jacques Stern and David Wagner for their review of a preliminary version of FOX.

References

1. AES Homepage. http://csrc.nist.gov/encryption/aes/.
2. E. Barkan and E. Biham. In how many ways can you write Rijndael? In Y. Zheng, editor, *Advances in Cryptology – ASIACRYPT'02*, volume 2501 of *Lecture Notes in Computer Science*, pages 160–175. Springer-Verlag, 2002.
3. E. Biham, A. Biryukov, and A. Shamir. Cryptanalysis of Skipjack reduced to 31 rounds using impossible differentials. In J. Stern, editor, *Advances in Cryptology - EUROCRYPT'99*, volume 1592 of *Lecture Notes in Computer Science*, pages 12–23. Springer-Verlag, 1999.
4. E. Biham, O. Dunkelman, and N. Keller. Enhancing differential-linear cryptanalysis. In Y. Zheng, editor, *Advances in Cryptology – ASIACRYPT'02*, volume 2501 of *Lecture Notes in Computer Science*, pages 254–266. Springer-Verlag.
5. E. Biham, O. Dunkelman, and N. Keller. The rectangle attack - rectangling the Serpent. In B. Pfitzmann, editor, *Advances in Cryptology – EUROCRYPT'01*, volume 2045 of *Lecture Notes in Computer Science*, pages 340–357. Springer-Verlag, 2001.
6. A. Biryukov and D. Wagner. Slide attacks. In L. Knudsen, editor, *Fast Software Encryption: 6th International Workshop, FSE'99*, volume 1636 of *Lecture Notes in Computer Science*, pages 245–259. Springer-Verlag, 1999.
7. A. Biryukov and D. Wagner. Advanced slide attacks. In B. Preneel, editor, *Advances in Cryptology - EUROCRYPT'00*, volume 1807 of *Lecture Notes in Computer Science*, pages 589–606. Springer-Verlag, 2000.
8. N. Courtois and J. Pieprzyk. Cryptanalysis of block ciphers with overdefined systems of equations. In Y. Zheng, editor, *Advances in Cryptology – ASIACRYPT'02*, volume 2501 of *Lecture Notes in Computer Science*, pages 267–287. Springer-Verlag, 2002.
9. H. Feistel. Cryptography and data security. *Scientific American*, 228(5):15–23, 1973.
10. N. Ferguson, R. Schroeppel, and D. Whiting. A simple algebraic representation of Rijndael. In S. Vaudenay and A. Youssef, editors, *Selected Areas in Cryptography: SAC 2001*, volume 2259 of *Lecture Notes in Computer Science*, pages 103–111. Springer-Verlag, 2001.
11. C. Harpes and J. Massey. Partitioning cryptanalysis. In E. Biham, editor, *Fast Software Encryption: 4th International Workshop, FSE'97*, volume 1267 of *Lecture Notes in Computer Science*, pages 13–27. Springer-Verlag.
12. S. Hong, S. Lee, J. Lim, J. Sung, D. Cheon, and I. Cho. Provable security against differential and linear cryptanalysis for the SPN structure. In B. Schneier, editor, *Fast Software Encryption: 7th International Workshop, FSE 2000*, volume 1978 of *Lecture Notes in Computer Science*, pages 273–283. Springer-Verlag, 2001.
13. T. Jakobsen and L. Knudsen. The interpolation attack against block ciphers. In E. Biham, editor, *Fast Software Encryption: 4th International Workshop, FSE'97*, volume 1267 of *Lecture Notes in Computer Science*, pages 28–40. Springer-Verlag, 1997.
14. P. Junod and S. Vaudenay. *FOX specifications version 1.1*. Technical Report EPFL/IC/2004/75, École Polytechnique Fédérale, Lausanne, Switzerland, 2004.
15. P. Junod and S. Vaudenay. Perfect diffusion primitives for block ciphers – building efficient MDS matrices. In *Proceedings of SAC'04*. Springer-Verlag, 2004.
16. L. Knudsen. Truncated and higher order differentials. In B. Preneel, editor, *Fast Software Encryption: Second International Workshop*, volume 1008 of *Lecture Notes in Computer Science*, pages 196–211. Springer-Verlag, 1995.

17. L. Knudsen and D. Wagner. Integral cryptanalysis (extended abstract). In J. Daemen and V. Rijmen, editors, *Fast Software Encryption: 9th International Workshop, FSE 2002*, volume 2365 of *Lecture Notes in Computer Science*, pages 112–127. Springer-Verlag, 2002.

18. X. Lai. *On the design and security of block ciphers*, volume 1 of *ETH Series in Information Processing*. Hartung-Gorre Verlag, 1992.

19. X. Lai and J. Massey. A proposal for a new block encryption standard. In I. Damgård, editor, *Advances in Cryptology - EUROCRYPT'90*, volume 473 of *Lecture Notes in Computer Science*, pages 389–404. Springer-Verlag, 1991.

20. K. Langford and E. Hellman. Differential-linear cryptanalysis. In Y. Desmedt, editor, *Advances in Cryptology - CRYPTO'94*, volume 839 of *Lecture Notes in Computer Science*, pages 17–25. Springer-Verlag, 1994.

21. M. Luby and C. Rackoff. How to construct pseudorandom permutations from pseudorandom functions. *SIAM Journal on Computing*, 17(2):373–386, 1988.

22. M. Matsui. New block encryption algorithm MISTY. In E. Biham, editor, *Fast Software Encryption: 4th International Workshop, FSE'97*, volume 1267 of *Lecture Notes in Computer Science*, pages 53–67. Springer-Verlag.

23. MediaCrypt AG. Website http://www.mediacrypt.com.

24. F. Muller. A new attack against Khazad. In C. Laih, editor, *Advances in Cryptology - ASIACRYPT'03*, volume 2894 of *Lecture Notes in Computer Science*, pages 347 – 358. Springer-Verlag, 2003.

25. S. Murphy and M. Robshaw. Essential algebraic structure within the AES. In M. Yung, editor, *Advances in Cryptology – CRYPTO'02*, volume 2442 of *Lecture Notes in Computer Science*, pages 1–16. Springer-Verlag, 2002.

26. S. Murphy and M. Robshaw. Comments on the security of the AES and the XSL technique. *Electronic Letters*, 39(1):36–38. 2003.

27. NESSIE Homepage. https://www.cryptonessie.org.

28. C. Schnorr and S. Vaudenay. Black box cryptanalysis of hash networks based on multipermutations. In A. De Santis, editor, *Advances in Cryptology - EUROCRYPT'94*, volume 950 of *Lecture Notes in Computer Science*, pages 47–57. Springer-Verlag, 1995.

29. S. Vaudenay. On the need for multipermutations: cryptanalysis of MD4 and SAFER. In B. Preneel, editor, *Fast Software Encryption: Second International Workshop*, volume 1008 of *Lecture Notes in Computer Science*, pages 286–297. Springer-Verlag, 1995.

30. S. Vaudenay. On the Lai-Massey scheme. In K. Lam, T. Okamoto, and C. Xing, editors, *Advances in Cryptology - ASIACRYPT'99*, volume 1716 of *Lecture Notes in Computer Science*, pages 8–19. Springer-Verlag, 2000.

31. S. Vaudenay. Decorrelation: a theory for block cipher security. *Journal of Cryptology*, 16(4):249–286, 2003.

32. D. Wagner. The boomerang attack. In L. Knudsen, editor, *Fast Software Encryption: 6th International Workshop, FSE'99*, volume 1636 of *Lecture Notes in Computer Science*, pages 156–170. Springer-Verlag, 1999.

33. H. Wu. Related-cipher attacks. In R. Deng, S. Qing, F. Bao, and J. Zhou, editors, *Information and Communications Security: 4th International Conference, ICICS 2002*, volume 2513 of *Lecture Notes in Computer Science*, pages 447–455. Springer-Verlag, 2002.

A   Test Vectors

An implementation of FOX can be validated using the following test vectors. The ciphertexts corresponding to the plaintext 0x0123456789ABCDEF, respectively 0x0123456789ABCDEFFEDCBA9876543210 are given for two different key lengths, for FOX64 and FOX128, respectively.

```
-----------------------------------------------------------------------------
FOX64/16/128 K  : 00112233 44556677 8899AABB CCDDEEFF
FOX64/16/128 C  : B85D6B76 6DCE952E
-----------------------------------------------------------------------------
FOX64/16/256 K  : 00112233 44556677 8899AABB CCDDEEFF FFEEDDCC BBAA9988 77665544 33221100
FOX64/16/256 C  : BB654D30 11DB367E
-----------------------------------------------------------------------------
FOX128/16/128 K : 00112233 44556677 8899AABB CCDDEEFF
FOX128/16/128 C : 849E0F06 82F50CD5 88AE0730 06A10BEE
-----------------------------------------------------------------------------
FOX128/16/256 K : 00112233 44556677 8899AABB CCDDEEFF FFEEDDCC BBAA9988 77665544 33221100
FOX128/16/256 C : 45CCB103 0F67B768 247F5302 66BC4996
-----------------------------------------------------------------------------
```

B   sbox Definition

The three small S-boxes S_1, S_2, and S_3, as well as the full S-box, are defined in the following tables:

x	0x0	0x1	0x2	0x3	0x4	0x5	0x6	0x7	0x8	0x9	0xA	0xB	0xC	0xD	0xE	0xF
$S_1(x)$	0x2	0x5	0x1	0x9	0xE	0xA	0xC	0x8	0x6	0x4	0x7	0xF	0xD	0xB	0x0	0x3
$S_2(x)$	0xB	0x4	0x1	0xF	0x0	0x3	0xE	0xD	0xA	0x8	0x7	0x5	0xC	0x2	0x9	0x6
$S_3(x)$	0xD	0xA	0xB	0x1	0x4	0x3	0x8	0x9	0x5	0x7	0x2	0xC	0xF	0x0	0x6	0xE

One should read the next table in that way: to compute sbox(0x4C), one selects first the row named 4. (i.e. the fifth row), and then one selects the column named .C (i.e. the thirteenth column) and we get finally sbox(0x4C) = 0x15.

sbox	.0	.1	.2	.3	.4	.5	.6	.7	.8	.9	.A	.B	.C	.D	.E	.F
0.	5D	DE	00	B7	D3	CA	3C	0D	C3	F8	CB	8D	76	89	AA	12
1.	88	22	4F	DB	6D	47	E4	4C	78	9A	49	93	C4	C0	86	13
2.	A9	20	53	1C	4E	CF	35	39	B4	A1	54	64	03	C7	85	5C
3.	5B	CD	D8	72	96	42	B8	E1	A2	60	EF	BD	02	AF	8C	73
4.	7C	7F	5E	F9	65	E6	EB	AD	5A	A5	79	8E	15	30	EC	A4
5.	C2	3E	E0	74	51	FB	2D	6E	94	4D	55	34	AE	52	7E	9D
6.	4A	F7	80	F0	D0	90	A7	E8	9F	50	D5	D1	98	CC	A0	17
7.	F4	B6	C1	28	5F	26	01	AB	25	38	82	7D	48	FC	1B	CE
8.	3F	6B	E2	67	66	43	59	19	84	3D	F5	2F	C9	BC	D9	95
9.	29	41	DA	1A	B0	E9	69	D2	7B	D7	11	9B	33	8A	23	09
A.	D4	71	44	68	6F	F2	0E	DF	87	DC	83	18	6A	EE	99	81
B.	62	36	2E	7A	FE	45	9C	75	91	0C	0F	E7	F6	14	63	1D
C.	0B	8B	B3	F3	B2	3B	08	4B	10	A6	32	B9	A8	92	F1	56
D.	DD	21	BF	04	BE	D6	FD	77	EA	3A	C8	8F	57	1E	FA	2B
E.	58	C5	27	AC	E3	ED	97	BB	46	05	40	31	E5	37	2C	9E
F.	0A	B1	B5	06	6C	1F	A3	2A	70	FF	BA	07	24	16	C6	61

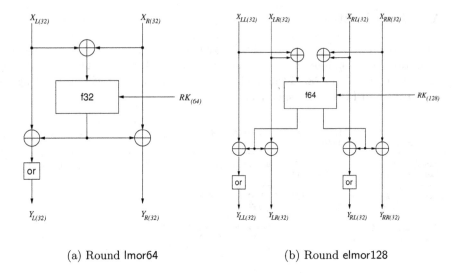

(a) Round Imor64   (b) Round elmor128

Fig. 1. Round Functions

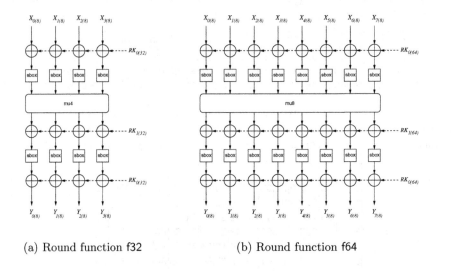

(a) Round function f32   (b) Round function f64

Fig. 2. Functions f32 and f64

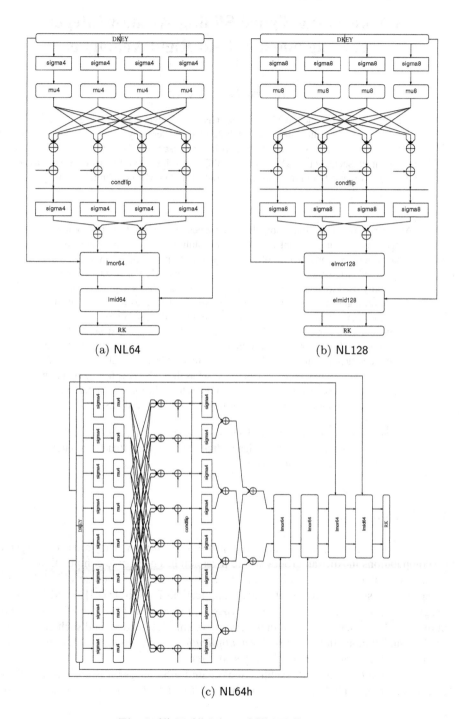

(a) NL64   (b) NL128

(c) NL64h

Fig. 3. NL64, NL64h, and NL128 Functions

A Note on the Signed Sliding Window Integer Recoding and a Left-to-Right Analogue

Roberto Maria Avanzi*

Institute for Experimental Mathematics (IEM) — Universität Duisburg–Essen
Ellernstraße 29, D-45326 Essen, Germany
mocenigo@exp-math.uni-essen.de
Communication Security (COSY) — Electrical Engineering and Information Technology
Ruhr-Universität Bochum, Universitätsstraße 150, D-44780 Bochum, Germany

Abstract. Addition-subtraction-chains obtained from signed digit recodings of integers are a common tool for computing multiples of random elements of a group where the computation of inverses is a fast operation. Cohen and Solinas independently described one such recoding, the w-NAF. For scalars of the size commonly used in cryptographic applications, it leads to the current scalar multiplication algorithm of choice. However, we could find no formal proof of its optimality in the literature. This recoding is computed right-to-left.

We solve two open questions regarding the w-NAF. We first prove that the w-NAF is a redundant radix-2 recoding of smallest weight among all those with integral coefficients smaller in absolute value than 2^{w-1}. Secondly, we introduce a left-to-right recoding with the same digit set as the w-NAF, generalizing previous results. We also prove that the two recodings have the same (optimal) weight. Finally, we sketch how to prove similar results for other recodings.

Keywords: Computer arithmetic, Integer Recoding, Non-adjacent form, Width-w non-adjacent form (w-NAF), Signed-digit representation, Redundant number representation, Left-to-right recoding.

1 Introduction

This paper deals with *signed sliding window integer recodings*. They are used to speed up computations in Abelian groups where inversion has negligible computational cost. Notable examples of such groups are: the rational point group of an elliptic curve, independently suggested for cryptographic applications by Koblitz [14] and Miller [16]; the group of rational divisor classes of a hyperelliptic curve [15]; and the XTR subgroup in its natural representation [24]. In the cryptosystems designed around such groups the fundamental computation is the *scalar multiplication*, *i.e.* the computation of the n-fold ng of a group element g for an arbitrary scalar $n \in \mathbb{Z}$.

An addition (resp. addition-subtraction) chain for an integer n is a sequence of integers beginning with 1 and ending with n such that each element is the sum (resp.

---

* The work described in this paper has been supported in part by the European Commission through the IST Programme under Contracts IST-2001-32613 (AREHCC).

H. Handschuh and A. Hasan (Eds.): SAC 2004, LNCS 3357, pp. 130–143, 2005.

sum or difference) of two previous elements of the sequence. For example $\{1, 2, 3, 6, 9\}$ and $\{1, 2, 4, 8, 9\}$ are addition chains for 9. The computation of ng for any element g of a group G can be done using an addition(-subtraction) chain for n. For example, $9g$ can be obtained by computing $g, 2g, 3g, 6g$ and finally $9g$. Methods for finding short addition(-subtraction) chains are very important: The shorter is a chain, the faster will be the corresponding scalar multiplication. An addition-subtraction can be shorter than the shortest addition chain for the same integer. A shortest addition chain for 31 is $\{1, 2, 3, 6, 7, 14, 28, 31\}$, but a shortest addition-subtraction chain is $\{1, 2, 4, 8, 16, 32, 31\}$.

Downey, Leong, and Sethi [6] proved that the decision problem whose instances are the tuples $(k, n_1, n_2, \ldots, n_k, \ell)$ such that there is an addition chain of length ℓ containing $n_1, n_2, \ldots, n_k$ is NP-complete. It is conjectured that the subset of instances with fixed k, such as $k = 1$, is also NP-complete. Even if it were so, and thus the problem of finding shortest chains were NP-hard, this would not necessarily rule out the existence of efficient algorithms to find near optimal chains. Erdős [7] proved that for almost all integers n the shortest addition chain for n has length $\lambda(n) + \lambda(n)/\lambda(\lambda(n))$ where $\lambda(n) = \lfloor \log_2(n) \rfloor$. The upper bound $\lambda(n) + (1 + o(1))\lambda(n)/\lambda(\lambda(n))$ is attained by means of Thurber's [25] *sliding windows* variation of Brauer's method [3] - which is therefore a concrete example of a method giving almost always near optimal addition chains. Similar considerations hold for addition-subtraction chains.

Let $n = \sum_{i=0}^{\ell} n_i 2^i$ be a *recoding* of the integer n, where the integers n_i belong to a digit set $\mathcal{S}$ with $\{0, 1\} \subseteq \mathcal{S} \subset \mathbb{Z}$, and $n_\ell \neq 0$. If digits other than zero and one are allowed, we have a *redundant representation*.

It is easy to build an addition-subtraction chain from such a recoding by a technique called *double-and-add*. The chain starts with $\{1, 2, \ldots, \max\{|n_i|\}\}$. For $i = \ell - 1, \ldots, 2, 1, 0$, we do the following: if $n_i = 0$ we append $a_i := 2a_{i+1}$ to the chain; if $n_i \neq 0$ we append both $2a_{i+1}$ and $a_i := 2a_{i+1} + n_i$. At the end, $a_0 = n$. If the non-zero coefficients are odd, to save some operations the chain can begin after 2 begin with $\{1, 2, 3, 5, 7, \ldots, \max\{|n_i|\}\}$ (the even numbers other than 2 are omitted). Apart from the cost of computing $2g, 3g, \ldots, \max\{|n_i|\}g$, the amount of doublings, resp. generic additions in G equals the length, resp. the weight of the recoding: We recall that the *length* of any expression $n = \sum_{i=0}^{\infty} n_i 2^i$ with only a finite number of non-vanishing terms, is $\ell + 1$, where ℓ is the highest index for which $n_\ell \neq 0$; its *weight* is the number of non-zero coefficients. It is then interesting to find recodings which minimize those quantities.

Cohen et al. [5] and Solinas [22] independently introduced the *width-w non-adjacent form*, or *w-NAF* of the scalar. This signed digit representation is defined in Section 2. For scalars of the size commonly used in cryptographic applications, it leads to the current scalar multiplication algorithm of choice. Cohen [4] analyzes weight and length of the w-NAF as a function of the input length.

A potential drawback of the w-NAF is that it scans the bits from the least significant to the most significant ones, *i.e.* from right to left. This means that the recoding must be completely known and stored in memory before the scalar multiplication in the group G is performed with a classical double-and-add scalar multiplication algorithm. This can be disadvantageous on a device with limited resources like a smart card. On the other hand, if the bits could be scanned and the digits of the recoding generated from left to right, one could *interleave* recoding and scalar multiplication: this is sometimes called *online recoding*. Of course one can interleave a right-to-left recoding with Yao's [26] scalar multiplication algorithm, but this method requires a few more operations than double-and-add even with the same recoding. (Surveys of scalar multiplication algorithms can be found in [8] (slightly outdated) and [2].)

Not only for its intrinsic practical interest, but also because the subject itself is challenging, the development of algorithms for left-to-right optimal recodings has recently attracted a lot of attention in the mathematical community [9, 12, 13]. Rizzo [21] has analyzed the left-to-right unsigned sliding window method.

The *non adjacent form* (NAF) [20] is the special case of the w-NAF with $w = 2$. It is known that the NAF is a recoding of minimal weight among all those having coefficients in $\{0, \pm 1\}$. As we started our research, there was no formal proof in the literature that the general w-NAF is a recoding of minimal weight among those having the same digit set. We provide this proof in Section 2, Theorem 2.3.

Joye and Yen [12] devised a left-to-right recoding using the digit set $\{0, \pm 1\}$, having the same weight as the NAF, and which can be used online. Their method does not apply to the w-NAF. We introduce a left-to-right analogue of the w-NAF in Section 3, and in Section 4 we prove that it has the same weight as the w-NAF. While proving our results, we in fact show that the two recodings parse their inputs essentially in the same way, and use the same function of $w + 1$ consecutive bits to generate the non-zero digits. Some remarks, including generalizations of our results to unsigned recodings and joint recodings of more integers, as well as references to related similar work, conclude the paper.

2   Optimality

For each integer n and for any value of the positive integral parameter $w \geq 2$, the w-NAF of n is a representation $n = \sum_{j=0}^{\ell} n_j 2^j$ where the integer coefficients n_j satisfy the following two conditions:

(**w-NAF-1**) Either $n_j = 0$ or n_j is odd and $|n_j| < 2^{w-1}$.
(**w-NAF-2**) If $n_j \neq 0$, then $n_{j+1} = \cdots = n_{j+w-1} = 0$.

Using the fact that the set of odd integers of absolute value smaller than 2^{w-1} is a complete residue set modulo 2^w for the odd integers, it is easy to write a simple algorithm to generate a w-NAF for each integer n and to prove that it is uniquely determined.

The algorithm works as follows: A temporary variable x is put equal to the input. If x is even, it is halved and a zero is output; otherwise the smallest residue r of x modulo 2^w is subtracted from x; x is then halved w times and the digit r is output followed by $w - 1$ zeros. This process is repeated until x reaches 0. Correctness and termination are obvious. For the applications we use a version that works directly on the binary representation of the input n and does not modify it, whence it needs (at least in theory) to keep a carry.

Algorithm 2.1 w-NAF Recoding

INPUT: An integer $n = \sum_{j=0}^{\ell-1} e_j\, 2^j$, and a parameter $w \geq 2$.

OUTPUT: The w-NAF $\sum_{j=0}^{\ell} n_j\, 2^j$ of n.

---

1.   Initialize $n_j \leftarrow 0$ for $0 \leq j \leq \ell$. Assume $e_\ell = 0$.

2. $i \leftarrow 0, c \leftarrow 0$.

3.   **while** $(i \leq \ell)$ **do** {

4.   **if** $e_i = c$ **then** {

5. $i \leftarrow i + 1$.

6.   } **else** {

7. $w' \leftarrow \min\{w, \ell - i + 1\}$.

8. $v \leftarrow c + \sum_{j=0}^{w'-1} e_{i+j} 2^j$.

9.   **if** $v \geq 2^{w-1}$ **then** $c \leftarrow 1, v \leftarrow v - 2^w$ **else** $c \leftarrow 0$.

10. $n_i \leftarrow v$.

11. $i \leftarrow i + w'$. } }

12. **return**

Note that, at Step 8 it is in fact $v = 1 + \sum_{j=1}^{w'-1} e_{i+j} 2^j$ because $c \neq e_j$ and the variables c, e_j can only take the values 0 and 1. This also guarantees that v, being odd, is non-zero.

Definition 2.2 *Let n, w be integers. A w-signed digit recoding, or w-SDR for short, is an expression of the type $n = \sum_{i=0}^{\ell} n_i 2^i$ where the digits n_i are integers with $|n_i| < 2^{w-1}$. (There is no restriction that the digits of a w-SDR either vanish or are odd.)*

We use the notation $\mathcal{H}(\cdot)$ to denote the Hamming weight of any recoding, where by Hamming weight of $\sum_{i=0}^{\ell} n_i 2^i$ we understand the number of non vanishing digits n_i.

The w-NAF of an integer n is a particular w-SDR.

Theorem 2.3 *Let n, w be integers. The w-NAF of n is a recoding of minimal weight among all the w-SDR's of n.*

Proof. We define *two* transformations of recodings. The first one, called *coefficient formation* (**CF**), takes as input any w-SDR of an integer n, and outputs another recoding of n. If n is odd, the least significant digit of the new recoding is non-zero, the next $w - 1$ digits are zero and the w-th digit (the coefficient of 2^w) may have absolute value possibly $\geq 2^{w-1}$ – in which case we say that an *overflow* has been generated – but still smaller than 2^w; all the other digits are equal to the corresponding ones of the input. If n is even, the least significant digit of the new recoding will be zero, and the second least significant digit may be an overflow. The Hamming weight of the output of **CF** is never greater than that of the input, and it is strictly smaller than that if an overflow has been generated. The second transformation, called *overflow propagation* (**OP**) is applied if only if **CF** has generated an overflow. Its output may have Hamming weight equal to that of the input, plus one.

We now describe in detail the two transformations, and prove some of their properties. Later we shall use them to prove the theorem.

Coefficient formation: If $n = \sum_{i=0}^{\ell} n_i 2^i$ is even, then n_0 is even. Put $n_0' = 0$ and $n_1' = n_1 + n_0/2$. If $n_1 = 0$, then $|n_1'| = |n_1| < 2^{w-1}$ and the Hamming weight does not change if we replace n_0, n_1 with n_0', n_1'. If $|n_1'| \geq 2^{w-1}$ then n_0 and n_1 were both non-zero and the Hamming weight decreases by one. Plainly $|n_1'| < \frac{3}{2} 2^{w-1} < 2^w$ and $n_0 + 2n_1 = n_0' + 2n_1'$, hence if we replace n_0, n_1 with n_0', n_1' we obtain a new recoding for n, which is also a w-SDR except for at most one overflow.

Let now n be odd. Define $M = \sum_{i=0}^{w-1} n_i 2^i$ (if the input recoding has length than w, we suitably pad it with zeros). Now,

$$|M| \leq (2^{w-1} - 1) \cdot \sum_{i=0}^{w-1} 2^i = (2^{w-1} - 1)(2^w - 1) = 2^{2w-1} - 3 \cdot 2^{w-1} + 1 \; ,$$

hence there exist integers c, r such that $M = c2^w + r$ with $|c| < 2^{w-1}$ and $|r| \leq 2^{w-1}$. Put now $n_w' = n_w + c$, $n_0' = r$ and $n_j' = 0$ for all j with $0 < j < w$.

Let $h = \mathcal{H}\left(\sum_{i=0}^{w} n_i 2^i\right)$ and $h' = \mathcal{H}\left(\sum_{i=0}^{w} n_i' 2^i\right)$. We want to show that $h \geq h'$.

First note that only one coefficient among the w least significant ones in $\sum_{i=0}^{w} n_i' 2^i$ is non-zero, namely n_0', whereas at least one of the integers $n_0, n_1, \dots, n_{w-1}$ is non-zero.

It can be $c \neq 0$ only if at least one of the digits $n_1, \dots, n_{w-1}$ is non-zero, because if these digits all vanish then $|M| < 2^{w-1}$ and $c = 0$. In the case where $c \neq 0$, it is therefore $h \geq 2$ and $h' \leq 2$.

If an overflow occurs, it must be $c \neq 0$ and $n_w \neq 0$, hence $h \geq 3$ but $h' \leq 2$ by construction.

If we replace n_j with n_j' for $0 \leq j \leq w$, we get a recoding for n whose w least significant digits satisfy the properties of the w-NAF.

Overflow propagation: Let t be the only index in a recoding (which is the output of **CF**) such that $|n_t| \geq 2^{w-1}$, but $|n_t| < 2^w$. Define $n_t' = \text{sign}(n_t)(n_t \bmod 2)$ and $n_{t+1}' = n_{t+1} + \frac{n_t - n_t'}{2}$. Replace then n_t and n_{t+1} by n_t' and n_{t+1}'. Clearly, $|n_{t+1}'| < 2^w$. If $|n_{t+1}'| \geq 2^{w-1}$, we repeat the procedure just described with $t+1$ in place of t, otherwise we stop. This process must terminate by the finiteness of the recoding, and it can increase the Hamming weight at most by one.

OP is performed after **CF** if and only if the latter generates an overflow and decreases the Hamming weight at least by one. Therefore the application of the two transformations will not increase the Hamming weight of the input.

We can now prove the theorem by induction.

For integers of absolute value at most 2^{w-1} it is obvious that the w-NAF has minimal weight. Let then $|n| > 2^{w-1}$ in the sequel.

We consider first the case where n is odd. Let $\sum_{i=0}^{\ell} n_i 2^i$ be original recoding, of weight h, and $\sum_{i=0}^{\ell'} n_i' 2^i$ be the output of **CF** and **OP**, which has weight not greater than h. Recall that $n_0' \neq 0$ and $n_1' = \dots = n_{w-1}' = 0$ by construction.

Consider $m = \frac{n - n_0'}{2^w}$. Its w-NAF $\sum_{i=0}^{\lambda} m_i 2^i$ (for some upper bound λ on the indices) has by the inductive assumption weight not greater than the weight of $\sum_{i=0}^{\ell' - w} n_{i+w}' 2^i$. Since $n_0' + \sum_{i=0}^{\lambda} m_i 2^{i+w}$ satisfies the defining properties of the w-NAF, it is the w-NAF of n and its weight satisfies

$$\mathcal{H}\left(n_0' + \sum_{i=0}^{\lambda} m_i 2^{i+w}\right) = 1 + \mathcal{H}\left(\sum_{i=0}^{\lambda} m_i 2^{i+w}\right) \leq$$

$$\leq 1 + \mathcal{H}\left(\sum_{i=0}^{\ell' - w} n_{i+w}' 2^i\right) = \mathcal{H}\left(\sum_{i=0}^{\ell'} n_i' 2^i\right) \leq h \ .$$

If n is even, proceed in a similar (but simpler) way, using the w-NAF of $n/2$ to complete the proof. $\qquad\square$

Remark 2.4 It is immediate to see that, upon repeated application of **CF** and **OP**, one can obtain the w-NAF of any integer from a w-SDR. Making some obvious simplifications and the overflow propagation implicit, we obtain the following algorithm:

Algorithm 2.5 w-SDR to w-NAF recoding

INPUT: An integer n given by a w-SDR $n = \sum_{j=0}^{\ell-1} e_j 2^j$.

OUTPUT: The w-NAF $\sum_{j=0}^{\ell+w-1} n_j 2^j$ of n.

---

1.   Initialize $n_j \leftarrow 0$ for $0 \leq j < \ell + w$.

2. $i \leftarrow 0, c \leftarrow 0$.

3.   **while** $(i < \ell)$ **do** {

4.   **if** $e_i + c$ is even **then** {

5. $i \leftarrow i + 1, c \leftarrow \dfrac{e_i + c}{2}$.

6.   } **else** {

7. $M \leftarrow c + \displaystyle\sum_{j=0}^{w-1} e_{i+j} 2^j$. $[|M| \leq 2^{2w-1} - 2^{w-1} + 1]$

8.   Write $M = c2^w + r$ with r odd, $|r| < 2^{w-1}$, and $|c| < 2^{w-1}$.

9.   Put $n_i \leftarrow r$.

10. $i \leftarrow i + w$. } }

11. **if** $c \neq 0$ **then** {

12.   **while** c is even **do** {

13. $i \leftarrow i + 1, c \leftarrow c/2$. }

14. $n_i \leftarrow c$. }

15. **return**

---

3   A Left-to-Right Recoding

We introduce a left-to-right recoding using the same digit set as the w-NAF. For $w = 2$, it is different from Joye and Yen's analogue of the NAF, but it produces the same output. (On the other hand, Joye and Yen's algorithm has no conditional tests and branches and is thus resistent against simple power analysis on the recoding of the scalar.) We shall then prove the correctness of our algorithm.

In the next Section we shall see that it scans its input essentially in the same way as Algorithm 2.1, but in reversed order and that its output has the same Hamming weight as the w-NAF.

Algorithm 3.1 w-LtoR: a left-to-right recoding

INPUT: An integer $n = \sum_{j=0}^{\ell-1} e_j 2^j$, with $e_{\ell-1} = 1$, and a parameter $w \geq 2$.

OUTPUT: A signed digit recoding of n as $\sum_{j=0}^{\ell} n_j 2^j$ where each digit n_j are either 0 or odd and $|n_j| < 2^{w-1}$.

1.   Put $n_j \leftarrow 0$ for $0 \leq j < \ell + w$. Assume $e_\ell = e_{-1} = 0$.

2. $i \leftarrow \ell$.

3.   **while** $(i \geq 0)$ **do** {

4.   **if** $(e_i = e_{i-1})$ **then** {

5. $i \leftarrow i - 1$.

6.   } **else** {

7. $w' \leftarrow \min\{w, i+1\}$.

8. $v \leftarrow -e_i 2^{w'-1} + \sum_{j=0}^{w'-2} e_{i-(w'-1)+j} 2^j + e_{i-w'}$.

9. $n_{i-(w'-1)+s} \leftarrow v/2^s$, where $2^s \| v$.

10. $i \leftarrow i - w'.$ } }

11.   **return**

Remark 3.2 We show that v as computed in Step 8 is non-zero. We are in the second branch of the if-then-else construct, in other words $e_i \neq e_{i-1}$. If $i = 0$ then $w' = 1$, but since the second branch has been taken, this means that $e_0 \neq 0$, and clearly $v = -1$. Let now be $w' > 1$. If $e_i = 1$ then $e_{i-1} = 0$ and the positive contributions to v are $\leq 2^{w'-2}$, therefore $v < 0$. (Of course, if in a summation the upper value of the index is smaller than the initial value, the sum is intended empty, hence 0.) If $e_i = 0$ then $e_{i-1} = 1$ and $v \geq 2^{w'-2} > 0$.

An useful way of interpreting the expression in Step 8 is the following one. The value of v is obtained considering the number represented by the string of w' consecutive bits whose most significant bit is the i-th bit, with the sign of the i-th bit itself changed, and adding the following bit to this number. For example, if $w = 3$ and the 3 bits starting from the i-th one are 1011, the value of v is $\bar{1}01 + 1 = -2$. If these bits had been 0111, v would have been $\bar{0}11 + 1 = 4$.

Remark 3.3 Algorithms 2.1 and 3.1 look very similar. In fact, they have been written intentionally that way, in order to make the proof that the recodings they generate have the same Hamming weight (Theorem 4.2) as straightforward as possible. Nevertheless, they can produce quite different outputs.

Theorem 3.4 *Algorithm 3.1 is correct, i.e. its output is an expression which evaluates to the integer represented by its input.*

Proof. Consider the expression

$$\sum_{j=0}^{i-1} e_j 2^j - e_i 2^i + \sum_{j=i+1}^{\ell} n_j 2^j . \tag{1}$$

At the beginning of the algorithm, before entering the loop with $i = \ell$, (1) equals n. Upon exiting the loop, (1) is the output of the algorithm. To prove the statement, we just need to show that (1) is an invariant of the algorithm.

Suppose first that the condition at Step 4 is evaluated to true, *i.e.* $e_i = e_{i-1}$. The only action is to decrement i by 1, and $n_i = 0$ is left as initialised, whence

$$\sum_{j=0}^{i-1} e_j 2^j - e_i 2^i + \sum_{j=i+1}^{\ell} n_j 2^j = \sum_{j=0}^{i-2} e_j 2^j + e_{i-1} 2^{i-1} - e_i 2^i + \sum_{j=i}^{\ell} n_j 2^j$$

$$= \sum_{j=0}^{i-2} e_j 2^j - e_{i-1} 2^{i-1} + \sum_{j=i}^{\ell} n_j 2^j .$$

Let now $i' = i - 1$, *i.e.* i' is the value that i will take after Step 5, we see that the last expression is in fact $\sum_{j=0}^{i'-1} e_j 2^j - e_{i'} 2^{i'} + \sum_{j=i'+1}^{\ell} n_j 2^j$, which proves that (1) is invariant in this case.

Suppose, on the other hand, that the second branch is taken. Before Step 9 we have $n_{i-(w'-1)+s} = 0$ for all s with $0 \le s \le w' - 1$ and

$$\sum_{j=0}^{i-1} e_j 2^j - e_i 2^i + \sum_{j=i+1}^{\ell} n_j 2^j =$$

$$= \left(\sum_{j=0}^{i-w'-1} e_j 2^j + e_{i-w'} 2^{i-w'} + \sum_{j=0}^{w'-2} e_{i-(w'-1)+j} 2^{i-(w'-1)+j} \right) - e_i 2^i + \sum_{j=i+1}^{\ell} n_j 2^j$$

$$= \sum_{j=0}^{i-w'-1} e_j 2^j - e_{i-w'} 2^{i-w'} + \left(-e_i 2^{w'-1} + \sum_{j=0}^{w'-2} e_{i-(w'-1)+j} 2^j + e_{i-w'} \right) 2^{i-(w'-1)} + \sum_{j=i+1}^{\ell} n_j 2^j$$

$$= \sum_{j=0}^{i-w'-1} e_j 2^j - e_{i-w'} 2^{i-w'} + \left(\sum_{j=i+1}^{\ell} n_j 2^j + v 2^{i-(w'-1)} \right) . \tag{2}$$

Putting $n_{i-(w'-1)+s} = v/2^s$ (note that $0 \le s \le w' - 1$) in Step 9 – and leaving $n_{i-(w'-1)+t} = 0$ for all $t \ne s$ with $0 \le t \le w' - 1$, as initialised at the beginning of the algorithm – we obtain that (2) equals

$$\sum_{j=0}^{i-w'-1} e_j 2^j - e_{i-w'} 2^{i-w'} + \sum_{j=i-w'+1}^{\ell} n_j 2^j .$$

Similarly to what we have done before, let now $i' = i - w'$, i.e. i' is the value that i will take after Step 10. The last expression becomes $\sum_{j=0}^{i'-1} e_j 2^j - e_{i'} 2^{i'} + \sum_{j=i'+1}^{\ell} n_j 2^j$, proving (1) invariant also in this case. $\square$

4   Equivalence

Definition 4.1 *For any integer n, denote by w-NAF(n) its w-NAF, i.e. the output of Algorithm 2.1, and by w-LtoR(n) the output of Algorithm 3.1.*

If $n = \sum_{i=0}^{\ell} n_i 2^i$ with $n_i \in \{0,1\}$ and $n_\ell = 1$, let $\mathrm{rev}(n)$ be the integer obtained by reversing the binary representation of n, i.e. $\mathrm{rev}(n) = \sum_{i=0}^{\ell} n_{\ell-i} 2^i$. If n is odd, $\mathrm{rev}(\mathrm{rev}(n)) = n$.

In this section we shall prove the following result.

Theorem 4.2 *For all integers n, and for every value of the parameter $w \ge 2$, the w-NAF of n and the output of Algorithm 3.1 always have the same Hamming weight. In other words $\mathcal{H}(w\text{-NAF}(n)) = \mathcal{H}(w\text{-LtoR}(n))$ for all n and w.*

In particular, the w-LtoR is a recoding of minimal weight among all the w-SDR's, besides the w-NAF.

Proof. The proof is based on a comparison of Algorithms 2.1 and 3.1, showing that they both scan their input in the same way.

At Step 8 of Algorithm 2.1 it is $v \ge 2^w$ (in which case, in fact, $v > 2^w$) if and only if $w = w'$ and $e_{i+w} = 1$. This implies that c in Step 9 is equal to e_{i+w}: In other words c contains the "last bit read" (in the previously formed window). Assuming $e_k = 0$ for $k < 0$, Step 4 can be written as "**if** $(e_i = e_{i-1})$ **then** ...", and in Step 9

$$v = -e_{i+w'-1} 2^{w'-1} + \sum_{j=0}^{w'-2} e_{i+j} 2^j + e_{i-1} .$$

We see that there is no need to store a carry bit to compute the w-NAF, exactly as for the w-LtoR.

In Algorithm 3.1 the test in Step 4 is also a comparison of the bit at the current position with the "last bit read" (becaue the bits between two windows are equal to each other).

We can rewrite Algorithm 3.1 by modifying a few steps as follows:

7.	$w' \leftarrow \min\{w, i+1\}, \; i \leftarrow i - (w' - 1)$
8.	$v \leftarrow -e_{i+w'-1}2^{w'-1} + \displaystyle\sum_{j=0}^{w'-2} e_{i+j}2^j + e_{i-1}.$
9.	$n_{i+s} \leftarrow v/2^s$, where $2^s \| v.$
10.	$i \leftarrow i - 1. \; \} \; \}$

We immediately see that *the expression for the value v is the same for both algorithms.* The expression is deceivingly simple, too: *consider a window of $w' + 1$ consecutive bits; add the least significant one to the number represented by the w' most significant ones but with the highest bit negated.* In fact, the algorithms also scan the bit pattern of the input using the same set of rules!

The algorithms' behaviour can be described by a simple finite state machine that reads the input (in the form of a string of zeros and ones) from a *finite* read-only tape. At the beginning a reading head is placed on one end of the tape and it can only advance towards the other end. The machine stops when the tape has been read completely. We shall also assume that the input string is padded with zeros at both ends in order to properly handle the termination and the cases when $w' < w$, yet using only the parameter w and ignoring the additional variable w'. (Putting $e_{-1} = e_\ell = 0$ in Algorithms 2.1 and 3.1 served the same purpose, yet only for the case $w' = 1$.) The machine has also two registers: c, holding the "last bit read"; and e, containing the bit at the current position, which decides whether a new window has to be formed from the current position. The machine might write something with a second head on a second tape (in fact the algorithms write on an *output* tape), but the details of this operation are not important here.

1.	$c \leftarrow 0$
2.	**while** (tape not finished) **do** {
3.	$e \leftarrow$ bit at current position
4.	**if** $(e = c)$ **then** {
5.	Advance head by one position.
6.	} **else** {
7.	Advance head by $w - 1$ positions.
8.	$c \leftarrow$ bit at current position.
9.	Advance head by one position.
10.	*(Output a non-zero digit.)*
11.	} }

The only difference which concerns us here is the following: Algorithm 2.1 scans the bit string corresponding to the input from right to left, whereas Algorithm 3.1 works left-to-right.

Let us now feed a bit sequence to the first algorithm, and then the reversing of the same bit sequence to the second algorithm. As far as only the number of non-zero digits in the output is concerned, the operations of the two algorithms can be described by two different runs of the machine, where the tape *and* the direction of the head have been reversed between the two runs. Clearly, the machine will perfom in the two runs exactly the same steps and in the same order.

The two algorithms will therefore output the same number of non-zero digits even though the values of the digits may differ. In other words: $\mathcal{H}(w\text{-}\mathrm{NAF}(n)) = \mathcal{H}(w\text{-}\mathrm{LtoR}(\mathrm{rev}(n)))$ and $\mathcal{H}(w\text{-}\mathrm{LtoR}(n)) = \mathcal{H}(w\text{-}\mathrm{NAF}(\mathrm{rev}(n)))$.

Suppose now that the Theorem is false. Then, being the w-NAF a w-SDR of minimal weight (Theorem 2.3), there exists a (without loss of generality) odd positive integer n for which $\mathcal{H}(w\text{-}\mathrm{NAF}(n)) < \mathcal{H}(w\text{-}\mathrm{LtoR}(n))$. This in turn implies that $\mathcal{H}(w\text{-}\mathrm{LtoR}(\mathrm{rev}(n))) < \mathcal{H}(w\text{-}\mathrm{NAF}(\mathrm{rev}(n)))$, a contradiction.   □

Note that not only the individual digits, but also the *lengths* of the w-NAF and of the w-LtoR of the same integer may differ. The 4-NAF and the 4-LtoR of 1971 (the author's year of birth) coincide and are equal to (100000050003). On the other hand, the 4-NAF of 2004 is (1000010000500) whereas its 4-LtoR is (100000005100) – here the two recodings differ but have the same length. Let us consider now 2359, the dreaded CET last minute for submitting papers to SAC (without the seconds): the 4-NAF is (10007000030007) but the 4-LtoR is (50030010001), which is shorter. Of course, in all examples shown, the w-NAF and the w-LtoR have the same Hamming weight. The recodings of 2004 and 2359 are examples of the fact that the w-LtoR does not necessarily satisfy the generalized non-adjacency property **w-NAF-2** of the w-NAF.

5   Additional Remarks

The approach presented in this paper can be used to show the corresponding results for the unsigned sliding window recodings. The only (marginal) difficulty is adapting the proof of the optimality to the right-to-left unsigned sliding window recoding. Then, the result can be interpreted at a purely combinatorial level: the problem is here *grouping and counting substrings of bounded length in strings of two symbols, say 0 and 1, where the zeros do not need to belong to a substring, but all ones must belong to some substring.* Then, it is obvious that the right-to-left and the left-to-right algorithms create the same number of windows on a bit sequence and on its reversing, respectively. From this, as in the concluding arguments of the proof of Theorem 4.2, it follows that they must form the same number of windows also on the same input. Therefore, it does not come as a surprise that Cohen's [4] analysis of the expected Hamming weight for the right-to-left unsigned sliding window method and Rizzo's [21] for the left-to-right method lead to the same result. Here, too, the *lengths* of the expansions can be different.

As another application of these ideas, let us consider the *Joint Sparse Form* (JSF), introduced by Solinas [23] to make *Shamir's trick* more effective for elliptic curves. It is a simultaneous recoding of two integers $n_i = \sum_{j=0}^{\ell} e_{i,j} 2^j$ for $i = 0, 1$ with digit set $\{0, \pm 1\}$, uniquely determined by the following properties:

(JSF-1) Of any three consecutive columns $\left(\begin{smallmatrix} e_{0,j} \\ e_{1,j} \end{smallmatrix} \right)$, at least one is zero.

(JSF-2) Adjacent non-zero bits have the same sign, *i.e.* $e_{i,j+1}e_{i,j} = 0$ or 1.

(JSF-3) If $e_{i,j+1}e_{i,j} \neq 0$ then $e_{1-i,j+1} \neq 0$ and $e_{1-i,j} = 0$.

Here the weight is the number of non-zero columns. The JSF has optimal weight and expected density $1/2$. Note that joining the NAFs of the two given integers produces a representation with expected density $5/9$. The JSF is computed right-to-left, but a left-to-right variant of the same weight exists [9]. Avanzi in [1] lets windows slide over a JSF to further speed-up the computation of linear combinations of elements of a group. The windows are formed distinguishing only between zero and non-zero columns, the actual content of the non-zero columns playing no role. The complexity of this method has been carefully analyzed in [10]. Constructing the windows from, say, right-to-left, produces a minimal number of windows: To prove this claim we reuse the result for the unsigned sliding windows recoding of one integer, in its combinatorial interpretation - where we have two symbols, say 0 and $\star$ in place of every zero, resp. non-zero column. By our arguments the number of windows obtained forming from right-to-left and from left-to-right must be the same. (The same clearly applies also to windows sliding over a joint recoding of more than two integers.)

During the preparation of the final version of the paper the author became aware of the fact that Muir and Stinson [17, 18] independently obtained similar results. In particular, they also proved the minimality of the w-NAF and found an optimal left-to-right recoding with the same digit set. Our Theorem 2.3 is slightly more general and our proofs are shorter. Their left-to-right algorithm is optimal, is different from ours and can output up to two different recodings of the same integer, one of which is equal to that of our algorithm, whereas the other one differs on some of the least significant digits. Okeya et al. [19] also have a left-to-right algorithm, do not prove equivalence to the w-NAF but only give asymptotic density estimates using Markov chains.

The w-NAF and the w-LtoR of an integer n can be computed also letting windows of length w slide (from right to left and from left to right respectively) on the *alternating greedy expansion* [10] of n. This is a representation $n = \sum_{i=0}^{\ell} \varepsilon_i 2^i$ with digits 0 and ± 1 satisfying the following two properties

(AGE-1) If $\varepsilon_j = \varepsilon_i \neq 0$ for some $j < i$, then there is an index k with $j < k < i$ such that
$$\varepsilon_j = -\varepsilon_k = \varepsilon_i.$$

(AGE-2) For $j_* := \min\{j : \varepsilon_j \neq 0\}$ and $j^* := \max\{j : \varepsilon_j \neq 0\}$, we have $\mathrm{sign}(n) = \varepsilon_{j^*} = -\varepsilon_{j_*}$.

The alternating greedy expansion is computed from the binary expansion $n = \sum_{i=0}^{\ell-1} e_i 2^i$ simply putting $\varepsilon_i = e_{i-1} - e_i$, where it is understood $e_{-1} = e_\ell = 0$.

To obtain the w-NAF and the w-LtoR, the windows slide on the alternate greedy expansion distinguishing only between zero and non-zero digits. This interpretation can be found in [11]. Using it and the results on the minimality of sliding window methods on string with two symbols, the fact that these representations have the same Hamming weight follows at once.

Acknowledgment. Many results in this paper have been discovered by the author in November 2002 traveling in a train to Oberwolfach with Tanja Lange and Preda Mihăilescu. The author acknowledges useful discussions with Henri Cohen, Matthijs Coster, Clemens Heuberger, Tanja Lange, Bodo Möller, James Muir, Helmut Prodinger and Ottavio Rizzo, and the support of Simonetta. Gratitude goes also to the anonymous reviewers for their comments.

References

1. R. M. Avanzi. *On the complexity of certain multi-exponentiation techniques in cryptography.* To appear in: J. of Cryptology.
2. D. J. Bernstein. *Pippenger's exponentiation algorithm*. Preprint. Available from http://cr.yp.to
3. A. Brauer. *On addition chains*. Bull. AMS. **45**, pages 736–739 (1939).
4. H. Cohen. *Analysis of the flexible window powering algorithm.* To appear in: J. of Cryptology.
5. H. Cohen, A. Miyaji, and T. Ono. *Efficient elliptic curve exponentiation.* In *Proceedings ICICS'97*, LNCS 1334, 282–290. Springer, 1997.
6. P. Downey, B. Leong, and R. Sethi. *Computing sequences with addition chains*. SIAM J. Computing **10**, 638–646 (1981). MR 82h:68064.
7. P. Erdős. *Remarks on number theory III. On addition chains*. Acta Arith., **6**, 77–81 (1960).
8. D. Gordon. *A Survey of Fast Exponentiation Methods*. J. of Algorithms, **27**, 129–146 (1998).
9. P. J. Grabner, C. Heuberger, and H. Prodinger. *Distribution results for low-weight binary representations for pairs of integers*. Theoretical Computer Science, to appear.
10. P. J. Grabner, C. Heuberger, H. Prodinger, and J. Thuswaldner. *Analysis of linear combination algorithms in cryptography*. Preprint. Available from:
    http://www.opt.math.tu-graz.ac.at/~cheub/publications/Windows.pdf
11. C. Heuberger, R. Katti, H. Prodinger, and X. Ruan. *The Alternating Greedy Expansion and Applications to Left-To-Right Algorithms in Cryptography*. Preprint.
12. M. Joye, and S.-M. Yen. *Optimal left-to-right binary signed-digit recoding*. IEEE Trans. on Comp. **49** (7), 740–748 (2000).
13. M. Joye, and S.-M. Yen. *New Minimal Modified Radix-r Representation*. In *Proceedings of PKC 2002*. LNCS 2274, 375–384. Springer, 2003.
14. N. Koblitz. *Elliptic curve cryptosystems*. Math. Comp. **48** (177), 203–209 (1987).
15. N. Koblitz. *Hyperelliptic cryptosystems*. J. of Cryptology **1**, 139–150 (1989).
16. V. S. Miller. *Use of elliptic curves in cryptography*. In: Proceedings of Crypto '85, LNCS 218, 417–426. Springer, 1986.
17. J. A. Muir, and D. R. Stinson. *Minimality and Other Properties of the Width-w Nonadjacent Form*. Technical Report CORR 2004-08, Centre for Applied Cryptographic Research. Available from http://www.cacr.math.uwaterloo.ca/techreports/2004/
18. J. A. Muir, and D. R. Stinson. *New Minimal Weight Representations for Left-to-Right Window Methods*. Technical Report CACR 2004-03, Centre for Applied Cryptographic Research. Available from http://www.cacr.math.uwaterloo.ca/techreports/2004/
19. K. Okeya, K. Schmidt-Samoa, C. Spahn, and T. Takagi. *Signed Binary Representations Revisited*. Proceedings of Crypto 2004.
20. G. W. Reitwiesner. *Binary arithmetic*. Advances in Computers **1**, 231–308 (1960).

21. O. Rizzo. *On the complexity of the 2^k-ary and of the sliding window algorithms for fast exponentiation*. To appear in: Rivista di Matematica dell'Universitá di Parma.

22. J. A. Solinas. *An improved algorithm for arithmetic on a family of elliptic curves*. In *Proceedings of CRYPTO '97*, LNCS 1294, 357–371. Springer, 1997.

23. J. A. Solinas. *Low-Weight Binary Representations for Pairs of Integers*. Centre for Applied Cryptographic Research, University of Waterloo, Combinatorics and Optimization Research Report **CORR 2001-41**, 2001. Available from:
http://www.cacr.math.uwaterloo.ca/techreports/2001/corr2001-41.ps

24. M. Stam and A. K. Lenstra. *Efficient subgroup exponentiation in quadratic and sixth degree extensions*. In *Proceedings of CHES 2002*. LNCS 2523, 318–332. Springer, 2003.

25. E. G. Thurber. *On addition chains $l(mn) \leq l(n)b$ and lower bounds for $c(r)$*. Duke Math. J. **40** 907–913 (1973).

26. A. C. Yao. *On the evaluation of powers*. SIAM J. Computing **5** 100–103 (1976).

Fast Irreducibility Testing for XTR
Using a Gaussian Normal Basis of
Low Complexity

Soonhak Kwon[1], Chang Hoon Kim[2], and Chun Pyo Hong[2]

[1] Inst. of Basic Science and Dept. of Mathematics, Sungkyunkwan University,
Suwon 440-746, Korea
shkwon@skku.edu
[2] Dept. of Computer and Information Engineering, Daegu University,
Kyungsan 712-714, Korea
chkim@dsp.taegu.ac.kr, cphong@daegu.ac.kr

Abstract. XTR appeared in 2000 is a very promising alternative to elliptic curve cryptosystem. Though the basic idea behind XTR is very elegant and universal, one needs to restrict the primes p such as $p \equiv 2$ (mod 3) for optimal normal bases since it involves many multiplications in $GF(p^2)$. Moreover the restriction $p \equiv 2$ (mod 3) is consistently used to improve the time complexity for irreducibility testing for XTR polynomials. In this paper, we propose that a Gaussian normal basis of type $(2, k)$ for small k can also be used for efficient field arithmetic for XTR when $p \not\equiv 2$ (mod 3). Furthermore we give a new algorithm for fast irreducibility testing and finding a generator of XTR group when $p \equiv 1$ (mod 3). Also we present an explicit generator of XTR group which does not need any irreducibility testing when there is a Gaussian normal basis of type $(2, 3)$ in $GF(p^2)$. We show that our algorithms are simple to implement and the time complexity of our methods are comparable to the best ones proposed so far.

Keywords: XTR cryptosystem, Gauss period, normal basis, roots of unity, cubic residue.

1 Introduction

XTR public key cryptosystem is introduced by Lenstra and Verheul [1], where it is shown that 170-bit XTR realizes a security of 1024-bit RSA. Therefore it is comparable to 160-bit ECC. In a series of paper, Lenstra and Verheul [2,3], and Stam and Lenstra [4,5] discuss various ideas and techniques to speed up XTR implementation where the condition $p \equiv 2$ (mod 3) is used for a faster arithmetic. The crucial steps of XTR are to test whether a given XTR polynomial over $GF(p^2)$ is irreducible or not and to compute a suitable trace of a zero of the polynomial to verify that the root is indeed a generator of XTR group. Stam and Lenstra [5] showed that, when $p \equiv 3$ (mod 4), one can also compute the trace of

H. Handschuh and A. Hasan (Eds.): SAC 2004, LNCS 3357, pp. 144–158, 2005.

the root as effectively as when $p \equiv 2 \pmod 3$. However for a fast irreducibility testing, the condition $p \equiv 2 \pmod 3$ is consistently used in [2,3,4].

Our aim in this paper is to give some evidence that the basic idea of XTR implementation is not so dependent on the choice of primes p. That is, by providing a few alternative bases for different primes p, we show that the field arithmetic in $GF(p^2)$ is as equally fast as the type I optimal normal basis which was originally proposed. Furthermore we present an algorithm for fast irreducibility testing which can be used when $p \equiv 1 \pmod 3$ and show that our algorithm performs as fast as the one proposed in [3,4]. Also we propose a method of finding a generator of XTR group without any irreducibility testing by using a Gaussian normal basis of type $(2,3)$ in $GF(p^2)$. Consequently one has much freedom to choose a prime p for fast XTR implementation. Also some possible known or unknown attacks (for example, variants of Number Field Sieve) which exploit properties of special primes p may be avoided because we can choose either $p \equiv 1 \pmod 3$ or $p \equiv 2 \pmod 3$.

This paper is organized as follows. In section 2, we study basic properties of XTR and Gauss periods. In section 3, We show that efficient field arithmetic can be obtained using a low complexity Gaussian normal basis. In section 4, we suggest a new irreducibility testing with Gauss period technique which can be used when $p \equiv 1 \pmod 3$ and show that our irreducibility testing is significantly faster than the irreducibility testings in [3,4]. In section 5, we propose an algorithm for finding an explicit generator of XTR group which does not need any irreducibility testing when there exists a type $(2,3)$ Gaussian normal basis. In section 6, we compare our methods with previously proposed algorithms. Finally, in section 7, we give concluding remarks.

2   Overview of XTR and Gaussian Normal Basis in $GF(p^n)$

2.1   XTR Cryptosystem

Let p be a prime. For $c \in GF(p^2)$, define a cubic polynomial $F(c,X) = x^3 - cX^2 + c^pX - 1$. It is well known [1] that $F(c,X)$ is irreducible over $GF(p^2)$ if and only if all zeros of $F(c,X)$ have order dividing $p^2 - p + 1$ and > 3. When $F(c,X)$ is irreducible, letting $h \in GF(p^6)$ be any zero of $F(c,X)$, we define c_n for any n as the trace of h^n over $GF(p^2)$, i.e. $c_n = Tr(h^n) = h^n + h^{np^2} + h^{np^4} = h^n + h^{n(p-1)} + h^{-np}$. Then the roots of $F(c_n, X)$ are h^n, h^{np^2}, h^{np^4}, and for any i and j, one has the following recurrence relation,

$$c_{i+j} = c_i c_j - c_j^p c_{i-j} + c_{i-2j}. \tag{1}$$

Let q be a prime such that q divides $p^2 - p + 1$. To realize a security comparable to 1024 bit RSA, it is suggested to choose primes $p, q \approx 170$ bit with $p \geq q$. Then $GF(p^6)$ has a unique multiplicative subgroup G of order q such that G is not contained in any proper subfield of $GF(p^6)$. XTR cryptosystem is based on the assumption that if $g \in GF(p^6)$ is a generator of G where both p and q are sufficiently large, solving $Tr(g^n) = c$ for unknown n is very difficult. It is shown [1] that finding such n is as difficult as solving a discrete logarithm problem in $GF(p^6)$. On the other hand, basic manipulations such as choosing a key of XTR are effectively done. Moreover one easily computes $Tr(g^n)$ for given $Tr(g)$ and n using the recurrence relation (1). Therefore efficient multiplication in $GF(p^2)$ is a core of XTR speed up. When one chooses $p \equiv 2 \pmod 3$, there exists a type I ONB (optimal normal basis) for $GF(p^2)$ over $GF(p)$ and using this basis, one has the time complexity for the field arithmetic in $GF(p^2)$ as follows [4].

Lemma 1. *Let* $p \equiv 2 \pmod 3$ *and let* $\{\alpha, \alpha^p\}$ *be a type I ONB (optimal normal basis) over* $GF(p)$ *where* α *is a zero of* $X^2 + X + 1$. *Then*

1. *Squaring in* $GF(p^2)$ *costs two multiplications in* $GF(p)$.
2. *Computing* $xy \in GF(p^2)$ *costs 2.5 multiplications in* $GF(p)$.
3. *Computing* $xz - z^p y \in GF(p^2)$ *costs 3 multiplications in* $GF(p)$.

We assumed in the above lemma that small number of additions in $GF(p^2)$ is free. Also it is assumed that the cost of one multiplication without reduction of two $x, y \approx p$ and one reduction of $x \approx p^2 \pmod p$ are roughly the same.

2.2   Gauss Periods of Type (n, k) in $GF(p^n)$

The theory of Gauss periods has been studied by S. Gao, J. von zur Gathen, D. Panario, I. Shparlinski, S. Vanstone, and many other people. We will briefly review the theory of Gauss periods and the corresponding Gaussian normal bases [16,17]. Let n, k be positive integers such that $r = nk + 1$ is a prime different from p. Let $K = \langle \tau \rangle$ be a unique subgroup of order k in $GF(r)^\times$. Let β be a primitive rth root of unity in $GF(p^{nk})$. The following element

$$\alpha = \sum_{j=0}^{k-1} \beta^{\tau^j} \tag{2}$$

is called a Gauss period of type (n, k) or k in $GF(p^n)$. Let $ord_r p$ be the order of $p \pmod r$ and assume $gcd(nk/ord_r p, n) = 1$. Then it is well known that α is a normal element in $GF(p^n)$. That is, letting $\alpha_i = \alpha^{p^i}$ for $0 \le i \le n - 1$, $\{\alpha_0, \alpha_1, \alpha_2, \cdots, \alpha_{n-1}\}$ is a basis for $GF(p^n)$ over $GF(p)$. It is usually called a Gaussian normal basis of type (n, k) or k in $GF(p^n)$. Since $K = \langle \tau \rangle$ is a subgroup of order k in $GF(r)^\times$, a cyclic group of order nk, the quotient group $GF(r)^\times / K$ is also a cyclic group of order n and the generator of the group is pK. Therefore we have a coset decomposition of $GF(r)^\times$ as a disjoint union,

$$GF(r)^\times = K_0 \cup K_1 \cup K_2 \cdots \cup K_{n-1}, \tag{3}$$

where $K_i = p^i K, 0 \le i \le n - 1$. Note that any element in $GF(r)^\times$ is uniquely written as $\tau^s p^t$ for some $0 \le s \le k - 1$ and $0 \le t \le n - 1$.

Now for each $0 \le i \le n - 1$, we have

$$\alpha\alpha_i = \sum_{s=0}^{k-1} \beta^{\tau^s} \sum_{t=0}^{k-1} \beta^{\tau^t p^i}$$

$$= \sum_{s=0}^{k-1}\sum_{t=0}^{k-1} \beta^{\tau^s(1+\tau^{t-s}p^i)} = \sum_{s=0}^{k-1}\sum_{t=0}^{k-1} \beta^{\tau^s(1+\tau^t p^i)}. \tag{4}$$

There are unique $0 \le u \le k-1$ and $0 \le v \le n-1$ such that $1+\tau^u p^v = 0 \in GF(r)$, that is, $-1 = \tau^u p^v \in K_v$. If $t \ne u$ or $i \ne v$, then we have $1 + \tau^t p^i \in K_{\sigma(t,i)}$ for some $0 \le \sigma(t,i) \le n - 1$ depending on t and i, and we may write $1 + \tau^t p^i = \tau^{t'} p^{\sigma(t,i)}$ for some t'. Therefore when $i \ne v$,

$$\alpha\alpha_i = \sum_{s=0}^{k-1}\sum_{t=0}^{k-1} \beta^{\tau^s(1+\tau^t p^i)} = \sum_{s=0}^{k-1}\sum_{t=0}^{k-1} \beta^{\tau^s(\tau^{t'} p^{\sigma(t,i)})}$$

$$= \sum_{t=0}^{k-1}\sum_{s=0}^{k-1} \beta^{\tau^{s+t'} p^{\sigma(t,i)}} = \sum_{t=0}^{k-1} \alpha^{p^{\sigma(t,i)}} = \sum_{t=0}^{k-1} \alpha_{\sigma(t,i)}. \tag{5}$$

Also when $i = v$,

$$\alpha\alpha_v = \sum_{s=0}^{k-1}\sum_{t=0}^{k-1} \beta^{\tau^s(1+\tau^t p^v)}$$

$$= \sum_{t \ne u}\sum_{s=0}^{k-1} \beta^{\tau^s(\tau^{t'} p^{\sigma(t,v)})} + \sum_{s=0}^{k-1} \beta^{\tau^s(1+\tau^u p^v)}$$

$$= \sum_{t \ne u}\sum_{s=0}^{k-1} \beta^{\tau^{s+t'} p^{\sigma(t,v)}} + \sum_{s=0}^{k-1} 1$$

$$= \sum_{t \ne u} \alpha^{p^{\sigma(t,v)}} + k = \sum_{t \ne u} \alpha_{\sigma(t,v)} + k. \tag{6}$$

Thus $\alpha\alpha_i$ is computed by the sum of at most k basis elements in $\{\alpha_0, \alpha_1, \cdots, \alpha_{n-1}\}$ for $i \ne v$ and $\alpha\alpha_v$ is computed by the sum of at most $k - 1$ basis elements and the constant term $k \in GF(p)$.

3   Efficient Field Arithmetic in $GF(p^2)$ with Gaussian Normal Basis

XTR cryptosystem involves many multiplications in $GF(p^2)$. Consequently, an appropriate choice of a basis for $GF(p^2)$ over $GF(p)$ is necessary. Our purpose is to show that a Gaussian normal basis of type $(2, k)$ for small k can be used for a fast arithmetic of XTR. Recall that a type $(2, 1)$ Gauss period is used in [1] where the corresponding irreducible polynomial is $X^2 + X + 1$, and such basis exists if and only if $p \equiv 2 \pmod 3$. Similar statements can be derived for any Gauss period of type $(2, k)$. In other words, a necessary and sufficient condition for the existence of such basis will be determined and the corresponding irreducible polynomial will also be given.

For XTR, We have $n = 2$ and $2k + 1 = r$ is a prime. Thus the possible choices of k are $k = 1, 2, 3, 5, 6, 8, 9, 11, \cdots$. From the formula (3), the coset decomposition of $GF(r)^\times$ is $GF(r)^\times = K \cup pK$ where $K = \langle \tau \rangle$ is a unique subgroup of $GF(r)^\times$ of order k.

Lemma 2. *Let $2k + 1 = r$ be a prime. Then a Gaussian normal basis $\{\alpha, \alpha^p\}$ of type $(2, k)$ exists in $GF(p^2)$ if and only if p is a quadratic nonresidue $\pmod r$. We have $\alpha + \alpha^p = -1$ and $\alpha\alpha^p = \frac{k+1}{2}$ if k is odd, $-\frac{k}{2}$ if k is even. That is, the corresponding irreducible polynomial of α is $X^2 + X + \frac{k+1}{2}$ if k is odd and $X^2 + X - \frac{k}{2}$ if k is even.*

Proof. It is easy to show that the given Gauss period forms a normal basis if and only if $gcd(2k/ord_r p, 2) = 1$. This condition is equivalent to say that p is an odd power of a primitive root $\pmod r$, i.e. p is a quadratic nonresidue $\pmod r$. Recall that $K = \langle \tau \rangle$ is a unique subgroup of order k in $GF(r)^\times$ and $GF(r)^\times = K \cup pK$ is a disjoint union. In particular $p \notin K$. Also from $\alpha = \sum_{j=0}^{k-1} \beta^{\tau^j}$ where β is a primitive rth root of unity over $GF(p)$, we have

$$\alpha + \alpha^p = \sum_{j=0}^{k-1} \beta^{\tau^j} + \sum_{j=0}^{k-1} \beta^{p\tau^j} = \sum_{t \in GF(r)^\times} \beta^t = \frac{\beta^r - 1}{\beta - 1} - 1 = -1. \tag{7}$$

Now from the formulas (5) and (6), we have the followings depending on whether $-1 \in K$ or $-1 \in pK$,

$$\alpha\alpha^p = \sum_{t=0}^{k-1} \alpha_{\sigma(t,1)} \quad or \quad \alpha\alpha^p = \sum_{t \neq u} \alpha_{\sigma(t,1)} + k, \tag{8}$$

where $\alpha_0 = \alpha, \alpha_1 = \alpha^p$, and $1 + \tau^t p \in p^{\sigma(t,1)} K$ with $\sigma(t, 1) = 0$ or 1. Let us consider the case $k = odd$ first. In this case, we have $-1 \in pK$ and $u \pmod k$ in the second equation of (8) is a unique value satisfying $1 + \tau^u p = 0$ in $GF(r)$. Using this, we have the following for any $j \not\equiv 0 \pmod k$,

$$\frac{1 + \tau^{u-j} p}{1 + \tau^{u+j} p} = \frac{1 - \tau^{-j}}{1 - \tau^j} = -\tau^{-j} = \tau^{u-j} p \in pK. \tag{9}$$

In other words, $1 + \tau^{u-j} p$ and $1 + \tau^{u+j} p$ are in different cosets for any $j \not\equiv 0 \pmod k$. Since $\{1 + \tau^{u+j} p | -\frac{k-1}{2} \leq j \leq \frac{k-1}{2}\} = \{1 + \tau^i p | 0 \leq i \leq k - 1\}$, we find

$$\alpha\alpha^p = \frac{k-1}{2}(\alpha + \alpha^p) + k = \frac{-k+1}{2} + k = \frac{k+1}{2}. \tag{10}$$

Now suppose that $k = even$. Then $-1 \in K$ and $1 + \tau^j p \neq 0 \in GF(r)$ for any j. Also we have

$$1 + \tau^j p = \tau^j p (1 + \tau^{i-j} p), \tag{11}$$

where $i \pmod{k}$ is a unique value satisfying $p^2 = \tau^{-i} \in K$. In particular we have $j \not\equiv i - j \pmod{k}$. Thus $1 + \tau^j p$ and $1 + \tau^{i-j} p$ are in different cosets for any j. By observing the residue system $\pmod{k}$ can be written as a disjoint union

$$\{0, 1, 2, \cdots, k-1\} = \{j_1, i-j_1\} \cup \{j_2, i-j_2\} \cup \cdots \cup \{j_{\frac{k}{2}}, i-j_{\frac{k}{2}}\}, \quad (12)$$

we easily deduce

$$\alpha\alpha^p = \frac{k}{2}(\alpha + \alpha^p) = -\frac{k}{2}. \quad (13)$$

$\square$

The case $k = 1$ is used in original XTR where a type I ONB exists if and only if $p \equiv 2 \pmod{3}$ with the corresponding irreducible polynomial $X^2 + X + 1$. Using a Gaussian normal basis $\{\alpha, \alpha^p\}$ of type $(2, k)$ where p is a quadratic nonresidue $\pmod{r}$ with $r = 2k + 1$, we have roughly the same computational complexity of the field arithmetic in $GF(p^2)$. That is,

Lemma 3. *If a Gaussian normal basis of type $(2, k)$ is used for small k, Lemma 1 is also true.*

Proof. This is a straightforward computation using Lemma 2. For example, letting $x = x_0\alpha + x_1\alpha^p$ and $y = y_0\alpha + y_1\alpha^p$ in $GF(p^2)$, the multiplication of xy is as follows when $k = odd$

$$xy = \{(x_0 - x_1)(y_0 - y_1)\frac{k+1}{2} - x_0 y_0\}\alpha + \{(x_0 - x_1)(y_0 - y_1)\frac{k+1}{2} - x_1 y_1\}\alpha^p, \quad (14)$$

and when $k = even$

$$xy = -\{(x_0 - x_1)(y_0 - y_1)\frac{k}{2} + x_0 y_0\}\alpha - \{(x_0 - x_1)(y_0 - y_1)\frac{k}{2} + x_1 y_1\}\alpha^p. \quad (15)$$

Thus the computation $xy \in GF(p^2)$ needs 3 multiplications (without reduction) of integers $\approx p$ and 2 reductions $\pmod{p}$ of integers $\approx p^2$. Therefore the total cost is 2.5 multiplications in $GF(p)$. Here we assumed that k is small and a small number of additions in $GF(p)$ is negligible compared with one multiplication in $GF(p)$. Also letting $z = z_0\alpha + z_1\alpha^p \in GF(p^2)$, we have the value of $xz - yz^p$ as

$$\{(s\frac{k+1}{2} - x_0)z_0 - (s\frac{k+1}{2} - y_0)z_1\}\alpha + \{(s\frac{k+1}{2} + y_1)z_0 - (s\frac{k+1}{2} + x_1)z_1\}\alpha^p, \quad (16)$$

when $k = odd$, and we have

$$\{(s\frac{k}{2} + y_0)z_1 - (s\frac{k}{2} + x_0)z_0\}\alpha + \{(s\frac{k}{2} - x_1)z_1 - (s\frac{k}{2} - y_1)z_0\}\alpha^p, \quad (17)$$

when $k = even$, where $s = x_0 - x_1 + y_0 - y_1$. Thus the cost of $xz - yz^p \in GF(p^2)$ is 4 integer multiplications plus 2 reductions $\pmod{p}$, which is approximately 3 multiplications in $GF(p)$.

$\square$

It is not difficult to see that, with a Gaussian normal basis of type k, the number of necessary additions for each of the basic operations increases roughly in proportion to $\log_2 \frac{k+1}{2}$ or $\log_2 \frac{k}{2}$ depending on whether $k = odd$ or $k = even$. The exact number of necessary additions with a type k Gaussian normal basis is shown in Table 1 in section 6.

Note that so far we have only considered classical Gauss periods and their implications. However one may repeat the same arguments as in Lemma 2 and 3 based on the more general Gauss periods [20] successfully developed by S. Feisel, J. von zur Gathen, and M. Shokrollahi. Since the irreducible polynomial of the (classical or general) Gauss period in $GF(p^2)$ is of the form $X^2 + aX + b$ and since the linear coefficient a contributes twice of a computational cost of the constant term b, one may not have a significant advantage of general Gauss periods over classical Gauss periods in this case.

4   New Irreducibility Testing and Finding a Generator of XTR Group

For a proper implementation of XTR, we need to find a generator of XTR group. That is, an element g of prime order q with $q|p^2 - p + 1$ should be determined. This g is a zero of the polynomial $F(c, X) = X^3 - cX^2 + c^p X - 1$ where $c = g + g^{p^2} + g^{p^4}$ and it can be found as follows. First one randomly chooses $c \in GF(p^2)$ until one finds $F(c, X)$ which is irreducible over $GF(p^2)$. Here we need a fast irreducibility testing. Next, from an irreducible $F(c, X)$, one computes $c_{(p^2-p+1)/q}$ using the recurrence relation (1). Here we need an efficient field arithmetic such as Lemma 1 or 3. If $c_{(p^2-p+1)/q} \neq 3$ (which is very probable), then the roots of $F(c_{(p^2-p+1)/q}, X)$ have order q.

In section 3, we showed that, with Gaussian normal bases of low weight, the computation of $c_{(p^2-p+1)/q}$ or c_i for any i can be done as equally fast as with the optimal normal basis of type I in [3,4]. On the other hand, the best of a few irreducibility testings of $F(c, X)$ is related to an irreducibility testing of a certain cubic polynomial over $GF(p)$ [3]. And the condition $p \equiv 2 \pmod 3$ is wisely used to determine whether a given cubic polynomial over $GF(p)$ is irreducible or not. If one follows the method in [3] in the case of $p \equiv 1 \pmod 3$, one instantly encounters with the problem of determining whether an element of the form $\frac{-f_0 \pm \sqrt{\Delta}}{2}$ is a cubic residue in $GF(p^2)$ or not, where Δ and f_0 are certain integers determined from the coefficients of the cubic polynomial and Δ is a quadratic residue $\pmod p$. It seems that the computational cost of determining whether $\frac{-f_0 \pm \sqrt{\Delta}}{2}$ is a cubic residue in $GF(p^2)$ when Δ is a quadratic residue $\pmod p$ is not so cheap compared with the computational cost of determining whether $\frac{-f_0 \pm \sqrt{\Delta}}{2}$ is a cubic residue in $GF(p^2)$ when Δ is a quadratic nonresidue $\pmod p$ (See [3].). So we devise another method which combines the idea of cubic residue $\pmod p$ and the idea [2] of presenting an explicit generator of XTR group without irreducibility testing.

Let us consider the following two irreducible polynomials over $GF(p)$,

$$X^2 + X + a = (X - \alpha)(X - \alpha^p) \quad \text{and} \quad X^3 - b = (X - \gamma)(X - \gamma^p)(X - \gamma^{p^2}), \quad (18)$$

where α and γ are zeros the corresponding polynomials. A necessary condition for the irreducibility of $X^3 - b$ is $p \equiv 1 \pmod 3$. So throughout this section we assume $p \equiv 1 \pmod 3$.

Lemma 4. *Let $s \neq 0 \in GF(p)$ and let $g = (s + \alpha\gamma)^{\frac{p^6 - 1}{p^2 - p + 1}}$. Then $X^3 - Tr(g)X^2 + Tr(g)^p X - 1$ is irreducible over $GF(p^2)$, where $Tr(g) = g + g^{p^2} + g^{p^4}$ is the trace of g over $GF(p^2)$. Moreover letting $w \equiv b^{\frac{p-1}{3}} \pmod p$, $Tr(g)$ has the following expression*

$$\frac{-3}{P(-s)} \{ (s^6 + b\{w(4a - 1) - a\}s^3 + a^3 b)\alpha$$

$$+ (s^6 - b\{w(4a - 1) + 5a - 1\}s^3 + a^3 b)\alpha^p \},$$

where $P(X) = X^6 + b(1 - 3a)X^3 + a^3 b^2$.

Proof. Note that $g = (s + \alpha\gamma)^{\frac{p^6 - 1}{p^2 - p + 1}} = (s + \alpha\gamma)^{p^4 + p^3 - p - 1}$. Clearly the order of g divides $p^2 - p + 1$. It is well known [1] that g has an order > 3 and dividing $p^2 - p + 1$ if and only if the corresponding cubic polynomial is irreducible over $GF(p^2)$. Therefore to prove the irreducibility of $X^3 - Tr(g)X^2 + Tr(g)^p X - 1$, it is enough to show that g has an order > 3. Suppose that g has an order ≤ 3. Then since $p \equiv 1 \pmod 3$, we have $g^p = g$. Thus

$$(s + \alpha\gamma)^{p^5 + p^4 - p^2 - p} = (s + \alpha\gamma)^{p^4 + p^3 - p - 1}, \quad (19)$$

which can be written as

$$(s + \alpha^p \gamma^{p^2})(s + \alpha\gamma) = (s + \alpha^p \gamma)(s + \alpha\gamma^{p^2}). \quad (20)$$

Cancelling common terms of both sides of (20) and since $s \not\equiv 0 \pmod p$, we get

$$(\alpha - \alpha^p)(\gamma - \gamma^{p^2}) = 0, \quad (21)$$

which is a contradiction because the polynomials in (18) are irreducible over $GF(p)$. Now let us calculate $Tr(g)$. Let

$$P(X) = \prod_{j=0}^{5} (X - (\alpha\gamma)^{p^j}) = X^6 + b(1 - 3a)X^3 + a^3 b^2 \quad (22)$$

be the irreducible polynomial of $\alpha\gamma$ over $GF(p)$. From this one easily get

$$(s + \alpha\gamma)^{-p-1} = \frac{1}{P(-s)}(s + \alpha\gamma^p)(s + \alpha\gamma^{p^2})(s + \alpha^p\gamma)(s + \alpha^p\gamma^{p^2})$$

$$= \frac{1}{P(-s)}\{s^4 - (\alpha\gamma + \alpha^p\gamma^p)s^3 + (\alpha^{2p}\gamma^{1+p^2} + \alpha^2\gamma^{p+p^2} + a\gamma^{1+p})s^2$$

$$- a(\alpha^p\gamma^{2+p^2} + \alpha\gamma^{2p+p^2})s + a^2 b\gamma^{p^2}\}.$$

$$(23)$$

Also we have

$$(s + \alpha\gamma)^{p^4+p^3} = (s + \alpha\gamma^p)(s + \alpha^p\gamma) = s^2 + (\alpha\gamma^p + \alpha^p\gamma)s + a\gamma^{1+p}. \quad (24)$$

On the other hand, from the equation $X^3 - b = 0$ in (18), we get $Tr(\gamma^j) = 0$ for any $j \not\equiv 0 \pmod 3$. This is obvious from the third order linear recurrence relation arising from the equation or one may directly show as follows. Letting $j = 3j' + j''$ with $j'' = 1, 2$, we have $Tr(\gamma^j) = Tr(\gamma^{3j'}\gamma^{j''}) = b^{j'}Tr(\gamma^{j''}) = 0$ since γ is a zero of the irreducible polynomial $X^3 - b$. From (23) and (24), though the complete expression of $(s+\alpha\gamma)^{p^4+p^3-p-1}$ is a little bit complicated, it is easy to see that the coefficients of s, s^2, s^4 and s^5 of $(s+\alpha\gamma)^{p^4+p^3-p-1}$ are polynomials of γ where each of the exponents of γ is not divisible by 3. For example, the coefficient of s^5 is $\alpha\gamma^p + \alpha^p\gamma - \alpha\gamma - \alpha^p\gamma^p$. Therefore the trace of these terms are 0 by the previous remark. Now since $w = b^{\frac{p-1}{3}} \in GF(p)$ and using

$$\gamma^{2+p} = \gamma^{2p+p^2} = bw, \quad \gamma^{1+2p} = \gamma^{2+p^2} = bw^2 \quad (25)$$

in the expression of the multiplication of the equations (23) and (24), we find that the coefficient of s^3 of $(s + \alpha\gamma)^{p^4+p^3-p-1}$ is

$$b\{w(-4a + 1) + a\}\alpha + b\{w(4a - 1) + 5a - 1\}\alpha^p. \quad (26)$$

Therefore the trace of $g = (s + \alpha\gamma)^{p^4+p^3-p-1}$ over $GF(p^2)$ is

$$\frac{-3}{P(-s)}\{(s^6 + b\{w(4a - 1) - a\}s^3 + a^3b)\alpha$$
$$+ (s^6 - b\{w(4a - 1) + 5a - 1\}s^3 + a^3b)\alpha^p\}. \quad (27)$$

$\square$

Lemma 4 implies that, if the irreducible polynomials $X^2 + X + a$ and $X^3 - b$ are given, one can find an element $Tr(g)$ where g is of order > 3 and dividing $p^2 - p + 1$. In view of Lemma 2, we may take $a = \frac{k+1}{2}$ if $k = odd$ and $a = -\frac{k}{2}$ if $k = even$. A Gaussian normal basis of type $(2, k)$, or simply of type k, in $GF(p^2)$ exists if and only if p is a quadratic nonresidue $\pmod{2k + 1}$. For example, there exists a Gaussian normal basis of type 2 if and only if $p \equiv 2, 3 \pmod 5$, type 3 if and only if $p \equiv 3, 5, 6 \pmod 7$, type 5 if and only if $p \equiv 2, 6, 7, 8, 10 \pmod{11}$, etc. On the other hand, $X^3 - b$ is irreducible over $GF(p)$ if and only if b is a cubic nonresidue $\pmod p$, that is, $b^{\frac{p-1}{3}} \not\equiv 1 \pmod p$. The cost of computing $b^{\frac{p-1}{3}}$ is $1.8 \log_2 p$ multiplications in $GF(p)$ if one use a square and multiply method using the same assumption in [3,4] saying that the cost of one squaring is roughly 80 percent of the cost of one multiplication. Note that one can reduce the cost of computation if one use more sophisticated argument on addition chains. For a simple example, let $\frac{p-1}{3} = \sum_{i=0}^{l-1} s_i 4^i$ be a 4-ary expansion of $\frac{p-1}{3}$ with $l = \lfloor \log_4 \frac{p-1}{3} \rfloor + 1$. Then a 4-ary window method says that

$$b^{\frac{p-1}{3}} = b^{\sum_{i=0}^{l-1} s_i 4^i} = (\cdots(((b^{s_{l-1}})^4 b^{s_{l-2}})^4 b^{s_{l-3}})^4 \cdots)^4 b^{s_0} \quad (28)$$

can be computed with $2.6 \log_4 p = 1.3 \log_2 p$ multiplications in $GF(p)$ using the precomputed values of b^2 and b^3. Please refer to [18,19] for more advanced window techniques and tricks of additions chains. Since one thirds of integers b are cubic residues (mod p), using the above mentioned 4-ary window method, it is expected that after $1.95 \log_2 p$ multiplications one finds a cubic nonresidue b (mod p) and an element g of order dividing $p^2 - p + 1$ with the irreducible polynomial $X^3 - Tr(g)X + Tr(g)^p X - 1$ over $GF(p^2)$. Now let q be a prime dividing $p^2 - p + 1$. Then $g^{\frac{p^2-p+1}{q}}$ is an element of order q if and only if $Tr(g^{\frac{p^2-p+1}{q}}) \neq 3$. One may use the recurrence relation (1) to compute the trace value and in view of Lemma 3, the computational cost is $7 \log_2(\frac{p^2-p+1}{q})$ multiplications in $GF(p)$.

Also the probability that $g^{\frac{p^2-p+1}{q}} = (s + \alpha\gamma)^{\frac{p^6-1}{q}}$ is an element of order q, for a randomly chosen s, is expected to $(p^6 - 1)(1 - \frac{1}{q})/(p^6 - 1) = \frac{q-1}{q}$. Of course, this is not really correct unless we assume that the choice of $s + \alpha\gamma$ is random in $GF(p^6)^\times$. Since q is very large, the (error) probability that $g^{\frac{p^2-p+1}{q}} = 1$ is extremely small from a practical point of view as is already explained in [2]. Therefore we have the following result.

Theorem 5. *Let $p \equiv 1$ (mod 3) and suppose that a Gaussian normal basis of type $(2, k)$ is given in $GF(p^2)$ for small k. Then one can find a generator of the XTR group, a trace of an element of order q, using approximately $1.95 \log_2 p + 7 \log_2(\frac{p^2-p+1}{q})$ multiplications in $GF(p)$ on average.*

Note that, compared with previous results, the computational cost of our algorithm has been improved from $2.7 \log_2 p + 7 \log_2(\frac{p^2-p+1}{q})$ in [3,4] to $1.95 \log_2 p + 7 \log_2(\frac{p^2-p+1}{q})$. This is because the methods in [3,4] have no other choice but to use the trace map $GF(p^2) \rightarrow GF(p)$ to avoid an exponentiation in $GF(p^2)$ with the condition $p \equiv 2$ (mod 3) during the irreducibility testing, while our method needs an exponentiation in $GF(p)$ not in $GF(p^2)$. It should be mentioned that our factor 1.95 can be improved further if we use more refined window techniques. Another good point (or the difference) is that our algorithm is applied to the primes p with $p \equiv 1$ (mod 3), whereas only the case $p \equiv 2$ (mod 3) is dealt in [3,4].

5   Gaussian Normal Basis of Type $(2, 3)$ and an Explicit Generator of XTR Group Without Irreducibility Testing

In section 4, assuming $p \equiv 1$ (mod 3), we explained how one can find a generator of XTR group where an explicit value of $b^{\frac{p-1}{3}}$ and the irreducibility of $X^3 - b$ need to be determined. However, as is already mentioned in [2], an irreducibility testing may be omitted if one has an explicit irreducible polynomial of degree 6 over $GF(p)$ with corresponding roots of low multiplicative order. For example, Lenstra and Verheul [2] used a primitive 9th root of unity with the irreducible polynomial $X^6 - X^3 + 1$ and a type I ONB. A necessary and sufficient condition for the irreducibility of $X^6 - X^3 + 1$ over $GF(p)$ is $p \equiv 2, 5 \pmod 9$, or equivalently $ord_9 p = 6$. In this section, we show that a similar argument also works if we use a primitive 7th root of unity with a Gaussian normal basis of type $(2, 3)$ over $GF(p)$. Our method is applicable when $p \equiv 3, 5 \pmod 7$ and no restriction of $p \pmod 3$ is necessary.

Let $\{\alpha, \alpha^p\}$ be a Gaussian normal basis of type $(2, 3)$, or more simply type 3, in $GF(p^2)$. That is, $\alpha = \beta + \beta^2 + \beta^4$ where β is a primitive 7th root of unity over $GF(p)$ and $\langle 2 \rangle$ is a unique multiplicative subgroup of order 3 in $GF(7)^\times$. Such basis exists if and only if p is a quadratic nonresidue $\pmod 7$, i.e. $p \equiv 3, 5, 6 \pmod 7$. Note that β is a zero of the polynomial

$$P(X) = \frac{X^7 - 1}{X - 1} = X^6 + X^5 + X^4 + X^3 + X^2 + X + 1. \qquad (29)$$

The above polynomial is irreducible over $GF(p)$ if and only if p is a primitive root $\pmod 7$, i.e. $p \equiv 3, 5 \pmod 7$. Therefore from now on, we assume $p \equiv 3, 5 \pmod 7$ to use the irreducibility of the polynomial in (29). Then using the relation

$$\{1, p^2, p^4\} \equiv \{1, 2, 4\} \pmod 7, \qquad \{p, p^3, p^5\} \equiv \{3, 5, 6\} \pmod 7, \qquad (30)$$

we get

$$\alpha = \beta + \beta^2 + \beta^4 = \beta + \beta^{p^2} + \beta^{p^4} = Tr(\beta), \qquad (31)$$

and

$$\alpha^p = \beta^3 + \beta^5 + \beta^6 = \beta^{p^3} + \beta^{p^5} + \beta^{p^6} = Tr(\beta^p). \qquad (32)$$

Lemma 6. *Let $s \neq 0, \pm 1 \in GF(p)$ and let $g = (s + \beta)^{\frac{p^6 - 1}{p^2 - p + 1}}$. Then $X^3 - Tr(g)X^2 + Tr(g)^p X - 1$ is irreducible over $GF(p^2)$, where $Tr(g) = g + g^{p^2} + g^{p^4}$ is the trace of g over $GF(p^2)$. Moreover $Tr(g)$ has the following expression if $p \equiv 3 \pmod 7$,*

$$Tr(g) = \frac{-1}{P(-s)} \{(s^3 - s)(3s^3 - 3s^2 - s - 2)\alpha + ((s^2 - s)(3s^4 - 4s^2 - 4s - 6) - 1)\alpha^p\},$$

and if $p \equiv 5 \pmod 7$,

$$Tr(g) = \frac{-1}{P(-s)} \{(s^3 - s)(3s^3 - 3s^2 - s - 2)\alpha^p + ((s^2 - s)(3s^4 - 4s^2 - 4s - 6) - 1)\alpha\}.$$

Proof. It is enough to show that g has an order > 3 to show the irreducibility of the cubic polynomial because g has an order dividing $p^2 - p + 1$. Recall that, from (29),

$$P(X) = X^6 + X^5 + X^4 + X^3 + X^2 + X + 1 \qquad (33)$$

is irreducible over $GF(p)$ if and only if $p \equiv 3, 5 \pmod 7$. If the order of g is ≤ 3, then using $g^{p^2 - 1} = 1$, we get

$$(s + \beta)^{p^6 + p^5 - p^3 - p^2} = (s + \beta)^{p^4 + p^3 - p - 1}, \qquad (34)$$

which is reexpressed as

$$(s + \beta)^{p^5 + p + 2} = (s + \beta)^{p^4 + 2p^3 + p^2}. \tag{35}$$

Using $\beta^7 = 1$ and $p \equiv 3, 5 \pmod 7$, we may express both sides of the above equations as polynomials of β of degree < 7. Comparing the coefficients of β^j, $0 \leq j \leq 6$, we get a contradiction. Now let us calculate the trace value of $g = (s + \beta)^{p^4 + p^3 - p - 1}$. The element g can be expressed as follows depending on whether $p \equiv 3 \pmod 7$ or $p \equiv 5 \pmod 7$,

$$g_0 = \frac{(s + \beta^4)(s + \beta^6)}{(s + \beta^3)(s + \beta)}, \quad or \quad g_1 = \frac{(s + \beta^2)(s + \beta^6)}{(s + \beta^5)(s + \beta)}. \tag{36}$$

Since it is trivial to show $Tr(g_0^p) = Tr(g_1)$ and $Tr(g_1^p) = Tr(g_0)$ regardless of the choice of $p \equiv 3, 5 \pmod 7$, we only need to find the trace in the case $p \equiv 3 \pmod 7$. One easily get

$$(s + \beta)^{-p-1} = \frac{1}{P(-s)}(s + \beta^2)(s + \beta^4)(s + \beta^5)(s + \beta^6)$$

$$= \frac{1}{P(-s)}\{s^4 - (1 + \beta + \beta^3)s^3 - \beta^5 s^2 - (1 + \beta^2 + \beta^3)s + \beta^3\}. \tag{37}$$

Also we have

$$(s + \beta)^{p^4 + p^3} = (s + \beta^4)(s + \beta^6) = s^2 + (\beta^4 + \beta^6)s + \beta^3. \tag{38}$$

Therefore g can be written as

$$g = (s + \beta)^{\frac{p^6 - 1}{p^2 - p + 1}} = (s + \beta)^{p^4 + p^3 - p - 1}$$

$$= \frac{1}{P(-s)}\{s^6 + (\beta^2 + 2\beta^4 + \beta^5 + 2\beta^6)s^5 \tag{39}$$

$$+ (-1 + \beta + 2\beta^3 - \beta^5)s^4 + (1 + 2\beta + 2\beta^5 + \beta^6)s^3$$

$$+ (-\beta + 2\beta^3 + \beta^5 - \beta^6)s^2 + (2 + \beta + 2\beta^2 + \beta^4)s + \beta^6\}.$$

Taking the trace of g and using the relation (31) and (32), we get

$$Tr(g) = \frac{-1}{P(-s)}\{(s^3 - s)(3s^3 - 3s^2 - s - 2)\alpha \tag{40}$$

$$+ ((s^2 - s)(3s^4 - 4s^2 - 4s - 6) - 1)\alpha^p\}.$$

$\square$

The condition $s \neq 0, \pm 1$ is necessary in view of the equation (40) for non obvious choices of g, since when $s = 0, \pm 1$, the trace value is α or α^p and, from the equations in (36), the corresponding g is of order 7, i.e. $g \in \langle \beta \rangle$. Note that one has the similar restriction on s in [2]. Since the irreducibility testing is not necessary in this case, we have

Theorem 7. Let $p \equiv 3, 5 \pmod 7$. Then using a Gaussian normal basis of type 3 in $GF(p^2)$, one can find a generator of the XTR group, a trace of an element of order q, using approximately $7 \log_2(\frac{p^2 - p + 1}{q})$ multiplications in $GF(p)$ on average.

6   Comparison with Previous Results

In section 3, we claimed that one can obtain equally fast arithmetic using a Gaussian normal basis of type k for small k. This is true if one can really ignore the cost of small number of additions of integers of bit size $\approx \log_2 p$. In fact, our method of Gaussian normal basis of type $k \geq 2$ slightly increases the number of necessary additions for each of the basic operations. Let A (resp. B) be the cost of one addition (resp. one doubling) of integers of bit size $\approx \log_2 p$ without reduction for each of the operations $x^2, xy, xz - yz^p$ in $GF(p^2)$. From the equations (14)–(17) in Lemma 3, the number of necessary additions and doublings with a Gaussian normal basis of type k can be computed easily and they are shown in Table 1.

Table 1. The number of necessary additions and doublings

Type k	1	2	3	5	6	8	9	11
x^2	$3A$	$5A+B$	$5A+2B$	$6A+2B$	$6A+2B$	$5A+3B$	$6A+3B$	$6A+3B$
xy	$3A$	$4A$	$4A+B$	$5A+B$	$5A+B$	$4A+2B$	$5A+2B$	$5A+2B$
$xz - yz^p$	$8A$	$9A$	$9A+B$	$10A+B$	$10A+B$	$9A+2B$	$10A+2B$	$10A+2B$

For example, compared with the original XTR (i.e. $k = 1$) in [3,4], the computation of xy needs one more addition of two integers of bit size $\approx \log_2 p$ with a Gaussian normal basis of type 2, and needs one more addition and a doubling with a Gaussian normal basis of type 3.

Typically, the cost of one addition (with or without reduction) is of linear complexity $O(\log_2 p)$ and the cost of one multiplication in $GF(p)$ is of $O(\log_2{}^2 p)$. Thus the cost of one addition is negligible compared with the cost of one multiplication in this point of view. The cost of computing $Tr(g^m)$ with g the generator of XTR group is $7 \log_2 m$ multiplications in $GF(p)$, where the constant 7 comes from the fact that two of x^2 and one of $xz - yz^p$ are computed for every iteration of the trace computation. Therefore compared with [3,4], our basis requires $c \log_2 m$ more additions for the computation of $Tr(g^m)$ where c is a small constant depending on k. For example, we have $c = 7$ (resp. $c = 10$) if we use a Gaussian normal basis of type 2 (resp. 3). Since the cost of $c \log_2 m$ (with $m < q \approx p$) additions is roughly equivalent to the cost of c multiplications in $GF(p)$, we conclude that c more multiplications in $GF(p)$ is needed for the computation of $Tr(g^m)$ compared with the original XTR with a type I ONB. This constant c is negligible compared with the total delay time of XTR implementation including parameter set up and irreducibility testing, since the worst case in Table 1 with a type 11 Gaussian normal basis requires only $c = 16$ more multiplications in $GF(p)$ for the computation of the trace value. Moreover Theorem 5 says that our method can find a generator of XTR group in $1.95 \log_2 p + 7 \log_2(\frac{p^2-p+1}{q})$ $GF(p)$-multiplications while the methods in [3,4] need $2.7 \log_2 p + 7 \log_2(\frac{p^2-p+1}{q})$ $GF(p)$-multiplications to find a generator. Thus $0.75 \log_2 p$ $GF(p)$-multiplications is saved using our method and this is a huge saving compared with c multiplications in $GF(p)$.

It should be mentioned that an explicit example of XTR polynomial is given in [12] using the assumption of $p \equiv 3, 5 \pmod 7$. However the given XTR polynomial needs another condition $p \equiv 3 \pmod 4$ to be irreducible over $GF(p^2)$. On the other hand, only the assumption $p \equiv 3, 5 \pmod 7$ is needed in our Theorem 7 and no further restriction (such as $p \equiv 2 \pmod 3$ or $p \equiv 3 \pmod 4$) is needed. Moreover our theorem of using a Gaussian normal basis of type 3 presents a method of finding a generator of XTR group whereas no explicit generator (nor the method of finding it) of XTR group is given in [12].

7   Conclusions

In this paper, we showed that an efficient implementation of XTR is not so dependent on the choice of prime p. Using a Gaussian normal basis of type $(2, k)$ for small k, we find that the field arithmetic for XTR is as efficient as that of the type I ONB used in [1]. Moreover, with the condition $p \equiv 1 \pmod 3$, we presented an algorithm which combines an efficient irreducibility testing and finding a generator of XTR group, and showed that our irreducibility testing is significantly faster than the methods in [3,4]. Also we proposed an efficient algorithm, with a Gaussian normal basis of type $(2, 3)$, which determines a generator of XTR group without any irreducibility testing. The time complexity of these algorithms are comparable to the best algorithms [3,4,5] proposed so far. Since the generality of the idea behind XTR does not restrict the choice of particular primes p and since no possible cryptographic weakness or strongness of choosing special $p \equiv 1$ or $2 \pmod 3$ is known at this moment, our result provides a meaningful improvement over the existing XTR implementations.

Acknowledgements. The authors would like to thank anonymous referees and Prof. J. von zur Gathen who made valuable suggestions on the preliminary version of this paper. Also, this work was supported by Korea Research Foundation Grant (KRF-2004-015-C00004).

References

1. A.K. Lenstra and E.R. Verheul, "The XTR public key system," *Crypto 2000, Lecture Notes in Computer Science*, vol. 1880, pp. 1–19, 2000.
2. A.K. Lenstra and E.R. Verheul, "Key improvements to XTR," *Asiacrypt 2000, Lecture Notes in Computer Science*, vol. 1976, pp. 220–233, 2000.
3. A.K. Lenstra and E.R. Verheul, "Fast irreducibility and subgroup membership testing in XTR," *PKC 2001, Lecture Notes in Computer Science*, vol. 1992, pp. 73–86, 2001.
4. M. Stam and A.K. Lenstra, "Speeding up XTR," *Asiacrypt 2001, Lecture Notes in Computer Science*, vol. 2248, pp. 125–143, 2001.
5. M. Stam and A.K. Lenstra, "Efficient subgroup exponentiation in quadratic and sixth degree extensions," *CHES 2002, Lecture Notes in Computer Science*, vol. 2523, pp. 318–332, 2003.

6. W. Bosma, J. Hutton, and E.R. Verheul, "Looking beyond XTR," *Asiacrypt 2002, Lecture Notes in Computer Science*, vol. 2501, pp. 46–63, 2002.

7. A.E. Brouwer, R. Pellikaan, and E.R. Verheul, "Doing more with fewer bits," *Asiacrypt 1999, Lecture Notes in Computer Science*, vol. 1716, pp. 321–332, 1999.

8. E.R. Verheul, "Evidence that XTR is more secure than supersingular elliptic curve cryptosystems," *Eurocrypt 2001, Lecture Notes in Computer Science*, vol. 2045, pp. 195–210, 2001.

9. G. Gong and L. Harn, "Public key cryptosystems based on cubic finite field extensions," *IEEE Trans. Information Theory*, vol. 45, pp. 2601–2605, 1999.

10. G. Gong, L. Harn, and H. Wu, "The GH Public key cryptosystem," *SAC 2001, Lecture Notes in Computer Science*, vol. 2259, pp. 284–300, 2001.

11. S. Lim, S. Kim, I. Yie, J. Kim, and H. Lee, "XTR extended to $GF(p^{6m})$," *SAC 2001, Lecture Notes in Computer Science*, vol. 2259, pp. 301–312, 2001.

12. J. Kim, I. Yie, S. Oh, H. Kim, and J. Ryu, "Fast generation of cubic irreducible polynomials for XTR," *Indocrypt 2001, Lecture Notes in Computer Science*, vol. 2247, pp. 73–78, 2001.

13. D. Han, K. Yoon, Y. Park, C. Kim, and J. Lim, "Optimal extension fields for XTR," *SAC 2002, Lecture Notes in Computer Science*, vol. 2595, pp. 369–384, 2002.

14. W.W. Li, M. Naslund, and I. Shparlinski "Hidden number problem with the trace and bit security of XTR and LUC," *Crypto 2002, Lecture Notes in Computer Science*, vol. 2442, pp. 433–448, 2002.

15. I. Shparlinski "On the generalized hidden number problem and bit security of XTR," *AAECC 2001, Lecture Notes in Computer Science*, vol. 2227, pp. 268–277, 2001.

16. A.J. Menezes, I.F. Blake, S. Gao, R.C. Mullin, S.A. Vanstone, and T. Yaghoobian, *Applications of Finite Fields*, Kluwer Academic Publisher, 1993.

17. S. Gao, J. von zur Gathen, and D. Panario, "Gauss periods and fast exponentiation in finite fields," *Latin 1995, Lecture Notes in Computer Science*, vol. 911, pp. 311–322, 1995.

18. D.E. Knuth, "The Art of Computer Programming, Third Edition," *Vol. 2, Seminumerical Algorithms*, Addison Wesley, 1997.

19. D.M. Gordon, "A survey of fast exponentiation methods," *J. of Algorithms*, vol. 27, pp. 129–146, 1998.

20. S. Feisel, J. von zur Gathen, M. Shokrollahi, "Normal bases via general Gauss periods," *Math. Comp.*, vol. 68, pp. 271–290, 1999.

Modular Number Systems:
Beyond the Mersenne Family

Jean-Claude Bajard[1], Laurent Imbert[1,2], and Thomas Plantard[1]

[1] LIRMM, CNRS UMR 5506,
161 rue Ada, 34392 Montpellier cedex 5, France
[2] ATIPS, CISaC, University of Calgary,
2500 University drive N.W, Calgary, T2N 1C2, Canada
{bajard, plantard, Laurent.Imbert}@lirmm.fr

Abstract. In SAC 2003, J. Chung and A. Hasan introduced a new class of specific moduli for cryptography, called the more generalized Mersenne numbers, in reference to J. Solinas' generalized Mersenne numbers proposed in 1999. This paper pursues the quest. The main idea is a new representation, called Modular Number System (MNS), which allows efficient implementation of the modular arithmetic operations required in cryptography. We propose a modular multiplication which only requires n^2 multiplications and $3(2n^2 - n + 1)$ additions, where n is the size (in words) of the operands. Our solution is thus more efficient than Montgomery for a very large class of numbers that do not belong to the large Mersenne family.

Keywords: Generalized Mersenne numbers, Montgomery multiplication, Elliptic curve cryptography

1   Introduction

Efficient implementation of modular arithmetic is an important prerequisite in today's public-key cryptography [6]. In the case of elliptic curves defined over prime fields, operations are performed modulo prime numbers whose size range from 160 to 500 bits [4].

For moduli p that are not of special form, Montgomery [7] or Barrett [1] algorithms are widely used. However, modular multiplication and reduction can be accelerated considerably when the modulus p has a special form. Mersenne numbers of the form $2^m - 1$ are well known examples, but they are not useful for cryptography because there are only a few primes (the first Mersenne primes are $3, 7, 31, 127, 8191, 131071, 524287, 2147483647$, etc). Pseudo-Mersenne of the form $2^m - c$, introduced by R. Crandall in [3], allow for very efficient modular reduction if c is a small integer. In 1999, J. Solinas [8] introduced the family of generalized Mersenne numbers. They are expressed as $p = f(t)$, where f is a well chosen monic integral polynomial and t is a power of 2, and lead to very fast modular reduction using only a few number of additions and subtractions.

H. Handschuh and A. Hasan (Eds.): SAC 2004, LNCS 3357, pp. 159–169, 2005.
© Springer-Verlag Berlin Heidelberg 2005

For example, the five NIST primes listed below, recommended in the FIPS 186-2 standard for defining elliptic curves over primes fields, belong to this class[1].

$$p_{192} = 2^{192} - 2^{64} - 1$$
$$p_{224} = 2^{224} - 2^{96} + 1$$
$$p_{256} = 2^{256} - 2^{224} + 2^{192} + 2^{96} - 1$$
$$p_{384} = 2^{384} - 2^{128} - 2^{96} + 2^{32} - 1$$
$$p_{521} = 2^{521} - 1$$

In 2003, J. Chung and A. Hasan, in a paper entitled "more generalized Mersenne numbers" [2], extended J. Solinas' concept, by allowing any integer for t.

In this paper we further extend the idea of defining new classes of numbers (possibly prime), suitable for cryptography. However, the resemblance with the previous works ends here. Instead of considering moduli of special form, we represent the integers modulo p in the so-called Modular Number System (MNS). By a careful choice of the parameters which define our MNS, we introduce the concept of Adapted Modular Number System (AMNS). We propose a modular multiplication which is more efficient than Montgomery's algorithm, and we explain how to define suitable prime moduli for cryptography. We provide examples of such numbers at the end of the paper.

2   Modular Number Systems

In positional number systems, we represent any nonnegative integer X in base β as

$$X = \sum_{i=0}^{k-1} d_i \, \beta^i, \qquad (1)$$

where the digits d_is belong to the set $\{0, \ldots, \beta - 1\}$. If $d_{k-1} \neq 0$, we call X a k-digit base-β number.

In cryptographic applications, computations have to be done over finite rings or fields. In these cases, we manipulate representatives of equivalence classes modulo P (for simplicity we use the set of positive integers $\{0, 1, 2, \ldots, P - 1\}$), and the operations are performed modulo P.

In the next definition, we extend the notion of positional number system to represent the integers modulo P.

Definition 1 (MNS). *A Modular Number System (MNS) $\mathcal{B}$ is defined according to four parameters (γ, ρ, n, P), such that all positive integers $0 \leq X < P$ can be written as*

$$X = \sum_{i=0}^{n-1} x_i \, \gamma^i \bmod P, \qquad (2)$$

---

[1] Note that p_{521} is also a Mersenne prime.

with $1 < \gamma < P$, and $x_i \in \{0, \ldots, \rho - 1\}$. The vector $(x_0, x_1, \ldots, x_{n-1})_\mathcal{B}$ denotes the representation of X in $\mathcal{B}$.

In the sequel of the paper, we shall omit the subscript $(.)_\mathcal{B}$ when it is clear from the context, and we shall consider X either as a vector or as a polynomial (in γ). In the later, the x_is correspond to the coefficients of the polynomial (note that we use a left-to-right notation; x_0 is the constant term).

Example 1. Let us consider the MNS defined with $\gamma = 7, \rho = 3, n = 3, P = 17$. Over this system, we represent the elements of $\mathbb{Z}_{17}$ as polynomials in γ of degree at most 3 with coefficients in $\{0, 1, 2\}$ (cf. Table 1).

Table 1. The elements of $\mathbb{Z}_{17}$ in $\mathcal{B} = MNS(7, 3, 3, 17)$

0	1	2	3	4	5
0	1	2	$\gamma + 2\gamma^2$	$1 + \gamma + 2\gamma^2$	$\gamma + \gamma^2$

6	7	8	9	10	11
$1 + \gamma + \gamma^2$	γ	$1 + \gamma$	$2 + \gamma$	$2\gamma + 2\gamma^2$	$1 + 2\gamma + 2\gamma^2$

12	13	14	15	16	
$2\gamma + \gamma^2$	$1 + 2\gamma + \gamma^2$	2γ	$1 + 2\gamma$	$2 + 2\gamma$	

We remark that this system is redundant. For example, we can write $5 = 2 + \gamma^3 = \gamma + \gamma^2$, or $14 = 1 + 2\gamma^2 = 2\gamma$. However, we do not take any advantage of this property in this paper.

Definition 2 (AMNS). *A modular number system* $\mathcal{B} = MNS(\gamma, \rho, n, P)$ *is called Adapted Modular Number System (AMNS) if* $\gamma^n \bmod P = c$ *is a small integer. In this case we shall denote* $\mathcal{B} = AMNS(\gamma, \rho, n, P, c)$.

Although c is given by $\gamma^n \bmod P$, we introduce it in the AMNS definition to simplify the notations.

Note that it is not obvious (see Section 5) to prove that a given set of parameters (γ, ρ, n, P) is an MNS. Algorithm 3, presented in the next section, gives sufficient conditions to prove that this is an AMNS.

In the rest of the paper, we shall consider $\mathcal{B} = AMNS(\gamma, \rho, n, P, c)$, unless otherwise specified.

3   Modular Multiplication

As in [2], modular multiplication is performed in three steps presented in Algorithm 1.

In order to evaluate the computational complexity of Algorithm 1, let us get into more details. In the first step we evaluate

$$U(X) = \sum_{i=0}^{2n-2} u_i X^i, \quad \text{where } u_i = \sum_{j=0}^{i} a_i b_{i-j}, \tag{3}$$

Algorithm 1 – Modular Multiplication

Input : An AMNS $\mathcal{B} = (\gamma, \rho, n, P, c)$, and $A = (a_0, ..., a_{n-1})$, $B = (b_0, ..., b_{n-1})$
Output : $S = (s_0, ..., s_{n-1})$ such that $S = A B \bmod P$
1: Polynomial multiplication in $\mathbb{Z}[X]$: $U(X) \leftarrow A(X) B(X)$
2: Polynomial reduction: $V(X) \leftarrow U(X) \bmod (X^n - c)$
3: Coefficient reduction: $S \leftarrow CR(V)$, gives $S \equiv V(\gamma) \pmod{P}$

---

where $a_t = b_t = 0$ for $t > n-1$. We have $u_0 = a_0 b_0 < \rho^2$, $u_1 = a_0 b_1 + a_1 b_0 < 2\rho^2$, etc. Clearly, the largest coefficient is $u_{n-1} < n\rho^2$. Then, for the coefficients of degree greater than $n - 1$, we have $u_n < (n - 1)\rho^2, \ldots, u_{2n-2} < \rho^2$.

The cost of the first step clearly depends on the size of ρ and n. It requires n^2 products of size $\log_2(\rho)$, and $(n - 1)^2$ additions of size at most $\log_2(n\rho^2)$.

In step 2, we compute

$$V(X) = \sum_{i=0}^{n-1} v_i X^i, \quad \text{where } v_i = u_i + c\, u_{i+n}. \tag{4}$$

This yields

$$v_i < cn\rho^2, \quad \text{for } i = 0 \ldots n - 1. \tag{5}$$

The cost of step 2 is $(n-1)$ products between the constant c and numbers of size $\log_2(n\rho^2)$, and $(n - 1)$ additions of size $\log_2(cn\rho^2)$. When c is a small constant, for example a power of 2, the $(n - 1)$ products can be implemented with only $(n - 1)$ shifts and additions.

In order to get a valid AMNS representation we must reduce the coefficients such that all the v_is are less than ρ. This is the purpose of the coefficient reduction.

3.1   Coefficient Reduction

For simplicity, we define $\rho = 2^{k+1}$. We reduce the elements of the vector V, obtained after step 2 of Algorithm 1, by iteratively applying Algorithm 2, presented below, which reduces numbers of size $\lceil \frac{3k}{2} \rceil$ bits to numbers of size $k + 1$, i.e. less than ρ.

So, let us first consider a vector V with elements of size at most $\lceil \frac{3k}{2} \rceil$ bits. Our goal is to find a representation of V where the elements are less than ρ, i.e. of size at most $k + 1$ bits.

If $V = (v_0, \ldots, v_{n-1})$, we define two vectors $\underline{V}$ and $\overline{V}$ such that

$$V = \underline{V} + \overline{V} \cdot 2^k I, \tag{6}$$

where the elements of $\underline{V}$ are less than 2^k and those of $\overline{V}$ are less than $2^{\lceil k/2 \rceil}$. In equation (6), I denotes the $n \times n$ identity matrix explicitly given by $I_{ij} = \delta_{ij}$ for $i, j = 0, \ldots, n - 1$ and δ_{ij} is the Kronecker delta.

If we can express $\overline{V} \cdot 2^k I$ as a vector with elements less than 2^k, then the sum of the two vectors in (6) is less than 2^{k+1}, and gives a valid AMNS representation of V. The idea is to find a matrix M with small coefficients which satisfies

$$M \cdot (1, \gamma, \ldots, \gamma^{n-1})^T \equiv 2^k I \cdot (1, \gamma, \ldots, \gamma^{n-1})^T \quad (\mathrm{mod}\ P). \tag{7}$$

Roughly speaking, the matrix M can be seen as a representation of $2^k I$ in the AMNS.

If $2^k = (\xi_0, \ldots, \xi_{n-1})_{\mathcal{B}}$, is a representation of 2^k in the AMNS, then by definition 1 we have

$$2^k \equiv \xi_0 + \xi_1 \gamma + \cdots + \xi_{n-1} \gamma^{n-1} \quad (\mathrm{mod}\ P). \tag{8}$$

Similarly the following congruences hold:

$$\gamma\, 2^k \equiv c\xi_{n-1} + \xi_0 \gamma + \cdots + \xi_{n-2} \gamma^{n-1} \quad (\mathrm{mod}\ P) \tag{9}$$

$$\gamma^2\, 2^k \equiv c\xi_{n-2} + c\xi_{n-1} \gamma + \xi_0 \gamma^2 + \cdots + \xi_{n-3} \gamma^{n-1} \quad (\mathrm{mod}\ P) \tag{10}$$

$$\vdots$$

$$\gamma^{n-1}\, 2^k \equiv c\xi_1 + c\xi_2 \gamma + \cdots + c\xi_{n-1} \gamma^{n-2} + \xi_0 \gamma^{n-1} \quad (\mathrm{mod}\ P). \tag{11}$$

Equations (8) to (11) allow us to define the matrix

$$M = \begin{pmatrix} \xi_0 & \xi_1 & \cdots & & \xi_{n-1} \\ c\xi_{n-1} & \xi_0 & \cdots & & \xi_{n-2} \\ \vdots & & & & \\ c\xi_1 & c\xi_2 & \cdots & c\xi_{n-1} & \xi_0 \end{pmatrix} \tag{12}$$

which satisfies equation (7). Thus $\overline{V} \cdot 2^k I \equiv \overline{V} \cdot M \pmod{P}$, and equation (6) becomes

$$V = \underline{V} + \overline{V} \cdot M. \tag{13}$$

If we impose $c \sum_{i=0}^{n-1} \xi_i < 2^{\lfloor k/2 \rfloor}$, then the elements of the vector $\overline{V} \cdot M$ are less than 2^k. Algorithm 2 implements equation (13) to reduce the elements of V to a valid AMNS representation, i.e. with $v_i < \rho = 2^{k+1}$ for $i = 0 \ldots n-1$.

Algorithm 2 – $\mathrm{Red}(V, \mathcal{B})$: reduction from $\lceil \frac{3k}{2} \rceil$ to $k+1$ bits

---

Input : $\mathcal{B} = (\gamma, \rho, n, P, c)$ an AMNS with $\rho = 2^{k+1}$; $2^k = (\xi_0, \ldots, \xi_{n-1})$ with $c \sum_{i=0}^{n-1} \xi_i < 2^{\lfloor k/2 \rfloor}$; a matrix M as defined in (12); a vector $V = (v_0, \ldots, v_{n-1})$ with $v_i < 2^{\lceil 3k/2 \rceil}$ for $i = 0 \ldots n-1$.
Output : $S = (s_0, \ldots, s_{n-1})$ with $s_i < \rho$ for all $i = 0 \ldots n-1$.
1: Define vectors $\underline{V}$ and $\overline{V}$ such that $V = \underline{V} + \overline{V} \cdot 2^k I$
2: Compute $S \leftarrow \underline{V} + \overline{V} \cdot M$

The cost of Algorithm 2 is n^2 multiplications of size $\frac{k}{2}$ and n additions of size k. However, since the M_{ij} in (12) are small constants, the n^2 products can be efficiently computed with only a small number of additions and shifts. For example, if c and the ξ_is are small powers of 2, then we can evaluate $\overline{V} \cdot M$ with $n(n-1)$ additions. In this case the total cost for Red is n^2 additions of size k.

In order to reduce polynomials with coefficients larger than $\frac{3k}{2}$ bits, we iteratively apply the previous algorithm until all the coefficients are less than ρ. The following theorem holds.

Theorem 1. *Let us define* $\mathcal{B} = AMNS(\gamma, \rho, n, P, c)$, *with* $\rho = 2^{k+1}$. *We denote* $(\xi_0, \ldots, \xi_{n-1})$ *a representation of* 2^k *in* $\mathcal{B}$, *and we assume* $V = (v_0, \ldots, v_{n-1})$ *with* $v_i < cn\rho^2$.

If $c \sum_{i=0}^{n-1} \xi_i < 2^{\lfloor k/2 \rfloor}$ *then there exists an algorithm which reduces* V *into a valid AMNS representation, in* $\frac{k+2+\lfloor \log_2(cn) \rfloor}{\lceil k/2 \rceil - 1}$ *calls to Red (algorithm 2).*

Proof. After step 2 of Algorithm 1, and under the condition $\rho = 2^{k+1}$, the elements of V satisfy $v_i < 2^{2k+2}cn$. Thus $|v_i| < 2k + 3 + \lfloor \log_2(cn) \rfloor$, where $|v_i|$ denotes the size of v_i. Since each step of Red eliminates $\lceil \frac{k}{2} \rceil - 1$ bits of v_i, the number of iteration is given by the value t which satisfy the equation $2k + 3 + \lfloor \log_2(cn) \rfloor - t \left(\lceil \frac{k}{2} \rceil - 1 \right) = k+1$, i.e. $t = \frac{k+2+\lfloor \log_2(cn) \rfloor}{\lceil k/2 \rceil - 1}$. This gives $t = 2 + \frac{8+2\lfloor \log_2(cn) \rfloor}{k-2}$ is k is even, and $t = 2 + \frac{6+2\lfloor \log_2(cn) \rfloor}{k-1}$ if k is odd.   □

Note that in practice, the number of iterations is very small. In the examples of section 5, the coefficient reduction step only requires 3 or 4 calls to algorithm Red. Algorithm 3 implements theorem 1.

Algorithm 3 – CR$(V, \mathcal{B})$, Coefficient reduction

Input : $\mathcal{B} = (\gamma, \rho, n, P, c)$ an AMNS with $\rho = 2^{k+1}$; $2^k = (\xi_0, ..., \xi_{n-1})$ with $c \sum_{i=0}^{n-1} \xi_i < 2^{\lfloor k/2 \rfloor}$; a vector $V = (v_0, ..., v_{n-1})$.
Output : $S = (s_0, ..., s_{n-1})$ with $s_i < \rho$ for all $i = 0 \ldots n - 1$.
1: $l \leftarrow \max(\lfloor \log_2(v_i) \rfloor + 1)$
2: $U \leftarrow V$
3: **while** $l > \frac{3k}{2}$ **do**
4:    Define $\underline{U}$ and $\overline{U}$ s.t. $U = \underline{U} + 2^{l-3k/2} \cdot \overline{U}$
5:    $\overline{U} \leftarrow Red(\overline{U}, \mathcal{B})$
6:    $U \leftarrow \underline{U} + 2^{l-3k/2} \cdot \overline{U}$
7:    $l \leftarrow \max(\lfloor \log_2(U_i) \rfloor + 1)$
8: **end while**
9: $S \leftarrow Red(U, \mathcal{B})$

---

4   Complexity Comparisons

In this section, we evaluate the number of elementary operations (word-length multiplications and additions) of our modular multiplication algorithm. Since the complexity of our algorithms clearly depends on many parameters we try to consider different interesting options. For simplicity, we assume $cn < \rho$ as this is the case in the examples presented in the next section.

For a large part, the moduli (possibly primes) we are able to generate do not belong neither to Solinas' [8] or Chung and Hasan's generalized Mersenne family [2]. Thus, we only compare our algorithm with Montgomery since it was the best known algorithm available for those numbers.

As explained in section 3, our modular multiplication requires three steps: polynomial multiplication, polynomial reduction, and coefficient reduction.

The polynomial multiplication only depends on n and ρ. If $\rho = 2^{k+1}$ ($k + 1$ is the word-size), the cost of the first step is $n^2 T_m$, where T_m is the delay of one word-length multiplication, and $(n-1)^2$ additions involving two-word operands, i.e. of cost less than $3(n-1)^2 T_a$, where T_a is the delay of one word-length addition. Thus, the cost of step 1 is

$$n^2 T_m + 3(n-1)^2 T_a.$$

The polynomial reduction depends on n, ρ, and c. In the general case, it requires $(n-1)$ multiplications of size $\log_2(n\rho^2)$. However, if $c = 1, 2, 4$ (resp. $c = 3, 5, 6$) it can be implemented in n shift-and-add of three-word numbers (resp. $2n$ shift-and-add). This yields a cost of $3n T_a$ (resp. $6n T_a$). Thus, for the second step, a careful choice of c can lead to

$$3n T_a.$$

The coefficient reduction depends on all the parameters. The cost of algorithm Red, for $\xi_i = 0, 1, 2$ and $c = 1, 2, 4$ is $n^2 T_a$ (it becomes $n^2 + \frac{(n-1)^2}{2} T_a$ if $c = 3, 5, 6$). From theorem 1, algorithm CR requires 3 calls to Red if $cn < 2^{(k-10)/2}$ (4 calls if $cn < 2^{k-10}$). Finally, step 3 requires $3n^2 T_a$ if $cn < 2^{(k-10)/2}$, $\xi_i = 0, 1, 2$, and $c = 1, 2, 4$ (we have $8n^2 T_a$ if $cn < 2^{k-10}$, $\xi_i = 0, 1, 2$, $c = 3, 5, 6$). As for the previous step, a good choice of c and the ξ_is gives a complexity of

$$3n^2 T_a.$$

The important point here is that we can perform the coefficient reduction without multiplications.

To summarize, our algorithm performs the modular multiplication, where the moduli do not belong to the generalized Mersenne families – introduced by Solinas, and Chung and Hasan – in

$$n^2 T_m + 3 \left(2n^2 - n + 1\right) T_a.$$

This is better than Montgomery which requires $2n^2 T_m$ (cf. [7], [5]).

In the next section we explain how we define such modulus and we give examples that reach this complexity.

5   Construction of Suitable Moduli

In this section we explain how to find γ and P which allow fast modular arithmetic.

Let us first fix some of the parameters. Since we represent numbers as polynomials of coefficients less than $\rho = 2^{k+1}$, it is advantageous to define ρ according to the word-size of the targeted architecture, i.e. by taking $k = 15, 31, 63$ for 16-bit, 32-bit, and 64-bit architectures respectively. We define n such that $(k+1)n$ roughly corresponds to the desired dynamic range. To get a very efficient reduction of the coefficients, we impose restrictions on the ξ_is, for example by only allowing values in $\{0, 1, 2\}$, and we choose very small values for c. Based on the previous choices, we now try to find suitable P and γ.

From equation (7), we deduce $V \cdot (2^k I - M) \equiv 0 \pmod{P}$, for all $V = (v_0, \ldots, v_{n-1})_\mathcal{B}$. Thus, it is clear that the determinant

$$d = \left| 2^k I - M \right| \equiv 0 \pmod{P}. \tag{14}$$

All the divisors of d, including d itself, can be chosen for P. If we need P to be prime, we can either try to find a prime factor of the determinant which is large enough (this is easier than factorization since it suffices to eliminate the small prime factors up to an arbitrary bound), or consider only the cases where the determinant is already a prime.

We remark that γ is a root, modulo P, of both $\gamma^n - c$ and $2^k - \sum_{i=0}^{n-1} \xi_i \gamma^i$. Thus γ is also a root of $\gcd(\gamma^n - c, 2^k - \sum_{i=0}^{n-1} \xi_i \gamma^i) \bmod P$.

5.1   Generating Primes for Cryptographic Applications

For elliptic curve defined over prime fields, P must be a prime of size at least 160 bits.

Let us assume a 16-bit architecture. We fix $\rho = 2^{16}$, and we see if we can generate good primes P with $n = 11$. Note that $nk = 176$ does not guaranty 176-bit primes for P. In practice, the candidates we obtain are slightly smaller. We impose strong restrictions on the other parameters, by allowing only $\xi_i \in \{0, 1\}$, and $2 \le c \le 6$.

As an example, we consider $c = 3$, and $2^k = (1, 0, 0, 0, 0, 1, 0, 0, 1, 1, 1)_\mathcal{B}$, which correspond to the polynomial $1 + x^5 + x^8 + x^9 + x^{10}$. Using (14), we compute

$$d = 4675235506507447448560271345735633771016191076 7327,$$

which has

$$P = 792412797713126686196656160294175215426473063853$$

as a prime factor of size 160 bits.

Then, we compute a root of $\gcd(x^{11} - 3, 2^{15} - 1 - x^5 - x^8 - x^9 - x^{10})$ modulo P, and we obtain

$$\gamma = 474796736496801627149092588633773724051936841406.$$

We have investigated different set of parameters and applied the same technique to define suitable prime moduli. In Table 2, we give the number of such primes and the corresponding parameters.

Table 2. Number of primes P greater than 2^{160} for use in elliptic curve cryptography, and the corresponding AMNS parameters

$k+1$	n	c	ξ_i	Number of primes of size ≥ 160 bits
16	11	$\{2,3\}$	$\{0,1\}$	132
16	11	$\{2,3,4,5,6\}$	$\{0,1\}$	306
16	11	2	$\{0,1,2\}$	3106
16	11	$\{2,3,4,5,6\}$	$\{0,1,2\}$	$\geq 7416\ (a)$
32	6	$\{2,3,4,5,6\}$	$\{0,1\}$	$\geq 12\ (b)$
32	6	$\{2,3,4,5,6\}$	$\{0,1,2\}$	$\geq 87\ (b)$
64	16	$\{2,3,4,5,6\}$	$\{0,1\}$	$\geq 1053\ (b)$

(a): the determinant d was already a prime in 7416 cases. We did not try to factorize it in the other cases.
(b): computation interrupted.

6   Others Operations in an AMNS

In this section we briefly describe the other basic operations in AMNS in order to provide a fully functional system for cryptographic applications. We present methods for converting numbers between binary and AMNS, as well as solutions for addition and subtraction. In the context of elliptic curve cryptography, it is important to notice that, except for the inversion which can be performed only once at the very end of the computations if we use projective coordinates, all the operations can be computed within the AMNS. Thus conversions are only required at the beginning and at the end of the process.

6.1   Conversion from Binary to AMNS

Theorem 2. *If X is an integer such that $0 \leq X < P$, given in classical binary representation, then a representation of X in the AMNS $\mathcal{B}$ is obtained with at most $2(n-1) + \frac{6(n-1)}{k-2}$ calls to Red.*

Proof. We simply remark that $P < 2^{n(k+1)}$ and that the size of the largest coefficient of X is reduced by $\lceil \frac{k}{2} \rceil - 1$ bits after each call to Red. Thus the reduction of $0 \leq X < P$ requires at least $\frac{(n-1)(k+1)}{\lceil \frac{k}{2} \rceil - 1}$ iterations, or more precisely $2(n-1) + \frac{6(n-1)}{k-2}$ is k is even, and $2(n-1) + \frac{4(n-1)}{k-1}$ if k is odd.   □

We use theorem 2 by applying the coefficient reduction CR (Algorithm 3) to the vector $(X, 0, \ldots, 0)$.

6.2   Conversion from AMNS to Binary

Given $X = (x_0, \ldots, x_{n-1})_{\mathcal{B}}$, we have to evaluate $X = \sum_{i=0}^{n-1} x_i \gamma^i \bmod P$. The binary representation of X can be obtained with Horner's scheme

$$X = x_0 + \gamma\left(x_1 + \gamma\left(x_2 + \cdots + \gamma\left(x_{n-2} + \gamma\,x_{n-1}\right)\cdots\right)\right) \bmod P.$$

Since γ is of the same order of magnitude as P, the successive modular multiplications must be evaluated with Barrett or Montgomery algorithms. The cost of the conversion is thus at most $3n^3 T_m$.

6.3 Addition, Subtraction

Given $X = (x_0, \ldots, x_{n-1})_{\mathcal{B}}$ and $Y = (y_0, \ldots, y_{n-1})_{\mathcal{B}}$, the addition is simply given by $S = (x_0 + y_0, \ldots, x_{n-1} + y_{n-1})_{\mathcal{B}^+}$, where $\mathcal{B}^+$ denotes an extension of the AMNS $\mathcal{B}$ where the elements are not necessarily less than ρ. Since the input vectors of our modular multiplication algorithm do not need to have their elements less than ρ, this is a valid representation. However, if the reduction to $\mathcal{B}$ is required, it can be done thanks to algorithm CR.

Subtraction $X - Y$ is performed by adding X and the negative of Y. We use $Z = (z_0, \ldots, z_{n-1})_{\mathcal{B}^+}$ as a representation of 0 in $\mathcal{B}^+$, i.e. with $z_i > \rho$ for $i = 0 \ldots n - 1$. From (12) and (13) we have

$$Z = \sum_{i=0}^{n-1} z_i \gamma^i \equiv 0 \bmod P,$$

with $z_i = 3\left[2^k - \left(\sum_{j=0}^{i} \xi_j + c\sum_{j=i+1}^{n-1} \xi_j\right)\right]$.

The negative of Y is thus given in $\mathcal{B}^+$ by the vector $(z_0 - y_0, \ldots, z_{n-1} - y_{n-1})_{\mathcal{B}^+}$. For the reduction in $\mathcal{B}$, the same remark as for the addition applies.

7 Conclusions

In this paper we defined a new family of moduli suitable for cryptography. In that sense, this research can be seen as an extension of the works by J. Solinas, and J. Chung and A. Hasan. We introduced a new system of representation for the integers modulo P, called Adapted Modular Number System (AMNS), and we proposed a modular multiplication in AMNS which is more efficient than Montgomery. We explained how to construct an AMNS which lead to moduli suitable for fast modular arithmetic, and we explicitly provided examples of primes for cryptographic sizes. Future researches on this subject will be dedicated to the problem of defining an AMNS for a given number p, and to the exploration of the potential advantages of the redundancy of this representation.

Acknowledgments

This work was done during L. Imbert leave of absence at the university of Calgary, with the ATIPS[2] and CISaC[3] laboratories. It was also partly supported by the French ministry of education and research under the ACI 2002, "OpAC, Opérateurs arithmétiques pour la Cryptographie", grant number C03-02.

[2] Advanced Technology Information Processing Systems, `www.atips.ca`
[3] Centre for Information Security and Cryptography, `cisac.math.ucalgary.ca`

References

1. P. Barrett. Implementing the Rivest Shamir and Adleman public key encryption algorithm on a standard digital signal processor. In A. M. Odlyzko, editor, *Advances in Cryptology - Crypto '86*, volume 263 of *LNCS*, pages 311–326. Springer-Verlag, 1986.

2. J. Chung and A. Hasan. More generalized mersenne numbers. In M. Matsui and R. Zuccherato, editors, *Selected Areas in Cryptography – SAC 2003*, volume 3006 of *LNCS*, Ottawa, Canada, August 2003. Springer-Verlag. (to appear).

3. R. Crandall. Method and apparatus for public key exchange in a cryptographic system. U.S. Patent number 5159632, 1992.

4. D. Hankerson, A. Menezes, and S. Vanstone. *Guide to Elliptic Curve Cryptography*. Springer-Verlag, 2004.

5. Ç. K. Koç, T. Acar, and B. S. Kaliski Jr. Analyzing and comparing montgomery multiplication algorithms. *IEEE Micro*, 16(3):26–33, June 1996.

6. A. J. Menezes, P. C. Van Oorschot, and S. A. Vanstone. *Handbook of applied cryptography*. CRC Press, 2000 N.W. Corporate Blvd., Boca Raton, FL 33431-9868, USA, 1997.

7. P. L. Montgomery. Modular multiplication without trial division. *Mathematics of Computation*, 44(170):519–521, April 1985.

8. J. Solinas. Generalized mersenne numbers. Research Report CORR-99-39, Center for Applied Cryptographic Research, University of Waterloo, Waterloo, ON, Canada, 1999.

Efficient Doubling on Genus Two Curves over Binary Fields

Tanja Lange[1,*] and Marc Stevens[2,*]

[1] Institute for Information Security and Cryptology (ITSC),
Ruhr-Universität Bochum Universitätsstraße 150 D-44780 Bochum Germany
lange@itsc.ruhr-uni-bochum.de
http://www.ruhr-uni-bochum.de/itsc/
[2] Department of Mathematics and Computer Science,
Eindhoven University of Technology,
P.O. Box 513, 5600 MB Eindhoven, The Netherlands
m.m.j.stevens@student.tue.nl

Abstract. In most algorithms involving elliptic and hyperelliptic curves, the costliest part consists in computing multiples of ideal classes. This paper investigates how to compute faster doubling over fields of characteristic two.

We derive explicit doubling formulae making strong use of the defining equation of the curve. We analyze how many field operations are needed depending on the curve making clear how much generality one loses by the respective choices. Note, that none of the proposed types is known to be weak – one only could be suspicious because of the more special types. Our results allow to choose curves from a large enough variety which have extremely fast doubling needing only half the time of an addition. Combined with a sliding window method this leads to fast computation of scalar multiples. We also speed up the general case.

Keywords: Hyperelliptic curves, fast arithmetic, explicit group operations, binary fields.

1 Introduction

Hyperelliptic curves of low genus obtained a lot of attention in the recent past for cryptographic applications. It is a rather recent result that they can compete with elliptic curves in terms of efficiency of the group law [Ava03, Lan04a]. The security of low genus hyperelliptic curves is assumed to be similar to that of elliptic curves of the same group size. Here, *low* really means genus $g \leq 3$ by [Gau00, Thé03, GT04, Nag04], and even for $g = 3$ some care has to be taken.

---

* The work described in this paper has been supported in part by the European Commission through the IST Programme under Contract IST-2002-507932 ECRYPT. The information in this document reflects only the author's views, is provided as is and no guarantee or warranty is given that the information is fit for any particular purpose. The user thereof uses the information at its sole risk and liability.

H. Handschuh and A. Hasan (Eds.): SAC 2004, LNCS 3357, pp. 170–181, 2005.
© Springer-Verlag Berlin Heidelberg 2005

The main operation in protocols based on the *discrete logarithm problem* in an additively written group is the computation of scalar multiples of a group element. Using standard scalar multiplication methods this boils down to additions, doublings, and perhaps some precomputations.

In this paper we concentrate on genus two curves over fields of characteristic two and in detail on doubling formulae for the different types of curves. Obviously, choosing curves defined over $\mathbb{F}_2$ allows very efficient scalar multiplication as shown in the publications on Koblitz curves [GLS00, Lan04b]. However, there are only 6 different isogenie classes and, hence, the choice of curves is rather limited. So there is a trade-off between speed-up and special parameters.

In this article, we give a complete study of all cases of defining equation of the curve where we allow the curve to be *defined over the extension field*. In combination with a windowing method the best case achieves a performance only twice as slow as for Koblitz curves, the reason being that additions remain costly in both cases and there are more of them in the Koblitz curve setting. Clearly, this again is a special choice but the number of non-isomorphic curves has grown considerably.

So far only one very special type of curves has been considered [PWP04] and shown to lead to efficient doubling formulae. Our results improve their formulae and provide clear tables with *all types of defining equations* together with the number of operations and also give the doubling formulae.

After the submission of this paper the authors found a further work in special curves [BD04]. They obtain less efficient doublings, but also do a complete study of all kinds of curves. Even more recently, Duquesne (see [ACD$^+$04]) made improvements for the case where $\deg h = 2$ and $h_0 \neq 0$.

We now briefly state the background needed on hyperelliptic curves and then give a complete study of the doubling formulae. Section 7 provides timings for the different cases giving evidence that the claimed speed up can actually be obtained. We end with some remarks on side channel attacks.

2   Basic Notations and Preliminaries

We refer the interested reader to [FL03, Lor96, MWZ98, Sti93] for mathematical background. For the scope of this paper we only try to motivate the representation of the group elements and the group law as this is what we concentrate on in the remainder of the paper.

Let $\mathbb{F}_q, q = 2^\ell$, be a finite field of characteristic 2 and let C be a hyperelliptic curve defined over $\mathbb{F}_q$. In cryptography one usually deals with curves C given by

$$C: \quad Y^2 + h(X)Y = f(X)$$
$$h, f \in \mathbb{F}_q[X], \ f \text{ monic}, \ \deg f = 2g + 1, \ \deg h \leq g \tag{1}$$

for which no point $(x, y) \in C$ satisfies both partial derivative equations. For characteristic 2 one needs to have a non-zero h to achieve this quality. The integer g appearing in (1) is called the *genus of C*. We concentrate on curves of genus 2.

The group one uses for cryptographic applications is the ideal class group $\mathrm{Cl}(C/\mathbb{F}_q)$ of C over $\mathbb{F}_q$. This is the quotient of the group of fractional ideals of $\mathbb{F}_q[X, Y]/(Y^2 + h(X)Y + f(X))$ by the group of principal ideals. Like in the case of quadratic imaginary fields in each ideal class one finds an ideal generated by two polynomials $\langle u(X), v(X) + Y \rangle$.

There is a unique ideal of minimal degree in each class. Actually, each element D of $\mathrm{Cl}(C/\mathbb{F}_q)$ can be represented by an ordered pair of polynomials $D = [u(X), v(X)]$, with $u, v \in \mathbb{F}_q, \deg v < \deg u \leq g$ and u monic satisfying $u | v^2 + hv + f$.

3   Group Law

The group operation in $\mathrm{Cl}(C/\mathbb{F}_q)$ is performed by first computing the product of the ideals and then reducing it modulo the principal ideals. This is the principle behind Cantor's algorithm [Can87, Kob89].

Obviously, this algorithm has to depend on the properties of the input – to derive explicit formulae one needs to study additions independently from doublings. For a complete study of all possible inputs together with formulae we refer to [Lan04a]. In this paper we concentrate on doublings for genus 2 curves in the most frequent case where the input $[u, v]$ has full degree and u and h do not have a root in common. Accordingly, we assume from now on

$$D = [u, v], \quad \deg u = 2, \quad \mathrm{res}(h, u) \neq 0.$$

Put $u = x^2 + u_1 x + u_0$, $v = v_1 x + v_0$. Composing $[u, v]$ with itself should result in a class $[u_{\text{new}}, v_{\text{new}}]$, where

$$u_{new} = u^2,$$
$$v_{new} \equiv v \mod u,$$
$$u_{new} \mid v_{new}^2 + v_{new}h + f.$$

Then this class is reduced to obtain $[u', v'] = 2[u, v]$.

We fix the notation to refer to the coefficient of X^i in a polynomial $p(X)$ as p_i.

The following expressions follow those in [Lan04a] and are explained there. We slightly modified them for the way we will apply them.

$$\tilde{v} \equiv h \mod u$$
$$r = \mathrm{res}(\tilde{v}, u)$$
$$inv' \equiv r\tilde{v}^{-1} \mod u \equiv \tilde{v}_1 x + \tilde{v}_0 + u_1 \tilde{v}_1 \mod u$$
$$k = (f + hv + v^2)/u = k' + u(x + f_4), \text{ with } k' \equiv k \mod u$$
$$s' \equiv k' \, inv' \mod u$$
$$s'' = s' \text{ made monic}$$
$$l'' = s''u$$
$$u' = s''^2 + (kr^2/s_1'^2 + hs''r/s_1')/u$$
$$v' \equiv h + (l''s_1'/r + v) \mod u'$$

Remark 1. In the actual formulae we do not follow these steps literally. It turns out to be more efficient to perform the inversion of r and s_1' jointly using Montgomery's trick.

Going into the details of these expressions one notices that the actual execution of the steps depends on the coefficients of the curve. We will present formulae for three different cases: $\deg h = 1$, $\deg h = 2$ with obtainable $h_0 = 0$ and $\deg h = 2$ in general. In the two first cases we have $h_0 = 0$ and r will simplify (to the form $r = u_0 \tilde{r}$ for some $\tilde{r}$). This allows us to cancel r in the expressions, so its inverse is not needed anymore. This is how the major speedup is obtained in the formulae. In the case of general h we need the inversion of r and perform the inversion of r and s_1' jointly as explained above.

We now study the different expressions for h separately, always performing isomorphic transformations first to achieve as many zero coefficients as possible. In characteristic 2, curves with constant h are known to be supersingular. This makes them weak under the Frey-Rück attack [FR94, Gal01] and, hence, they should be avoided for DL systems.[1] Note, that in any case one needs to make sure that the extension field of $\mathbb{F}_q$ the Tate pairing maps to has large enough degree to avoid this attack.

4   Case deg $h = 1$

In this section we assume $\deg h = 1$. One can obtain an isomorphic curve where $f_4 = h_0 = 0$ and h_1 is divided by any cube a^3. In this case it is much more useful to have h_0 zero (at the cost of a non-zero f_3) as mentioned above. It is suggested to choose the cube a^3 such that $\frac{a^3}{h_1}$ is 'small'. This allows the multiplications with it to be performed via additions and thus they are almost for free. If, as usual, one chooses $\mathbb{F}_{2^n}$ with n odd there are no non-trivial cube roots of unity. Hence, there is always an a such that $a^3 = h_1$. For even n this happens with probability $1/3$. This isomorphic curve is obtained using the following change of variables and dividing the equation by a^{10}:

$$Y \leftarrow a^5 \tilde{Y} + a^4 \sqrt{f_4 + \frac{h_0}{h_1} \tilde{X}^2}, \quad X \leftarrow a^2 \tilde{X} + \frac{h_0}{h_1}$$

Hence, we obtain a curve of the form $Y^2 + h_1 XY = X^5 + f_3 X^3 + f_2 X^2 + f_1 X + f_0$, usually with $h_1 = 1$. Adding a linear factor to the substitution of $\tilde{Y}$ one can achieve $f_2 = 0$ with probability $1/2$. A constant term leads to $f_1 = 0$. Hence, there are only two free parameters f_3, f_0 as opposed to three in the general case showing that the type is indeed special.

---

[1] These curves have found an application in pairing based cryptography. The explicit formulae for this case together with information necessary to compute the pairing are the topic of an upcoming paper.

Table 1. Doubling $\deg h = 1$, $\deg u = 2$

	Doubling $\deg h = 1$, $\deg u = 2$			
Input	$[u, v], u = x^2 + u_1 x + u_0, v = v_1 x + v_0; h_1^2, h_1^{-1}$			
Output	$[u', v'] = 2[u, v]$			
Step	Expression	$h_1 = 1$	h_1^{-1} small	h_1 arbitrary
1	compute rs_1: $z_0 = u_0^2, k_1' = u_1^2 + f_3;$ $w_0 = f_0 + v_0^2 (= rs_1'/h_1^3);$ If $w_0 = 0$ see below	3S	3S	3S
2	compute $1/s_1$ and s_0'': $w_1 = (1/w_0)z_0(= h_1/s_1);$ $z_1 = k_1'w_1, s_0'' = z_1 + u_1;$	I, 2M	I, 2M	I, 2M
3	compute u': $w_2 = h_1^2 w_1, u_1' = w_2 w_1;$ $u_0' = s_0''^2 + w_2;$	2S	S, 2M	S, 2M
4	compute v': $w_3 = w_2 + k_1';$ $v_1' = h_1^{-1}(w_3 z_1 + w_2 u_1' + f_2 + v_1^2);$ $v_0' = h_1^{-1}(w_3 u_0' + f_1 + z_0);$	S, 3M	S, 3M	S, 5M
total		I, 6S, 5M	I, 5S, 7M	I, 5S, 9M
	Special case $s = s_0$			
2'	compute s and precomputations: $s_0 = (1/h_1)k_1', w_1 = u_0 s_0 + v_0;$	1M	1M	2M
3'	compute u': $u_0' = s_0^2;$	S	S	S
4'	compute v': $w_2 = s_0(u_1 + u_0') + v_1 + h_1;$ $v_0' = u_0' w_2 + w_1;$	2M	2M	2M
total		4S, 3M	4S, 3M	4S, 4M

With the new curve coefficients the expressions r and s will simplify to:

$$r = h_1^2 u_0,$$
$$s_1' = h_1 k_0',$$
$$s_0' = u_1 s_1' + h_1 u_0 u_1.$$

Since $f + hv + v^2 = uk' + u^2 x$ we also have that

$$f_0 + v_0^2 = u_0 k_0' \quad (= rs_1'/h_1^3)$$
$$f_1 + u_0^2 + h_1 v_0 = u_1 k_0' + u_0 k_1'$$
$$f_2 + v_1(h_1 + v_1) = k_0' + u_1 k_1'$$
$$u_1^2 + f_3 = k_1'$$

making it very cheap to calculate rs_1' as the exact coefficients of k' are not necessary. We present the doubling formulae for this case in Table 1. The operations are counted for the case that $h_1 = 1$, h_1^{-1} is 'small' (multiplications with h_1^{-1} are not counted), and arbitrary h_1. Both h_1^2 and h_1^{-1} are precomputed. In Step 2 the inversion and multiplication with z_0 can also be replaced by a division as the inverse is not used later on.

5   Case deg $h = 2$

If h is of degree two then in general we cannot make any of its coefficients zero, however, it is possible to make a change of coordinates to obtain $h_2 = 1$ and $f_3 = f_2 = 0$. The case $h_0 = 0$ allows for a significant speedup, however, we can only obtain h_0 zero if there exists a b such that $b^2 + bh_1 = h_0$ and this will be at the cost of a non-zero f_4. If there is no such b, i.e. $\text{Tr}(h_0/h_1^2) \neq 0$, then choose $b = f_4$ making f_4 zero. This can be done by the following change of variables and dividing the resulting equation by h_2^{10}.

$$Y \leftarrow h_2^5 \tilde{Y} + f_3 h_2 \tilde{X} + \frac{f_3(f_3 + h_1 h_2 + f_3 h_2^2) + f_2 h_2^2}{h_2^3}, \quad X \leftarrow h_2^2 \tilde{X} + b$$

5.1   Case deg $h = 2, h_0 = 0$

First, we assume that we have obtained $h_0 = 0$ leading to an equation

$$Y^2 + (X^2 + h_1 X)Y = X^5 + f_4 X^4 + f_1 X + f_0,$$

Using a quadratic term in the transformation of Y, one can additionally obtain $f_4 = 0$ with probability $1/2$, namely if $\text{Tr}((b + f_4)/h_2^2) = 0$, with b as above. If, as usual, one chooses $\mathbb{F}_{2^n}$ with n odd then one can always obtain either $f_4 = 0$ or $f_4 = 1$. Accordingly, one has three free parameters h_1, f_1, f_0.

Then the expressions for r and s will simplify to:

$$r = u_0(u_0 + h_1^2 + h_1 u_1)$$
$$s_1' = h_1 k_0' + u_0 k_1' + u_1 k_0'$$
$$s_0' = u_1 s_1' + u_0 k_0' + h_1 u_0 k_1'$$

And since $f + hv + v^2 = uk' + u^2(x + f_4)$ we also have that

$$f_0 + v_0^2 + h_0 v_0 + f_4 u_0^2 = u_0 k_0'$$
$$f_1 + u_0^2 + h_1 v_0 + h_0 v_1 = u_1 k_0' + u_0 k_1'$$
$$v_0 + v_1(h_1 + v_1) + f_4 u_1^2 = k_0' + u_1 k_1'$$
$$u_1^2 + v_1 = k_1'.$$

Table 2. Doubling, $\deg h = 2$, $h_0 = 0$, $\deg u = 2$

\multicolumn{2}{l}{**Doubling, $\deg h = 2$, $h_0 = 0$, $\deg u = 2$**}	h_1 small	h_1 arbitrary

| \multicolumn{2}{l}{Input $[u, v]$, $u = x^2 + u_1 x + u_0$, $v = v_1 x + v_0$; h_1^2} | | |
| \multicolumn{2}{l}{Output $[u', v'] = 2[u, v]$} | | |

Step	Expression	h_1 small	h_1 arbitrary
1	compute k_1' and precomputations: $z_0 = u_0^2$, $z_1 = u_1^2$, $w_0 = v_1(h_1 + v_1)$; $k_1' = z_1 + v_1$, $z_2 = h_1 u_1$, $z_3 = f_4 u_1$;	3S, M	2S, 3M
2	compute resultant $r = \mathrm{res}(\tilde{v}, u)$: $\tilde{r} = u_0 + h_1^2 + z_2 = (r/u_0)$;		
3	compute s_1' and almost s_0': $w_2 = u_1(k_1' + z_3) + w_0$, $w_3 = v_0 + h_1 k_1'$; $s_1' = f_1 + z_0 + h_1 w_2$; $m_0 = w_2 + w_3 (= (s_0' - u_1 s_1')/u_0)$; If $s_1' = 0$ see below	M	3M
4	compute $s'' = x + s_0/s_1$ and s_1: $w_2 = 1/(s_1')(= 1/r s_1)$, $w_3 = u_0 w_2$; $w_4 = \tilde{r} w_3 (= 1/s_1)$, $w_5 = w_4^2$; $s_0'' = u_1 + m_0 w_3$;	I, S, 3M	I, S, 3M
5	compute u': $z_4 = f_4 w_4$, $u_1' = w_4 + w_5$; $u_0' = s_0''^2 + w_4(s_0'' + h_1 + u_1 + z_4)$;	S, 2M	S, 2M
6	compute v': $z_5 = w_2(m_0^2 + k_1'(s_1' + h_1 m_0))$; $z_6 = s_0'' + h_1 + z_4 + z_5$; $v_0' = v_0 + z_2 + z_1 + w_4(u_0' + z_3) + s_0'' z_6$; $v_1' = v_1 + w_4(u_1' + s_0'' + f_4 + u_1) + z_5$;	S, 5M	S, 6M
total		I, 6S, 12M	I, 5S, 17M

\multicolumn{2}{c}{Special case $s = s_0$}		
3'	compute s and precomputations: $w_1 = 1/\tilde{r}$, $s_0 = m_0 w_1$; $w_2 = u_0 s_0 + v_0 + h_0$;	I, 2M	I, 2M
4'	compute u': $u_0' = s_0^2 + s_0$;	S	S
5'	compute v': $w_1 = s_0(u_1 + u_0') + u_0' + v_1 + h_1$; $v_0' = u_0' w_1 + w_2$;	2M	2M
total		I, 4S, 6M	I, 3S, 10M

Table 2 presents the operations for the case of $h_0 = 0$. In the formulae there are two counted multiplications with f_4 and five with h_1 which are cheaper or for free when f_4 resp. h_1 is 'small'. Furthermore, h_1^2 is precomputed.

Table 3. Doubling, $\deg h = 2$, $\deg u = 2$

\multicolumn{2}{c}{**Doubling, $\deg h = 2$, $\deg u = 2$**}		h_1, h_0 small	h_1 small	h_i arbitrary
Input	$[u, v], u = x^2 + u_1 x + u_0, v = v_1 x + v_0; h_0^2$			
Output	$[u', v'] = 2[u, v]$			
Step	Expression	h_1, h_0 small	h_1 small	h_i arbitrary
1	compute k_1' and precomputations:	3S	3S	2S,2M
	$z_0 = u_0^2,\ z_1 = u_1^2,\ w_0 = v_1(h_1 + v_1);$			
	$k_1' = z_1 + v_1,\ w_1 = h_1 u_0;$			
2	compute resultant $r = \mathrm{res}(\tilde{v}, u)$:	1M	2M	2M
	$w_2 = h_0 u_1,\ r = h_0^2 + z_0 + (h_1 + u_1)(w_1 + w_2);$			
3	compute s_1' and almost s_0':	1S,2M	1S,4M	1S,5M
	$s_1' = f_1 + z_0 + h_0 z_1 + h_1(u_1 k_1' + w_0);$			
	$m_0 = f_0 + w_1 k_1' + h_0 w_0 + v_0^2 (= s_0' - u_1 s_1');$			
	If $s_1' = 0$ see below			
4	compute $s'' = x + s_0/s_1$ and s_1:	I, 2S, 5M	I, 2S, 5M	I, 2S, 5M
	$w_1 = 1/(rs_1')(= 1/r^2 s_1),\ w_2 = rw_1(= 1/s_1');$			
	$w_3 = s_1'^2 w_1(= s_1);$			
	$w_4 = rw_2(= 1/s_1),\ w_5 = w_4^2,\ s_0'' = u_1 + m_0 w_2;$			
5	compute l':	2M	2M	2M
	$l_2' = u_1 + s_0'',\ l_1' = u_1 s_0'' + u_0,\ l_0' = u_0 s_0'';$			
6	compute u':	S, M	S, M	S, M
	$u_0' = s_0''^2 + w_4(s_0'' + u_1 + h_1);$			
	$u_1' = w_4 + w_5;$			
7	compute v':	4M	4M	4M
	$w_1 = l_2' + u_1',\ w_2 = u_1' w_1 + u_0' + l_1';$			
	$v_1' = w_2 w_3 + v_1 + h_1 + u_1';$			
	$w_2 = u_0' w_1 + l_0',\ v_0' = w_2 w_3 + v_0 + h_0 + u_0';$			
total		I,7S,15M	I,7S,18M	I, 6S, 21 M
\multicolumn{5}{c}{Special case $s = s_0$}				
3'	compute s and precomputations:	I,2M	I,2M	I,2M
	$w_1 = 1/r,\ s_0 = m_0 w_1,\ w_2 = u_0 s_0 + v_0 + h_0;$			
4'	compute u':	S	S	S
	$u_0' = s_0^2 + s_0;$			
5'	compute v':	2M	2M	2M
	$w_1 = s_0(u_1 + u_0') + u_0' + v_1 + h_1,\ v_0' = u_0' w_1 + w_2;$			
total		I,5S,7M	I,5S,10M	I,4S,13M

5.2   Case $\deg h = 2, h_0 \neq 0$

For completeness we include the formulae for the general case $\deg h = 2, h_2 = 1, h_0 \neq 0$. Compared to the doubling formulae in [Lan04a] we manage to trade one multiplication for a squaring which is usually more efficient in characteristic 2. To this aim we need to include one fixed precomputation h_0^2 to the curve parameters.

For h of full degree with non-zero h_0 we can transform to

$$Y^2 + (X^2 + h_1 X + h_0)Y = X^5 + f_1 X + f_0.$$

Accordingly h_2 and f_4 are not mentioned in the formulae.

If one is willing to choose either (or both) h_1 or h_0 'small', we can get much more operations for free.

Here we only used that $f + hv + v^2 = uk' + u^2(x + f_4)$ to calculate s' cheaper and that $s_0' = u_1 s_1' + m_0$ for some relatively simple m_0:

$$s_1' = f_1 + u_0^2 + h_0 u_1^2 + h_1(u_1 k_1' + v_1(h_1 + v_1))$$
$$m_0 = f_0 + h_1 u_0 k_1' + h_0 v_1(h_1 + v_1) + v_0^2$$

6 Summary

The previous sections showed a complete study of doubling formulae depending on the type of h. We summarize the findings in Table 4 listing only the general cases; for h of degree 1 and general h the case f_4 not small does not apply since then $f_4 = 0$.

Table 4. Overview

	$h = X$	$h = h_1 X$		$h = X^2 + h_1 X$		$h = X^2 + h_1 X + h_0$		
		h_1^{-1} small		h_1 small		h_1, h_0 small	h_1 small	
f_4 small	I, 6S, 5M	I, 5S, 7M	I, 5S, 9M	I, 6S, 10M	I, 5S, 15M	I, 7S, 15M	I, 7S, 18M	I, 6S, 21M
f_4 arb.	n. a.	n. a.	n. a.	I, 6S, 12M	I, 5S, 17M	n. a.	n. a.	n. a.

7 Experimental Results

We implemented our new formulae using the NTL library. We used a simple sliding windows method with window size 3 to perform the scalar multiplication in all tests. The extension fields over $\mathbb{F}_2$ were all defined by means of a trinomial. Magma was used to create good random curve equations.

We tested the different cases for $F = \mathbb{F}_{2^{83}}$ and $F = \mathbb{F}_{2^{97}}$ and we used 1 as synonym for 'small' which means that for $\deg h = 1$ the two cases $h_1 = 1$ and h_1 'small' were combined. We also included the elliptic curve case where the field is twice as big to have comparable security, here we also used the same sliding windows method.

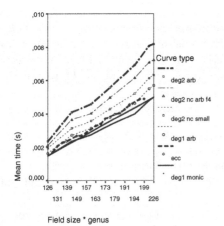

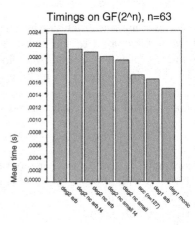

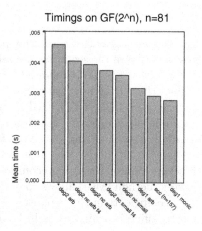

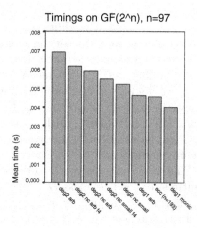

All tests were performed on a AMD Athlon XP 2500+ laptop running Gentoo linux. We used the NTL library to perform the field arithmetic. For all field extensions we used a trinomial or a pentanomial for the field arithmetic. Specifically for $n = 63, 81, 97, 127, 193$ we used a trinomial and for $n = 157$ a pentanomial. For the three bar graphs we have chosen field sizes for HEC and ECC such that the group orders were very close and that the arithmetic could be done with a trinomial to make a fair comparison. However for $n = 81$ there was no such comparable field extension for ECC. Therefore we have chosen for a smaller group order ($n = 157$) and arithmetic based upon a pentanomial. The cases included in the graphs are:

deg2 arb: The case where $\deg h = 2$ and $h_0 \neq 0$
deg2 nc arb f4:   The case where $\deg h = 2$, $h_0 = 0$, $f_4 \neq 0$;
deg2 nc arb: The case where $\deg h = 2$, $h_0 = 0$, $f_4 = 0$;
deg2 nc small f4: The case where $\deg h = 2$, $h_0 = 0$, $f_4 \neq 0$ and h_1 small;
deg2 nc small: The case where $\deg h = 2$, $h_0 = 0$, $f_4 = 0$ and h_1 small;
deg1 arb: The case where $\deg h = 1$;
deg1 monic: The case where $\deg h = 1$ and $h_1 = 1$;
ecc: ECC on the according field extension.

8   Conclusion and Outlook

We have given a complete study of doubling formulae reaching the minimal number of field operations in the respective cases and achieving a lower operation count compared to the special cases [PWP04, BD04] published so far.

The addition formulae depend far less on the equation of h and not on that of f. One can save one multiplication in case of $h_1 \in \{0, 1\}$; all other special choices allow to save at most some additions.

Accordingly, the operation counts for addition and doubling differ quite significantly, especially in the case of $h = X$, making sidechannel attacks feasible.

Following Coron's double-and-always-add countermeasure would lead to including many of the costly additions.

We assume first the setting of rather low storage capacities such that pre-computations cannot be made. Then one uses the NAF of the scalar to minimize the Hamming weight. This means that every addition (ADD) is followed by at least two doublings. As doublings have become rather cheap now, we propose to follow the strategy of putting the fixed sequence of ... DBL, ADD, DBL, DBL, DBL, ADD, DBL, DBL, DBL, ... (or even four doublings following an addition). This can be achieved by inserting several dummy doublings and only very few dummy additions.

The situation looks much more friendly if we are allowed to store precomputed multiples of the base class D. Möllers windowing method [Mö1] allows to obtain a uniform side channel by using only non-zero coefficients in the expansion.

In this article we restricted our attention to affine coordinates as in binary fields an inversion is not prohibitively expensive. It is planned to extend the formulae to inversion-free coordinate systems as well; our findings give new insight in even more efficient choices of the additional coordinates. Furthermore, the lower operation count obtained here for the special choices applies also to other coordinate systems. Projective and new coordinates bear the additional advantage that randomization techniques [Ava04] can be applied to avoid DPA, e. g. all coordinates can be multiplied by (powers of) a random integer leading to a different representation of the same ideal class. For affine coordinates one can randomize the curve equation by making a transformation to an isomorphic curve. This leaves invariant the classes of $\deg h = 1$ and $\deg h = 2$ but one cannot keep all best choices made above and hence, cannot achieve the lowest number of operations. As our publication details all possible cases one now has the choice to trade efficiency for a larger class of curves and hence better randomization.

References

[ACD+04] R. Avanzi, H. Cohen, C. Doche, G. Frey, T. Lange, K. Nguyen, and F. Ver-cauteren. *The Handbook of Elliptic and Hyperelliptic Curve Cryptography.* CRC, 2004. to appear.

[Ava03] R. M. Avanzi. Aspects of Hyperelliptic Curves over Large Prime Fields in Software Implementations. Cryptology ePrint Archive, Report 2003/253, 2003. to appear in CHES 2004.

[Ava04] R. M. Avanzi. Countermeasures Against Differential Power Analysis for Hyperelliptic Curve Cryptosystems. In *Proceedings of CHES 2003*, volume 2779 of *LNCS*, pages 366–381, 2004.

[BD04] B. Byramjee and S. Duqesne. Classification of genus 2 curves over $\mathbb{F}_{2^n}$ and optimization of their arithmetic. Cryptology ePrint Archive, Report 2004/107, 2004. http://eprint.iacr.org/.

[Can87] D. G. Cantor. Computing in the Jacobian of a hyperelliptic curve. *Math. Comp.*, 48:95–101, 1987.

[FL03] G. Frey and T. Lange. Mathematical Background of Public Key Cryptography. Technical Report 10, IEM Essen, 2003.

[FR94]   G. Frey and H. G. Rück. A remark concerning m-divisibility and the discrete logarithm problem in the divisor class group of curves. *Math. Comp.*, 62:865–874, 1994.

[Gal01]   S. D. Galbraith. Supersingular Curves in Cryptography. In *Advances in Cryptology – Asiacrypt 2001*, volume 2248 of *Lect. Notes Comput. Sci.*, pages 495–513. Springer, 2001.

[Gau00]   P. Gaudry. An algorithm for solving the discrete log problem on hyperelliptic curves. In *Advances in Cryptology – Eurocrypt'2000*, Lect. Notes Comput. Sci., pages 19–34. Springer, 2000.

[GLS00]   C. Günther, T. Lange, and A. Stein. Speeding up the Arithmetic on Koblitz Curves of Genus Two. In *Selected Areas in Cryptography – SAC 2000*, volume 2012 of *Lect. Notes Comput. Sci.*, pages 106–117. Springer, 2000.

[GT04]   P. Gaudry and E. Thomé. A double large prime variation for small genus hyperelliptic index calculus. Cryptology ePrint Archive, Report 2004/153, 2004.

[Kob89]   N. Koblitz. Hyperelliptic cryptosystems. *J. Cryptology*, 1:139–150, 1989.

[Lan04a]   T. Lange. Formulae for Arithmetic on Genus 2 Hyperelliptic Curves. http://www.itsc.ruhr-uni-bochum.de/tanja/preprints.html, 2004. to appear in J. AAECC.

[Lan04b]   T. Lange. Koblitz curve cryptosystems. *Finite Fields and Their Applications*, 2004. to appear.

[Lor96]   D. Lorenzini. *An Invitation to Arithmetic Geometry*, volume 9 of *Graduate studies in mathematics*. AMS, 1996.

[Mö1]   B. Möller. Securing elliptic curve point multiplication against side-channel attacks. In *Proc. of ISC 2001*, pages 324–334, 2001.

[MWZ98]   A. J. Menezes, Y.-H. Wu, and R. Zuccherato. An Elementary Introduction to Hyperelliptic Curves. In N. Koblitz, editor, *Algebraic Aspects of Cryptography*, pages 155–178. Springer, 1998.

[Nag04]   K. Nagao. Improvement of Thériault Algorithm of Index Calculus for Jacobian of Hyperelliptic Curves of Small Genus. Cryptology ePrint Archive, Report 2004/161, 2004.

[PWP04]   J. Pelzl, T. Wollinger, and C. Paar. Special Hyperelliptic Curve Cryptosystems of Genus Two: Efficient Arithmetic and Fast Implementation. In *Embedded Cryptographic Hardware: Design and Security*, 2004. to appear.

[Sti93]   H. Stichtenoth. *Algebraic Function Fields and Codes*. Springer, 1993.

[Thé03]   N. Thériault. Index calculus attack for hyperelliptic curves of small genus. In *Advances in cryptology – Asiacrypt 2003*, volume 2894 of *Lect. Notes Comput. Sci.*, pages 75–92. Springer, 2003.

About the Security of Ciphers
(Semantic Security and Pseudo-Random
Permutations)

Duong Hieu Phan and David Pointcheval

CNRS/ENS – Dépt d'informatique – 45 rue d'Ulm, 75230 Paris Cedex 05, France
{duong.hieu.phan, david.pointcheval}@ens.fr

Abstract. Probabilistic symmetric encryption have already been widely studied, from a theoretical point of view. Nevertheless, many applications require length-preserving encryption, to be patched at a minimal cost to include privacy without modifying the format (e.g. encrypted filesystems). In this paper, we thus consider the security notions for length-preserving, deterministic and symmetric encryption schemes, also termed *ciphers*: semantic security under lunchtime and challenge-adaptive adversaries. We furthermore provide some relations for this notion between different models of adversaries, and the more classical security notions for ciphers: pseudo-random permutations (PRP) and super pseudo-random permutations (SPRP).

1 Introduction

The main goal for any encryption scheme is secrecy: ideally, such a notion means that a ciphertext should not reveal any information about the plaintext, however powerful is the adversary. This had been defined under "perfect secrecy" [11], but also showed to be impossible, unless one uses one-time pad, which is a symmetric encryption that uses a secret key as long as the messages to be encrypted. That is, if one wants to use a small symmetric key in order to protect many plaintexts or a long message, or asymmetric encryption, such perfect secrecy is impossible.

To overcome this theoretical impossibility, but which has no real practical impact since adversaries are computationally limited, several security notions have thereafter been defined, and namely the polynomial security [4], *a.k.a.* indistinguishability of ciphertexts or semantic security. This intuitively means that no *polynomially* bounded adversary can extract any information about the plaintext, given the ciphertext.

However, in practice, an adversary is not only given the challenge ciphertext about which plaintext it wants to learn some information. It may also have access to extra information, such as plaintext-ciphertext pairs. According to the way these pairs are obtained, several kinds of attacks may be mounted: known pairs, chosen-plaintext or chosen-ciphertext attacks, in an adaptive way or not. Furthermore, when considering semantic security, the choice of the plaintexts or the ciphertexts may be allowed before the adversary has been given the challenge ciphertext (lunchtime attacks [8]), or unlimited (*challenge*-adaptive attacks [10]).

H. Handschuh and A. Hasan (Eds.): SAC 2004, LNCS 3357, pp. 182–197, 2005.

1.1   Some Wordings

In order to make things clear, let us note that all the adversaries considered in this paper are implicitly *adaptive*, in the sense that their queries to any oracle may depend on previous answers, but not necessarily on the challenge ciphertext they want to break (when such a specific challenge exists, as in the semantic security game, or the indistinguishability one). To make the distinction between whether the challenge ciphertext may impact the queries or not, we will use the terms "adaptive attacks" and "lunchtime attacks" respectively: in lunchtime attacks the adversary has a full and adaptive access to oracles but before the challenge ciphertext is known only, while in adaptive attacks this access is unlimited in time.

1.2   Motivation

Relations between various security notions for symmetric encryption, under different kinds of attacks, have been deeply studied by Bellare *et al.* [1] and Katz and Yung [6]. But they were mainly restricted to the probabilistic case. Nevertheless, many applications of encryption require length-preserving schemes. For compatibility, one may indeed want the message format to be similar, whatever it is in clear (no privacy) or encrypted (enhanced with privacy). Another famous application of encryption is for encrypted filesystems [5], which need encryption schemes able to encipher the sectors of a disk in-place, while sectors have a fixed length. Length-preserving symmetric encryption thus means *deterministic* encryption schemes. In the following we thus focus on length-preserving, deterministic and symmetric encryption schemes, also termed *ciphers*. However, from our knowledge, no analysis of *ciphers* has ever been done so far. The main reason may be that, while the security goal is privacy, no semantic security definition fits the deterministic case: it is clear that the straightforward extension of the usual notion fails when considering deterministic encryption (probabilistic encryption is a basic requirement for semantic security, when an oracle —encryption and decryption— is available at least once). As a consequence, other notions are used: pseudo-random permutation or super pseudo-random permutation properties [3, 7].

The security notion one usually requires from a block cipher is indeed to look like perfectly random permutations for random keys (family of pseudo-random permutations if one just considers chosen-plaintext attacks, or family of super pseudo-random permutations if decryption queries are also possible). This is a very strong security notion useful when the block cipher is seen as a all-purpose primitive (for providing stream ciphers with encryption modes, message authentication codes, etc.). But for confidentiality, the useful notion is secrecy only: the view of the ciphertext does not leak any useful information about the plaintext to a (polynomial) adversary. While the former notion of super pseudo-random permutations is clearly stronger than the latter, the actual relations have never been studied.

1.3   Previous Work

Security notions for encryption have been defined a long time ago, namely with the definition of polynomial security [4] (*a.k.a.* semantic security or indistinguishability). Bellare *et al.* [1] studied several variants of the latter, for symmetric encryption, under the names of *find-then-guess*, *left-or-right* and *real-or-random*, and relations in the concrete setting. Katz and Yung [6] studied the actual difference between these various kinds of attacks, against probabilistic symmetric encryption. Indeed, whereas in the public-key setting chosen-plaintext attack is the basic scenario for an adversary, since it can encrypt any plaintext of its choice granted the public key, in the symmetric setting, simply some known plaintext-ciphertext pairs may give extra information. However, they showed that an adaptive chosen-plaintext attack (where queries are allowed even after the challenge ciphertext is known) does not help more than a lunchtime attack (where oracle accesses are limited up to the reception of the challenge ciphertext.)

As already noted, the security notion usually required from a block cipher is the (super) pseudo-randomness, which means to look like *perfectly random permutations*, for randomly chosen keys. Depending on whether a decryption oracle is available or not, one indeed considers either the super pseudo-randomness or the pseudo-randomness only, respectively. The latter notion (the weakest) has been recently studied by Desai and Miner [2]. They claimed the equivalence between this notion and the semantic security under lunchtime chosen-plaintext attacks. Halevy and Rogaway [5] showed the equivalence between the super pseudo-randomness and the *left-or-right* indistinguishability, with (almost) unlimited oracle accesses, for tweakable ciphers.

1.4   Contributions

In this paper, we study the security notions of secrecy for ciphers, namely semantic security (indistinguishability of ciphertext) and (super) pseudo-randomness, with the existing relations between them.

We first show that the usual indistinguishability, modeled by the *find-then-guess* game, (with some natural restrictions) is still equivalent to the natural definition of semantic security (adapted for symmetric and deterministic encryption).

We then show that some results relative to the probabilistic case remain true for ciphers. Namely, adaptive chosen-plaintext attacks do not provide significant advantage against lunchtime attacks. More interestingly, we also consider the relation between adaptive and lunchtime chosen-ciphertext attacks, and prove that an adaptive access does not help either in the case where the cipher and its inverse are already both secure against lunchtime attacks.

Finally, for completeness, we provide relations between the above notions and the notion of (super) pseudo-random permutations. We namely prove that indistinguishability against lunchtime adversaries is equivalent to the notion of super pseudo-random permutations, when the cipher and its inverse have the same security level against lunchtime attacks: challenge-adaptive security level is not necessary. All the proofs and some additional relations, under various assumptions, are provided in the full version [9].

We believe that these results have concrete applications for practical ciphers, since the encryption and the decryption algorithms are often very similar, and thus with a similar security level. For example, when considering DES possibly using some mode of operation, under the conjecture that a slight modification of the key schedule (replacement of the left rotation by a right rotation) does not affect the security against at least lunchtime adversaries, we can show that the above results hold without any additional assumption (see the full version [9] for the application.)

2   Security Notions for Encryption

2.1   Symmetric Encryption Schemes

Let us first review the formal definition of a symmetric encryption scheme $\pi = (k, \ell, \mathcal{E}, \mathcal{D})$. It is defined by two algorithms, parameterized by a key k that is assumed to be uniformly distributed in $\{0,1\}^k$. Note that the two main data in practice are k, the bit-length of the keys, and ℓ the bit-length of the block to be encrypted:

- the encryption algorithm $\mathcal{E}_k$, which on a message m from the set $\{0,1\}^\ell$, and random coins r from $\{0,1\}^\mu$, outputs a ciphertext c in $\{0,1\}^\nu$;
- the decryption algorithm $\mathcal{D}_k$, which on a ciphertext c outputs the corresponding plaintext m, or $\perp$ if there is no corresponding plaintext.

2.2   Ciphers: Length-Preserving, Deterministic and Symmetric Encryption Schemes

In the particular case of deterministic encryption, the encryption scheme does not use any random coin, since it is furthermore length-preserving, any ciphertext is valid: it is a permutation for each key (and thus $\mu = 0$ and $\nu = \ell$.) For a given cipher $\pi = (k, \ell, \mathcal{E}, \mathcal{D})$, we can denote the inverse cipher by:

$$\pi^{-1} = (k, \ell, \mathcal{E}^{-1} = \mathcal{D}, \mathcal{D}^{-1} = \mathcal{E}).$$

2.3   Semantic Security

The natural security notion for encryption is the computational variant of perfect secrecy: the view of the ciphertext does not help to learn any information about the plaintext. This has been formalized by the notion of *semantic security* [4], for which a SEM-adversary $\mathcal{A} = (\mathcal{A}_1, \mathcal{A}_2)$ plays the following game, in two steps:

- a key k is first uniformly drawn from $\{0,1\}^k$;
- Stage 1: $\mathcal{A}_1$ outputs a samplable distribution D on the set $\{0,1\}^\ell$, together with a state information s to be forwarded to the second step of the attack;

- a message m is drawn from $\{0,1\}^\ell$ according to the distribution D (denoted $m \overset{D}{\leftarrow} \{0,1\}^\ell$), and a random tape r is uniformly drawn from $\{0,1\}^\mu$ (denoted $r \overset{R}{\leftarrow} \{0,1\}^\mu$) then one computes $c = \mathcal{E}_k(m;r)$;
- Stage 2: $\mathcal{A}_2$ is given the state information s and the ciphertext c. It outputs a computable predicate f.

The adversary is said to be successful if $f(m)$ is true. It means that it has been able to learn at least one bit of information about m, from the ciphertext c. However it is easy for an adversary to win all the time, by outputting a constant predicate f. Then we say that $\mathcal{A}$ breaks the semantic security if the predicate f holds on m with probability significantly greater than for another random plaintext m' (following the same "a priori" distribution D).

Therefore, we define the advantage $\mathsf{Adv}^{\mathsf{sem}}_\pi(\mathcal{A})$ of an adversary $\mathcal{A}$, against the semantic security of an encryption scheme π, by $\Pr[f(m) = 1] - \Pr[f(m') = 1]$ on the distribution space $\mathcal{D} = \{k \overset{R}{\leftarrow} \{0,1\}^k; (D,s) \leftarrow \mathcal{A}_1(); m, m' \overset{D}{\leftarrow} \{0,1\}^\ell; r \overset{R}{\leftarrow} \{0,1\}^\mu; c = \mathcal{E}_k(m;r); f \leftarrow \mathcal{A}_2(s,c)\}$

Definition 1. *An encryption scheme π is said to be (ε, t)-semantically secure if for any adversary $\mathcal{A}$, that runs within time t, $\mathsf{Adv}^{\mathsf{sem}}_\pi(\mathcal{A}) \leq \varepsilon$.*

Adversaries. Adversary $\mathcal{A}$ may be given extra information than just the challenge ciphertext, such as plaintext-ciphertext pairs. According to the way these pairs are defined, several kinds of attacks may be mounted: known pairs, chosen-plaintext and/or chosen-ciphertext attacks. Furthermore, the choice of the plaintexts or the ciphertexts may be allowed before the adversary has been given the challenge ciphertext only, or unlimited.

Such additional information is modeled by (un)limited access to oracles that compute encryptions or decryptions. A (t, e_1, d_1, e_2, d_2)-adversary $\mathcal{A} = (\mathcal{A}_1^{\mathcal{E}_k, \mathcal{D}_k}, \mathcal{A}_2^{\mathcal{E}_k, \mathcal{D}_k})$ is a 2-stage adversary $\mathcal{A}$ where $\mathcal{A}_1$ (resp. $\mathcal{A}_2$) can ask up to e_1 and d_1 (resp. e_2 and d_2) queries to the encryption and decryption oracles $\mathcal{E}_k$ and $\mathcal{D}_k$, with a running time bounded by t. We cover this way the passive adversary, where $e_1 = e_2 = d_1 = d_2 = 0$ that is denoted P0-C0, or any active adversary that is denoted PX-CY, according to the oracles access:

$X = \text{'1'} - e_1 > 0$ but $e_2 = 0$,   lunchtime chosen-plaintext (P1-CY);
$Y = \text{'1'} - d_1 > 0$ but $d_2 = 0$,   lunchtime chosen-ciphertext (PX-C1);
$X = \text{'2'} - e_2 > 0$ whatever e_1 is, adaptive chosen-plaintext (P2-CY);
$Y = \text{'2'} - d_2 > 0$ whatever d_1 is, adaptive chosen-ciphertext (PX-C2).

We remind that all the adversaries are adaptive w.r.t. the previous oracle answers, and thus by "adaptive" we mean "challenge-adaptive", while "lunchtime" stands for "challenge-non-adaptive".

Such a PX-CY adversary can play the attack game against semantic security, but there are natural restrictions in case of oracle access. Let us denote by $\Lambda_\mathcal{E}$ ($\Lambda_\mathcal{D}$ resp.) the lists of plaintext-ciphertext (m, c) pairs obtained from the encryption oracle (and the decryption oracle resp.). The superscript m (resp.

c) will be used to restrict these lists to the first coordinates (resp. the second coordinates), which thus leads to two lists of plaintexts $\Lambda_{\mathcal{E}}^m$ and $\Lambda_{\mathcal{D}}^m$, and two lists of ciphertexts $\Lambda_{\mathcal{E}}^c$ and $\Lambda_{\mathcal{D}}^c$. The restrictions are thus:

- if the adversary has access to the decryption oracle (that is C1 or C2), it is restricted not to ask the challenge ciphertext c in the second stage;
- in the deterministic case, if the adversary has access to the encryption oracle (that is P1 or P2), the support S_D of D (the set of plaintexts that have a non-zero probability in D) must be disjoint with the list of the plaintexts asked to the encryption oracle at any time, or obtained from the decryption oracle during the first stage.

The former restriction is the classical one, and the latter one is quite natural for deterministic encryption. We show later (by proving equivalence with the *find-then-guess* notion) that it is a minimal restriction.

Definition 2. *An encryption scheme π is said to be $(\varepsilon, t, e_1, d_1, e_2, d_2)$-semantically secure if for any (t, e_1, d_1, e_2, d_2)-SEM adversary $\mathcal{A}$, that asks at most e_1 and d_1 (resp. e_2 and d_2) encryption and decryption queries in the first stage (resp. in the second stage) within time t,* $\mathsf{Adv}_\pi^{\mathsf{sem}}(\mathcal{A}) \leq \varepsilon$.

2.4   Indistinguishability: Find-Then-Guess

The *indistinguishability* security notion (also known as *find-then-guess* [1]) involves a (t, e_1, d_1, e_2, d_2)-IND adversary $\mathcal{A} = (\mathcal{A}_1^{\mathcal{E}_k, \mathcal{D}_k}, \mathcal{A}_2^{\mathcal{E}_k, \mathcal{D}_k})$ that plays the following game:

- a key k is first uniformly drawn from $\{0,1\}^k$;
- Stage 1 (find): $\mathcal{A}_1^{\mathcal{E}_k, \mathcal{D}_k}$ outputs two plaintexts (m_0, m_1) together with a state information s;
- a bit b is randomly drawn, and a random tape r is uniformly drawn from $\{0,1\}^\mu$ then one computes $c = \mathcal{E}_k(m_b; r)$;
- Stage 2 (guess): $\mathcal{A}_2^{\mathcal{E}_k, \mathcal{D}_k}$ is given the state information s and the ciphertext c. It outputs its guess b' for b.

The adversary is said to be successful if $b' = b$. It means that it has been able to distinguish the encryption of m_0 from the encryption of m_1. However it is easy for an adversary to win half the time, by simply flipping a random coin. Then we say that $\mathcal{A}$ breaks the *find-then-guess* security if $b' = b$ with probability significantly greater than $1/2$. Therefore, we define the advantage of an adversary $\mathcal{A}$, against the *find-then-guess* security, or *indistinguishability*, of an encryption scheme π, by the following formula:

$$\mathsf{Adv}_\pi^{\mathsf{ind}}(\mathcal{A}) = 2 \times \Pr \left[\begin{array}{l} k \xleftarrow{R} \{0,1\}^k; (m_0, m_1, s) \leftarrow \mathcal{A}_1^{\mathcal{E}_k, \mathcal{D}_k}(); b \xleftarrow{R} \{0,1\}; \\ r \xleftarrow{R} \{0,1\}^\mu; c = \mathcal{E}_k(m_b; r); b' \leftarrow \mathcal{A}_2^{\mathcal{E}_k, \mathcal{D}_k}(s, c) : b' = b \end{array} \right] - 1.$$

As above, there are also natural restrictions in case of oracle access:

- if the adversary has access to the decryption oracle (that is C1 or C2), it is restricted not to ask the challenge ciphertext c in the second stage;
- in the deterministic case, if the adversary has access to the encryption oracle (that is P1 or P2) it is restricted not to ask m_0 or m_1 to the encryption oracle at any time, or to have obtained m_0 or m_1 from the decryption oracle during the first stage.

Since we focus this paper on the deterministic case, one can note that the above restrictions sum up to

$$m_0, m_1 \notin \Lambda_{\mathcal{E}}^m \qquad c \notin \Lambda_{\mathcal{D}}^c.$$

Definition 3. *An encryption scheme π is said to be $(\varepsilon, t, e_1, d_1, e_2, d_2)$-indistinguishable if for any (t, e_1, d_1, e_2, d_2)-IND adversary $\mathcal{A}$, that asks at most e_1 and d_1 (resp. e_2 and d_2) encryption and decryption queries in the first stage, a.k.a. the find stage (resp. in the second stage, a.k.a. the guess stage) within time t, $\mathsf{Adv}_{\pi}^{\mathsf{ind}}(\mathcal{A}) \leq \varepsilon$.*

2.5   Pseudo-Random and Super Pseudo-Random Permutations

Pseudo-Random Permutation. The usual security notion one requires from a block cipher is to look like perfectly random permutations, for the keys uniformly drawn. This notion can be formalized as follows: any adversary accessing an oracle $\mathcal{O}_b$ ($\mathcal{O}_0$ corresponds to the perfectly random permutation $\mathcal{P}$ —a permutation randomly chosen in the set $\mathcal{SP}_\ell$ of the permutations onto $\{0,1\}^\ell$— and $\mathcal{O}_1$ corresponds to an encryption permutation $\mathcal{E}_k$, for a random key k) cannot guess b (i.e, it cannot distinguish if it accesses the perfectly random permutation $\mathcal{P}$ or the actual encryption algorithm $\mathcal{E}_k$, with a random key):

$$\mathsf{Adv}_{\pi}^{\mathsf{prp}}(\mathcal{A}) = 2 \times \Pr \left[\begin{array}{l} \mathsf{k} \xleftarrow{R} \{0,1\}^k; \mathcal{P} \xleftarrow{R} \mathcal{SP}_\ell; \mathcal{O}_0 = \mathcal{P}; \mathcal{O}_1 = \mathcal{E}_k; \\ b \xleftarrow{R} \{0,1\}; b' \leftarrow \mathcal{A}^{\mathcal{O}_b}() : b' = b \end{array} \right] - 1.$$

Definition 4. *An encryption scheme π is said to be a (ε, t, n)-pseudo-random permutation, denoted (ε, t, n)-PRP if for any (t, n)-PRP adversary $\mathcal{A}$, that asks at most n encryption queries within time t, $\mathsf{Adv}_{\pi}^{\mathsf{prp}}(\mathcal{A}) \leq \varepsilon$.*

Super Pseudo-Random Permutation. The above notion does not take into account the decryption oracle access. Hence the stronger notion: as above, one requires that no adversary can distinguish if it accesses the perfectly random permutation $\mathcal{P}$ or the actual cipher. But in this case, the adversary not only accesses the permutation $\mathcal{O}_b$ itself, which is either $\mathcal{P}$ or $\mathcal{E}_k$, but also its inverse $\mathcal{O}_b^{-1}$, which is thus either $\mathcal{P}^{-1}$ or $\mathcal{D}_k$:

$$\mathsf{Adv}_{\pi}^{\mathsf{sprp}}(\mathcal{A}) = 2 \times \Pr \left[\begin{array}{l} \mathsf{k} \xleftarrow{R} \{0,1\}^k; \mathcal{P} \xleftarrow{R} \mathcal{SP}_\ell; \\ (\mathcal{O}_0, \mathcal{O}_0^{-1}) = (\mathcal{P}, \mathcal{P}^{-1}); (\mathcal{O}_1, \mathcal{O}_1^{-1}) = (\mathcal{E}_k, \mathcal{D}_k); \\ b \xleftarrow{R} \{0,1\}; b' \leftarrow \mathcal{A}^{\mathcal{O}_b, \mathcal{O}_b^{-1}}() : b' = b \end{array} \right] - 1.$$

Definition 5. *An encryption scheme π is said to be a (ε, t, n, m)-super pseudo-random permutation, denoted (ε, t, n, m)-SPRP if for any (t, n, m)-SPRP adversary $\mathcal{A}$, that asks at most n encryption queries and m decryption queries within time t, $\mathsf{Adv}_\pi^{\mathsf{sprp}}(\mathcal{A}) \le \varepsilon$.*

2.6   Equivalences

For completeness, let us briefly recall a well-known result: indistinguishability and semantic security are equivalent security notions, if D is required to be efficiently samplable, and the predicate f to be efficiently computable. From a more concrete point of view, we can state the following theorem.

Theorem 6. *For any encryption scheme $\pi = (k, \ell, \mathcal{E}, \mathcal{D})$:*

$$\frac{1}{2} \times \mathsf{Adv}_\pi^{\mathsf{ind}}(t, e_1, d_1, e_2, d_2) \le \mathsf{Adv}_\pi^{\mathsf{sem}}(t, e_1, d_1, e_2, d_2) \le \mathsf{Adv}_\pi^{\mathsf{ind}}(t', e_1, d_1, e_2, d_2),$$

where $t' \le t + 2T_D + T_f$, if the sampling time for D is bounded by T_D and the time to evaluate predicate f is bounded by T_f.

3   About the Indistinguishability of Ciphers

First, as already remarked, contrary to the probabilistic case, restrictions do not exist for the challenge only, which should not have been asked to the decryption oracle, but also for m_0 and m_1: they should not have been asked to the encryption oracle either, hence $m_0, m_1 \notin \Lambda_\mathcal{E}^m$ and $c \notin \Lambda_\mathcal{D}^c$.

3.1   Normal Adversary

Moreover, in the following, we restrict any adversary to behave like a *normal* adversary, which means that

- each query is asked at most once;
- if m has been asked as an encryption query (or to $\mathcal{O}_b$), with answer c, the query c will never be asked to the decryption oracle (or to $\mathcal{O}_b^{-1}$) later;
- if c has been asked as a decryption query (or to $\mathcal{O}_b^{-1}$), with answer m, the query m will never be asked to the encryption oracle (or to $\mathcal{O}_b$) later;
- for a (t, n)-PRP adversary (or (t, n, m)-SPRP adversary, respectively), the adversary makes exactly n queries to $\mathcal{O}_b$ (n queries to $\mathcal{O}_b$ and m queries to $\mathcal{O}_b^{-1}$, respectively) .

Proposition 7. *Any adversary can be made normal (with just additional look up in tables.)*

3.2   Adaptive Adversaries

Since we consider general adversaries, with possible oracle access, according to the values e_1, d_1, e_2 and d_2, for simpler notations we omit the oracle notation $\mathcal{A} = (\mathcal{A}_1^{\mathcal{E}_k, \mathcal{D}_k}, \mathcal{A}_2^{\mathcal{E}_k, \mathcal{D}_k})$ but simply use $\mathcal{A} = (\mathcal{A}_1, \mathcal{A}_2)$. Oracle access is now implicit.

Adaptive Chosen-Plaintext Attacks. First, we review the property showed by Katz and Yung [6] about probabilistic symmetric encryption schemes. By the Corollary 10 below, we prove that it still holds for ciphers: an adaptive access to the encryption oracle after the challenge ciphertext is known does not significantly increase the power of an adversary which already had adaptive access to this oracle in the first stage.

Theorem 8. *For any cipher* π:

$$\mathsf{Adv}_\pi^{\mathsf{ind}}(t, e_1, d_1, e_2, d_2) \leq (2e_2 + 1) \times \mathsf{Adv}_\pi^{\mathsf{ind}}(t, e_1 + e_2, d_1 + d_2, 0, d_2).$$

Proof. Let $\mathcal{A}$ be a (t, e_1, e_2, d_1, d_2)-normal adversary against indistinguishability. We denote by $\mathcal{A}[e_2]$ the new adversary $\mathcal{B}$ we build using $\mathcal{A}$, by restricting the interactions $\mathcal{A}$ actually has with the world. We indeed filter the queries it asks: all the queries asked by $\mathcal{A}_1$ are forwarded (as well as the answers); however, only the first ϵ_2 encryption queries are forwarded in the second stage, extra encryption queries are answered at random, but different from any previously involved ciphertext (the decryption queries, the ciphertext answers to encryption queries, and the challenge ciphertext.) We easily see that $\mathcal{A}[e_2]$ is normal. Note that $\mathcal{A}[e_2] = \mathcal{A}$ since in this case all the queries are forwarded, as well as the answers, whereas $\mathcal{A}[0]$ is in fact an adversary who makes no encryption query in the second stage, since the queries asked by $\mathcal{A}_2$ are answered at random, without querying $\mathcal{E}_k$.

Lemma 9. *For any* $1 \leq \epsilon_2 \leq e_2$:

$$\mathsf{Adv}_\pi^{\mathsf{ind}}(\mathcal{A}[\epsilon_2]) - \mathsf{Adv}_\pi^{\mathsf{ind}}(\mathcal{A}[\epsilon_2 - 1]) \leq 2 \times \mathsf{Adv}_\pi^{\mathsf{ind}}(t, e_1 + e_2, d_1 + d_2, 0, d_2).$$

The proof of this lemma is quite similar but simpler than the proof of the Lemma 12 below. The full proof of the Lemma 12 is included below. By applying e_2 times this lemma, using a classical hybrid argument, one gets

$$\mathsf{Adv}_\pi^{\mathsf{ind}}(\mathcal{A}) \leq \mathsf{Adv}_\pi^{\mathsf{ind}}(t, e_1, d_1, 0, d_2) + 2e_2 \times \mathsf{Adv}_\pi^{\mathsf{ind}}(t, e_1 + e_2, d_1 + d_2, 0, d_2),$$

which implies the claimed result.   □

In the particular case where $d_2 = 0$, one gets the following corollary which means that adaptive chosen-plaintext attacks do not give any additional power to an adversary.

Corollary 10. *For any cipher* π:

$$\mathsf{Adv}_\pi^{\mathsf{ind}}(t, e_1, d_1, e_2, 0) \leq (2e_2 + 1) \times \mathsf{Adv}_\pi^{\mathsf{ind}}(t, e_1 + e_2, d_1, 0, 0).$$

Adaptive Chosen-Plaintext and Chosen-Ciphertext Attacks. This result was already known. But the particular case of deterministic encryption admits improvements: under specific assumptions, an adaptive access to both the encryption oracle and the decryption oracle after the challenge ciphertext is known does not significantly increase the power of an adversary which already had access to these oracles in the first stage. Interestingly, the cost of the reduction is only linear in the (total) number of queries.

Theorem 11. *For any cipher π: $\mathsf{Adv}_\pi^{\mathsf{ind}}(t, e_1, d_1, e_2, d_2)$ is upper-bounded by*

$$\left(2(e_2 + d_2) + 1\right)\left(\begin{array}{c}\mathsf{Adv}_\pi^{\mathsf{ind}}(t, e_1 + e_2, d_1 + d_2, 0, 0) \\ +\mathsf{Adv}_{\pi^{-1}}^{\mathsf{ind}}(t, d_1 + d_2 - 1, e_1 + e_2 + 2, 0, 0)\end{array}\right).$$

Proof. Let $\mathcal{A}$ be a (t, e_1, e_2, d_1, d_2)-normal adversary against indistinguishability. As above, we denote by $\mathcal{A}[n]$ the new adversary $\mathcal{B}$ we build using $\mathcal{A}$, by restricting the interactions $\mathcal{A}$ actually has with the world: all the queries in the first stage are forwarded, and the answers too, but only the first n queries are answered correctly in the second stage, while extra queries are answered at random but different from any message which previously appeared in the same category: if it is an encryption query, the answer must be different from any previously involved ciphertext (the decryption queries, the ciphertext answers to encryption queries, and the challenge); if it is a decryption query, the answer must be different from any previously involved plaintext (the encryption queries, the plaintext answers to decryption queries, and the two plaintexts output of $\mathcal{A}_1$). We easily see that $\mathcal{A}[n]$ is normal. Note that $\mathcal{A}[e_2 + d_2] = \mathcal{A}$, since there are at most $e_2 + d_2$ oracle queries in the second stage. However, $\mathcal{A}[0]$ is a lunchtime adversary, since all the queries in the second stage are answered at random, without querying any oracle.

Lemma 12. *For any $n \le e_2 + d_2$: the difference $\mathsf{Adv}_\pi^{\mathsf{ind}}(\mathcal{A}[n]) - \mathsf{Adv}_\pi^{\mathsf{ind}}(\mathcal{A}[n-1])$ is upper-bounded by*

$$2 \times \left(\mathsf{Adv}_\pi^{\mathsf{ind}}(t, e_1 + e_2, d_1 + d_2, 0, 0) + \mathsf{Adv}_{\pi^{-1}}^{\mathsf{ind}}(t, d_1 + d_2 - 1, e_1 + e_2 + 2, 0, 0)\right),$$

where t is the running time of $\mathcal{A}$.

Proof. We construct two adversaries $\mathcal{B}$ and $\mathcal{C}$, such that for each successful execution of $\mathcal{A}$, one of $\mathcal{B}$ or $\mathcal{C}$ is successful. The former is a $(t, e_1 + e_2, d_1 + d_2, 0, 0)$-IND adversary against π, while the latter is a $(t, d_1 + d_2 - 1, e_1 + e_2 + 2, 0, 0)$-IND adversary against π^{-1}.

Description of $\mathcal{B}$ and $\mathcal{C}$. Our adversaries $\mathcal{B}$ and $\mathcal{C}$ actually restrict the interactions $\mathcal{A}$ has, the same way as $\mathcal{A}[n-1]$ or $\mathcal{A}[n]$ would do: $\mathcal{B}_1$ and $\mathcal{C}_1$ run $\mathcal{A}_1$, forwarding any query/answer to their corresponding encryption/decryption oracles[1]. When $\mathcal{A}_1$ outputs (m_0, m_1), $\mathcal{B}_1$ and $\mathcal{C}_1$ choose a random bit b and get $c = \mathcal{E}_k(m_b)$. This value requires one more encryption query to π for $\mathcal{B}_1$, while it requires one more decryption query to π^{-1} for $\mathcal{C}_1$. Then $\mathcal{B}_1$ and $\mathcal{C}_1$ run $\mathcal{A}_2(c)$ up to the nth query q, still forwarding any query/answer to their corresponding oracles, except that last q one (the nth query of $\mathcal{A}_2$). In the case that $\mathcal{A}_2$ makes less than n queries, $\mathcal{B}$ and $\mathcal{C}$ complete randomly their games by choosing immediately two random plaintexts different from any previous plaintext and outputting randomly the guesses. The advantages are thus exactly zero in this case. We thus now turn to the case where such a query q exists:

---

[1] Note that a query to $\mathcal{E}_k$ corresponds to an encryption query to π (for $\mathcal{B}_1$), while it corresponds to a decryption query to π^{-1} (for $\mathcal{C}_1$), and similarly for a query to $\mathcal{D}_k$.

- If q is an encryption query, $\mathcal{C}$ completes randomly its game in the above sense with a random answer since we do not care about it but only about $\mathcal{B}$, which attacks π as follows. $\mathcal{B}_1$ chooses a random plaintext q_0 for π, different from any previous plaintext (encryption queries and decryption answers), and then outputs $(q_0, q_1 = q)$. Thereafter, the challenge ciphertext $a = \mathcal{E}_k(q_d)$ is produced, for a random bit d. On input a, $\mathcal{B}_2$ resumes $\mathcal{A}_2$ using a for answering the query q (note that $\mathcal{B}_2$ does not query on q). When $\mathcal{A}_2$ outputs its guess b' for the bit b, $\mathcal{B}_2$ outputs its guess d', for the bit d, that is defined by the boolean value of the test $b' = b$ (in other words, if $b' = b$, then $d' = 1$, else $d' = 0$).
- If q is a decryption query, $\mathcal{B}$ completes randomly its game in the above sense with a random answer since we do not care about it but only about $\mathcal{C}$, which attacks π^{-1} as follows. $\mathcal{C}_1$ chooses a random plaintext q_0 for π^{-1} (and thus a ciphertext for π), different from any previous plaintext for π^{-1} ($\mathcal{D}_k$ queries and $\mathcal{E}_k$ answers) but also from $\mathcal{E}_k(m_{\bar{b}})$ ($\mathcal{C}_1$ must ask this further query —a decryption query for π^{-1}— to learn this value and avoid the collision), and then outputs $(q_0, q_1 = q)$. Thereafter, the challenge $a = \mathcal{D}_k(q_d)$, a ciphertext for π^{-1}, is produced for a random bit d. On input a, $\mathcal{C}_2$ resumes $\mathcal{A}_2$ using a for answering the query q. When $\mathcal{A}_2$ outputs its guess b' for the bit b, $\mathcal{C}_2$ outputs its guess d', for the bit d, that is defined by the boolean value of the test $b' = b$ (in other words, if $b' = b$, then $d' = 1$, else $d' = 0$).

Advantages of $\mathcal{B}$ and $\mathcal{C}$. We first check that $\mathcal{B}$ and $\mathcal{C}$ satisfy the access restriction to the oracles, which is easy. Indeed, in the case $\mathcal{B}_1$ and $\mathcal{C}_1$ choose a random plaintext q_0 (when $\mathcal{A}$ makes the nth query), they choose it different from any previous plaintext. Then, we know that $\mathcal{B}_2$ and $\mathcal{C}_2$ do not ask any other query, the access restriction to the decryption oracle is then satisfied. Let us now evaluate the number of queries:

- Algorithm $\mathcal{B}_1$ makes at most $e_1 + e_2$ encryption queries (all the encryption queries that $\mathcal{A}$ makes up to the nth query q excepted q itself and it must make one more encryption query to get $c = \mathcal{E}_k(m_b)$), and $d_1 + d_2$ decryption queries (all the decryption queries that $\mathcal{A}$ makes up to the nth query);
- Algorithm $\mathcal{C}_1$ makes at most $d_1 + d_2 - 1$ encryption queries (all the decryption queries that $\mathcal{A}$ makes up to the nth query q excepted the query q itself) and $e_1 + e_2 + 2$ decryption queries (all the encryption queries that $\mathcal{A}$ makes up to the nth query, one more query to get $c = \mathcal{E}_k(m_b)$, and one more query to learn the value $\mathcal{E}_k(m_{\bar{b}})$).

About the running time, no extra computation has to be perform by either $\mathcal{B}$ or $\mathcal{C}$. We thus get the following upper-bounds, where t is the running time of $\mathcal{A}$:

$$\mathsf{Adv}_\pi^{\mathsf{ind}}(\mathcal{B}) \le \mathsf{Adv}_\pi^{\mathsf{ind}}(t, e_1 + e_2, d_1 + d_2, 0, 0),$$
$$\mathsf{Adv}_{\pi^{-1}}^{\mathsf{ind}}(\mathcal{C}) \le \mathsf{Adv}_{\pi^{-1}}^{\mathsf{ind}}(t, d_1 + d_2 - 1, e_1 + e_2 + 2, 0, 0).$$

Let us now analyze the relation between the advantages of $\mathcal{B}$ and $\mathcal{C}$, and those of $\mathcal{A}[n]$ and $\mathcal{A}[n-1]$. We denote by Enc^q the event in which q is an encryption query and we also denote by $\mathsf{Adv}_\pi^{\mathrm{ind}}(\mathcal{A}\,|\,\mathsf{Enc}^q)$ the conditional advantage of $\mathcal{A}$ providing the event Enc^q holds, that is

$$\mathsf{Adv}_\pi^{\mathrm{ind}}(\mathcal{A}\,|\,\mathsf{Enc}^q) = \Pr[\mathcal{A}() = 1\,|\,b = 1 \wedge \mathsf{Enc}^q] - \Pr[\mathcal{A}() = 1\,|\,b = 0 \wedge \mathsf{Enc}^q].$$

- if q is an encryption query, we have a non trivial adversary $\mathcal{B}$:

$$\mathsf{Adv}_\pi^{\mathrm{ind}}(\mathcal{B}) = 2\Pr[d' = d] - 1 = \Pr[d' = 1\,|\,d = 1] - \Pr[d' = 1\,|\,d = 0].$$

When $d = 1$, the distribution of b and b' used by $\mathcal{B}$ is exactly the same as the usual attack game for $\mathcal{A}[n]$, since a is the correct answer of $q_1 = q$. When $d = 0$, the answer of the encryption query q (w.r.t. π) is a, the encryption of q_0 (a random distinct message), and thus a random ciphertext different from any previously involved ciphertext because of the permutation propriety of the cipher. The last remark shows that $\mathcal{B}$ is identical to $\mathcal{A}[n-1]$. Since $d' = 1$ means $b' = b$, we have[2]:

$$\begin{aligned}
\mathsf{Adv}_\pi^{\mathrm{ind}}(\mathcal{B}\,|\,\mathsf{Enc}^q) &= \Pr[d' = 1\,|\,d = 1 \wedge \mathsf{Enc}^q] - \Pr[d' = 1\,|\,d = 0 \wedge \mathsf{Enc}^q] \\
&= \frac{1}{2}\cdot\left(\mathsf{Adv}_\pi^{\mathrm{ind}}(\mathcal{A}[n]\,|\,\mathsf{Enc}^q) - \mathsf{Adv}_\pi^{\mathrm{ind}}(\mathcal{A}[n-1]\,|\,\mathsf{Enc}^q)\right).
\end{aligned}$$

- if q is a decryption query, a similar argument can be provided for the adversary $\mathcal{C}$: when $d = 1$, $\mathcal{C}$ is identical to $\mathcal{A}[n]$ and when $d = 0$, $\mathcal{C}$ is identical to $\mathcal{A}[n-1]$ because the encryption of q_0 (a random distinct message) for $\mathcal{C}$ is a random plaintext different from any previous plaintext (included m_0 and m_1.) Therefore, we have[2]:

$$\begin{aligned}
\mathsf{Adv}_\pi^{\mathrm{ind}}(\mathcal{C}\,|\,\overline{\mathsf{Enc}^q}) &= \Pr[d' = 1\,|\,d = 1 \wedge \overline{\mathsf{Enc}^q}] - \Pr[d' = 1\,|\,d = 0 \wedge \overline{\mathsf{Enc}^q}] \\
&= \frac{1}{2}\cdot\left(\mathsf{Adv}_\pi^{\mathrm{ind}}(\mathcal{A}[n]\,|\,\overline{\mathsf{Enc}^q}) - \mathsf{Adv}_\pi^{\mathrm{ind}}(\mathcal{A}[n-1]\,|\,\overline{\mathsf{Enc}^q})\right).
\end{aligned}$$

In the above formula, $\overline{\mathsf{Enc}^q}$ denotes the negation of event Enc^q. With the remark that $\mathsf{Adv}_\pi^{\mathrm{ind}}(\mathcal{B}\,|\,\overline{\mathsf{Enc}^q}) = 0$ and $\mathsf{Adv}_\pi^{\mathrm{ind}}(\mathcal{C}\,|\,\mathsf{Enc}^q) = 0$, we have:

$$\Pr[\mathsf{Enc}^q] \times \mathsf{Adv}_\pi^{\mathrm{ind}}(\mathcal{B}\,|\,\mathsf{Enc}^q) = \mathsf{Adv}_\pi^{\mathrm{ind}}(\mathcal{B}) \le \mathsf{Adv}_\pi^{\mathrm{ind}}(e_1 + e_2, d_1 + d_2, 0, 0),$$
$$\Pr[\overline{\mathsf{Enc}^q}] \times \mathsf{Adv}_\pi^{\mathrm{ind}}(\mathcal{C}\,|\,\overline{\mathsf{Enc}^q}) = \mathsf{Adv}_\pi^{\mathrm{ind}}(\mathcal{C}) \le \mathsf{Adv}_{\pi-1}^{\mathrm{ind}}(d_1 + d_2 - 1, e_1 + e_2 + 2, 0, 0).$$

Combined with the two above equations, this leads to the expected result.   □

Starting from $\mathcal{A} = \mathcal{A}[e_2 + d_2]$, and applying $e_2 + d_2$ times the above relation, one gets:

$$\mathsf{Adv}_\pi^{\mathrm{ind}}(\mathcal{A}) \le \mathsf{Adv}_\pi^{\mathrm{ind}}(\mathcal{A}[0]) + 2(e_2 + d_2)\left(\begin{array}{l}\mathsf{Adv}_\pi^{\mathrm{ind}}(t, e_1 + e_2, d_1 + d_2, 0, 0) \\ + \mathsf{Adv}_{\pi-1}^{\mathrm{ind}}(t, d_1 + d_2 - 1, e_1 + e_2 + 2, 0, 0)\end{array}\right).$$

Since $\mathcal{A}[0]$ is a $(t, e_1, d_1, 0, 0)$-IND adversary, and thus its advantage is bounded by $\mathsf{Adv}_\pi^{\mathrm{ind}}(t, e_1 + e_2, d_1 + d_2, 0, 0)$, one gets the result.   □

---

[2] We remind that $\mathsf{Adv}_\pi^{\mathrm{ind}}(\mathcal{A}\,|\,\mathrm{E})$ denotes the conditional advantage of any adversary $\mathcal{A}$ providing the event E holds.

In many ciphers, the encryption algorithm and the decryption algorithm are similar. Therefore, if the cipher is secure against any lunchtime adversary (IND-P1-C1), its inverse achieves a similar security level. The above theorem implies that the cipher is actually secure against any adaptive adversary (IND-P2-C2): thus, adaptive attacks do not help against symmetric and deterministic encryption schemes.

4   Indistinguishability and Pseudo-Randomness

In this section, we give a relation between the notion of indistinguishability defined above and the classical security notions for ciphers, namely to provide a pseudo-random permutation family or a super pseudo-random permutation family.

4.1   IND-P1-C0 is Equivalent to Pseudo-Randomness

In [2], Desai and Miner claimed that:

Proposition 13. *For any cipher π:*

$$\frac{1}{2} \times \mathsf{Adv}_\pi^{\mathsf{ind}}(t, e_1, 0, 0, 0) \leq \mathsf{Adv}_\pi^{\mathsf{prp}}(t, e_1 + 1) \leq (e_1 + 1) \times \mathsf{Adv}_\pi^{\mathsf{ind}}(t, e_1 + 1, 0, 0, 0).$$

We prove this proposition (which has not been published anywhere) in the following two theorems whose results are more general. In fact, the left relation is a particular case of Theorem 14 where $d_1 = e_2 = d_2 = 0$, while the right relation is a particular case of the proof of Theorem 15 where $n = e_1 + 1$ and $m = 0$. Since we know that the last query is always an encryption query, the second term disappears. We just have to build the adversary $\mathcal{B}$.

4.2   IND-P2-C2 is "Almost" Equivalent to Super Pseudo-Randomness

The first theorem is the intuitive and easy direction:

Theorem 14. *For any cipher π:*

$$\mathsf{Adv}_\pi^{\mathsf{ind}}(t, e_1, d_1, e_2, d_2) \leq 2 \times \mathsf{Adv}_\pi^{\mathsf{sprp}}(t, e_1 + e_2 + 1, d_1 + d_2).$$

Proof. We are assuming that π is SPRP-secure. We then show that π is also secure in the sense of IND-P2-C2. Let $\mathcal{A}$ to be a (t, e_1, d_1, e_2, d_2)-IND adversary attacking π. We want to show that $\mathsf{Adv}_\pi^{\mathsf{ind}}(\mathcal{A})$ is negligible. To this end, we describe a SPRP adversary $\mathcal{B}$ which attacks π by using $\mathcal{A}$ as a sub-program.

Description of $\mathcal{B}^{\mathcal{O}_b, \mathcal{O}_b^{-1}}$. Our adversary $\mathcal{B}$ runs $\mathcal{A}_1$ by answering its encryption/decryption queries, which are simply forwarded to the oracles $\mathcal{O}_b$ and $\mathcal{O}_b^{-1}$, respectively. When $\mathcal{A}_1$ outputs (m_0, m_1), $\mathcal{B}$ chooses a random bit d and gets

$y_d = \mathcal{O}_b(m_d)$. $\mathcal{B}$ then runs $\mathcal{A}_2(y_d)$, still forwarding all the encryption/decryption queries of $\mathcal{A}$ to the oracles $\mathcal{O}_b$ and $\mathcal{O}_b^{-1}$, respectively. When $\mathcal{A}_2$ outputs its guess d' for the bit d, $\mathcal{B}$ outputs its guess b', for the bit b, that is defined by the boolean value of the test $d' = d$ (i.e, if $d' = d$, then $b' = 1$, else $b' = 0$).

Advantage of $\mathcal{B}$. We now consider the relation between the advantage of $\mathcal{B}$ and the advantage of $\mathcal{A}$.

- in the case $b = 1$, this game is exactly the game in which $\mathcal{A}$ plays against π. The probability that $\mathcal{B}$ outputs $b' = 1$ is therefore the probability that $d' = d$: $(\mathsf{Adv}_\pi^{\mathsf{ind}}(\mathcal{A}) + 1)/2$.
- in the case $b = 0$, because $\mathcal{A}$ queries a random permutation, and $y_d = \mathcal{P}(m_d)$ is perfectly independent with m_0 and m_1, $\mathcal{A}_2$ therefore gives an answer $d' = d$ with probability $1/2$. Consequently, $\mathcal{B}$ gives $b' = 1$ with probability $1/2$.

Combining these two cases, in which $\mathcal{A}$ is a (t, e_1, d_1, e_2, d_2)-IND adversary and $\mathcal{B}$ is a $(t, e_1 + e_2 + 1, d_1 + d_2)$-SPRP adversary, we get the expected result. $\mathcal{B}$ indeed asks $e_1 + e_2 + 1$ queries to $\mathcal{O}_b$, because of the extra query to get y_d. □

The other direction is less natural, and much more surprising:

Theorem 15. *For any cipher π:*

$$\mathsf{Adv}_\pi^{\mathsf{sprp}}(t, n, m) \leq (n + m) \times \left(\mathsf{Adv}_\pi^{\mathsf{ind}}(t, n, m, 0, 0) + \mathsf{Adv}_{\pi^{-1}}^{\mathsf{ind}}(t, m, n, 0, 0) \right).$$

Proof. Let $\mathcal{A}$ be a (t, n, m)-SPRP normal adversary against π. We denote by $\mathcal{A}[\eta]$ the hybrid adversary $\mathcal{B}$, built using $\mathcal{A}$ by restricting its interactions: the first η queries to the oracles are answered by $\mathcal{E}_k$ (for an encryption query – oracle $\mathcal{O}$) and by $\mathcal{D}_k$ (for a decryption query – oracle $\mathcal{O}^{-1}$), the following queries are answered by $\mathcal{P}$ and $\mathcal{P}^{-1}$ respectively. The goal of the adversary is always to output a bit b'. We define $\mathsf{Pl}(\mathcal{B})$ to be the probability that any adversary $\mathcal{B}$ gives the answer $b' = 1$. We thus have:

$$\mathsf{Adv}_\pi^{\mathsf{sprp}}(\mathcal{A}) = \Pr[\mathcal{A}() = 1 \mid b = 1] - \Pr[\mathcal{A}() = 1 \mid b = 0]$$
$$= \mathsf{Pl}[\mathcal{A}^{\mathcal{E}_k, \mathcal{D}_k}() = 1] - \Pr[\mathcal{A}^{\mathcal{P}, \mathcal{P}^{-1}}() = 1] = \mathsf{Pl}(\mathcal{A}[n + m]) - \mathsf{Pl}(\mathcal{A}[0]).$$

Lemma 16. *For any $\eta \leq n + m$:*

$$\mathsf{Pl}(\mathcal{A}[\eta]) - \mathsf{Pl}(\mathcal{A}[\eta - 1]) \leq \mathsf{Adv}_\pi^{\mathsf{ind}}(n, m, 0, 0) + \mathsf{Adv}_{\pi^{-1}}^{\mathsf{ind}}(m, n, 0, 0).$$

This proof is similar to the one of the Lemma 12. The idea is that we construct two adversaries, a $(t, n, m, 0, 0)$-adversary $\mathcal{B}$ against π and a $(t, m, n, 0, 0)$-adversary $\mathcal{C}$ against π^{-1} such that one of their advantages is exactly equal to the left-hand side. These two adversaries run $\mathcal{A}$ up to the ηth query of $\mathcal{A}[\eta]$ using $\mathcal{E}_k$ for answering a query to $\mathcal{O}_b$ and using $\mathcal{D}_k$ for answering a query to $\mathcal{O}_b$. According to the type of the ηth query of $\mathcal{A}[\eta]$ (an encryption query or a decryption query), $\mathcal{B}_1$ or $\mathcal{C}_1$ outputs this query as one of its two chosen messages (the other is chosen randomly) and then $\mathcal{B}_1$ or $\mathcal{C}_1$ gives its received challenge as the answer to the ηth query of $\mathcal{A}$. $\mathcal{B}_2$ or $\mathcal{C}_2$ then outputs its guess according to the guess of $\mathcal{A}$ without making any query.

Applying $n + m$ times this lemma, we obtain the expected result. $\square$

From these two theorems, we see that a cipher is a super pseudo-random permutation if and only if itself and its inverse achieve semantic security against any lunchtime adversary (IND-P1-C1). In other words, under the conjecture that a cipher and its inverse achieve a similar security level secure against any lunchtime adversary, SPRP and IND-P1-C1 are equivalent with a linear-cost reduction.

The more intuitive equivalence, between IND-P2-C2 and SPRP, can be obtained under a weaker condition: if π^{-1} is just IND-P1-C0. This result is given in details in the full version [9].

Acknowledgement

The work described in this paper has been supported in part by the European Commission through the IST Programme under Contract IST-2002-507932 ECRYPT. The information in this document reflects only the authors' views, is provided as is and no guarantee or warranty is given that the information is fit for any particular purpose. The user thereof uses the information at its sole risk and liability.

References

1. M. Bellare, A. Desai, E. Jokipii, and P. Rogaway. A Concrete Security Treatment of Symmetric Encryption: Analysis of the DES Modes of Operation. In *Proc. of the 38th FOCS*. IEEE, New York, 1997.
2. A. Desai and S. Miner. Concrete Security Characterization of PRFs and PRPs: Reduction and Applications. In *Asiacrypt '00*, LNCS 1976, pages 503–516. Springer-Verlag, Berlin, 2000.
3. O. Goldreich, S. Goldwasser, and S. Micali. On The Cryptographic Applications of Random Functions. In *Crypto '84*, LNCS 196. Springer-Verlag, Berlin, 1985.
4. S. Goldwasser and S. Micali. Probabilistic Encryption. *Journal of Computer and System Sciences*, 28:270–299, 1984.
5. S. Halevi and P. Rogaway. A Tweakable Enciphering Mode. In *Crypto '03*, LNCS 2729, pages 482–499. Springer-Verlag, Berlin, 2003.
6. J. Katz and M. Yung. Complete Characterization of Security Notions for Probabilistic Private-Key Encryption. In *Proc. of the 32nd STOC*. ACM Press, New York, 2000.
7. M. Luby and Ch. Rackoff. How to Construct Pseudorandom Permutations from Pseudorandom Functions. *SIAM Journal of Computing*, 17(2):373–386, 1988.
8. M. Naor and M. Yung. Public-Key Cryptosystems Provably Secure against Chosen Ciphertext Attacks. In *Proc. of the 22nd STOC*, pages 427–437. ACM Press, New York, 1990.

9. D. H. Phan and D. Pointcheval. About the Security of Ciphers (Semantic Security and Pseudo-Random Permutations). In *SAC '04*. Springer-Verlag, Berlin, 2004. Full version available from `http://www.di.ens.fr/users/pointche/`.

10. C. Rackoff and D. R. Simon. Non-Interactive Zero-Knowledge Proof of Knowledge and Chosen Ciphertext Attack. In *Crypto '91*, LNCS 576, pages 433–444. Springer-Verlag, Berlin, 1992.

11. C. E. Shannon. Communication Theory of Secrecy Systems. *Bell System Technical Journal*, 28(4):656–715, 1949.

A Subliminal Channel in Secret Block Ciphers

Adam Young[1] and Moti Yung[2]

[1] Cigital, Inc.
ayoung@cigital.com
[2] Dept. of Computer Science, Columbia University
moti@cs.columbia.edu

Abstract. In this paper we present the first general purpose subliminal channel that can be built into a secret symmetric cipher by a malicious designer. Subliminal channels traditionally exploit randomness that is used in probabilistic cryptosystems. In contrast, our channel is built into a *deterministic* block cipher, and thus it is based on a new principle. It is a broadcast channel that assumes that the sender and the receiver know the subliminal message m_s (i.e., something derived from their common key). We show that the designer can expect to be able to read m_s when $O(|m_s|log|m_s|)$ plaintext/ciphertext pairs are obtained. Here $|m_s|$ is the length of m_s in bits. We show how to turn the channel into a narrowcast channel using a deterministic asymmetric cipher and then present an application of the narrowcast channel. In this application, the secret block cipher securely and subliminally transmits the symmetric key of the sender and receiver to the malicious designer and confidentiality holds even when the cipher is made public.

1   Introduction

One of the central concerns, from a user's standpoint, of using a black-box cryptographic device is the possibility that the output might maliciously expose private data. Cryptosystems that contain subliminal channels allow this type of information leakage to occur. Subliminal channels have been shown to exist in digital signing algorithms, asymmetric key generation algorithms, and so forth. These channels traditionally exploit randomness in the algorithms they are built into, and more recently it has been shown how to exploit redundancies in plaintext to create such channels. The methodology behind identifying a subliminal channel within a particular cryptosystem involves identifying these features wherever they are present. However, to date, no general-purpose subliminal channel has been shown to exist in a block cipher which is a deterministic function (this holds for published as well as secret designs). In this paper we present the first general-purpose subliminal channel in secret block ciphers.

We stress again that this channel is built into a *deterministic* function, which contrasts with traditional subliminal channels that have been identified in *probabilistic* cryptosystems. Subliminal channels typically use acceptance/rejection on the random bits that are available to the cryptosystem in order to transmit

H. Handschuh and A. Hasan (Eds.): SAC 2004, LNCS 3357, pp. 198–211, 2005.
© Springer-Verlag Berlin Heidelberg 2005

the subliminal message m_s in the output. A deterministic channel within a deterministic cryptosystem does not have the luxury of using random bits in this fashion, so it may seem somewhat counter-intuitive that subliminal information can be encoded in the output ciphertext.

This brings us to the nature of our channel, which is atypical and suggests that the definition of a subliminal channel should be broadened. A typical subliminal channel allows, e.g., a sender to send a subliminal message (through digital signatures for example) to a receiver unbeknownst to a passive eavesdropper. Our channel allows a sending device to send a subliminal message to a receiving device *that already knows the subliminal message* such that the subliminal message can be read by a known-plaintext attacker that is privy to secret information (a particular private key). Our main application is a backdoor attack against a secret block cipher that covertly leaks the *asymmetric* encryption of the sender and receiver's symmetric key to the cipher designer. Furthermore, the channel employed this way is robust against reverse-engineering (robust meaning that the confidentiality of encryptions still holds even if the cipher becomes public).

Due to space limitations only an overview of the other applications will be given. A second application is an attack on operating systems that share the same decryption private key within the security kernel (e.g., to decrypt encrypted programs before running them). The attack subliminally leaks the private key. A third application is an attack that subliminally leaks the private signing symmetric key of Russia to the U.S. within the Salt II Treaty verification protocol [23].

1.1   Modern Motivations for Backdoor Research

In the past, the motivation for studying backdoors in symmetric secret ciphers was simple. The U.S. government had endorsed Skipjack, a classified block cipher [16]. RC4 is another cipher that was initially a trade secret (of RSA Data Security Inc.). Companies still engage in the practice of marketing secret ciphers under the premise that they are proprietary. So, the chief motivation for this research has not changed with time.

Also, digital rights management efforts have sought to utilize software obfuscation and hardware implementations to protect digital content ([4] obfuscated a published cipher). In fact, recently Boneh et al. described a technique akin to differential fault analysis to cryptanalyze a simplied version of a software obfuscation package [10]. They suggested countermeasures to their attack and mentioned the possibility of using secret designs prior to obfuscating the code. So, the hazards of secret ciphers are still not fully observed.

1.2   Subliminal Channels and Backdoor Ciphers

To show that the notion of a subliminal channel was applicable in practice, the *prisoner's problem* was devised [21]. In this problem, two prisoners want to communicate *subliminal messages* to each other within digital signatures so that the warden, who verifies all signatures, will not know this is taking place. Solutions to this problem have been given for DSA, ElGamal, and others. Progress has been slow in subliminal channel research [6, 1] in both identifying attack possibilities as well as in formally defining the subject. Progress has also been slow, yet steady, in researching robust backdoors in cryptosystems [24, 26]. Previously, no subliminal channel of a general nature was known to exist in secret block ciphers nor in publishable block ciphers.

Rijmen and Preneel gave a methodology for designing a backdoor cipher where the cipher that results has a *public* specification [19]. The recovery ability is based on a specific trapdoor that allows the designer to break the encryption using linear cryptanalysis. Security issues with this methodology were subsequently addressed [25]. Related work includes [17] which was cryptanalyzed in [3, 7].

Earlier work on building backdoors into symmetric ciphers showed that a shared string between the sender and receiver (the symmetric encryption key) could be subliminally leaked. However, these designs left room for improvement. The cipher in [27] reveals multiple plaintext bits (in particular bit positions) in every ciphertext to the reverse-engineer. The backdoor presented in [28] only leaks subliminal information when the input plaintext is highly redundant and also reveals an upper or lower bound on the entropy of every plaintext to the reverse-engineer. The non-trivial security goal that we achieve in this paper is the construction of a backdoor cipher that does not leak plaintext bits to the reverse-engineer nor one that requires redundancy in plaintexts to operate correctly.

A fundamental difference between the cipher we present here and Monkey [27] is the use of *pre-processing symmetric decryption* in the block encryption function (Monkey uses only a post-processing encryption during block encryption). Thus, the block encryption function presented here involves *both* post and pre-processing tranformations in the block encryption function. This is an integral part of the mechanism that prevents the reverse-engineer from learning plaintext bits in individual bit positions.

2   Notation and Definitions

$A \parallel B$ denotes the concatenation of strings A and B. $A \oplus B$ denotes the bitwise XOR of A with B. The symbol $\triangleq$ is used to define a function. For example, $f(x) \triangleq x^2 + 3x - 7$. $\{0, 1\}^\infty$ is the set of all bit strings that are each countably infinite in length. A random oracle is defined [2] as:

Definition 1. *A* **random oracle** *R is a function from $\{0, 1\}^*$ to $\{0, 1\}^\infty$ such that for a given query s to R, each and every output bit of $R(s)$ is chosen uniformly at random and independent of every bit in s.*

If R is given query s twice, R will respond with the same bit string.

A random function is similar to a random oracle except that the range is defined to be a finite set. It is possible to instantiate a random function F_θ :

$\{0,1\}^* \rightarrow S$ where $S = \{0, 1, 2, ..., \theta - 1\}$ using a random oracle R as follows. Let s be a binary string. Let t be the first $|\theta|$ bits of the infinitely long string $R(s)$. If $t \in S$ then $F_\theta(s) = t$. Otherwise, consider the next $|\theta|$ bits of $R(s)$. If this string is contained in S then this string is $F_\theta(s)$, and so on. So, $F_\theta(s)$ maps to an element drawn uniformly at random from S.

In practice, cryptographic hash functions are used to instantiate random oracles (and random functions). However, when a public and private string are supplied to a random function it may be desirable to use a pseudorandom function [9] instead.

A *block cipher* is a pair of algorithms (ENC, DEC) that is used to encrypt and decrypt plaintext messages m that are w bits in length. The encryption is performed using a key k such that for all m, the equality $m = DEC(k, ENC(k, m))$ holds. The function ENC must therefore be injective to allow unambiguous decryption. In a block cipher, $\{0, 1\}^w$ is both the set of plaintexts as well as the set of ciphertexts. The encryption function for a block cipher is therefore a bijection (and must be deterministic). There are $2^w!$ possible bijections in total over $\{0, 1\}^w$. This implies that about $w2^w$ bits are needed to represent each possible bijection. An *ideal random cipher* is a w-bit block cipher that implements all $2^w!$ bijections on 2^w elements. Each of the $2^w!$ keys specifies one such permutation [15]. However, a key size of about $w2^w$ bits is highly impractical. So, a weaker definition of a cipher is needed for practical purposes.

An *ideal classic cipher* implements a randomly chosen subset of all $2^w!$ permutations from the message space onto the ciphertext space. They are secure against chosen-plaintext attacks. It is standard practice to make the cardinality of the key space exponential in some security parameter. A design principle for a block cipher is to make the cipher as close to an ideal classic cipher as possible. A block cipher is "secure" in some sense, if the encryption function corresponding to a randomly selected key appears to be a randomly chosen invertible function (pseudorandom permutation). The notion of choosing a block cipher at random is as follows. If the subset of permutations can be chosen randomly, then a w-bit ideal classic cipher can be chosen randomly.

Kerckhoffs' basic principle is that the adversary will somehow learn the details of the cipher. So in principle, all of the secrecy should reside in the key. A *secret* block cipher, in contrast, is a block cipher in which ENC and DEC are known only to the designer, unless an implementation of the cipher is reverse-engineered. However, the key space, message space, and ciphertext space are publicly known. A secret block cipher is a gross violation of Kerckhoffs' principle, and it is this that motivates the present investigation. Namely, we strive to justify this principle from the perspective of information leakage attacks.

Recall that IND-CPA stands for *Indistinguishability - chosen-plaintext attack*. In an IND-CPA attack, the adversary first mounts a CPA attack. The adversary then submits two plaintexts of his choice to the encryption oracle and is then given the encryption of one of the two at random and is asked to guess which plaintext was encrypted. A cipher is IND-CPA secure if the adversary guesses correctly with probability negligibly greater than $1/2$.

3   New Definitions and Building Blocks

Informally, a *broadcast block cipher* is a block cipher that broadcasts a subliminal message m_s to everyone that knows the algorithm for the cipher. The bit string m_s must be supplied as input (e.g., internally) to the broadcast encryption algorithm as well as the broadcast decryption algorithm. Define $BENC(k, m, k_s, m_s)$ to be a broadcast block cipher with a w-bit block size, where m is the plaintext, k is the symmetric key used to encrypt m, m_s is the subliminal message, and k_s is a secret key. Algorithm $BDEC(k, c, k_s, m_s)$ decrypts the output of $BENC$ using k. Define algorithm $ENC(k, m) \triangleq BENC(k, m, k_s, m_s)$ and define algorithm $DEC(k, c) \triangleq BDEC(k, c, k_s, m_s)$ for some pair (k_s, m_s).

Our threat model involves four entities that we define informally yet intuitively (a more formal definition will be given in the full version). The role of each of these entities is as follows.

The **designer** is a malicious entity that is permitted to design and deploy the black-box device. Therefore, the designer only has write-once and oracle access to the device. The goal of the designer is to learn m_s. The designer supplies the secret key k_s and the collected plaintext/ciphertext pairs to an algorithm called $BREC$ which then returns the subliminal message m_s.

The **reverse-engineer** has only oracle access to the device (i.e., the cipher can't be changed). The reverse-engineer mounts a chosen-plaintext attack. Upon completion of the attack the reverse-engineer knows α plaintext/ciphertext pairs denoted by $(m_1, c_1), (m_2, c_2), ..., (m_\alpha, c_\alpha)$ computed using $BENC(k, \cdot, k_s, m_s)$. It is assumed that these ciphertexts subliminally transmit m_s. So, the reverse-engineer knows $BENC, BDEC, m_s, k_s$ as well as the pairs $(m_1, c_1), ..., (m_\alpha, c_\alpha)$. The goal of the reverse-engineer is to break the cipher by learning a non-negligible amount of plaintext information.

The **inquirer** and **sampler** have only oracle access to the cipher. The inquirer is a boolean function. An output of true indicates a guess that the cipher is an ideal classic cipher. An output of false indicates a guess that it is not an ideal classic cipher (e.g., that it contains a subliminal channel and as a result appears less than ideal).

There exists a set of weak probability distributions in the broadcast block cipher that breaks the confidentiality of encryptions with respect to the reverse-engineer. The purpose of formalizing the sampler is to show that with overwhelming probability a weak distribution will not be selected (by users in practice). The sampler chooses a probability distribution over the message space and returns plaintexts sampled accordingly.

So, the inquirer is a user (adversary) that tries to distinguish between "good" and "bad" ciphers and the sampler is a user (adversary) that tries to choose a probability distribution that allows the reverse-engineer to violate the confidentiality of encryptions. It is assumed that the reverse-engineer, inquirer, and sampler are computationally bounded.[1]

---

[1] i.e., they are probabilistic poly-time Turing machines.

Definition 2. *A secure w-bit* **broadcast block cipher** *is a 3-tuple* $(BENC, BDEC, BREC)$ *that satisfies the following:*

1. *(inquirer indistinguishability) It is computationally intractable for the inquirer to distinguish a black-box implementation of (ENC, DEC) from a randomly chosen ideal classic cipher.*
2. *(completeness) For all plaintexts m, for all symmetric keys k, for all subliminal messages m_s, and for all secret keys k_s, the following equality holds, $m = BDEC(k, BENC(k, m, k_s, m_s), k_s, m_s)$.*
3. *(reverse-engineer confidentiality) After completing a chosen-plaintext attack, the reverse-engineer learns at most W pairs of random plaintexts and corresponding ciphertexts (computed using k) where W is bounded by a polynomial in the length of $((m_1, c_1), ..., (m_\alpha, c_\alpha), k_s)$.*
4. *(designer completeness) For sufficiently large α, for all m_s, and for all distinct plaintexts $(m_1, m_2, ..., m_\alpha)$, the subliminal message m_s is equal to $BREC((m_1, m_2, ..., m_\alpha, c_1, c_2, ..., c_\alpha), k_s)$ with overwhelming probability where each ciphertext $c_i = BENC(k, m_i, k_s, m_s)$ for $i = 1, 2, ..., \alpha$. The probability is over the random choice of k and k_s.*

Property (2) guarantees that decryption will always yield the original plaintext. The secret key k_s is fixed and is contained in all of the black-box devices. This value must be kept secret (hence, the subscript "s") by the designer to prevent users from being able to read the channel. The reverse-engineer knows k_s and so the reverse-engineer can read the subliminal channel. So, it is a broadcast channel. It is made narrowcast using the deterministic asymmetric encryption function E. In our main application we set $m_s = E(y, k)$ where y is the designer's public key. Clearly $E(y, k)$ can be reconstructed by $BENC$ and $BDEC$ on input k. Since only the designer knows the decryption private key corresponding to y, only the designer (and not the reverse-engineer) can learn k.

Property (4) implies that a sufficient number of known plaintext-ciphertext pairs under a common key k are required in order to read m_s. Observe that this construction constitutes a cipher within a cipher. The secret key k_s acts like a symmetric key that decrypts the "ciphertext" $(m_1, m_2, ..., m_\alpha, c_1, c_2, ..., c_\alpha)$ to reveal m_s.

Building Blocks. Let s be a bit string. The function $GetBit(s, i)$ returns the bit at position i of s where $0 \le i \le |s| - 1$. The bits are ordered from right to left starting with 0. For example, if $s = 0001$ then $GetBit(s, 0) = 1$, $GetBit(s, 1) = 0$, $GetBit(s, 2) = 0$, and $GetBit(s, 3) = 0$. Let $H_{\delta-1} : \{0, 1\}^* \to \{0, 1\}^{\delta-1}$ be a random function. Also, let $F_1 : \{0, 1\}^* \to \{0, 1\}$ and $GetRandPos_\theta : \{0, 1\}^* \to \{0, 1, 2, ..., \theta - 1\}$ be random functions. These random functions are publicly known.

The pair $(ENC1, DEC1)$ is a secret ideal classic cipher with a w-bit block size. Let δ be a constant. The pair $(ENC2, DEC2)$ is a secret ideal classic cipher with block size $w - \delta$ bits. We are somewhat lax about specifying the set from which the symmetric keys k are drawn. The set is typically, say $\{0, 1\}^{128}$ or an even larger set.

These ciphers can be instantiated using a pseudorandom invertible permutation generator that will make the outputs secure against chosen plaintext attacks [13]. In practice, symmetric ciphers often utilize Feistel transformations. Luby and Rackoff have provided some theoretical justification for Feistel's construction [12, 11].

4   The Broadcast Block Cipher

The broadcast block encryption algorithm is given in Fig. 1.

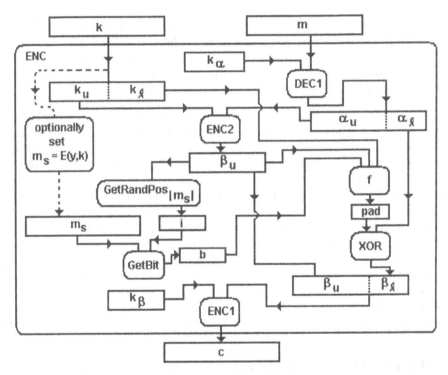

Fig. 1. Subliminal Channel in Block Encryption Algorithm

(**Intuitive Description**). The channel transmits one pseudorandomly chosen bit of the subliminal message in each ciphertext block that is output. First, a large portion of the block is simply encrypted using a secure block cipher. The resulting ciphertext is recoverable under a known plaintext attack by the reverse-engineer. This block is used as the "public" input to a random function.[2] This

---

[2] It is not really a public input, but when pseudorandom functions are used to instantiate these random functions, they correspond to the "public input."

public input is used to select a bit position randomly in the subliminal message. The problem that remains is to display the subliminal bit in this bit position.

This is accomplished by embedding this bit in the encryption of the remaining plaintext that has not been enciphered. To do so, the public input is again supplied to a random function, but this time the user's symmetric key is supplied to the random function as well. The result is a random pad that is used to XOR encrypt all but the last remaining plaintext bit. This bit is also XOR encrypted. This is accomplished by supplying the pad along with the public input to yet another random function, to obtain a one bit pad. The idea is that the larger pad is secret due to the secrecy of the user's symmetric key, and so this larger pad can be used to derive a secret one-bit pad to XOR encrypt the final plaintext bit. An initial permutation and a final permutation are also performed for reasons that will become clear later on.

(**Detailed Description**). The pair $k_s = (k_\alpha, k_\beta)$ is randomly chosen by the designer *and is placed in the black-box device* that implements $BENC$ and $BDEC$ (so k_s may become known to a reverse-engineer but the symmetric key k that the user supplies to the device will not). For simplicity it is assumed that w is even. The value δ is an integer constant used in the broadcast block cipher. The function f is defined as follows.

$$f(b, \beta_u, k_\ell) \triangleq H_{\delta-1}(k_\ell \, || \, \beta_u) \, || \, (b \, \oplus \, F_1(H_{\delta-1}(k_\ell \, || \, \beta_u) \, || \, \beta_u))$$

$\Pi_1(k, m, k_\alpha, m_s)$:   /* subroutine for encryption algorithm */
1. let k_u and k_ℓ be strings such that $k = k_u \, || \, k_\ell$ and $|k_u| = |k_\ell|$
2. compute $\alpha = DEC1(k_\alpha, m)$ /* yes, we want to decrypt */
3. let α_u and α_ℓ be strings such that $\alpha = \alpha_u \, || \, \alpha_\ell$ and $|\alpha_\ell| = \delta$
4. $\beta_u = ENC2(k_u, \alpha_u)$
5. compute $i = GetRandPos_{|m_s|}(\beta_u)$ and then $b = GetBit(m_s, i)$
6. compute $pad = f(b, \beta_u, k_\ell)$, $\beta_\ell = pad \oplus \alpha_\ell$, and return $\beta = \beta_u \, || \, \beta_\ell$

$BENC(k, m, (k_\alpha, k_\beta), m_s)$:
Input: w-bit plaintext m, symmetric key k where $|k|$ is even,
        subliminal message m_s, secret key (k_α, k_β)
Output: w-bit ciphertext c
1. $\beta = \Pi_1(k, m, k_\alpha, m_s)$
2. compute $c = ENC1(k_\beta, \beta)$ and then output c

$\Pi_{-1}(k, c, k_\alpha, m_s)$:   /* subroutine for decryption algorithm */
1. let k_u and k_ℓ be strings such that $k = k_u \, || \, k_\ell$ and $|k_u| = |k_\ell|$
2. compute $\beta = DEC1(k_\beta, c)$
3. let β_u and β_ℓ be strings such that $\beta = \beta_u \, || \, \beta_\ell$ and $|\beta_\ell| = \delta$
4. $\alpha_u = DEC2(k_u, \beta_u)$
5. compute $i = GetRandPos_{|m_s|}(\beta_u)$ and then $b = GetBit(m_s, i)$
6. compute $pad = f(b, \beta_u, k_\ell)$, $\alpha_\ell = pad \oplus \beta_\ell$, and return $\alpha = \alpha_u \, || \, \alpha_\ell$

$BDEC(k, c, (k_\alpha, k_\beta), m_s)$:

Input: w-bit ciphertext c, symmetric key k where $|k|$ is even,
        subliminal message m_s, secret key (k_α, k_β)
Output: w-bit plaintext m
1. $\alpha = \Pi_{-1}(k, c, k_\alpha, m_s)$
2. compute $m = ENC1(k_\alpha, \alpha)$ and then output m

It is clear that property (2) of Definition 2 holds (completeness).

$\quad$ $BRECBIT$ recovers a single bit of m_s from a plaintext/ciphertext pair. $BREC$ invokes this subroutine for each plaintext/ciphertext pair that it is given in order to recover m_s.

$BRECBIT((k_\alpha, k_\beta), m, c)$:

Input: w-bit plaintext m, w-bit ciphertext c,
        secret key (k_α, k_β)
Output: (i, b) where b is the bit at bit position i of m_s
1. compute $\alpha = DEC1(k_\alpha, m)$
2. let α_u and α_ℓ be strings such that $\alpha = \alpha_u \,||\, \alpha_\ell$ and $|\alpha_\ell| = \delta$
3. compute $\beta = DEC1(k_\beta, c)$
4. let β_u and β_ℓ be strings such that $\beta = \beta_u \,||\, \beta_\ell$ and $|\beta_\ell| = \delta$
5. compute $pad = \alpha_\ell \oplus \beta_\ell$
6. let z and t be strings such that $pad = z \,||\, t$ and $|t| = 1$
7. compute $r = F_1(z \,||\, \beta_u)$ and then set $b = t \oplus r$
8. compute $i = GetRandPos_{|m_s|}(\beta_u)$ and then output (i, b)

$\quad$ Since each bit is selected uniformly at random from the $|m_s|$ bit positions, the designer (and the reverse-engineer) can expect to have to obtain $O(|m_s|log|m_s|)$ plaintext/ciphertext pairs under a common key k in order to recover m_s. This results from analyzing the first moment of the *coupon collector's problem* [8]. It follows that property (4) of Definition 2 holds (designer completeness). We call this the insignis channel, named after the carnivorous plant Nepenthes Insignis Danser.

5   Security

The following claim is used to show that indistinguishability (i.e., property (1) of Definition 2) holds.

Claim 1. $\forall\, k$, m_s, and k_α, $\Pi_1(k, \cdot, k_\alpha, m_s)$ *is a permutation over* $\{0, 1\}^w$.

Proof. Assume for the sake of contradiction that this does not hold. Then there exists k, m_s, k_α, m_1, and m_2 where $m_1 \neq m_2$ such that $\beta_1 = \Pi_1(k, m_1, k_\alpha, m_s) = \Pi_1(k, m_2, k_\alpha, m_s) = \beta_2$.

$\quad$ Observe that α is a permutation of the input message. So, m_1 maps to α_1 and m_2 maps to α_2 where $\alpha_1 \neq \alpha_2$. Define $\alpha_{u,1}$, $\alpha_{\ell,1}$, $\alpha_{u,2}$, $\alpha_{\ell,2}$, $\beta_{u,1}$, $\beta_{\ell,1}$, $\beta_{u,2}$, and $\beta_{\ell,2}$ as follows:

$$\alpha_1 = \alpha_{u,1} \parallel \alpha_{\ell,1} \qquad \alpha_2 = \alpha_{u,2} \parallel \alpha_{\ell,2} \qquad |\alpha_{\ell,1}| = |\alpha_{\ell,2}| = \delta$$
$$\beta_1 = \beta_{u,1} \parallel \beta_{\ell,1} \qquad \beta_2 = \beta_{u,2} \parallel \beta_{\ell,2} \qquad |\beta_{\ell,1}| = |\beta_{\ell,2}| = \delta$$

Suppose that $\alpha_{u,1} \neq \alpha_{u,2}$. Since $ENC2(k_u, \cdot)$ is a permutation it follows that $\beta_{u,1} \neq \beta_{u,2}$. Hence, $\beta_1 \neq \beta_2$ in this case. So, it remains to consider the case that $\alpha_{u,1} = \alpha_{u,2}$.

Since $\alpha_1 \neq \alpha_2$ it must be the case that $\alpha_{\ell,1} \neq \alpha_{\ell,2}$. It is not hard to show that pad is the same for m_1 and m_2. Since $\alpha_{\ell,1} \neq \alpha_{\ell,2}$ it follows that the strings resulting from the bitwise XOR operation differ. Therefore, $\beta_{\ell,1} \neq \beta_{\ell,2}$. It follows that $\beta_1 \neq \beta_2$. Therefore, in all cases $\beta_1 \neq \beta_2$ which is a contradiction. ◇

Let m_s be any subliminal message and let k_s be any secret key. Claim 1 shows that $ENC(k, m)$ maps each $m \in \{0, 1\}^w$ under k to one and only one $\beta \in \{0, 1\}^w$. ENC then encrypts β using a randomly chosen key k_β in a randomly chosen ideal classic cipher. Hence, this last operation is a randomly chosen permutation from among the set of possible random permutations in the ideal classical cipher. Since the composition of two permutations is a permutation and since k_β is secret, we have therefore shown the following.

Claim 2. *A secret implementation of (ENC, DEC) is indistinguishable from an ideal classic cipher.*

It follows that property 1 of Definition 2 holds. The following corollary follows from Claim 2 and the notion of security for an ideal classic cipher.

Corollary 1. *With only oracle access, ENC appears like a randomly chosen invertible function.*

(ENC, DEC) is as secure as $ENC1$ against attacks mounted by a user since the key k_β is secret from the user. Therefore, since $(ENC1, DEC1)$ is secure against chosen-plaintext attacks mounted by the user (note that it is first [14]) (ENC, DEC) is secure against chosen-plaintext attacks mounted by the user. We will now consider the security of (ENC, DEC) when attacks are carried out by the reverse-engineer who knows k_β, among other things. Thus, the remainder of this section is devoted to showing that property (3) of Definition 2 holds.

First, note that β_u is the block encryption of α_u. So, the encryption using $ENC2$ will not compromise k_u unless $ENC2$ is itself vulnerable to a chosen plaintext attack. Now consider the confidentiality of α_ℓ.

Observe that in (ENC, DEC) there exist non-trivial distributions M_p that compromise plaintexts. These M_p's lead to a non-negligible probability of collision in β_u. A collision in β_u implies a collision in pad. So, we must first show that the chances that the sampler compromises its own plaintexts is negligible.

Define p_c to be the probability that two messages m_1 and m_2 that are chosen according to M_p lead to the same value for β_u in the corresponding encryptions c_1 and c_2. If p_c is not negligible then the sampler may produces messages that are compromised. This results from the fact that the random functions in f would be given the same β_u thereby resulting in a selection of pads for c_1 and c_2 that are not only dependent, but identical.

Claim 3 utilizes a fact that is related to the *birthday paradox*. An urn has u balls numbered from 1 to u. Suppose that v balls are drawn from the urn one at a time, with replacement, and their numbers are listed. (**Fact 1**) A well-known fact is that as $u \to \infty$, the expected number of draws before a coincidence is $\sqrt{(\pi u)/2}$.

Claim 3. *(random oracle model) If $ENC2$ is an ideal classic cipher and $w - \delta$ is sufficiently large then p_c is negligible.*

Proof. Assume that $ENC1$ is an ideal classic cipher for sufficiently large w. It follows that $DEC1$ is a bijection and so every message maps to one and only one α. Also, assume that $w - \delta$ is sufficiently large.

Since $ENC2$ is an ideal classic cipher, each α_u is assigned randomly to a β_u under the random permutation $ENC2(k_u, \cdot)$. It follows from Corollary 1 that the sampler can do no better than guess a value for M_p that has a non-negligible probability of yielding a collision in β_u when sampled. So, it remains to consider the probability of a collision for randomly chosen β_u's.

The value β_u is selected randomly from a set with cardinality $2^{w-\delta}$. It follows from Fact 1 that the expected number of ciphertexts needed to have a collision in β_u is close to $2^{(w-\delta)/2}\sqrt{\pi/2}$. Since $w - \delta$ is sufficiently large it follows that with overwhelming probability the β_u's will be unique. Hence, p_c is negligible. $\diamond$

This analysis implies that $w - \delta$ should be at least 128.

Observe that the function f is known to the reverse-engineer since $H_{\delta-1}$ and F_1 are public. From property (4) of Definition 2 it follows that m_s is known to the reverse-engineer. It is not hard to show that b and β_u are known to the reverse-engineer for every ciphertext. This implies that k_ℓ is a private input and (b, β_u) is a public input (from the reverse-engineer's perspective) to f.

Claim 4. *(random oracle model) If p_c is negligible and k_ℓ is secret then with overwhelming probability the values for pad that result (from the sampler's choice of plaintexts) in the resulting ciphertexts are independently random and secret.*

Proof. Assume that k_ℓ is secret from the reverse-engineer. Also, assume that p_c is negligible. It follows from the latter assumption that the β_u's are different with overwhelming probability. Consider the event that the β_u's differ.

Since the β_u's differ, the $\delta - 1$ uppermost bits of *pad* are selected uniformly at random and independent of every other plaintext. This follows from the fact that β_u is supplied as input to the random function $H_{\delta-1}$. Furthermore, the $\delta - 1$ uppermost bits $H_{\delta-1}(k_\ell \parallel \beta_u)$ of *pad* are secret due to the secret k_ℓ that is supplied as input to $H_{\delta-1}$ in f.

Since the β_u's differ, for each β_u, the least significant bit of *pad* is selected uniformly at random and independent of every other plaintext. This follows from the fact that β_u is supplied as input to the random function F_1. Furthermore, the least significant bit of *pad* is secret since it was shown that $H_{\delta-1}(k_\ell \parallel \beta_u)$ is secret and this value is supplied as input to F_1 in f. $\diamond$

This analysis implies that δ should not be less than 64. The assumption here is that 64 is an acceptable security parameter, which even today is arguably cutting it close. We remark that Rijndael has block sizes of 128, 192, and 256 bits [5]. So, a block size of 192 bits or larger is not unreasonable. Also, the bits that comprise *pad* are the outputs of a random oracle, so they will not compromise k_ℓ. Claims 3 and 4 show that even if the computationally bounded sampler wants to find an M_p that compromises plaintexts, the probability that the sampler finds such an M_p is negligible.

Now consider the case that the reverse-engineer mounts a known-plaintext attack. Recall that in a known plaintext attack the reverse-engineer queries an encryption oracle (the sampler) and receives $S = \{(m_1, c_1), (m_2, c_2),..., (m_\gamma, c_\gamma)\}$. Here c_i is the ciphertext of m_i for $1 \leq i \leq \gamma$. The encryption key k that is generately randomly is used to compute all the ciphertexts, and is kept secret by the sampler. The sampler samples the m_i from the message space according to M_p. The reverse-engineer is not permitted to query the sampler again.

Consider the problem for the reverse-engineer to learn information relating to the plaintext in c where $c \neq c_i$ for $1 \leq i \leq \gamma$. This is possible in the following known plaintext attack. The reverse-engineer computes *pad*, α_ℓ, β_u, α_u, etc. used in (m_1, c_1). The reverse-engineer begins to iterate through the possible values for α_ℓ (there are 2^δ possible values in total). The values $\alpha = \alpha_u \mathbin{\|} \alpha_\ell$ are encrypted using k_α in the cipher $ENC1$. This yields a set of new plaintexts for ENC. The reverse-engineer computes the corresponding ciphertexts in the same way that ENC would. The number of plaintext/ciphertext pairs that can be learned by the reverse-engineer is bounded by a polynomial in the length of $((m_1, c_1), ..., (m_\gamma, c_\gamma), k_s)$ which is provided as "input" to the computationally bounded reverse-engineer.

This attack also applies to IND-CPA attacks. Note that when the encryption oracle $ENC(k, \cdot)$ is taken away, the reverse-engineer is able to make oracle queries to $ENC1(k_\alpha, \cdot)$ and learn more plaintext/ciphertext pairs. The reverse-engineer can take one of the new plaintext/ciphertext pairs, make the IND-CPA oracle request with the new plaintext, and then distinguish perfectly. For this reason we use a weaker notion of confidentiality than IND-CPA in Definition 2.

However, by taking the probability over the coin tosses of when $ENC1$ was generated, it follows that the new plaintexts that are learned are random ($ENC1$ is an ideal classic cipher). So, the reverse-engineer can only sample the new plaintext/ciphertext pairs *randomly*. Under these arguments, property (3) of Definition 2 holds.

Theorem 1. ($BENC, BDEC, BREC$) *is a broadcast block cipher.*

6   Kleptographic Attack

This section describes how to carry out a kleptographic attack that leaks k exclusively to the designer. Let (E, D) be a deterministic asymmetric cryptosystem, let y be the public key of the malicious designer and let x be the corresponding private key. The ciphertext $c = E(y, m)$ denotes the encryption of m. To decrypt we compute $m = D(x, c)$.

In the attack, the cipher computes $m_s = E(y, k)$. The designer computes $k = D(x, m_s)$. The reverse-engineer has access to (m_s, y, E) but does not have access to x. So, the broadcast subliminal channel is tranformed into a narrowcast channel using y and E. Clearly other information besides k can be leaked this way as well. The notion of a SETUP is given in [26]. We have therefore shown the following.

Lemma 1. *The subliminal transmission of $E(y, k)$ is a SETUP attack against the secret w-bit block cipher (ENC, DEC).*

7   Conclusion

The notion of a broadcast subliminal channel in a block cipher was introduced and an instantiation was given for secret block ciphers. The channel broadcasts a subliminal message to the reverse-engineer and the malicious designer. It was shown how to turn the broadcast channel into a narrow cast channel using a deterministic asymmetric cipher. In the narrowcast construction, only the malicious designer can obtain the plaintext message. An application of the narrowcast channel was given that constitutes the first secretly embedded trapdoor attack against a deterministic block cipher.

References

1. R. Anderson, S. Vaudenay, B. Preneel, K. Nyberg. The Newton Channel. In *Workshop on Information Hiding*, pages 151–156, 1996.
2. M. Bellare, P. Rogaway. Random Oracles are Practical: A Paradigm for Designing Efficient Protocols. In *Conference on Computer and Communications Security*, pages 62–73, ACM, 1993.
3. E. Biham. Cryptanalysis of Patarin's 2-Round Public Key System S Boxes (2R). In *Advances in Cryptology—Eurocrypt '00*, pages 408–416, 1999.
4. S. Chow, P. Eisen, H. Johnson, P. C. van Oorshot. A White-Box DES Implementation for DRM Applications. Workshop on Digital Rights Management, ACM, 2002.
5. J. Daemen, V. Rijmen. The Block Cipher Rijndael. In *Smart Card Research and Applications*, pages 288–296, 2000.
6. Y. Desmedt. Abuses in Cryptography and How to Fight Them. In *Advances in Cryptology—Crypto '88*, pages 375–389, 1988.
7. Y. Ding-Feng, L. Kwok-Yan, D. Zong-Duo. Cryptanalysis of the "2R" schemes. In *Advances in Cryptology—Crypto '99*, pages 315–325, 1999.
8. W. Feller. An Introduction to Probability Theory and its Applications. John Wiley & Sons, Inc., pages 210–212, 1957.
9. O. Goldreich, S. Goldwasser, S. Micali. How to Construct Random Functions. *J. of the ACM*, 33(4), pages 210–217, 1986.
10. M. Jacob, D. Boneh, E. Felten. Attacking an obfuscated cipher by injecting faults. ACM Workshop on Digital Rights Management, 2002.
11. L. Knudsen. DEAL: A 128-bit block cipher. Technical Report 151, Department of Informatics,University of Bergen, Norway, Feb. 1998.

12. M. Luby, C. Rackoff. How to Construct Pseudorandom Permutations from Pseudorandom Functions. In *SIAM J. Comput.*, v. 17, 1988, pages 373–386.
13. M. Luby. Pseudorandomness and Cryptographic Applications. Princeton Computer Science Notes, Princeton University Press, Lectures 13 & 14, pages 128–145, 1996.
14. U. Maurer, J. Massey. Cascade Ciphers: The Importance of Being First. In *Journal of Cryptology*, vol. 6, no. 1, pages 55–61, 1993.
15. A. J. Menezes, P. C. van Oorschot, S. A. Vanstone. Handbook of Applied Cryptography. CRC Press, pages 224–225, 1997.
16. Skipjack Symmetric Cipher. Declassified on June 23, 1998. Appeared on NIST website on June 24, 1998 at http://csrc.nist.gov/encryption/skipjack-1.pdf and http://csrc.nist.gov/encryption/skipjack-2.pdf (no author).
17. J. Patarin, L. Goubin. Asymmetric Cryptography with S-Boxes. In *Proceedings of ICICS*, pages 369–380, 1997.
18. M. Rabin. Digitalized Signatures as Intractable as Factorization. MIT Laboratory for Computer Science, MIT/LCS/TR-212, Jan, 1979.
19. V. Rijmen, B. Preneel, A Family of Trapdoor Ciphers. Fast Software Encryption, pages 139–148, 1997.
20. R. Rivest, A. Shamir, L. Adleman. A Method for Obtaining Digital Signatures and Public-Key Cryptosystems. CACM, v. 21, n. 2, pages 120–126, Feb. 1978.
21. G. J. Simmons. The Prisoners' Problem and the Subliminal Channel. In *Advances in Cryptology—Crypto '83*, pages 51–67, Plenum Press, 1984.
22. G. J. Simmons. Subliminal Communication is Easy Using the DSA. In *Advances in Cryptology—Eurocrypt '93*, pages 218–232, 1993.
23. G. J. Simmons. The History of Subliminal Channels. *IEEE Journal on selected areas in communication*, v. 16, n. 4, pages 452–462, 1998.
24. R. Weis, S. Lucks. "All Your Key Bit Are Belong to Us" The True Story of Blackbox Cryptography. In *Proceedings of the 3rd International System Administration and Networking Conference—SANE '02*, Maastricht, 2002.
25. H. Wu, F. Bao, R. Deng, Q. Ye. Cryptanalysis of Rijmen-Preneel Trapdoor Ciphers. In *Advances in Cryptology—Asiacrypt '98*, pages 126–132, 1998.
26. A. Young, M. Yung. The Dark Side of Black-Box Cryptography, or: Should we trust Capstone? In *Advances in Cryptology—Crypto '96*, pages 89-103, 1996.
27. A. Young, M. Yung. Monkey: Black-Box Symmetric Ciphers Designed for MONopolizing KEYs. In *Fast Software Encryption*, pages 122–133, 1998.
28. A. Young, M. Yung. Backdoor Attacks on Black-Box Ciphers Exploiting Low-Entropy Plaintexts. In *Proceedings of ACISP*, pages 297–311, 2003.

Blockwise Adversarial Model for On-line Ciphers and Symmetric Encryption Schemes

Pierre-Alain Fouque[1], Antoine Joux[2], and Guillaume Poupard[2]

[1] École normale supérieure, Département d'Informatique, 45 rue d'Ulm,
75230 Paris 5, France
`Pierre-Alain.Fouque@ens.fr`
[2] DCSSI CryptoLab, 51, rue de Latour-Maubourg, 75007 Paris SP, France
{`Antoine.Joux, Guillaume.Poupard`}`@m4x.org`

Abstract. This paper formalizes the security adversarial games for *on-line* symmetric cryptosystems in a unified framework for deterministic and probabilistic encryption schemes. On-line encryption schemes allow to encrypt messages even if the whole message is not known at the beginning of the encryption. The new introduced adversaries better capture the on-line properties than *classical* ones. Indeed, in the new model, the adversaries are allowed to send messages block-by-block to the encryption machine and receive the corresponding ciphertext blocks on-the-fly. This kind of attacker is called *blockwise* adversary and is stronger than standard one which treats messages as atomic objects.

In this paper, we compare the two adversarial models for on-line encryption schemes. For probabilistic encryption schemes, we show that security is not preserved contrary to for deterministic schemes. We prove in appendix of the full version that in this last case, the two models are polynomially equivalent in the number of encrypted blocks. Moreover in the blockwise model, a polynomial number of *concurrent accesses* to encryption oracles have to be taken into account. This leads to the strongest security notion in this setting. Furthermore, we show that this notion is valid by exhibiting a scheme secure under this security notion.

1   Introduction

In 2002, Joux, Martinet and Valette introduce the *blockwise adaptive attacks* (BA) in [17], in order to better model attackers in the real world. This adversarial model is particularly relevant to study the security of *on-line* schemes where output blocks are viewed gradually by the adversary since for example the whole encrypted message cannot be stored by the encryption machine. Indeed, usually in order to encrypt a message M with a symmetric scheme, M is first split into blocks of the length of the block cipher: $M = M[1]M[2]\dots M[l]$. An encryption scheme is said to be *on-line* if the encryption of the block $M[i]$ only depends on the previous blocks $M[1], M[2], \dots, M[i]$ and not on the next ones $M[i+1]\dots M[l]$. Consequently, the encryption function can compute and return $C[i]$ before the introduction of $M[i+1]\dots M[l]$. There exist a lot of *on-line* encryption

H. Handschuh and A. Hasan (Eds.): SAC 2004, LNCS 3357, pp. 212–226, 2005.

schemes such as ECB, CBC, OFB, CFB [19] or OCB [1]. However, some schemes require a pre-treatment on the whole plaintext before the encryption process [20] or require two encryption passes in two directions [16], and thus are not *on-line*.

In this paper, we propose to study the relations between the security notions in the standard and blockwise models for probabilistic and deterministic on-line encryption schemes.

1.1   Standard Versus Blockwise Adversarial Model

The standard attack model for the CPA security is *message oriented*: *i.e.* the messages are viewed as atomic object which cannot be split into blocks. Thus, adversaries can only be adaptive between the messages. This model correctly captures the interactions of an adversary with an encryption machine for schemes which require the whole plaintext before to start the encryption process or implementations that can record the entire plaintext before the beginning of the encryption.

However, sometimes the encryption process has to be started even if the entire plaintext is not known. For example, in real-time applications, the cryptographic device cannot store the whole plaintext before the starting of the encryption. Consequently, on-line encryption schemes are useful in such scenario. Moreover, in many practical applications, cryptographic devices (smart cards) are memory restricted. Then, if messages are too large, they cannot be stored in the cryptographic module before the beginning of the encryption process. Therefore, the message must be sent block by block to the cryptographic module which returns on-the-fly the output block $C[i]$, say just after the query of the input block $M[i]$ in some implementations. As a consequence, the adversary model needs to be changed to take into account attackers querying messages block by block. In the BA model, attackers are more adaptive than standard adversaries: they are *adaptive during the encryption query*, *i.e.* between each block of messages, and not only *between the encryption queries*, *i.e.* between the messages. Hence the name of "blockwise" adversaries. Obviously the BA model is stronger than the standard one. In the sequel, we respectively denote BCPA and CPA adversaries in the BA and standard models.

It is important to thwart such adversaries since they can lead to theoretical attacks on traditional cryptosystems, such as on the CBC encryption mode or on the authenticated encryption mode presented by Jutla [17]. In [3], Bellare *et al.* have proved that the CBC encryption scheme is secure in the standard model up to the encryption of $2^{n/2}$ blocks, where n denotes the block length of a block cipher. However, in [17], Joux, Martinet and Valette have presented a new simple attack showing that the CBC encryption scheme is not secure in the BA model after only two encrypted blocks. This kind of adversary is mainly meaningful in the private-key setting when long messages are encrypted. It is worth noticing that blockwise adversaries are not only of theoretical interest as the attacks in [17] seem to show. In [17], the attacks invalidate the security proof by building distinguisher but do not allow to recover the secret key or to totally break the scheme. However, it is easy to show that for example the

CBC encryption scheme in the BA model is as sensible as the ECB mode in the standard model against a key recovery attack since the adversary can adapt his queries to the block cipher by xoring its queries to the previous output blocks.

1.2   Backgrounds and Previous Results

Usually, in cryptography, *security notions* are defined by combining a *security goal* and an *attack model* [4]. Different security goals have been proposed so far, such as *indistinguishability of ciphertexts* (IND), *one-wayness*, *non-malleability*,... For example, semantic security [14] formalizes the adversary's inability to learn any information about a plaintext M underlying a challenge ciphertext C. This captures a strong notion of privacy and is also defined as indistinguishability of ciphertexts. In the symmetric setting of interest to us, IND has been redefined as left-or-right (LOR), real-or-random (ROR), and find-then-guess (FTG) indistinguishability. All these latter notions, described in [3], encompass the same security definition. Bellare *et al.* in [3] have defined several security goals, while Katz and Yung, in [18], present a complete characterization of the security notions for encryption scheme in the standard model. Based on these two works, we examine the relations between the standard and the blockwise models.

The blockwise model has been introduced at Crypto 2002 by Joux, Martinet and Valette in [17]. They show that several encryption schemes such as the CBC and IACBC are not secure in the BA model. At FSE 2003, Fouque, Martinet and Poupard in [10] show that a slight variant of the on-line CBC encryption scheme, and the CFB mode of operation can be proved secure against blockwise chosen plaintext attack. For this, they introduce a strong security model. We show here that this model is the strongest one. At SAC 2003, Fouque *et al.* in [9] study the security of authenticated on-line encryption mode against blockwise chosen ciphertext attacks. Finally, at RSA Conf 2004, Boldyreva and Taesombut introduced new security notions for chosen-ciphertext attacks in [6]. We will not here take into account such adversaries due to lack of places.

1.3   Our Results

Several papers have considered blockwise adversaries either in order to attack some schemes such as in [17] or in order to prove security against such adversaries as in [10, 9, 7]. Our aim is to study the relations between the security notions in the standard model and in the blockwise model. Therefore, in section 2 we define more formally several security notions in order to study the relationship between these notions and the related notions in the standard attacker model. Then, in section 3, we study relations between the FTG and LOR security goals for blockwise adaptive chosen plaintext attacks (BCPA) and standard chosen plaintext attacks (CPA). First of all, in theorem 1, we generalize the result stating that security in the standard model does not imply security in the blockwise model. We also show that an equivalence for probabilistic schemes does not hold for on-line encryption schemes against the new adversarial model. In [18], Katz and Yung have mainly analyzed the relations between the non-malleability and the FTG notions for different adversaries having access or not to encryption or decryption oracles. For the FTG security game, they have proved that oracle accesses only before the challenge phase is equivalent to oracle accesses before and after this phase. We show in theorems 2 and 3 that this equivalence no longer holds in the BA model.

Furthermore, the equivalence of the LOR and FTG security goal is not security preserving. In fact, the main results of Bellare *et al.* in [3] of interest for us about probabilistic schemes are that LOR is the strongest security notion and that LOR and FTG are not security preserving but are polynomially-equivalent in the number of messages. We show in theorem 5 (section 3) that LOR and FTG are *not* security preserving in the BA model. We show that in the BA model two definitions of LOR exist. The stronger one corresponds to adversaries which can *concurrently* access the oracles. This is the strongest security notion we define. Moreover, we also exhibit in section 4 a special class of encryption schemes for which the weakest LOR definition and FTG are exactly equivalent in both models and not only polynomially related (theorems 4 and 6). This allows better reductions for these schemes since security is preserved once we have a security proof under the FTG security notion. Finally, in section 5, we show that the security under concurrent blockwise adversarial can be achieved with the counter mode for example.

In appendix A of the full version [11], we fully characterize the relations between the security of ciphers in the BA model and in the standard one and prove that for on-line ciphers, also known as deterministic schemes, the two models are polynomially-equivalent in the number of encrypted blocks. However, this reduction does not preserve the security since it is quadratic in the number of encrypted blocks. Furthermore, we show that the bound is tight by exhibiting an on-line cipher for which the security in the BA adversary model is not guaranteed if the cipher encrypts more than N blocks although the security in the standard model is preserved up to the encryption of $(N-1)(N-2)/2$ blocks.

1.4   Notations

In the rest of this paper, we use standard notations and conventions for writing probabilistic algorithms and experiments. If A is a probabilistic algorithm, then $A(x_1, x_2, \ldots; r)$ is the result of running A on inputs $x_1, x_2, \ldots$ and coins r. We let $y \leftarrow A(x_1, x_2, \ldots; r)$ denote the experiment of picking r at random and letting y be $A(x_1, x_2, \ldots; r)$. If S is a finite set then $x \leftarrow S$ is the operation of picking an element uniformly from S. We say that y *can be output by* $A(x_1, x_2, \ldots)$ if there is some r such that $A(x_1, x_2, \ldots; r) = y$. If $p(x_1, x_2, \ldots)$ is a predicate, the notation $\Pr[x_1 \leftarrow S; x_2 \leftarrow A(x_1, y_2, \ldots); \ldots : p(x_1, x_2, \ldots)]$ denotes the probability that $p(x_1, x_2, \ldots)$ is true after ordered execution of the listed experiments. In the sequel, q denotes the number of message queries and μ denotes the total number of blocks queried. We note by $D_{d,n}$ the set of d-bit strings, where d is a multiple of n, and by Perm_n, the set of permutations on n-bit blocks.

2   Security Notions for On-line Encryption Schemes

2.1   Description of On-line Encryption Schemes

We assume that if $C = C[0] \ldots C[l]$ is the encryption of $M = M[1]M[2] \ldots$, then $C[0]$ represents some information used to randomize the encryption process such as the initialization vector in the CBC encryption mode. Encryption of $M[i]$ is denoted by $C[i]$. This formalism is not restrictive and most of the encryption schemes satisfy it. Moreover, it can be adapted to more exotic schemes.

A *(symmetric) on-line encryption scheme* $\mathcal{SE} = (\mathcal{K}, \mathcal{E}, \mathcal{D})$ consists in three algorithms.

- The randomized *key generation* algorithm $\mathcal{K}$ takes as input a security parameter $k \in \mathsf{N}$ and returns a key k; we write $\mathsf{k} \xleftarrow{R} \mathcal{K}(k)$.
- The *encryption* algorithm $\mathcal{E}$ can be randomized or stateful. It takes the key k and a *plaintext* M and returns a *ciphertext* C; we write $C \xleftarrow{R} \mathcal{E}_\mathsf{k}(M)$. (If randomized it flips new coins on each invocations. If stateful, it uses and then updates a state that is maintained across invocations such as a counter.) Moreover, *on-line* encryption schemes can encrypt block $M[i]$ using only $M[1], M[2], \ldots, M[i]$.
- The *decryption* algorithm $\mathcal{D}$ is deterministic and stateless. It takes the key k and a string C and returns either the corresponding plaintext M or the symbol $\perp$; we write $x \leftarrow \mathcal{D}_\mathsf{k}(C)$ where $x \in \{0,1\}^* \cup \{\perp\}$. We require that $\mathcal{D}_\mathsf{k}(\mathcal{E}_\mathsf{k}(M)) = M$ for all $M \in \{0,1\}^*$. Moreover, on-line decryption can decrypt $C[i]$ only using $C[0], \ldots, C[i]$.

2.2   Security Notions for On-line Encryption Schemes

In this section, we adapt the standard security notions for symmetric encryption schemes to the BA model. FIND-THEN-GUESS. Semantic security captures the intuitive notion of privacy for an encrypted text. The formulation of semantic security stipulates that given a ciphertext, a polynomially-bounded adversary cannot gain any information about the corresponding plaintext (except maybe its length). The Find-Then-Guess (FTG) goal is an equivalent security notion, as shown in [3]. The adversary A, viewed as three sub-adversaries $A = (A_1, A_c, A_2)$, tries to win the following game: in the find phase, A_1 tries to get some information and returns some state information in s_0. Then in the challenge phase, A_c gradually submits two messages M_0 and M_1 to the encryption oracle which chooses a random bit b at the beginning of the encryption process, encrypts the blocks of M_b and returns the corresponding blocks C_b to A_c in an interactive manner. Finally in the guess phase, A_2 tries to distinguish whether C_b is the encryption of M_0 or M_1. In the standard model, the adversary A_1 chooses the messages M_0 and M_1. In the BA model, we need to assume that in some cases, the two messages are chosen by the adversary A_c since this new attacker is more adaptive and can choose the two messages either at the beginning of the challenge phase or during it. We add the adversary A_c in order to take into account the two adversarial models in a single definition.

In the FTG game, A may have access to different oracles during each phase. To avoid obfuscating security notions, we only define the three most representative notions: if A is blockwise adaptive in the find phase, then we write BCPA-P1, or in the find and guess phases, then we write BCPA-P2, or during the challenge phase and in the find and guess phases, and then we write BCPA-D. The adversary advantage in winning the FTG game in these different settings for a symmetric scheme Π is given by:

$$\mathsf{Adv}^{\mathrm{ftg-atk}}_{\Pi,A}(k) \stackrel{\mathrm{def}}{=} \left| 2 \cdot \Pr \left[\begin{array}{c} k \leftarrow \mathcal{K}(1^k); b \leftarrow \{0,1\}; s_0 \leftarrow A_1^{\mathcal{O}_1}(1^k); \\ (M_0, M_1, s_1, C) \leftarrow A_c^{\mathcal{O}_c}(s_0) : \\ A_2^{\mathcal{O}_2}(s_1, M_0, M_1, C) = b \end{array} \right] - 1 \right|$$

where

if atk=BCPA-P1,	then $\mathcal{O}_1 = \mathcal{E}_k^{\mathrm{bl}}(.)$	and $\mathcal{O}_c = \mathcal{E}_k(.,.,b)$	and $\mathcal{O}_2 = \varepsilon$
if atk=BCPA-P2,	then $\mathcal{O}_1 = \mathcal{E}_k^{\mathrm{bl}}(.)$	and $\mathcal{O}_c = \mathcal{E}_k(.,.,b)$	and $\mathcal{O}_2 = \mathcal{E}_k^{\mathrm{bl}}(.)$
if atk=BCPA-D,	then $\mathcal{O}_1 = \mathcal{E}_k^{\mathrm{bl}}(.)$	and $\mathcal{O}_c = \mathcal{E}_k^{\mathrm{bl}}(.,.,b)$	and $\mathcal{O}_2 = \mathcal{E}_k^{\mathrm{bl}}(.)$

We measure as $\mathsf{Adv}^{\mathrm{ftg-atk}}_{\Pi}(k, t, q, \mu) = \max_A \{\mathsf{Adv}^{\mathrm{ftg-atk}}_{\Pi,A}(k)\}$ the security of the scheme Π, where the maximum is over all legitimate A having time-complexity t, making to the oracle at most q encryption queries totaling μ blocks. A secret-key encryption scheme is said to be FTG *-secure against blockwise adaptive chosen plaintext attack* in the FTG sense if for all polynomial-time probabilistic adversaries, the advantage in this guessing game is negligible as a function of the security parameter k.

LEFT-OR-RIGHT INDISTINGUISHABILITY. In the LOR security goal, the adversary is allowed to make queries of the form (M_0, M_1) where M_0 and M_1 are equal-length messages. Two experiments are considered. In the first one, each query is answered with the encryption of the left message; in the second, the right message is encrypted. Formally, the adversary has access to the *left-or-right* oracle $\mathcal{E}_K(\mathcal{LR}(.,.,b))$, where $b \in \{0,1\}$: it takes as input pairs of messages (M_0, M_1) and, if $b = 0$, it computes $C \leftarrow \mathcal{E}_K(M_0)$ and returns C; else it computes $C \leftarrow \mathcal{E}_K(M_1)$ and returns C. We consider an encryption scheme to be "good" if a "reasonable" adversary cannot obtain "significant" advantage in distinguishing the cases $b = 0$ and $b = 1$ given access to the left-or-right oracle.

In the BA model, adversaries are allowed to feed the oracle block by block. This introduces new interactions since the adversary can interleave encryption blocks for different messages. Consequently, we present two LOR games. In the first game, called LORS, for LOR with sequential message queries, the adversary has to finish an encryption query before requesting the next message. In the second game, called LORC, for LOR with concurrent accesses, the adversary can interleaved the block queries of different messages.

The $\mathcal{E}_k^{\mathrm{bl},s}(M_0[i], M_1[i], b)$ oracle is a LOR-block encryption oracle: the adversary is allowed to query multiple pairs of messages (M_0^j, M_1^j) with the restriction that it begins the encryption of a new pair of messages only if it has finished the encryption of the previous pair. In the $\mathcal{E}_k^{bl,c}(M_0^j[i], M_1^j[i], b)$ oracle, we add a session identifier sid since the adversary is not limited to sequence its pairs of messages but can interleaved the session queries. The session identifier will be the first element in the query. Equivalently, we can say that the adversary can run multiple $\mathcal{E}_k^{bl,c}(\text{sid}, M_0^j[i], M_1^j[i], b)$ oracles concurrently.

$$\mathsf{Adv}_{\Pi,A}^{\text{lors}-\text{bcpa}}(k) = \left| 2 \cdot \Pr\left[k \leftarrow \mathcal{K}(1^k); b \leftarrow \{0,1\} : A^{\mathcal{E}_k^{bl,s}(\mathcal{LR}(.,.,b))}(k) = b \right] - 1 \right|$$

$$\mathsf{Adv}_{\Pi,A}^{\text{lorc}-\text{bcpa}}(k) = \left| 2 \cdot \Pr\left[k \leftarrow \mathcal{K}(1^k); b \leftarrow \{0,1\} : A^{\mathcal{E}_k^{bl,c}(\mathcal{LR}(.,.,b))}(k) = b \right] - 1 \right|$$

Therefore, we define the $\mathsf{Adv}_{\Pi}^{\text{lors}-\text{bcpa}}(k, t, q, \mu) = \max_A \{\mathsf{Adv}_{\Pi,A}^{\text{lors}-\text{bcpa}}(k)\}$, where the maximum is over all legitimate A having time-complexity t, making to the concurrent oracles at most q encryption queries totaling μ blocks (resp. $\mathsf{Adv}_{\Pi}^{\text{lorc}-\text{bcpa}}(k, t, q, \mu) = \max_A \{\mathsf{Adv}_{\Pi,A}^{\text{lorc}-\text{bcpa}}(k)\}$). A secret-key encryption scheme is said to be *LOR-secure against blockwise adaptive chosen plaintext attack* in the LORS sense (resp. LORC) if, for all polynomial-time probabilistic adversaries, the advantage in this guessing game is negligible as a function of the security parameter k.

3   Relations Between the Standard and Blockwise Models

In this section, we study relations between the BA and standard models for probabilistic schemes. Figure 1 presents the main relations we prove in the sequel. First, it is easy to see that FTG-BCPA-P1 implies FTG-CPA-P1, FTG-BCPA-P2 implies FTG-CPA-P2, and LORS-BCPA implies LOR-CPA since the standard model can be easily simulated in the BA model. Secondly, it is also clear from the definitions of FTG-BCPA-P1, FTG-BCPA-P2, FTG-BCPA-D, LORC and LORS, that FTG-BCPA-P2 implies FTG-BCPA-P1, FTG-BCPA-D implies FTG-BCPA-P2, and LORC-BCPA implies LORS-BCPA. Thirdly, using hybrid arguments, it is easy to prove the implication between LORS-BCPA and FTG-BCPA-D (see in appendix of the full version).

In a lot of counterexamples, we use encryption schemes Π that treat the blocks such that there is no way to distinguish an input block from an output (in particular no redundancy is added on the input blocks): $\forall i \geq 1, n = |C[0]| = |M[i]| = |C[i]|$.

We use the notation $A \Rightarrow B$ to indicate a security-preserving reduction from notion A to notion B. $A \xrightarrow{q} B$ indicates a reduction (not necessarily security-preserving) from A to B. We also assume that $\mathcal{E}$ is a symmetric encryption scheme operating on n-bit blocks with a k-bit secret key k.

3.1   Blockwise Adversaries are Stronger Than Standard Ones

The following theorem shows the separation between BCPA and CPA adversaries for the goals FTG-P1, FTG-P2 and LORS. It is a generalization of a result of paper [17] which only state that FTG-CPA-P2 $\not\Rightarrow$ FTG-BCPA-P2.

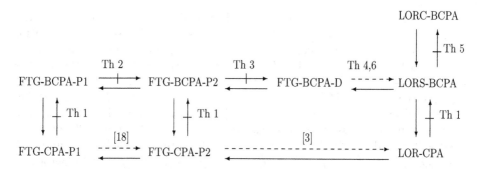

Fig. 1. Relations between the FTG and LOR security goals in the standard and BA models. In the figure, a plain arrow means that security in the first notion implies security in the second, a hatched arrow means that the first notion does not imply the second, and a dashed arrow indicates that the security between the two notions is not preserved

Theorem 1. *[FTG-CPA-P1 $\not\Rightarrow$ FTG-BCPA-P1 and FTG-CPA-P2 $\not\Rightarrow$ FTG-BCPA-P2 and LOR-CPA$\not\Rightarrow$ LORS-BCPA] If there exists an on-line encryption scheme Π which is secure in the sense of FTG-CPA-P1 (resp. FTG-CPA-P2 or LOR-CPA), then there exists an on-line encryption scheme Π' which is also secure in the sense of FTG-CPA-P1 (resp. FTG-CPA-P2 or LOR-CPA) but which is not FTG-BCPA-P1 secure (resp. FTG-BCPA-P2 or BCPA-LORS) assuming the existence of pseudo-random permutations.*

Proof. Assume that there exists some FTG-CPA-P1 secure on-line encryption scheme $\Pi = (\mathcal{K}, \mathcal{E}, \mathcal{D})$, since otherwise the theorem is vacuously true. We now modify Π to a new on-line encryption scheme $\Pi' = (\mathcal{K}, \mathcal{E}', \mathcal{D}')$ which is also FTG-CPA-P1 secure but not secure in the FTG-BCPA-P1 sense:

```
Algorithm E'_k(M[i])                     Algorithm D'_k(C[i]‖v)
    If i = 2 and M[2] = C[1]                 return D_k(C[i])
        then return E_k(M[2])‖k
    else return E_k(M[i])‖0^k
```

In the description of Π', 0^k denotes the concatenation of k zeros, and v denotes a k-bit value.

A BCPA adversary can choose the message blocks so that the relation $M[2] = C[1]$ holds with probability 1. Hence a BCPA adversary obtains the secret key and easily wins the FTG game. Thus Π' is not FTG-BCPA-P1 secure.

However a CPA adversary cannot choose the blocks. Then the relation holds with probability $1/2^n$ for each message queried if $\mathcal{E}_k$ is a pseudo-random permutation. Indeed, except if the relation $M[2] = C[1]$ holds, the CPA adversary gains no additional advantage in winning the FTG game against Π' than against Π. Therefore, it is easy to show that if Π is secure, then so is Π': $\mathsf{Adv}_{\Pi'}^{\text{ftg-cpa-p1}}(k, t, q, \mu) \leq \mathsf{Adv}_{\Pi}^{\text{ftg-cpa-p1}}(k, t, q, \mu) + 2q/2^n$. We can prove this result using different games as in [21]. The first game G_0 is the real security game and in the next game G_1, the simulation is stopped as soon as the relation $M[2] = C[1]$ holds. The difference between the two games can be analyzed using the probability of collision. Let F be the event $M[2] = C[1]$, S be the event of the adversary wins the FTG security game against Π and S' be the event the adversary wins the FTG security game against Π'. As long as F does not occur, $\Pr[S] = \Pr[S']$ so $\Pr[S \wedge \neg F] = \Pr[S' \wedge \neg F]$. Therefore, $|\Pr[S] - \Pr[S']| \leq \Pr[F]$ as a lemma in [21] shows. Then, it is easy to upper bound $\Pr[F]$ by $q/2^n$ since each call will be independent (a new random value is used for each message query) and $\mathsf{Adv}_{\Pi'}^{\mathrm{ftg-cpa-p1}}(k, t, q, \mu) \leq \mathsf{Adv}_{\Pi}^{\mathrm{ftg-cpa-p1}}(k, t, q, \mu) + 2q/2^n$. The factor of 2 comes from the fact that the advantage is twice the probability of success minus 1. Consequently, Π' is FTG-CPA-P1 secure but is not FTG-BCPA-P1 secure. This conversion can be adapted to prove the separation between FTG-BCPA-P2 and FTG-CPA-P2, and between LORS-BCPA and LOR-CPA.

3.2   Adaptive Adversaries Can be More Powerful in the Blockwise Model

ADAPTIVE ADVERSARIES. Katz and Yung show in [18] that accesses to an adaptive encryption oracle after the challenge phase do not help an CPA adversary. Formally, they show that FTG-CPA-P1 is polynomially-equivalent in the number of message queries to FTG-CPA-P2. In the BA model, this equivalence is no longer valid and we prove that BCPA-P2 adversaries are strictly stronger than BCPA-P1 ones since the CBC encryption mode is FTG-BCPA-P1 but not FTG-BCPA-P2 according to [17]. Finally, it is worth noticing in the following proof that if the condition $M[4] = C[3]$ is not present, the scheme Π' is not FTG-CPA-P1. Thus, as one could believe at first glance, the counterexample we use in the proof cannot be applied in the standard model.

Theorem 2. *[FTG-BCPA-P1 $\not\Rightarrow$ FTG-BCPA-P2] If there exists an on-line encryption scheme Π which is FTG-BCPA-P1 secure, then there exists an on-line encryption scheme Π' which is also secure FTG-BCPA-P1 secure but not FTG-BCPA-P2 secure assuming the existence of pseudo-random permutations.*

Proof. Assume that there exists some FTG-BCPA-P1 secure on-line encryption scheme $\Pi = (\mathcal{K}, \mathcal{E}, \mathcal{D})$, since otherwise the theorem is vacuously true. We now modify Π to a new on-line encryption scheme $\Pi' = (\mathcal{K}, \mathcal{E}', \mathcal{D}')$ which is also FTG-BCPA-P1 secure but not secure in the FTG-BCPA-P2 sense. The new on-line encryption scheme $\Pi' = (\mathcal{K}, \mathcal{E}', \mathcal{D}')$ is defined as follows:

```
Algorithm E'ₖ(M[i])                                          |  Algorithm D'ₖ(C[i]‖b')
  If (i = 4) ∧ (M[4] = C[3]) ∧ (Dᵐₖ(M[2]‖M[3]) = M[1])       |     return Dₖ(C[i])
      then return Eₖ(M[4])‖1                                  |
  else return Eₖ(M[i])‖0                                      |
```

where $\mathcal{D}_k^m(C)$ denotes the decryption of the whole ciphertext C using the secret key k and not only as the decryption of one block of the ciphertext. More precisely, in the above description, the block $M[2]$ is treated for example as the initialization vector $C[0]$ and $M[3]$ is the encryption of the first block.

Every BCPA adversary can choose the blocks of messages such that the relation $M[4] = C[3]$ holds with probability 1. We show that a FTG-BCPA-P2 adversary A, can win its FTG game, *i.e.* distinguish between the encryption of M_0 and M_1. Now A tries to correctly guess the bit b. In the challenge phase, A chooses two different random blocks $\{0,1\}^n$, $M_0[1]$ and $M_1[1]$ and sends them to the encryption oracle which returns $C_b[0]\|C_b[1]$. In the guess phase, A sends $M[1] = M_0[1]$ and receives $C[0]\|C[1]$. Then, A sends $M[2] = C_b[0]$, receives $C[2]$, and sends $M[3] = C_b[1]$ except the last bit and receives $C[3]$. Finally, A sends $M[4] = C[3]$ and the encryption oracle returns $\mathcal{E}_k(M[4])\|d$. If $d = 1$, then A has correctly guessed the bit $b = 0$, since $\mathcal{D}_k^m(M[2]\|M[3]) = M[1]$ (because if $b = 0$, then $\mathcal{D}_k^m(C_b[0]\|C_b[1]) = M_0[1]$). Therefore A wins the FTG game with probability 1. Hence a FTG-BCPA-P1 adversary B, which has not access to a blockwise encryption oracle after the challenge phase cannot win the game with significant advantage. Indeed, assume that there exists a FTG-BCPA-P1 adversary A against scheme Π', then we will construct a FTG-BCPA-P1 attacker B against scheme Π. The attacker B will simulate the challenger to the adversary A. The event $\mathcal{D}_k^m(M[2]\|M[3]) = M[1]$ can appear in two situations: either at random with probability $1/2^n$ for each message, if $\mathcal{E}_k$ is a pseudo-random permutation, or since the attacker B knows all encryption queries of A, he can decide when this event occurs in the second case. Consequently, B is able to simulate the encryption process to A except in the first case which appears with small probability. Consequently, Π' is FTG-BCPA-P1 secure but is not FTG-BCPA-P2 secure.

ADAPTIVE ADVERSARIES DURING THE CHALLENGE PHASE. We also prove that adversaries adaptive before, during and after the challenge phase, BCPA-D, are stronger than adversary, BCPA-P2 adaptive before and after. The notion of BCPA-D adversaries is equivalent to BCPA-P2 in the standard adversarial model since messages are treated as atomic objects.

Theorem 3. *[FTG-BCPA-P2 $\not\Rightarrow$ FTG-BCPA-D] If there exists an on-line encryption scheme Π which is FTG-BCPA-P2 secure, then there exists an on-line encryption scheme Π' which is also FTG-BCPA-P2 secure but not FTG-BCPA-D secure assuming the existence of pseudo-random permutations.*

Proof. Assume that there exists some FTG-BCPA-P2 secure on-line encryption scheme $\Pi = (\mathcal{K}, \mathcal{E}, \mathcal{D})$, since otherwise the theorem is vacuously true. We now modify Π to a new on-line encryption scheme $\Pi' = (\mathcal{K}, \mathcal{E}', \mathcal{D}')$ which is also FTG-BCPA-P2 secure but not FTG-BCPA-D secure. The new on-line encryption scheme $\Pi' = (\mathcal{K}, \mathcal{E}', \mathcal{D}')$ is a slight modification of the encryption function $\mathcal{E}$ defined as follows:

```
Algorithm E'_k(M[i])              Algorithm D'_k(C[i])
    If i = 3 and M[2] = C[1]          If i = 3 and M[2] = C[1]
        then return M[3]                  then return C[3]
    else return E_k(M[i])            else return D_k(C[i])
```

Clearly Π' is FTG-BCPA-P2 secure as Π as shown in the previous proofs. A BCPA adversary can choose the blocks of messages such that the relation $M[2] = C[1]$ holds with probability 1 during the challenge phase. Therefore a FTG-BCPA-D adversary A can distinguish between the encryption of M_0 and M_1: A first sends $(M_0[1], M_1[1])$, gets $C[0]\|C[1]$, and then queries $(M_0[2], M_1[2])$ where $M_0[2] = C[1]$ and $M_0[2] \neq C[1]$. Finally, he queries $(M_0[3], M_1[3])$ such that $M_0[3] \neq M_1[3]$. Consequently, if he receives $C[3] = M_0[3]$, then $b = 0$, otherwise $b = 1$. Hence Π' is FTG-BCPA-P2 secure but is not FTG-BCPA-D secure.

RELATION BETWEEN FTG AND LOR IN THE BA MODEL. In [3] Bellare *et al.* prove that in the standard model FTG and LOR are polynomially-equivalent in the number of encrypted queries. We prove here in the BA model that this relation holds between FTG-BCPA-D and LORS-BCPA. The proof is an adaptation of [3] and uses the same hybrid argument (introduced in [12]) in the blockwise setting. It is given in appendix of the full version.

Theorem 4. *[LORS-BCPA $\Rightarrow$ FTG-BCPA-D $\xrightarrow{q}$ LORS-BCPA] For any scheme $\mathcal{SE} = (\mathcal{K}, \mathcal{E}, \mathcal{D})$,*

$$\mathsf{Adv}_{\mathcal{SE}}^{\mathrm{ftg-bcpa-d}}(k, t, q, \mu) \leq \mathsf{Adv}_{\mathcal{SE}}^{\mathrm{lors-bcpa}}(k, t, q, \mu) \leq q \times \mathsf{Adv}_{\mathcal{SE}}^{\mathrm{ftg-bcpa-d}}(k, t, q, \mu)$$

3.3   Concurrent Adversaries

Finally, we show that LORC-BCPA is the strongest security notion in the blockwise model. Concurrent adversaries have already been considered in other contexts such as zero-knowledge proofs in [8]. According to our knowledge, it is the first time that concurrent adversaries appear in encryption schemes. In the BA model and for the LOR game, this notion is natural.

Theorem 5. *[LORS-BCPA$\nRightarrow$ LORC-BCPA] If there exists an on-line encryption scheme Π which is LORS-BCPA secure, then there exists an on-line encryption scheme Π' which is also LORS-BCPA secure but not LORC-BCPA secure assuming the existence of pseudo-random permutations.*

Proof. Assume that there exists some LORS-BCPA secure on-line encryption scheme $\Pi = (\mathcal{K}, \mathcal{E}, \mathcal{D})$, since otherwise the theorem is vacuously true. We now modify Π to a new on-line encryption scheme $\Pi' = (\mathcal{K}', \mathcal{E}', \mathcal{D}')$ which is also LORS-BCPA secure but not secure in the LORC-BCPA sense. The new on-line encryption scheme $\Pi' = (\mathcal{K}, \mathcal{E}', \mathcal{D}')$ is a slight modification of the functions $\mathcal{E}$ and $\mathcal{D}$:

```
Algorithm E'ₖ(M[i])
    If i = 3 and C[1] = Dᵐₖ(M[2]‖M[3])
        then return M[3]
    else return Eₖ(M[i])
```

where $\mathcal{D}_{\mathsf{k}}^{\mathrm{m}}(M)$ denotes the decryption of the whole message M using the key k and the decryption can be easily adapted.

Clearly Π' is LORS-BCPA secure as the initial scheme Π. Indeed, assume for the sake of contradiction that there exists a LORS-BCPA adversary A' against Π'. We must show that there also exists a LORS-BCPA adversary A against Π. We have to simulate the challenger against A'. The only difference between the two schemes is in the encryption of the third block if some relation occurs. The relation can hold either by a correct guess of the adversary which is negligible if $\mathcal{E}_k$ behaves as a pseudo-random permutation or if a collision occurs with previous encryption queries. The last event is easily detectable by adversary A since all encryption queries goes through A which forwards them to its challenger. Hence, it is easy for A to not encrypt the third block if the relation occurs. In this case, the simulation is quite perfect.

Any LORC-BCPA adversary can choose the message blocks such that the relation $C[1] = \mathcal{D}_k^m(M[2]\|M[3])$ holds with probability 1. Indeed, a LORC-BCPA adversary A begins the encryption of a pair of messages (M_0, M_1) by sending $(M_0[1], M_1[1])$ to a first instance of the LOR-block encryption oracle which returns $C_b[0]\|C_b[1]$. Then, he sends $(M'_0[1], M'_1[1])$ where $M'_0[1] = C_b[1]$ to a second instance running concurrently and gets $C'_b[0]\|C'_b[1]$. He continues the encryption of (M_0, M_1) by sending $(M_0[2], M_1[2])$ such that $M_0[2] = C'_b[0]$ and $M_1[2]$ is a random block. Finally, he queries $(M_0[3], M_1[3])$ with $M_0[3] = C'_b[1]$. A simple manipulation shows that if $b = 0$, then $C_0[1] = \mathcal{D}_k^m(C'_0[0]\|C'_0[1])$ and consequently $\mathcal{E}_k(M_0[3]) = M_0[3]$. Therefore Π' is LORS-BCPA secure but is not LORC-BCPA secure.

4   On-line Encryption Schemes with a Special Property

In this section we define a new property for on-line encryption schemes, called *Resettable-Or-Continuous* (ROC). For these schemes, the two security notions LORS-BCPA and FTG-BCPA-D are exactly equivalent.

The Resettable-Or-Continuous property can be defined informally as follows: it is computationally hard for a polynomial-time adversary to distinguish with non-negligible advantage between the encryption of the concatenation of a polynomial number of messages, $\mathcal{E}(M_1\|M_2\|\ldots\|M_{\ell(k)})$, and the concatenation of the encryptions of the same messages $\mathcal{E}(M_1)\|\mathcal{E}(M_2)\|\ldots\|\mathcal{E}(M_{\ell(k)})$ for stateful encryption schemes such as the counter mode or for a stateless encryption scheme between $\mathcal{E}(M_1\|r_1\|M_2\|r_2\ldots\|r_{\ell(k)-1}\|M_{\ell(k)})$, where the r_i's denote random blocks such that the length of the two bitstring be the same. This special class captures many important on-line encryption schemes such as the CBC and CTR mode [3].

Formally, we define the *resettable-or-continuous* oracle $ROC(\mathcal{E}_k^{bl}(.), b)$, taking as input a message M and working as follows for a stateful encryption scheme such as the CBC. At the beginning of the game, the ROC oracle chooses a random bit b. The first message $M = M[1]M[2]\ldots M[l]$ is encrypted by the ROC oracle which returns $C[0]C[1]\ldots C[l]$. The adversary is free to stop this encryption by using the stop command or to submit a new message block by block. When the adversary submits the stop command and if $b = 0$, the ROC encryption oracle stops the encryption of M and starts the encryption of the new message $M'[1], \ldots M[l']$ under the key k and a new random value $C'[0]$ and returns $C' = C'[0]C'[1] \ldots C'[l']$. However if $b = 1$, the ROC oracle does not stop the encryption of the first message. He takes a random block $r_1 \in \{0,1\}^n$, encrypts it into $C'[0]$ as if r_1 was the next block in M. Then, he encrypts the message $M'[1]M'[2] \ldots M'[l']$ block by block and returns gradually $C'[0]C'[1]C'[2] \ldots C'[l']$. In the case $b = 1$, the ROC encryption oracle has encrypted the concatened message $M[1] \ldots M[l]\|r_1\|M'[1] \ldots M'[l']$. This game continues for the other queries. This simulation can be made for any stateless encryption scheme such as the CBC mode. For a stateful encryption scheme such as the CTR mode, the random block is not present when $b = 1$. This property can also be defined in the standard model.

$$\mathsf{Adv}_{\Pi,A}^{\mathrm{ind-roc}}(k,t,q,\mu) \overset{\mathrm{def}}{=} \left| 2 \cdot \Pr\left[\mathsf{k} \leftarrow \mathcal{K}(1^k); b \leftarrow \{0,1\} : A^{ROC(\mathcal{E}_k^{\mathrm{bl}}(.),b)}(k) = b \right] - 1 \right|$$

Therefore, the security bound for the scheme Π is given by $\mathsf{Adv}_{\Pi}^{\mathrm{ind-roc}}(k,t,q,\mu) = \max_A\{\mathsf{Adv}_{\Pi,A}^{\mathrm{ind-roc}}(k)\}$, where the maximum is over all legitimate A having time-complexity t, making to the oracle at most q encryption queries totaling μ blocks. A secret-key encryption scheme is said to be *IND-secure against blockwise adaptive chosen plaintext attack* in the ROC sense if for all polynomial-time probabilistic adversaries, the advantage in this game is negligible as a function of the security parameter. The ROC class is the set of encryption schemes satisfying the ROC property.

Theorem 6. *[FTG-BCPA-D $\overset{ROC}{\Rightarrow}$ LORS-BCPA] For any ROC scheme $\mathcal{SE}$,*

$$\mathsf{Adv}_{\mathcal{SE}}^{\mathrm{lors-bcpa}}(k,t,q,\mu) \leq \mathsf{Adv}_{\mathcal{SE}}^{\mathrm{ftg-bcpa-d}}(k,t,q,\mu) + \mathsf{Adv}_{\mathcal{SE}}^{\mathrm{ind-roc}}(k,t,q,\mu)$$

Proof. The proof goes by contradiction. Let $\mathcal{SE}$ be a ROC encryption scheme. Assume for the sake of contradiction that a LORS-BCPA adversary A wins the LORS game against $\mathcal{SE}$ with non-negligible advantage. Then it can be used to build a BCPA-D attacker B winning a FTG game against $\mathcal{SE}$ with non-negligible advantage. The FTG adversary B does not use his find phase and begins the challenge phase by running A. To simulate the LORS encryption queries of A, B forwards the pairs of messages block by block and does not send the stop command at the end of a message query. All messages are chained. The messages are separated with a random block chosen by B in the case of stateless schemes and are not separated for stateful schemes. This simulation is perfect for schemes having the ROC property. Therefore, A wins the LORS game with non-negligible advantage and B forwards the bit guessed by A and also wins the FTG game with non-negligible advantage.

5   Security Under Concurrent Adversary

In this section, we prove that security against concurrent adversaries can be achieved. We prove that the randomized counter mode, called XOR in [3] is secure. We note that encryption with XOR or CTR mode of operation does not require permutations. Therefore we use only functions. We prove such scheme and not the standard counter mode where the counter is incremented between each message since in the concurrent scenario, the adversary can begin the encryption of several messages in parallel.

We consider several attacker games such that the distance between each game can be easily shown. In the last game, it will be clear that the adversary has no way to get some information about the random bit b in the LORC security game.

Theorem 7. *For any adversary $\mathcal{A}$ running within time bound t, with less than $q < 2^{n/2}$ calls to the function F, totalling at most μ blocks,*

$$\mathsf{Adv}^{\mathsf{lorc-bcpa}}_{\mathsf{XOR},A}(k,t,q,\mu) \leq \mathsf{Adv}^{\mathsf{prf}}_{F,A}(k,t,q) + \frac{q(q-1)}{2^n}$$

where n denotes the block length, $\mathsf{Adv}^{\mathsf{prf}}_{F,A}(k,t,q)$, the advantage of the adversary A in distinguishing a function taken from F to a random function with at most q black-box queries within time bounded by t. The same kind of definition can be given for $\mathsf{Adv}^{\mathsf{lorc-bcpa}}_{\mathsf{XOR},A}(k,t,q,\mu)$.

The proof is in the full version [11].

6   Conclusion

In this paper we have analyzed the relations between the block adversary and the standard models for probabilistic and deterministic schemes. For probabilistic schemes, the relations are modified and we introduce new security notions. The resettable-or-continuous property extends the result of Bellare *et al.*. Moreover, we also prove that concurrent accesses lead to the strongest security notion and we show that some schemes can be secure in this setting. Finally, we show that the models are equivalent for deterministic schemes in appendix of the full version.

References

1. M. Bellare, J. Black, T. Krovetz, and P. Rogaway. OCB : A Block-Cipher Mode of Operation for Efficient Authenticated Encryption. Available at http://www.cs.ucdavis.edu/users/~rogaway, 2001.
2. M. Bellare, A. Boldyreva, L. Knudsen, and C. Namprempre. On-Line Ciphers and the Hash-CBC Constructions. In *Crypto '01*, LNCS 2139, pages 292–309. Springer-Verlag, 2001.
3. M. Bellare, A. Desai, E. Jokipii, and P. Rogaway. A Concrete Security Treatment for Symmetric Encryption. In *Proc. 38th of FOCS*, pages 394–403. IEEE, 1997.

4. M. Bellare, A. Desai, D. Pointcheval, and P. Rogaway. Relations Among Notions of Security for Public-Key Encryption Schemes. In *Crypto '98*, LNCS 1462, pages 26–45. Springer-Verlag, 1998.

5. M. Bellare and P. Rogaway. On the Construction of Variable-Input-Length Ciphers. In *FSE '99*, LNCS 1636. Springer-Verlag, 1999.

6. A. Boldyreva and N. Taesombut. On-line Encryption Schemes: New Security Notions and Constructions. In *RSA Conf 2004*, LNCS, pages –. Springer-Verlag, Berlin, 2003.

7. Y. Dodis and J. H. An. Concealment and Its Applications to Authenticated Encryption. In *Eurocrypt '03*, LNCS 2656, pages 312–329. Springer-Verlag, 2003.

8. C. Dwork, M. Naor, and A. Sahai. Concurrent Zero-Knowledge. In *Proc. of the 30th STOC*, pages 409–418. ACM Press, New York, 1998.

9. P. A. Fouque, A. Joux, G. Martinet, and F. Valette. Authenticated On-line Encryption. In *Selected Areas in Cryptography '03*, LNCS. Springer-Verlag, 2003. *To appear*.

10. P. A. Fouque, G. Martinet, and G. Poupard. Practical Symmetric On-line Encryption. In *Fast Software Encryption '03*, LNCS. Springer-Verlag, 2003. *To appear*.

11. P. A. Fouque, A. Joux, and G. Poupard. Blockwise Adversarial Model for On-line Ciphers and Symmetric Encryption Schemes. In *Selected Areas in Cryptography '04*, LNCS. Springer-Verlag, 2004. http://www.di.ens.fr/~fouque/pubs/.

12. O. Goldreich. *Foundations of Cryptography*. Cambridge University Press, Weizmann Institute of Science, 2001. Basic Tools.

13. O. Goldreich, S. Goldwasser, and S. Micali. How to Construct Random Functions. *Journal of the ACM*, 33(4):210–217, 1986.

14. S. Goldwasser and S. Micali. Probabilistic encryption. *Journal of Computer and System Sciences*, 28:270–299, 1984.

15. A. Herzberg, S. Jarecki, H. Krawczyk, and M. Yung. A Tweakable Enciphering Mode. In *Crypto '03*, LNCS. Springer-Verlag, 2003.

16. R. Housley. Cryptographic message syntax. S/MIME Working Group of the IETF, Internet-draft draft-ietf-smime-cms-12.txt, March 1999.

17. A. Joux, G. Martinet, and F. Valette. Blockwise-Adaptive Attackers: Revisiting the (in)security of some provably secure Encryptions Modes: CBC, GEM, IACBC. In *Crypto '02*, LNCS 2442, pages 17–31. Springer-Verlag, 2002.

18. J. Katz and M. Yung. Complete characterization of security notions for probabilistic private-key encryption. In *STOC '00*. ACM Press, 2000.

19. NBS. FIPS PUB 81 - DES Modes of Operation, December 1980.

20. R. Rivest. All-or-nothing encryption and the package transform. In *FSE '97*, LNCS 1267. Springer-Verlag, 1997.

21. V. Shoup. OAEP Reconsidered. In *Crypto '2001*, LNCS 2139, pages 239–259. Springer-Verlag, Berlin, 2001.

Cryptanalysis of a White Box AES Implementation

Olivier Billet, Henri Gilbert, and Charaf Ech-Chatbi

France Télécom R&D
38–40, rue du Général Leclerc
92794 Issy les Moulineaux Cedex 9 — France
{olivier.billet, henri.gilbert}@francetelecom.com
charaf_echchatbi@yahoo.fr

Abstract. The white box attack context as described in [1, 2] is the common setting where cryptographic software is executed in an untrusted environment—i.e. an attacker has gained access to the implementation of cryptographic algorithms, and can observe or manipulate the dynamic execution of whole or part of the algorithms. In this paper, we present an efficient practical attack against the obfuscated AES implementation [1] proposed at SAC 2002 as a means to protect AES software operated in the white box context against key exposure. We explain in details how to extract the whole AES secret key embedded in such a white box AES implementation, with negligible memory and worst time complexity 2^{30}.

Keywords: white box, AES, block ciphers, tamper resistance, software piracy, implementation.

1   Introduction

One of the consequences of the ever spreading use of cryptology within mass applications e.g. email, web servers access, digital content distribution, and so on implemented in software on standard terminals, like PCs, PDAs, or mobile phones, is that cryptologic algorithms are quite often executed in an untrusted environment. The usual "black box" model, where keys and cryptographic algorithms are confined and executed in a logically protected and tamper resistant cryptographic module, like a smart card, is no longer applicable. This situation motivated the introduction of a new setting, coined "white box" context of execution: the software representing cryptographic algorithms, cryptographic keys when separate from the cryptographic software, and dynamic data produced during the execution of all or part of the cryptographic algorithms, are exposed to being accessed or even manipulated by malicious processes hosted by the same machine which may be controlled either by an outsider or by the legitimate user of the host terminal. Cryptographic applications running in the white box context of execution are highly vulnerable to the most severe form

---

Work performed at France Télécom R&D

H. Handschuh and A. Hasan (Eds.): SAC 2004, LNCS 3357, pp. 227–240, 2005.

of attack, namely the leakage of the cryptographic keys. Thus, the protection cryptographic algorithms would offer in the black box model of execution vanish.

This security issue is at the origin of the introduction, in a pair of seminal articles [2, 1] S. Chow, P. Eisen, . Johnson, and P.C. van Oorschot, of a new protection technique preventing from key leakage for cryptographic software run in the white box context. It consists in implementing key-instantiated versions of an algorithm, as the composition of a series of lookup tables, each look-up table concealing some components of the algorithm. Implementations of an algorithm resulting from this protection technique are named white-box implementations. White box implementations of the ES and AES blockciphers were respectively described in [2] and [1]. Short after the publication of [2], it was shown by M. Jacob, . Boneh and . Felten in [3], that the obfuscation technique applied in [2] was insecure, i.e. that a low complexity attack requiring few accesses (with partly chosen input values) to lookup tables representing external ES rounds, allowed to extract the key from a white box ES implementation. owever, the attack technique of [3] is not applicable to the white box implementation of AES described in [1] due to the additional protection provided by some extra features introduced by [1]. More precisely, a fundamental difference between both implementations results from the application, in the case of AES, of so-called external encodings. One of the main security consequences of this extra feature which description is provided in Sec. 2 is that in the case of AES, and unlike ES, the protection of external rounds is not weaker than the protection of internal rounds. Since the attack strategy of [3] is essentially based upon the extra weakness of external rounds, it is not applicable to the AES implementation described in [1]. To the best of our knowledge, no realistic attack against the white box implementation of [1] has been proposed so far.

In this paper, we present a practical low complexity attack i.e. with negligible memory, and work factor $3 \cdot 2^{28} < 2^{30}$ of the AES white box implementation proposed in [1]. The conducting idea of the attack is that though none of the lookup tables, when considered individually, leaks sensitive information related to the AES key in an obvious way, the analysis (based on the observation of related input output values) of lookup tables composition, reveals information on the encodings embedded in those lookup tables. We show that the information provided by the analysis of such tables during three consecutive encoded rounds, allows an attacker to entirely recover the AES 128-bit secret key of an obfuscated AES implementation. The key steps of the proposed attack were successfully implemented in C++, and confirmed by computer experiments.

This paper is organized as follows. In Section 2, we describe the white box AES implementation as proposed by [1]. In Section 3 we show how to extract the secret key. The last section concludes the paper.

2   Description of the White Box AES Implementation

We now describe the implementation proposed in [1]. The general strategy is to merge several steps of the AES round function into table lookups, blended by input output encodings, and mixing bi ections.

Internal encodings (resp. mixing bi ections) are non-linear (resp. GF(2)-linear) and introduce confusion (resp. diffusion) in the representation of the intermediate blocks of the computation. Their inclusion in the implementation must respect the fact that two consecutive tables in the data flow have matching output and input encodings, as well as matching mixing bi ections, at their boundary.

Apart from the above pairwise canceling internal transformations, another obfuscation technique called external encoding is used. It consists in feeding the obfuscated implementation with AES inputs in an encoded form. At the same time, the implementation also outputs the AES encrypted values in an encoded form. Thus, the implementation does not exactly achieve an AES computation $Y = \quad (X)$, but a modified computation $Y = \quad ' (X) = \quad \circ \quad \circ F^{-1}(X)$. The external input output encodings $\quad$ and F^{-1} have to be annihilated on the peer site e.g. a server when the AES obfuscated implementation is embedded in a software player in order to compute $\quad '^{-1}$. Though the encodings $\quad$ and F^{-1} suggested in [1] are hereafter taken into account, our attack is not highly dependent upon their exact specification. One of the main consequences of using external encodings is that internal input output encodings can be used to blend the first and last round, in addition to inner rounds' blending. This prevents attackers from exploiting specific weaknesses one would otherwise encounter against external rounds of obfuscated implementations [3].

Let us hereafter denote AES-128 the AES version operating on 128 bits blocks. Recall [4,5] that the AES-128 round function is made of the four steps described in Fig. 1 operating on the 16 bytes of a 4×4 state array. The AES-128

Fig. 1. tracking four bytes during an AES round

considered in [1] consists of 10 such rounds; a preliminary AddRoundKey step is performed before the first round, and MixColumns is omitted in the final round. Let us index the state bytes by their row and column numbers (i, j) in the state array. If the S-box function operating on bytes during the SubBytes step is denoted by S, define for any round r and any byte (i, j) with indexes taken modulo 4:

$$1 \leq r \leq 9 \qquad T_{i,j}^r(x) := S\left(x \oplus \quad_{i,j}^r\right) ,$$
$$T_{i,j}^{10}(x) := S\left(x \oplus \quad_{i,j}^{10}\right) \oplus \quad_{i,j-i}^{11} .$$

(Note that we shifted the round index of the original AES-128 by 1, and that the post-whitening key $\quad_{i,j}^{11}$ occuring in the last round is absorbed by the definition of the last function $T_{i,j}^{10}$.) Now each 4-byte column of the output of the SubByte plus ShiftRows steps will contribute to the 4-byte column of the state array after MixColumns, and those four bytes are related to the former by a 32×8

submatrix MC_i of the 32×32 matrix MC representing `MixColumns`. Now the entire function can be described by a lookup table. owever, it is necessary to obfuscate this table, which leads to encode its 4-bit input and output nibbles using concatenated non-linear permutations ▯in▯ and ▯out▯ respectively.

To add to the diffusion, 8×8 affine "mixing" bi ection is inserted before $T^r_{i,j}$ and a 32×32 affine bi ection MB is inserted after the `MixColumn` part. The resulting lookup table is depicted in Fig. 2 as the `sub` table. The 32×8 linear mapping of Fig. 2 is associated with $MB \times MC_i$.

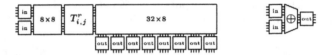 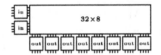

Fig. 2. `sub` table (type II) and `xor` table (type IV)

To cancel the effect of MB, a lookup table takes care of the inversion. owever, instead of constructing a huge table for the entire 32×32 matrix, the mapping MB^{-1} is split into four submatrices $\left(MB^{-1}\right)_{.i}$, ust like with the `MixColumns` matrix MC. This results in the lookup table depicted in Fig. 3.

Fig. 3. `untwist` table (type III)

Finally, external input and output encodings are implemented, using two sets of sixteen 8-bit to 128-bit lookup tables depicted in Fig. 4. Each external input encoding table represents the linear mapping associated with one 128×8 vertical stripe of a 128×128 matrix   the composition of $_F$ and the concatenation of the input mixing bi ections for $T^1_{i,j}$'s inverses   surrounded by 4-bit to 4-bit non-linear encodings. Each external output encoding table represents one 128×8 vertical stripe of a 128×128 parasitic matrix   the composition of one round 10's output mixing bi ection's inverse, one of the mappings $T^{10}_{i,j}$, and 128×8 vertical stripe of a 128×128 parasitic matrix   surrounded by 4-bit to 4-bit non linear encodings. The outputs of the 16 **external input encoding** tables have to be decoded, xored together and reencoded to complete the implementation. This is done by using 15×32 additional **xor** tables per 128-block. The same number of xor tables is needed to support the 16 **extern_encode** tables.

Thus, in order to implement a white box instance of AES-128 associated with a key   , $9 \cdot 4 \cdot 4$ **sub** tables, $9 \cdot 4 \cdot 4$ **untwist** tables, $9 \cdot 4 \cdot 3 \cdot 8$ **xor** tables supporting **sub** tables, $9 \cdot 4 \cdot 3 \cdot 8$ xor tables supporting **untwist** tables, $2 \cdot 16$ **extern_encode** tables, and $2 \cdot 15 \cdot 32$ xor tables supporting **extern_encode** tables are needed. Therefore, the total size of lookup tables in an AES-128 white box implementation is 770 048 bytes.

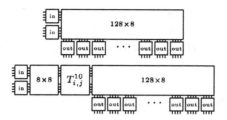

Fig. 4. extern_encode tables for input and output respectively (type I)

3   Cryptanalysis of the White Box AES Implementation

We now describe a very efficient attack against the white box AES implementation of [1]. The leading idea is that, though recovering information about the key by a local inspection of the lookup tables seems difficult lookup tables were designed to satisfy so-called diversity and ambiguity criteria recovering information by analyzing compositions of lookup tables corresponding to one encoded AES round is easier. More precisely, it is convenient to analyze each of the four mappings between four bytes of the input state array, and the four corresponding bytes of the output state array, which together form an encoded AES round. Each such mapping can be conceptualized by the box in Fig. 5, where we can choose inputs and observe outputs, whereas intermediate values remain concealed. Let us denote this box by R_j^r. Each R_j^r box is made of four 8-bit to 8-bit parasitic input permutations $_{i,j}^r$ (resp. output permutations $_{i,j}^r$) constructed as the composition of two concatenated 4-bit to 4-bit input (resp. output) encodings, and one 8-bit to 8-bit linear mixing bi ection. ue to the fact that internal input encodings plus linear mixing bi ections and linear mixing bi-ections plus output encodings mutually cancel out at the boundary between two rounds r and $r + 1$, each $_{i,j}^r$ is the inverse of $_{i,j}^{r+1}$.

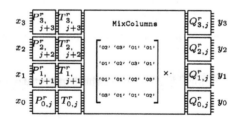

Fig. 5. One of the four   mappings,   = 0   3

The attack proceeds in three steps. First of all, we recover the non-affine part of the parasites $_i^r$ in round $r = 1, \ldots, 9$, i.e. we determine $_i^r$ up to unknown affine bi ections, and thus get at the same time the non-affine part of the inverse $_i^{r+1}$ of round $r + 1$, $r = 1, \ldots, 9$. At this stage we are in the setting depicted in Fig. 5, but this time the permutations $_i$ and $_i$ are now GF(2)-affine, except for the permutation $_{i,j}^1$ whose non-affine part has not been determined. In a second step, we recover those $GF(2)$-affine mappings (but $\overset{1}{_{i,j}}$ and $\overset{1}{_{i,j}}$), first up to an unknown $GF(2^8)$-affine bi ection, and then entirely. Eventually combining all this information in a third step, we extract the AES-128 key.

3.1   Recovering Non-linear Parts

Consider the mapping R_j^r. We are trying to remove the non-linearity in the parasites ($\overset{r}{_i})_{i=0,\ldots,3}$. To this end consider y_0 as a function of (x_0, x_1, x_2, x_3), and fix the values of x_1, x_2, and x_3 to some constants, say c_1, c_2, and c_3. One easily checks that there exists two constants in $GF(2^8)$, namely   independent of c_1, c_2, c_3, and $_{1, 2, 3}$, such that

$$y_0(x, c_1, c_2, c_3) = \overset{r}{_{0,j}} \left(T_{0,j}^r \left(\overset{r}{_{0,j}}(x) \right) \oplus \quad _{1, 2, 3} \right) .$$

Since x only takes 256 values, those mappings are known by input output, as well as their inverses. Also, varying one constant (say c_3) into the whole $GF(2^8)$, and keeping the other one fixed, has the effect that $_{1, 2, 3}'$ takes all the values in $GF(2^8)$. We are thus able to produce   as lookup tables, of course   all the functions

$$y_0(x, c_1, c_2, c_3) \circ y_0(x, c_1, c_2, c_3')^{-1} = {}_0 \left({}_0^{-1}(x) \oplus \quad \right) , \tag{1}$$

where $= {}_{1, 2, 3}' \oplus {}_{1, 2, 3}$ takes all the values in $GF(2^8)$. This leads to the problem of recovering $_0$, or at least its non-linear part from the set of all those lookup tables. Note that since functions are given as lookup tables, we are not provided with the underlying translations: we only know the unordered set of functions corresponding to the 256 translations. As this problem is of independent interest, we state it, along with a solution, in a standalone context.

Theorem 1. *Given a set of functions $= \{ \circ \oplus \circ {}^{-1} \}_{\in GF(2^8)}$ given by values, where   is a permutation of $GF(2^8)$ and $\oplus$ is the translation by   in $GF(2^8)$, one can construct a particular solution $\widetilde{}$ such that there exists an affine mapping A so that $\widetilde{} = \circ A$.*

Proof. There is an isomorphism between the commutative groups $\left(GF(2)^8, \oplus\right)$ and $(, \circ)$, given by

$$
\begin{array}{c}
: \qquad\qquad\qquad \longrightarrow GF(2)^8 \\
\circ \oplus \circ \quad {}^{-1} \longrightarrow [\ ] ,
\end{array}
$$

where $[\ ]$ denotes the embedding of the element   into the vector space $GF(2)^8$ with canonical base $([\ _i])_{i=1,\ldots,8}$. The issue is we do not know this isomorphism. The general idea of the proof is to recover this isomorphism up to an unknown linear bi ection, i.e. to recover a known isomorphism ψ equal to   up to an unknown linear bi ection. To this end, first select from   a tuple $(f_1, \ldots, f_8)$ of 8 functions such that their images through   constitute a base of $GF(2)^8$. Although we do not know   and thus the underlying translations $[\ _i] = (f_i)$

for each $f_i = \ \circ \oplus \ \circ \ ^{-1}$ this can easily be done by gradually selecting f_1 to f_8 so that they span the whole set   through composition, that is

$$\forall f \in \ , \quad !(\ _1, \ldots, \ _8) \in \{0,1\}^8, \qquad f = f_8^{\ _8} \circ f_7^{\ _7} \circ \cdots \circ f_1^{\ _1} , \qquad (2)$$

where $f_i^1 = f_i$ and f_i^0 denotes the identity function. An efficient algorithm to compute such a tuple of functions $(f_1, \ldots, f_8)$ is described at the end of this paragraph.

Now since $([\ _i])_{i=1 \ldots 8}$ is a base of $GF(2)^8$, there exists a unique one-to-one linear change of base L mapping $[\ _i]$ onto $[\ _i]$ for all $i = 1, \ldots, 8$. Also define the isomorphism $\psi \stackrel{\text{def}}{=} L^{-1} \circ \ $ between $(\ , \circ)$ and $\big(GF(2)^8, \oplus\big)$. One checks that ψ can be efficiently recovered, by using the unique decomposition given by Eq. 2. Indeed, for any $f \in \ $ the unique tuple of binary values $(\ _1, \ldots, \ _8)$ verifying Eq. 2 is easily computed   an exhaustive search would be quick enough, but we give a better algorithm at the end of this paragraph. By successively applying

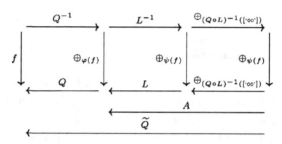

Fig. 6. Relating   , $(\ )$, and $\tilde{\ }$

and L^{-1} to f, one obtains

$$\psi(f) = L^{-1}(\ (f)) = L^{-1}\left(\bigoplus_{i=1\ldots8} \ _i[\ _i] \right) = \bigoplus_{i=1\ldots8} \ _i[\ _i] .$$

Thus the isomorphism ψ is entirely determined.

Let us explain how to recover   from the knowledge of ψ, up to an unknown affine transformation A. For that purpose, consider the commutative diagram of Fig. 6, and define the $GF(2)$-affine one-to-one mapping A by

$$A(x) \stackrel{\text{def}}{=} L\big(x \oplus (\ \circ L)^{-1}([\ 00'])\big) = L(x) \oplus \ ^{-1}([\ 00']) ,$$

and let us set

$$\tilde{\ } \stackrel{\text{def}}{=} \ \circ A .$$

One verifies that $\tilde{\ }^{-1}(\ 00') = [\ 00']$. By applying the above definition of $\tilde{\ }$, or equivalently by inspecting the commutative diagram of Fig.6, one checks that $f = \tilde{\ } \circ \oplus_{(f)} \circ \tilde{\ }^{-1}$.   ence,

$$f(\ 00') = \tilde{\ }(\psi(f)) .$$

From our knowledge of ψ and f, we can therefore compute $\tilde{\ } = \ \circ A$.

Now, we propose an efficient algorithm   time complexity is at most 2^{24} that chooses a tuple $(f_1, \ldots, f_8)$ on the fly, and computes the corresponding mapping ψ. It was successfully implemented in C++.

INPUT : $\mathcal{S}$

OUTPUT : $\mathcal{R} \subset \mathcal{S} \times \mathrm{GF}(2^8)$ such that $\forall(\quad) \in \mathcal{R}$ $(\quad) = [\;]$

ALGORITHM : $\mathcal{R} \leftarrow \{(i \;\; `00')\}$
$(i\;\;) = [`00']$
$\leftarrow `01'$
while $\#\mathcal{R}$ 2^8 **do**
$\quad \mathcal{S} \leftarrow \mathcal{S} \setminus \{\;\;\}$
$\quad$ **if** $(\;\; \cdot) \notin \mathcal{R}$ **then**
$\quad\quad \leftarrow `02' \times$
$\quad\quad (\;\;) = [\;]$
$\quad\quad$ **foreach** $(\quad) \in \mathcal{R}$ **do**
$\quad\quad\quad \mathcal{R} \leftarrow \mathcal{R} \cup \{(\;\; \circ \;\; [\;] \oplus [\;])\}$
$\quad\quad\quad (\;\; \circ \;\;) = [\;] \oplus [\;]$
$\quad\quad$ **enddo**
$\quad$ **endif**
endwhile

Going back to our initial motivation, Theorem 1 enables us to recover for any round $r = 1, \ldots, 9$, the non-linear part $\tilde{\quad}^r_{i,j}$ of $\quad^r_{i,j}$, i.e. such that $\tilde{\quad}^{r}_{i,j}{}^{-1} \circ \quad^r_{i,j}$ is an affine mapping $A^r_{i,j}{}^{-1}$. Given the fact that for the next round, the input encoding $\quad^{r+1}_{i,j}$ must match the output encoding $\quad^r_{i,j}$ of the previous round that is $\quad^{r+1}_{i,j} \circ \quad^r_{i,j}$ must be the identity   we have that $\quad^{r+1}_{i,j} \circ \tilde{\quad}^r_{i,j}$ is exactly the mapping $A^r_{i,j}$. Thus, we have reduced the original problem depicted in Fig. 5 where all   and   are non-linear and matching, to one where they are affine and still matching. The next step is to recover those affine mappings, which is the sub ect of next sections.

3.2   Relations Between Affine Parasites

So let us start again with the setting depicted in Fig.5, except for the fact that all parasitic mappings $\quad^r_{i,j}$ and $\quad^r_{i,j}$ are now affine. Since the problem is identical for each round, we drop the subscripts r and j without loss of generality. We have access to the following functions as lookup tables

$$
\begin{cases}
{}_0(\;_0 \;\;_1 \;\;_2 \;\;_3) = \;_0 \left(`02' \cdot \;'_0(\;_0) \oplus `03' \cdot \;'_1(\;_1) \oplus `01' \cdot \;'_2(\;_2) \oplus `01' \cdot \;'_3(\;_3) \right) \\
{}_1(\;_0 \;\;_1 \;\;_2 \;\;_3) = \;_1 \left(`01' \cdot \;'_0(\;_0) \oplus `02' \cdot \;'_1(\;_1) \oplus `03' \cdot \;'_2(\;_2) \oplus `01' \cdot \;'_3(\;_3) \right) \\
{}_2(\;_0 \;\;_1 \;\;_2 \;\;_3) = \;_2 \left(`01' \cdot \;'_0(\;_0) \oplus `01' \cdot \;'_1(\;_1) \oplus `02' \cdot \;'_2(\;_2) \oplus `03' \cdot \;'_3(\;_3) \right) \\
{}_3(\;_0 \;\;_1 \;\;_2 \;\;_3) = \;_3 \left(`03' \cdot \;'_0(\;_0) \oplus `01' \cdot \;'_1(\;_1) \oplus `01' \cdot \;'_2(\;_2) \oplus `02' \cdot \;'_3(\;_3) \right)
\end{cases}
$$

with the shortcut $T'_i = T_i \circ {}_i$. Actually there is one more issue, which is that we do know the set $\{y_i\}_{i=0,\ldots,3}$ but we do not know the labels to put on each function. Put in another way, we know those functions have the general form

$$
{}_i(\;_0 \;\;_1 \;\;_2 \;\;_3) = \left({}_{i0} \cdot \;'_0(\;_0) \oplus {}_{i1} \cdot \;'_1(\;_1) \oplus {}_{i2} \cdot \;'_2(\;_2) \oplus {}_{i3} \cdot \;'_3(\;_3) \right)
$$

but we do not know what the underlying coefficients $\alpha_{i,j}$ occurring from the MixColumn step are. Let us hereafter denote by the matrix over $GF(2)^8$ of the multiplication by .

Before going any further, let us state a very useful property. Though simple, it is a corner stone in the strategy we designed for the affine parasites' recovery, as well as in resolving the above mentioned renaming issue.

Proposition 1. *For any pair (y_i, y_j) as introduced above, there exists a unique linear mapping L and a unique constant c such that,*

$$\forall x_0 \in GF(2^8), \quad y_i(x_0,\ 00',\ 00',\ 00') = L\left(y_j(x_0,\ 00',\ 00',\ 00')\right) \oplus c. \quad (3)$$

Proof. ecompose the affine maps $_i(x) = A_i(x) \oplus\ _i$ and $_j(x) = A_j(x) \oplus\ _j$, where A_i and A_j are linear, $_i$ and $_j$ constants. ence,

$$y_i(x,\ 00',\ 00',\ 00') = A_i(\ _{i,0} \cdot T_0'(x) \oplus c_i) \oplus\ _i,$$
$$y_j(x,\ 00',\ 00',\ 00') = A_j(\ _{j,0} \cdot T_0'(x) \oplus c_j) \oplus\ _j.$$

Thus, by taking $L = A_i \circ\ _{0/}\ _0 \circ A_j^{-1}$ and $c =\ _i \oplus A_i(c_i) \oplus L[\ _j \oplus A_j(c_j)]$, Eq. 3 holds, which shows the existence of a solution.

The other way round, assuming there is a linear mapping L and a constant c such that Eq. 3 holds, amounts to saying that $(A_i \circ\ _0 \oplus L \circ A_j \circ\ _0) \circ T_0'$ is a constant mapping. Since $T_0' = T_0 \circ\ _0$ is one-to-one, and $(A_i \circ\ _0 \oplus L \circ A_j \circ\ _0)$ is a linear mapping, this constant must be $00'$. Thus $L = A_i \circ\ _{0/}\ _0 \circ A_j^{-1}$, which uniquely defines L. Then $_{i,0} \cdot y_i \oplus L \circ\ _{j,0} \cdot y_j$ is constant, and this constant uniquely defines c.

Obviously, there are analogous statements where one varies the second, third, or fourth variable and keep the other one constant. Also note that given two functions y_i and y_j, there is a straightforward practical algorithm to get the corresponding affine mapping (L, c) connecting their affine parts together. Indeed, considering the 64 entries of the matrix L as well as the 8 entries of the constant vector of c as unknowns over $GF(2)$, and using our knowledge of the functions y_i and y_j by values, one can form a highly overdefined linear system of $2^8 \times 8$ equations involving the 72 unknowns and solve it with time complexity much lower than 2^{16}.

3.3   Recovering the Affine Parasites

We note that Prop. 1 of the previous section enables us to directly compute the linear parts of $_1$, $_2$, and $_3$ from the knowledge of $_0$'s linear part. We will therefore focus on $_0$'s determination. This section is organized in two steps. First, we show how to recover the linear part of $_0$ up to , for some non-zero in $GF(2^8)$. Then we show how this information can be used to recover both and the constant part $_0$ of $_0$.

About Q_0's Linear Part. Let us recall that we decompose each affine transformation φ_i into its linear and constant parts: $\varphi_i(x) = A_i(x) + c_i$. Applying Prop. 1 with $i = 0$ and $j = 1$, we get $L_0 = A_0 \circ \lambda_{0\,0}/\lambda_{1\,0} \circ A_1^{-1}$. Then, using the variant of Prop. 1 with $i = 0$ and $j = 1$, but where one varies x_1 instead of x_0, we obtain $L_1 = A_0 \circ \lambda_{0\,1}/\lambda_{1\,1} \circ A_1^{-1}$. We are thus able to compute $L = L_0 \circ L_1^{-1}$, that is $L = A_0 \circ \mu \circ A_0^{-1}$ where $\mu = \lambda_{0,0}\lambda_{1,1}/\lambda_{0,1}\lambda_{1,0}$. Remembering that λ values are standing for the `MixColumn` coefficients i.e., taking their values in the set $\{$ `01'`, `02'`, `03'` $\}$ only 16 values for μ remain possible, which are collected in the following set

$$B = \{\text{`02', `d8', `03', `6f', `04', `bc', `06', `b7', `05', `25', `4a', `f8', `7f', `c8', `64', `5f'}\}.$$

(One checks that no element of B is contained in any subfield of $\mathrm{GF}(2^8)$.)

Thus, the new starting point is a matrix L, with the form $A_0 \circ \mu \circ A_0^{-1}$, and we want to retrieve both μ and A_0. Given that μ is chosen from B, computing the characteristic polynomial of L reduces the number of possibilities for μ to at most 2; actually, either μ is already determined, or $\mu \in \{\nu, \nu^2\} \subset B$. To ease the exposition, we assume that μ is known, for instance by testing the two possibilities, and using Prop. 3 of the next section to determine the correct one.

Proposition 2. *Given an element μ of $\mathrm{GF}(2^8)$ not in any subfields of $\mathrm{GF}(2^8)$ and its corresponding matrix $L = A_0 \circ \mu \circ A_0^{-1}$, we can compute with time complexity lower than 2^{16}, a matrix $\tilde{A}_0$ such that there exists a unique non-zero constant κ in $\mathrm{GF}(2^8)$, so that $\tilde{A}_0 = A_0 \circ \kappa$.*

Proof. We seek for $\tilde{A}_0$ such that $L \circ \tilde{A}_0 = \tilde{A}_0 \circ \mu$. Considering $\tilde{A}_0$'s entries as unknowns, this equation gives 64 equations in the 64 unknowns. Some non-trivial solution can be computed in time complexity $64^3 < 2^{16}$, which we hereafter denote by $\tilde{A}_0$. Then, define $A = A_0^{-1} \circ \tilde{A}_0$. The equation $L \circ \tilde{A}_0 = \tilde{A}_0 \circ \mu$ also reads $\mu \circ A = A \circ \mu$. The only $\mathrm{GF}(2)$-affine mappings that commutes with the multiplication by μ, are the multiplications by a $\mathrm{GF}(2^8)$ element. (To see this, write $A(x) = \sum_{i=0}^{7} \alpha_i \cdot x^{2^i}$. The commutativity constraint is then expressed by $\sum_{i=0}^{7} \alpha_i \mu^{2^i} \cdot x^{2^i} = \sum_{i=0}^{7} \mu \alpha_i \cdot x^{2^i}$ for all $x \in \mathrm{GF}(2^8)$. Since μ is not contained in any subfield of $\mathrm{GF}(2^8)$, this in turn implies $\alpha_i = $ `00'` for all i but $i = 0$. Therefore, as announced, $A(x) = \alpha_0 x$.) Thus, there exists a unique $\kappa \in \mathrm{GF}(2^8)$ such that $A = \kappa$, and remembering that $A = A_0^{-1} \circ \tilde{A}_0$, we have computed $\tilde{A}_0 = A_0 \circ \kappa$. $\square$

Now we only have to recover μ of Prop. 2 in order to fully determine A_0, the linear part of φ_0. In the following paragraph we explain how to compute it, as well as the constant part c_0 of φ_0, that is to recover φ_0 entirely.

Recovering P_i up to the Key, and Q_0. Let us return to the function we originally studied, namely

$$y_0(x_0, x_1, x_2, x_3) = \varphi_0\left(\bigoplus_{i=0}^{3} \lambda_{0,i} \cdot T_i \circ \varphi_i(x_i)\right). \tag{4}$$

Remember that T_i stands for the key addition, followed by the AES-128's S-box application, that is $T_i(\ ) = S(\ \oplus\ _i)$. ence, the mapping $x \to S^{-1} \circ T_i \circ\ _i(x) =\ _i(x) \oplus\ _i$ is affine. Now, from Prop. 2 we get some matrix $\widetilde{A}_0 = A_0 \circ\ _{1/}$. We have the following:

Proposition 3. *There exists unique pairs* $(\ _i, c_i)_{i=0,\dots,3}$ *of elements in* $\mathrm{GF}(2^8)$, $_i$ *being non-zero, such that*

$$\tilde{}_0\ :\ x \longrightarrow (S^{-1} \circ\ _0 \circ \widetilde{A}_0^{-1})\ \big(y_0(x,\ 00',\ 00',\ 00') \oplus c_0\big)\ ,$$
$$\tilde{}_1\ :\ x \longrightarrow (S^{-1} \circ\ _1 \circ \widetilde{A}_0^{-1})\ \big(y_0(\ 00',x,\ 00',\ 00') \oplus c_1\big)\ ,$$
$$\tilde{}_2\ :\ x \longrightarrow (S^{-1} \circ\ _2 \circ \widetilde{A}_0^{-1})\ \big(y_0(\ 00',\ 00',x,\ 00') \oplus c_2\big)\ ,$$
$$\tilde{}_3\ :\ x \longrightarrow (S^{-1} \circ\ _3 \circ \widetilde{A}_0^{-1})\ \big(y_0(\ 00',\ 00',\ 00',x) \oplus c_3\big)\ ,$$

are affine mappings. Any pair $(\ _i, c_i)$ *can be computed with time complexity* 2^{24}. *Moreover, those mappings are exactly* $\tilde{}_i =\ _i(x) \oplus\ _i$.

Proof. The proposition amounts to saying that $x \to S^{-1}(\ \cdot S(x) \oplus c)$ is affine and non-constant. Since S represent the AES-128 S-box, and in non-zero, this is only possible if $(\ ,c) = (\ 01',\ 00')$, hence the existence and uniqueness of $(\ _i, c_i)$. (This is also very easy to verify by an exhaustive search, which we have done.)

Since c is $00'$, we have $c_0 = y_0(x,\ 00',\ 00',\ 00') \oplus\ _{0,0} \cdot T_0(\ _0(x))$, and since $\widetilde{A}_0 = A_0 \circ\ _{1/}$, we get $\tilde{}_0(x) = S^{-1} \circ\ _0 \cdot\ _{0\ 0} \circ S(\ _0(x) \oplus\ _0)$, where $_0$ is a byte of the corresponding round key. As shown above, $_0 \cdot\ \tilde{}\ _{0,0}$ must be $01'$, hence $\tilde{}_0(x) =\ _0(x) \oplus\ _0$. The proof goes the same for $\tilde{}_1$, $\tilde{}_2$, and $\tilde{}_3$.

For every possible values for the pairs $(\ _i, c_i)$ there are 2^{16} possible pairs we test if the corresponding mapping is affine. The lookup table has to be evaluated 2^8 times, and then 8 systems of 9 unknowns over $\mathrm{GF}(2)$, or equivalently one system of 72 unknowns which can be precomputed, has to be solved. Since the mapping evaluation through the lookup table dominates, the total time complexity is bounded by 2^{24}.

Since $_i^{-1} =\ \cdot\ _{0,i}$, and given the fact that two of those $_{0,i}$ are $01'$, another is $02'$ and the last one is $03'$, exactly two of the $_i^{-1}$ are equal and share the common value $\ $. Therefore we know $\ $, and thus the matrix $A_0 = \widetilde{A}_0 \circ\ $, as well as the underlying MixColumn coefficients $_{0,i}$.

Also note that we recover at the same time the constant $_0$ of the affine mapping $_0$. Indeed, let us define $c_4 = y_0(\ 00',\ 00',\ 00',\ 00')$. Considering Eq. 4, it can also be written as

$$c_4 = \left(\bigoplus_{i=0}^{3}\ _{0,i} \cdot T_i \circ\ _i(\ 00')\right) \oplus\ _0 .$$

Then, remembering that

$$c_0 = y_0(x,\ 00',\ 00',\ 00') \oplus\ _{0,0} \cdot T_0(\ _0(x)),$$
$$c_1 = y_0(\ 00',\ x,\ 00',\ 00') \oplus\ _{0,1} \cdot T_1(\ _1(x)),$$
$$c_2 = y_0(\ 00',\ 00',\ x,\ 00') \oplus\ _{0,2} \cdot T_2(\ _2(x)),$$
$$c_3 = y_0(\ 00',\ 00',\ 00',\ x) \oplus\ _{0,3} \cdot T_3(\ _3(x)),$$

which holds for every x and thus in particular for $00'$, we easily check that the constant part of $_0$ is given by $_0 = c_0 \oplus c_1 \oplus c_2 \oplus c_3 \oplus c_4$, which achieves to fully recover the mapping $_0$.

3.4   Putting Everything Together

Let us now summarize the whole process of recovering the white box AES-128 implementation's original parasites. In Sec. 3.1 we have shown how to compute, for any round $r = 1, \ldots, 9$ and any index $j = 0, \ldots, 3$, with time complexity 2^{24}, the non-linear part of any parasitic mapping $_{i,j}^r$, $i = 0, \ldots, 3$ and thus at the same time, the non-linear part of its inverse parasitic mapping $_{i,j}^{r+1}$ up to some affine application $x \to A_i^r(x) \oplus\ _i^r$. Section 3.2 showed how to recover A_1, A_2, and A_3 from the knowledge of A_0, with time complexity lower than $3 \cdot 2^{16}$. Finally, Sec. 3.3 explained how to recover the affine mapping $x \to A_0^r(x) \oplus\ _0^r$, for $r = 2, \ldots, 9$, with time complexity lower than 2^{16}. At the same time, Sec. 3.3 also retrieved the missing affine part of $_{i,j}^r$ up to the key addition, which will allow us, as explained in the next section, to extract the key embedded in the AES-128 white box implementation.

ence the time complexity to compute the parasites for a complete obfuscated AES-128 round, is bounded by $4 \cdot 4 \cdot 2^{24} = 2^{28}$.

3.5   Key Extraction

We now give the procedure for the key extraction. The white box implementation of AES-128 key embeds round keys produced by the AES-128 key derivation algorithm. Thus the keys for two different rounds are related to each other. Using this property, one can obviously ease the recovery of the keys.

In a first step, we determine $_{i,j}^r$'s non-linear part for some round plus the entire parasites of two consecutive AES-128 obfuscated rounds. For instance, recover the parasitic mappings $_{i,j}^2$, as well as $\tilde{}_{i,j}^3$, $_{i,j}^3$, and $\tilde{}_{i,j}^4$, for $i = 0, \ldots, 3$ and $j = 0, \ldots, 3$ as described in Sec. 3.4. Then, since $_{i,j}^{r+1} \circ\ _{i,j}^r$ must be the identity, we get the round key bytes as the composition of the affine mappings and the affine part of which is denoted here by , that is $_{i,j}^3 = \tilde{}_{i,j}^3 \circ\ _{i,j}^2$, and $_{i,j}^4 = \tilde{}_{i,j}^4 \circ\ _{i,j}^3$.

We now have the key bytes $_{i,j}^3$ and $_{i,j}^4$, however they are not necessarily in the right order. Still, the data flow exposed by the implementation, rules the way each round r key bytes relates to the next round $r + 1$ key bytes. If we assume according to Sec. 3.1 of [1] that the round keys were generated using the key derivation algorithm of AES-128, the added constraint between the 16 bytes $\frac{3}{i,j}$ and the 16 bytes $\frac{4}{i,j}$ allows us to rearrange them the right way. Thus, having correctly recovered an AES-128 round key, we are able to derive the whole set of round keys.

4 Conclusion

This paper explained how to extract, in a very efficient way, the whole secret key of a white box AES-128 implementation suggested in [1]. Some of our attack methods, for instance the technique of Sec. 3.1 used to recover the non linear parts of the encodings, are potentially applicable to other iterated blockciphers white box implementations using similar encoding and linear mixing techniques.

owever, parts of our attack take advantage from AES specificities. Therefore, no general conclusion can be drawn about the possibility to construct a strong white box AES implementation, or a strong white box implementations of other iterated blockciphers. espite the general impossibility results concerning obfuscation [6], there is no evidence so far that strong white box implementation of blockciphers is unachievable; there is only some practical evidence that this is not an easy task. An interesting avenue for further research on obfuscation techniques might consist in developing a dedicated blockcipher, designed bottom-up with white box implementation in mind.

Acknowledgements

The authors thank the anonymous referees for their valuable comments.

References

1. Chow, S., Eisen, P.A., Johnson, H., van Oorschot, P.C.: White-Box Cryptography and an AES Implementation. In Nyberg, K., Heys, H.M., eds.: Selected Areas in Cryptography – SAC 2002. Volume 2595 of Lecture Notes in Computer Science., Springer Verlag (2003) 250–270
2. Chow, S., Eisen, P.A., Johnson, H., van Oorschot, P.C.: A White-Box DES Implementation for DRM Applications. In Feigenbaum, J., ed.: Digital Rights Management Workshop – DRM 2002. Volume 2696 of Lecture Notes in Computer Science., Springer Verlag (2003) 1–15
3. Jacob, M., Boneh, D., Felten, E.W.: Attacking an Obfuscated Cipher by Injecting Faults. In Feigenbaum, J., ed.: Digital Rights Management – DRM 2002. Volume 2696 of Lecture Notes in Computer Science., Springer Verlag (2003) 16–31
4. Daemen, J., Rijmen, V.: The Design of Rijndael. Springer Verlag (2002)
5. National Institute of Standards and Technology: Advanced encryption standard. FIPS publication 197 (2001)
   http://csrc.nist.gov/publications/fips/fips197/fips-197.pdf.

6. Barak, B., Goldreich, O., Impagliazzo, R., Rudich, S., Sahai, A., Vadhan, S.P., Yang, K.: On the (Im)possibility of Obfuscating Programs. In Kilian, J., ed.: Advances in Cryptology – CRYPTO 2001. Volume 2139 of Lecture Notes in Computer Science., Springer Verlag (2001) 1–18
7. Biryukov, A., Preneel, B., Braeken, A., de Cannire, C.: A Toolbox for Cryptanalysis: Linear and Affine Equivalence Algorithms. In Biham, E., ed.: Advances in Cryptology – EUROCRYPT 2003. Volume 1267 of Lecture Notes in Computer Science., Springer Verlag (2003) 33–50

Predicting Subset Sum
Pseudorandom Generators

Joachim von zur Gathen[1] and Igor E. Shparlinski[2]

[1] Fakultät für Elektrotechnik, Informatik und Mathematik,
Universität Paderborn,
33095 Paderborn, Germany
gathen@upb.de
http://www-math.upb.de/~aggathen
[2] Department of Computing, Macquarie University,
NSW 2109, Australia
igor@comp.mq.edu.au
http://www.comp.mq.edu.au/~igor

Abstract. We consider the subset sum pseudorandom generator, introduced by Rueppel and Massey in 1985 and given by a linearly recurrent bit sequence u_0, u_1, ... of order n over $\mathbb{Z}_2$, and weights $w = (w_0, \ldots, w_{n-1}) \in R^n$ for some ring R. The rings $R = \mathbb{Z}_m$ are of particular interest. The ith value produced by this generator is $\sum_{0 \leq j < n} u_{i+j} w_j$. It is also recommended to discard about $\log n$ least significant bits of the result before using this sequence. We present several attacks on this generator (with and without the truncation), some of which are rigorously proven while others are heuristic. They work when one "half" of the secret is given, either the control sequence u_j or the weights w_j. Our attacks do not mean that the generator is insecure, but that one has to be careful in evaluating its security parameters.

1 Introduction

Let $u_0, u_1, \ldots$ be a linear recurrence sequence of order n over the field $\mathbb{Z}_2$ of two elements; see [12–Chapter 8]. We may also consider each u_j as an integer, namely 0 or 1, and multiply by it an element z of an arbitrary ring R, so that $u_j z \in R$.

We consider the following *subset sum* generator of pseudorandom elements. Given an n-dimensional vector $w = (w_0, \ldots, w_{n-1}) \in R^n$, its output is the sequence

$$v_i = \sum_{0 \leq j < n} u_{i+j} w_j, \qquad \text{for } i = 0, 1, \ldots, \tag{1}$$

of elements of R. A popular choice is to take $R = \mathbb{Z}_m$, the residue ring modulo $m \geq 2$. The choice $m = 2^k$ with some integer k is recommended, and in particular, it is natural to choose $k = n$; see [14–Section 6.3.2]. We also consider the

H. Handschuh and A. Hasan (Eds.): SAC 2004, LNCS 3357, pp. 241–251, 2005.

case where $m = p$ is prime. We call (u_j) the *control sequence* and $w_0, \ldots, w_{n-1}$ the *weights*.

This generator, which is also known as the *knapsack generator*, was introduced in [19] and studied in [17], see also [14–Section 6.3.2] and [18–Section 3.7.9]. The generation algorithm is multiplication-free and involves only Boolean operations, integer additions and one modular reduction; in the case $R = \mathbb{Z}_{2^k}$, the reduction modulo $m = 2^k$ is essentially for free in the binary representation. Thus it presents a very attractive alternative to pseudorandom number generators based on Boolean functions. On the other hand, its close relation to the subset sum problem could make it cryptographically strong and suitable for using in stream ciphers.

For cryptographic applications, it is usually recommended to use a linear recurrence sequence of maximal period $2^n - 1$, however here we consider more general settings.

The linear complexity and distribution of this generator have been studied in [6, 17, 18] and have turned out to be rather attractive. Furthermore, [14–page 220] states that no weaknesses of this generator have been reported in the literature. This paper presents some weaknesses. We do not, however, consider them as lethal.

We study predictability properties of the subset sum generator and show that its security is smaller than has been assumed previously, but presumably still large enough, with appropriate parameters. In the simplest cases our attacks are based on linear algebra. In more practical settings we use lattice algorithms, namely algorithms for the *short vector problem* which essentially go back to the seminal paper of Lenstra, Lenstra and Lovász [11]. Thus our results add one more example to the substantial list of cryptographic constructions which have been successfully attacked by such algorithms, see [13, 15, 16].

We note that our results resemble those about predictability of various recursive pseudorandom number generators; see [2, 3, 4, 5, 8, 9, 10] and references therein.

In general, if $R = \mathbb{Z}_m$, the whole generator is defined by about $n(2 + \log m)$ bits, where $\log z$ denotes the binary logarithm of $z > 0$. Indeed, one needs n bits to describe the characteristic polynomial of the control linear recurrence sequence (u_j), n bits for its initial values, and about $n \log m$ bits to describe the weight vector w. Thus a brute force search through the space of all possible parameters takes about $(4m)^n$ steps.

In our attacks we use polynomial time and assume that some partial information about the generator is known. However, one might as well "guess" this information; in this formulation our attacks lead to a substantial reduction of the cost of brute force search. In the same vein, some of our results deal with the generator before truncation, but one may simply "guess" the truncated parts and then apply our attacks. For example, as we have mentioned, it is suggested to discard about $\log n$ bits of each output v_i, see [14–Section 6.3.2]. Usually our attacks need only $O(n)$ consecutive outputs, so that the total number of guesses for the discarded bits is $2^{O(n \log n)}$ which, for the typically recommended values of m near 2^n, is substantially smaller than $(4m)^n \asymp 2^{n^2}$. On the other hand, in some cases our attacks, empowered by lattice basis reduction algorithms, apply to truncated outputs directly.

The upshot is that when n is large enough and both controls and weights are kept secret, we still consider the generator to be secure. A simple observation is that $2n$ outputs give away the linear recurrence of the control bits if m is even. This leads to an exhaustive search with cost 2^n, and for odd m, we can mount an exhaustive search attack with cost 2^{2n}. Thus it is not clear in how far larger values of m make the generator much more secure than $m = 3$. (Our short vector attack becomes more expensive with growing m, but only by a polynomial factor.)

2   Attacks with Known Control Sequence

We first consider the case when the linear recurrence sequence (u_j) is known. It is equivalent to know the characteristic polynomial and n initial values, or just $2n$ initial values; the characteristic polynomial can then be computed by the Berlekamp-Massey algorithm (see, for example, [7–Section 12.3]).

2.1   Exact Outputs

It is useful to express (1) in terms of the power series

$$h_u = \sum_{i \geq 0} u_i x^i, \quad h_v = \sum_{i \geq 0} v_i x^i, \quad h_w = \sum_{0 \leq i < n} w_{n-i-1} x^i$$

in $R[[x]]$. We show that the power series $h_u \cdot h_w$ and $x^{n-1} h_v$ agree at all but the small-order coefficients.

Lemma 1. *Let $r = h_u \cdot h_w$ rem x^{n-1} be the remainder of $h_u \cdot h_w$ on division by x^{n-1}. Then*

$$h_u \cdot h_w - r = x^{n-1} h_v. \tag{2}$$

Proof. We have

$$x^{n-1} h_v = \sum_{i \geq 0} v_i x^{i+n-1} = \sum_{i \geq 0} \sum_{0 \leq j < n} u_{i+j} w_j x^{i+n-1}$$

$$= \sum_{\substack{i \geq 0 \\ 0 \leq j < n}} u_{i+j} x^{i+j} \cdot w_j x^{n-j-1} = \sum_{\substack{k+l \geq n-1 \\ 0 \leq l < n}} u_k x^k \cdot w_{n-l-1} x^l.$$

The bijective correspondence

$$(i, j) = (k + l - n + 1, n - l - 1) \leftrightarrow (k, l) = (i + j, n - j - 1)$$

is responsible for the last equation. The condition $i \geq 0$ means that $k + l \geq n - 1$. Thus the coefficient of the terms of degree at least $n - 1$ in the products $x^{n-1} h_v$ and $h_u \cdot h_w$ coincide.   □

When we take the weights as unknowns, the equations (1), or, equivalently, (2) yield a Hankel system of linear equations with the matrix

$$H = (u_{i+j})_{0 \leq i,j < n}. \tag{3}$$

In a finite prime field, the Hankel matrix (3) is not guaranteed to be non-singular. Our attack works by building up matrices of maximal rank from lines of the Hankel matrix (3). Accordingly, we may have to use n arbitrary outputs, not necessarily the first ones. More precisely, we consider algorithms that for $i = 0, 1, \ldots$ either output v_i or query v_i. The following result shows that we can do with few queries.

Theorem 2. *Over a finite field $R = \mathbb{F}_q$ of q elements, given a control sequence (u_j) of order n, there is a deterministic algorithm to compute the sequence v_i for $i = 0, 1, \ldots$, in polynomial time per element, making no more than n queries in total.*

Proof. The algorithm builds up $l \times n$ matrices U_l consisting of rows

$$r_i = (u_i, u_{i+1}, \ldots, u_{i+n-1}) \in \mathbb{F}_q^n$$

for growing values of l, up to n. The matrix U_l has rank l over $\mathbb{F}_q$. We also store the values v_i for the rows r_i that appear in U_l.

We start with $U_0 = I_0 = \emptyset$, and consider $i = 0, 1, \ldots$. If r_i is not linearly dependent over $\mathbb{F}_q$ on the rows of the current U_l (this is the case in the first step, where $i = 0$, unless $r_0 = 0$), then we set $I_{l+1} = I_l \cup \{i\}$ and add the row r_i to U_l to obtain U_{l+1}, of rank $l + 1$. We also query and store v_i.

Otherwise we can write

$$r_i = \sum_{k \in I_l} c_k r_k$$

as a linear combination of the rows r_k of U_l, with $k \in I_l$ and coefficients $c_k \in \mathbb{F}_q$. Then we output

$$\sum_{k \in I_l} c_k v_k = \sum_{k \in I_l} c_k \sum_{0 \leq j < n} u_{k+j} w_j$$
$$= \sum_{0 \leq j < n} w_j \sum_{k \in I_l} c_k u_{k+j} \sum_{0 \leq j < n} w_j\, u_{i+j} = v_i.$$

We have to make at most n queries for values v_i, since once we have n linearly independent (over $\mathbb{F}_q$) rows r_i, then we can actually compute the weight vector w, and predict correctly ever after. $\qquad\square$

In characteristic 2, the Hankel matrix (3) is guaranteed to be nonsingular, and the algorithm simplifies as follows.

Corollary 3. *Given an integer $k \geq 1$, a control sequence (u_j) of order n over $\mathbb{Z}_2$, and n consecutive outputs v_i for $0 \leq i < n$ over $R = \mathbb{Z}_{2^k}$, one can find the unknown weight vector $w \in R^n$ in deterministic polynomial time.*

Proof. Because (u_j) is of order n in $\mathbb{F}_2$, the integer Hankel matrix (3) is nonsingular modulo 2, see [12–Section 8.6], and hence also modulo 2^k. □

The algorithm also works over rings $R = \mathbb{Z}_m$ with squarefree $m \geq 2$, by using a "lazy" variant of Gaussian elimination. Here, whenever an element is to be inverted, one calculates its greatest common divisor with the current moduli (which initially is just m). If the greatest common divisor is nontrivial, one obtains a factorization of the modulus, and continues with the factors separately as new moduli. In fact, one should use the finest factorization of the moduli which is easy to calculate from these partial factorizations (see [1]).

2.2   Truncated Outputs

We now consider the case where a certain number ℓ of low-order bits of each value v_i gets discarded before the rest is output, that is, only the "truncated" value $\lfloor v_i/2^\ell \rfloor$ is known. Intuitively, it is clear that if the weights $w_0, \ldots, w_{n-1}$ are known up to the 2^s least significant bits, with $2^s = o(2^l/n)$, then these approximate values can be used to produce a sequence which with high probability equals the truncated output of the original generator.

Following this intuition, we now use algorithms for the short vector problem in lattices to find the truncations $\widetilde{w}_j = \lfloor w_j/2^s \rfloor$ for $0 \leq j < n$. Although our method also works in other situations, we make various simplifying assumptions about the parameters m, n, ℓ, and s. They always include the case when $\log m \sim n$, which is of greatest practical interest.

Given k consecutive values $\lfloor v_i/2^\ell \rfloor$ for $0 \leq i < k$, we define a lattice $\mathcal{L}_k$ as the set of all integer solutions $x = (x_{-1}, x_0, x_1, \ldots x_{n-1}, y_0, \ldots, y_{k-1}) \in \mathbb{Z}^{k+n+1}$ of the system of congruences

$$x_{-1} + y_i 2^\ell \left\lfloor v_i/2^\ell \right\rfloor x_{-1} + y_i - \sum_{0 \leq j < n} 2^s u_{i+j} x_j \equiv 0 \bmod m \qquad \text{for } 0 \leq i < k.$$

We use the celebrated algorithm of Lenstra, Lenstra and Lovász [11] for computing short vectors in lattices. This has become a central tool in cryptography; see [13, 15, 16] for outlines of recent progress in this area since the original result. Standard heuristic arguments, as in [16–Section 3.4], imply that the discriminant D_k of $\mathcal{L}_k$ is likely to be m^k. Furthermore, the standard heuristics suggest that if a vector $\widetilde{w} \in \mathcal{L}_k$ is such that $\|\widetilde{w}\|$ is substantially smaller than $D_k^{1/(k+n)}$, then any vector in $\mathcal{L}_k$ of length substantially smaller than $D_k^{1/(k+n)}$ is likely to be proportional to $\widetilde{w}$.

We observe that $\mathcal{L}_k$ contains a very short vector

$$z = (1, \widetilde{w}_0, \ldots, \widetilde{w}_{n-1}, z_0, \ldots, z_{k-1}),$$

where

$$z_i = v_i - 2^\ell \left\lfloor v_i/2^\ell \right\rfloor + \sum_{0 \leq j < n} u_{i+j} \left(2^s \lfloor w_j/2^s \rfloor - w_j \right) \qquad \text{for } 0 \leq i < k.$$

We may assume that our parameters satisfy $n2^s \leq 2^\ell$; otherwise the approximate weights cannot be used. Under this condition we have

$$|z_i| \leq n2^s + 2^\ell \leq 2^{\ell+1} \qquad \text{for } 0 \leq i < k.$$

To simplify our calculations we also assume that

$$k^{1/2}2^{2\ell+1} \leq m \qquad \text{and} \qquad 2^s \geq n + 1;$$

otherwise we either discard too many bits (and the generator is inefficient) or try to use a lattice of very high dimension (and the attack is infeasible). In this case,

$$k2^{2\ell+2} \leq m^2 2^{-2\ell} \leq m^2 2^{-2s} \qquad \text{and} \qquad (n+2)^{1/2}2^{-s} < n^{-1/2}.$$

Then the Euclidean norm of the vector z satisfies

$$\|z\| \leq \left(1 + nm^2 2^{-2s} + k2^{2\ell+2}\right)^{1/2} \leq (n+2)^{1/2}m2^{-s} < mn^{-1/2}.$$

Now if we assume that $\log m \sim n$, then for $k = n^2 - n$ we deduce

$$D_k^{1/(k+n)} = m^{k/(k+n)} = m^{1-1/n},$$

which is much larger than $\|z\| \leq mn^{-1/2}$ as long as, say, $\log m = O(n)$. Hence a nonzero multiple of z is likely to be recovered by a short vector problem algorithm. Because the first component of z is known, this allows us to find z.

3   Attacks with Known Weights

We now consider the dual question, where the linear recurrence sequence (u_n) is unknown but the vector of weights $w = (w_0, \dots, w_{n-1}) \in \mathbb{Z}_m^n$ is given. When we are given only a single output of the generator, then this is a subset sum problem and NP-complete. However, having several consecutive outputs allows us to mount efficient linear algebra attacks.

3.1   Exact Outputs

We start with even characteristic and present our results in the case when the characteristic polynomial of the control linear recurrence sequence (u_j) is irreducible, which includes the most interesting cases of such sequences. In the general case one can obtain similar results, which however hold only for almost all weights rather than for all $w \in \mathbb{Z}_m^n$.

Theorem 4. *Given an integer $k \geq 1$, the weights $w = (w_0, \dots, w_{n-1}) \in R^n$ over $R = \mathbb{Z}_m$ with even m, and $2n$ consecutive outputs v_i for $0 \leq i < 2n$, not all even, one can find the controls $u = (u_0, \dots, u_{2n-1}) \in \mathbb{Z}_2^{2n}$ in deterministic polynomial time, provided that the (unknown) characteristic polynomial of degree n over $\mathbb{Z}_2$ of the control linear recurrence sequence (u_j) is irreducible.*

Proof. The reduction of the sequence (v_i) modulo 2 satisfies the same linear recurrent relation as the control sequence (u_j). By assumption, this reduction is not identical to zero modulo 2. We use the Berlekamp–Massey algorithm, see [7–Chapter 7] or [12–Section 8.6], to recover the characteristic polynomial

$$f = \sum_{0 \le i \le n} f_i x^i \in \mathbb{Z}_2[x]$$

of this sequence, so that

$$\sum_{0 \le i \le n} f_i u_{k+i} = 0$$

for all $k \ge 0$. The first n equations in (2) plus the $n-1$ equations for the control values $u_n, \ldots, u_{2n-2}$ lead to the following system of $2n-1$ linear equations in the $2n-1$ unknowns $u_0, \ldots, u_{2n-2}$:

$$
\begin{pmatrix}
w_0 & w_1 & \cdots & w_{n-1} & 0 & \cdots & 0 \\
0 & w_0 & \cdots & w_{n-2} & w_{n-1} & \cdots & 0 \\
\vdots & \ddots & \ddots & \ddots & & \ddots & \vdots \\
0 & \cdots & \cdots & w_0 & w_1 & \cdots & w_{n-1} \\
f_0 & f_1 & \cdots & f_{n-1} & f_n & \cdots & 0 \\
\vdots & \ddots & \ddots & \ddots & & \ddots & \vdots \\
0 & \cdots & f_0 & f_1 & f_2 & \cdots & f_n
\end{pmatrix}
\begin{pmatrix}
u_0 \\ u_1 \\ \vdots \\ u_{n-1} \\ u_n \\ u_{n+1} \\ \vdots \\ u_{2n-2}
\end{pmatrix}
=
\begin{pmatrix}
v_0 \\ v_1 \\ \vdots \\ v_{n-1} \\ 0 \\ 0 \\ \vdots \\ 0
\end{pmatrix}.
$$

We denote the matrix of the above system of equations by $A \in R^{(2n-1) \times (2n-1)}$, and observe that A is the (transpose of the) Sylvester matrix of the two polynomials f and

$$w = \sum_{0 \le i < n} w_i x^i \in \mathbb{Z}_2[x].$$

The outputs are not all even, and hence also the weights, and thus w is nonzero of degree less than n. Since f is irreducible of degree n, we have $\gcd(w, f) = 1$ and hence A is nonsingular. Thus we can solve the system for $u_0, \ldots, u_{2n-2}$. $\square$

When the characteristic polynomial f is not irreducible, the characteristic polynomial g of $v_0, v_1, \ldots$ is a divisor of f. If the weights are chosen at random, we expect $g = f$ to hold with high probability; see [7–Section 12.4]. Furthermore, for random w the condition $\gcd(w, f) = 1$ (so that A is nonsingular) holds with probability

$$\Phi(f)/2^n = \prod_{j=1}^{s}(1 - 2^{-d_j}),$$

where $d_1, \ldots, d_s$ are the degrees of the distinct irreducible factors of f. Thus, $\Phi(f)$ is the polynomial analogue of Euler's φ function. Using the fact that the number of irreducible polynomials of degree d over $\mathbb{Z}_2[x]$ is $2^d/d + O(2^{d/2})$, one can show that this probability is also reasonably large.

We now consider the case of an arbitrary modulus m. Given k consecutive values v_i for $0 \leq i < k$, we may define the lattice $\mathcal{L}_k$ as the set of all integer solutions $x = (x_{-1}, x_0, x_1, \ldots x_{k+n-2}) \in \mathbb{Z}^{k+n}$ of the system of congruences

$$\sum_{0 \leq j < n} x_{i+j} w_j + v_i x_{-1} \equiv 0 \bmod m \qquad \text{for } 0 \leq i < k.$$

By (1), it contains a very short vector $\mathbf{u} = (-1, u_0, \ldots, u_{k+n-2})$ with Euclidean norm at most $\|\mathbf{u}\| \leq (k+n)^{1/2}$. Standard heuristic arguments, as in [16–Section 3.4], imply that the discriminant D_k of $\mathcal{L}_k$ is likely to be m^k.

On the other hand, also standard heuristic arguments suggest that if $\|\mathbf{u}\|$ is substantially smaller than $D_k^{1/(k+n)}$, then any nonzero vector $x \in \mathcal{L}_k$ of length substantially smaller than $D_k^{1/(k+n)}$ is likely to be proportional to $\mathbf{u}$. Thus applying any of the algorithms for the shortest vector problem, we can hope to recover x.

If $k \geq n+1$, then the vector x gives us the values u_j for $0 \leq j < 2n$. By the Berlekamp-Massey algorithm, one can find the characteristic polynomial of the linear recurrence sequence (u_j) over $\mathbb{Z}_2$ and thus continue to generate the sequence (v_i).

Furthermore, with $k = n+1$ we expect

$$D_k^{1/(k+n)} \sim m^{k/(k+n)} \geq m^{1/2}$$

which is much larger than $(k+n)^{1/2} = (2n+1)^{1/2}$ for all practically interesting situations.

3.2   Truncated Outputs

We now consider the case when some bits of the output are discarded before exhibiting the remaining bits. Although our approach works in more general settings, here consider only the case which is outlined in [14–Section 6.5.6]. In this case $t = 2^n - 1$, $m = 2^n$ and $\ell = \lceil \log n \rceil$ bits of each value v_i get discarded before the rest is output, that is, only the "truncated" values $\lfloor v_i/2^\ell \rfloor$ are known.

Given k consecutive values $\lfloor v_i/2^\ell \rfloor$ for $0 \leq i < k$, we define a lattice $\mathcal{L}_k$ as the set of all integer solutions $x = (x_{-1}, x_0, x_1, \ldots x_{k+n-2}, y_0, \ldots, y_{k-1}) \in \mathbb{Z}^{2k+n}$ of the system of congruences

$$\sum_{0 \leq j < n} x_{i+j} w_j + 2^\ell \lfloor v_i/2^\ell \rfloor x_{-1} + y_i \equiv 0 \bmod m \qquad \text{for } 0 \leq i < k.$$

Again we observe that the discriminant of $\mathcal{L}_k$ is likely to be $D_k = m^k$. We also see that it contains a very short vector

$$z = (-1, u_0, \ldots, u_{k+n}, z_0, \ldots, z_{k-1}),$$

where $z_i = 2^\ell \lfloor v_i/2^\ell \rfloor - v_i$ for $0 \leq i < k$, whose Euclidean norm satisfies

$$\|z\| \leq \left(k + n + k\left(2^\ell - 1\right)\right)^{1/2} = \left(k2^\ell + n\right)^{1/2} \leq (2kn + n)^{1/2}.$$

We see that if $k = \lceil \log n \rceil$, then $\|z\| \leq (2n \log n + O(n))^{1/2}$, while

$$D_k^{1/(2k+n)} = 2^{kn/(2k+n)} \geq n^{n/(2k+n)} = n^{1+o(1)}, \qquad \text{for } n \to \infty,$$

is much larger. Certainly increasing the value of k increases the chances that z is much shorter than any other non-parallel vectors in $\mathcal{L}_k$ and thus can be found by an appropriate algorithm for the shortest vector problem.

We have conducted several tests for values of n up to $n = 100$ with m a 100-bit prime. In each case, the short vector computed provided correctly the control sequence. In all cases, there have not been other "smallish" short vectors in the lattice. These experiments confirm that the algorithm always finds the control sequence, at least for sufficiently large problems of cryptographically interesting sizes.

4   Final Remarks

As noted before, our results do not rule out the possibility of successfully using the subset sum generator for cryptographic purposes. They merely imply that the security is less than its naive estimate based on counting unknown bits in the parameters defining the generator. Thus with a careful choice of these parameters this generator might turn out to be very useful and reliable.

It would be very interesting to obtain rigorous proofs for the heuristic attacks described in this paper. Besides being of theoretic value, this may also give further insight on the structure and thus security of the subset sum generator.

For convenience, we have assumed that R is a ring, so that we could use the language of the power series ring $R[[x]]$. But the construction of the generator applies to any semigroup R. Now if, for example, R is a finite cyclic group of order m and the output sequence is given "as is", without discarding any information, then the prediction problem over R can be reduced to a prediction problem over $\mathbb{Z}_m$ by computing the discrete logarithms of $v_0, v_1, \ldots$. At the small key sizes for which we already expect security, the discrete logarithm problem is not hard. Similar arguments apply also to groups which are not necessarily cyclic. However, this reduction to discrete logarithms does not work if some information about each generated value v_i is discarded before the generator outputs the rest of v_i.

For example, one can use this idea in one of the cryptographically most interesting groups, namely the group of rational points of an elliptic curve over a finite field $\mathbb{F}_p$, where p is a prime. We may choose the size $m \approx p \approx 2^n$ of the group sufficiently large, and discard the $\log n$ low-order bits of the x-coordinate of the point before using it as pseudorandom output. Then none of our attacks works, and at the current state of knowledge the only available attack on this generator is the brute force search over all parameters defining this generator. Certainly this construction deserves a further study.

With our attacks, an exhaustive search to break a subset sum generator requires about 2^u many values, where u is the following "effective key size", and $m \approx 2^n$:

group	key size u
$\mathbb{Z}_m$, m even	n
$\mathbb{Z}_m$, m odd	$2n$
elliptic curve, truncated output	n^2

We conclude with an observation which may seem somewhat paradoxical. While we believe that truncation of the output sequence is a good idea, it must be applied with great care. Indeed, although truncation provides less information to the attacker, he only has to solve the simpler task of finding suitable approximations to the weights. This is exactly the observation that underlies our attack in Section 2.2. This attack does not work if the number of truncated bits ℓ is too small. On the other hand, if this value is too large, the attack becomes prohibitively expensive. It is an interesting question to estimate the "hardest" value of ℓ (as a function of m and n), which takes into account the cost of algorithms for the short vector problem, both theoretic and heuristic.

References

1. E. Bach, J. Driscoll and J. Shallit, 'Factor refinement', J. Algorithms, **15** (1993), 199–222.
2. S. R. Blackburn, D. Gomez-Perez, J. Gutierrez and I. E. Shparlinski, 'Predicting the inversive generator', Lect. Notes in Comp. Sci., Springer-Verlag, Berlin, **2898** (2003), 264–275.
3. S. R. Blackburn, D. Gomez-Perez, J. Gutierrez and I. E. Shparlinski, 'Predicting nonlinear pseudorandom number generators', Math. Comp., (to appear).
4. S. R. Blackburn, D. Gomez-Perez, J. Gutierrez and I. E. Shparlinski, 'Reconstructing noisy polynomial evaluation in residue rings', J. Algorithms, (to appear).
5. E. F. Brickell and A. M. Odlyzko, 'Cryptoanalysis: A survey of recent results', Contemp. Cryptology, IEEE Press, NY, 1992, 501–540.
6. A. Conflitti and I. E. Shparlinski, 'On the multidimensional distribution of the subset sum generator of pseudorandom numbers', Math. Comp., **73** (2004), 1005–1011.
7. J. von zur Gathen and J. Gerhard, Modern computer algebra, Cambridge University Press, Cambridge, 2003.
8. A. Joux and J. Stern, 'Lattice reduction: A toolbox for the cryptanalyst', J. Cryptology, **11** (1998), 161–185.
9. H. Krawczyk, 'How to predict congruential generators', J. Algorithms, **13** (1992), 527–545.
10. J. C. Lagarias, 'Pseudorandom number generators in cryptography and number theory', Proc. Symp. in Appl. Math., Amer. Math. Soc., Providence, RI, **42** (1990), 115–143.
11. A. K. Lenstra, H. W. Lenstra and L. Lovász, 'Factoring polynomials with rational coefficients', Mathematische Annalen, **261** (1982), 515–534.
12. R. Lidl and H. Niederreiter, Finite fields, Cambridge University Press, Cambridge, 1997.
13. D. Micciancio and S. Goldwasser, Complexity of lattice problems, Kluwer Acad. Publ., 2002.

14. A. J. Menezes, P. C. van Oorschot and S. A. Vanstone, *Handbook of applied cryptography*, CRC Press, Boca Raton, FL, 1996.
15. P. Q. Nguyen and J. Stern, 'Lattice reduction in cryptology: An update', *Lect. Notes in Comp. Sci.*, Springer-Verlag, Berlin, **1838** (2000), 85–112.
16. P. Q. Nguyen and J. Stern, 'The two faces of lattices in cryptology', *Lect. Notes in Comp. Sci.*, Springer-Verlag, Berlin, **2146** (2001), 146–180.
17. R. A. Rueppel, *Analysis and design of stream ciphers*, Springer-Verlag, Berlin, 1986.
18. R. A. Rueppel, 'Stream ciphers', *Contemporary cryptology: The science of information integrity*, IEEE Press, NY, 1992, 65–134.
19. R. A. Rueppel and J. L. Massey, 'Knapsack as a nonlinear function', *IEEE Intern. Symp. of Inform. Theory*, IEEE Press, NY, 1985, 46.

Collision Attack and Pseudorandomness of Reduced-Round Camellia[1]

Wu Wenling, Feng Dengguo, and Chen Hua

State Key Laboratory of Information Security, Institute of Software,
Chinese Academy of Sciences, Beijing 100080, P. R. China
{wwl, feng, chenhua}@is.iscas.ac.cn

Abstract. Camellia is the final winner of 128-bit block cipher in NESSIE. In this paper, we construct some efficient distinguishers between 4-round Camellia and random permutation of the blocks space. By using collision-searching techniques, the distinguishers are used to attack 6,7,8 and 9 rounds of Camellia with 128-bit key and 8,9 and 10 rounds of Camellia with 192/256-bit key. The attack on 6-round of 128-bit key Camellia is more efficient than known attacks. The complexities of the attack on 7(8,9,10)-round Camellia without FL/FL^{-1} functions are less than that of previous attacks. Furthermore, we prove that the 4-round primitive-wise idealized Camellia is not pseudorandom permutation and the 5-round primitive-wise idealized Camellia is super-pseudorandom permutation for non-adaptive adversaries.

Keywords: Block cipher; Camellia; Data complexity; Time complexity; Pseudorandomness.

1 Introduction

Camellia[1] is a 128-bit block cipher which was published by NTT and Mitsubishi in 2000 and selected as the final selection of the NESSIE[2] project. The security of Camellia has been studied by many researchers using various cryptanalytic methods, for instance: higher-order differential attack[3,4], truncated differential attack[5], truncated and impossible differential attacks[6], differential attack[7], square attack[8,9], integral attack[10]. In this paper we present collision attacks on reduced-round variants of Camellia without FL/FL^{-1} and whitening function layers. The attack on 6-round of 128-bit key Camellia is more efficient than known attacks. The complexities of the attack on 7(8,9,10)-round Camellia without FL/FL^{-1} functions are less than that of previous attacks.

In addition to cryptanalytic methods mentioned above, pseudorandomness is also an important cryptographic criterion of iterated block ciphers. In their celebrated paper[11], Luby and Rackoff introduced a theoretical model for the

---

[1] This work was supported by Chinese Natural Science Foundation (Grant No.60373047 and 60025205) and 863 Project (Grant No. 2003AA14403).

H. Handschuh and A. Hasan (Eds.): SAC 2004, LNCS 3357, pp. 252–266, 2005.

security of block ciphers by using the notion of pseudorandom and super-pseudorandom permutations, which was later developed by Patarin[12], Maurer[13], Vaudenay[14], and other researchers. This approach studies the pseudorandomness of block cipher by assuming that each round function is ideally random. Luby and Rackoff idealized DES by replacing each round function with one large random function, then they proved that the idealized three round DES yields a pseudorandom permutation and the idealized four round DES yields a super-pseudorandom permutation. For this kind of idealization, the three round idealized Camellia is a pseudorandom permutation and the four round idealized Camellia is a super-pseudorandom permutation because Camellia has the same Feistel structure as DES. Iwata and Kurosawa[15] introduced a primitive-wise idealization in which some of the primitive operations of the round function(e.g., linear transformation and etc.) are left untouched and some of them (e.g., S-boxes and etc.) are replaced with small random functions or permutations. It is not known whether such a primitive-wise idealization DES is pseudorandom (or super-pseudorandom). Similarly, the same problem has been open for Camellia, which is solved in this paper. In section 6, Camellia is idealized by replacing only the S-boxes with small random functions. We then prove that the 4-round primitive-wise idealized Camellia is not pseudorandom permutation and the 5-round primitive-wise idealized Camellia is super-pseudorandom permutation for non-adaptive adversaries.

This paper is organized as follows: Section 2 briefly introduces the structure of Camellia and the basic definitions on pseudorandomness. 4-round distinguishers are explained in section 3. In section 4, we show how to use the 4-round distinguishers to attack 6 ,7,8 and 9 rounds of Camellia with 128-bit key. In section 5, we describe attacks on 9 and 10 rounds of Camellia with 192/256-bit key. Section 6 present our results on the pseudorandomness and super-pseudorandomness of Camellia, and Section 7 concludes the paper.

2   Preliminaries

2.1   Description of Camellia

Camellia has a 128 bit block size and supports 128,192 and 256 bit keys. The design of Camellia is based on the Feistel structure and its number of rounds is 18(128 bit key) or 24(192/256 bit key). The FL/FL^{-1} function layer is inserted at every 6 rounds. Before the first round and after the last round, there are pre- and post-whitening layers which use bitwise exclusive-or operations with 128 bit subkeys, respectively. But we will consider camellia without FL/FL^{-1} function layer and whitening layers and call it modified camellia.

Let L_{r-1} and R_{r-1} be the left and the right halves of the rth round inputs, and k_r be the rth round subkey. Then the Feistel structure of Camellia can be written as

$$L_r = R_{r-1} \oplus F(L_{r-1}, k_r),$$
$$R_r = L_{r-1},$$

here F is the round function defined below:

$$F : \{0,1\}^{64} \times \{0,1\}^{64} \longrightarrow \{0,1\}^{64}$$
$$(X_{64}, k_{64}) \longrightarrow Y_{(64)} = P(S(X_{(64)} \oplus k_{(64)})).$$

where S and P are defined as follows:

$$S : \{0,1\}^{64} \longrightarrow \{0,1\}^{64}$$
$$l_{1(8)}||l_{2(8)}||l_{3(8)}||l_{4(8)}||l_{5(8)}||l_{6(8)}||l_{7(8)}||l_{8(8)}$$
$$\longrightarrow l_{1(8)}^*||l_{2(8)}^*||l_{3(8)}^*||l_{4(8)}^*||l_{5(8)}^*||l_{6(8)}^*||l_{7(8)}^*||l_{8(8)}^*$$

$$l_{1(8)}^* = s_1(l_{1(8)}), \qquad l_{2(8)}^* = s_2(l_{2(8)}), \qquad l_{3(8)}^* = s_3(l_{3(8)}),$$
$$l_{4(8)}^* = s_4(l_{4(8)}), \qquad l_{5(8)}^* = s_2(l_{5(8)}), \qquad l_{6(8)}^* = s_3(l_{6(8)}),$$
$$l_{7(8)}^* = s_4(l_{7(8)}), \qquad l_{8(8)}^* = s_1(l_{8(8)}).$$

$$P : \{0,1\}^{64} \longrightarrow \{0,1\}^{64}$$
$$Z_{1(8)}||Z_{2(8)}||Z_{3(8)}||Z_{4(8)}||Z_{5(8)}||Z_{6(8)}||Z_{7(8)}||Z_{8(8)}$$
$$\longrightarrow Z_{1(8)}^*||Z_{2(8)}^*||Z_{3(8)}^*||Z_{4(8)}^*||Z_{5(8)}^*||Z_{6(8)}^*||Z_{7(8)}^*||Z_{8(8)}^*$$

$$Z_1^* = Z_1 \oplus Z_3 \oplus Z_4 \oplus Z_6 \oplus Z_7 \oplus Z_8, \qquad Z_5^* = Z_1 \oplus Z_2 \oplus Z_6 \oplus Z_7 \oplus Z_8,$$
$$Z_2^* = Z_1 \oplus Z_2 \oplus Z_4 \oplus Z_5 \oplus Z_7 \oplus Z_8, \qquad Z_6^* = Z_2 \oplus Z_3 \oplus Z_5 \oplus Z_7 \oplus Z_8,$$
$$Z_3^* = Z_1 \oplus Z_2 \oplus Z_3 \oplus Z_5 \oplus Z_6 \oplus Z_8, \qquad Z_7^* = Z_3 \oplus Z_4 \oplus Z_5 \oplus Z_6 \oplus Z_8,$$
$$Z_4^* = Z_2 \oplus Z_3 \oplus Z_4 \oplus Z_5 \oplus Z_6 \oplus Z_7, \qquad Z_8^* = Z_1 \oplus Z_4 \oplus Z_5 \oplus Z_6 \oplus Z_7.$$

Below briefly describes the key schedule of Camellia. First two 128-bit variables K_L and K_R are generated from the user key. Then two 128-bit variables K_A and K_B are generated from K_L and K_R. The round subkeys are generated by rotating K_L, K_R, K_A and K_B. Details are shown in [1]

2.2   Pseudorandomness and Super-Pseudorandomness

Let $\{0,1\}^n$ denote the set of binary strings of length n, let F_n denote the set of functions from $\{0,1\}^n$ to $\{0,1\}^n$ and P_n denote the set of permutations from $\{0,1\}^n$ to $\{0,1\}^n$. A n-bit block cipher can be regarded as a subset of permutations $B_n \subset P_n$ obtained from all the keys. Let $\mathcal{A}$ be a computationally unbounded distinguisher with an oracle $\mathcal{O}$. The oracle chooses randomly a permutation π from P_n or B_n. The aim of the distinguisher $\mathcal{A}$ is to distinguish if the oracle $\mathcal{O}$ implements P_n or B_n. Let p_0 denote the probability that $\mathcal{A}$ outputs 1 when $\mathcal{O}$ implements P_n and p_1 denote the probability that $\mathcal{A}$ outputs 1 when $\mathcal{O}$ implements B_n. That is $p_0 = Pr(\mathcal{A} \ outputs \ 1 \ | \ \mathcal{O} \leftarrow P_n)$ and $p_1 = Pr(\mathcal{A} \ outputs \ 1 \ | \ \mathcal{O} \leftarrow B_n)$. Then the advantage of the distinguisher $\mathcal{A}$ is defined as

$$Adv_A = | \ p_1 - p_0 \ |$$

Assume that the distinguisher $\mathcal{A}$ is restricted to make at most q queries to the oracle $\mathcal{O}$, where q is some polynomial in n. We say that $\mathcal{A}$ is pseudorandom distinguisher if it queries x and the oracle answers $y = \pi(x)$, where π is randomly chosen permutation by $\mathcal{O}$. We say that $\mathcal{A}$ is super-pseudorandom distinguisher if it is also allowed to query y and receives $x = \pi^{-1}(y)$ from the oracle.

Definition 1. A function $h : N \to R$ is negligible if for any constant $c > 0$ and all sufficiently large $n \in N$, $h(n) < \frac{1}{n^c}$.

Definition 2. Let B_n be an efficiently computable permutation ensemble. B_n is called a pseudorandom permutation ensemble if Adv_A is negligible for any pseudorandom distinguisher $\mathcal{A}$.

Definition 3. Let B_n be an efficiently computable permutation ensemble. B_n is called a super-pseudorandom permutation ensemble if Adv_A is negligible for any super-pseudorandom distinguisher $\mathcal{A}$.

In definition 2 and 3, a permutation ensemble is efficiently computable if all permutations in the ensemble can be computed efficiently. See[16] for the rigorous definition of this. It is reasonable assumption that B_n is an efficiently computable permutation ensemble if it is obtained from an n-bit block cipher. In Section 6 , we consider a non-adaptive distinguisher which sends all the queries to the oracle at the same time.

3   4-Round Distinguishers

Choose

$$L_0 = (\alpha_1, \alpha_2, \cdots, \alpha_8), \qquad\qquad R_0 = (x, \beta_2, \cdots, \beta_8).$$

where x take values in $\{0,1\}^8$, α_i and β_j are constants in $\{0,1\}^8$. Thus, the input of 2nd round can be written as follows:

$$L_1 = (x \oplus \gamma_1, \gamma_2, \cdots, \gamma_8), \qquad\qquad R_1 = (\alpha_1, \alpha_2, \cdots, \alpha_8),$$

where γ_i are entirely determined by $\alpha_i(1 \leq i \leq 8), \beta_j(2 \leq j \leq 8)$ and k_1, so γ_i are constants when the user key is fixed. In the 2nd round a transformation on L_1 using $F(\bullet, k_2)$ is as follows:

$$L_1 = (x \oplus \gamma_1, \gamma_2, \cdots, \gamma_8) \xrightarrow{F(\bullet, k_2)} (y \oplus \theta_1, y \oplus \theta_2, y \oplus \theta_3, \theta_4, y \oplus \theta_5, \theta_6, \theta_7, y \oplus \theta_8)$$

where $y = s_1(x \oplus \gamma_1 \oplus k_{2,1})$, $k_{2,1}$ is the first byte of k_2, θ_i are entirely determined by $\gamma_i(1 \leq i \leq 8)$ and k_2, thus θ_i are constants when the user key is fixed. Therefore, the output of 2nd round is

$$L_2 = (y \oplus \varpi_1, y \oplus \varpi_2, y \oplus \varpi_3, \varpi_4, y \oplus \varpi_5, \varpi_6, \varpi_7, y \oplus \varpi_8),$$
$$R_2 = L_1 = (x \oplus \gamma_1, \gamma_2, \cdots, \gamma_8),$$

where $\varpi_i = \theta_i \oplus \alpha_i$ are constants. In the 3rd round a transformation on L_2 using $F(\bullet, k_3)$ is as follows:

$$L_2 = (y \oplus \varpi_1, y \oplus \varpi_2, y \oplus \varpi_3, \varpi_4, y \oplus \varpi_5, \varpi_6, \varpi_7, y \oplus \varpi_8) \xrightarrow{F(\bullet, k_3)} (z_1, z_2, \cdots, z_8).$$

Thus,we have the left half of output for the 3rd round:

$$L_3 = (z_1 \oplus x \oplus \gamma_1, z_2 \oplus \gamma_2, z_3 \oplus \gamma_3, \cdots, z_8 \oplus \gamma_8).$$

So the right half of output for the 4th round is as follows:

$$R_4 = L_3 = (z_1 \oplus x \oplus \gamma_1, z_2 \oplus \gamma_2, z_3 \oplus \gamma_3, \cdots, z_8 \oplus \gamma_8).$$

Now we analyze the relations among bytes of R_4. By observing the equation $(z_1, z_2, \cdots, z_8) = F(L_2, k_3)$, we get the following equations

$$z_3 \oplus z_4 \oplus z_5 \oplus z_6 \oplus z_7 = s_4(\varpi_7 \oplus k_{3,7})$$

$$z_2 \oplus z_3 \oplus z_4 \oplus z_6 \oplus z_7 \oplus z_8 = s_1(y \oplus \varpi_1 \oplus k_{3,1})$$

$$z_2 \oplus z_3 \oplus z_5 \oplus z_6 \oplus z_8 = s_3(\varpi_6 \oplus k_{3,6})$$

$$z_1 \oplus z_7 \oplus z_8 = s_4(\varpi_4 \oplus k_{3,4}) \oplus s_3(\varpi_6 \oplus k_{3,6})$$

$$z_3 \oplus z_4 \oplus z_5 = s_4(\varpi_4 \oplus k_{3,4}) \oplus s_2(y \oplus \varpi_2 \oplus k_{3,2}) \oplus s_3(\varpi_6 \oplus k_{3,6})$$

$$z_2 \oplus z_4 \oplus z_5 \oplus z_6 \oplus z_7 = s_4(\varpi_4 \oplus k_{3,4}) \oplus s_3(y \oplus \varpi_3 \oplus k_{3,3}) \oplus s_3(\varpi_6 \oplus k_{3,6})$$

$$z_2 \oplus z_5 = s_4(\varpi_4 \oplus k_{3,4}) \oplus s_2(y \oplus \varpi_5 \oplus k_{3,5}) \oplus s_3(\varpi_6 \oplus k_{3,6})$$

$$z_4 \oplus z_6 = s_4(\varpi_4 \oplus k_{3,4}) \oplus s_1(y \oplus \varpi_8 \oplus k_{3,8}) \oplus s_3(\varpi_6 \oplus k_{3,6})$$

Because s_1 is a permutation, $y = s_1(x \oplus \gamma_1 \oplus k_{2,1})$ differs when x takes different values. As a consequence, $s_1(y \oplus \varpi_1 \oplus k_{3,1})$ will have different values. Similarly, $s_2(y \oplus \varpi_2 \oplus k_{3,2})$, $s_3(y \oplus \varpi_3 \oplus k_{3,3})$, $s_2(y \oplus \varpi_5 \oplus k_{3,5})$ and $s_1(y \oplus \varpi_8 \oplus k_{3,8})$ have the same property as $s_1(y \oplus \varpi_1 \oplus k_{3,1})$. Obviously, $s_4(\varpi_4 \oplus k_{3,4})$, $s_3(\varpi_6 \oplus k_{3,6})$ and $s_4(\varpi_7 \oplus k_{3,7})$ are constants, Thus, from the above discussion we know that $z_3 \oplus z_4 \oplus z_5 \oplus z_6 \oplus z_7$, $z_2 \oplus z_3 \oplus z_5 \oplus z_6 \oplus z_8$ and $z_1 \oplus z_7 \oplus z_8$ are constants, and $z_2 \oplus z_3 \oplus z_4 \oplus z_6 \oplus z_7 \oplus z_8$, $z_3 \oplus z_4 \oplus z_5$, $z_2 \oplus z_4 \oplus z_5 \oplus z_6 \oplus z_7$, $z_2 \oplus z_5$ and $z_4 \oplus z_6$ each will have different values when x takes different values. Therefore we get the following theorem by considering $R_4 = L_3 = (z_1 \oplus x \oplus \gamma_1, z_2 \oplus \gamma_2, z_3 \oplus \gamma_3, \cdots, z_8 \oplus \gamma_8)$.

Theorem 1. *Let $P = (L_0, R_0)$ and $P_0^* = (L_0^*, R_0^*)$ be two plaintexts of 4-round Camellia, $C = (L_4, R_4)$ and $C_4^* = (L_4^*, R_4^*)$ be the corresponding ciphertexts, $R_{0,i}$ denote the ith byte of R_0. If $L_0 = L_0^*, R_{0,1} \neq R_{0,1}^*, R_{0,j} = R_{0,j}^* (2 \leq j \leq 8)$, then R_4 and R_4^* satisfy:*

$$R_{4,3} \oplus R_{4,4} \oplus R_{4,5} \oplus R_{4,6} \oplus R_{4,7} = R_{4,3}^* \oplus R_{4,4}^* \oplus R_{4,5}^* \oplus R_{4,6}^* \oplus R_{4,7}^* \tag{1}$$

$$R_{4,2} \oplus R_{4,3} \oplus R_{4,5} \oplus R_{4,6} \oplus R_{4,8} = R_{4,2}^* \oplus R_{4,3}^* \oplus R_{4,5}^* \oplus R_{4,6}^* \oplus R_{4,8}^* \tag{2}$$

$$R_{4,2} \oplus R_{4,3} \oplus R_{4,4} \oplus R_{4,6} \oplus R_{4,7} \oplus R_{4,8}$$
$$\neq R_{4,2}^* \oplus R_{4,3}^* \oplus R_{4,4}^* \oplus R_{4,6}^* \oplus R_{4,7}^* \oplus R_{4,8}^* \tag{3}$$

$$R_{4,1} \oplus R_{4,7} \oplus R_{4,8} \neq R_{4,1}^* \oplus R_{4,7}^* \oplus R_{4,8}^* \tag{4}$$

$$R_{4,3} \oplus R_{4,4} \oplus R_{4,5} \neq R_{4,3}^* \oplus R_{4,4}^* \oplus R_{4,5}^* \tag{5}$$

$$R_{4,2} \oplus R_{4,4} \oplus R_{4,5} \oplus R_{4,6} \oplus R_{4,7} \neq R_{4,2}^* \oplus R_{4,4}^* \oplus R_{4,5}^* \oplus R_{4,6}^* \oplus R_{4,7}^* \tag{6}$$

$$R_{4,2} \oplus R_{4,5} \neq R_{4,2}^* \oplus R_{4,5}^* \tag{7}$$

$$R_{4,4} \oplus R_{4,6} \neq R_{4,4}^* \oplus R_{4,6}^* \tag{8}$$

The above (in)equations in the theorem 1 provide some efficient 4-round distinguishers,which will be used to attack and show the pseudorandomness of reduced-round Camellia.

4   Attacks on Reduced-Round Camellia with 128 Bit Key

4.1   Attacking 6-Round Camellia with 128 Bit Key

This section explains the attack on 6-round Camellia with 128-bit key in some detail. First we recover the first byte $k_{1,1}$ of k_1 and the seventh byte $k_{6,7}$ of k_6. From the key schedule for 128-bit key, we know that $k_{6,7}[2 \sim 8] = k_{1,1}[1 \sim 7]$, so we only need to guess 9 bits. Using the equation (1) of theorem 1, we construct the following algorithm to recover$(k_{1,1}, k_{6,7})$:

Algorithm 1
Step1. For each possible value t of $k_{1,1}$, choose two plaintexts $P0^t = (L0_0^t, R0_0^t)$ and $P1^t = (L1_0^t, R1_0^t)$ as follows:

$$L0_0^t = (i_0, \alpha_2, \cdots, \alpha_8),$$
$$R0_0^t = (s_1(i_0 \oplus k_{1,1}), s_1(i_0 \oplus k_{1,1}), s_1(i_0 \oplus k_{1,1}), \beta_4, s_1(i_0 \oplus k_{1,1}), \beta_6, \beta_7, s_1(i_0 \oplus k_{1,1})),$$
$$L1_0^t = (i_1, \alpha_2, \cdots, \alpha_8),$$
$$R1_0^t = (s_1(i_1 \oplus k_{1,1}), s_1(i_1 \oplus k_{1,1}), s_1(i_1 \oplus k_{1,1}), \beta_4, s_1(i_1 \oplus k_{1,1}), \beta_6, \beta_7, s_1(i_1 \oplus k_{1,1})).$$

where α_i and β_j are constants, $0 \le i_0 < i_1 \le 255$. The corresponding ciphertexts are $C0^t = (L0_6^t, R0_6^t)$ and $C1^t = (L1_6^t, R1_6^t)$.
Step2. For each possible value of $(t, k_{6,7})$, compute

$$\triangle_0 = s_4(R0_{6,7}^t \oplus k_{6,7}) \oplus (L0_{6,3}^t \oplus L0_{6,4}^t \oplus L0_{6,5}^t \oplus L0_{6,6}^t \oplus L0_{6,7}^t),$$
$$\triangle_1 = s_4(R1_{6,7}^t \oplus k_{6,7}) \oplus (L1_{6,3}^t \oplus L1_{6,4}^t \oplus L1_{6,5}^t \oplus L1_{6,6}^t \oplus L1_{6,7}^t).$$

Check if $\triangle_0$ equals $\triangle_1$. If so, record the corresponding value of $(t, k_{6,7})$. Otherwise, move to next value of $(t, k_{6,7})$.
Step3. For the recorded value of $(t, k_{6,7})$ in Step2, choose some other plaintexts $P2^t (\ne P0^t, P1^t)$, compute $\triangle_2$, and check if $\triangle_2$ equals $\triangle_0$, if so, record the corresponding value of $(t, k_{6,7})$, otherwise, discard the value of $(t, k_{6,7})$. If there are more than one recorded value, then repeat Step 3 on the newly recorded values.

Take q values at random over $\{0, 1\}^8$, the probability of that they are the same is $2^{-8(q-1)}$. So invalid subkey will pass step2 with a probability 2^{-8}, and there are about $2^9 \times 2^{-8} = 2$ remaining values after step2. So the attack requires less than 3×2^8 chosen plaintexts. The main time complexity of attack is from step2, where the time complexity of computing each $\triangle$ is about the same as the 1-round encryption, so the time complexity of attack is less than 2^9 encryptions.

Knowing $k_{1,1}$, we can choose plaintexts such that the outputs of the first round meet the requirement of Theorem 1. Thus, R_5 satisfies Theorem 1, and from $R_5 = L_6 \oplus F(R_6, k_6)$ and that $s_1(R_{6,1} \oplus k_{6,1})$ is the result of $\oplus$ of the 2nd ,3rd ,4th ,6th,7th and 8th byte of $F(R_6, k_6)$, we have

$$R_{5,2} \oplus R_{5,3} \oplus R_{5,4} \oplus R_{5,6} \oplus R_{5,7} \oplus R_{5,8} = L_{6,2} \oplus L_{6,3} \oplus L_{6,4} \oplus L_{6,6} \oplus L_{6,7} \oplus L_{6,8} \oplus s_1(R_{6,1} \oplus k_{6,1}).$$

Using this equation and inequation (3) in Theorem 1, we can construct the following algorithm to recover $k_{6,1}$:

Algorithm 2

Step1. Choose 64 plaintexts $P^i = (L_0^i, R_0^i)(0 \leq i \leq 63)$ as follows:

$$L_0^i = (i, \alpha_2, \cdots, \alpha_8),$$
$$R_0^i = (s_1(i \oplus k_{1,1}), s_1(i \oplus k_{1,1}), s_1(i \oplus k_{1,1}), \beta_4, s_1(i \oplus k_{1,1}), \beta_6, \beta_7, s_1(i \oplus k_{1,1})).$$

where α_i and β_j are constants. Denote by $C^i = (L_6^i, R_6^i)$ the corresponding ciphertexts of the above plaintexts.

Step2. For each possible value of $k_{6,1}$, compute

$$\triangle_i = s_1(R_{6,1}^i \oplus k_{6,1}) \oplus (L_{6,2}^i \oplus L_{6,3}^i \oplus L_{6,4}^i \oplus L_{6,6}^i \oplus L_{6,7}^i \oplus L_{6,8}^i).$$

Check if there are collisions among $\triangle_i$. If so, discard the value of $k_{6,1}$. Otherwise, output $k_{6,1}$.

Step3. From the output values of $k_{6,1}$ in Step2, choose some other plaintexts, and repeat Step2.

The probability of at least one collision occurs when we throw 64 balls into 256 buckets at random is larger than $1 - e^{-64(64-1)/2 \times 2^8} \geq 1 - 2^{-11}$. So the probability of wrong output (invalid subkey) in Step2 is less than 2^{-11}. For the 256 possible values of $k_{6,1}$, at most 64 more plaintexts are needed in Step3. Thus, the attack requires less than 2^7 chosen plaintexts and 2^{12} encryptions.

Similarly, using equation (2) in Theorem 1 and the plaintexts chosen in Algorithm 2, we can recover $k_{6,6}$ by computing

$$\triangle_i = s_3(R_{6,6}^i \oplus k_{6,6}) \oplus (L_{6,2}^i \oplus L_{6,3}^i \oplus L_{6,5}^i \oplus L_{6,6}^i \oplus L_{6,8}^i).$$

Check if $\triangle_i$ is a constant. If so, output the value of $k_{6,6}$, otherwise, discard the value of $k_{6,6}$. Here the attack requires 2^{10} encryptions.

And using $k_{6,6}$, inequation (4) in Theorem 1 and the plaintexts chosen in Algorithm 2, we can recover $k_{6,4}$ by computing

$$\triangle_i = s_4(R_{6,4}^i \oplus k_{6,4}) \oplus s_3(R_{6,6}^i \oplus k_{6,6}) \oplus (L_{6,1}^i \oplus L_{6,7}^i \oplus L_{6,8}^i).$$

and the attack requires 2^{12} encryptions.

And using inequation (5) in Theorem 1 and the plaintexts chosen in Algorithm 2, we can recover $k_{6,2}$ by computing

$$\triangle_i = s_4(R_{6,4}^i \oplus k_{6,4}) \oplus s_2(R_{6,2}^i \oplus k_{6,2}) \oplus s_3(R_{6,6}^i \oplus k_{6,6}) \oplus (L_{6,3}^i \oplus L_{6,4}^i \oplus L_{6,5}^i).$$

and the attack requires 2^{12} encryptions.

And using inequation (6) in Theorem 1 and the plaintexts chosen in Algorithm 2, we can recover $k_{6,3}$ by computing

$$\triangle_i = s_4(R_{6,4}^i \oplus k_{6,4}) \oplus s_3(R_{6,3}^i \oplus k_{6,3}) \oplus s_3(R_{6,6}^i \oplus k_{6,6}) \oplus (L_{6,2}^i \oplus L_{6,4}^i \oplus L_{6,5}^i \oplus L_{6,6}^i \oplus L_{6,7}^i).$$

and the attack requires 2^{12} encryptions.

And using inequation (7) in Theorem 1 and the plaintexts chosen in Algorithm 2, we can recover $k_{6,5}$ by computing

$$\triangle_i = s_4(R_{6,4}^i \oplus k_{6,4}) \oplus s_2(R_{6,5}^i \oplus k_{6,5}) \oplus s_3(R_{6,6}^i \oplus k_{6,6}) \oplus (L_{6,2}^i \oplus L_{6,5}^i).$$

and the attack requires 2^{12} encryptions.

And using inequation (8) in Theorem 1 and the plaintexts chosen in Algorithm 2, we can recover $k_{6,8}$ by computing

$$\triangle_i = s_4(R^i_{6,4} \oplus k_{6,4}) \oplus s_1(R^i_{6,8} \oplus k_{6,8}) \oplus s_3(R^i_{6,6} \oplus k_{6,6}) \oplus (L^i_{6,4} \oplus L^i_{6,6}).$$

and the attack requires 2^{12} encryptions.

Now we have recovered $k_{1,1}$ and k_6, using less than 2^{10} chosen plaintexts and $6 \times 2^{12} + 2^{10} + 2^9$ encryptions. Similarly, by decrypting the 6th round, we can recover k_5. Therefore, the attack on the 6-round Camellia requires less than 2^{10} chosen plaintexts and 2^{15} encryptions.

Similarly we can get the user key of 7(8)-round Camellia. For 7-round Camellia, the attack requires less than 2^{12} chosen plaintexts and $2^{54.5}$ encryptions. For 8-round Camellia, the attack requires less than 2^{13} chosen plaintexts and $2^{112.1}$ encryptions.

4.2   Attacking 9-Round Camellia with 128 Bit Key

If we use the 4-round distinguisher from the 2nd to the 5th round of encryption as in the case of 8-round, then the time complexity of recovering 9-round Camellia key is larger than 2^{128} which is apparently useless. So we will use the 4-round distinguisher only from the 4th to the 7th round. First guess $k_1, k_{2,1}, k_{2,2}, k_{2,3}, k_{2,5}, k_{2,8}, k_{3,1}, k_{8,7}, k_{9,3}, k_{9,4}, k_{9,5}, k_{9,6}, k_{9,8}$, When $(k_1, k_{2,1}, k_{2,2}, k_{2,3}, k_{2,5}, k_{2,8})$ is given, we only need to guess 3 bits of $(k_{9,3}, k_{9,4}, k_{9,5}, k_{9,6}, k_{9,8})$.

Algorithm 3
Step1. For each possible value t of $(k_1, k_{2,1}, k_{2,2}, k_{2,3}, k_{2,5}, k_{2,8}, k_{3,1})$, Choose 3 plaintexts $Pj^t = (Lj^t_0, Rj^t_0)(1 \le j \le 3)$ such that

$$Lj^t_2 = (i_j, \alpha_2, \cdots, \alpha_8),$$
$$Rj^t_2 = (s_1(i_j \oplus k_{3,1}), s_1(i_j \oplus k_{3,1}), s_1(i_j \oplus k_{3,1}), \beta_4, s_1(i_j \oplus k_{3,1}), \beta_6, \beta_7, s_1(i_j \oplus k_{3,1})).$$

where α_i and β_j are constants, $0 \le i_j \le 255$, and the the corresponding ciphertexts are $Cj^t = (Lj^t_9, Rj^t_9)$.
Step2. For each fixed value of t, and for each possible value of $(k_{8,7}, k_{9,3}, k_{9,4}, k_{9,5}, k_{9,6}, k_{9,8})$, compute $\triangle_1$ and $\triangle_2$, where

$$\triangle_j = s_4(Rj^t_{8,7} \oplus k_{8,7}) \oplus (Rj^t_{9,3} \oplus Rj^t_{9,4} \oplus Rj^t_{9,5} \oplus Rj^t_{9,6} \oplus Rj^t_{9,7}),$$
$$Rj^t_{8,7} = Lj^t_{9,7} \oplus s_3(Rj^t_{9,3} \oplus k_{9,3}) \oplus s_4(Rj^t_{9,4} \oplus k_{9,4}) \oplus s_2(Rj^t_{9,5} \oplus k_{9,5})$$
$$\oplus s_3(Rj^t_{9,6} \oplus k_{9,6}) \oplus s_1(Rj^t_{9,8} \oplus k_{9,8}).$$

Check if $\triangle_1$ equals $\triangle_2$. If so, output the value of $(k_{8,7}, k_{9,3}, k_{9,4}, k_{9,5}, k_{9,6}, k_{9,8})$. Otherwise, discard the value of $(k_{8,7}, k_{9,3}, k_{9,4}, k_{9,5}, k_{9,6}, k_{9,8})$.

For the output values of $(k_{8,7}, k_{9,3}, k_{9,4}, k_{9,5}, k_{9,6}, k_{9,8})$, compute $\triangle_3$, check if $\triangle_3$ equals $\triangle_1$. If so, output the value of $(k_{8,7}, k_{9,3}, k_{9,4}, k_{9,5}, k_{9,6}, k_{9,8})$. Otherwise, discard the value of $(k_{8,7}, k_{9,3}, k_{9,4}, k_{9,5}, k_{9,6}, k_{9,8})$.

Step3. For the output values of $(t, k_{8,7}, k_{9,3}, k_{9,4}, k_{9,5}, k_{9,6}, k_{9,8})$ in Step2, Choose some other plaintexts $P4^t (\neq Pj^t, 1 \leq j \leq 3)$, compute $\triangle_4$, check if $\triangle_4$ equals $\triangle_1$. If so, output the value of $(t, k_{8,7}, k_{9,3}, k_{9,4}, k_{9,5}, k_{9,6}, k_{9,8})$. Otherwise, discard the value of $(t, k_{8,7}, k_{9,3}, k_{9,4}, k_{9,5}, k_{9,6}, k_{9,8})$. If there are more than one output value, then repeat Step3.

Wrong values will pass step2 successfully with probability 2^{-16}. Thus there are about $2^{123} \times 2^{-16} = 2^{107}$ output values in step2. So, the attack requires less than $3 \times 2^{112} + 2^{108}$ chosen plaintexts. The main time complexity of the attck is in Step2, the time of computing each $\triangle$ is about the 1-round encryption, so the time complexity of the attck is less than $(2 \times 2^{112} \times 2^{11} + 2^{116}) \times 1/9 < 2^{120} + 2^{119} + 2^{118} + 2^{117}$ encryptions.

Now we know $k_1, k_{2,1}, k_{2,2}, k_{2,3}, k_{2,5}, k_{2,8}, k_{3,1}, k_{8,7}, k_{9,3}, k_{9,4}, k_{9,5}, k_{9,6}, k_{9,8}$, we can recover the other bytes of k_9 and get the user key of 9-round Camellia. The attack requires less than $2^{113.6}$ chosen plaintexts and 2^{121} encryptions.

5   Attacks Reduced-Round Camellia with 192/256 Bit Key

5.1   Attacking 9-Round Camellia with 192/256 Bit Key

First guess $k_{1,1}, k_{6,7}, k_{7,3}, k_{7,4}, k_{7,5}, k_{7,6}, k_{7,8}, k_8, k_9$. When $k_{1,1}$ is given, we can get 8 bits of k_8 from the key schedule. So we need guess 176 bits subkey. Using equation (1) in Theorem 1, we can construct the following algorithm:

Algorithm 4
Step1. For each possible value t of $k_{1,1}$, Choose 22 plaintexts $Pj^t = (Lj_0^t, Rj_0^t)$ $(1 \leq j \leq 22)$ as follows:

$$Lj_0^t = (i_j, \alpha_2, \cdots, \alpha_8),$$
$$Rj_0^t = (s_1(i_j \oplus k_{1,1}), s_1(i_j \oplus k_{1,1}), s_1(i_j \oplus k_{1,1}), \beta_4, s_1(i_j \oplus k_{1,1}), \beta_6, \beta_7, s_1(i_j \oplus k_{1,1})).$$

where α_i and β_j are constants, $0 \leq i_j \leq 255$, and the the corresponding ciphertexts are $Cj^t = (Lj_9^t, Rj_9^t)$.
Step2. For each fixed value of t, for each possible value of $(k_{6,7}, k_{7,3}, k_{7,4}, k_{7,5}, k_{7,6}, k_{7,8}, k_8, k_9)$, First compute $\triangle_1$ and $\triangle_2$, where

$$\triangle_j = s_4(Rj_{6,7}^t \oplus k_{6,7}) \oplus (Rj_{7,3}^t \oplus Rj_{7,4}^t \oplus Rj_{7,5}^t \oplus Rj_{7,6}^t \oplus Rj_{7,7}^t),$$
$$Lj_7^t = Rj_8^t, \quad Rj_7^t = Lj_8^t \oplus F(Rj_8^t, k_8), \qquad Lj_8^t = Rj_9^t, \quad Rj_8^t = Lj_9^t \oplus F(Rj_9^t, k_9),$$
$$Rj_{6,7}^t = Lj_{7,7}^t \oplus s_3(Rj_{7,3}^t \oplus k_{7,3}) \oplus s_4(Rj_{7,4}^t \oplus k_{7,4}) \oplus s_2(Rj_{7,5}^t \oplus k_{7,5})$$
$$\oplus s_3(Rj_{7,6}^t \oplus k_{7,6}) \oplus s_1(Rj_{7,8}^t \oplus k_{7,8}).$$

Check if $\triangle_1$ equals $\triangle_2$. If so, output the value of $(k_{6,7}, k_{7,3}, k_{7,4}, k_{7,5}, k_{7,6}, k_{7,8}, k_8, k_9)$. Otherwise, discard the value of $(k_{6,7}, k_{7,3}, k_{7,4}, k_{7,5}, k_{7,6}, k_{7,8}, k_8, k_9)$.
For the output values of $(k_{6,7}, k_{7,3}, k_{7,4}, k_{7,5}, k_{7,6}, k_{7,8}, k_8, k_9)$, compute $\triangle_3$, check if $\triangle_3$ equals $\triangle_1$. If so, output the value of $(k_{6,7}, k_{7,3}, k_{7,4}, k_{7,5}, k_{7,6}, k_{7,8},$

k_8, k_9). Otherwise, discard the value of $(k_{6,7}, k_{7,3}, k_{7,4}, k_{7,5}, k_{7,6}, k_{7,8}, k_8, k_9)$. Similar process will go through $\triangle_4$ up to $\triangle_{22}$.

Step3. For the output values of $(t, k_{6,7}, k_{7,3}, k_{7,4}, k_{7,5}, k_{7,6}, k_{7,8}, k_8, k_9)$ in Step2, choose some other plaintexts $P23^t (\neq Pj^t, 1 \le j \le 22)$, compute $\triangle_{23}$, check if $\triangle_{23}$ equals $\triangle_1$. If so, output the value of $(t, k_{6,7}, k_{7,3}, k_{7,4}, k_{7,5}, k_{7,6}, k_{7,8}, k_8, k_9)$. Otherwise, discard the value of$(t, k_{6,7}, k_{7,3}, k_{7,4}, k_{7,5}, k_{7,6}, k_{7,8}, k_8, k_9)$. If there are more than one output value, then repeat Step3.

Invalid values of $(k_{6,7}, k_{7,3}, k_{7,4}, k_{7,5}, k_{7,6}, k_{7,8}, k_8, k_9)$ that can pass Step2 will be successful with probability 2^{-168}. Thus it is likely that there is only one output value for any fixed t after Step2, so there are about 2^8 different values after step2. Thus, the attack requires $22 \times 2^8 + 2^8 + 2^8 = 3 \times 2^{11}$ chosen plaintexts. The main time complexity of the attack is in Step2, and the time of computing each $\triangle$ is about the same as 3-round encryption, so the time complexity of an attack is less than that of $(2 \times 2^8 \times 2^{168} + 2^8 \times 2^{160} + 2^8 \times 2^{153}) \times 1/3 < 2^{175} + 2^{174}$ encryptions.

Now we have known $(k_{1,1}, k_{6,7}, k_{7,3}, k_{7,4}, k_{7,5}, k_{7,6}, k_{7,8}, k_8, k_9)$, we can decrypt the ninth and eighth round and recover the other bytes of k_7 and get the user key of 9-round Camellia. The attack requires less than 2^{13} chosen plaintexts and $2^{175.6}$ encryptions.

5.2   Attacking 10-Round Camellia with 256 Bit Key

First guess $k_{1,1}, k_{6,7}, k_{7,3}, k_{7,4}, k_{7,5}, k_{7,6}, k_{7,8}, k_8, k_9, k_{10}$. When $k_{1,1}$ is given, we can get 8 bits of k_8 from the key schedule. So we need guess 240 bits subkey. Using equation (1) in Theorem 1, we construct the following algorithm:

Algorithm 5
Step1. For each possible value t of $k_{1,1}$, Choose 30 plaintexts $Pj^t = (Lj_0^t, Rj_0^t)$ $(1 \le j \le 30)$ as follows:

$$Lj_0^t = (i_j, \alpha_2, \cdots, \alpha_8),$$
$$Rj_0^t = (s_1(i_j \oplus k_{1,1}), s_1(i_j \oplus k_{1,1}), s_1(i_j \oplus k_{1,1}), \beta_4, s_1(i_j \oplus k_{1,1}), \beta_6, \beta_7, s_1(i_j \oplus k_{1,1})).$$

where α_i and β_j are constants, $0 \le i_j \le 255$, and the the corresponding ciphertexts are $Cj^t = (Lj_{10}^t, Rj_{10}^t)$.
Step2. For each fixed value of t, for each possible value of $(k_{6,7}, k_{7,3}, k_{7,4}, k_{7,5}, k_{7,6}, k_{7,8}, k_8, k_9, k_{10})$, First compute $\triangle_1$ and $\triangle_2$, where

$$\triangle_j = s_4(Rj_{6,7}^t \oplus k_{6,7}) \oplus (Rj_{7,3}^t \oplus Rj_{7,4}^t \oplus Rj_{7,5}^t \oplus Rj_{7,6}^t \oplus Rj_{7,7}^t).$$

$$Lj_7^t = Rj_8^t, \quad Rj_7^t = Lj_8^t \oplus F(Rj_8^t, k_8),$$
$$Lj_8^t = Rj_9^t, \quad Rj_8^t = Lj_9^t \oplus F(Rj_9^t, k_9),$$
$$Lj_9^t = Rj_{10}^t, \quad Rj_9^t = Lj_{10}^t \oplus F(Rj_{10}^t, k_{10}),$$
$$Rj_{6,7}^t = Lj_{7,7}^t \oplus s_3(Rj_{7,3}^t \oplus k_{7,3}) \oplus s_4(Rj_{7,4}^t \oplus k_{7,4}) \oplus s_2(Rj_{7,5}^t \oplus k_{7,5})$$
$$\oplus s_3(Rj_{7,6}^t \oplus k_{7,6}) \oplus s_1(Rj_{7,8}^t \oplus k_{7,8}).$$

Check if $\triangle_1$ equals $\triangle_2$. If so, output the value of $(k_{6,7}, k_{7,3}, k_{7,4}, k_{7,5}, k_{7,6}, k_{7,8},$ $k_8, k_9, k_{10})$. Otherwise, discard the value of $(k_{6,7}, k_{7,3}, k_{7,4}, k_{7,5}, k_{7,6}, k_{7,8}, k_8, k_9,$ $k_{10})$.

For the output values of $(k_{6,7}, k_{7,3}, k_{7,4}, k_{7,5}, k_{7,6}, k_{7,8}, k_8, k_9, k_{10})$, compute $\triangle_3$, check if $\triangle_3$ equals $\triangle_1$. If so, output the value of $(k_{6,7}, k_{7,3}, k_{7,4}, k_{7,5}, k_{7,6}, k_{7,8},$ $k_8, k_9, k_{10})$. Otherwise, discard the value of $(k_{6,7}, k_{7,3}, k_{7,4}, k_{7,5}, k_{7,6}, k_{7,8}, k_8, k_9,$ $k_{10})$. Similar process will go through $\triangle_4$ up to $\triangle_{30}$.

Step3. For the output values of $(t, k_{6,7}, k_{7,3}, k_{7,4}, k_{7,5}, k_{7,6}, k_{7,8}, k_8, k_9, k_{10})$ in Step2, choose some other plaintexts $P31^t (\neq Pj^t, 1 \leq j \leq 30)$, compute $\triangle_{31}$, check if $\triangle_{31}$ equals $\triangle_1$. If so, output the value of $(t, k_{6,7}, k_{7,3}, k_{7,4}, k_{7,5}, k_{7,6}, k_{7,8},$ $k_8, k_9, k_{10})$. Otherwise, discard the value of $(t, k_{6,7}, k_{7,3}, k_{7,4}, k_{7,5}, k_{7,6}, k_{7,8}, k_8, k_9,$ $k_{10})$. If there are more than one output value, then repeat Step3.

Invalid values of $(k_{6,7}, k_{7,3}, k_{7,4}, k_{7,5}, k_{7,6}, k_{7,8}, k_8, k_9, k_{10})$ that can pass Step2 will be successful with probability 2^{-232} . Thus it is likely that there is only one output value for any fixed t after Step2, so there are about 2^8 different values after step2. Thus, the attack requires $30 \times 2^8 + 2^8 + 2^8 = 2^{13}$ chosen plaintexts. The main time complexity of the attack is in Step2, and the time of computing each $\triangle$ is about the same as 4-round encryption, so the time complexity of an attack is less than that of $(2 \times 2^8 \times 2^{232} + 2^8 \times 2^{224} + 2^8 \times 2^{217}) \times 4/10 < 2^{239} + 2^{238} + 2^{237}$ encryptions.

Now we have known $(k_{1,1}, k_{6,7}, k_{7,3}, k_{7,4}, k_{7,5}, k_{7,6}, k_{7,8}, k_8, k_9, k_{10})$, we can decrypt the tenth, ninth and eighth round and recover the other bytes of k_7 and get the user key of 10-round Camellia. The attack requires less than 2^{14} chosen plaintexts and $2^{239.9}$ encryptions.

6   Pseudorandomness of Primitive-Wise Idealized Camellia

6.1   Primitive-Wise Idealization of Camellia

Let n denote the length of a plaintext which can be written as $n = 16m$, where m is an integer. Now we idealize Camellia as shown in Fig.1, where each f_{ij} is an independent random function from $\{0, 1\}^m$ to $\{0, 1\}^m$.

6.2   Pseudorandomness of Primitive-Wise Idealized Camellia

Let $P = (L_0, R_0)$ denote the plaintext, (L_i, R_i) denote the output of the ith round primitive-wise idealized Camellia. Let $L_i = (L_{i,1}, L_{i,2}, \ldots, L_{i,8})$ and $R_i = (R_{i,1}, R_{i,2}, \ldots, R_{i,8})$, where each of $L_{i,j}$ and $R_{i,j}$ is m bits long.

Theorem 2. *The four round primitive-wise idealized Camellia is not a pseudorandom permutation.*

Proof. Let B_n be the set of permutations over $\{0, 1\}^n$ obtained from the four round primitive-wise idealized Camellia. We consider a distinguisher $\mathcal{A}$ as follows.

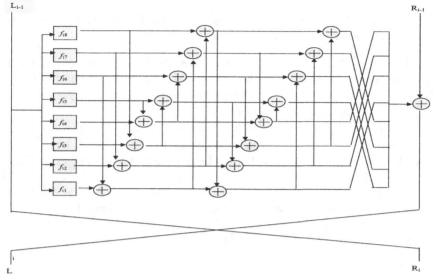

Fig. 1. The i-th round of the primitive-wise idealized Camellia

1. $\mathcal{A}$ randomly chooses two plaintexts $P = (L_0, R_0)$ and $P^* = (L_0^*, R_0^*)$ such that

$$L_0 = L_0^* \ \text{and} \ R_{0,1} \neq R_{0,1}^*, \ R_{0,j} = R_{0,j}^* (2 \leq j \leq 8) \tag{9}$$

2. $\mathcal{A}$ sends them to the oracle and receives the ciphertexts $C = (L_4, R_4)$ and $C^* = (L_4^*, R_4^*)$ from the oracle.
3. Finally, $\mathcal{A}$ outputs 1 if and only if

$$R_{4,3} \oplus R_{4,4} \oplus R_{4,5} \oplus R_{4,6} \oplus R_{4,7} = R_{4,3}^* \oplus R_{4,4}^* \oplus R_{4,5}^* \oplus R_{4,6}^* \oplus R_{4,7}^*$$
$$R_{4,2} \oplus R_{4,3} \oplus R_{4,5} \oplus R_{4,6} \oplus R_{4,8} = R_{4,2}^* \oplus R_{4,3}^* \oplus R_{4,5}^* \oplus R_{4,6}^* \oplus R_{4,8}^*$$

Suppose that the oracle implements the truly random permutation ensemble P_n. Then it is clear that $p_0 = 2^{-2m}$. Next suppose that the oracle implements the four round primitive-wise idealized Camellia. Using Theorem 1, we get $p_1 = 1$. Therefore, we obtained that

$$Adv_A = | \, p_1 - p_0 \, | \geq 1 - 2^{-2m} \tag{10}$$

which is non-negligible. Hence, the four round primitive-wise idealized Camellia is not a pseudorandom permutation.

We will use the following lemma of which the proof is trivial:

Lemma 1. *Let* $f_1, f_2, \ldots, f_t$ *be random functions from* $\{0,1\}^m$ *to* $\{0,1\}^m$. *If* $x = (x_1, x_2, \ldots, x_t)$ *and* $y = (y_1, y_2, \ldots, y_t)$ *are two distinct t-uple of* $\{0,1\}^m$, *and* δ *is a given value of* $\{0,1\}^m$, *then*

$$Pr[f_1(x_1) \oplus \ldots f_t(x_t) \oplus f_1(y_1) \oplus \ldots f_t(y_t) = \delta] \leq 2^{-m}$$

We next prove the following theorem.

Theorem 3. *The five round primitive-wise idealized Camellia is a pseudoran-dom permutation for non-adaptive adversaries.*

Proof. Suppose that $\mathcal{A}$ makes q oracle calls. In the ith oracle call, $\mathcal{A}$ sends a plaintexts $P^i = (L_0^i, R_0^i)$ to the oracle and receives the ciphertexts $C^i = (L_5^i, R_5^i)$. Let $L_3^i = (L_{3,1}^i, \ldots, L_{3,8}^i)$ denote the inputs to $(f_{41}, \ldots, f_{48})$ and $L_4^i = (L_{4,1}^i, \ldots, L_{4,8}^i)$ denote the inputs to $(f_{51}, \ldots, f_{58})$.

Without loss of generality, we assume that $P^1, \ldots, P^q$ are all distinct. Let T_{3l} be the event that $L_{3,l}^1, L_{3,l}^2, \ldots, L_{3,l}^q$ are all distinct for $l = 1, \ldots, 8$, and T_3 be the event that all $T_{31}, \ldots, T_{38}$ occur. Let T_{4l} be the event that $L_{4,l}^1, L_{4,l}^2, \ldots, L_{4,l}^q$ are all distinct for $l = 1, \ldots, 8$, and T_4 be the event that all $T_{41}, \ldots, T_{48}$ occur. If T_3 and T_4 occur, then $C^1, \ldots, C^q$ are completely random since $f_{41}, \ldots, f_{48}, f_{51}, \ldots, f_{58}$ are truly random functions. Therefore, $Adv_{\mathcal{A}}$ is upper bounded by

$$Adv_{\mathcal{A}} = \mid p_1 - p_0 \mid \leq 1 - Pr(T_3 \cap T_4) \tag{11}$$

Further, it is easy to see that

$$1 - Pr(T_3 \cap T_4) \leq \sum_{1 \leq i < j \leq q} Pr(L_{3,1}^i = L_{3,1}^j) + \ldots + \sum_{1 \leq i < j \leq q} Pr(L_{3,8}^i = L_{3,8}^j) +$$

$$\sum_{1 \leq i < j \leq q} Pr(L_{4,1}^i = L_{4,1}^j) + \ldots + \sum_{1 \leq i < j \leq q} Pr(L_{4,8}^i = L_{4,8}^j) \tag{12}$$

Fix $i \neq j$ arbitrarily. We show that all $Pr(L_{3,1}^i = L_{3,1}^j), \ldots, Pr(L_{3,8}^i = L_{3,8}^j)$, $Pr(L_{4,1}^i = L_{4,1}^j), \ldots, Pr(L_{4,8}^i = L_{4,8}^j)$ are sufficiently small. First we show $Pr(L_{3,1}^i = L_{3,1}^j)$ is sufficiently small.

Let E_{2l} be the event that $L_{2,l}^i = L_{2,l}^j$ for $l = 1, \ldots, 8$. Since $P^i \neq P^j$, by Lemma 1 we have $Pr(L_1^i = L_1^j) \leq 2^{-m}$. If $L_1^i \neq L_1^j$, then $(L_{1,1}^i, L_{1,3}^i, L_{1,4}^i, L_{1,6}^i, L_{1,7}^i, L_{1,8}^i) \neq (L_{1,1}^j, L_{1,3}^j, L_{1,4}^j, L_{1,6}^j, L_{1,7}^j, L_{1,8}^j)$ or $(L_{1,1}^i, L_{1,2}^i, L_{1,3}^i, L_{1,5}^i, L_{1,6}^i, L_{1,8}^i) \neq (L_{1,1}^j, L_{1,2}^j, L_{1,3}^j, L_{1,5}^j, L_{1,6}^j, L_{1,8}^j)$. From the 2nd round function of idealized Camellia, we have that

$$L_{2,1}^i = L_{0,1}^i \oplus f_{21}(L_{1,1}^i) \oplus f_{23}(L_{1,3}^i) \oplus f_{24}(L_{1,4}^i) \oplus f_{26}(L_{1,6}^i) \oplus f_{27}(L_{1,7}^i) \oplus f_{28}(L_{1,8}^i)$$

$$L_{2,3}^i = L_{0,3}^i \oplus f_{21}(L_{1,1}^i) \oplus f_{22}(L_{1,2}^i) \oplus f_{23}(L_{1,3}^i) \oplus f_{25}(L_{1,5}^i) \oplus f_{26}(L_{1,6}^i) \oplus f_{28}(L_{1,8}^i)$$

Therefore, by using Lemma 1 we get $Pr(E_{21} \mid L_1^i \neq L_1^j) \leq 2^{-m}$ or $Pr(E_{23} \mid L_1^i \neq L_1^j) \leq 2^{-m}$, hence $Pr(E_{21}) \leq Pr(L_1^i = L_1^j) + Pr(E_{21} \mid L_1^i \neq L_1^j) \leq 2^{-m+1}$ or $Pr(E_{23}) \leq Pr(L_1^i = L_1^j) + Pr(E_{23} \mid L_1^i \neq L_1^j) \leq 2^{-m+1}$, and therefore, $Pr(E_{21} \cap E_{23}) \leq 2^{-m+1}$.

Similarly, from Lemma 1 and the following equation

$$L_{3,1}^i = L_{1,1}^i \oplus f_{31}(L_{2,1}^i) \oplus f_{33}(L_{2,3}^i) \oplus f_{34}(L_{2,4}^i) \oplus f_{36}(L_{2,6}^i) \oplus f_{37}(L_{2,7}^i) \oplus f_{38}(L_{2,8}^i)$$

we have $Pr(L_{3,1}^i = L_{3,1}^j \mid \overline{E_{21} \cap E_{23}}) \leq 2^{-m}$. Hence, we have

$$Pr(L_{3,1}^i = L_{3,1}^j)$$
$$= Pr(L_{3,1}^i = L_{3,1}^j \mid E_{21} \cap E_{23})Pr(E_{21} \cap E_{23}) + Pr(L_{3,1}^i = L_{3,1}^j \mid \overline{E_{21} \cap E_{23}})Pr(\overline{E_{21} \cap E_{23}})$$
$$\leq Pr(E_{21} \cap E_{23}) + Pr(L_{3,1}^i = L_{3,1}^j \mid \overline{E_{21} \cap E_{23}})$$
$$\leq 2^{-m+1} + 2^{-m} = 3 \times 2^{-m} \tag{13}$$

Similarly for $l = 2, \ldots, 8$, we can get $Pr(L_{3,l}^i = L_{3,l}^j) \leq 3 \times 2^{-m} (l = 2, \ldots, 8)$.

Next we show $Pr(L_{4,l}^i = L_{4,l}^j)$ is sufficiently small for $l = 1, \ldots, 8$. For simplicity, we only consider the case $Pr(L_{4,1}^i = L_{4,1}^j)$.

Let E_{3l} be the event that $L_{3,l}^i = L_{3,l}^j$ for $l = 1, \ldots, 8$. Let $W_1 = E_{31} \cap E_{33} \cap E_{34} \cap E_{36} \cap E_{37} \cap E_{38}$. Because

$$L_{4,1}^i = L_{2,1}^i \oplus f_{41}(L_{3,1}^i) \oplus f_{43}(L_{3,3}^i) \oplus f_{44}(L_{3,4}^i) \oplus f_{46}(L_{3,6}^i) \oplus f_{47}(L_{3,7}^i) \oplus f_{48}(L_{3,8}^i)$$
$$L_{4,1}^j = L_{2,1}^j \oplus f_{41}(L_{3,1}^j) \oplus f_{43}(L_{3,3}^j) \oplus f_{44}(L_{3,4}^j) \oplus f_{46}(L_{3,6}^j) \oplus f_{47}(L_{3,7}^j) \oplus f_{48}(L_{3,8}^j)$$

we have $Pr(L_{4,1}^i = L_{4,1}^j \mid \overline{W_1}) \leq 2^{-m}$. Therefore, we obtain

$$Pr(L_{4,1}^i = L_{4,1}^j) = Pr(L_{4,1}^i = L_{4,1}^j \mid W_1)Pr(W_1) + Pr(L_{4,1}^i = L_{4,1}^j \mid \overline{W_1})Pr(\overline{W_1})$$
$$\leq Pr(W_1) + Pr(L_{4,1}^i = L_{4,1}^j \mid \overline{W_1})$$
$$\leq Pr(L_{3,1}^i = L_{3,1}^j) + 2^{-m} \leq 4 \times 2^{-m} \tag{14}$$

Similarly for $l = 2, \ldots, 8$, we have $Pr(L_{4,l}^i = L_{4,l}^j) \leq 4 \times 2^{-m}$.

Since we have $\binom{q}{2}$ choices of (i, j) pairs, so we have

$$1 - Pr(T_3 \cap T_4) \leq \sum_{1 \leq i < j \leq q} Pr(L_{3,1}^i = L_{3,1}^j) + \ldots + \sum_{1 \leq i < j \leq q} Pr(L_{3,8}^i = L_{3,8}^j) +$$
$$\sum_{1 \leq i < j \leq q} Pr(L_{4,1}^i = L_{4,1}^j) + \ldots \sum_{1 \leq i < j \leq q} Pr(L_{4,8}^i = L_{4,8}^j)$$
$$\leq \binom{q}{2} \times 8 \times 3 \times 2^{-m} + \binom{q}{2} \times 8 \times 4 \times 2^{-m}$$
$$< \frac{28q^2}{2^m} \tag{15}$$

Since $q = poly(n), m = \frac{n}{16}$, we have that Adv_A is negligible for any $\mathcal{A}$. This shows that the five round primitive-wise idealized Camellia is a pseudorandom permutation for non-adaptive adversaries.

Similar to the above, we can prove the following corollary.

Corollary 1. *The five round primitive-wise idealized Camellia is a super-pseudorandom permutation for non-adaptive adversaries.*

7 Concluding Remarks

In this paper we have proposed some 4-round distinguishers of Camellia, and discussed the security of Camellia by using the 4-round distinguishers and collision-searching techniques. The 128-bit key of 6 rounds Camellia can be recovered with 2^{10} chosen plaintexts and 2^{15} encryptions. The 128-bit key of 7 rounds Camellia can be recovered with 2^{12} chosen plaintexts and $2^{54.5}$ encryptions. The 128-bit key of 8 rounds Camellia can be recovered with 2^{13} chosen plaintexts and $2^{112.1}$ encryptions. The 128-bit key of 9 rounds Camellia can be recovered with $2^{113.6}$ chosen plaintexts and 2^{121} encryptions. The 192/256-bit key of 8 rounds Camellia can be recovered with 2^{13} chosen plaintexts and $2^{111.1}$ encryptions. The 192/256-bit key of 9 rounds Camellia can be recovered with 2^{13} chosen plaintexts and $2^{175.6}$ encryptions. The 256-bit key of 10 rounds Camellia can be recovered with 2^{14} chosen plaintexts and $2^{239.9}$ encryptions. Furthermore, we have shown that the four round primitive-wise idealized Camellia is not pseudorandom permutation and the five round primitive-wise idealized Camellia is super-pseudorandom permutation for non-adaptive adversaries.

References

1. K.Aoki,T.Ichikawa,M.Kanda,M.Matsui,S.Moriai,J.Nakajima and T.Tokita, "Specification of Camellia-a 128-bit Block Cipher," *Selected Areas in Cryptography - SAC'2000*, Springer-Verlag 2000,pp. 183-191.
2. http://www.cryptonessie.org
3. T.Kawabata, T.Kaneko, "A study on higher order differential attack of Camellia," *Proceedings of the 2nd NESSIE workshop*,2001.
4. Y.Hatano,H.Sekine, and T.Kaneko, "Higher order differential attack of Camellia(II)," *Selected Areas in Cryptography-SAC'02*, LNCS 2595,Springer-Verlag 2002, pp.39-56.
5. S. Lee, S. Hong, S. Lee, J. Lim and S. Yoon, "Truncated Differential Cryptanalysis of Camellia", *Information Security and Cryptology-ICISC'01*,LNCS 2288, Springer-Verlag,2001,pp.32-38.
6. M.Sugita,K.Kobara, and H.Imai, "Security of reduced version of the block cipher Camellia against truncated and impossible differential cryptanalysis," *Advances in Cryptology– Asiacrypt'01*,LNCS 2248,Springer-Verlag 2001, pp.193-207.
7. T.Shirai,S.Kanamaru,and G.Abe, "Improved upper bounds of differential and linear characteristic probability for Camellia," *Fast Software Encryption-FSE'02*,LNCS 2365,Springer-Verlag 2002,pp.128-142.
8. He Ye-ping and Qing Si-han, "Square attack on Reduced Camellia Cipher," *Information and Communication Security-ICICS'01*,LNCS 2229, Springer-Verlag 2001,pp.238-245.
9. Y.Yeom, S.Park, and I. Kim, "On the security of Camellia against the square attack," *Fast Software Encryption-FSE'02*,LNCS 2356, Springer-Verlag 2002,pp.89-99.
10. Y.Yeom, I. Park, and I. Kim, "A study of Integral type cryptanalysis on Camellia," *The 2003 Symposium on Cryptography and Information Security-SCIS'03*.
11. M. Luby and C. Rackoff, " How to construct pseudorandom permutations from pseudorandom functions," *SIAM Journal on Computing*, Vol.17,No.2,(1988),pp.373-386.
12. J.Patarin, " New results on pseudorandom permutation generators based on the DES Scheme," *Advances in Cryptology–Crypto'91*, Springer-Verlag 1991,pp.72-77.
13. U.M.Maurer, "A simplified and generalized treatment of Luby-Rackoff pseudorandom permutation generators," *Advances in Cryptology-Eurocrypt'92*, LNCS 658,Springer-Verlag 1992,pp.239-255.
14. S. Vaudenay, "Provable security for block ciphers by decorrelation," *In Proc. of STACS'98*, LNCS 1373, Springer-Verlag 1998,pp.249-275.
15. T.Iwata and K. Kurosawa, "On the Pseudorandomness of the AES Finalists-RC6 and Serpent," *Fast Software Encryption–FES'2000*, LNCS 1978, Springer-Verlag 2000,pp.231-243,.
16. M.Naor and O.Reingold, "On the construction of pseudorandom permutations Luby-Rackoff revisited," *Journal of Cryptology*, Vol.12, No.1,pp.29-66,1999.

Password Based Key Exchange with Mutual Authentication

Shaoquan Jiang and Guang Gong

Department of Electrical and Computer Engineering,
University of Waterloo,
Waterloo, Ontario N2L 3G1, Canada
{jiangshq, ggong}@calliope.uwaterloo.ca

Abstract. A reasonably efficient password based key exchange (KE) protocol with provable security without random oracle was recently proposed by Katz, *et al.* [17] and later by Gennaro and Lindell [13]. However, these protocols do not support mutual authentication (MA). The authors explained that this could be achieved by adding an additional flow. But then this protocol turns out to be 4-round. As it is known that a high entropy secret based key exchange protocol with MA[1] is optimally 3-round (otherwise, at least one entity is not authenticated since a replay attack is applicable), it is quite interesting to ask whether such a protocol in the password setting (without random oracle) is achievable or not. In this paper, we provide an affirmative answer with an efficient construction in the common reference string (CRS) model. Our protocol is even simpler than that of Katz, *et al.* Furthermore, we show that our protocol is secure under the DDH assumption (*without* random oracle).

1   Introduction

In the area of secure communications, key exchange (KE) is one of the most important issues. In this scenario, two interactive parties are assumed to hold long-term secrets. Through an interactive procedure, they establish a temporary session key and then use it to encrypt and authenticate the subsequent communication. There are two types of KE protocols in the literature. In the first case, each party holds a high entropy secret (e.g., a signing key of a digital signature). Research along this line has been well studied, see [1, 6, 8, 12]. The other case is a password authenticated key exchange protocol (see [19] for a detailed description), in which it is assumed that the two parties only share a human-memorable (low entropy) password. Unlike a high entropy secret, it is believed that an exhaustive search attack (or a dictionary attack) is feasible. In fact, it is

---

[1] We do not consider a protocol with a time stamp or a stateful protocol (e.g., a counter based protocol). In other words, we only consider protocols in which a session execution within an entity is independent of its history, and in which the network is asynchronous.

H. Handschuh and A. Hasan (Eds.): SAC 2004, LNCS 3357, pp. 267–279, 2005.

this attack that makes a construction of a secure password based KE protocol more difficult than the high entropy secret based one.

1.1 Related Work

Password authenticated key exchange was first studied by Bellovin and Merritt [4]. Since then, it has been extensively studied in literature [5, 16]. However, none of these solutions had provable security. The first effort to achieve provable security was due to Lucks [18]. Halevi and Krawczyk [15] proposed a password KE protocol in an asymmetric setting: a user only holds a password while the server additionally has a *private key* of a public key cryptosystem. Password KE protocols without this asymmetric assumption were proposed in [2, 7]. However, these protocols including [18] were proved in the random oracle model. It is known [9] that a random oracle based cryptographic construction could be insecure when the oracle is replaced by any real function. In the password setting, it is even worse since a minor weakness of the real function might open the door to a dictionary attack. The first solution without random oracle was due to Goldreich and Lindell [14]. Actually, their protocol was based on a general assumption only (i.e., the existence of trapdoor permutation). But this solution is very inefficient. A reasonably efficient construction in CRS model without random oracle was proposed by Katz, *et al.* [17]. We shall refer to this as the KOY protocol. An abstract framework for this protocol was proposed by Gennaro and Lindell [13]. Nevertheless, these protocols do not support mutual authentication (MA). Katz, *et al.* mentioned in their paper that a mutual authentication can be made by adding an additional flow. This is indeed true. However, the resulting protocol is then 4-round. It is known that a high entropy secret based KE protocol with MA is optimally 3-round. Thus, it is quite interesting to ask whether there exists such a protocol in the password setting *without* random oracles.

1.2 Contribution

In this paper, we provide an affirmative answer to the above problem with an explicit construction. Our construction is in the CRS model (as in [13, 17]), where all the parties have access to a set of public parameters drawn from a predetermined distribution, but nobody knows the corresponding secret key if any. Our construction is optimally 3-round. Comparing with work in [13, 17], it additionally supports mutual authentication and is also simpler than KOY protocol in the sense of exponentiation cost. Nevertheless, their work has been instructive to us. In fact, one technique in their construction helps us in authenticating the initiator. As our important contribution, we formally prove the security under the Decisional Diffie-Hellman (DDH) assumption (*without random oracles*).

2 Security Model

In this section, we introduce a formal model of security. This model is mainly adopted from Bellare, *et al.* [2] and [3]. Our difference is in the mutual authentication where we feel our definition is more reasonable. Details are provided later.

The basic security model without MA was previously adopted by Katz, *et al.* [17] and Gennaro and Lindell [13]. We start with the following notations, which will be used throughout the paper.

- D: a password dictionary with a polynomial size (otherwise, it becomes a KE problem with high entropy secrets). WOLG, we assume that $D = \{1, \cdots, N\}$ with a uniform distribution for some $N > 0$.
- P_i: party i, either a client or a server. If it is a server, then it could individually share a password with a set of clients.
- $\Pi_i^{l_i}$: protocol instance l_i within party P_i. We require that l_i be unique within P_i in order to distinguish local instances. However, we do not require it is globally unique, which reflects the practical concern for possible independence of different parties.
- $Flow_i$: The ith message exchanged between two particular instances.
- $\mathbf{sid}_i^{l_i}$: the session identifier of a particular instance $\Pi_i^{l_i}$.
- $\mathbf{pid}_i^{l_i}$: the party with which instance $\Pi_i^{l_i}$ *believes* that he has been interacting.

Partnering. We say two protocol instances $\Pi_i^{l_i}$ and $\Pi_j^{l_j}$ are partnered if (1) $\mathbf{pid}_i^{l_i} = P_j$ and $\mathbf{pid}_j^{l_j} = P_i$; (2) $\mathbf{sid}_i^{l_i} = \mathbf{sid}_j^{l_j}$.

Adversarial Model. Roughly speaking, the adversary is allowed to fully control the external network. He can inject, modify, block and delete messages at will. He can also request any session keys adaptively. Formally, he can adaptively query the following oracles.

- **Execute**(i, l_i, j, l_j): When this oracle is called, it checks whether instances $\Pi_i^{l_i}$ and $\Pi_j^{l_j}$ are fresh. If either of them is old, it outputs $\perp$. Otherwise, a protocol execution between $\Pi_i^{l_i}$ and $\Pi_j^{l_j}$ takes place. At the end of the execution, a complete transcript (messages exchanged between the two instances) is returned. This oracle call models a threat from an eavesdropping adversary.
- **Send**(d, i, l_i, M) : When this oracle is called, message M is sent to instance $\Pi_i^{l_i}$ as $Flow_d$. If instance $\Pi_i^{l_i}$ does not exist but $d \geq 2$, or if oracle **Send**$(d, i, l_i, *)$ was called before, or if instance $\Pi_i^{l_i}$ already exists but either **Send**$(d - 2, i, l_i, *)$ was not previously called or its output was $\perp$ if called, then the oracle output is set to $\perp$; otherwise, the oracle output is whatever $\Pi_i^{l_i}$ returns. We stress that the oracle response needs to be consistent with **Send**$(d - 2t, i, l_i, *)$ for all $t > 0$. Furthermore, when **Send**$(0, i, l_i, null)$ is called, it first checks whether instance $\Pi_i^{l_i}$ is fresh. If it is old, then the output is set to $\perp$; otherwise, $\Pi_i^{l_i}$ is initiated within P_i, and the output is whatever $\Pi_i^{l_i}$ returns as $Flow_1$. Similarly, when **Send**$(1, i, l_i, M)$ is called, it first checks whether instance $\Pi_i^{l_i}$ is fresh. If it is old, then the output is set to $\perp$; otherwise, an instance $\Pi_i^{l_i}$ is initiated within party P_i as a responsor with input M. The output is whatever $\Pi_i^{l_i}$ outputs as $Flow_2$. The oracle call reflects a threat from man-in-the-middle attack.

- **Reveal**(i, l_i) : When this oracle is called, it outputs the session key of instance $\Pi_i^{l_i}$ if it has accepted and completed with a session key derived; otherwise, it outputs $\perp$. This oracle reflects the threat from a session key loss.
- **Test**(i, l_i) : This oracle does not reflect any real concern. However, it provides a security test. The adversary is allowed to query it once. The queried session must be completed and accepted. Furthermore, this session as well as its partnered session (if it exists) should not be issued a **Reveal** query. When this oracle is called, it flips a fair coin b. If $b = 1$, then the session key of $\Pi_i^{l_i}$ is provided to adversary; otherwise, a random number of the same length is provided. The adversary then tries to output a guess bit b'. He is successful if $b' = b$.

Having defined adversary behavior, we come to define the protocol security. It contains two conditions: correctness and privacy. The mutual authentication is considered in the privacy condition.

Correctness. If two partnered instances both accept, then they conclude with the same session key except for a negligible probability.

Privacy. We define two types of adversary success:

- ⋄ If at any moment, an instance $\Pi_i^{l_i}$ with $\mathbf{pid}_i^{l_i} = P_j$ has accepted and completed with a session key derived while there does not exist an instance $\Pi_j^{l_j}$ with $\mathbf{pid}_j^{l_j} = P_i$ such that the exchanged messages seen by $\Pi_i^{l_i}$ and $\Pi_j^{l_j}$ prior to this moment (especially not including the currently generated message by $\Pi_i^{l_i}$ if any) are equal, then we announce the success of adversary. Furthermore, if such an instance $\Pi_j^{l_j}$ indeed exists, then we require it is unique except for a negligible probability.
- ⋄ If the above event does not happen but the adversary succeeds in the test session, we also announce its success.

We use random variable **Succ** to denote the above success events. We define the advantage of adversary $\mathcal{A}$ as $\mathbf{Adv}(\mathcal{A}) := 2 \Pr[\mathbf{Succ}] - 1$.

Now we are ready to provide a formal definition of security.

Definition 1. *A password authenticated key exchange protocol with mutual authentication is said to be secure if it satisfies*

- *Correctness.*
- *Privacy.*
  *If adversary $\mathcal{A}$ makes Q_{send} queries to **Send** oracle, then*

$$\mathbf{Adv}(\mathcal{A}) < \frac{Q_{send}}{|D|} + \mathbf{negl}(n), \tag{1}$$

where D is the password dictionary, n is the security parameter.

Remarks. Here we give two comments on our definition and that in [2].

1. From our first privacy condition, whenever an instance $\Pi_i^{l_i}$ with $\mathbf{pid}_i^{l_i} = P_j$ accepts and completes, there exists an (essentially) unique instance in P_j (say, $\Pi_j^{l_j}$) with $\mathbf{pid}_j^{l_j} = P_i$ interacting with it and also the exchanged messages prior to the moment $\Pi_i^{l_i}$ accepts are not tampered. This is indeed our intuition about "$\Pi_j^{l_j}$ is authenticated".

2. In Bellare, *et al.* [2], MA is said to be violated if one instance terminates while no partner instance exists. This definition is not always satisfactory. Indeed, *session identifier* $\mathbf{sid}_i^{l_i}$ for instance $\Pi_i^{l_i}$ is popularly [13, 17] defined as a complete transcript seen by $\Pi_i^{l_i}$. Under this SID, their version of MA is always violated since once the adversary holds on the last message the partnership is never established. However, this problem does not occur for our version of MA since we only consider the messages exchanged before the considered instance (i.e., $\Pi_i^{l_i}$) accepts and completes. We stress that a provable MA property of a particular protocol in [2] does not contradict our remark here since their SID is defined as a *partial* transcript. More discussions on the definition appear in the full paper [11].

3 Our Protocol

In this section, we introduce our 3-round construction under the common reference string (CRS) model, where all the parties have access to the public parameters that are drawn from a predetermined distribution. In reality, this condition could be realized by a trusted third party or a threshold scheme. Assume p, q are large primes with $q|(p-1)$; G_q is the (unique) multiplicative subgroup of F_p^* of order q; g, h are uniformly random generators of G_q; H is a collision resistant hash function; $e \leftarrow \mathcal{G}enPK(1^n)$ is the public key for a chosen ciphertext attack (in the postprocessing model) (CCA2) secure public key cryptosystem E (we stress that *nobody* knows the secret key of E_e); $\mathcal{F}$ is a pseudorandom function family and its realization with secret key σ is denoted by $F_\sigma()$. Our protocol is presented as Figure 1. Assume that password π_{ij} is ideally shared between party P_i and P_j. In order to establish a session key, P_i and P_j interact as follows. Assume P_i speaks first. He picks $x \leftarrow Z_q$ uniformly, computes a plain ElGamal ciphertext $A|C$ and sends it together with id P_i to P_j as $Flow_1$. When P_j receives $Flow_1$, he chooses $\lambda_1, \lambda_2 \leftarrow Z_q$, and computes $\mu, C', \sigma, r, \omega, \Sigma$ properly, where r is used as the random input in encryption of Σ, and if it requires a longer string, r can be defined as $F_\sigma(3)|F_\sigma(4)| \cdots$ until it is long enough. We prefer the simple case since the security proof under this modification is essentially identical. Then he sends $\mu|\omega|P_j$ back to P_i (as $Flow_2$). Using μ, P_i is able to compute σ since $\sigma = \mu^x$. Then he verifies whether ω is a ciphertext of $H(\mu|A|C'|P_j|P_i)$ using random bits r. If the verification is successful, then he believes P_j is authentic and therefore returns an authentication tag $\tau = F_\sigma(2)$ as $Flow_3$. Furthermore, he outputs a session key $sk = F_\sigma(1)$ and terminates. When P_j receives τ, he checks whether τ is correct. If the verification succeeds, he believes P_i is

$P_i(\pi_{ij})$ $P_j(\pi_{ij})$

Pub: $g, h, H, \mathcal{F}, e, p, q$

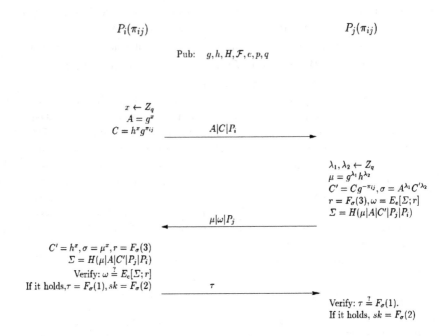

Fig. 1. Key Exchange Protocol Execution between P_i and P_j

authentic. Therefore, he accepts and outputs a session key $sk = F_\sigma(1)$. If the verification fails, it rejects. Note in the above interaction, *implementation issues (e.g., a validity check whether appropriate elements belong to G_q) are omitted for simplicity.*

3.1   Comparison with KOY Protocol

Now we provide a more detailed comparison with KOY protocol. As mentioned before, KOY protocol does not support MA, or it is 4-round if an additional flow is added. In contrast, our protocol is 3-round with MA. Each party in their construction needs 15 exps while ours needs at most 4 exps plus one ciphertext of a CCA2-secure PKE(note it is easy to find such a PKE with a ciphertext cost less than 11 exps). Their construction employs a one-time signature to "bind" the whole transcript while we do not use such a technique since it requires the responsor to store the whole transcript, which might be more vulnerable to denial of service (DoS) attack. However, we stress their construction is instructive to us. Specifically, in authentication of initiator, we use a technique that if $A|C$ is not an ElGamal ciphertext of $g^{\pi_{ij}}$, then σ is uniformly random in G_q. This technique is essentially from KOY protocol with a relaxation of Cramer-Shoup ciphertext [10] to ElGamal ciphertext.

4   Security

In this section, we prove the security of our protocol.

Theorem 1. *Let Γ be the password authenticated key exchange protocol in Figure 1. Let a, b, c be polynomially related to the security parameter n. Assume $e \leftarrow \mathcal{G}enPK(1^n)$ is the public key of a CCA2 secure public key cryptosystem E; $H : \{0,1\}^* \to \{0,1\}^a$ is a collision resistant hash function uniformly taken from a family $\mathcal{H}$; p, q are large primes with $q|(p-1)$; $\mathcal{F}$ is a pseudorandom function family from $\{0,1\}^b$ to $\{0,1\}^c$; G_q is the (unique) multiplicative subgroup of order q in F_p^*; g, h are random generators of G_q. Then under DDH assumption, protocol Γ is secure.*

Proof. Define $\mathbf{sid}_i^{l_i}$ to be the whole transcript seen by instance $\Pi_i^{l_i}$. Assume $\Pi_i^{l_i}$ and $\Pi_j^{l_j}$ are partnered and both accept. Then, $\mathbf{pid}_i^{l_i}$ and $\mathbf{pid}_j^{l_j}$ are consistent and the messages are faithfully exchanged. Thus, P_i and P_j derive the same σ: $\sigma = \mu^x = A^{\lambda_1} C'^{\lambda_2}$. Thus, the correctness follows.

In the rest, we concentrate on the proof of the privacy condition. We look the protocol execution as a game between a simulator and an adversary $\mathcal{A}$. The simulator picks large prime p, q with $q|(p-1)$ and takes $g \leftarrow G_q, u \leftarrow Z_q$, $(e, d) \leftarrow \mathcal{G}en(1^n)(= (\mathcal{G}enPK, \mathcal{G}enSK)(1^n))$, $\mathcal{F}$ a pseudorandom function family from $\{0,1\}^b$ to $\{0,1\}^c$ and H uniformly from a family of a collision resistant hash function (CRHF). He lets $h = g^u$. Then he sets the public parameters as $g, h, H, \mathcal{F}, e, p, q$ and assigns passwords to parties as in the real protocol. He simulates the protocol execution with adversary $\mathcal{A}$.

We construct a sequence of slightly modified protocols $\Gamma_1, \Gamma_2, \cdots$ from Γ and show that the success probability of $\mathcal{A}$ in Γ_i is no less than that in Γ_{i-1} except for a negligible gap for any $i \geq 1$, where $\Gamma_0 := \Gamma$. And then we bound the success probability of $\mathcal{A}$ in the last variant. Before our actual proof, *we assume that in response to any oracle query, the basic validity check in its definition has already been successfully verified thus the output is never $\perp$.*

For given two parties P_i and P_j with common password π_{ij}, we say $A|C$ is *inconsistent* if $\log_g A \neq \log_h Cg^{-\pi_{ij}}$. We first introduce the following simple fact, where the proof is mainly due to the fact that λ_1, λ_2 are both uniform in Z_q (independent of anything else).

Fact 1. *If $A|C$ is inconsistent, then σ is uniformly random in G_q, given $A|C|\mu$ where σ and μ are derived according to the responsor's execution.*

Game Γ_1. Now we modify Γ_0 to Γ_1 with the only difference in **Execute** query, where C in Γ_1 is chosen uniformly random. Using a hybrid argument or a better proof similar to Lemma 2 in [17], both with reduction to DDH assumption, we have

Lemma 1. *Under DDH assumption in G_q, the success probabilities of $\mathcal{A}$ in Γ and Γ_1 are negligibly close.*

Game Γ_2. We modify Γ_1 to Γ_2 with only difference in **Execute** queries where r, τ and $sk_i^{l_i}(= sk_j^{l_j})$ in any **Execute**(i, l_i, j, l_j) are chosen uniformly random from

$\{0,1\}^{3c}$. Note $A|C$ is inconsistent in **Execute** queries of Γ_1 (and Γ_2) except for a negligible probability. By **Fact 1**, one can conclude the following lemma using a standard hybrid argument with reduction to the pseudorandomness of $\mathcal{F}$.

Lemma 2. *The success probabilities of $\mathcal{A}$ in Γ_1 and Γ_2 are negligibly close.*

Game Γ_3. Now we modify Γ_2 to Γ_3 with the only difference in computing ω in **Execute** query, where Simulator picks $C^* \leftarrow G_q$ randomly and defines $\omega = E_e(H(\mu|A|C^*|P_j|P_i); r)$ instead of a ciphertext of $\Sigma = H(\mu|A|C'|P_j|P_i)$. Here r is uniformly random (as in Γ_2). By a standard hybrid argument with reduction to the semantic security[2] of cryptosystem E (note the challenge template should be set according to the above modification), we have the following lemma.

Lemma 3. *The success probabilities of $\mathcal{A}$ in Γ_2 and Γ_3 are negligibly close.*

Game Γ_4. Till now, we have finished modifying **Execute** oracle. Next, let us consider **Send** oracle. Before that, we introduce some notations. We say that a message is *adversary-generated* if it is not exactly equal to the output of a **Send** oracle or a *Flow* in a response of an **Execute** oracle; otherwise, we say it is an *oracle-generated* message. Consider any query **Send**$(2, i, l_i, \mu|\omega|P_j)$. If there *exists* **Send**$(1, j, l_j, A|C|P_i)$ such that it outputs $\mu|\omega|P_j$ and that $A|C|P_i$ is exactly the output of **Send**$(0, i, l_i, null)$, then we say that **Send**$(2, i, l_i, \mu|\omega|P_j)$ *matches* with **Send**$(1, j, l_j, A|C|P_i)$; otherwise, we say that a *none-match* event happens to **Send**$(2, i, l_i, \mu|\omega|P_j)$. Now we modify Γ_3 to Γ_4 with the only difference: upon any query **Send**$(2, i, l_i, \mu|\omega|P_j)$, if a *none-match event* happens to it (note Simulator can check this since it controls all the oracles), then deciding accept/reject only depends on whether ω can be decrypted to $\Sigma = H(\mu|A|C'|P_j|P_i)$ or not, where $A|C|$ is in the output of **Send**$(0, i, l_i, null)$ and $C' = Cg^{-\pi_{ij}}$. If it accepts in this case, it announces the success of $\mathcal{A}$ and halts. Note in case of a *match event* it responses as in Γ_3.

Lemma 4. *The success probability of $\mathcal{A}$ in Γ_4 is no less than that in Γ_3.*

Proof. Note in case of a none-match event, if **Send**$(2, i, l_i, \mu|\omega|P_j)$ in Γ_4 rejects, then it rejects in Γ_3 too. Therefore, before a none-match event is accepted in Γ_4, adversary view in Γ_4 is identically distributed as that in Γ_3. On the other hand, an accepted none-match event in Γ_4 already announces the success of $\mathcal{A}$. Thus, the conclusion follows.   □

Game Γ_5. Now we modify Γ_4 to Γ_5 such that C in any **send**$(0, i, l_i, null)$ is taken uniformly random from G_q. In order of consistency (in view of $\mathcal{A}$), we need to take care of other oracle definitions. **Send**$(1, j, l_j, M)$ remains unchanged. Since there does not exist x in $A|C$ such that the normal action can be executed, **Send**$(2, i, l_i, A|C|P_j)$ is modified as follows.

i) If there exists a unique l_j such that **Send**$(2, i, l_i, \mu|\omega|P_j)$ matches with **Send**$(1, j, l_j, M)$, then it *accepts* (without verification of ω) and computes

---

[2] Here semantic security suffices and CCA2 security will be required later to deal with **Send** oracle.

$\tau = F_\sigma(2)$ using σ defined in **Send**$(1, j, l_j, M)$. Then, he outputs τ and defines the session key $sk_i^{l_i} = F_\sigma(1)$. If there are two or more $l_j, l'_j, \cdots$ such that the above match event holds simultaneously (in the future, we call it a *multi-match* event), then it chooses one match randomly and follows the same procedure.

ii) If a none-match event happens to **Send**$(2, i, l_i, \mu|\omega|P_j)$, then it responses as in Γ_4 (i.e. it decrypts ω, and decides to announce the success of $\mathcal{A}$ or to reject).

The **Send**$(3, j, l_j, M)$ answers normally. The rest oracles remain unchanged (note the validity follows from the fact that their actions do not depend on the above modification).

Lemma 5. *The success probabilities of $\mathcal{A}$ in Γ_4 and Γ_5 are negligibly close.*

Proof. To relate Γ_4 and Γ_5, we define a slightly modified Γ_4 as Γ'_4. The only difference is that in case of a *match event* in Γ'_4, **Send**$(2, i, l_i, \mu|\omega|P_i)$ responses as i) in definition of Γ_5. On the one hand, if l_j is always unique (whenever a match event happens), then adversary views in Γ_4 and Γ'_4 are identically distributed since a unique match event is always accepted in Γ_4. On the other hand, the probability that a multi-match event happens throughout the simulation is negligible since μ is uniform in G_q. Thus, the success probabilities of $\mathcal{A}$ in Γ_4 and Γ'_4 are negligibly close. Notice that executions of Games Γ'_4 and Γ_5 are different only in that C is real or random. Thus, if the conclusion were wrong, a standard hybrid argument directly would reduce to break DDH assumption, a contradiction. Details are omitted.   □

Game Γ_6. Now we modify Γ_5 to Γ_6 with the only difference in oracle **Send**$(1, j, l_j, A|C|P_i)$. If $A|C$ is consistent: $C = A^u g^{\pi_{ij}}$, it announces the success of adversary $\mathcal{A}$ and exits (recall Simulator knows $u := \log_g h$; recall normally $C \neq A^u g^{\pi_{ij}}$ since C is chosen uniformly random in oracle **Send**$(0, *, *, null)$); otherwise, it answers normally (as in Γ_5). The rest oracle definitions remain unchanged as in Γ_5. Note this modification only increases the success probability of $\mathcal{A}$. Indeed, if $A|C$ is always inconsistent, then the adversary view in Γ_6 is identically distributed as in Γ_5; otherwise, $\mathcal{A}$ already succeeds in Γ_6. Thus, we have

Lemma 6. *The success probability of $\mathcal{A}$ in Γ_6 is no less than that in Γ_5.*

Game Γ_7. Γ_7 is modified from Γ_6 as follows. In order to answer oracle **Send**$(1, j, l_j, A|C|P_j)$ in Γ_7, Simulator chooses σ uniformly random from G_q instead of $A^{\lambda_1} C'^{\lambda_2}$. Other oracle definitions remain unchanged as in Γ_6 (here the validity is due to the fact that the state information λ_1, λ_2 is not required in these oracle definitions).

Lemma 7. *The success probabilities of $\mathcal{A}$ in Γ_6 and Γ_7 are equal.*

Proof. Whenever σ is defined in Γ_6 (and Γ_7), this implies that $\mathcal{A}$ is not announced to succeed in **Send**$(1, j, l_j, A|C|P_i)$ and thus $A|C$ is inconsistent. Thus, from **Fact 1**, the adversary view in Γ_6 and Γ_7 is identically distributed. The conclusion follows immediately.   □

Game Γ_8. Now we modify Γ_7 to Γ_8 with the only difference: $(r, \tau, sk_i^{l_i})$ in **Send** oracles are chosen uniformly random from $\{0,1\}^{3c}$, which is the range of $\mathcal{F}$. Details are as follows. Whenever any **Send**$(1, j, l_j, A|C|P_i)$ is called, Simulator follows the oracle definition in Γ_7 except r is random in $\{0,1\}^c$. When any **Send**$(2, i, l_i, \mu|\omega|P_j)$ oracle is called, Simulator responses as in $\Gamma_5 - \Gamma_7$ with the following exception: in case of a match event, $\tau, sk_i^{l_i}$ are taken uniformly random in $\{0,1\}^c$ and furthermore he saves tuple $(\mu, \tau, sk_i^{l_i}, i, j)$ in his memory. Whenever any **Send**$(3, j, l_j, \tau')$ is called, Simulator searches for $(\tau, *, *, *, j)$ in his memory. If a unique tuple is found, then it recovers $(\tau, sk_i^{l_i}, i)$ from this tuple and checks whether $\tau' = \tau$. If it holds, **Send**$(3, j, l_j, \tau')$ accepts and concludes the session key $sk_j^{l_j} := sk_i^{l_i}$. If more than one such a tuple are found, then it chooses one randomly and follows the same procedure. Otherwise, if either of the above two checks (i.e., search and comparison) fails, it rejects. The rest oracle definitions (**Reveal, Test, Execute**) remain unchanged (the validity follows since such definitions are independent of the way **Send** chooses $(r, \tau, sk_i^{l_i})$).

Lemma 8. *The success probabilities of $\mathcal{A}$ in Γ_7 and Γ_8 are negligibly close.*

Proof Sketch. Consider a slightly modified Γ_7, denoted as Γ_7'. Oracle definitions in Game Γ_7' are identical to those in Γ_8 except that $(r, \tau, sk_i^{l_i}(= sk_j^{l_j}))$ is computed as $F_\sigma(3), F_\sigma(2), F_\sigma(1)$. We show that the success probabilities of $\mathcal{A}$ in Γ_7 and Γ_7' are negligibly close. Indeed, for **Send**$(1, *, *, *)$ and **Send**$(2, *, *, *)$, adversary views in Γ_7' and Γ_7 are identical since their *outgoing* messages are computed from the same definitions. In the full paper [11], we show that **Send** $(3, j, l_j, \tau')$ in Γ_7' can be answered consistently with Γ_7 except for a negligible probability.

   Other oracle definitions in Γ_7' and Γ_7 are identical. Thus, the success probabilities of $\mathcal{A}$ in Γ_7 and Γ_7' are negligibly close. Furthermore, the success probabilities of $\mathcal{A}$ in Γ_7' and Γ_8 are negligibly close, because their executions are identical only except that $(r, \tau, sk_i^{l_i})$ in Γ_8 are taken uniformly random and thus a standard hybrid argument with reduction to the pseudorandomness of $\mathcal{F}$ can be applied. □

Game Γ_9. Γ_8 is modified to Γ_9 so that ω in **Send**$(1, j, l_j, A|C|P_i)$ is defined as $E_e[\Sigma'; r]$, where r is uniform in $\{0,1\}^c$ and $\Sigma' = H(\mu|A|C^*|P_j|P_i)$ for $C^* \leftarrow G_q$. The rest oracles are unchanged. We have the following result.

Lemma 9. *The success probabilities of $\mathcal{A}$ in Γ_8 and Γ_9 are negligibly close.*

Proof Sketch. We define $\Gamma_8^{(l)}$ to be the variant of Γ_8 such that the first l **Send**$(1, *, *, *)$ queries are answered according to Γ_9 and the rest queries are answered according to Γ_8. It follows $\Gamma_8^{(0)} = \Gamma_8$ and $\Gamma_8^{(\eta_9)} = \Gamma_9$, where η_9 is the upperbound of number of queries **Send**$(1, *, *, *)$. If the success gap in Γ_8 and Γ_9 were non-negligible, then there would exist $z \in \{1, \cdots, \eta_9\}$ such that the success gap between $\Gamma_8^{(z-1)}$ and $\Gamma_8^{(z)}$ would be non-negligible. We build a CCA2 breaker $\mathcal{D}_9$ for E_e as follows. He takes l randomly from $\{1, \cdots, \eta_9\}$ and initializes public parameters as done by Simulator except e provided by his challenger. Then, $\mathcal{D}_9$ simulates $\Gamma_8^{(l)}$ except for the lth $\mathbf{Send}(1, *, *, *)$ query, say $\mathbf{Send}(1, j, l_j, A|C|P_i)$. In this case, he computes Σ and gives $(\Sigma, \mu|A|P_j|G_q)$ to his encryption oracle, requesting that a random message has a pattern $\Sigma' = H(\mu|A|C^*|P_j|P_i)$ for $C^* \leftarrow G_q$. Then, he will receive ω^*, that is an encryption of either Σ or a random message Σ' of that pattern. $\mathbf{Send}(1, j, l_j, A|C|P_i)$ outputs $\mu|\omega^*|P_j$. Different from Simulator, $\mathcal{D}_9$ does not have a private key d for E. In the full paper, we show that any $\mathbf{Send}(2, s, l_s, \mu'|\omega'|P_t)$ can be consistently answered except for a negligible error probability.

The rest oracles are answered normally as in Γ_8 (or Γ_9) since no decryption is required any more. Thus, in case ω^* is a ciphertext of Σ, then adversary view in the simulation is negligibly close to that in $\Gamma_8^{(l-1)}$; otherwise it is negligibly close to $\Gamma_8^{(l)}$. Thus, a correct guess for z, which is non-negligible, immediately implies non-negligible advantage of $\mathcal{D}_9$, a contradiction. $\square$

Bounding Success Probability in Γ_9. Now let us consider protocol Γ_9. The adversary succeeds only possibly (1) at $\mathbf{Send}(1, j, l_j, A|C|P_i)$ where he inputs a consistent ElGamal ciphertext $A|C$, or (2) at oracle $\mathbf{Send}(2, i, l_i, \mu|\omega|P_j)$ where a none-match event occurs, but the oracle decrypts ω to $\Sigma = H(\mu|A|C''|P_j|P_i)$, or (3) at $\mathbf{Send}(3, j, l_j, \tau)$, where the oracle accepts but τ is not the output by a $\mathbf{Send}(2, i, l_i, *)$ that is matched to $\mathbf{Send}(1, j, l_j, *)$, or (4) at $\mathbf{Test}$ query. Here we stress that mutual authentication in Definition 1 is fully covered by (2) and (3). For case (3), since τ will be compared with the value in the memory, success here happens only when there are two $\mathbf{Send}(2, *, *, *)$ that match with $\mathbf{Send}(1, j, l_j, *)$. This implies that $\exists$ two $\mathbf{Send}(0, *, *, null)$ generate the same output. This happens with only negligible probability since A is uniform in G_q. We thus only consider cases (1), (2), and (4). We say the adversary attempt to succeed in cases (1) (2) is an impersonation trial, denoted by $\mathbf{ITri}$. In case (1), no input can be successful in two protocol executions with different password candidates (recall that $D = \{1, \cdots, N\}$ with $N < q$). In case (2), no input can be accepted with non-negligible probability in two password candidates (otherwise, we can break H in two steps: Step 1. Simulate the protocol execution and record all the events in case (2); Step 2. Check whether the collision in case (2) happens by trying to find two passwords that accept some recorded event simultaneously)[3]. Thus, we assume each input at case (1) or (2) can be accepted by at most one password candidate. Notice that just before $\mathbf{ITri}$ happens, the adversary view in Γ_9 is completely independent of password. Thus, immediately after the first $\mathbf{ITri}$ is rejected, the adversary view is distributed identically among a password dictionary of size at least $|D| - 1$. The reason is: it has the same reject

---

[3] Here in order for our attack to be polynomial time, we use the fact that $|D|$ is polynomially bounded. If $|D|$ is super polynomial, although it is not the setting for password KE protocol, a similar conclusion holds, see the full paper [11].

event for at least $|D| - 1$ password candidates. Furthermore, using a simple induction, we have the probability that the first l **ITri** events are rejected but it succeeds in $l + 1$th **ITri** event is $\frac{1}{|D|-l} \prod_{i=1}^{l}(1 - \frac{1}{|D|-(i-1)}) = \frac{1}{|D|}$. Thus, suppose the number of **Send** queries is upperbounded by Q_{send}. Then the success in **ITri** happens with probability at most $\frac{Q_{send}}{|D|}$ except for a negligible gap. Now we consider case (4), this success event happens only if the success event in **ITri** does not happen. In this case, since the session key is chosen uniformly random independent of anything else. Thus, the success probability is exactly $\frac{1}{2}$ except that the session key was seen at a previous moment, which is only possible by **Reveal** query. Note the test session is not allowed to issue **Reveal** query. We show the revealed session must be its partnered session, which is not allowed by definition. To this end, let $\Pi_i^{l_i}$ be the test session with $\mathbf{pid}_i^{l_i} = P_j$. Since $\mathbf{Send}(2, i, l_i, *)$ accepts with $sk_i^{l_i}$ derived, there must exist a matched $\mathbf{Send}(1, j, l_j, *)$ and a tuple $(\mu, \tau, sk_i^{l_i}, i, j)$ is stored in the memory. And later only $\mathbf{Send}(3, j, l'_j, \tau')$ with μ in the output of $\mathbf{Send}(1, j, l'_j, M)$ will access this tuple and define $sk_j^{l'_j} = sk_i^{l_i}$. Note in this case, $l_j = l'_j$ except for a negligible probability since μ is uniform in G_q. The exchanged messages seen by $\Pi_i^{l_i}$ and $\Pi_j^{l_j}$ (unique except for negligible probability) are identical by definition of *match*, and they see the same τ (as in the tuple). Thus, $\mathbf{pid}_i^{l_i} = P_j$, $\mathbf{pid}_j^{l_j} = P_i$ and $\mathbf{sid}_i^{l_i} = \mathbf{sid}_j^{l_j}$. That is, they are partnered sessions.

As a summary, the success probability of adversary in **Test** session is exactly $\frac{1}{2}$. Let α be the probability of **ITri** event. Then the total success probability of adversary is $\alpha + (1 - \alpha)\frac{1}{2} \leq \frac{1}{2} + \frac{Q_{send}}{2|D|}$.

Proof of Theorem 1. Summarizing the results in Lemmas 1- 9 and success probability of $\mathcal{A}$ in Γ_9, we have $\mathbf{Adv}(\mathcal{A}) < \frac{Q_{send}}{|D|} + \mathbf{negl}(n)$.   ♠

Acknowledgement. The authors would like to thank anonymous referees for valuable comments. S. Jiang would like to thank Mihir Bellare for kind response upon query on mutual authentication, and he especially feels grateful to David Pointcheval for an instructive discussion on the definition of mutual authentication.

References

1. Mihir Bellare, Ran Canetti, and Hugo Krawczyk, A Modular Approach to the Design and Analysis of Authentication and Key Exchange Protocols, *STOC 98*: 419-428.
2. Mihir Bellare, David Pointcheval, Phillip Rogaway: Authenticated Key Exchange Secure against Dictionary Attacks. *EUROCRYPT 2000*: 139-155.
3. Mihir Bellare, Phillip Rogaway: Entity Authentication and Key Distribution. *CRYPTO 1993*: 232-249.
4. Bellovin, S.M.; Merritt, M., Encrypted key exchange: password-based protocols secure against dictionary attacks, *IEEE S&P'92*, 72-84.

5. Steven M. Bellovin, Michael Merritt: Augmented Encrypted Key Exchange: A Password-Based Protocol Secure against Dictionary Attacks and Password File Compromise. *ACM CCS'93*: 244-250.
6. Simon Blake-Wilson, Don Johnson, Alfred Menezes: Key Agreement Protocols and Their Security Analysis. *IMA Int. Conf.* 1997: 30-45.
7. Victor Boyko, Philip D. MacKenzie, Sarvar Patel: Provably Secure Password-Authenticated Key Exchange Using Diffie-Hellman. *EUROCRYPT 2000*: 156-171.
8. Ran Canetti and Hugo Krawczyk, Analysis of Key-Exchange Protocols and Their Use for Building Secure Channels, *Eurocrypt 2001*: 453-474.
9. Ran Canetti, Oded Goldreich, Shai Halevi: The Random Oracle Methodology, Revisited (Preliminary Version). *STOC 1998*: 209-218.
10. Ronald Cramer, Victor Shoup: A Practical Public Key Cryptosystem Provably Secure Against Adaptive Chosen Ciphertext Attack. *CRYPTO 1998*: 13-25.
11. Shaoquan Jiang and Guang Gong, Password Based Key Exchange with Mutual Authentication, Available at http://calliope.uwaterloo.ca/~jiangshq/
12. W. Diffie, P.C. van Oorschot, and M.J. Wiener, Authentication and Authenticated Key Exchanges, *Designs, Codes and Cryptography,* vol. 2, no. 2, 1992, pp. 107-125.
13. Rosario Gennaro, Yehuda Lindell: A Framework for Password-Based Authenticated Key Exchange. *EUROCRYPT 2003*: 524-543.
14. Oded Goldreich, Yehuda Lindell: Session-Key Generation Using Human Passwords Only. *CRYPTO 2001*: 408-432.
15. Shai Halevi, Hugo Krawczyk: Public-Key Cryptography and Password Protocols. *ACM CCS'98*: 122-131.
16. David P. Jablon, Extended Password Key Exchange Protocols Immune to Dictionary Attacks. *WETICE 1997*: 248-255.
17. Jonathan Katz, Rafail Ostrovsky, Moti Yung: Efficient Password-Authenticated Key Exchange Using Human-Memorable Passwords. *EUROCRYPT 2001*: 475-494.
18. Stefan Lucks, Open Key Exchange: How to Defeat Dictionary Attacks Without Encrypting Public Keys. *Security Protocols Workshop* 1997: 79-90.
19. Alfred Menezes, Paul C. van Oorschot, Scott A. Vanstone: *Handbook of Applied Cryptography*. CRC Press 1996.

Product Construction of Key Distribution Schemes for Sensor Networks

Reizhong Wei and Jiang Wu

Department of Computer Science, Lakehead University,
Thunder Bay, Ontario P7B 5E1, Canada
wei@ccc.cs.lakeheadu.ca
jwu1@lakeheadu.ca

Abstract. Wireless sensor networks are composed of a large number of randomly deployed sensor nodes with limited computing ability and memory space. These characteristics give rise to much challenge to key agreement. General key agreement schemes like KDC, PKI and the Diffie-Hellman key exchange schemes are not applicable to sensor networks. Recently several key distribution schemes have been proposed specifically for sensor networks, aimed to provide high connectivity and resilience while keeping low memory usage in the sensor nodes. In this paper, we formularize and analyze these methods, and deduce general conditions for a scheme to be optimal in terms of connectivity, resilience and memory usage. The result provides guideline to design optimal schemes. Based on the result, we proposed 2 schemes that can achieve optimal connectivity and resilience with the restriction of memory space.

1 Introduction

A distributed sensor network is composed of a large number of sensor nodes that are densely deployed. The position of sensor nodes usually are not predetermined. This allows random deployment in inaccessible terrains or disaster relief operations. This means that sensor network protocols and algorithms must possess self-organizing capabilities. In general, a sensor node is battery powered and equipped with integrated sensors, data processing capabilities, and short-range radio communications. Examples of sensor network protocols include SmartDust [9] and WINS [1]. There is a wide range of applications for sensor networks. Some examples of the application areas are health, military, and smart environment (see, e.g., [2]).

To secure communications for a sensor network is extremely important, as the network is prone to different types of malicious attacks when it is deployed in a hostile environment. An adversary can compromise sensor nodes much easier than to compromise computers. However, since the limitation in both the memory resources and computing capacity of a sensor node, it is impractical to use public-key cryptosystems to secure sensor networks. Using a traditional Internet style key exchange and key distribution protocols based on trusted third parties are also impractical.

H. Handschuh and A. Hasan (Eds.): SAC 2004, LNCS 3357, pp. 280–293, 2005.

To solve the key management problem for sensor networks, several researchers considered special key pre-distribution schemes. In [7], Eschnauer and Gligor used random methods to distribute keys. In their scheme, each sensor node received a random subset of keys from a large key pool before deployment. Any two nodes able to find one common key within their respective subsets can use that key as their shared secret to initiate communication. Some theory of random graphs was used to analyze their scheme. Based on this scheme, Chan, Perrig and Song in [4] proposed a q-composite random key pre-distribution scheme. In their scheme, q common key instead of just one common key are used to establish secure communications between two nodes, which increases the security (resilience) of the network. Recently, Du, Deng, Han and Varshney in [6] and Liu and Ning in [10] used a new method to construct key distribution schemes, which we will call it product construction. In their method, they combined traditional pairwise key distribution scheme with other schemes to construct new key distribution schemes. Their methods improved network resilience comparing to previous key pre-distribution schemes. The purpose of this paper is to formularize and analyze their methods in order to optimize this method. Upon these analysis, some combinatorial methods are then used to improve their constructions.

When we design a key distribution scheme for a distributed sensor network, the following key characteristics of the design must be considered.

- *Small key size*: Since the limited resource of a sensor node, key storage should be small. For example, if there are b nodes in the network, then we cannot expect that a node can store $b - 1$ keys to share a secrete key with each of the other nodes.
- *Resilience of the network*: Even quite a large amount of sensor nodes are compromised by an adversary, the communications among other nodes should be still secure. In other words, a coalition of certain number of sensor nodes cannot compute other secrete keys used by other sensor nodes.
- *Local connectivity*: A sensor node should be able to securely communicate with its local neighbors. Here a local neighbor means a sensor node physically located within transmission range.
- *Global connectivity*: Any two nodes of the sensor network are connected. So for any two nodes u and v in the network, there are notes $c_1, c_2 \cdots c_t$ such that u and c_1 share a secret key, c_i and c_{i+1} share a secret key for $i = 1, \cdots, t - 1$ and c_t and v share a secret key.

We will only consider schemes satisfying all these properties. The main contributions of this paper are as follows. First we use a uniformed method to generalize the methods used in [6, 10]. We define a product of a key distribution scheme and a set system and use that definition to construct new key distribution schemes. Then we use combinatorial methods to analyze the product construction and give some necessary conditions to optimize the product construction. Finally, we propose new constructions which meet all of these necessary conditions.

The rest of this paper is organized as follows. Section 2 defines production construction. In Section 3, set system used in the production construction is analyzed using combinatorial methods. Section 4 describes our proposed schemes which is then compared with the previous schemes. Section 5 concludes the paper.

2   Product Construction

In this section, we give a generalized description of the schemes in [6] and [10], which used a similar method to construct key pre-distribution schemes for sensor networks. We start with a definition of a *pairwise key pre-distribution scheme*.

Definition 1. A pairwise key pre-distribution scheme D is a triple $(\mathcal{U}, \mathcal{F}, \mathcal{K})$, where $\mathcal{U}$ is a set of nodes, $\mathcal{F}$ is a set of algorithms and $\mathcal{K}$ is a set of keys, which satisfies the following conditions:

1. For each $u \in \mathcal{U}$ an $f_u \in \mathcal{F}$ is assigned to u;
2. For any $u, v \in \mathcal{U}$ there is a unique key $K_{u,v} \in \mathcal{K}$ shared between u and v, which can be obtained from f_u and from f_v;
3. For any other $w \in \mathcal{U}$, no information about $K_{u,v}$ can be obtained by f_w.

The above definition shows that we are considering unconditional secure schemes (not for computational secure ones).

If a pairwise key pre-distribution scheme has the property that even λ nodes are compromised the system is still secure, then we say that the scheme is λ-secure, or the scheme is λ resilience. More formally, in a λ-secure pairwise key pre-distribution scheme, for any $w_1, w_2, \cdots, w_\lambda \in \mathcal{U}, K_{u,v}$ cannot be computed by $f_{w_1}, f_{w_2}, \cdots, f_{w_\lambda}$ where u, v are different from $w_1, w_2 \cdots, w_\lambda$.

Note that it is not necessary to use a pairwise key pre-distribution scheme to a sensor network, because even two nodes shared a common key, they may not be able to communicate each other when their distance is beyond transmission range. For a sensor network, local communications are more important. So we will consider both the local connectivity and the global connectivity of a key distribution scheme for our purpose.

An example of λ-secure key pre-distribution scheme is the Blom's scheme [3] in which each node stores $\lambda + 1$ keys.

The Blom's scheme can be described as follows. Suppose there are b nodes $u_1, u_2, \cdots, u_b$ in a network. To distribute keys, an *authorized center* (AC) chooses a random bivariate symmetric polynomial in a finite field $GF(q)$:

$$f(x,y) = \sum_{i=0}^{\lambda} \sum_{j=0}^{\lambda} a_{i,j} x^i y^j,$$

where $a_{i,j} = a_{j,i}$. Then the CA gives $P_i(x) = f(x, i)$ to u_i as its personal key. The common key between u_i and u_j is $P_i(j) = P_j(i) = f(i, j)$. It is proved using a linear algebra method that a Blom's scheme is λ-secure.

To formularize the methods used in [6, 10], we need some concepts from combinatorics which we introduce below.

A *set system* S is a pair $(X, \mathcal{B})$ where X is a set of points and $\mathcal{B}$ is a collection of k-subsets (called blocks) of X. For our purpose, same blocks are allowed in a set system.

Suppose there is a map from the set of nodes $\mathcal{U}$ to the set of blocks $\mathcal{B}$ of a set system so that for a $u_i \in \mathcal{U}$ there is a unique $B_i \in \mathcal{B}$ corresponding to it. Then we can define a product of D and S as follows.

Definition 2. Suppose $D = (\mathcal{U}, \mathcal{F}, \mathcal{K})$ is a pairwise key pre-distribution scheme and $S = (X, \mathcal{B})$ is a set system, where $|\mathcal{B}| \geq |\mathcal{U}|$. Suppose there is also a map from $\mathcal{U}$ to $\mathcal{B}$ such that a $u_i \in \mathcal{U}$ is mapped to a $B_i \in \mathcal{B}$. A product of D and S, $D \times S$, is defined as a triple $(\mathcal{U}, \mathcal{F} \times \mathcal{B}, \mathcal{K} \times X)$ such that the algorithm assigned to u_i is $f_{u_i} \times B_i$.

The method used in [6] and [10] for key establishment of sensor networks actually is the above product method. Both of the papers used Blom's scheme as D. [10] proposed two set systems. One is random subset assignment. In this assignment, each node gains a random τ-subset of X, so $\mathcal{B}$ contains u random τ-subsets (by this setting, repeated blocks are allowed). The other proposed set system in [10] is grid-based system. In this system, $X = M_1 \cup M_2 \cup \cdots \cup M_t$, where $M_1, M_2, \cdots M_t$ are disjoint m-sets for $m \geq u^{1/t}$. The set $\mathcal{B}$ contains all the blocks from $\{(i_1, i_2, \cdots, i_t) : i_1 \in M_1, \cdots, i_t \in M_t\}$. [6] used the random subset assignment.

As an example, in the following we give a brief description of the random subset assignment used in both [6] and [10].

To distribute keys, the AC chooses a set X where $|X| = v$. Then for each element $i \in X$, the AC generates a random symmetric polynomial $f_i(x, y)$ as in a Blom's scheme. So v polynomials are generated. For a node $u_j \in \mathcal{U}$, the AC chooses a random k-subset of X. Denote the subset as $B = \{i_1, i_2, \cdots, i_k\}$. The keys given to u_j are $f_{i_s}(x, j)$, for $1 \leq s \leq k$. The choice of v and k depends on the connectivity of the network. To form a secret key between u_i and u_j, they will try to find a common element in the subset assigned to them. If they found the element, say i_0, then the secret key is $f_{i_0}(i, j)$.

Sometimes we also can view the product construction as using different copies of a pairwise key distribution scheme D and denote it as $D \times X$. So (D, i) will be used to denote the ith scheme. It's also called a *key space* in this paper.

The main purpose of using a set system is to add resilience of the key distribution scheme. However, [6] and [10] only discussed the specific set systems used in their schemes. In next section, we will discuss how a set system effects the resilience and connectivity of the product scheme in general.

3   Analysis of the Set System

For a better key pre-distribution system, we should consider several things: the resilience of the system, the storage space requested for a node, the connectivity of the network, etc. Basically, the storage space requested for a node depends on the size of a block in the set system. In this section, we discuss how the set system used in the product construction effects the resilience and connectivity of the network if the size of block is fixed.

3.1   Resilience

Suppose the resilience of the original key pre-distribution scheme D is λ. When a set system S is used in the product construction, we need to consider the probability that one of the schemes in the product system $D \times S$ is broken. For example we consider the probability that $(D, 1)$ is broken (We denote this event as D_1). Let p_j^1 denote the probability that exact j blocks out of s blocks contain 1. Let C_s denote the event that s nodes were compromised. Then we have

$$Pr(D_1|C_s) = \sum_{j=\lambda+1}^{s} p_j^1. \tag{1}$$

Therefore we want to keep p_j^1 as small as possible. On the other hand, since D_i and D_j are independent and we want the probability that any space is broken as small as possible, we have the following result about the structure of D, which gives some necessary condition for D.

Theorem 1. *In a product scheme $D \times S$, suppose D, the size of X, the size of $\mathcal{B}$ and the size of a block are fixed. Then each element of X should appear in equal number of blocks to keep the optimal resilience of the scheme.*

Proof. Suppose all the parameters of the set system mentioned in the theorem are fixed. Let $b = |\mathcal{B}|$, k be the size of a block. Suppose $X = \{1, 2, \cdots, v\}$ and $i \in X$ appears in r_i blocks. Then the probability that exact j out of s blocks contain i is

$$p_j^i = \frac{\binom{r_i}{j}\binom{b-r_i}{s-j}}{\binom{b}{s}},$$

which depends on the value of r_i. Since $\sum_{i=1}^{v} r_i = kb$ is fixed, if there are some i such that the value of $\sum_{j=\lambda+1}^{s} p_j^i$ is small, then there must be some t such that $\sum_{j=\lambda+1}^{s} p_j^t$ is larger. That means (D, t) is easier to break.   □

In intuition, if an element in X appears in more blocks, then the corresponding key space is weaker. So we want the elements distributed evenly.

It is easy to check that the grid-based system satisfies the condition of Theorem 1 (However, we will see later that its local connectivity is not good). Theoretically, the random subset assignment also satisfies the condition of Theorem 1 in a sense of probability. However, in practice the random subset assignment may violate that condition. For example the worst case of the random subset assignment will not fit the condition of Theorem 1. So we want some deterministic method to find a set system that has even distributions of elements.

Suppose each element appears in r blocks. Then we have

$$p_j^i = \frac{\binom{r}{j}\binom{b-r}{s-j}}{\binom{b}{s}}. \tag{2}$$

Therefore the value of $Pr(D_i|C_s)$ is determined by the values of r and b.

To obtain a set system satisfying the condition of Theorem 1, we need a definition from combinatorial design theory. For general information about combinatorial design theory used in this paper, see [11].

Definition 3. *A 1-design $S_r(1, k, v)$ is a set system $(X, \mathcal{B})$ such that each element $x \in X$ is contained in exactly r blocks, where $v = |X|$, k is the block size.*

The following construction is from [11–Theorem 9.10].

Theorem 2. *There exists an $S_r(1, k, v)$ with b blocks if $b = vr/k$ is an integer.*

Proof. Let $u = \gcd(k, r)$. Then $r = ur'$ and $k = uk'$ where $\gcd(r', k') = 1$. Since $b = vr/k = vr'/k'$ and $\gcd(r', k') = 1$, it must be the case that $v \equiv 0 \pmod{k'}$. Let $v = sk'$ where s is a positive integer. Then $b = sr'$.

Let Y be a set of cardinality k', and define $X = Y \times \mathbb{Z}_s$. Let $A_1, A_2, \cdots, A_{r'}$ be r' arbitrary u-subsets of $\mathbb{Z}_s$. For $1 \leq i \leq r'$, define $B_i = Y \times A_i$. Then each B_i is a k-subset of X. Now for each B_i, we develop s blocks B_i^j as follows. Suppose $B_i = Y \times \{s_1, s_2, \cdots, s_{r'}\}$. Then for each $j, 1 \leq j \leq s - 1$, let $B_i^j = Y \times \{s_1', s_2', \cdots, s_{r'}'\}$, where $s_t' = s_t + j \pmod{s}, 1 \leq t \leq r'$. The result is an $S_r(1, k, v)$. □

When $r = \binom{v}{k}$, we have a easy way to construct a 1-design.

Theorem 3. *There exists an $S_r(1, k, v)$ for $r = \binom{v-1}{k-1}$ and $b = \binom{v}{k}$.*

Proof. Let the set of blocks contains all the k-subsets of a v-set. □

Suppose we fix $|X| = v$, and the size of block is k. Then we want each element belongs to $\frac{kb}{v}$ blocks so that the condition of Theorem 1 is satisfied. In practice, we let b be multiples of v and $r = \frac{kb}{v}$.

3.2   Connectivity

To consider the connectivity of a sensor network, we consider the graph $G(\mathcal{U}, E)$, where two nodes are connected by an edge if and only if these two nodes share at least one common secret key. Following from the method used in [7], we view a sensor network as a random graph. Since the connectivity of a random graph is a monotone property (when the number of nodes are fixed, the probability of connectivity is increasing when the number of edges is increasing), according to a theory of [8], the expected node degree d can be computed as follows:

$$d = \frac{b-1}{b}(\ln b - \ln(-\ln P_c)),$$

where $b = |\mathcal{U}|$ and P_c is the probability that the random graph is connected. Therefore the connectivity of the network depends on the degree d when the number of nodes are fixed.

In the product construction, two nodes share a common secret key if and only if their blocks have at least one common element. Suppose in the set system, each block intersects t other blocks. For a given density of sensor network deployment, if the expected value of number of neighbors is n, then $d = \frac{nt}{b}$. So we have the following result.

Lemma 1. *The connectivity of the product scheme depends on the number of blocks which share at least one element with a block in the set system.*

From Lemma 1, we know that the connectivity of the scheme from grid-based system in [10] is not good. In that system, each block intersects $tv^{1/t} - t$ other blocks. However, we will see later that using other set system will improve the connectivity of the network a lot.

Suppose $X = \{1, 2, \cdots, v\}$ and $\mathcal{B} = \{B_1, B_2, \cdots, B_b\}$. An incidence matrix of the set system $(X, \mathcal{B})$ is a $b \times v$ 0-1 matrix $A = (a_{i,j})$, where

$$a_{i,j} = \begin{cases} 1 & \text{if } j \in B_i, \\ 0 & \text{otherwise.} \end{cases}$$

Let $C = AA^T = (c_{i,j})$. Then C is a symmetric $b \times b$ matrix. Suppose each element of X appears in r blocks. Then we have $c_{i,i} = k$, $0 \leq c_{i,j} \leq k$ and

$$\sum_{i=1, i \neq j}^{b} c_{i,j} = k(r - 1). \tag{3}$$

The number of blocks which intersect block B_i equals to the number of nonzero elements in the ith row of C. So if we want to keep the local connectivity as large as possible, we need to let the number of nonzero elements in C as large as possible. In other words, we want to keep the individual $c_{i,j}$ as small as possible. In intuition, we don't want repeat blocks to avoid the case that $c_{i,j} = k$ for some $i \neq j$.

Remark 1. From (2) and (3) we can see that there is a trade-off between the resilience and connectivity of the network. For the connectivity, we want r to be large. However, when r is larger the probability that a scheme is broken is increasing.

The following result indicates that the construction of Theorem 3 is optimal.

Theorem 4. *When $b = \binom{v}{k}$, $r = \binom{v-1}{k-1}$ and $v > 2k$, the set system constructed in Theorem 3 has the largest number of intersections for a block.*

Proof. It is easy to know that a block intersects

$$I = \binom{v}{k} - \binom{v-k}{k} - 1$$

other blocks in the set system of Theorem 3. We are going to prove that if there are repeated blocks in an $S_r(1, v, k)$, then a block intersects less blocks.

Suppose there are two identical blocks. Then each element in that block appears in $r-2$ other blocks. So that block can intersect at most $I' = k(r-2)+1$ other blocks. Since $\binom{v}{k} = \frac{v}{k}\binom{v-1}{k-1}$ and $r = \binom{v-1}{k-1}$ we have

$$I = \frac{v}{k}\binom{v-1}{k-1} - \binom{v-k}{k} - 1,$$

and

$$I - I' = \frac{v-k}{k}\binom{v-1}{k-1} - \binom{v-k}{k} + 2k - 2$$

$$= \frac{(v-1)(v-2)\cdots(v-k)}{(v-k)(v-k-1)\cdots(v-2k+1)}\binom{v-k}{k} - \binom{v-k}{k} + 2k - 2$$

$$= \left(\frac{(v-1)(v-2)\cdots(v-k)}{(v-k)(v-k-1)\cdots(v-2k+1)} - 1\right)\binom{v-k}{k} + 2k - 2$$

$$> 0.$$

The conclusion follows.   □

In order to use construction of Theorem 2, we need to consider how to choose the sets $A_1, A_2, \cdots, A_{r'}$. Suppose $S \subseteq \mathbb{Z}_s$, where $\mathbb{Z}_s$ is the additive group of order s. Define the differences of S as:

$$\triangledown S = \{x - x' \pmod{s} : x, x' \in S, x \neq x'\}.$$

If an element of $\mathbb{Z}_s \setminus \{0\}$ appears t times in $\cup_i \triangledown S_i$ for some subsets S_i, then we say that the element has $t-1$ *repeatings*. The sum of the repeatings of all elements is called the repeatings of $\cup_i \triangledown S_i$.

Theorem 5. *The 1-design constructed from Theorem 2 has the largest local connectivity, if the collection*

$$\cup_{i=1}^{r'} \triangledown (A_i)$$

contains least repeatings.

Proof. If an element $g \in \mathbb{Z}_s \setminus \{0\}$ has $t-1$ repeatings in $\cup_{i=1}^{r'} \triangledown (A_i)$, then pairs (x_i, x_j) appear in t blocks, where $x_i - x_j = g$. Since each element appears in r blocks, we want to reduce the number of blocks containing a same pair of elements to maximize the number of blocks which intersect a fixed block.   □

Definition 4. *Let G be an additive abelian group of order v. A set system $(G, \mathcal{B})$ is called a (v, k, λ) difference family if every nonzero element of G occurs λ times in*

$$\cup_{B \in \mathcal{B}} \triangledown B.$$

For example, a $(13, 3, 1)$ difference family contains blocks $\{0, 1, 4\}$ and $\{0, 2, 7\}$.

There are many results about the construction of difference families in literature (see i.e., [5]). From Theorem 5 we know that we can use blocks in a (v, k, λ) difference family with smallest λ to construct 1-design and then obtain a good product scheme.

4   Proposed Schemes

Several recently proposed key distribution schemes used random distribution method [4, 6, 7, 10]. There are reasons that deterministic method should be developed as well. For example, the theoretical analysis shows scheme in [6] can provides good connectivity, resilience and memory consuming attributes to sensor networks. But the random distribution of the keys leaves open issues in practical implementation. We can view this scheme as a $D \times S$ scheme. Here S is a set system (X, B), where $X = \{A_1, A_2, \cdots, A_v\}$, $B = \{B_1, B_2, \cdots, B_b\}$, and each B_i contains k elements randomly selected from X. As we analyzed in Section 3, in a sense of probability this scheme meets Theorem 1 and 5 to achieve optimal connectivity and resilience. But in real implementation, it may produce worse result. The result also depends on the random number generating function used to generate the S set system. Different random number generators may result in different S systems. It is necessary to design a deterministic distribution scheme that always meets Theorem 1 and 5 for the purpose of real applications.

In this section we consider the construction of set systems used in the key distribution scheme. Given the scale and connectivity of the sensor networks, the memory space of each sensor node, we need to determine which set system to be used, what are the parameters of the selected set system, and how to construct the set system.

The predefined requirements and restriction on the sensor network include:

- b, the number of nodes in the sensor network,
- M, the memory space of a sensor node to store the keys,
- P_c, the probability that the random graph of the sensor nodes are connected, and
- n, the estimated number of neighbors of a sensor node after deployment.

The constructed set systems should meet the above requirements and restrictions and at the same time achieve optimal resilience. Analysis in Section 3 shows that set systems that meet Theorem 1 and 5 can obtain optimal resilience and connectivity. In the next parts we give construction using 2 such set systems.

4.1   Construction with $(v, k, 1)$ Difference Families

From Definition 4 we know that $(v, k, 1)$ Difference Families meet conditions of Theorem 1 and 5. In this subsection, we give the construction using $(v, k, 1)$ Difference Families, and analyze its performance.

First we compute $P_{connect}$, which is the probability that a pair of nodes share at least one common key space:

$$P_{connect} = \frac{b-1}{nb}(\ln b - \ln(-\ln P_c)). \tag{4}$$

Next we choose a proper $(v, k, 1)$ difference family that can provide the desired connectivity. We compute P_{vk1}, the probability that a pair of blocks from the $(v, k, 1)$ shares an element:

$$P_{vk1} = \frac{k^2(r'-1) + k(k-1)}{vr'-1},$$

where r' is the number of basic blocks of the chosen family. Also we can compute the number of blocks of the $(v, k, 1)$:

$$r = kr'$$

The following table chooses a sample collection of $(v, k, 1)$ difference families from [5] and computes their parameters:

v	k	r'	r	P_{vk1}
25	3	4	100	0.33
27	3	5	135	0.31
31	3	5	155	0.27
33	3	6	198	0.25
37	3	6	222	0.23
39	3	7	273	0.22
43	3	7	301	0.20
40	4	4	160	0.38
49	4	6	196	0.31

Usually there are more than one families whose connectivity are better than and close to $P_{connect}$. We choose the one with least blocks that is larger than b, and assign each block to a sensor node.

The third step is to construct v key spaces. We computer the security threshold λ of the key space:

$$\lambda = \left\lfloor \frac{M}{k} \right\rfloor - 1$$

The construction of the key spaces is the same as that in [6] which is equivalent to a Blom's scheme. We briefly introduce an example as follows.

1. Select a primitive element s from a finite field $GF(q)$, where q is the least prime larger than the key size, then generate the following $(\lambda+1) \times b$ matrix G:

$$G = \begin{bmatrix} 1 & 1 & 1 & 1 & 1 \\ s & s^2 & s^3 & \cdots & s^b \\ s^2 & (s^2)^2 & (s^3)^2 & \cdots & (s^b)^2 \\ \vdots & \vdots & \vdots & \cdots & \vdots \\ s^\lambda & (s^2)^\lambda & (s^3)^\lambda & \cdots & (s^b)^\lambda \end{bmatrix}$$

2. Randomly generate v symmetric matrix $D_1, \ldots, D_v$ of size $(\lambda+1) \times (\lambda+1)$, then compute the matrixes $A_i = (D_i \cdot G)^T$, for $1 \le i \le v$. Here we get v key spaces $A_1, \cdots, A_v$. Every key space is λ-secure.

Finally, the key spaces are assigned to the sensor nodes according to the blocks. For example, if a block {2,3,4} was assigned to node 5, the 5th rows of matrixes A_2, A_3 and A_4 are assigned to node 5.

We give an illustration of the resilience of the scheme using $(v, k, 1)$ (we call it $(v, k, 1)$ scheme). We use the $P_{break} = Pr(D_1|C_s)$ defined in (1) as an indication of resilience, and plot it as a function of number of compromised node in Figure 1. In the figure, M is set to 200, 3 schemes with different parameters and connectivity are shown. We see that to achieve a probability of 0.5 to break 1

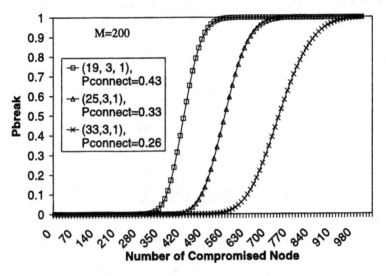

Fig. 1. Probability that one key space is broken

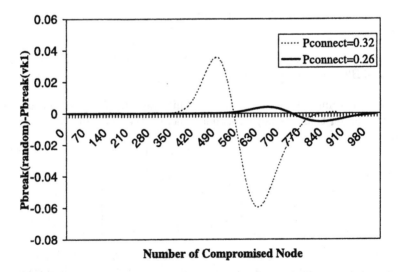

Fig. 2. Difference between P_{break} of $(v, k, 1)$ scheme and random scheme

key space, more than 200 nodes are to be compromised. The lower the $P_{connect}$ of the $(v, k, 1)$, the more compromised nodes are needed. This is the same attribute that the scheme in [6] (we call it random scheme in the following parts) provides.

Now we compare the $(v, k, 1)$ scheme with the random scheme in Figure 2. Figure 2 shows the difference between P_{break} of pairs of $(v, k, 1)$ and random schemes with same M and similar $P_{connect}$. The figure shows the difference is very small, and generally, the 2 schemes risk similar compromise possibility.

4.2   Construction Using all k-Subsets

One potential drawback of the $(v, k, 1)$ scheme is that its number of blocks is limited. So when the network size is large, we consider using all k-subsets which provides large block size easily. As proved in Theorem 3 and 4, the set system of all k-subsets meets Theorem 1 and 5, and can provide optimal connectivity and resilience. We give construction steps using that set system as follows.

First, we compute $P_{connect}$ using (4), then we need to find the v and k so that the set system meets the requirement on the scale and connectivity. The next 2 conditions need to be met:

$$P_{connect} \geq 1 - \frac{\binom{n-k}{k}}{\binom{n}{k} - 1}$$

$$b \leq \binom{v}{k}$$

The above functions produce a list of tables for v, k, $P_{connect}$ and b. From the tables, given $P_{connect}$ and b, we can get corresponding v and k. Following is a sample table for $Pconnect = 0.3$:

v	k	b
20	3	1140
21	3	1330
22	3	1540
23	3	1771

With v and k, it is easy to construct the set system of all k-subsets. For the all k-subsets scheme, the resilience is

$$P_{break} = \sum_{j=\lambda+1}^{s} \frac{\binom{d}{j}\binom{x-d}{s-j}}{\binom{x}{s}}$$

where $x = \binom{v}{k}$, $d = \binom{v-1}{k-1}$ and $\lambda = \lfloor \frac{M}{k} \rfloor - 1$.
The $P_{connect}$ of all k-subsets scheme is

$$P_{connect} = 1 - \frac{\binom{v-k}{k}}{\binom{v}{k} - 1},$$

which is very close to that of random scheme.

We compare the all k-subsets scheme with random scheme with the same v and k in Figure 3. M is set to 200 here. The figure shows the difference between P_{break} of all k-subsets and random sets is very small.

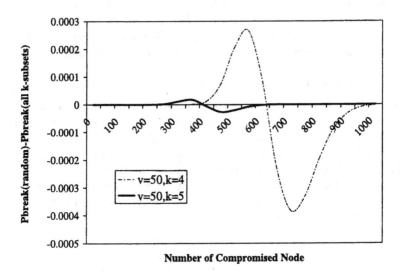

Fig. 3. Difference between P_{break} of all k-subsets and random scheme

5   Conclusion

In this paper, we introduced a generalized $D \times S$ key pre-distribution scheme for sensor networks. We deduced conditions of the set system used in the scheme that can provide optimal connectivity and resilience to the sensor network. Based on the result we analyzed some existing key pre-distribution schemes and evaluated their strength and weakness. Then we proposed 2 specific schemes and their constructions that can achieve optimal connectivity and resilience.

This paper is focused on optimal connectivity and resilience of the key distribution scheme. Another important property of the schemes is scalability. In real implementation, the scale of the sensor networks often impacts connectivity and resilience. In the future research, we are going to focus on scalability and its relationship with connectivity and resilience, and look for optimal schemes.

Acknowledgements

The authors wish to thank D.R. Stinson for informing us the construction in Theorem 2. R. Wei's research is supported by NSERC grant 239135-01.

References

1. Wireless Integrated Network Sensors, University of California,
   http://www.janet.ucla.edu/WINS.

2. I.F. Akyildiz, W. Su, Y. Sankarasugramaniam and E. Cayirci, A survey on sensor networks, IEEE Communications Magzine, 40(2002), 102-114.

3. R. Blom, An optimal class of symmetric key generation systems, Advances in Cryptology: EUROCRYP 84 (T. Beth, N. Cot and I. Ingemarsson, eds.) LNCS 209 (1985), 335-338.

4. H. Chan, A. Perrig and D. Song, Random key predistribution schemes for sensor networks, IEEE Sumposium on Research in Security and Privacy, (2003), 197-213.

5. C. J. Colbourn and J.H. Dinitz, The CRC Handbook of Combinatorial Designs, CRC Press, 1996.

6. W. Du, J. Deng, Y. S. Han and P. K. Varshney, A pairwise key pre-distribution scheme for wireless sensor networks, Proc. of the 10th ACM conf. on Computer and communications Security, (2003), 42-51.

7. L. Eschenauer and V. D. Gligor, A key-management scheme for distributed sensor networks, Proc. of the 9th ACM conf. on Computer and communications Security, (2002), 41-47.

8. Erdös and Rényi, On random graphs I. Publ.Math. Debrecen, 6(1959), 290-297.

9. J.M. Kahn, R.H. Katz and K.S.J. Pister, Next century challenges: Mobile networking for smart dust, In: Proceedings of the 5th Annual ACM/IEEE Internation Conference on Mobile Computing and Networking, (1999), 483-492.

10. D. Liu and P. Ning, Establishing pairwise keys in distributed sensor networks, Proc. of the 10th ACM conf. on Computer and communications Security, (2003), 52-61.

11. D.R. Stinson, Combinatorial Designs: Constructions and Analysis, Springer, New York, 2003.

Deterministic Key Predistribution Schemes for Distributed Sensor Networks

Jooyoung Lee[1] and Douglas R. Stinson[2]

[1] Department of Combinatorics and Optimization
[2] School of Computer Science,
University of Waterloo, Waterloo, Ontario, Canada N2L 3G1
{j3lee, dstinson}@uwaterloo.ca

Abstract. It is an important issue to establish pairwise keys in distributed sensor networks (DSNs). In this paper, we present two key predistribution schemes (KPSs) for DSNs, ID-based one-way function scheme (IOS) and deterministic multiple space Blom's scheme (DMBS). Our schemes are deterministic, while most existing schemes are based on randomized approach. We show that the performance of our schemes is better than other existing schemes in terms of resiliency against coalition attack. In addition we obtain perfectly resilient KPSs such that the maximum supportable network size is larger than random pairwise keys schemes.

1 Introduction

Distributed sensor networks (DSNs) are ad-hoc mobile networks that include sensor nodes with limited computation and communication capabilities. They are mainly used for military purposes but they also have wide applications in civilian areas. In military operations, sensor nodes are distributed in a hostile territory in order to monitor and collect various information (e.g., acoustic, seismic, magnetic). Since they are typically carried by soldiers or spread from airplanes, we assume that sensor nodes have no information on where they are located, that is, they are distributed in a random way. Once deployed, they operate unattended for extended periods without any movement. They have no external power supply during their operation. Therefore the most essential requirement is that each sensor should consume as small power as possible.

The sensor nodes in DSNs should be able to communicate with each other in order to relay or accumulate secret information. There are three ways to establish pairwise keys between sensor nodes. First is to establish secret keys using a public key infrastructure. However, asymmetric cryptographic primitives are not suitable due to expensive computational cost as well as storage constraints in each node. In another strategy, a sensor node is chosen to be a *trusted authority* (TA), which all other nodes in the network are assumed to trust. The TA shares a long-lived key with every node and transmit session keys between sensor nodes on request. This method can result in expensive costs for message relay. Arbitrated

H. Handschuh and A. Hasan (Eds.): SAC 2004, LNCS 3357, pp. 294–307, 2005.

protocols are also vulnerable to a single compromise of the TA. Therefore it is natural that we are interested in key predistribution schemes (KPSs), where a set of secret keys is installed in each node before each sensor node is deployed. After being deployed, it sets up a secret key with every node in certain neighborhood using their common information.

There are two simple strategies for KPSs. One is to use a single secret key over the entire network. This scheme is obviously efficient in terms of the cost of computation and memory. However the compromise of only a single node exposes all communications over the entire network, which is a serious deficiency. The other approach is to use distinct keys for all possible pairs of nodes. Then every node is preloaded with $n - 1$ keys, where n is the network size. This scheme guarantees perfect resiliency in that links between noncompromised nodes are secure against any coalition of compromised nodes. However this scheme is not suitable for large networks since the storage required per node increases linearly with the network size. In a classic paper by Blom [1], a tradeoff between key storage and security is presented. Given a security parameter $1 < t < n$, each node is deployed with $t + 1$ keys. This scheme provides perfect security against any coalition of up to t compromised nodes, while the compromise of $t + 1$ nodes would totally break the system. We briefly review this scheme in Sect. 5.

Recently, Eschenauer and Gliger [6] proposed a probabilistic key predistribution scheme. This scheme consists of three phases: *key predistribution, shared-key discovery*, and *path-key establishment*. We briefly describe these phases since our scheme also follow the same framework. In key predistribution phase, a large pool of keys and their key identifiers are generated. Every sensor node is equipped with a fixed number of keys randomly chosen from the key pool with their key identifiers. After deployment, the shared-key discovery phase takes place, where two nodes in a wireless communication range look for their common keys. If they share common keys in their key rings, they can pick one of them as their secret key. Sensor nodes can exchange the key identifiers of their keys, for example, to discover if they share a common key. The path-key establishment phase takes place in case there is no common key between a pair of nodes in a wireless communication range. They look for multiple secure links (hops) to reach each other so that one of them can choose an arbitrary key and relay it through the links. In our paper, we focus on the key predistribution phase which is given by a deterministic way.

The Eschenauer-Gliger scheme is generalized by Chan, Perrig and Song [3], where two nodes compute a pairwise key only if they share at least q common keys. They also presented a random-pairwise keys scheme, where a random graph is generated as the network layer and each link receives a unique key. In [5] and [9], the Eschenauer-Gligor schemes are combined with Blom's schemes, resulting in better performance compared with existing schemes.

DSNs can be regarded as superposition of a physical layer and a network layer. Due to resource constraints, a sensor node can communicate with only nodes within a limited radius. Hence the physical layer is represented by a *random geometric graph*. On the other hand, the network layer is represented by a graph such that two nodes are adjacent if they share a secret key, which is called a *network graph*. The network graph is determined by the KPS, independent of the distribution of sensor nodes. The network graphs have been given by random graphs since Eschenauer and Gliger's work. In this paper, we propose to use strongly regular graphs as network graphs. This means that the assignment of keys is deterministic. We can reduce the storage per node without loss of resiliency by introducing public one-way functions in our KPSs. We describe this method in Sect. 3 and 4. In Sect. 5, we modify Blom's scheme by allowing asymmetric matrices when generating keys, which yields a tradeoff between the connectivity of the network and the resiliency. In a similar way as Du-Deng-Han-Varsheney/Liu-Ning schemes [5], we use the modified Blom's schemes on strongly regular graphs at a network layer. Our schemes show better resiliency than Du-Deng-Han-Varsheney/Liu-Ning schemes.

2   Preliminaries

In this section we present some basic terminologies and facts on combinatorial objects. These notions turn out to be useful to describe deterministic KPSs.

2.1   Set Systems and KPSs

We begin with the following definition.

Definition 2.1. *A* set system *is a pair* $(X, \mathcal{A})$, *where* $\mathcal{A}$ *is a finite set of subsets of* X, *called* blocks. *The* degree *of a point* $x \in X$ *is the number of blocks containing the point* x. $(X, \mathcal{A})$ *is* regular *(of degree* d*) if all points have the same degree,* d. *The* rank *of* $(X, \mathcal{A})$ *is the size of the largest block. If all blocks have the same size, say* r, *then* $(X, \mathcal{A})$ *is said to be* uniform *(of rank* r*).*

Balanced incomplete block designs (BIBDs) are widely studied set systems. For extensive survey, we refer to [4] and [10].

Definition 2.2. *A* (v, r, λ)*-BIBD is a uniform set system* $(X, \mathcal{A})$ *of rank* r *with* $|X| = v$ *such that every pair of points in* X *occurs in exactly* λ *blocks.*

In the context of KPS, the set X corresponds to a key pool and each block to a sensor node. Thus a node is loaded with the keys in the corresponding block. If any two blocks have nonempty intersection, then they can establish their secret key. We can obtain Eschenauer-Gliger schemes choosing blocks of the same size randomly from a key pool. Each block is required to have size as small as possible in view of limited memory of a sensor node. In a KPS based on a regular set system of degree d, the exposure of one key in a node compromises d nodes. Hence we also wish the degree of each node to be as small as possible.

Example 2.1. An $(n^2 + n + 1, n + 1, 1)$-BIBD is called a *projective plane* of order n. A projective plane of order n exists for a prime power n. It is a symmetric BIBD, which means that the number of blocks is equal to the number of points. If the network chooses a projective plane of order 32 for KPS, it can accommodate 1057 nodes. Each node has 33 keys loaded in it. This scheme is deterministic and needs no path-key establishment.

For a set system $(X, \mathcal{A})$, the network graph of the corresponding KPS is given by the *intersection graph* $(\mathcal{A}, E)$ of the set system, where two blocks are adjacent if they have nonempty intersection. In the above example, the intersection graph is a complete graph.

2.2   Strongly Regular Graphs and KPSs

Once a set system is defined, we can check the connectivity of the corresponding KPS through its intersection graph. On the other hand, we can first specify an intersection graph, and then construct a corresponding KPS as follows: Given a graph G on n nodes, we use $E(G)$ as a key pool. A set of keys

$$K(v) = \{e \in E : \ e \text{ is incident with } v\}$$

are predeployed in a node v. In this scheme, each node has a set of $\leq \Delta(G)$ keys, where $\Delta(G)$ is the maximal degree of G. No matter how many nodes are captured, any link between noncompromised nodes remains secure. When we take G as a random graph on n nodes, the KPS is reduced to the random pairwise keys scheme [3]. We want small degrees at the nodes and short paths between nonadjacent nodes of G. For this reason, we are interested in strongly regular graphs [4] (though they have stronger properties than we require).

Definition 2.3. *A strongly regular graph with parameters (n, r, λ, μ) is a graph on n vertices, without loops or multiple edges, regular of degree r (with $0 < r < n - 1$), and such that any two distinct vertices have λ common neighbors when they are adjacent, and μ common neighbors when they are nonadjacent.*

Any pair of nonadjacent nodes in a strongly regular graph are connected by μ paths of length two. There are various ways to construct strongly regular graphs using combinatorial objects. We define an orthogonal array, a latin square and mutual orthogonality [10] to describe a construction.

Definition 2.4. *An orthogonal array $OA(t, n)$ is an $n^2 \times t$ array A on an alphabet X of n symbols such that every ordered pair of symbols occur in every set of two columns of A exactly once.*

Definition 2.5. *A latin square of order n is an $n \times n$ array L on an alphabet X of n symbols such that every symbol occurs exactly once in each row and each column of L.*

Definition 2.6. *Let L and M be two latin squares of order n on alphabets X and Y, respectively. L and M are orthogonal if their superposition contains every ordered pair of symbols. A set of latin squares $L_1, \ldots, L_s$, all of the same order n are mutually orthogonal if L_i and L_j are orthogonal for all $i \neq j$.*

The *block graph* of a (t, n)-orthogonal array A is a graph with the rows of A as vertices, where two rows are adjacent if there exists a position in which they have the same symbol. Such a graph is an $(n^2, t(n-1), n+t^2-3t, t(t-1))$-strongly regular graph. The following results are well-known.

Theorem 2.1. *An $OA(t+2, n)$ exists if and only if t mutually orthogonal latin squares (MOLS) of order n exist, for positive integers n and t.*

Theorem 2.2. *Let $N(n)$ denote the largest number of MOLS of order n. Then $N(n) \leq n-1$, and if n is a prime power, then $N(n) = n-1$.*

We can construct $n-1$ MOLS of prime power order n from a projective plane of order n. The construction of a projective plane and the corresponding MOLS and orthogonal array is described in [10] in detail. To summarize, we have

Construction 2.3. *Let n be a prime power and let $3 \leq t \leq n+1$. Then we can construct an $(n^2, t(n-1), n+t^2-3t, t(t-1))$-strongly regular graph.*

Consider a KPS whose intersection graph is an (n, r, λ, μ)-strongly regular graph G. We assume that sensor nodes are distributed on a plane in a random way and the range where a node can reach physically forms a circle, as shown in Fig. 1. We call this circle a *neighborhood* of the sensor node. The probability that a node shares a common key with another node in a neighborhood is $p = r/(n-1)$. Let d denote the average number of nodes in a neighborhood and d' the number of nodes in the common neighborhood of two nodes u and v within a wireless communication range. The probability that u and v are connected within two hops is given by

$$p^2(u, v) = p + (1-p)\left(1 - \binom{n-\mu-2}{d'-2}\Big/\binom{n-2}{d'-2}\right)$$

$$\approx p + (1-p)\left(1 - \left(1 - \frac{\mu}{n}\right)^{d'-2}\right)$$

$$\geq p + (1-p)\left(1 - \left(1 - \frac{\mu}{n}\right)^{\frac{d}{3}}\right).$$

The last inequality follows from the fact that two circles of the same radius has the intersection whose area is at least $1/3$ the area of the circle if the distance between the centres is less than the radius.

Example 2.2. Suppose that 1000 nodes are to be distributed and each neighborhood contains about $d = 40$ nodes. By taking $n = 32$ and $t = 14$ in Construction 2.3, we obtain a $(1024, 434, 186, 182)$-strongly regular graph G. In the corresponding KPS, we have $p^2(u, v) \geq 0.9547$ for any two nodes u and v within a wireless communication range.

Example 2.3. Consider a *complete bipartite graph* $K_{n,n}$. It is a $(2n, n, 0, n)$-strongly regular graph. In the corresponding KPS, we have

$$p^2_{K_{n,n}}(u, v) \approx 0.5 + 0.5(1 - (0.5)^{d'-2}) = 1 - (0.5)^{d'-1}$$

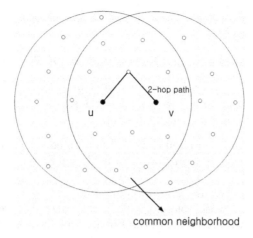

Fig. 1. A 2-hop path between two sensor nodes u and v

for any two nodes u and v within a wireless communication range. If we choose a random graph $G_{2n,p}$ with $p = 0.5$ as a network graph, the network layer has the same local connectivity. However, we have

$$p^2_{G_{2n,p}}(u, v) = 0.5 + (1 - 0.5)(1 - (1 - (0.5)^2)^{d'-2}) = 1 - (0.5)(0.75)^{d'-2},$$

which is smaller than $p^2_{K_{n,n}}(u, v)$. Hence the complete bipartite graph $K_{n,n}$ performs better than a random graph.

3   Basic ID-Based One-Way Function Schemes

In this section we use a public one-way hash function h in order to reduce the number of keys stored in a node. The KPSs presented here are ID-based since a unique ID is assigned to each sensor node and the ID is used to compute secret keys. First we determine a network graph G and construct a key pool $\mathcal{K} = \{K_v : v \in G\}$. Next we decompose the edges of graph G into star-like subgraphs. A sensor node u receives a secret key K_u and 'hashed' keys $h(K_v \parallel ID(u))$ if it is contained in a star-like subgraph centred at v. Since a node v can compute $h(K_v \parallel ID(u))$ by evaluating the public one-way function h at the concatenation of its unique key K_v and public ID, $ID(u)$, both of u and v can establish their secret key $h(K_v \parallel ID(u))$. In case v is a leaf of a star-like subgraph centred at u, $h(K_u \parallel ID(v))$ is established as their secret key.

Now we consider an edge decomposition of a regular graph into star-like subgraphs. We begin with the following definition.

Definition 3.1. *An* Euler circuit *of G is a circuit in a graph G containing all the edges.*

Theorem 3.1. *A nontrivial connected graph has an Euler circuit if and only if each vertex has even degree.*

There is an algorithm to find Euler circuits in $O(|E|)$-time [7].

Theorem 3.2. *A connected regular graph G of order n and even degree r has an edge decomposition into star-like subgraphs such that each vertex is a centre of one star and a leaf of $r/2$ distinct stars.*

Proof. By using an Euler circuit, we will find an edge colouring of G such that the edges with the same colour form a star-like subgraph.

Note that $|E(G)| = nr/2$. Let $v_0 E_0 v_1 E_1 \cdots v_{\frac{nr}{2}-2} E_{\frac{nr}{2}-2} v_{\frac{nr}{2}-1} (= v_0)$ be an Euler circuit of G. We use a set of colours labeled by vertices in G. Now we colour each edge E_i with colour v_i. Then the edges coloured by v is the $r/2$ edges coming from the vertex v in the Euler circuit, which form a star-like subgraph centred at v. Thus this colouring yields an edge decomposition of G into star-like subgraphs such that each vertex is a centre of one star and a leaf of $r/2$ distinct stars. □

Each node v stores one secret key K_v and $r/2$ hashed keys for the nodes u such that v is contained in a star-like subgraph centred at u. Therefore the total number of keys stored in a sensor node is given by $r/2 + 1$. This scheme reduces the number of keys per node by almost 50% as compared with the method discussed in the previous section.

Security Analysis. When a node u is revealed to an adversary, he obtains K_u as well as $h(K_{v_i} \| ID(u))$ for $r/2$ adjacent nodes v_i. It is infeasible to compute K_{v_i} even though he knows the key $h(K_{v_i} \| ID(u))$ since h is a one-way function. It follows that an adversary cannot compromise any link between two noncompromised nodes. Under the restriction of perfect resiliency, random pairwise keys schemes [3] exhibited the highest performance in terms of maximum supportable network size. However the basic ID-based one-way function schemes (IOSs) with regular network graphs (of even degree r) have maximum supportable network size two times larger than the random pairwise keys scheme, for a fixed probability p of sharing a common key, as shown in Fig. 2. Assuming each node contains k secret keys, the maximum supportable network size n is estimated as

$$n = \frac{2(k-1)}{p} + 1 \approx \frac{2k}{p},$$

since $p = r/(n-1)$ and $k = r/2 + 1$. In random pairwise keys schemes, the maximum supportable network size is given by $n = k/p$.

4   Multiple ID-Based One-Way Function Schemes

Basic IOSs are not suitable for a network of large size since they can accommodate only $O(k)$ sensor nodes for the node storage of k keys. In this section, we

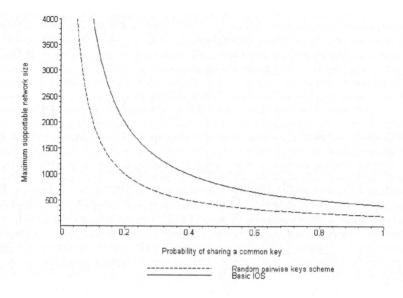

Fig. 2. The relationship between the probability of sharing a common key and the maximum supported network size for perfect resilience against node compromise. Each node is assumed to have $k = 200$ keys

use multiple copies of a single basic IOS to increase the network size relative to available memory. In exchange, the resiliency of multiple IOSs is weakened. In order to deploy $n = ml$ sensor nodes, we first determine an (m, r, λ, μ)-strongly regular graph G which is decomposed by star-like subgraphs. Each vertex u of G corresponds to l sensor nodes, say $u_1, \ldots, u_l$, of the network. We say the sensor nodes $u_1, \ldots, u_l$ are contained in a class u. Every node in a class u receives a common key K_u. If a vertex u is contained in a star-like subgraph centred at a vertex v in G, each sensor node u_i in a class u receives $h(K_v \parallel ID(u_i))$. Since any node v_j in a class v can compute $h(K_v \parallel ID(u_i))$, two nodes u_i and v_j can establish their session key using this hashed key. We assume that the duplicates $u_1, \ldots, u_l$ share no common key (even though we can set up an arbitrary key among them). The number of keys stored in a node is $k = r/2 + 1$, which is $1/l$ times smaller than using a single graph with the same probability of sharing a common key. The probability that two nodes share a common key is given by $p = rl/(n-1) \approx r/m$.

Security Analysis. Consider a DSN of size $n = ml$ which adopts an l-multiple IOS based on an (m, r, λ, μ)-strongly regular graph G. Suppose that an adversary compromises s nodes randomly in the network. We compute the probability that an arbitrary link $u_i v_j$ ($u \neq v$) between two noncompromised nodes is compromised. It also estimates the fraction of compromised links between noncompromised nodes in the total network. Let u and v be the vertices (classes) of G containing u_i and v_j, respectively, such that v is a leaf of a star-like subgraph centred at u. Then $h(K_u \| ID(v_j))$ is established as a secret key between two nodes u_i and v_j. In order to compute $h(K_u \| ID(v_j))$ without capturing u_i or v_j, the coalition have to contain at least one node in class u different from the node u_i. Therefore the probability is estimated as

$$P(s) = 1 - \frac{\binom{n-l-1}{s}}{\binom{n-2}{s}} \approx 1 - \left(1 - \frac{l-1}{n-2}\right)^s \approx 1 - \left(1 - \frac{p}{2k}\right)^s. \qquad (1)$$

Figure 3 shows the performance of a multiple IOS compared with other existing schemes.

Example 4.1. Let $G = K_{\frac{m}{2},\frac{m}{2}}$ be a complete bipartite graph, where $4|m$. It is an $(m, m/2, 0, m/2)$-strongly regular graph. Using l copies of the graph G, we can accommodate lm sensor nodes. The number of keys per node is $m/4+1$. If a node u_i in a class u is compromised, then $ml(l-1)/4$ links between noncompromised nodes are compromised. These are the links between the other $l-1$ duplicates in the class u and the nodes whose class is a leaf of a star-like subgraph centred at u in G. Note that we do not consider physical constraints in this analysis.

Key Revocation. If a node u_i is detected as being compromised, a controller node (which has a large communication range and may be mobile) broadcasts $ID(u_i)$ so that secure nodes can stop communicating with u_i. Nevertheless the other duplicates u_j, $i \neq j$ can still use the links established by the keys of the form $h(K_v \| ID(u_j))$.

In order to replace the captured node u_i, a new node u_{new} is installed with a new key $K_{u_{new}}$ and $h(K_v \| ID(u_{new}))$ for $r/2$ node classes v, where the node classes v are randomly chosen among secure classes. Alternatively, we can choose the same classes v as the hashed keys of the revoked node u_i has. Now the controller node broadcasts $ID(u_{new})$ so that every node v_i can compute $h(K_{v_i} \| ID(u_{new}))$. After deployment, the node u_{new} can communicate with a (physical) neighbor v_j of a class v for which u_{new} has $h(K_v \| ID(u_{new}))$. Shared-key discovery and path-key establishment phase should be restarted.

5   Deterministic Multiple Space Blom's Schemes

In this section, we briefly describe Blom's KPSs and present modified schemes for DSNs. First we consider original Blom's KPSs which are secure against up to coalition of size t. Let n be the size of a network and q a prime power large enough to assume that keys of $\ln q$ bits in length are secure. In order to accommodate n sensor nodes, the TA constructs a public $(t+1) \times n$ matrix M over $GF(q)$ such that any $t+1$ columns of M are linearly independent. A well-known example of such a matrix M is a Vandermonde matrix

$$M = \begin{pmatrix} 1 & 1 & 1 & \ldots & 1 \\ 1 & 2 & 3 & \ldots & n \\ 1 & 2^2 & 3^2 & \ldots & n^2 \\ & & \vdots & & \\ 1 & 2^t & 3^t & \ldots & n^t \end{pmatrix}.$$

Each node u receives a unique $(t+1) \times 1$ column vector x_u from the matrix M, which is public. Using a Vandermonde matrix, a node given the j-th column vector can store only a seed $j \in GF(q)$ to generate the other elements [5]. In the next step, the TA generates a secret random $(t+1) \times (t+1)$ symmetric matrix D over $GF(q)$ and assigns secret information $K_u = x_u^T D$ to each node u. Any two nodes u and v can compute their secret key $K_{uv} = x_u^T D x_v$ from one's secret information and the other's public column vector. Note that $x_u^T D x_v = x_v^T D x_u$ due to the symmetry of the matrix D.

5.1   Modified Blom's KPSs on Complete Bipartite Graphs

As described above, any pair of nodes can establish a secret key in Blom's schemes. Thus the network layer is represented by a complete graph. We can weaken the connectivity of the network graph in order to improve resiliency against node compromise. We choose a complete bipartite graph K_{m_1, m_2} instead of a complete graph as a network graph in this modification. We divide the set of nodes into two sets U and V such that $|U| = m_1$ and $|V| = m_2$. The initial assignment of public column vectors is the same as the original schemes. The difference is that the TA generates a random $(t+1) \times (t+1)$ matrix D, which is *not necessarily symmetric*. Secret information $x_u^T D$ is assigned to each node $u \in U$ and $D x_v$ is assigned to each node $v \in V$, given their public column vectors x_u and x_v. Now both of the nodes x_u and x_v can compute their secret key $x_u^T D x_v$. The following theorem supports the stronger resiliency of this modification.

Theorem 5.1. *Let* $U = \{u_1, \ldots, u_{m_1}\}$ *and* $V = \{v_1, \ldots, v_{m_2}\}$ *be sets of* $(t+1) \times 1$ *column vectors over* $GF(q)$ *such that any* $t+1$ *vectors, either all in* U *or all in* V, *are linearly independent. Let* D *be a* $(t+1) \times (t+1)$ *matrix. Then*

1. *D is determined by $t+1$ row vectors $u_{l_i}^T D$, $i = 1, \ldots, t+1$ or $t+1$ column vectors Dv_{l_i}, $i = 1, \ldots, t+1$, and*
2. *for any $t+1$ vectors $u_{l_i} \in U$, $(i = 1, \ldots, t+1)$, and for any $t+1$ vectors $v_{l_i} \in V$, $(i = 1, \ldots, t+1)$, and for any scalar $k \in GF(q)$, there exists a $(t+1) \times (t+1)$ matrix D' such that*

$$u_{l_i}^T D' = u_{l_i}^T D, \text{ and } D' v_{l_i} = D v_{l_i} \ (i = 1, \ldots, t), \text{ and } u_{l_{t+1}}^T D' v_{l_{t+1}} = k.$$

Proof. Let

$$U = \begin{pmatrix} u_{l_1}^T \\ u_{l_2}^T \\ \vdots \\ u_{l_{t+1}}^T \end{pmatrix} \text{ and } V = \begin{pmatrix} v_{l_1} & v_{l_2} & \cdots & v_{l_{t+1}} \end{pmatrix}.$$

Then U and V are invertible $(t+1) \times (t+1)$ matrices over $GF(q)$. Given UD or DV, we can compute D by multiplying by the inverse matrix U^{-1} or V^{-1}, which proves the first part of the theorem.

Now we define

$$(\hat{D})_{i,j} = \begin{cases} k, & \text{if } i = j = t+1, \\ (UDV)_{i,j}, & \text{otherwise.} \end{cases}$$

and

$$D' = U^{-1}\hat{D}V^{-1}.$$

Then we have

$$e_i^T UD'V = e_i^T \hat{D} = e_i^T UDV$$

and

$$UD'Ve_i = \hat{D}e_i = UDVe_i,$$

for every elementary vector e_i (with a "1" in position i and "0"s in all other positions), $i = 1, \ldots, t$. Since $e_i^T UD' = e_i^T UD$ and $D'Ve_i = DVe_i$ for $i = 1, \ldots, t$, it follows that

$$u_{l_i}^T D' = e_i^T UD' = e_i^T UD = u_{l_i}^T D,$$

and

$$D'v_{l_i} = D'Ve_i = DVe_i = Dv_{l_i}$$

for $i = 1, \ldots, t$, and

$$u_{l_{t+1}}^T D'v_{l_{t+1}} = e_{t+1}^T UD'Ve_{t+1} = e_{t+1}^T \hat{D}e_{t+1} = k,$$

as desired.   □

Theorem 5.1 means that an adversary cannot obtain any information on the keys of the links between noncompromised nodes unless it compromise at least $t+1$ nodes, either all in U or in V. In the original Blom's scheme with the same threshold parameter t, the compromise of any $t+1$ keys breaks the total system. However, in our modification, the probability of a total break is reduced to

$$P(t+1) = \frac{\binom{m_1}{t+1} + \binom{m_2}{t+1}}{\binom{m_1+m_2}{t+1}}.$$

In general, when s nodes are captured randomly, the probability $P(s)$ of total break is estimated as

$$P(s) = 1 - \frac{\sum_{\substack{i+j=s \\ 0 \le i,j \le t}} \binom{m_1}{i}\binom{m_2}{j}}{\binom{m_1+m_2}{s}}. \tag{2}$$

We will use this modification as building blocks to construct new KPSs in the next section.

5.2   Deterministic Multiple Space Blom's Schemes (DMBSs)

We consider l copies of an (m, r, λ, μ)-strongly regular graph G to accommodate $n = ml$ nodes. We regard each vertex of G as a class of l nodes. Every sensor node u_i receives its public column vector x_{u_i} from a Vandermonde matrix M and every edge e of G is associated with a random $(t + 1) \times (t + 1)$ matrix D_e, not necessarily symmetric.

Now an arbitrary direction is assigned to every edge of G. For every edge $e \in E(G)$ incident to a vertex (class) u, each node u_i of class u receives row vector $x_{u_i}^T D_e$ if e starts from u, or column vector $D_e x_{u_i}$ if e ends at u. Suppose that an edge $uv \in E(G)$ begins at u. Then two sensor nodes $u_i \in u$ and $v_j \in v$ can compute their secret key $K_{u_i v_j} = x_{u_i}^T D_{uv} x_{v_j}$ using each other's public vector. Since each vector has size equivalent to $t+1$ keys, the total amount of information per node is given by $r(t + 1)$. The probability that two nodes share a common key is $p = rl/(n - 1) \approx r/m$.

Security Analysis. Suppose that s nodes are captured by an adversary in a random way. Consider a link between two noncompromised nodes u_i and v_j, contained in classes u and v, respectively. In order to compute their secret key $K_{u_i v_j} = x_{u_i}^T D_{uv} x_{v_j}$, the coalition has to contain at least $t + 1$ nodes, either all in the class of u or the class of v. Therefore the probability $P(s)$ that the link is compromised is estimated as

$$P(s) = 1 - \frac{\sum_{i=0}^{t} \sum_{j=0}^{t} \binom{l-1}{i} \binom{l-1}{j} \binom{n-2l}{s-i-j}}{\binom{n-2}{s}}. \tag{3}$$

Figure 3 illustrates the graph of $P(s)$ as a function of the number of compromised nodes for various schemes. In this plot, we assume that

1. the total network size is $n = 1200$,
2. each node has 200 pieces of secret information,
3. the probability of sharing a common key between two nodes is $p = 0.5$.

We briefly describe the graphs and parameters used in this plot as follows:

(a) is from Fig. 2 in [9], where we take $s' = 2$, $s = 7$, and $t = 99$.
(b) shows the resiliency of a modified Blom's scheme with threshold parameter $t = 199$ and network graph $K_{600,600}$. We use (2) in Sect. 5.1.
(c) shows the resiliency of a deterministic multiple space Blom's scheme based on 300 copies of a $(4, 2, 0, 2)$-strongly regular graph, where we take threshold parameter $t = 99$. We use (3) in Sect. 5.2.
(d) shows the resiliency of a basic scheme such that 200 keys are chosen from a pool of size 58000 [6].
(e) shows the resiliency of a q-composite scheme with $q = 1$ [3].
(f) is given by (1) in Sect. 4.

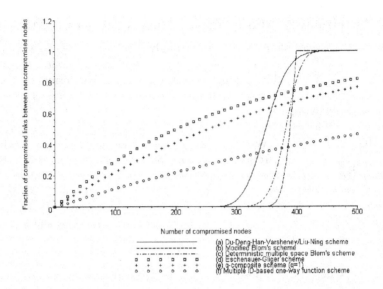

Fig. 3. Fraction of compromised links between noncompromised nodes v.s. number of compromised nodes

6   Conclusion

We presented two KPSs for distributed sensor networks in this paper. We can determine network graphs in both schemes. ID-based one-way function schemes allow each node to reduce the storage by using one-way functions in generating secret keys. Using a single copy of a network graph, we obtain a KPS with perfect resiliency. A basic IOS has the maximum supportable network size larger than a random pairwise keys scheme [3]. A multiple IOS provides a trade-off between node storage (or total network size) and resiliency against coalition attack. MBSs are based on modified Blom's schemes and Du-Deng-Han-Varsheney/Liu-Ning schemes. MBSs show stronger resiliency than Du-Deng-Han-Varsheney/Liu-Ning schemes.

References

1. R. Blom. An Optimal Class of Symmetric Key Generation Systems, In *Advances in Cryptology - Eurocrypt '84*, pages 335-338, 1985. Lecture Notes in Computer Science Volume 209.
2. D.W. Carmen, P.S. Kruus and B.J. Matt. Constraints and Approaches for Distributed Sensor Network Security. *NAI Labs Technical Report #00-010*, September 2000.
3. H. Chan, A. Perrig, and D. Song. Random Key Predistribution Schemes for Sensor Networks, In *IEEE Symposium on Research in Security and Privacy*, pages 197-213, May 2003.

4. C.J. Colbourn, J.H. Dinitz (editors). *The CRC Handbook of Combinatorial Designs*, CRC Press, Boca Raton, 1996.
5. W. Du, J. Deng, Y.S. Han, and P.K. Varsheney. A Pairwise Key Pre-distribution Scheme for Wireless Sensor Networks, In *Proceedings of the 10th ACM Conference on Computer and Communications Security (CCS)*, October 2003.
6. L. Eschenauer and V.D. Gligor. A Key-Management Scheme for Distributed Sensor Networks, In *Proceedings of the 9th ACM conference on Computer and communications security*, pages 41-47, November 2002.
7. A. Gibbons. *Algorithmic Graph Theory*, Cambridge Univ. Press, Cambridge, 1985.
8. R.L. Graham, M. Grötschel and L. Lovász (editors). *Handbook of Combinatorics*, vol. 2, North-Holland, Amsterdam, 1995.
9. D. Liu and P. Ning, Establishing Pairwise Keys in Distributed Sensor Networks, In *Proceedings of the 10th ACM Conference on Computer and Communications Security (CCS)*, October 2003.
10. D.R. Stinson, *Combinatorial Designs: Constructions and Analysis*, Springer-Verlag, New York, 2003.

On Proactive Secret Sharing Schemes

Ventzislav Nikov[1] and Svetla Nikova[2,*]

[1] Department of Mathematics and Computing Science,
Eindhoven University of Technology,
P.O. Box 513, 5600 MB, Eindhoven, the Netherlands
`v.nikov@tue.nl`
[2] Department Electrical Engineering, ESAT/COSIC,
Katholieke Universiteit Leuven, Kasteelpark Arenberg 10,
B-3001 Heverlee-Leuven, Belgium
`svetla.nikova@esat.kuleuven.ac.be`

Abstract. This paper investigates the security of Proactive Secret Sharing Schemes. We start with revision of the mobile adversary model of Herzberg's *et al.* imposing less restriction to the adversary. We first investigate the approach of using commitment to 0 in the renewal phase in order to renew the player's shares. In the considered model some well known computationally secure protocols (which use this approach) turns out to be vulnerable to a specific attack. We show that this type of attack is applicable also in the unconditional case. Then we extend the attack of D'Arco and Stinson to non-symmetric polynomials, which is applicable even in the mobile adversary model of Herzberg *et al*. Next the conditions for the security of a proactive scheme using this approach are shown. We also investigate another approach to add proactivity, namely using re-sharing instead of commitment to 0. Two protocols using this approach are described and it is shown that both are not secure against a mobile adversary. The main contribution of the paper is to show specific weaknesses, when a mobile adversary is considered.

1 Introduction

Verifiable secret sharing (VSS) schemes are secret sharing schemes (SSSs) dealing with possible misbehaving of the participants. Proactive security was first suggested by Ostrovsky and Yung in [14]. This concept was applied to the secret sharing schemes by Herzberg *et al.* in [9]. Basically the idea is that, if the information stored by the servers in order to share a given secret stays the same for all lifetime of the system, then an adversary can eventually break into a sufficient number of servers, to learn and destroy the secret. On the other hand,

---

* The work described in this paper has been supported in part by the European Commission through the IST Programme under Contract IST-2002-507932 ECRYPT, IWT STWW project on Anonymity and Privacy in Electronic Services and Concerted Research Action GOA-MEFISTO-666 of the Flemish Government.

H. Handschuh and A. Hasan (Eds.): SAC 2004, LNCS 3357, pp. 308–325, 2005.

let the time is divided into periods. At the beginning of each period the information stored by the servers in a given time period changes, while the shared secret stays the same. Then the adversary probably does not have enough time to break into necessary number of servers. Moreover, the information he learns during the period t is useless during the period $t + i$, for $i = 1, 2, \ldots$. So, he has to start a new attack from scratch during each time period.

We revise the mobile adversary model from [9], imposing less restriction to the adversary. In the model of Herzberg's *et al.* the players corrupted during an update phase were considered corrupt for both (adjacent) periods. We propose a model in which these corrupt players are considered corrupt only in one of the adjacent periods. As a result in the new model some well known computationally secure protocols e.g. [9, 10, 8] became vulnerable to a specific attack, which we call attacks of first type.

The first unconditionally secure proactive VSS was proposed by Stinson and Wei [16]. In [12] a generalization of the scheme has been given, but D'Arco and Stinson [2, 3] showed that these two proactive schemes can be broken. We refer to their attack as of second type. The authors also proposed two new variations of the schemes to add proactive security to VSS, based on two different approaches, one using symmetric polynomials and another one using non-symmetric polynomials. However, in [12] an attack on the scheme with symmetric polynomials were described and slightly modified solution were proposed.

We next show that the first type attack is applicable also in the unconditional case in the considered model. Then we extend the second type of attack to the non-symmetric case. Note that the second type attack is successful even in the mobile adversary model of Herzberg's *et al.* We point out that a specific problem arises in the renewal phase, namely we need a distributed commitment protocol in which the committer is committed to 0 and the players are able to check that the commitment is indeed 0 without revealing their auxiliary shares. In order for this protocol to be secure against a mobile adversary we need to reduce the number of cheating players. The necessary and sufficient condition for security are consequently given in Theorem 3.

Last we investigate another approach [5, 6] to make an SSS proactively secure, namely using re-sharing protocol instead of commitment to 0 in order to renew and re-randomize the player's shares. We describe two protocols using this approach and show that both are subject to a modification of the second type attack. Our goal is to show specific weaknesses when mobile adversary is considered. Note that all unconditionally secure protocols we describe in this paper remain secure if the adversary is not mobile. Our aim throughout the paper is to learn more from the systems that fail in order to build systems that succeed.

2   Preliminary

2.1   Notations

Denote the *participants* (players) of the scheme by P_i, $1 \le i \le n$, and the set of all *players* by $\mathcal{P} = \{P_1, \ldots, P_n\}$. Denote the *dealer* of the scheme by $\mathcal{D}$. The role of the dealer is to share a secret s to all participants in the scheme. For the sake of simplicity we will consider only the threshold case in this paper. The simplest access structure Γ is called (k, n)-threshold if all subsets of players $\mathcal{P}$ with at least $k + 1$ participants are *qualified* to reconstruct the secret and any subset of up to k players are *forbidden* of doing it. Accordingly we will call a Secret Sharing Scheme (SSS) (k, n)-threshold if the access structure Γ associated with it is (k, n)-threshold.

2.2   Verifiable Secret Sharing Schemes

Verifiable Secret Sharing (VSS) schemes guarantee the robustness of the sharing and the detection of corrupt players. Informally, there are n players, some of them may be corrupt and deviate from the protocol. One of the players, the dealer, possesses a value s as a secret input. In the first stage, the dealer commits to a unique value $\tilde{s}$ (no matter what corrupt players may do); moreover, $\tilde{s} = s$ whenever the dealer is not corrupt. In the second stage, the already committed value $\tilde{s}$ will be recovered by all good players (no matter what the corrupt players may do).

It is common to model cheating by considering an *adversary* $\mathcal{A}$ who may corrupt some of the players (up to k players). One can distinguish between *passive* and *active* corruption. Passive corruption means that the adversary obtains the complete information held by the corrupt players, but the players execute the protocol correctly. Active corruption means that the adversary takes full control of the corrupt players. Active corruption is strictly stronger than passive corruption. Both passive and active adversaries may be *static*, meaning that the set of corrupt players is chosen once and for all before the protocol starts, or *adaptive* meaning that the adversary can at any time during the protocol choose to corrupt a new player based on all the information he has at the time, as long as the total number of corrupt players is less or equal to k.

In the Appendix certain VSS schemes are given. Most of the used computationally secure schemes are based on Feldman's or Pedersen's VSS. We chose to consider only Feldman's scheme since it is simpler, but our attacks work against all these schemes. Also in the Appendix we present unconditionally secure VSS protocols, one based on symmetric and one based on asymmetric bivariate polynomials. We will refer to the unconditional secure sub-protocols described in the Detection phase also as "pair-wise" checking, for obvious reasons. These protocols ensure the consistency of the shares. We will refer to $h_v(0)$ and $g_v(0)$ as "true parts" of the shares since they are used to reconstruct the secret. The following result is classic for VSS theory.

Theorem 1. *A computationally secure (k, n)-threshold VSS exists if and only if $2k < n$. An unconditional secure (k, n)-threshold VSS exists if and only if $3k < n$.*

3   Computational Secure Proactive VSS Schemes

The concept of *proactive security* was introduced by Ostrovsky and Yung in [14] and applied by Herzberg *et al.* in [9] to secret sharing schemes. Proactive security refers to security and availability in the presence of a so-called *mobile adversary*. Herzberg *et al.* [9] have further specialized this notion to robust secret sharing schemes and have given a detailed efficient proactive secret sharing scheme.

Consider the following problem: if the information stored by the players in order to share a given secret stays the same for a long period of time (e.g. the lifetime of the system), then an adversary may gradually break into a sufficient number of players, to learn and destroy the secret. A way to address this problem is to divide the time into periods. At the beginning of each period the information stored by the players in that period changes, while the shared secret stays the same. The system is set up in such a way that the adversary does not have enough time to break into a required set of players. Moreover, the information that the adversary learns during a particular period is useless during later periods. So, he has to start a new attack from scratch during each time period.

Proactive security provides enhanced protection to long-lived secrets against a *mobile adversary*, i.e. the adversary which is allowed to potentially move among players over time with the limitation that it can only control some subset of players at a time unit. In fact, proactive security adds protection by "time diffusion". Namely, all shares are periodically refreshed. This renders useless the knowledge obtained by the mobile adversary in the past. Proactive systems also use robustness techniques to enhance availability by tolerating (detecting and correcting) malicious players. Moreover, it also allows *recoveries* of the previously corrupt players, by "removing" the adversary influence and restoring their (correct) information. This gives the system a *self-healing* nature. As a result, the system can tolerate a mobile adversary.

We will follow the settings of the schemes in [14, 9]. In general they coincide with the settings of the VSS except that we consider a more powerful adversary - a mobile one. In situations when the secret value needs to be maintained for a long period of time, in order to protect the secret against a mobile adversary, the life time is divided into time periods which are determined by the global clock. At the end of each time period the players engage in an interactive update protocol. The update protocol will not reveal the value of the secret. At the beginning of the next period the players hold new shares of the secret.

We assume that the adversary intruding player P_i is "removable", through a "reboot" procedure, when the adversary influence is detected. By "rebooting" the player we mean that the adversary's influence over this player is stopped and all player's information is erased. That is why after this procedure the correct share should be recovered. It is important to note that in proactive protocols some information (e.g. the check values, the old share, etc.) should be "erased". This operation, to be performed by honest players, is essential for the proactive security. Not doing so would provide an adversary that attacks a player at a given time period with information from a previous period that later could enable the adversary to break the system.

The following new phases *Recovery* and *Renewal* can be distinguished [9], compare to a VSS scheme. In [9] the update phase (also called update protocol) is separated from the time frames in a sense that if a player is corrupt during an update phase the authors consider it corrupt during both (adjacent) periods to that update phase. We consider the following

MOBILE ADVERSARY MODEL

At the beginning and at the end of the life time of the system we have *Share-Detection* respectively *Reconstruction*. At the end of each time period we have *Detection* followed by *Recovery* after that the next period begins with *Renewal*. Together Detection, Recovery and Renewal form an update phase, but we do not restrict additionally the adversary to corrupt players in this phase as in [9]. In fact the "rebooting" of the corrupt players finishes the current time frame and new time period begins.

The shares computed in period t for player P_u are denoted by using superscript (t), i.e. $s_u^{(t)}$, $h_u^{(t)}(x)$ or $g_u^{(t)}(y)$, $t = 0, 1, \ldots$. Dealer's polynomials corresponding to these shares are denoted by $f^{(t)}(x)$ and $f^{(t)}(x, y)$. Let us describe the Recovery and Renewal protocols given in [9].

We first briefly describe the idea how the player's shares are renewed at period $t = 1, 2, \ldots$. When the secret s is distributed as a value $f^{(t-1)}(0) = s$ of a k degree polynomial $f^{(t-1)}(x)$, we can update this polynomial by adding it to a k degree random polynomial $\delta^{(t-1)}(x)$, where $\delta^{(t-1)}(0) = 0$, so that $f^{(t)}(0) = f^{(t-1)}(0) + \delta^{(t-1)}(0) = s$. Thus we can renew the shares $f^{(t)}(\alpha_u) = f^{(t-1)}(\alpha_u) + \delta^{(t-1)}(\alpha_u)$ thanks to the linearity.

Renewal Phase:
1. Each player P_u plays the role of the dealer.
2. P_u runs the Share-Detection Phase of Feldman's VSS with a random polynomial $\delta_u(x) = \sum_{j=0}^{k} \delta_{u,j} x^j$ subject to $\delta_u(0) = 0$. The following broadcast values are used $A_{u,j} = g^{\delta_{u,j}}$.
3. As a result of this Share-Detection Phase every player P_v has a temporary share $\delta_u(\alpha_v)$ if the player P_u is not blamed as a corrupt dealer.
4. Let A be the set of uncorrupt players.
5. Each player P_v updates its own share by performing

$$s_v^{(t)} = s_v^{(t-1)} + \sum_{u \in A} \delta_u(\alpha_v).$$

6. The new verification values are set $A_j^{(t)} = A_j^{(t-1)} \prod_{u \in A} A_{u,j}$.

Note that $\delta^{(t-1)}(x) = \sum_{u \in A} \delta_u(x)$ and that $A_j^{(t)}$ corresponds to the j-th coefficient in $f^{(t)}(x)$.

Now we describe the idea how the player's shares are recovered at period $t = 1, 2, \ldots$. Let the players in a set B are detected as corrupt and thus their shares should be recovered. Set $A = \mathcal{P} \setminus B$ to be the set of uncorrupt players. In general an analogous way to that used for re-randomization in the renewal phase is applied. First all corrupt players $P_v \in B$ are "rebooted". In order to recover the share of player $P_v \in B$ every player $P_u \in A$ share a random k-degree polynomial $\delta_u(x)$, such that $\delta_u(\alpha_v) = 0$. By adding $\delta_u(x)$ to $f^{(t)}(x)$ (for $u \in A$) a new random polynomial $\delta(x)$ is obtained. Now the players $P_u \in A$ send their temporary shares $\delta(\alpha_u)$ to P_v, which allow him to recover the whole polynomial $\delta(x)$ and to compute his share $\delta(\alpha_v)$.

Theorem 2. *[9] A computationally secure (k,n)-threshold proactive VSS exists if and only if $2k < n$.*

3.1   The First Type of Attack

Proactive secret sharing [9] and proactive signature schemes [10] were introduced to cope with mobile adversary who may corrupt more than k servers during the life time of the secret. In both papers the proactive scheme is build on top of Feldman's VSS scheme [4]. In [8] the authors showed a specific attack against Feldman's VSS scheme and proposed a distributed key generation protocol build on top of Pedersen's VSS scheme [15]. The authors in [8] then claimed that their protocol is secure against a mobile adversary which can corrupt up to k players in given time frame.

In this section we will illustrate an attack against the renewal phase, in the schemes of Feldman, Pedersen and Genarro *et al.* We will show that even a passive, but mobile adversary can break these schemes in the considered model. For the sake of simplicity we will illustrate the attack only for Feldman's scheme.

Suppose that the attacker has corrupted a set B of players in some time frame $t - 1$, i.e. he knows their shares $f^{(t-1)}(\alpha_u)$ for $u \in B$. All players $P_u \in B$ being detected as corrupt are "rebooted" and the new period t starts with the renewal phase, when all shares are updated. Now let the adversary corrupt k players (not in B) in this period and note that any k corrupt players can uniquely reconstruct the polynomial $\delta(x)$ since they have the additional information that $\delta(0) = 0$. Thus the adversary which gets information from k corrupt players in this period is able to compute the new player's shares $f^{(t)}(\alpha_u)$ for $u \in B$. Note that in this period the players $P_u \in B$ are no more corrupt. Therefore, incrementally breaking different sets of players the attacker is able to compute the secret. Actually the attacker needs to know only one share from the previous period which together with k player's shares from the current time frame will allow him to reconstruct the secret.

Note that the proposed attack applies if the renewal phase is considered as the beginning of the next period. However a slightly modified attack can be applied if we consider the renewal phase as the end of the previous period.

Therefore the first solution of Herzberg *et al.* allows even a passive, mobile adversary to break the scheme in the considered adversary model. Also most of the consecutive schemes, we will cite only some of them [9, 7, 10, 8], are subject to this kind of attack in the considered adversary model.

4   Unconditionally Secure Proactive VSS Schemes

The first unconditionally secure proactive VSS was proposed by Stinson and Wei [16]. A generalization of this scheme to general access structures has later been given in [11]. Recently D'Arco and Stinson [2, 3] showed that some existing unconditionally secure proactive schemes [11, 16] can be broken.

In [16, 2, 3] the authors consider different model in which all subsets of players with at least $k + 1$ participants are qualified, but any subset of up to b ($b < k$) players is forbidden, where the restriction is due to the fact that some information is broadcast. So, we will consider (k, n) access structure where up to b ($b < k$) players are corrupt and will denote it by (b, k, n). Again we will present only Recovery and Renewal Phases. Recall that as a result of the previous phases all players maintain a set A of honest (not corrupt) players and possess shares $h_u^{(t)}(x)$. The shares $h_u^{(t)}(x)$ are derived from a symmetric polynomial $f^{(t)}(x, y)$ by setting $y = \alpha_u$. Set $B = \mathcal{P} \setminus A$ to be the set of corrupt players.

Recovery Phase:
1. Every corrupt player $P_v \in B$ is "rebooted".
2. Every good player P_u computes and sends to every corrupt player $P_v \in B$ a check-value $C_{u,v} = h_u^{(t)}(\alpha_v)$.
3. Upon receiving the data, P_v computes $h_v^{(t)}(x)$, such that $h_v^{(t)}(\alpha_u) = C_{u,v}$ holds for certain subset of honest, qualified players $P_u \in \widetilde{A}$, $\widetilde{A} \subseteq A$.
4. Player P_v sets $h_v^{(t)}(x)$ as his share.

Renewal Phase:
1. In this phase each player P_u plays the role of the dealer.
2. Each player P_u selects a random symmetric polynomial $\delta_u(x, y)$ of degree k, subject to $\delta_u(0, 0) = 0$.
3. Player P_u sends $\delta_{u;v}(x) = \delta_u(x, \alpha_v)$ to P_v for $1 \le v \le n$ and broadcasts $\delta_{u;0}(x) = \delta_u(x, 0)$.
4. Player P_v checks whether $\delta_{u;v}(0) = \delta_{u;0}(\alpha_v)$ and whether $\delta_{u;0}(0) = 0$.
5. If these relations are satisfied, then P_v computes and sends to P_w the usual check value $C_{u;v,w} = \delta_{u;v}(\alpha_w)$. Otherwise P_v broadcasts an accusation to P_u.
6. All players perform the (usual) pair-wise checking with accusations protocol. At the end they update the set of good players A.
7. Each player P_v updates his share by putting

$$h_v^{(t)}(x) = h_v^{(t-1)}(x) + \sum_{u \in A} \delta_{u;v}(x).$$

Set $\delta(x, y) = \sum_{u \in A} \delta_u(x, y)$, then $f^{(t)}(x, y) = f^{(t-1)}(x, y) + \delta(x, y)$ holds. Note that in Step 2 of the renewal phase additional information is broadcast, that we do not have in the standard Share-Detection phase. This information allows the players (in Step 4) to check that the value committed by P_u in Renewal phase is indeed 0. The latter ensures that the secret will not be changed.

4.1   The Second Type of Attack

Notice that the attack proposed in the previous section (the first type) is not applicable in this setting, since this attack is successfully mounted only when the number of corrupt players $b = k$. Obviously any k players using their temporary shares $\delta_v(x)$ together with the broadcast value $\delta_0(x)$ are able to compute $\delta(x, y)$. Therefore in case $b = k$ the first type of attack is applicable to the unconditional model.

But, it turns out that the broadcast information in the renewal phase allows the attacker to break the system even when $b < k$. We will demonstrate briefly the attack against the proactivity, proposed by D'Arco and Stinson [2], which we call second type attack.

Note that $\delta_{u;v}(0) = \delta_{u;0}(\alpha_v)$ holds. Suppose that the attacker has corrupted player P_v in some time frame $t - 1$, i.e. he knows his share $h_v^{(t-1)}(x)$. Then P_v being detected as corrupt is "rebooted". In the renewal phase his share is updated by

$$h_v^{(t)}(x) = h_v^{(t-1)}(x) + \sum_{u \in A} \delta_{u;v}(x).$$

But since $\delta_{u;0}(x)$ is public the attacker is able to compute $\sum_{u \in A} \delta_{u;v}(0) = \sum_{u \in A} \delta_{u;0}(\alpha_v)$. Thus he knows the "true part" of the P_v's new share, namely $h_v^{(t)}(0) = h_v^{(t-1)}(0) + \sum_{u \in A} \delta_{u;v}(0)$. Recall that the knowledge of the "true part" of the shares is enough for reconstructing the secret. Therefore, incrementally breaking different sets of players the attacker is able to compute the secret.

4.2   Patching Stinson and Wei's Scheme

D'Arco and Stinson [2, 3] proposed two new variations of the unconditional schemes to add proactive security to VSS, based on two different approaches, one using symmetric polynomials and another one using asymmetric polynomials.

However, in [12] an attack on the proactive scheme with symmetric polynomials from [2] were described and a slightly modified scheme was proposed that solves this problem (see also [3]). For the sake of completeness we will provide here the solution for the symmetric case. The Recovery Phase is the same as in Stinson and Wei scheme.

Renewal Phase:
1. Each player P_u plays the role of the dealer.
2. Each player P_u selects a random symmetric polynomial $\delta_u(x, y)$ of degree $k - 1$.
3. Player P_u sends $\delta_{u;v}(x) = \delta_u(x, \alpha_v)$ to P_v for $1 \leq v \leq n$.
4. Then P_v computes and sends to P_w the usual check value $C_{u;v,w} = \delta_{u;v}(\alpha_w)$.
5. All players perform the (usual) pair-wise checking with accusations protocol. At the end they update the set of good players A.
6. Each player P_v updates his share by putting

$$h_v^{(t)}(x) = h_v^{(t-1)}(x) + (x + \alpha_v) \sum_{u \in A} \delta_{u;v}(x).$$

Note that $\delta(x,y) = \sum_{u \in A} \delta_u(x,y)$ is a polynomial of degree $k-1$, but since at most b $(b < k)$ players are corrupt the adversary can not compute $\delta(x,y)$.

4.3   D'Arco and Stinson's Scheme - The Asymmetric Case

In this section we will consider the second solution of D'Arco and Stinson (using asymmetric polynomials) proposed in [2,3]. As in the previous section, we will consider (b,k,n) access structure where up to b $(b < k)$ players are corrupt.

Recall that as a result of the previous phases all players maintain a set A of "good" (not corrupt) players and have shares $h_u^{(t)}(x)$ and $g_u^{(t)}(y)$. The shares are derived from an asymmetric polynomial $f^{(t)}(x,y)$ by setting $y = \alpha_u$ for $h_u^{(t)}(x)$ and by setting $x = \alpha_u$ for $g_u^{(t)}(y)$. Let $B = \mathcal{P} \setminus A$ be the set of corrupt players.

Recovery Phase:
1. Every corrupt player $P_v \in B$ is "rebooted".
2. Every good player $P_u \in A$ computes and sends to every corrupt player $P_v \in B$ the values $C_{u,v} = g_u^{(t)}(\alpha_v)$ and $D_{u,v} = h_u^{(t)}(\alpha_v)$.
3. Upon receiving the data, P_v computes $h_v^{(t)}(x)$ and $g_v^{(t)}(y)$, such that $h_v^{(t)}(\alpha_u) = C_{u,v}$, $g_v^{(t)}(\alpha_u) = D_{u,v}$ and $h_v^{(t)}(\alpha_v) = g_v^{(t)}(\alpha_v)$ hold for certain subset of honest, qualified players $P_u \in \tilde{A}$ and $\tilde{A} \subseteq A$.
4. Player P_v sets $h_v^{(t)}(x)$ and $g_v^{(t)}(y)$ as his shares.

Renewal Phase:
1. Each player P_u plays the role of the dealer.
2. Each player P_u selects a random polynomial $\delta_u(x,y)$ of degree k, subject to $\delta_u(0,0) = 0$.
3. Player P_u sends $h_{u;v}(x) = \delta_u(x, \alpha_v)$ and $g_{u;v}(y) = \delta_u(\alpha_v, y)$ to P_v for $1 \leq v \leq n$ and broadcasts $h_{u;0}(x) = \delta_u(x,0)$.
4. Player P_v checks whether $g_{u;v}(0) = h_{u;0}(\alpha_v)$ and $h_{u;0}(0) = 0$.
5. If the conditions are satisfied, then P_v computes and sends to P_w the (usual) check value $C_{u;v,w} = g_{u;v}(\alpha_w)$. Otherwise P_v broadcasts an accusation to P_u.
6. All players perform the usual pair-wise checking with accusations protocol and update the set of good players A.
7. Each player P_v updates his shares by putting

$$h_v^{(t)}(x) = h_v^{(t-1)}(x) + \sum_{u \in A} h_{u;v}(x)$$

$$g_i^{(t)}(y) = g_v^{(t-1)}(y) + \sum_{u \in A} g_{u;v}(y).$$

4.4   The Second Type of Attack - Asymmetric Case

We will show now that the above described protocol has a flaw. The idea is to apply a similar attack as described in [2,3] for [16] (see also the previous section) but now applied to $g_u^{(t)}(y)$ instead of $h_u^{(t)}(x)$.

Suppose that the attacker has corrupted player P_v at some time frame $t-1$, i.e. he knows his shares $h_v^{(t-1)}(x)$ and $g_v^{(t-1)}(y)$. Then P_v being detected as corrupt is "rebooted". In the renewal phase his share is updated by

$$h_v^{(t)}(x) = h_v^{(t-1)}(x) + \sum_{u \in A} h_{u;v}(x) \qquad g_v^{(t)}(y) = g_v^{(t-1)}(y) + \sum_{u \in A} g_{u;v}(y).$$

Note that $g_{u;v}(0) = h_{u;0}(\alpha_v)$ holds. But since $h_{u;0}(x)$ is public the attacker is able to compute $\sum_{u \in A} g_{u;v}(0) = \sum_{u \in A} h_{u;0}(\alpha_v)$. Thus he knows the "true part" of the P_v's new share, namely $g_v^{(t)}(0) = g_v^{(t-1)}(0) + \sum_{u \in A} g_{u;v}(0)$. Note that the knowledge of the "true part" of the share of either $g_v(y)$ or $h_v(x)$ is enough for reconstructing the secret (see Remark 2 in the Appendix). Also it does not matter whether $h_{u;0}(x) = \delta_u(x,0)$ or $g_{u;0}(y) = \delta_u(0,y)$ is broadcast since the attack is symmetric. Therefore incrementally breaking different set of players the attacker is able to compute the secret.

4.5   Conditions for Security of Proactive VSS

Now we are ready to refine the conditions for security of proactive VSS (Theorem 2), based on the considered approach to renew player's shares by sharing 0.

Theorem 3. *A computationally secure (b, k, n) (for $b < k$) proactive VSS exists if and only if $k + b < n$. An unconditionally secure (b, k, n) (for $b < k$) proactive VSS exists if and only if $k + 2b < n$.*

The first proactive protocols [9, 10] were applied to threshold access structures in the cryptographic setting. Since it was quite easy in that case to add the functionality of proactivity it was a common expectation that it would also be easy to add this functionality to all existing distributed protocols like VSS. But it turns out that a specific problem arises, namely in the renewal phase we need a distributed commitment protocol in which the committer is committed to 0 and the players are able to check that the commitment is indeed 0 without revealing their auxiliary shares. As a result of this specific problem several attacks against the Renewal phase that break the proactive security have been found. Thus the approach to refresh the shares by sharing 0 as a secret in the renewal phase seems to have a drawback, i.e. in order for the protocols to be secure against b cheating players we need to use polynomials of degree $k - 1$ (instead of k) and hence we impose the requirement $b < k$.

Remark 1. The Renewal phase protocol in which 0 is shared as a secret is used as a stand alone sub-protocol in several other distributed protocols. Note that the weaknesses we pointed out here to these protocols arise only when mobile adversary is considered.

For the unconditional case all described attacks work even in the Herzberg *et al.* mobile adversary model.

5   Another Approach to Add Proactivity

Another approach to refresh (renew) the shares of the players is to re-share each share amongst the participants and then to combine the auxiliary shares in a special way. This approach was first applied to proactive SSS in [5, 6] divided there in two sub-protocols called sum-to-poly and poly-to-sum. These two sub-protocols together achieve the re-sharing goal. In general, every player first shares his own share (re-sharing) and then computes his new share as a certain linear combination of the auxiliary shares he receives from the other players, in such a way that at the end the players have new shares for the same secret as required in the renewal phase.

The approach of re-sharing the players shares is well known is SSS and it could be applied to change dynamically the access structure associated with the scheme. For example let $f(x)$ be k-degree polynomial such that $f(0) = s$ and let every player P_u has a share $s_u = f(\alpha_u)$. Then every player P_u chooses an ℓ-degree polynomial $g_u(x)$ such that $g_u(0) = s_u$, i.e. he re-shares his share sending auxiliary shares $g_u(\alpha_v)$ to player P_v. A set A of at least $k + 1$ good players is determined. For such a set A there exist constants r_w (which depends only on A, but not on player's shares) such that $\sum_{w \in A} r_w s_w = s$. Now every player P_v combines the auxiliary shares he has received to compute his new share, i.e. $\tilde{s}_u = \sum_{w \in A} r_w g_w(\alpha_v)$. It is easy to check that the new shares correspond to the same secret s and that the access structure is changed from (k, n) to (ℓ, n). Nearly the same protocol works in the computational secure VSS setting, e.g. Feldman's VSS.

On the other hand in the unconditionally secure VSS setting re-sharing and especially changing the access structure is more subtle. We will consider two protocols, which do not allow changing the access structure, since it is out of scope. Our goal is to show that the usual ways of doing re-sharing are not secure against a mobile adversary. First we will describe the straightforward way to re-share the shares. Then we will show that this protocol is not secure against a mobile adversary. Second we will describe another (more complex) protocol and will show that it is also not secure.

5.1   A Simple Re-sharing Protocol

Let us consider the protocol on Fig. 1 proposed in [13]. Every player P_u holds a share $h_u(x)$. The shares are derived from a symmetric polynomial $f(x, y)$ by setting $y = \alpha_u$. In the renewal phase the new shares are computed by $h_v^{(t)}(x) = \sum_{u \in A} r_u \, \delta_{u;v}(x)$. It is not difficult to verify that indeed **A.** We have new sharing for the same secret and **B.** The "symmetry" is not destroyed, i.e. the pair-wise check $h_v^{(t)}(\alpha_u) = h_u^{(t)}(\alpha_v)$ still holds for every u, v. The latter implies that there exists a symmetric polynomial $f^{(t)}(x, y)$ such that $f^{(t)}(0, 0) = s$ and $h_v^{(t)}(x) = f^{(t)}(x, \alpha_v)$.

Suppose now that the attacker has corrupted player P_v in some time frame $t - 1$, i.e. he knows his share $h_v^{(t-1)}(x)$. Then P_v being detected as corrupt is "rebooted" and in the renewal phase his share is updated. Note that $\delta_{u;v}(0) =$

Re-sharing Phase:

1. Each player P_u re-shares the "true part" of his share, i.e. $h_u(0)$, by choosing a symmetric polynomial $\delta_u(x, y)$ of degree k such that $\delta_u(x, 0) = h_u(x)$.
2. Player P_u sends to P_v $(1 \le v \le n)$ temporary shares $\delta_{u;v}(x) = \delta_u(x, \alpha_v)$.
3. Each pair of players P_v and P_w exchange and then performs the usual pairwise-check: $\delta_{u;v}(\alpha_w) = \delta_{u;w}(\alpha_v)$.
4. In addition, each P_v checks his "true part" of the temporary share

$$\delta_{u;v}(0) = \delta_u(0, \alpha_v) = h_u(\alpha_v) = h_v(\alpha_u).$$

   The last equality is the pair-wise check in the VSS used to distribute the secret s. Note that this additional check ensures that player P_u really re-shares his share, i.e., he is an honest "dealer", and that player P_v has a consistent "true part" of the temporary share.
5. All players agree on a set of "good" players $A \in \Gamma$, which were not accused as corrupt dealers. Let r_u be the constants which correspond to players $P_u \in A$.
6. Each player P_v computes his new-share as follows:

$$h_v(x) \longleftarrow \sum_{u \in A} r_u \, \delta_{u;v}(x).$$

Fig. 1. A Simple Re-sharing Protocol [13]

$h_v(\alpha_u)$ holds. But since the attacker is able to compute $\sum_{u \in A} r_u \, \delta_{u;v}(0) = \sum_{u \in A} r_u \, h_v^{(t-1)}(\alpha_u)$, thus he knows the "true part" of the P_v's new share, namely $h_v^{(t)}(0) = \sum_{u \in A} r_u \, \delta_{u;v}(0)$. Recall that the knowledge of the "true part" of the shares is enough for reconstructing the secret. Therefore, again incrementally breaking different sets of players the attacker is able to compute the secret.

5.2   Re-sharing Protocol with Randomization

Another drawback of the protocol described in the previous section (on Fig. 1) is that the "true parts" of the shares are not re-randomized. That is why in this section we will avoid this drawback using a *commitment transfer protocol* [1] and proposing a kind of *commitment sharing protocol* [1] (see Fig. 2). As in the previous section we consider the following scenario. Every player P_u holds a share $h_u(x)$. The shares are derived from a symmetric polynomial $f(x, y)$ by setting $y = \alpha_u$. The protocol is on Fig. 2. Note that again the new shares are computed by $h_v^{(t)}(x) = \sum_{u \in A} r_u \, \delta_{u;v}(x)$. In the same way it is not difficult to verify that the conditions **A** and **B** are satisfied.

   Suppose now that the attacker has corrupted player P_v in some time frame $t - 1$, i.e. he knows his share $h_v^{(t-1)}(x)$. Then P_v being detected as corrupt is "rebooted" and in the renewal phase his share is updated. Note that $\delta_{u;v}(0) = h_v^{(t-1)}(\alpha_u) - g_u(\alpha_v)$ and that $g_u(x)$ is public. Thus the attacker is able to compute $\sum_{u \in A} r_u \delta_{u;v}(0) = \sum_{u \in A} r_u \, (h_v^{(t-1)}(\alpha_u) - g_u(\alpha_v))$. He knows the "true part" of the P_v's new share, namely $h_v^{(t)}(0) = \sum_{u \in A} r_u \, \delta_{u;v}(0)$. Therefore, again incrementally breaking different sets of players the attacker is able to compute the secret.

On the negative side we do not know secure perfect proactive VSS protocols, based on the considered approach to re-share the player's shares. On the positive side we can improve the conditions for security of proactive VSS (Theorem 3).

Re-sharing Phase:

1. Each player P_u re-shares the "true part" of his share, i.e. $h_u(0)$, by choosing a symmetric polynomial $\delta_u(x,y)$ of degree k.
2. Player P_u plays the role of the dealer executing Share-Detection phase.
3. As a result every player P_v posses a share $\delta_{u;v}(x)$ polynomial of degree k, if P_u is not blamed as a corrupt dealer.
4. In order to prove that the shared secret is indeed $h_u(0)$, P_u broadcasts a k-degree polynomial $g_u(x) = h_u(x) - \delta_u(x,0)$. Note that if P_u is honest dealer then $g_u(0) = 0$ holds.
5. Each player P_v verifies that $g_u(0) = 0$ and that

$$g_u(\alpha_v) = h_u(\alpha_v) - \delta_u(\alpha_v, 0) = h_v(\alpha_u) - \delta_{u;v}(0).$$

   If these relations are satisfied he accepts his auxiliary share, otherwise an accusation against P_u is broadcast.
6. Let A be the set of uncorrupt players. Let r_u be the constants which correspond to players $P_u \in A$.
7. Each player P_v computes his new-share as follows:

$$h_v(x) \longleftarrow \sum_{u \in A} r_u \, \delta_{u;v}(x).$$

Fig. 2. Re-sharing Protocol with Randomization

Theorem 4. *A computationally secure (k, n) proactive VSS exists if and only if $2k < n$.*

6   A Remark on the General Access Structure Case

We first want to point out that all threshold protocols and attacks described in this paper can be easily generalized for the general access structure case using Monotone Span Programs (see [11, 12]). We choose not to do it just for the sake of simplicity, now we will only state the corresponding result to Theorem 3.

Denote the set of all subsets of $\mathcal{P}$ (i.e. the power set of $\mathcal{P}$) by $P(\mathcal{P})$. The set of qualified groups is denoted by Γ and the set of forbidden groups by Δ. The set Γ is called *monotone increasing* if for each set A in Γ also each set containing A is in Γ. Similarly, Δ is called *monotone decreasing*, if for each set B in Δ also each subset of B is in Δ. A monotone increasing set Γ can be efficiently described by the set Γ^- consisting of the *minimal elements (sets)* in Γ, i.e. the elements in Γ for which no proper subset is also in Γ. Similarly, the set Δ^+ consists of the *maximal elements (sets)* in Δ, i.e. the elements in Δ for which no proper superset is also in Δ. The tuple (Γ, Δ) is called an *access structure* if $\Gamma \cap \Delta = \emptyset$. If the union of Γ and Δ is equal to $P(\mathcal{P})$ (so, Γ is equal to Δ^c, the complement of Δ), then we say that access structure (Γ, Δ) is *complete* and we denote it just by Γ. The adversary is characterized by a particular subset Δ_A of Δ, which is itself monotone decreasing structure. The set Δ_A is called *adversary structure* while the set Δ is called *privacy structure* The players which belong to Δ are also called *curious* and the players which belong to Δ_A are called *corrupt*. An (Δ, Δ_A)-adversary is an adversary who can (adaptively) corrupt some players passively and some players actively, as long as the set A of actively corrupt players and the set B of passively corrupt players satisfy both $A \in \Delta_A$ and $(A \cup B) \in \Delta$. For any two monotone *decreasing* sets Δ_1, Δ_2 operation *element-wise union* $\uplus$ is defined as follows: $\Delta_1 \uplus \Delta_2 = \{A = A_1 \cup A_2; A_1 \in \Delta_1, A_2 \in \Delta_2\}$.

Now we give a formal definition of a Monotone Span Program.

Definition 1. *A* Monotone Span Program *(MSP)* $\mathcal{M}$ *is a quadruple* $(\mathbb{F}, M, \boldsymbol{\varepsilon}, \psi)$, *where* $\mathbb{F}$ *is a finite field,* M *is a matrix (with m rows and $d \leq m$ columns) over* $\mathbb{F}$, $\psi : \{1, \ldots, m\} \to \{1, \ldots, n\}$ *is a surjective function and* $\boldsymbol{\varepsilon} = (1, 0, \ldots, 0)^T \in \mathbb{F}^d$ *is called* target vector. *The size of* $\mathcal{M}$ *is the number m of rows and is denoted as* $size(\mathcal{M})$.

As ψ labels each row with a number i from $[1, \ldots, m]$ that corresponds to player $P_{\psi(i)}$, we can think of each player as being the "owner" of one or more rows. Let M_A denote the restriction of M to the rows i with $i \in A$. An MSP is said *to compute* a (complete) access structure Γ when $\boldsymbol{\varepsilon} \in \text{im}(M_A^T)$ if and only if A is a member of Γ. We denote such an access structure by $\Gamma(\mathcal{M})$. We say that A is *accepted* by $\mathcal{M}$ if and only if $A \in \Gamma$, otherwise we say A is *rejected* by $\mathcal{M}$. In other words, the players in A can reconstruct the secret precisely if the rows they own contain in their linear span the target vector of $\mathcal{M}$, and otherwise they get no information about the secret.

Theorem 5. *Let* $\mathcal{M} = (\mathbb{F}, M, \boldsymbol{\varepsilon}, \psi)$ *be an MSP and M be an $m \times d$ matrix. Let* $\widetilde{\Delta}^c = \Gamma(\mathcal{M})$ *and let* $\widetilde{\Delta} \supseteq \Delta$. *Then there exist a perfect proactive VSS scheme secure against* (Δ, Δ_A)-*adversary if the following conditions are satisfied:*

1. $rank(M_A) = d$, *for any group* $A \in \Gamma(\mathcal{M})^-$; *(Recovery)*
2. $rank(M_B) \lneqq d - 1$, *for any group* $B \in \Delta^+$; *(Renewal)*
3. $\mathcal{P} \notin \Delta_A \uplus \Delta_A \uplus \widetilde{\Delta}$. *(VSS)*

Note that the Vandermonde matrix is the matrix for MSP in the threshold case. Hence conditions 1. and 2. imply that $\widetilde{\Delta} \supsetneq \Delta$, i.e. $b < k$.

7   Conclusions

In this paper we have revised the mobile adversary model of Herzberg *et al.* and showed that the first scheme as well as most of the consecutive computationally secure schemes are subject to a kind of attack in the new adversary model. We have shown that several unconditionally secure schemes can be broken when mobile adversary is considered (even in the Herzberg *et al.* adversary model), while the same protocols remain secure in case the adversary is not mobile. In conclusion we have shown several specific weaknesses. It is an open question whether we can do better than Theorem 3 (and Theorem 5), using for example the re-sharing approach instead of commitment to 0.

Acknowledgements

The authors would like to thank the anonymous referees for the valuable comments and remarks.

References

1. R. Cramer, I. Damgard, U. Maurer, General Secure Multi-Party Computation from any Linear Secret Sharing Scheme, *EUROCRYPT'2000*, LNCS 1807, Springer-Verlag 2000, pp. 316-334.
2. P. D'Arco, D. Stinson, On Unconditionally Secure Proactive Secret Sharing Scheme and Distributed Key Distribution Centers, *Manuscript*, May 2002.
3. P. D'Arco, D. Stinson, On Unconditionally Secure Robust Distributed Key Distribution Centers, *ASIACRYPT'2002*, LNCS 2501, Springer-Verlag 2002, pp. 346-363.
4. P. Feldman, A practical scheme for non-interactive verifiable secret sharing, *FOCS'1987*, pp. 427-437.
5. Y. Frankel, P. Gemmell, P. MacKenzie, M. Yung, Proactive RSA, *CRYPTO'1997*, LNCS 1294, Springer-Verlag 1997, pp. 440-454.
6. Y. Frankel, P. Gemmell, P. MacKenzie, M. Yung, Optimal-resilience proactive public-key cryptosystems, *FOCS'1997*, pp. 384-393.
7. S. Jarecki, Proactive Secret Sharing and Public Key Cryptosystems, *M.Sc. Thesis*, 1995, MIT.
8. R. Gennaro, S. Jarecki, H. Krawczyk, T. Rabin, Secure Distributed Key Generation for Discrete-Log Based Cryptosystems, *EUROCRYPT'1999*, LNCS 1592, Springer-Verlag 1999, pp. 295-310.
9. A. Herzberg, S. Jarecki, H. Krawczyk, M. Yung, Proactive secret sharing or: How to cope with perpetual leakage, *CRYPTO'1995*, LNCS 963, Springer-Verlag 1995, pp. 339-352, (extended version 1998).
10. A. Herzberg, M. Jakobsson, S. Jarecki, H. Krawczyk, M. Yung, Proactive Public Key and Signature Systems, *ACM'1997 - Computer and Communication Security*, pp. 100-110.
11. V. Nikov, S. Nikova, B. Preneel, J. Vandewalle, Applying General Access Structure to Proactive Secret Sharing Schemes, *Proc. Benelux*, Springer-Verlag 2002, pp. 197-206, *Cryptology ePrint Archive:* Report 2002/141.
12. V. Nikov, S. Nikova, B. Preneel, J. Vandewalle, On Distributed Key Distribution Centers and Unconditionally Secure Proactive Verifiable Secret Sharing Schemes based on General Access Structure, *INDOCRYPT'2002*, LNCS 2551, Springer-Verlag 2002, pp. 422-437.

13. V. Nikov, S. Nikova, B. Preneel, Multi-Party Computation from any Linear Secret Sharing Scheme Unconditionally Secure against Adaptive Adversary: The Zero-Error Case, *ACNS'2003*, LNCS 2846, Springer-Verlag 2003, pp. 1-15.
14. R. Ostrovsky, M. Yung, How to withstand mobile virus attack, *PODC'1991*, pp. 51-59.
15. T. Pedersen, Non-Interactive and Information-Theoretic Secure Verifiable Secret Sharing, *CRYPTO'1991*, LNCS 547, Springer-Verlag 1991, pp. 129-140.
16. D. Stinson, R. Wei, Unconditionally Secure Proactive Secret Sharing Scheme with combinatorial Structures, *SAC'1999*, LNCS 1758, Springer-Verlag 1999, pp. 200-214.

A   Appendix

We first present Feldman's computational secure VSS protocol.

Sharing Phase:

Let s be a secret from a finite field $\mathbb{F} = \mathbb{Z}_p$ and g is primitive element in $\mathbb{F}$. Each player P_u is associated publicly with different non-zero element $\alpha_u \in \mathbb{F}$.

1. Dealer $\mathcal{D}$ chooses a random polynomial $f(x)$ over $\mathbb{F}$ of degree k subject to the condition $f(0) = s$.
2. Each share s_u is computed by $\mathcal{D}$ as $s_u = f(\alpha_u)$ and then transmitted *secretly* to participant P_u.
3. Let $f(x) = \sum_{j=0}^{k} a_j x^j$. The dealer broadcasts the values $A_j = g^{a_j}$ for $j = 0, 1, \ldots, k$.

Detection Phase:

1. Each player P_u verifies his own share by checking the following equation: $g^{s_u} = \prod_{j=0}^{k} A_j^{\alpha_u^j}$. If the equation does not hold the player broadcasts an accusation to the dealer.
2. If there are more than k accusations to the dealer then $\mathcal{D}$ is blamed corrupt, and the protocol is stopped.

Reconstruction Phase:

1. Each player P_u broadcasts $f(\alpha_u)$.
2. Take $k + 1$ broadcast values for which $g^{f(\alpha_u)} = \prod_{j=0}^{k} A_j^{\alpha_u^j}$ holds.
3. Determine $\widetilde{f}(x)$ of degree at most k that passes through these points and output $\widetilde{f}(0)$.

Next we present two unconditional secure VSS protocols. The first one is based on symmetric bivariate polynomials.

Sharing Phase:

Let s be a secret from some finite field $\mathbb{F}$. Each player P_u is associated publicly with different non-zero element $\alpha_u \in \mathbb{F}$.

1. $\mathcal{D}$ chooses a random symmetric polynomial $f(x,y) = \sum_{i=0}^{k} \sum_{j=0}^{k} a_{i,j} x^i y^j$ over $\mathbb{F}$, where $a_{0,0} = s$ and $a_{i,j} = a_{j,i}$.
2. Then, for each player P_u, $\mathcal{D}$ sends $h_u(x) = f(x, \alpha_u)$ to P_u through a private channel.

Detection Phase:

1. Player P_u sends a check-value $C_{u,v} = h_u(\alpha_v)$ to P_v for $1 \leq v \leq n$, $(v \neq u)$.
2. Each player P_v checks whether $h_v(\alpha_u) = C_{u,v}$ for $1 \leq v \leq n$, $(v \neq u)$. If P_v finds that this is not true, then P_v broadcasts an accusation to P_u in the form $(v; u)$.
3. For each player P_w, who has been accused by a qualified group of players, the dealer must broadcast his share $h_w(x)$. Then each player again performs all relevant verifications on the values broadcast by the dealer and those known to him and accuses $\mathcal{D}$ if there is an inconsistency. The dealer defends himself by broadcasting back the share of the accusing player. This process continues until no new accusations are made.
4. Each player P_w computes the minimum subset $A \subseteq \mathcal{P}$, such that any ordered pair $(v; u) \in A \times A$ is not broadcast (i.e. is consistent). If $|A| \geq n - k$, then P_w accepts his share. Otherwise, P_w accuses the dealer.
5. If there are more than k accusations to the dealer then $\mathcal{D}$ is blamed corrupt, and the protocol is stopped.

Reconstruction Phase:

1. Each player $P_v \in A$ sends $h_v(x)$ to each $P_u \in A$.
2. After having received the polynomials $h_v(x)$, each $P_u \in A$ again applies non-interactive pair-wise checking for all received polynomials, namely: filling the consistency matrix with a 1 on position (v, w) if $h_v(\alpha_w) = h_w(\alpha_v)$ holds and with a 0 otherwise. Then P_u computes a subset of consistent shares $\tilde{A} \subseteq A$, $\tilde{A} \in \Gamma$.
3. Next, player P_u computes a polynomial $f_u(0, y)$, such that $f_u(0, \alpha_v) = h_v(0)$, for those v with $P_v \in \tilde{A}$. Finally, the player P_u computes and outputs $s' = f_u(0, 0)$.

The second protocol is based on non-symmetric bivariate polynomials.

Sharing Phase:

Let s be a secret from some finite field $\mathbb{F}$. Each player P_i is associated publicly with different non-zero element $\alpha_i \in \mathbb{F}$.

1. $\mathcal{D}$ chooses a random polynomial $f(x, y) = \sum_{i=0}^{k} \sum_{j=0}^{k} a_{i,j} x^i y^j$, where $a_{i,j} \in \mathbb{F}$ and $a_{0,0} = s$.
2. Then, for each player P_u, $\mathcal{D}$ sends $h_u(x) = f(x, \alpha_u)$ and $g_u(y) = f(\alpha_u, y)$ to P_u through a private channel.

Detection Phase:

1. Player P_u checks whether $h_u(\alpha_u) = g_u(\alpha_u)$. If this condition is not satisfied he broadcasts an accusation on the dealer.
2. Next, player P_u sends a check value $C_{u,v} = g_u(\alpha_v)$ to P_v for $1 \leq v \leq n$, $(v \neq u)$.
3. Each player P_v checks whether $h_v(\alpha_u) = C_{u,v}$ for $1 \leq v \leq n$, $(v \neq u)$. If P_v finds that this is not true, then P_v broadcasts an accusation to P_u in the form $(v; u)$.
4. For each player P_w, who has been accused by a qualified group of players, the dealer must broadcast his share $h_w(x)$. Then each player again performs all relevant verifications on the values broadcast by the dealer and those known to him and accuses $\mathcal{D}$ if there is an inconsistency. The dealer defends himself by broadcasting back the share of the accusing player. This process continues until no new accusations are made.
5. Each player P_w computes the minimum subset $A \subseteq \mathcal{P}$, such that any ordered pair $(v; u) \in A \times A$ is not broadcast (i.e. is consistent). If $|A| \geq n - k$, then P_w accepts his share. Otherwise, P_w accuses the dealer.
6. If there are more than k accusations to the dealer then $\mathcal{D}$ is blamed corrupt, and the protocol is stopped.

Reconstruction Phase:

1. Each player $P_v \in A$ sends $h_v(x)$ and $g_v(y)$ to each $P_u \in A$.
2. After having received the polynomials $h_v(x)$ and $g_v(y)$, each $P_u \in A$ again applies non-interactive pair-wise checking for all received polynomials, namely: filling the consistency matrix with a 1 on position (v, w) if $h_v(\alpha_w) = g_w(\alpha_v)$ holds and with a 0 otherwise. Then P_u computes a subset of consistent shares $\widetilde{A} \subseteq A$, $\widetilde{A} \in \Gamma$.
3. Next, P_u computes a polynomial $f_u(0, y)$, such that $f_u(0, \alpha_v) = h_v(0)$, for those v with $P_v \in \widetilde{A}$. Finally, P_u computes and outputs $s' = f_u(0, 0)$.

Remark 2. Notice that the roles of the polynomials $h_v(x)$ and $g_v(y)$ are symmetric. Indeed, in the reconstruction phase a player P_u can also compute a polynomial $f_u(x, 0)$, such that $f_u(\alpha_v, 0) = g_v(0)$ for those v with $P_v \in \widetilde{A}$ and then he can again compute $s' = f_u(0, 0)$.

Efficient Constructions of Variable-Input-Length Block Ciphers

Sarvar Patel[1], Zulfikar Ramzan[2] and Ganapathy S. Sundaram[1]

[1] Lucent Technologies
{sarvar, ganeshs}@bell-labs.com
[2] DoCoMo Communications Laboratories, USA**
ramzan@docomolabs-usa.com

Abstract. Existing block ciphers operate on a fixed-input-length (FIL) block size (e.g., 64-bits for DES). Often, one needs a variable-input-length (VIL) primitive that can operate on a different size input; it is, however, undesirable to construct this primitive from "scratch." This paper contains two constructions that start with a fixed-input-length block cipher and show how to securely convert it to a variable-input-length block cipher without making any additional cryptographic assumptions. Both constructions model the FIL block cipher as a pseudorandom permutation (PRP) – that is, indistinguishable from a random permutation against adaptive chosen plaintext attack. The first construction converts it to a VIL PRP and is an efficiency improvement over the scheme of Bellare and Rogaway [4]. The second construction converts it to a VIL super pseudorandom permutation (SPRP) – that is, the resulting VIL block cipher is indistinguishable from a random permutation against adaptive chosen *plaintext and ciphertext* attack.

1 Introduction

A cryptographic primitive which operates on an input of fixed size is called a fixed-input-length (FIL) primitive. For example, block ciphers typically operate on messages of fixed size (64 bits in the case of DES [18]). But often in practice, one is faced with the situation of applying a cryptographic primitive on data of varying lengths. A striking example is the need for an encryption algorithm which deals with messages of varying sizes but at the same time preserves the property that the length of ciphertext equals the length of the plaintext. This situation is very common in Internet applications where traffic consists of "packets" of varying sizes. If a block cipher is being used for encryption, then the blocks that need to be encrypted could be of varying lengths. Differential packet sizes are also prevalent in wireless applications: this is due to the fact that the frames of data that are sent to each user may be different from user to user because of the difference in the so called path-loss of the users relative to the base station.

** Work done while the author was a visiting member at Lucent Technologies.

H. Handschuh and A. Hasan (Eds.): SAC 2004, LNCS 3357, pp. 326–340, 2005.

Moreover, channel conditions are a function of time, thereby forcing a change in the transmission rates (and hence block sizes). This calls for the development of variable-input-length (VIL) cryptographic primitives.

In general, one wants to avoid having to construct new primitives "from scratch" to deal with specific applications, since this approach might be prone to error. Instead, one can attempt to utilize a FIL primitive as a building block in order to build a VIL primitive. In this paper, we take this approach and provide *efficient constructions* for the conversion of a FIL block cipher to a VIL block cipher. We also provide proofs of security relating the security of the VIL primitive to the security of the underlying FIL primitive.

1.1   Related Work

FIL TO VIL FOR BLOCK CIPHERS. The first formal treatment for converting a fixed-input-length block cipher to a variable-input-length block cipher is due to Bellare and Rogaway [4]. They formalized the problem and gave a generic technique for constructing a block cipher which operates on any arbitrary length input from a block cipher that works on a fixed length input; they used the idea of a parsimonious pseudorandom function and parsimonious encryption scheme. In addition, their cipher possesses the customary requirement, initially due to Luby and Rackoff [15], of being a secure "pseudorandom permutation (PRP)" as long as the original cipher is.

A number of other papers could also be used as partial solutions towards converting FIL block ciphers into VIL block ciphers. For example, the celebrated paper of Luby and Rackoff [15] showed how to convert a n-bit to n-bit pseudorandom function (PRF) into a block cipher operating on $2n$-bits. The subsequent work by Naor and Reingold [17], provided constructions for converting block ciphers operating on n-bits to block ciphers on cn-bits for a constant $c \geq 1$. Bleichenbacher and Desai [7] have a construction that potentially converts a FIL SPRP to a VIL SPRP, though they do not provide a formal security proof. More recently, Halevi and Rogaway [12, 13] have provided constructions of tweakable enciphering schemes that operate on mn bits where m can be any positive integer and n is the size of the underlying block cipher. It was initially unclear how to use the techniques of [15] and [17] to attain provably-secure ciphers that operate on lengths which are not a multiple of n. One of the contributions of the present paper is to utilize these previous results to achieve such a construction.

FIL TO VIL FOR OTHER PRIMITIVES. The FIL to VIL problem has been addressed for Message Authentication Codes (MACs) and for PRFs. The elegant FIL-MAC to VIL-MAC work of An and Bellare [1] is a Damgård-like [10] nested iteration construction. Numerous works implicitly address the issue of converting a fixed-input-length PRF into a variable-input-length one; to name a few: Bellare, Kilian and Rogaway's CBC-MAC analysis [3] (which assumes messages are fixed length, but arbitrarily large), Petrank and Rackoff's [21] extension to variable-length messages, Bellare, Canetti, and Krawzyck's [16] cascade construction, and Bernstein's [5] protected counter sum construction.

1.2   Meaning of FIL to VIL

There is some ambiguity in the meaning of a FIL to VIL construction which we would like to clarify. A VIL primitive operates on messages $x \in \{0, 1\}^*$ or some large set containing strings of various lengths. The VIL construction can only use the given FIL primitive in conjunction with other non-cryptographic operations, but it cannot use other types of FIL cryptographic primitives. For example, if a VIL MAC is being constructed then only the given FIL MAC primitive can be used, but other cryptographic primitives like a PRG or PRF cannot be used. There are two possible meanings of using the FIL cryptographic primitive:

- Oracle Model: In this model, we only have oracle access to the FIL cryptographic primitive. We can query the FIL primitive with an input and get back an output. But, we cannot look inside the primitive for a key or run many instances of the primitive. This is a restrictive model which is useful to model certain scenarios; e.g., a smartcard or an assistant server which can answer our queries without giving internal access.
- Keyed Model: Unlike the Oracle model, here we are given a FIL cryptographic primitive which takes a single fixed key and message as input. Next, we can run various instances of the FIL primitive each keyed with its own key. However, any other key material must be derived from the single given key and using the FIL primitive itself without making any additional cryptographic assumption other than what is implied by the FIL primitive. The restriction of not having extra key material is appropriate because it would not be an apples to apples comparison of VIL constructions which take large keys with those that do not. Next, it is interesting and important to see if an efficient construction can be so achieved. Practically speaking, in existing systems, layer and functionality separation may mean, for example, that after a session key agreement, a key of fixed size may be handed to the encryption layer to encrypt the messages. As designers of the encryption layer we may be able to use a VIL construction, but we cannot request more key material from the session key agreement protocol because that may be a standardized protocol over which we have no control. So, if we need more keys for the VIL construction we have to create them using the given key and the FIL primitive. Bellare-Rogaway [4] used this keyed model and both of our constructions do as well.

1.3   Our Results

In this work, our goal is to provide very efficient VIL constructions for block ciphers. We utilize various classes of universal hash functions together with the existing cryptographic primitives to attain very efficient constructions; using such hash functions in conjunction with cryptographic primitives is a well-studied idea, but the novelty of this paper is their use in constructing block ciphers in the variable-input-length setting. Moreover, for our constructions we provide an exact security analysis. In some cases we utilize a technique / framework due to Naor and Reingold [17] that enables us to provide clean proofs of security in the presence of adaptive adversaries. We obtain the following results:

- Sections 3 and 4 give a FIL to VIL Block Cipher construction that is almost twice as fast as the Bellare-Rogaway construction [4]. Here we model the block cipher as a pseudorandom permutation.
- Section 5 gives a FIL to VIL Block Cipher that is *super pseudorandom*. We provably achieve an open goal suggested by Bellare-Rogaway [4].

In both cases, the concrete security of our schemes are limited by birthday bounds, so $2^{n/2}$ should be sufficiently large, where n is the starting block size.

2 Definitions

We introduce the notions of pseudorandom functions (PRFs) and pseudorandom permutations (PRPs). Although these primitives are often treated asymptotically, we model them in the concrete security framework. This is necessary since we deal with *fixed-input-length* primitives; as a result, meaningful security results are not captured by an asymptotic treatment. The exposition borrows freely from [3], [16].

NOTATION. For a bit string x, we denote its length by $|x|$. If $a, b > 0$ are integers, and $a \leq b$, then the substring of x starting at bit position a and ending at bit position b (counting from the left) is denoted $x[a, \ldots, b]$. Let S be a probability space, then the process of picking an element from S according to the underlying probability distribution is denoted $x \xleftarrow{R} S$. We use I_n to denote $\{0,1\}^n$ (the set of bit strings of length n). The set of all functions mapping I_n to I_m is denoted $\mathcal{F}_{n,m}$, and set of permutations on I_n is denoted $\mathcal{P}_n$.

COMPUTATIONAL MODEL. We follow the convention in [3] and model our adversary $\mathcal{A}$ as a program for a Random Access Machine. This adversary will have access to an oracle for computing a specified function f; it can make black-box queries to this oracle, and we assume that it will receive a correct response in unit time. We denote by $\mathcal{A}^f$ an adversary with access to an oracle for computing function f. Following the convention of [3], we define the running time of the adversary to be its execution time plus the length of its description.[1] The query complexity of $\mathcal{A}$ is defined as the number of queries it makes to its oracle.

FINITE FUNCTION FAMILIES. A finite function family $\mathcal{F}$, is a collection of functions, all of which have domain $Dom(\mathcal{F})$ and range $Range(\mathcal{F})$. Our focus is on function families in which each function in the family can be formally specified by (by at least one) "key." Typically, the key for a function family will be a pre-defined fixed-length bit string. And for a function family $\mathcal{F}$, and a key k, we let $\mathcal{F}_k$ denote the function associated with the given key, and we assume that computing $\mathcal{F}_k$ at any given point of $Dom(\mathcal{F})$ is easy given the key k.

EXAMPLES. Perhaps the simplest example is the set of all functions with domain I_k and range I_ℓ, under the uniform distribution. We denote this family by

---

[1] By defining the running time as such, we prevent anomalies that may arise from embedding arbitrarily large lookup tables in $\mathcal{A}$'s description.

$\mathsf{Rand}^{k \to \ell}$. A function in this family can be represented by $k2^\ell$ bits – hence an appropriate key space is I_{k2^ℓ}. Another simple example is the set of all *permutations* on I_ℓ. We denote this family by Perm^ℓ. Any block cipher constitutes a keyed family of permutations. For example, DES [18] has key space I_{56}, with domain and range I_{64}, and the AES algorithm (Rijndael [9]) is typically instantiated with a key space, a domain, and a range of I_{128} (though the specification accommodates alternate lengths).

DISTINGUISHABILITY. The concept of distinguishability, due to Goldreich, Goldwasser, and Micali [11], helps capture the idea of a "computational distance" between two function families. This notion will be useful when we discuss pseudorandom functions and permutations. Suppose that $\mathcal{F}^0$ and $\mathcal{F}^1$ are two function families that have both identical domains and identical ranges. An adversary $\mathcal{A}$ will get oracle access to either a function sampled from $\mathcal{F}^0$, or a function sampled from $\mathcal{F}^1$. The adversary will not, however, be told whether the oracle really sampled from $\mathcal{F}^0$ or $\mathcal{F}^1$. The adversary's goal is to determine which function family was actually sampled. Informally, distinguishability corresponds directly to the adversary's success rate in making this determination. In particular, let $\mathsf{Adv}_\mathcal{A}(\mathcal{F}^0, \mathcal{F}^1) \triangleq \Pr[f \overset{R}{\leftarrow} \mathcal{F}^0 : \mathcal{A}^f = 1] - \Pr[f \overset{R}{\leftarrow} \mathcal{F}^1 : \mathcal{A}^f = 1]$, where the probabilities are taken over the choice of f and $\mathcal{A}$'s internal coin tosses. Now, we say that $\mathcal{A}$ (t, q, n, ϵ)-distinguishes $\mathcal{F}^0$ from $\mathcal{F}^1$ if $\mathcal{A}$ runs for time at most t, makes at most q queries to its oracle each length at most n, and $\mathsf{Adv}_\mathcal{A}(\mathcal{F}^0, \mathcal{F}^1) \geq \epsilon$.

PSEUDORANDOM FUNCTIONS AND PERMUTATIONS. Pseudorandomness captures the computational distance between $\mathsf{Rand}^{k \to \ell}$, and another function family $\mathcal{F}$ with domain I_k and range I_ℓ.

Definition 1. *Let $\mathcal{F}$ be a keyed function family with domain I_k and range I_ℓ. Let $\mathcal{A}$ be an adversary that is equipped with an oracle. Then, $\mathsf{Adv}_\mathcal{F}^{\mathsf{prf}}(\mathcal{A}) \triangleq \Pr[f \overset{R}{\leftarrow}$ $\mathcal{F} : \mathcal{A}^f = 1] - \Pr[f \overset{R}{\leftarrow} \mathsf{Rand}^{k \to \ell} : \mathcal{A}^f = 1]$. For any integers $q, t \geq 0$, we define an insecurity function $\mathsf{Adv}_\mathcal{F}^{\mathsf{prf}}(q, t) \triangleq \max_\mathcal{A}\{\mathsf{Adv}_\mathcal{F}^{\mathsf{prf}}(\mathcal{A})\}$. Where the maximum is taken over choices of adversary $\mathcal{A}$ that are restricted to running time at most t, and q oracle queries.*

We employ the convention due to [3] and incorporate the amount of time it takes to sample f from $\mathcal{F}$ into the running time of $\mathcal{A}$.

We now consider the concept of a pseudorandom permutation family, which was originally defined by Luby and Rackoff [15]. The original notion considered the computational indistinguishability between a given family of permutations and the family of all *functions*. Following the treatment of Bellare et al. [3], we measure the pseudorandomness of a permutation family on I_ℓ in terms of its indistinguishability from Perm^ℓ.

Definition 2. *Let $\mathcal{F}$ be a keyed permutation function family with domain and range I_ℓ. Let $\mathcal{A}$ be an adversary that is equipped with an oracle. Then,*

$$\mathsf{Adv}_\mathcal{F}^{\mathsf{prp}}(\mathcal{A}) \triangleq \Pr[f \overset{R}{\leftarrow} \mathcal{F} : \mathcal{A}^f = 1] - \Pr[f \overset{R}{\leftarrow} \mathsf{Perm}^\ell : \mathcal{A}^f = 1].$$

We define an insecurity function $\mathsf{Adv}^{\mathsf{prp}}_{\mathcal{F}}(q, t) \triangleq \max_{\mathcal{A}}\{\mathsf{Adv}^{\mathsf{prp}}_{\mathcal{F}}(\mathcal{A})\}$, *for any integers* $q, t \geq 0$. *The maximum is taken over choices of adversary* $\mathcal{A}$ *that are restricted to running time at most* t, *and* q *oracle queries.*

Luby and Rackoff [15] also considered the notion of a super pseudorandom permutation (SPRP). In this setting, the adversary is given access to both an oracle that computes the permutation for a given element, and an oracle that computes the inverse of the permutation.

Definition 3. *Let* $\mathcal{F}$ *be a keyed permutation function family with domain and range* I_ℓ. *Let* $\mathcal{A}$ *be an adversary that is given access to two oracles. Then,*

$$\mathsf{Adv}^{\mathsf{sprp}}_{\mathcal{F}}(\mathcal{A}) \triangleq \Pr[f \xleftarrow{R} \mathcal{F} : \mathcal{A}^{f, f^{-1}} = 1] - \Pr[f \xleftarrow{R} \mathsf{Perm}^\ell : \mathcal{A}^{f, f^{-1}} = 1].$$

We define an insecurity function $\mathsf{Adv}^{\mathsf{sprp}}_{F}(q, t) \triangleq \max_{\mathcal{A}}\{\mathsf{Adv}^{\mathsf{prp}}_{\mathcal{F}}(\mathcal{A})\}$, *for any integers* $q, t \geq 0$. *The maximum is taken over choices of adversary* $\mathcal{A}$ *that are restricted to running time at most* t, *and* q *oracle queries.*

The security of a Block Cipher against chosen plaintext attacks can be understood by examining it as a pseudorandom permutation, whereas the security against chosen plaintext and ciphertext attacks can be understood by examining it as a super pseudorandom permutation.

UNIVERSAL HASH FUNCTIONS. Let H be a family of functions with domain D and range S [2] that comes with an induced distribution (e.g., uniform); functions can be sampled from H according to this distribution. Let ϵ be a "small" constant such that $1/|S| \leq \epsilon \leq 1$.

- We call H an ϵ-almost universal family of hash functions if, for all $x \neq y \in D$, $\Pr_{h \in H}[h(x) = h(y)] \leq \epsilon$.
- We call H ϵ-almost-Δ-universal family of hash functions if, for all $x \neq y \in D$, $\Pr_{h \in H}[h(x) - h(y) = \delta] \leq \epsilon$.
- We call H an ϵ-almost-strongly-universal family of hash functions if, for all $x \neq y \in D$, $\Pr_{h \in H}[h(x) = a, h(y) = b] \leq \epsilon/|S|$. If H consists only of permutations, we say that H is a strongly universal family of permutations.

The above definitions are due to [8] [22]. As an example, the linear congruential hash $h(x) = ax + b \bmod p$ where a is non-zero and p is a prime, meets the above criteria. For simplicity, we often say that h is a certain type of universal hash function to mean that h was drawn from the family H according to its equipped distribution. We will later need universal and Δ-universal hash functions to operate on variable-length domains. Standard techniques of padding and length appending to create variable-input-length universal hash functions can be used (e.g., UMAC [6]) and we do not discuss them further.

---

[2] S is a usually a finite group with '+' and '−' as the addition and subtraction operators respectively.

3   FIL to VIL PRP: An Example Construction

Before presenting our general construction, we provide a concrete instantiation which takes the DES block cipher [18] with key K and creates a variable-input-length block cipher for block sizes larger than 64 bits. This example is primarily pedagogical – in practice, one should apply our construction on a longer starting block length to avoid birthday-type attacks. As depicted in Figure 1, we need several keys. We use key K_1 in DES in the second round, we use K_2 in the last round where DES is called in counter mode, and we need a key for the universal hash function h in round 1. To generate these keys, we run DES with key K and inputs $1, 2, \ldots, i$ and label the outputs $K_1, K_2, \ldots, K_i$. We can then use key K_1 to key DES in round 2 and we can use key K_2 to key DES in round 3. The rest of the keys can be used as the hash keys. This key expansion step will take place only once. The exact hash key size we need in order to deal with large inputs depends upon the exact nature of the hash function. For concreteness, we will use the Δ-universal hash function utilized in UMAC [6] which can work with a limited size hash key and specifies methods (e.g., padding, length appending, and a well-known Toeplitz key-scheduling trick) to deal with variable-length inputs.

Encryption

1. The message M is divided into two parts M_{pref} of size $|M| - n$ bits and M_{suff} of size $n = 64$ bits.
2. In round 1, the universal hash function h is applied on M_{pref} and the result is added to M_{suff} to create S. M_{pref} is also carried forward to round 2.
3. In round 2, S is encrypted using the DES block cipher keyed with key K_1 resulting in output T. M_{pref} is carried forward.
4. In round 3, T is carried forward. T is also used as the initial counter value used to encrypt M_{pref} using DES in counter mode; i.e., DES is keyed with K_2 and called with as many inputs $T, T + 1, \ldots$ as needed to create enough stream bits to XOR with M_{pref} to create C_{pref}. The output is (T, C_{pref}).

To see that the above procedure yields a variable-input-length block cipher it suffices to note that each round yields an invertible permutation. Round 1 is a Feistel permutation where the universal hash function is the underlying round function, so it is invertible. Round 2 block encrypts S and is invertible by the nature of block ciphers. Finally, round 3 uses T as the initial value for counter mode encryption, and so is also invertible. The details for decryption follow.

Decryption

1. The ciphertext C is divided into two parts, T of size n bits and C_{pref} of size $|M| - n$ bits.
2. $T, T + 1, \ldots$ are fed through DES block cipher keyed with K_2 to create a stream of output bits which are XORed with C_{pref} to recover M_{pref}. We have now inverted round 3 to recover (T, M_{pref}).
3. T is decrypted using DES block cipher keyed with K_1 to recover S. We have now inverted round 2 to recover (S, M_{pref}).

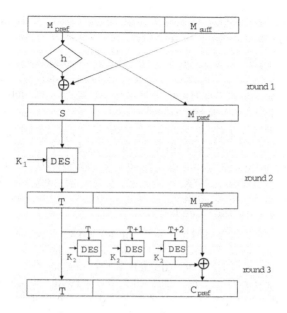

Fig. 1. An example of our construction for FIL to VIL conversion of DES

4. M_{pref} is fed to the universal hash function h and the result is XORed with S to recover M_{suff}. We have now recovered the plaintext $M = (M_{pref}, M_{suff})$.

As we describe next, we can instantiate the above example with any block cipher (not just one with a 64-bit block length) and any Δ-universal hash function. Furthermore, round 3 can employ other encryption schemes besides counter mode.

4   FIL to VIL PRP: Generalization and Security

The problem of constructing a variable-input-length encryption mode for block ciphers was considered by Bellare and Rogaway [4]. They give a generic approach for solving this problem, and then instantiate it with a specific construction. The generic approach involves utilizing a *parsimonious pseudorandom function* together with a *parsimonious encryption scheme*. It turns out that the CBC-MAC is a parsimonious PRF. In addition, both CBC-mode encryption and counter-mode encryption (with a random initial counter) serve as examples of parsimonious encryption schemes. In this section, we give an efficient construction for taking an existing fixed-input-length pseudorandom permutation, and building a variable-input-length parsimonious PRF (this is equal to round 1 and round 2 in figure 1). Our construction is more efficient than the CBC-MAC. Overall the construction in [4] requires two cryptographic passes on the entire input, whereas our construction requires one cryptographic pass and one non-cryptographic pass using a computationally lightweight universal hash function.

We now describe the Bellare-Rogaway framework [4] which we use to generalize our construction and analyze its security.

PARSIMONIOUS PRF. Let $\mathcal{F}$ be a keyed function family with domain I_k and range I_n, where $k \geq n$. We call $\mathcal{F}$ a parsimonious family if, for any key $a \in Keys(\mathcal{F})$, and any input $x \in I_k$, the last n bits of x are uniquely determined by: the remaining bits of x, the key a, and $\mathcal{F}_a(x)$.

PARSIMONIOUS ENCRYPTION. Following Bellare-Rogaway [4] we define a parsimonious encryption scheme via three algorithms $S = (\mathcal{K}, \mathcal{E}, \mathcal{D})$. The algorithm $\mathcal{K}$ is a key-generation algorithm, and returns a random key κ to be used for the encryption. The algorithm $\mathcal{E}$ takes this key κ and the message M, picks a random, fixed-length IV, and then encrypts M to get a ciphertext $C = (IV; C^*)$, where C^* and M have the same length.

GENERAL SCHEME FOR VIL BLOCK CIPHERS. Given a parsimonious PRF and encryption scheme, we can construct a general VIL scheme $\mathcal{F}$ as follows. We let G be the parsimonious PRF whose domain is the message space and whose range is I_n. Let Recover denote G's corresponding recovery algorithm that obtains the last n bits of the message M given the key to G, the first $|M| - n$ bits of M, and the output of G. Let $S = (\mathcal{K}, \mathcal{E}, \mathcal{D})$ be a parsimonious encryption scheme. Let K_{prf} and K_{enc} be the secret keys for the parsimonious PRF and encryption schemes respectively. Let M_{pref} be the first $|M| - n$ bits of M.

Algorithm Encrypt K_{prf}, K_{enc} (M)	**Algorithm Decrypt** K_{prf}, K_{enc} (C)
$T = G_{K_{prf}}(M)$	Let T be the first n bits of C.
$C_{pref} = \mathcal{E}_{K_{enc}}(M_{pref}; T)$	$M_{pref} = \mathcal{D}_{K_{enc}}(C)$
return $C = (T; C_{pref})$	$M_{suff} = \text{Recover}_{K_{prf}}(M_{pref}, T)$
	return $M = (M_{pref}; M_{suff})$

SECURITY FOR VIL MODE ENCRYPTION. Before giving any security analysis for general VIL Mode block cipher encryption, we discuss security for parsimonious encryption. The security for a parsimonious encryption scheme is defined by the adversary's inability to distinguish the encryption of a message from the encryption of a randomly chosen string of equal length. This definition was given in [4], but follows a definition given by [2]. More formally, if $S = (\mathcal{K}, \mathcal{E}, \mathcal{D})$ is a parsimonious encryption scheme, and $\mathcal{A}$ is a distinguishing adversary, then

$$\text{Adv}_{\mathcal{A}}^{\text{priv}}(S) \triangleq \Pr[K \leftarrow \mathcal{K} : \mathcal{A}^{\mathcal{E}_K(\cdot)} = 1] - \Pr[K \leftarrow \mathcal{K} : \mathcal{A}^{\mathcal{E}_K(\$^{|\cdot|})} = 1].$$

In the first experiment, the oracle returns a random encryption of the message under the given key K, and in the second, a random encryption of a random string of the same length as the message (under the key K) is returned. We define $\text{Adv}_S^{\text{priv}}(t, q, \mu)$ as $\max_{\mathcal{A}}\{\text{Adv}_S^{\text{priv}}(\mathcal{A})\}$. Here the maximum is taken over all adversaries $\mathcal{A}$ who are restricted to time t, and make at most q oracle queries whose total length is no more than μ bits. Now, Bellare-Rogaway [4] proved the following theorem relating the security of their general VIL block cipher construct in terms of its constituent parsimonious PRF and encryption scheme.

Theorem 1 (Bellare-Rogaway [4]). *Let $\mathcal{B}$ denote the VIL block cipher constructed from the parsimonious PRF family $\mathcal{F}$ and the parsimonious encryption scheme S. Moreover, suppose that the functions in $\mathcal{F}$ have range I_n. Then*

$$\mathsf{Adv}_{\mathcal{B}}^{\mathsf{prp}}(t, q, \mu) \leq \mathsf{Adv}_{\mathcal{F}}^{\mathsf{prf}}(t', q, \mu) + \mathsf{Adv}_{S}^{\mathsf{priv}}(t', q, \mu) + \frac{q^2}{2^n},$$

where $t' = t + O(qn + \mu)$.

VIL PARSIMONIOUS PRF. We now show how to efficiently construct a parsimonious PRF that can handle variable input lengths. As pointed out above, our construction is the most efficient known parsimonious PRF. Combining our parsimonious PRF with an existing parsimonious encryption scheme (see [4] for examples) we get a very efficient scheme for VIL block cipher encryption. For now, we assume that we have a PRP over I_n (any block cipher will work). We show how to construct a *parsimonious* PRF family with domain I_{n+b} and range I_n, where $n \leq b$. Referring to figure 1, $b = |M| - n = |M_{pref}|$.

Construction 1. *Let $\mathcal{P}$ be any pseudorandom permutation family on I_n, and let H be an ϵ-almost Δ-universal family of hash functions with domain I_b and range I_n. We construct a parsimonious PRF ParG with domain I_{n+b} and range I_n as follows: A key of a function sampled from ParG is a pair $\langle h, g \rangle$ where h is sampled from H and g is sampled from $\mathcal{P}$. For every input $x \in I_{n+b}$, we define the value of $ParG_{h,g}$ as $ParG_{h,g}(x) = g(h(x[1 \ldots b]) \oplus x[b+1 \ldots n+b])$.*

REMARK. We observe that $ParG$ is parsimonious: given the output T and $x[1 \ldots b]$, it is easy to see $x[b+1 \ldots n+b] = g^{-1}(T) \oplus h(x[1 \ldots b])$.

Note that if $b < n$, we can simply append a fixed padding to the input x, to achieve total length $2n$; the security bounds we prove remain the same, and almost the exact same security proof will go through. Our construction is more efficient than [4] because, the CBC pass on the input in the first round in [4] has been replaced by a non-cryptographic Δ-universal hash applied to the input. We note that one can use this idea of applying a Δ-universal hash function to all but the last block to speed-up some MAC constructions in the Wegman-Carter paradigm [23] (e.g., UMAC [6]), especially for shorter messages.

At this point, the reader may feel that something is amiss because the task of dealing with variable input has been passed to the Δ-universal hash function without adequately dealing with all the issues. We deal with them individually:

- Variable Input Length: As previously mentioned, Δ-universal hash functions can be made to handle variable-length inputs by using standard techniques of padding and length appending; e.g., see UMAC [6].
- Large Universal Hash Keys: There are some universal hash functions whose key size grows linearly with the input, but not all suffer from this problem. Tree hashing makes the key size grow much slower (about logarithmic in the

input size). There are other universal hash function constructions whose key sizes are not dependent on the input size, but are rather dependent on the output size [14]. Again UMAC [6] is an example of how one can limit the key size of a universal hash function without compromising efficiency.

- Single Key: In the keyed model that we are working in, we are only given a single key K, yet we need keys for the universal hash function, a key for the block cipher g in $ParG_{h,g}$ and a key for the block cipher in the parsimonious encryption scheme S. To generate the needed keys, we run the FIL PRP or block cipher with key K and inputs $1, 2, \ldots, i$ and label the outputs $K_1, K_2, \ldots, K_i$. We can then use K_1 to key the block cipher g, and use K_2 to key the block cipher in the parsimonious encryption scheme S. The rest of the keys can be used as the hash keys. We note that this key expansion step takes place once, so the amortized cost is minimal.

We state the security theorem, but leave the detailed proof for the full version of this paper.

Theorem 2. *Define ParG as in construction 1. Let ϵ_1 be the parameter associated with the Δ-universal family of hash functions in the construction, and suppose that the underlying pseudorandom permutation family $\mathcal{P}$ utilized by ParG is (t, q, n, ϵ_2)-secure. Then, for any adversary $\mathcal{A}$ restricted to t time steps, and q oracle queries of length at most $n + b$:*

$$\mathsf{Adv}^{\mathsf{prf}}_{ParG}(\mathcal{A}) = \Pr[g \xleftarrow{R} ParG : \mathcal{A}^g = 1] - \Pr[g \xleftarrow{R} \mathsf{Rand}^{n+b \to n} : \mathcal{A}^g = 1]$$

$$\leq \binom{q}{2} \cdot \epsilon_1 + \epsilon_2.$$

PROOF SKETCH. We use the standard argument of demonstrating that the transcripts resulting from interacting with an idealized $ParG$ oracle are distributed identically to those from interacting with a truly random function so long as certain "bad" conditions do not occur. These bad conditions are related to the likelihood that the g component does not see the same input from two distinct queries. By the Δ-universal property of H, this happens with low probability.

5   FIL PRP to VIL SPRP

We now show how to convert a fixed-input-length block cipher that is secure against chosen plaintext attacks to a variable-input-length block cipher that is secure against both chosen plaintext and ciphertext attacks. This construction achieves an open goal stated in [4]. The VIL SPRP construction requires about 5 cryptographic passes over the input, thus it should be considered a first step in constructing more efficient VIL SPRPs. The idea is to first treat the original PRP as a PRF and create two different variable-input-length PRFs of specific lengths from it. Finally, we use these PRFs in an *unbalanced* Feistel network together with universal hash functions in the right places to yield the desired result (see figure 2). The construction we outline works when one needs to convert a block

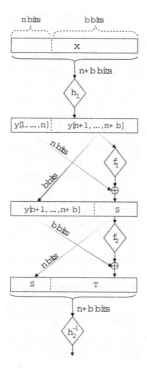

Fig. 2. Constructing a VIL SPRP from a PRP

cipher on I_n to a cipher on I_{n+b} where $b \geq n$. We can extend the ideas to work for the case when $b < n$, but there is a loss in security.

Construction 2. *Let $\mathcal{P}$ be any pseudorandom permutation family on I_n, and let H be a family of pairwise independent permutations on I_{n+b}, and let H' be a universal family of hash functions with domain I_b and range I_n. Define f_1 and f_2 as follows:*

$$f_1(x) \triangleq p_{k_0}(h'_1(x)), \tag{1}$$
$$f_2(x) \triangleq (p_{k_1}(x), p_{k_2}(x), \ldots, p_{k_r}(x))[1, \ldots, b] \tag{2}$$

where $r = \lceil \frac{b}{n} \rceil$ and $p_{k_0}, p_{k_1}, \ldots, p_{k_r}$ are independently keyed permutations drawn from $\mathcal{P}$, and h'_1 is drawn from H'. Now, we define a new permutation family $\mathcal{P}'$ which maps input $x \in I_{n+b}$ to $h_2^{-1}(S(x), T(x))$, where

$$y \triangleq h_1(x),$$
$$S(x) \triangleq y[1, \ldots, n] \oplus f_1(y[n+1, \ldots, n+b]), \text{ and}$$
$$T(x) \triangleq y[n+1, \ldots, n+b] \oplus f_2(S(x)),$$

where h_1, h_2 are drawn from H.

We state the security theorem. Due to space constraints, we sketch the proof.

Theorem 3. *Let $\mathcal{P}$ be a $(t, (1 + \lceil \frac{b}{n} \rceil)q, n, \epsilon_1)$-secure pseudorandom permutation family on I_n, let H be a family of pairwise independent permutations on I_{n+b}, let H' be an ϵ_2 universal family of hash functions with domain I_b and range I_n, and let $\mathcal{P}'$ be the permutation family defined above. Then $\mathcal{P}'$ is $(t, q, n + b, \epsilon')$ secure where: $\epsilon' = \binom{q}{2}(2/2^n + 1/2^b + 1/2^{n+b-1} + \epsilon_2) + \epsilon_1$.*

PROOF SKETCH. The proof easily follows by first utilizing theorem 4.1 from the paper of Naor and Reingold [17]. We first assume that the underlying round functions are truly random (from which the final advantage can be bounded by several applications of the triangle inequality in a series of hybrid arguments in which we eventually replace the truly random functions with f_1 and f_2 as above). In order to invoke theorem 4.1 of [17], we need to identify the "BAD" conditions (as a function of h_1 and h_2 on the transcript of the adversary's interaction with the block cipher). Letting the input-output pairs be denoted (x_k, c_k) for $1 \le k \le q$ (where the adversary makes q queries), the condition $BAD(h_1, h_2)$ occurs whenever $h_1(x_i)[n + 1, \ldots, n + b] = h_1(x_j)[n + 1, \ldots, n + b]$ or $h_2(c_i)[1, \ldots, n] = h_2(c_j)[1, \ldots, n]$ for $1 \le i < j \le q$. By the strongly-universal property of the h_1, the first condition occurs with probability 2^{-b} and the second occurs with probability 2^{-n}. To complete the proof, one merely has to form the hybrid argument by showing that f_1 and f_2 are pseudorandom functions. To do so, one should first replace the PRP p with a PRF. Then, the proof that f_1 is pseudorandom is very similar to the proof that our parsimonious function from the previous construction is pseudorandom. It is also clear that f_2 is pseudorandom since it is the concatenation of invocations of a pseudorandom function on random and independently chosen keys. Now, the final hybrid step involves showing that PRPs are statistically close to PRFs, which is well known.

A few remarks are in place:

- Single Key Model: Since we only have a single key K for a block cipher, we need to specify how the rest of the keys are created. There are 4 rounds in our construction and keys are needed in each round. The first and fourth rounds need keys for the pairwise independent permutation h_1 and h_2. The second round needs keys for the universal hash h'_1 and k_0. The third round needs keys $k_1, \ldots, k_r$. We create the other keys from the permutation, $p_K()$ by having arguments $p_K(roundnumber, index)$; for round 2, we set $k_0 = p_K(2, 0)$ and use index values 1 and higher to create the keys for the universal hash h'_1. For round 3, $k_1 = p_K(3, 1) \ldots k_i = p_K(3, i)$. For rounds 1 and 4, we cannot reuse keys created for a specific length input message as part of the keys for another larger length input message. The keys have to be independent. We achieve this by including a length parameter in the argument. To create keys for h_1 we would run $p_K(1, length, 1) \ldots p_K(1, length, i)$. Similarly for h_2 we would run $p_K(4, length, 1) \ldots p_K(4, length, i)$.
- Efficiency: In rounds two and three we have to basically do a cryptographic pass over the entire input. The keys $k_0, \ldots, k_r$ and the keys for h'_1 are generated once and can be reused, hence their cost is not dominant when amortized over multiple runs. However, the keys for h_1 and h_2 cannot be reused

and they have to be created again for each separate message length. Since a pairwise independent permutation takes a key whose size is twice the message length, we need to do effectively two cryptographic passes for round one and another two cryptographic passes for round 4. Thus, for the Strong VIL construction we effectively need five cryptographic passes.

- Optimizations: Note that when a message length has been previously used, then the keys of h_1 and h_2 previously calculated for that length can be reused. Thus, a table of keys can be kept for each length. This makes sense in applications that only involve a few specific message lengths. We also note that the above construction can be optimized in several ways using some standard tricks from [17, 19, 20]. First, the pairwise independent functions can be replaced by Δ-universal hash functions; the security proof is very similar to the ones in [17] and the full version of [19] (but we can no longer simply use theorem 4.1 from [17]). We may further use the same key material in the PRF in rounds 2 and 3 by strengthening the condition on the hash function as was done in [19]. Finally, we can in some cases recycle the key material used in the outer round hash functions by considering Feistel group operations other than XOR as was done in [20]. If we were to replace the pairwise independent permutation in the first round with a Feistel-permutation with a pseudorandom round function (as we did in the third round), and use a Feistel-permutation with a Δ-universal round function for the last round, we can eliminate the need for any additional key generation phase, thereby allowing us to handle dynamic block lengths efficiently (i.e., we generate keys once and they can be used for any block length). These types of tricks are fairly standard, so we omit a full discussion due to space constraints.

6   Conclusion and Open Problems

The constructions in this paper have been motivated by one dominant thought: push the application of universal hash functions in all directions to create VIL primitives from FIL primitives. The harder part has been to know exactly which cryptographic operations can be replaced by universal hashes, what kind of universal hashes should be used (e.g., universal vs. Δ-universal hashes), and providing security proofs. Specifically:

1. We show how to construct a VIL PRP from a FIL PRP which is almost twice as fast as the previous construction [4].
2. We show how to construct a VIL SPRP from a FIL PRP which solves an open problem in [4].

There are many open problems remaining in constructing VIL block ciphers including the construction of a VIL PRP and a VIL SPRP from a FIL PRP in the oracle model and a more efficient VIL SPRP construction in either model. The problem of creating efficient and secure VIL PRPs and VIL SPRPs for messages smaller than two block lengths remains open.

References

[1] J. An and M. Bellare. Constructing VIL-MACs from FIL-MACs: Message authentication under weakened assumptions. In *Proc. CRYPTO 99*.

[2] M. Bellare, A. Desai, E. Jokipii, and P. Rogaway. A concrete security treatment of symmetric encryption: Analysis of the DES modes of operation. *FOCS 1997*.

[3] M. Bellare, J. Kilian, and P. Rogaway. The security of cipher block chaining. In *Proc. CRYPTO 94*.

[4] M. Bellare and P. Rogaway. On the construction of Variable-Input-Length ciphers. In *Proc. Fast Software Encryption*, 1999.

[5] D. J. Bernstein. How to stretch random functions: The security of protected counter sums. *J. Cryptology*, 12(3):185–192, Summer 1999.

[6] J. Black, S. Halevi, H. Krawczyk, T. Krovetz, and P. Rogaway. UMAC: fast and secure message authentication. In *Proc. CRYPTO 99*.

[7] D. Bleichenbacher and A. Desai. A construction of a super-pseudorandom cipher. Manuscript, February 1999.

[8] J. L. Carter and M. N. Wegman. Universal classes of hash functions. *JCSS*, 18(2):143–154, April 1979.

[9] J. Daemen and V. Rijmen. AES proposal Rijndael. NIST AES Proposal, 6/98.

[10] I. Damgård. A design principle for hash functions. In *Proc. CRYPTO 89*.

[11] O. Goldreich, S. Goldwasser, and S. Micali. How to construct random functions. *Journal of the ACM*, 33(4):792–807, October 1986.

[12] S. Halevi and P. Rogaway. A tweakable enciphering mode. In *Proc. CRYPTO '03*.

[13] S. Halevi and P. Rogaway. A parallelizable enciphering mode. In *Proc. RSA Conference, Cryptographer's Track '04*.

[14] H. Krawczyk. LFSR-based hashing and authentication. In *Proc. CRYPTO 94*.

[15] M. Luby and C. Rackoff. How to construct pseudorandom permutations from pseudorandom functions. *SIAM J. Computing*, 17(2):373–386, April 1988.

[16] M.Bellare, R. Canetti, and H. Krawczyk. Pseudorandom functions revisited: The cascade construction and its concrete security. In *Proc. FOCS 1996*.

[17] M. Naor and O. Reingold. On the construction of pseudo-random permutations: Luby-Rackoff revisited. *J. of Cryptology*, 12:29–66, 1999. Previously in STOC 97.

[18] National Bureau of Standards. FIPS publication 46: Data Encryption Standard, 1977. Federal Information Processing Standards Publication 46.

[19] S. Patel, Z. Ramzan, and G. Sundaram. Towards making Luby-Rackoff ciphers optimal and practical. In *Proc. Fast Software Encryption*, 1999. Full version available from http://theory.lcs.mit.edu/~zulfikar/MyResearch/homepage.html.

[20] S. Patel, Z. Ramzan, and G. Sundaram. Luby-Rackoff ciphers: XOR is not so exclusive. In *Proc. Selected Areas of Cryptography*, 2002.

[21] E. Petrank and C. Rackoff. CBC MAC for Real Time Data Sources. Technical Report 97-26, Dimacs, 1997.

[22] D. R. Stinson. Universal Hashing and Authentication Codes. *Design, Codes, and Cryptography*, 4:369–380, 1994. Preliminary version appeared at CRYPTO 1991.

[23] Mark N. Wegman and J. Lawrence Carter. New hash functions and their use in authentication and set equality. *JCSS*, 22(3):265–279, June 1981.

A Sufficient Condition for Optimal Domain Extension of UOWHFs

Mridul Nandi

Applied Statistics Unit,
Indian Statistical Institute
mridul_r@isical.ac.in

Abstract. In this paper we will provide a non-trivial sufficient condition for UOWHF-preserving (or valid) domain extension which can be very easy to verify. Using this result we will prove very that all known domain extension algorithms are valid. This would be a nice technique to prove and to construct a valid domain extension. We also propose an optimal (with respect to both time complexity and key size) domain extension algorithm based on an incomplete binary tree.

Keywords: Hash function, UOWHF, Domain Extension Algorithm, masking assignment.

1 Introduction

A **UOWHF** or Universal One-Way Hash Function is a family of (n, m)-hash functions $\{h_k\}_{k \in \mathcal{K}}$ with $h_k : \{0,1\}^n \to \{0,1\}^m$, where the following task is hard: adversary has to commit an n-bit string x and then given a random key k he has to find another n-bit string $x' \neq x$ such that $h_k(x) = h_k(x')$. The pair (x, x') with $x \neq x'$ and $h_k(x) = h_k(x')$ is known as *collision pair*. More precisely, $\{h_k\}$ is (ϵ, t)-UOWHF if every adversary with runtime at most t has success probability (i.e. probability of finding the collision pair in the above task) at most ϵ. We say the above hash family $\{h_k\}_{k \in \mathcal{K}}$ is (n, m, K) hash family if $\mathcal{K} = \{0,1\}^K$ and for each k, h_k is an (n, m) hash function. $\mathcal{K}$ and K are known as the *key space* and *key size* respectively. Here, we are mainly interested in *valid* or *UOWHF-preserving domain extension* which means that given a (n, m, K) hash family $\{h_k\}_{k \in \mathcal{K}}$ (called *base hash family*) which is (ϵ, t)-UOWHF we want to construct another (N, m, P) (ϵ', t')-UOWHF $\{H_p\}_{p \in \mathcal{P}}$ (called *extended hash family*) based on $\{h_k\}$ where $N > n$ and ϵ', t' are constant multiples of ϵ, t respectively. We will be interested in valid domain extensions where the key expansion i.e. $(P - K)$ is as small as possible. Also we will try to reduce the time complexity by considering parallel domain extension algorithms.

Brief History. To sign a big message it is always better to compress the message first and then run a short domain signing algorithm on the compressed message. To have the security of signature scheme we need a Collision Resistant

H. Handschuh and A. Hasan (Eds.): SAC 2004, LNCS 3357, pp. 341–353, 2005.
© Springer-Verlag Berlin Heidelberg 2005

Hash Function or CRHF in which given a random key k it is hard to find a collision pair. But, Bellare and Rogaway (BR) [1] constructed a generic signature scheme where a UOWHF is sufficient to prove the security of the signature scheme. In their algorithm, $sig_{sk}(h_k(M)||k)||k$ is a signature of the message M. If the key size is large then one can use $sig_{sk}(h_{k_2}(h_{k_1}(M)||k_1)||k_2)||k_1||k_2$ as a signature of the message M. Usually the key size is $O(log(|M|))$ so input size of $sig_{sk}(\cdot)$ is $m + O(log(log|M|))$ which is very small. UOWHF is first introduced by Naor and Yung [7] and they constructed a UOWHF based on a one-way function. But the construction is much theoretical and slow. To construct a UOWHF of arbitrary domain we start with a construction of UOWHF with smaller domain from scratch and then extend it to an arbitrary domain. Natural domain extension method is MD construction which works for CRHF. But unfortunately, Bellare and Rogaway in the same paper [1] showed that MD construction will not work in case of UOWHF. They proposed a binary tree based construction with the notion of XOR-ing masks (parts of the key). Then Shoup [10] constructed a sequential domain extension and Mironov [4] proved that it is optimum in key size among all sequential construction (say $\mathcal{S}$ denotes set of all sequential construction). Sarkar [9] gave another binary tree based construction where the number of masks or key size is less than that of BR but it is more than that of Shoup. But this algorithm (also the BR algorithm) can be implemented in parallel. So these will be much faster than Shoup's algorithm. Sarkar considered a general class of domain extension algorithm (say $\mathcal{C}$, $\mathcal{S} \subset \mathcal{C}$) which includes all known UOWHF-preserving domain extension algorithm and provided a lower bound for the number of masks (or key size) to have a valid domain extension from $\mathcal{C}$. In $\mathcal{S}$ the both bounds given by Sarkar and Mirinov agree. Nandi [5] modified the Sarkar's algorithm with less number of masks. Lee et al [6] constructed an optimum algorithm in the general class $\mathcal{C}$ but parallelism is much smaller than binary tree based algorithm because they used incomplete l-ary tree. Finally in this paper we have an algorithm which has maximum possible parallelism and minimum key size.

Motivation. It is clear that UOWHF is a weaker notion than CRHF in the sense that a hash family is UOWHF whenever it is CRHF but the converse need not be true. In fact, Simon [11] proved that there exists an oracle relative to which UOWHF exists but CRHF does not exist. Unlike CRHF the birth-day attack will not work in the case of UOWHF. So roughly, to have a collision in UOWHF one needs $O(2^m)$ many computations whereas in CRHF one can find a collision pair in $O(2^{m/2})$ computations. So one can use the signature scheme proposed by BR using any standard hash functions e.g. SHA-256 or RIPEMD-160. Till now, we believe that those hash functions are CRHF and we can study the security of the signature scheme under the assumption of UOWHF. We can treat SHA-256, RIPEMD-160 as a hash family keyed by the initial values. Even if somebody finds a collision for the above hash functions it would not give any immediate threat to the signature scheme. One disadvantage for UOWHF is that if the signer himself is dishonest then the signature scheme proposed by Bellare and Rogaway will not be secure. Suppose $\{h_k\}_k$ is UOWHF but not CRHF. So, there exists a collision pair M_1 and M_2 for h_k. The signer can sign the message M_1 with the key k and then one can forge the signature of the message M_2. This problem could be solved if the signer does not have any control to choose the key k or the key is output of some random function depending on the message M.

General Domain Extension Algorithm. The general class of domain extension algorithm $\mathcal{C}$ is described in detail in [9]. Here we give a brief discussion on this. It is very natural that to extend the domain of a function we have to apply the function repeatedly. The question is how we will combine this iteration. If the output of one invocation of h_k is completely fed into the input of another invocation then the method of combination can be completely captured by a rooted directed tree. $T = (V, E, q)$ is called a rooted directed tree where $V = [1, r] := \{1, \ldots, r\}$ is the set of vertices, E is the set of arcs and $q \in V$ is a special vertex called the *root* of the tree with the property that, $outdeg(q) = 0$ whereas $outdeg(i) = 1$ for other vertices i. Here, $outdeg(i) = |\{j : (i,j) \in E\}|$. A hash function $h_k(\cdot)$ is placed on each node of T. The output of $h_k(\cdot)$ is passed through the arc i.e. if $(i, j) \in E$ then the output of $h_k(\cdot)$ at node i is fed into the input of $h_k(\cdot)$ at node j. For example, a sequential domain extension i.e. MD construction can be viewed by a sequential tree. As this is not UOWHF-preserving domain extension the notion of XOR-ing mask (a part of the key) is introduced. So, after each invocation the output is XOR-ed with some mask before feeding into next invocation. To determine the algorithm we have to specify which mask will be XOR-ed for every invocation. So we have a function $\psi : E \rightarrow [1, l] := \{1, \ldots, l\}$ known as *masking assignment*. We also say that ψ is a l-masking assignment. So, if $\psi((i, j)) = a$ then output of h_k at node i is at first XOR-ed with the mask μ_a and then it is fed into the input of h_k at node j. The domain extension algorithm is described in detail in the next section. It is clear that the above algorithm is completely determined by the rooted directed tree and the masking assignment on it. We will say the above algorithm is based on (T, ψ). The pair (T, ψ) is known as the **structure** of the domain extension algorithm. The class $\mathcal{C}$ consists of all such above algorithms based on any pair (T, ψ) where ψ is a masking assignment on a rooted tree T.

Our Contributions and Future Work. In this paper we provide a non trivial sufficient condition for valid domain extensions in the general class $\mathcal{C}$ defined by Sarkar [9]. More precisely, a domain extension algorithm based on (T, ψ) is UOWHF-preserving or valid if ψ is strongly even-free (See Definition 1). We show that all known valid domain extensions belong to the class $\mathcal{C}$ and satisfy the sufficient condition viz. the masking assignments are strongly even-free. Hence one can try to prove that the condition is also a necessary condition which will completely characterize the UOWHF-preserving domain extension algorithm. This sufficient condition would be very easy tool to prove that a domain extension is valid. It also helps to construct an optimal (with respect to both time complexity and key size) valid domain extension for the general class.

In fact, we construct an optimum domain extension algorithm for the general class.

2   The General Domain Extension Algorithm

Some Notes on Rooted Directed Tree. In any rooted directed tree $T = (V, E, q)$, from any vertex i there is one and only one path from that vertex i to the root q. So, we can define $l(i)$ (called *level* of the vertex i) by the number of vertices in the unique path from i to q. Note, $l(q) = 1$. Write, $V[k] = \{i \in V : l(i) = k\}$ for each $k \geq 1$. Define $h(T)$ (called *height* of the tree T) by $max_{i \in V} \, l(i)$. We also use the notation $h(i)$ (called height of i) for $t - l(i) + 1$ when T is a complete binary tree of height t. A sub-tree T_1 of T is the tree induced by a subset of the vertex set V. Root of a sub-tree $T_1 = (V_1, E_1)$ is the vertex with minimum level. More precisely, i is called a root of the sub-tree T_1 if $i \in V_1$ and $l(i) = min_{j \in V_1} l(j)$. If $i \in V$, define $V(i)$ by the set of all vertices from which there is a path to the vertex i i.e. $V(i) = \{j \in V : \text{there is a path from } j \text{ to } i\}$. We will say the induced full sub-tree rooted at i by the sub-tree induced by $V(i)$ (in notation $T(i)$). Note that i becomes the root of the sub-tree $T(i)$. Define $son(i) = \{j : (j, i) \in E\}$. In the next paragraph we state the general algorithm in the class $\mathcal{C}$ defined by Sarkar [9].

Domain Extension Algorithm (to compute $H_p(X)$)
Let ψ be a l-masking assignment on $T = (V, E, q)$ where $V = [1, r]$ for some positive integers l and r. We want to define (N, m, P) hash family $\{H_p\}_{p \in \mathcal{P}}$ given a (n, m, K) hash family $\{h_k\}_{k \in \mathcal{K}}$ where, $N = (n - m)r + m$ and $P = K + m.l$. Write, $p = k||\mu_1|| \ldots ||\mu_l$ and $X = x_1|| \ldots ||x_r$ where, $|p| = P$, $|k| = K$, $|\mu_i| = m$, $|X| = N$ and $|x_i| = n - indeg(i) \times m$. We need to assume that, $n \geq \delta(T) \times m$ where, $\delta(T) = max_{i \in V} indeg(i)$. Note, $|X| = \sum_{i=1}^{r} |x_i| = (n - m)r + m$. Here, p is a key of extended hash family and X is any input of that hash family. We will treat k as a key of base hash family. We use the term *mask* for μ_i's. Now we are ready to define $H_p(X)$ using the hash function h_k.

1. For $i \in V[t]$ $(t = h(T))$
   Compute $z_i = h_k(x_i)$.
2. For $j = t - 1$ down to 1
   For $i \in V[j]$ do in parallel
   $z_i = h_k((z_{i_1} \oplus \mu_{\psi(i_1)})|| \ldots ||(z_{i_d} \oplus \mu_{\psi(i_d)})||x_i)$ where $son(i) = \{i_1, \ldots, i_d\}$ and $i_1 < \ldots < i_d$.
3. z_q is the output of $H_p(X)$.

Main Parameters of the Above Domain Extensions

1. Key expansion is most important parameter in practical point of view. For above type of domain extension algorithms (key expansion) = (number of masks) × (size of range). So we need to have valid domain extension with smallest possible number of masks. In [8] author showed that at least $\lfloor log_2 r \rfloor$

many masks are necessary to have a valid domain extension where r is the total number of invocation i.e. number of vertices in the tree. Later we will construct a parallel algorithm called opt which needs t many masks for 2^t many invocations which is minimum possible.

2. The algorithm from above class can be implemented in parallel (unless the tree is a sequential tree i.e. a path). If we run the algorithm in parallel, number of rounds is same as the height of the tree. If we have $n \geq 2m$ then we can consider binary trees. So number of rounds should be at least $[log_2(r + 1)]$ where r is the number of vertices of the the binary tree. A complete binary tree of height t has $2^t - 1$ many vertices and hence a domain extension algorithm based on a complete binary tree needs t rounds only. Note that, this will have maximum possible parallelism if we only assume that $n \geq 2.m$. Later we will show that our construction opt needs $t + 1$ rounds for 2^t invocation which is minimum possible for binary tree based domain extensions.

3 Sufficient Condition of UOWHF-Preserving Domain Extension

In [8] it was proved that every valid domain extension should be based on even-free masking assignment (See Definition 1). In this section we will prove that any domain extension based on a strongly even-free masking assignment (See Definition 1) is valid. We also show that all known valid domain extensions satisfy this sufficient condition.

Definition 1. *A l-masking assignment ψ on $T = (V, E)$ is called an **even-free** masking assignment if for any non-trivial sub-tree $T_1 = (V_1, E_1)$ of T there exists $i \in [1, l]$ such that i appears odd many times in the multi-set $\psi(E_1) = \{\psi(e) : e \in E_1\}$. Similarly, ψ on $T = (V, E)$ is called **strongly even-free** masking assignment if for any non-trivial sub-tree $T_1 = (V_1, E_1)$ of T there exists $i \in [1, l]$ such that i appears exactly once in the multi-set $\psi(E_1) = \{\psi(e) : e \in E_1\}$. This i is called a single man for that sub-tree T_1.*

Theorem 1. *If a domain extension algorithm is based on a strongly even-free masking assignment ψ on T then it is a valid domain extension. More precisely, if for any (ϵ, t)-strategy for $\{H_p\}$ there is an (ϵ', t')-strategy for $\{h_k\}$ where $\epsilon' = \epsilon/r$ and $t' = t + O(r)$ where r is the size of the tree i.e. $r = |V|$.*

Proof. Let $\mathcal{A}$ be an adversary with runtime at most t and success probability at least ϵ for $\{H_p\}$. Now we will define an adversary $\mathcal{B}$ for $\{h_k\}$ with runtime atmost t' and success probability at least ϵ'.
$\mathcal{B}$**guess** :

1. $(X, s') \leftarrow \mathcal{A}$guess . $(|X| = N)$
2. Choose $i \in_R V = [1, r]$ (i is chosen randomly from $[1, r]$).
   If $i \in V[h]$, set $y = x_i$, $s = (s', i, y)$. Output (y, s) and stop.

Else $r_{i_1}, \ldots r_{i_d} \in_R \{0,1\}^m$ (randomly) where $son(i) = \{i_1, \ldots, i_d\}$, $y = r_{i_1}||\ldots||r_{i_d}||x_i$ and $s = (s', i, y)$ where, $i_1 < \ldots < i_d$. Output (y, s) and stop.

At this point the adversary is given a k which is chosen uniformly at random from the set $\mathcal{K} = \{0,1\}^K$. The adversary then runs $\mathcal{B}^{\text{find}}$ which is described below.

$\mathcal{B}^{\text{find}}(y, k, s)$: (Note $s = (s', i, y)$.)

1. $\mu_1||\ldots||\mu_l \leftarrow Mdef(X, k, i, r_{i_1}||\ldots||r_{i_d}, T, \psi)$ (see the algorithm $Mdef$ below).
2. $X' \leftarrow \mathcal{A}^{\text{find}}(X, p, s')$ where $p = k||\mu_1||\ldots||\mu_l$. Let y' be the input to processor at node i while computing $H_p(X')$. Output y'.

Now we state a lemma which says that there exists an algorithm $Mdef(\cdot)$ which outputs random string where input of a specified node is predefined random string. More precisely,

Lemma 1. *There exists an algorithm $Mdef(X, k, i, r_{i_1}||\ldots||r_{i_d}, T, \psi)$ which always returns a random string $\mu_1 ||\ldots||\mu_l$ whenever $r_{i_1}||\ldots||r_{i_d}$ is a random string. Also input of node i while computing $H_p(x)$ is $r_{i_1}||\ldots||r_{i_d}||x_i$ if $i \notin V[h]$.*

Proof of the Lemma: First we describe the algorithm below.

Algorithm. $Mdef(X, k, i, r_{i_1}||\ldots||r_{i_d}, T, \psi)$ (Note $|r_i| = m$ and $d = indeg(i)$)

1. We can assume that $i = q$ the root of the tree (otherwise we can do the same thing for the induced full sub-tree rooted at i, $T(i)$). Suppose, $\psi(e_u) = l$ (say) is a single man for T. Let $T' = T - (T(u) \cup \{e_u\}) = (V', E')$. If $r' = |E'|$ then, $r' < r$. Assume, $u \in son(j)$ and $son(j) = \{j_1, \ldots, j_c = u\}$ where $j_1 < \ldots < j_c$. If $j = q$ then $R = r_u = r_{i_d}$ otherwise it is a random string. Define, $x'_j = R||x_j, x'_k = \varepsilon$ (empty string) if $k \in V' - \{j\}$, otherwise $x'_k = x_k$. Now, we define $X' = x'_1||\ldots x'_r$. Run recursively $Mdef(X', k, q, r_{i_1}||\ldots||r_{i_{d-1}}, T', \psi')$ if $j = q$ or $Mdef(X', k, q, r_{i_1}||\ldots||r_{i_d}, T', \psi')$ if $j \neq q$ to define the masks where ψ' is ψ restricted on T'. Note $Mdef$ will always define those masks which are in the range of masking assignment. When we call $Mdef(., ., \psi')$ it will not define μ_l as l is not in the range of ψ'.
2. If $|E| = 1$ then $\mu = \mu_1$ where $\mu_1 = h_k(x) \oplus r_u$.
3. Define all other yet undefined masks except l by random strings. Compute the output at vertex u, call it by z. Define $\mu_l = R \oplus z$. This will completely define all masks.

Note that we assume that $j_c = u$ which need not be true. To avoid this problem we can redefine the general tree based domain extension by considering any order of the input at all nodes. Previously the input at node i is $s_{i_1}||\ldots||s_{i_c}||x_i$ but we can modify it to $\sigma_i(s_{i_1}||\ldots||s_{i_c}||x_i)$ where σ_i is some permutation of n-bit strings. In that case we have to redefine the permutation accordingly when we recursively call $Mdef$. For simplicity of the proof we can ignore this. We can check easily that all the masks are random strings as either they are random strings or they are XOR of two strings one of which is a random string. So, we can prove the first part of the lemma by using induction on size of the tree. We also prove the second part of the lemma by induction. So, if input at node j contributed by node u is R then input of node i will be $r_{i_1}||\ldots||r_{i_d}||x_i$ by the induction hypothesis. The mask μ_l is defined by $\mu_l = z \oplus R$. As output of node u be z (see step-3 in the algorithm $Mdef$) the input at node j contributed by node u is R . Note that μ_l is a single-man so it is not used any where else. This proves the lemma. □

So, by above lemma input of node i while computing $H_p(X)$ will be y which is already committed in $\mathcal{B}^{\text{guess}}$. Also note that p is a randomly chosen key from the set $\mathcal{P}$ as both k and μ_i's are random strings. Now We now lower bound the winning probability. Suppose X and X' collide for the function H_p. Then there must be a $v \in V$ such that at vertex v there is a collision for the function h_k. (Otherwise it is possible to prove by a backward induction that $X = X'$.) The probability that $i = v$ is $\frac{1}{|V|}$. Hence, if the winning probability of $\mathcal{A}$ is at least ϵ, then the winning probability of $\mathcal{B}$ is at least $\frac{\epsilon}{|V|}$ as two events $i = v$ and $\mathcal{A}$ wins are independent (the value of i is not known to $\mathcal{A}$). Also the number of invocation of h_k by $\mathcal{B}$ is equal to the number of invocation of h_k by $\mathcal{A}$ plus at most $2|V|$. (the number $2|V|$ is coming from the fact that in $Mdef$ algorithm we need at most $|V|$ many invocations and we may need at most $|V|$ many invocations of h_k again to compute y'). We skip the checking of time parameter as it is easy to verify. This completes the proof of the theorem. □

3.1   Sufficient Condition and Some of Known Previous Constructions

One can check easily that all previously known domain extension algorithms belong to the class $\mathcal{C}$. We will prove some of previous constructions are valid using the above sufficient condition. The same technique will also work for other known secure domain extensions. So, we reduce a problem of computational reduction to verifying strongly even-free property of a function (i.e. whether a masking assignment is strongly even-free or not) which would be much easier task. We list some known algorithms in terms of their structures.

1. **Shoup** [10] : $V = [1,r]$, $E = \{(i, i+1) : 1 \le i \le r-1\}$, $q = r$ is the root and $\psi(i) = \nu_2(i) + 1$. $\nu_2(i) = j$ means that $2^j|i$ but $2^{j+1} \nmid i$.
2. **Bellare-Rogaway** [1] , **Sarkar** [9], **Nandi** [5]: The tree is full binary tree of height t and the masking assignments are given below. The complete binary tree of height t has a set of vertices $[1, 2^t - 1]$ and a set of edges $E = \{e_i = (i, \lfloor i/2 \rfloor) : 2 \le i < 2^t\}$.
3. **Lee et al** [6] : In their paper a 4-dimensional construction is given which can be generalized to l-dim construction. Here we will describe 2-dimensional construction for simplicity. For integer t, $g(t) = (a, b)$, where $a = \lfloor t/2 \rfloor$, $b = \lfloor (t+1)/2 \rfloor$. $T_t = (V_t, E_t, 1)$ be a rooted binary tree, where $V_t = [1, 2^t]$

and $E_t = \{e_i : 2 \leq i \leq 2^t\}$ where $e_i = (i, i-1)$ for $2 \leq i \leq 2^a$, $e_i = (i, i-2^a)$ for $2^a < i \leq 2^{a+b} = 2^t$ (note, $a+b = t$).

The authors defined two functions α_t, β_t as follows.

(a) $\alpha_t : [1, 2^a - 1] \rightarrow [1, a]$ is defined by $\alpha_t(i) = 1 + \nu_2(2^a - i)$.

(b) $\beta_t : [1, 2^b - 1] \rightarrow [a+1, a+b]$ is defined by $\beta_t(i) = a+1+\nu_2(2^b - i)$.

The masking assignment $\psi_t(e_i)$ is defined as follow:

(a) $\psi_t(e_i) = \alpha_t(j)$ if $2 \leq i \leq 2^a$ and $j = i - 1$.

(b) $\psi_t(e_i) = \beta_t(j)$ if $2^a < i \leq 2^{a+b}$ and $j2^a < i \leq (j+1)2^a$.

To define the masking assignment used in $[1, 9, 5]$ we have to define level-uniform masking assignments.

Definition 2. (Level-Uniform Masking Assignment)
*A masking assignment ψ is said to be a **level-uniform** masking assignment on a complete binary tree $T_t = (V_t, E_t)$ of height t if there are two functions α_t and $\beta_t : [2, t] \rightarrow [1, l]$ such that $\psi(2i+1) = \alpha(j)$ and $\psi(2i) = \beta(j)$ where $2^{t-j} \leq i < 2^{t-j+1}$ i.e. $l(i) = t - j + 1$. The edge $(2i+1, i)$ (or $(2i, i)$) will be known as α-edge (or β-edge).*

In every complete binary tree all nodes except leave (the vertices i where $2^{t-1} \leq i < 2^t$) have two sons called left or right son. So, a level-uniform masking assignments depends on the level of the vertex and type of son i.e. whether it is a left or right son of its father. Also the values of masking assignment of α-edges (or β-edges) are determined by the functions α_t (or β_t). The masking assignments for Sarkar [9], BR [1] and Nandi [5] are level-uniform so we only describe the functions α_t and β_t.

1. **Bellare-Rogaway** [1] : $\beta_t(i) = i - 1$ and $\alpha_t(i) = t + i - 2$. no. of masks $= 2(t-1)$.

2. **Sarkar** [9] : $\alpha_t(i) = i-1$ and $\beta_t(i) = t+\nu(i-1)$. no. of masks $= t + \lfloor log_2(t-1) \rfloor$.

3. **Nandi** [5,6] : Define two sequences $\{l_k\}_{k \geq 0}$ and $\{m_t\}_{t \geq 2}$ as follow : $l_{k+1} = 2^{l_k+k} + l_k$ where, $l_0 = 2$ and if $k \geq 1$, $m_t = t + k$ for all $t \in [l_{k-1}+1, l_k]$. Define $m_2 = 2$. Note that, both l_k and m_t are strictly increasing sequences and if $t = l_k$ for some k then $m_{t+1} = m_t + 2$ and if for some k, $l_k < t < l_{k+1}$ then $m_{t+1} = m_t + 1$. It is proved in [5] that no of masks $= m_t = t + O(\log_2^* t)$. Here, $\log_2^* t = j$ means that after applying log function j many times for t it becomes less than 1 for first time. The recursive definitions of α_t and β_t are given below :

   (a) $\alpha_2(2) = 2$ and $\beta_2(2) = 1$.

   (b) For $t \geq 3$, $\alpha_t(i) = \alpha_{t-1}(i)$ and $\beta_t(i) = \beta_{t-1}(i)$ whenever $2 \leq i \leq t-1$.

   (c) $\alpha_t(t) = \alpha_{t-1}(t-1) + 2$, $\beta_t(t) = \beta_{t-1}(t-1) + 1$ if $t = l_k + 1$ for some k and $\alpha_t(t) = \alpha_{t-1}(t-1) + 1$, $\beta_t(t) = \nu_2(t-1-l_k) + 1$ if $l_k < t-1 < l_{k+1}$.

Now we can use the above theorem to prove the UOWHF-preserving property for the domain extension algorithms presented in this Section. In fact, one can check that all other known valid domain extensions are based on strongly even-free masking assignments.

Theorem 2. *The domain extension algorithms [1, 10, 9, 5, 6] presented above are valid domain extensions. In fact, all these domain extension algorithms are based on strongly even-free masking assignments.*

Proof. We only prove that all these domain extensions are based on strongly even-free masking assignments. So the theorem follows from Theorem 1. We will prove only in two cases. other cases are very easy to prove so we skip the proofs.

(1) (**Nandi** [5]) : Take a sub-tree say S rooted at height t' and $l_{k+1} \geq t' \geq l_k + 1$ then from height l_{k+1} to $l_k + 1$ no α-edge can be in S (otherwise first such one i.e. the α edge having maximum height will be a single-man so we are done). So, T' can contain at most one β edge at height $l_k + 1$. If it contain that then $\beta_t(l_k + 1)$ is a single-man for that sub-tree. So, if S does not contain that β edge then again it is a sequential sub-tree consists of only β-edges from height t' to at least height $l_k + 1$. But on that tree masking assignment is define by ν_2 function which is itself strongly even-free masking assignment. So, the above masking assignment is strongly even-free.

(2)(**Lee et al** $(l - dim)$) [6] : Let $T' = (V', E')$ be any sub-tree. Note that, $[1, 2^a] \cap V'$ is an interval say, $[c, d]$. If $d > c$ then from the definition of the masking assignment it is clear that on $[1, 2^a]$ is same as Shoup's assignment which is strongly even-free. Also note that the masks used on $[1, 2^a]$ are totally different with the masks used in other parts. So the single man on $[c, d]$ is also a single man of T'. Now if $c = d$ or $[1, 2^a] \cap V' = \phi$ then T' is a sequential sub-tree of the tree induced by the vertices $\{i, i + 2^a, \ldots, 2^a(2^b - 1) + i\}$ for some $2 \leq i \leq 2^a$. Again along this tree the masking assignment is determined by β_t which is strongly even-free (which is same as Shoup's assignment). So the masking assignment is strongly even-free.   □

Remark : The fact that all known valid domain extensions satisfy the sufficient condition may lead us to try to prove that strongly even-free is a necessary condition of valid domain extensions. If somehow we can prove that the minimum number of masks for existence of even-free is same as that for existence of strongly even-free then we can completely find out the best algorithm based on a given tree. Because, given a rooted directed tree one can find recursively the strongly even-free masking assignment with minimum number of masks. This idea will helps us to construct an optimum domain extension presented in Section 4.

4   Optimal Parallel Domain Extension

In this section we will construct valid and optimum with respect to both parallelism and key expansion (See Table 1) domain extension algorithm. Here, we will consider a rooted binary tree (not complete) instead of directed rooted binary tree. It is easy to correspond a directed binary tree to a binary tree and vice-versa. Let $T = (V, E, v_0)$ be a rooted binary tree i.e. $v_0 \in V$ and $deg(v) \leq 3$ for all $v \in V$ and $deg(v_0) \leq 2$. v_0 is called the root of the binary tree. To construct a valid domain extender it is enough to construct a strongly even-free masking assignment on a tree by our sufficient condition in the section 3.

Definition 3. (*i-binary tree*) $T = (V, E, v_1)$ *is called i-binary tree if there exists a binary sub-tree* $T_1 = (V_1, E_1, v_i)$ *of* T *such that* $E = E_1 \cup \{v_1 v_2, \ldots v_{i-1} v_i\}$ *and* v_k *are not in* V_1 *for* $1 \le k \le i - 1$. *The path* $v_1 v_2 \ldots v_i$ *is called the i-path of the i-binary tree* T.

See examples of i-binary trees are given in Figure 2. A i-binary tree of size i is a sequential tree i.e. a path of length $i - 1$. Given two disjoint binary tree (vertex sets are disjoint) $T_1 = (V_1, E_1)$ and $T_2 = (V_2, E_2)$ we can concatenate as follow: $T = T_1 +_{uv} T_2$ (notation) where, $T = (V, E)$, $V = V_1 \cup V_2$, $u \in V_1$, $v \in V_2$ and $E = E_1 \cup E_2 \cup \{uv\}$. Like concatenation of two trees we can define concatenation of two masking assignments as follow (see figure 1). Suppose, ψ_i is a k-masking assignment on T_i for $i = 1, 2$ then, we can define ψ a $(k+1)$-masking assignment on $T_1 +_{uv} T_2$ where, ψ on T_i is same as ψ_i on T_i and $\psi(uv) = k + 1$. We will denote ψ as $\psi_1 +_{uv} \psi_2$. If both ψ_1 and ψ_2 are strongly even-free then so is ψ.

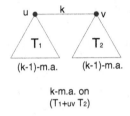

Fig. 1. Concatenation of two masking assignments

Some Useful Observations : We know that if ψ is even-free (also for strongly even-free) m-masking assignment then, $2^m \ge |V|$ (proved in [8]). A m-masking assignment ψ on $T = (V, E)$ is called an optimal masking assignment if it is strongly even-free and $2^m \ge |V| > 2^{m-1}$. So, an optimal masking assignment is a strongly even-free masking assignment whose size of image is minimum possible. One such example is given by Shoup's [10] sequential construction. If both ψ_1 and ψ_2 are optimal then so is ψ.

Definition 4. *A m-masking assignment is called* (m, l, i)-**optimal masking assignment** *if it is optimal masking assignment on a i-binary tree* T *such that* $l(T) = l$ *and* $|V| = 2^m$.

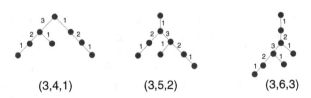

Fig. 2. some optimal masking assignments (the numbers besides edges denote the values of masking assignment)

Table 1. Specific comparison of domain extenders for UOWHF 1:seq/par, 2:message length, 3:# invocation of h_k, 4:# masks, 5:# rounds, 6:speed-up, 7:rank in parallelism, 8:rank in key expansion

Param	Shoup [10]	l-DIM($l \geq 2$)	Sarkar[9]	Nandi[5]	**Opt**
1	sequential	parallel	parallel	parallel	parallel
2	$2^t n$ $-(2^t-1)m$	$2^t n$ $-(2^t-1)m$	$2^t n$ $-(2^t-1)m$	$(2^t-1)n$ $-(2^t-2)m$	$2^t n$ $-(2^t-1)m$
3	2^t	2^t	2^t-1	2^t-1	2^t
4	t	t	$t+O(\log_2 t)$	$t+O(\log_2^* t)$	t
5	2^t	$l2^{t/l}-l+1(t\equiv 0 \bmod l)$	t	t	$t+1$
6	1	$\dfrac{2^t}{l2^{t/l}-l+1}(t\equiv 0 \bmod l)$	$\dfrac{2^t}{t+1}$	$\dfrac{2^t}{t+1}$	$\dfrac{2^t}{t+1}$
7	3	2	1	1	1
8	1	1	3	2	1

Theorem 3. *There exists an $(n, n+i, i)$-optimal masking assignment if $i \leq 2^n$.*

Proof. Let $f(k) = 2^k + k + 1$ for $k \geq 0$. It is strictly increasing function, So, given positive integers n and i there exists a unique $k \geq 1$ such that $f(k) > (n+i) \geq f(k-1)$. We will prove the theorem by induction on $n+i$. For small values of $n+i$ we have shown some examples in Figure 2. Now given n and i we assume that the theorem is true for any i_1 and n_1 such that $i_1 \leq 2^{n_1}$ and $i_1 + n_1 < i + n$. Choose k as above for these n and i. First assume that, $f(k) > (n+i) > f(k-1)$. Let $j = (n+i) - f(k-1) \geq 1$. By induction hypothesis there is a $(k-1, k-1+j, j)$-optimal masking assignment $(2^{k-1} \geq j$ as $f(k) > n+i)$. Call this by ψ_{k-1}. Now, ψ_{k-1} is a masking assignment on a j-binary tree $T_{k-1} = (V_{k-1}, E_{k-1}, v_1)$ where, $\{v_1, \ldots, v_j\}$ is the i-path. Now take the sequential $(k-1)$-optimal masking assignment ψ on $T = (V, E)$ and define $\psi_k = \psi_{k-1} +_{v_j v_{j+1}} \psi$ where, $V = \{v_{j+1}, \ldots v_{j+2^{k-1}}\}$. Now we can add optimal masking assignment one by one with ψ_k at v_i's. More precisely, let ψ'_l be a $(l-1, 1, l)$-optimal masking assignment on $T_l = (V_l, E_l, u_l)$ for $k+1 \leq l \leq n$. Define $\psi_l = \psi_{l-1} +_{v_{l-k+1} u_l} \psi'_l$ recursively for $k+1 \leq l \leq n$. Now it can be checked easily that ψ_n is $(n, n+i, i)$-optimal masking assignment.

We leave with other possible case where $n + i = f(k)$ for some k. In this case construct a k-sequential optimal masking assignment ψ on a sequential tree $T_k = (V_k, E_k)$ where, $V_k = \{v_1, \ldots, v_{2^k}\}$ For each l, $k \leq l \leq n-1$ we have $(l, l+1, 1)$-optimal masking assignment psi_l. We can concatenate ψ_l with ψ one by one. Finally we will have $(n, n+i, i)$-optimal masking assignment. $\square$

One immediate corollary is given below which tells that we have a domain extension algorithm which needs t many masks and $t + 1$ many rounds for 2^t many invocations of base hash function. Note that both number of rounds and number of keys are minimum possible.

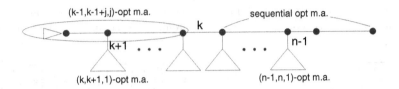

Fig. 3. Construction of $(n, n + i, i)$-optimal masking assignment

Corollary 1. *There exists an $(m, m + 1, 1)$-optimal masking assignment i.e. there exists a binary tree T of size 2^m with $l(T) = m + 1$ which is minimum possible (a complete binary tree of level m has size $2^m - 1$) so that an optimal masking assignment ψ on T exists.*

5   Conclusion

This paper has both theoretical and practical interests. Here, we will construct a UOWHF-preserving domain extension algorithm which is optimum in both key size and number of rounds. In this paper we also study how to check UOWHF-preserving property of a domain extension algorithm by just verifying a simple property called strongly even-free. It is very interesting to note that all known UOWHF-preserving domain extension algorithms satisfy the sufficient condition. So one can try to prove that the condition is also a necessary condition. The sufficient condition makes it easy to construct a UOWHF-preserving domain extension algorithm.

References

1. M. Bellare and P. Rogaway. Collision-resistant hashing: towards making UOWHFs practical. *Proceedings of CRYPTO 1997*, pp 470-484.
2. I. B. Damgård. A design principle for hash functions. *Lecture Notes in Computer Science*, 435 (1990), 416-427 (Advances in Cryptology - CRYPTO'89).
3. R. C. Merkle. One way hash functions and DES. *Lecture Notes in Computer Science*, 435 (1990), 428-226 (Advances in Cryptology - CRYPTO'89).
4. I. Mironov. Hash functions: from MD to Shoup. *Lecture Notes in Computer Science*, 2045 (2001), 166-181 (Advances in Cryptology - EUROCRYPT'01).
5. M. Nandi. A New Tree based Domain Extension of UOWHF. *IACR e-print server* *http://eprint.iacr.org/2003/142*.
6. W. Lee, D. Chang, S. Lee, S. Sung and M. Nandi. New Parallel Domain Extenders for UOWHF. *Lecture Notes in Computer Science* Advances in Cryptology - ASIACRYPT'03).
7. M. Naor and M. Yung. Universal one-way hash functions and their cryptographic applications. *Proceedings of the 21st Annual Symposium on Theory of Computing*, ACM, 1989, pp. 33-43.
8. P. Sarkar. Masking Based Domain Extenders for UOWHFs: Bounds and Constructions *IACR preprint server, http://eprint.iacr.org/2003/225*.

9. P. Sarkar. Construction of UOWHF : Tree Hashing Revisited . *IACR preprint server, http://eprint.iacr.org/2002/058.*

10. V. Shoup. A composition theorem for universal one-way hash functions. *Proceedings of Eurocrypt 2000*, pp 445-452, 2000.

11. D. Simon. Finding collisions on a one-way street: Can secure hash function be based on general assumptions?, *Lecture Notes in Computer Science - EUROCRYPT'98*, pp 334-345, 1998.

Author Index

Lecture Notes in Computer Science

For information about Vols. 1–3262

please contact your bookseller or Springer

Printed in the United States
by Baker & Taylor Publisher Services